ALSO BY BARBARA GOLDSMITH

The Straw Man

Little Gloria...

Happy at Last

Barbara Goldsmith

Alfred A. Knopf
New York 1980

LITTLE GLORIA... HAPPY AT LAST

THIS IS A BORZOI BOOK
PUBLISHED BY ALFRED A. KNOPF, INC.

Grateful acknowledgment is made to the following for permission to reprint excerpts from previously published material:

Doubleday & Company, Inc.: Excerpts from GERTRUDE VANDERBILT WHITNEY: A BIOGRAPHY by B. H. Friedman, with Flora Irving. Copyright © 1978 by B. H. Friedman. Reprinted by permission of Doubleday & Company, Inc.

David McKay Co., Inc.: Excerpts from DOUBLE EXPOSURE: A TWIN AUTOBIOGRAPHY by Gloria Vanderbilt and Thelma Furness. Copyright © 1958 by Gloria Vanderbilt and Thelma Furness. Reprinted by permission of David McKay Co., Inc.

Warner Bros. Music and Chappell & Co. Ltd.: Excerpt from lyrics of ANYTHING GOES by Cole Porter. © 1934 Warner Bros. Inc. Copyright Renewed. All Rights Reserved. Used by Permission.

LIBRARY OF CONGRESS CATALOGING IN PUBLICATION DATA
Goldsmith, Barbara.
Little Gloria . . . happy at last.
Bibliography: p. Includes index.
1. Vanderbilt, Gloria, 1924– 2. Artists—United States—Biography. I. Title.
N6537.V33G64 1980 700'.92'4 [B] 79-3483
ISBN 0-394-42836-0

Manufactured in the United States of America
First Edition

For these women

my mother, Evelyn
my sister, Ann
my daughter, Alice

Contents

Contents

The Trial

Since Then

Introduction

THE *Matter of Vanderbilt* was the most sensational custody trial in the history of the United States. It exploded into headlines on the first day of October 1934, and didn't leave the front pages of newspapers across the country until the year was out. The sensation lay in the clash of wills between two internationally famous women, Gertrude Vanderbilt Whitney and her sister-in-law Gloria Morgan Vanderbilt, over the custody of solemn, ten-and-a-half-year-old Gloria Laura Vanderbilt. At the time of the trial, Gertrude Vanderbilt Whitney was known as "the richest woman in America." She was seen by the press as a "haughty . . . austere . . . matriarch," the bearer of two mighty social names, the owner of vast estates, a mother and grandmother, a sculptor and art patron, founder of the Whitney Museum of American Art. Gloria Morgan Vanderbilt was a famous international beauty, a widow still in her twenties who was to be seen frolicking in the most fashionable places and who numbered among her friends the most impressive titles in Europe.

This trial took place during the Great Depression—a time when bright dreams had been shattered, and poverty, misery, hunger, and disillusionment were the order of the day—and a glamour-starved public eagerly consumed the accusations against Gloria Morgan Vanderbilt involving a German prince, a member of the British royal family, and an adulterous relationship with a flamboyant, married, playboy-businessman, a Jew and therefore automatically barred from the Society world of the Whitneys and Vanderbilts. Gloria Morgan Vanderbilt found herself accused of neglecting her child while she danced till dawn, of drinking alcohol, of reading pornography, of total indifference to her child's welfare, and of one thing more that so shocked the judge that he cleared the courtroom and conducted the rest of the trial in secrecy—a secrecy he was powerless to maintain.

Then there was the child herself, whom the press snatched up and immediately designated The Poor Little Rich Girl. Here was a perfect Depression symbol, a "gold child," a "Vanderbilt heiress" worth millions who was "dressed in rags," lonely, sick, neglected. These people might be rich, but they seemed emotionally impoverished, with no love to give. It was a consoling thought that this little girl, for all her money, seemed worse off than the poorest Depression child. And this was a time when children had become extraordinarily important as symbols of hope and optimism. At that moment, life held only misery and frustration, but children represented a limitless, untarnished future in which things would surely come right. People responded passionately to Little Orphan Annie's smile and optimism, to Shirley Temple's bobbing bright curls, to the phenomenon of the Dionne quintuplets in their temperature-controlled nursery behind their one-way glass.

For the entire last quarter of 1934, the *Matter of Vanderbilt* shared the spotlight with another trial—the extradition proceedings against Bruno Richard Hauptmann, the alleged kidnapper-murderer of the infant son of Colonel Charles Augustus Lindbergh. There was a hidden link between these two proceedings, but no one connected them at the time. At the center of the *Matter of Vanderbilt* was a mystery: during the trial one question—the crucial one—remained unanswered. No one could adequately explain little Gloria's hysterical, bizarre behavior. Clearly, the child was frightened to death, but no one could discover the root of her fear—not her mother, not her nurse (who had never left her for a single day in her life), not her grandmother, not her Aunt Ger (Gertrude Whitney), not a battery of competent doctors and lawyers, all of whom had questioned her. But I believe I discovered it.

Not immediately—at first, reading little Gloria's testimony in the voluminous trial transcript, I realized only that I was feeling edgy and uneasy; threatened, really. Certain phrases she had used sparked my earliest memories. "I was afraid she would *take me away . . . do something to me* . . . then IT would happen." Reading and rereading little Gloria's testimony, a secret language that I knew from my own childhood flooded back on me. I felt I knew exactly what she was saying. And I knew what IT was. She was speaking the language of kidnapping, and IT was death.

It came as a shock to me that I could understand something that all the people surrounding little Gloria had not understood (for if they had, the entire notorious and damaging trial might never have taken place); and I realized that I possessed this basic, emotional knowledge because, like little Gloria, I had been a child while "The Crime of the Century" was unfolding. (Had I been born even a few years earlier or later, I might have been as mystified by little Gloria's behavior as everyone else was.) I too had experienced—as a child—the terrible force of the Lindbergh case. It was a crime that shocked the world, but it held a special significance for children. From the moment the baby son of America's greatest hero was snatched from his crib (on the night of March 1, 1932), terror came rushing into American homes. If this could happen to so exalted a personage, then who was safe? In fact, from 1930 to 1932 there had been more than two thousand kidnappings in America, but this one was to become the quintessential American kidnapping, and later, many people would incorrectly assume that it had also been the first.

It was not the first, but it was the one that put fear into the hearts of a generation of children; little Gloria Vanderbilt knew about the Lindbergh kidnapping and so did I. I could recite the details like a litany. The kidnapper put a ladder up to the second-story nursery window. It was dark when he took the baby from his crib. His mommy and daddy were in the house and so was his nanny, but someone got him anyway. His daddy paid the kidnapper a lot of money—but it didn't help. The baby was found in a shallow grave in a densely wooded area. His skull had been bashed in. IT had happened.

The hysteria attendant upon the Lindbergh kidnapping-murder swept the nation, and kidnapping became an epidemic from which parents tried to protect their children. They taught them the rules of survival. Never take candy from a stranger. Never get into a car with a stranger. If anyone tells you your mommy or daddy is sick, or has had an accident and needs you, don't believe him. If a stranger asks you the time—keep walking. Many children of the time felt fear all around them and they assimilated it as their own. When I was a small child my family lived in an eleventh-story apartment on New York City's Central Park West. At night, after I'd been tucked into bed, I would lie awake waiting—knowing that this was the night when the ladder would go thwack against my bedroom window and I'd be *taken away*. I'd wait for that dull sound and while I waited I'd think about how my daddy would pay a lot of money, but it wouldn't matter because I would end up in a shallow grave in a densely wooded area. IT would happen.

But while I trembled each night from what was a pure fantasy of being kidnapped, little Gloria had real reason to be afraid. My emotional recognition of the root of her fear was soon substantiated with hard facts. On March 2, 1932, eight-year-old Gloria boarded the *Majestic* to return to America after more than six years abroad. On the previous evening, the Lindbergh infant had been kidnapped. Little Gloria and her mother existed in the glare of publicity: their arrival in New York City and residence at the Sherry-Netherland Hotel was announced in five newspapers which simultaneously stated that little Gloria Vanderbilt was the richest child in the United States. When the body of the infant Charles Augustus Lindbergh, Jr., was found on the afternoon of May 12, 1932, little Gloria lay sick in bed at the Sherry-Netherland Hotel with detectives guarding her around the clock. She had become the target of a kidnap and murder threat.

The lack of communication between little Gloria and the adults who surrounded her seemed incomprehensible to me until I carefully studied her particular family situation and realized that both her mother and her aunt were, for different reasons, unusually distant and emotionally removed women. But I was to discover in my research of the period that the prevailing philosophy reinforced this distance. Indeed, many well-to-do women of the thirties completely abandoned their children to the ministrations of nannies, the most obvious reason being that this marked their removal from monetary concerns and aped the pattern of European Society. And Dr. John B. Watson, the most eminent child psychologist of the thirties, recommended total detachment in child-rearing and warned, "Never hug and kiss them, never let them sit on your lap. If you must, kiss them once on the forehead when you say good night. . . . If you expected a dog to grow up and be useful as a watchdog, a bird dog, or a fox hound . . . you wouldn't dare treat it in the way you treat your child." Watson also advocated toilet training by six months (a physical impossibility) and recommended that babies who did not comply should be punished and forced to drink castor oil.

Of course, I have had the advantage of more than forty-five years' distance to look back and understand certain patterns which at the time were so much a part of the atmosphere that they were invisible. The automatic anti-Semitism displayed during this trial can now be seen as consistent with other patterns. At the time of the trial, newspapers invariably referred to Carol of Rumania's mistress, Magda Lupescu, as "the Titian-haired Jewess," and the dean of Wesleyan wrote that "We have difficulty placing the students of the Jewish faith in medical schools." In Germany, Jews were barred from the practice of medicine and law and Dr. Alfred Rosenberg, Nazi cultural commissioner, demanded a new score to *A Midsummer Night's Dream* to replace Felix Mendelssohn-Bartholdy's "decadent Jewish music."

By saturating myself with the atmosphere of each period I was exploring, I came to understand such phenomena as headline stories about marrying out of one's class, and an excuse in *The New York Times* for killing someone with your motorcar—*if* your name was Vanderbilt. In examining the generations of Vanderbilt women, I began to understand what it was like to live in the world they lived in and abide by the rules they abided by. I began to look at Society, not as a sociological observer but rather as one who empathized with the plight of these women who were powerless either to control their environment or to move beyond it. In her time, Alice Gwynne Vanderbilt was transformed from a puritanical Sunday School teacher into the most wantonly wasteful and grandiose woman in America. In hers, Gertrude Vanderbilt Whitney, a brilliant, lonely, talented woman with a desperate passion for life, dissipated her energies by leading a secret double life, a dual existence that became so painful to her that sometimes she thought she might go mad. Gloria Morgan Vanderbilt was totally formed by Society; she had absolutely no identity save that which others thrust upon her. Finally, there was little Gloria herself, a winsome, loving child who craved affection but instead found glittering coldness and luxurious isolation in the Society environment which constituted the boundaries of her world.

Through these women, I learned about Society in all its permutations—International Society, Café Society, Old Guard Society—and I came to think of these groups as separate tribes, each with its inflexible rules and regulations; self-created prisons for the spirit. Often I wonder how, without the constraints of Society, these women might have soared, and what they might have become.

Over a period of months, I read and reread more than 7,000 pages of testimony. Then I moved from the trial transcript into the world of that time, following the witnesses on an extended journey that took me over four years and led me across the country, from the pseudorustic 85,000-acre Whitney "camp" in the Adirondacks to the palatial estates of Newport—The Breakers and Marble House (a walk through these houses tells more of the loss of human scale than any research can convey), to Portsmouth's Oakland Farm, Sandy Point Farm; to California—Hollywood and William Randolph Hearst's pleasure palace at San Simeon.

The restless Gloria Morgan Vanderbilt shuttled between New York, Cherbourg, and Southampton the way someone else might drive to the country for a weekend. (By the time she was fifty-three years old, she had crossed the Atlantic more than 120 times, spending almost two years of her life at sea!) I traced Gloria's path to Prince Hohenlohe's castles in Germany; to villas in Monte Carlo, Cannes, and Biarritz; to opulent dwellings in Paris; to a hunting mansion in Leicestershire, England, a town house on Grosvenor Square, a secluded country estate in Sunningdale; and into the innermost circle surrounding Edward, Prince of Wales (who in 1936 became King Edward VIII and in that same year abdicated to marry "the woman I love").

Time after time, common sense became my best guide to truth. At the Vanderbilt trial, Gloria's former fiancé, Prince Gottfried Hohenlohe-Langenburg, crossed the Atlantic to testify to the purity of their relationship. His wife of two and a half years, Princess Margarita, also volunteered to testify as a character witness for Gloria Vanderbilt. While Prince Hohenlohe's gesture struck me as honorable, Princess Margarita's seemed unmotivated—why would someone rush to the defense of her husband's former love? I discovered the answer when I found out that Princess Margarita was not the "German woman" the American press thought her to be. She was, in fact, a princess of Greece and Denmark, granddaughter of Great Britain's Dowager Marchioness of Milford Haven, a niece of George, the second Marquis of Milford Haven, and of Louis Mountbatten—who was to become the world-renowned Earl Mountbatten of Burma and who died in 1979 when his small motorboat was blown up by Irish terrorists. Milford Haven had become the key name at the Vanderbilt custody trial, and it was this name that Margarita had come to defend.

Through a comparison of the American and European newspaper coverage of the Vanderbilt trial, I discovered that there had been a European cover-up of accusations concerning the Milford Haven involvement, due, no doubt, to the fact that the Marquis and Marchioness of Milford Haven were very close to the British royal family. Now, almost fifty years later, the Milford Haven connection to the royal family is stronger than ever. Margarita's brother, the exiled

Prince Philip who appears in this book as a boy, has become Philip, Duke of Edinburgh, married to Elizabeth II, Queen of England.

The setting for this story falls in a strange territory, located somewhere between history and memory. In addition to the usual research methods, this unique location in time has provided me with extraordinary research tools. By deep-blue, oxygen-free light I spent days looking at 1930s nitrate newsreels of the great ocean liners, of the cities and of the people whose lives connected and shaped the story of this custody case. I have seen Edward, Prince of Wales, escorting Gloria Morgan Vanderbilt and her twin sister Thelma, Lady Furness on his arms like matched gems. There is one extraordinary film never shown to the public of Gloria and Thelma showing dresses they have designed. It is the same scene, shot over and over again; and with each take, Gloria becomes more and more despondent while her twin tries to take command of the situation. I have seen people attending sessions of the trial and the crowds that block their way. And finally, I have seen the child herself, at the Supreme Court, at church, at a horse show, being escorted—*carried*—through the frenzied mobs.

In newspaper archives I have seen the power of the Vanderbilt name come clear. Here is Vanderbilt memorabilia dating back to the early 1800s (some of it in such bad condition that it turned to powder in my hands) that again and again pays homage to the Vanderbilts as America's royal family. I have seen the original George B. Post architectural drawings for Alice and Cornelius Vanderbilt's New York palace, and have read Vanderbilt wills and court cases starting with those pertaining to the Commodore, Cornelius Vanderbilt. These documents of men long dead breathe life and tell us much about the appetites and obsessions of those concerned. And in the *Sun* newspaper morgue, I found Whitney documents and affidavits illegally leaked to the newspapers during the trial in an effort to destroy Gloria Morgan Vanderbilt's reputation.

My main resource, however, has been people. The hundreds of interviews conducted for this book often made the past seem more vivid to me than the real world in which I was living. Many people can now speak freely because death has removed their last reason for silence. Time itself has given us the answers to questions unresolved during the trial. We know now that Gloria Morgan Vanderbilt's mother indeed was the "miser" her daughter accused her of being. Other information has worked its way into the light: the second Marquis of Milford Haven was alleged to possess a collection of pornography, and evidence pertaining to pornographic books was introduced at the trial, but at the time no one could prove the collection existed. Today, in the Private Case of the British Museum, is Album 7 from the pornography collection of George Milford Haven, an ordinary blue, leatherette, Army-Navy-store-type photograph album, in which, meticulously hand-mounted and cross-indexed, are some eighty-one items of pornography, illuminating something of George Milford Haven's sexual proclivities, as well as his orderly mind.

Once I had completed a study of the transcript of the *Matter of Vanderbilt*, I assembled from the testimony of the thirty-two witnesses a chronology of the lives and events leading to this trial. By noting dates and locations, a vivid picture of a life began to emerge from seemingly dry data. (We can visualize the nomadic life of Gloria Morgan Vanderbilt when we realize that six months was the longest time she stayed in any one place after her daughter's birth. In one year she made twelve ocean voyages and visited in six countries; during the year 1929 she employed twenty servants and maintained residences in England, France, and Switzerland.) After a chronology was completed, I then assembled each witness's testimony concerning each event. Often one witness held a piece of a puzzle the others knew nothing about. By a parallel study of the various versions of one event I was able to ascertain, for example, that in a six-week period eight physicians had attended little Gloria for a total of more than fifty (unnecessary) visits, and often one physician was unaware that the others were simultaneously treating the child.

There are many mysteries in this story, and it is my intention to take the reader along with me to discover each clue as I discovered it. Together we journey from the seemingly trivial incident of one hysterical little girl who ran away one October afternoon, into a world of wealth and Byzantine complications, and together we come to realize how the past affects the future—irrevocably. And because this story is true, there are no simple explanations of why people act the way they do: the elements that form character and behavior can only partially be illuminated.

At first, I had assumed that if Gloria Morgan Vanderbilt was telling the truth, then Gertrude Vanderbilt Whitney must be lying, or the other way around. But once I had finished my research I realized that they were both telling the truth as they grasped it. The lines of communication between them had broken down to such an extent that neither would tell the other the hard realities of what she thought or felt. These two women found themselves stranded in an emotional and intellectual vacuum of their own creation. Numerous Whitney and Vanderbilt relatives and acquaintances have given me their personal accounts of this conflict; their views differ radically from those of people sympathetic to Gloria Morgan Vanderbilt. Yet both views accurately reflect the positions sincerely held at the time of the trial.

Eventually, I obtained two different copies of the court transcript. One belonged to Herman Finkelstein, who prepared Gloria Morgan Vanderbilt's appeal brief; another to Judge Joseph Proskauer, who performed the same service for Gertrude Vanderbilt Whitney. At one point in the testimony Proskauer wrote a note in the margin that reads, "Child pathetic and neglected," and at exactly the same point Finkelstein wrote a note that reads, "Never alone for a night in her life—nurse or grandmother always there." Another Proskauer note reads, "Child an obstacle in Relator's life." Finkelstein's reads, "Battling for over two years to get her baby back." Where Proskauer wrote, "Relator had lost child's affections," Finkelstein wrote, "Ridiculous! Why did she write,

'if you love me
as I love you
no knife can cut
our love in two.' "

In presenting this story, the only liberty I've taken with the written dialogue is to correct inaccurate spellings and to contract certain words in the quoted material, when it seemed obvious that these words were not actually spoken in the formal manner in which they were recorded ("I am" to "I'm," etc.).

Today there exists a fifty-six-year-old international celebrity, a highly successful woman, Gloria Vanderbilt di Cicco Stokowski Lumet Cooper. I have met this woman (although not in relation to this book) and I admire her for what I have come to know of her talents, her courage, and her genius for survival. But it is little Gloria, the ten-and-a-half-year-old child of the thirties, who obsesses me; a child caught in a tragedy that transcended its own boundaries and whose elements reveal a world that has now vanished. A world where desperation was everywhere and the pathetic Poor Little Rich Girl had an incredible appeal. Where the name Vanderbilt stood for Croesus-like wealth, for immense power, and for a class superiority that at that very moment was slipping away. But that is my story.

HOW & WHY

The Visit: Gloria Morgan Vanderbilt's Version

Then little Gloria will come to me for good and ever.

GLORIA MORGAN VANDERBILT

SATURDAY, SEPTEMBER 15, 1934, 4:00 P.M. The North German Lloyd liner *Europa* docked at Pier 86 at Forty-sixth Street and the Hudson River. The day was gray and overcast, obscuring the sand-castle spires of New York City's skyline, as Gloria Morgan Vanderbilt, the glamorous young widow of Reginald Vanderbilt, emerged from her stateroom with her older sister Consuelo Morgan Thaw following close behind her. Gloria's image had been captured in newspapers scores of times, embarking and disembarking from ocean liners—she was an International Society celebrity, her willowy figure always clothed in the height of fashion, her magnolia-white skin accentuated by dark eyes, dark hair, and vermilion lips. But standing beside her, Consuelo saw nothing glamorous. Gloria was thinner than ever, her stammer more pronounced, and although Consuelo could point to no specific symptom, she was certain that her sister was close to a general nervous breakdown. It was no wonder either; for more than two years, Gloria had been fighting her sister-in-law—her late husband Reginald's sister, the vastly wealthy and powerful Gertrude Vanderbilt

Whitney—to get her own daughter, little Gloria Vanderbilt, returned to her.

Gloria had gone to Germany this time for the specific purpose of obtaining from Prince Gottfried Hohenlohe-Langenburg—her former fiancé, her dear Friedel—affidavits stating that their relationship had been an honorable one. In August, the lawyers for both sides had reached an agreement whereby Gloria was to regain her child within the year, and if Gertrude Whitney honored this agreement Gloria would have no need of these affidavits. But "if" was the operative word. Gloria's lawyer, Nathan Burkan, had heard that Gertrude was still contemplating a court battle. Well, if she wanted a court fight, Gloria was prepared to give it to her!

Gloria's chauffeur was waiting at the pier in her newly purchased Rolls-Royce to drive the sisters to their rented town house on East Seventy-second Street, and as soon as they got home, Gloria rushed to the telephone; her immediate concern was to have little Gloria with her, but the child was still at the Whitney estate, Wheatley Hills, in Old Westbury, Long Island. It was Gertrude Whitney herself who answered the phone, and their conversation began pleasantly enough. "I'm so glad an agreement has been reached," Gloria said cordially.

And Gertrude replied, "Yes, I am too."

Then Gloria explained that her ship had just docked and asked, "What has happened to little Gloria? Everyone is out of town, it's Saturday and I can't get any news."

"Our agreement stands exactly as it did before you went away," Gertrude answered. "That is, I am to have the child for the next year . . . you are to see the child any time you want to . . . you are to have the child for one month during the child's vacation. . . . After that, the question of the child's future will be reopened before Surrogate Foley." Gertrude's voice took on a soothing tone. "Won't you come down tomorrow—any time—to see [little] Gloria?"

Gloria felt herself growing angry. Furious! She didn't want to visit her daughter at Gertrude's—she wanted her baby back. Couldn't that woman understand? God knows she'd told her enough times! And just as she and Burkan had feared, Gertrude was lying about the agreement—changing it to suit her own purpose. Did Gertrude really imagine she would allow herself to be put through this crucifixion *every* year? But Gloria controlled her emotions as she stated *her* understanding: that her daughter would stay with Gertrude for eleven months, that she was to have little Gloria for one month during the child's summer vacation, and then Surrogate Foley would grant to Gloria sole guardianship of the person of her own child and joint guardianship of the child's property. "Then," she concluded firmly, "little Gloria will come to me for good and ever."

Gertrude answered her politely but coldly. "I disagree with you, but I will call my lawyer, Mr. Crocker, and check with him." In any event, Gertrude said, she would send the child in to town for lunch the following day.

It had been a year since little Gloria was at her mother's house, and Gloria felt that whenever she saw the child there was an awkwardness between them; it always took time—and a weaning away from Gertrude's influence—to establish their old relationship. But when little Gloria arrived for lunch on Sunday, she seemed warm and friendly. Gloria noted with satisfaction that her ten-and-a-half-year-old daughter was thin—Gloria detested fat people—and that her dark hair was carefully cropped, bangs barely brushing the top of her winged eyebrows. The child's gray eyes slanted in an almost Oriental fashion, a typical Vanderbilt feature that had particularly pleased the child's grandmother, Alice Gwynne Vanderbilt. As soon as she arrived, little Gloria begged to see the jewelry her mother was keeping for her, so Gloria took her by the hand and led her into the bedroom and opened the safe. Soon mother and daughter were poring over the trinkets and miniature gold cups with the shared enthusiasm of two delighted children discovering a pirate's treasure.

Little Gloria's nurse, Emma Sullivan Keislich, who never left her side, had accompanied the child to her mother's house. After lunch, Gloria noticed that nurse Keislich seemed very eager to leave. This doughy woman with close-cropped gray hair looked a decade older than her forty-three years. Her pigeon breast and wide hips were concealed in a shapeless white uniform; she wore black lace-up shoes. The nurse kept checking her watch and peering out the window to see if the Whitney limousine had returned. The nurse's attitude annoyed Gloria; she hadn't seen her daughter for so long, and now the woman couldn't wait to drag her away. Little Gloria, on the other hand, seemed perfectly happy playing Old Maid with her Aunt Consuelo. Wanting her child so much and thinking what a good time they were having, Gloria rang up Gertrude and asked if little Gloria might stay on for a few days. Gertrude's reply was almost curt. "The child has made no preparations to stay."

"I can send and get her clothes," Gloria said, resenting the fact that she was having to plead for her own child.

But Gertrude held firm; she had "promised" the child that she would be returning to Wheatley Hills that day.

"All right, I'll send her back, but will you send her in over Monday or Tuesday to stay with me for a few days?" asked Gloria.

Gertrude said that she would, but—and Gloria felt there was always a but—the child must be back on the following Sunday because her school opened two days later.

As her daughter and the nurse headed toward the door, Gloria felt a wrenching sense of frustration and loss. She kissed little Gloria goodbye and assured her, "I will see you Tuesday."

And the child looked up and replied simply, "Okay."

Gloria promised herself that this would be the last time she'd let Gertrude Whitney treat her in this high-handed fashion. Gertrude was one of the richest women in America, and she was used to taking whatever she wanted, but she wasn't going to take Gloria's child away from her. Gloria had come to think of Gertrude as unfeeling, willful, cold, and possessed of the same "granite hardness as the sculptures she executed," yet she could remember a time when she had trusted this woman completely, when, in fact, Gertrude had been her favorite member of the Vanderbilt family. How easily, how unsuspectingly, Gloria had been sucked into this terrible situation.

In the spring of 1932, the child's guardians had insisted that Gloria abandon her house in Paris and her beautiful life abroad so that little Gloria could go to school in New York City and be brought up as "an American heiress." Gloria did what the guardians wanted; she rented the house on Seventy-second Street and entered the child in the Chapin School. Late in June, little Gloria had her tonsils out, and since it was then summer, Gertrude Vanderbilt Whitney invited her niece to convalesce at her Long Island estate. That was when Gloria made her fatal mistake—she accepted Gertrude's hospitality. After that summer, Gertrude asked Gloria's permission to have the child stay on until Christmas. Gloria, with no child at home, went abroad. When she returned, Gertrude again asked that little Gloria be permitted to stay on. A pattern had been established. But as time went by, Gloria began to grow uneasy—her child was now surrounded by an almost impenetrable guard of doctors and lawyers who kept advising Gloria to leave the child in Mrs. Whitney's care. Gertrude herself periodically met with Gloria to tell her of the marked improvement in little Gloria's health, how good the country air was for her, how well she was doing in her new school, how many friends she had made. Even Gloria's own mother, Laura Kilpatrick Morgan, kept telling her she must leave the child with Gertrude. It seemed that an army of powerful people had lined up to bar her from her baby. And then, little by little, she began to realize that she might never get little Gloria back; that Gertrude

Vanderbilt Whitney, for reasons Gloria could not fathom, wanted to keep her child.

In all likelihood, Gloria would have fought to regain her daughter sooner had it not been for the love and respect she bore her mother-in-law, Gertrude's mother, Alice Gwynne Vanderbilt, who had been so unstintingly generous to Gloria with her frequent gifts and large checks. When little Gloria first went to stay with Gertrude Whitney, during the summer of 1932, the dowager Vanderbilt had been eighty-eight years old, and Gloria did not want to antagonize her or endanger any legacy that might be coming to herself or her daughter. Then in April of 1934 Alice Gwynne Vanderbilt died and bequeathed Gloria $100,000—not a fortune, but enough to begin a legal battle to get her baby back.

It seemed unimaginable that Gloria was a Vanderbilt without any money to call her own, but that was indeed the case, and Gloria reflected that "the humiliations that grew out of the singular disposal of the Vanderbilt fortune were, at times, unbelievable and insupportable." Since her husband Reginald's death, her only regular means of support had come to her through a Vanderbilt trust fund assigned to her small daughter. Now—after nine years—Gloria still had to go begging to her child's guardians for what she considered was rightfully her own. She could make no decision independently, her every action was questioned, and her resentment was palpable. As Gloria saw her situation, these guardians had been leading her by a halter—but no longer! She didn't care what Gertrude Whitney or the doctors or the lawyers or Mamma Morgan wanted—Gloria wanted her own child and her own life. Her lawyer, Nathan Burkan, had a plan, and she was about to put it into motion.

Tuesday, September 18, 1934, 11:00 a.m. As the Whitney limousine was once more heading toward New York City with little Gloria and her nurse, two police detectives stopped to question Walter Lyle, an attendant at the Warner-Quinlan gas station on 127th Street and Lexington Avenue. Lyle told them exactly what they wanted to know: the man had driven up in a black Dodge sedan last Saturday morning at 10:00 a.m. and had asked for five gallons of gas. "That'll be ninety-eight cents," said Lyle, and the man had handed him a ten-dollar gold certificate. President Franklin D. Roosevelt had called in all gold and gold notes the previous year, so Lyle remarked, "You don't see many of these anymore."

The sandy-haired, dour-looking driver replied, "Oh no? I guess you're right. I only got about a hundred left at home."

Something sounded phony. Lyle took a good look at the man, and when he went inside to make change he wrote the license number of the car on the face of the certificate—4U-13-41.

Two days later the garage owner, Walter Quinlan, made his bank deposit, and a clerk checked the serial number of the certificate. It was part of the $50,000 ransom that had been paid in the Lindbergh kidnapping on the night of April 2, 1932. Forty days after this payment, the body of twenty-one-month-old Charles Augustus Lindbergh, Jr., had been found in a shallow grave in a densely wooded area. His skull had been bashed in.

Tuesday morning's unusually heavy rainfall had left New York City's streets flooded, and it was almost noon when the Whitney limousine finally delivered little Gloria and her nurse to the Seventy-second Street house. Little Gloria left nurse Keislich standing in the entrance hall and bounded up the narrow staircase to her mother's bedroom carrying her tiny puppy in her arms. Her mother was seated at her dressing table, and the child put the dog down and ran across the room, holding her arms out. "Oh, Mummy," she cried, as she wrapped her arms around her mother's long, swanlike neck, and kissed her.

Elizabeth Wann—Mrs. Vanderbilt's personal maid, called Wann by her mistress—was there helping Mrs. Vanderbilt to change her dress. Wann watched the child press her head close to that of her beautiful, fragile mother. Their rich brown hair, the child's only a shade lighter, glowed in the soft, late morning light. (Wann, a slim, spry, forty-three-year-old Scottish woman, had been in Mrs. Vanderbilt's service fourteen months, and in that time had established herself as the most fiercely loyal and sympathetic member of the Vanderbilt staff. Gloria, responding to this attachment, confided in Wann in a manner that was most unusual. She hardly noticed most of her servants; she wasn't even sure how many there had been at her Paris triplex, but once when Wann found her still in bed in the middle of the afternoon, she said, "If I had my child living with me I would have such a different life. . . . What is there to get up for? If I stay in bed I can read a book.")

Little Gloria drew back from the kiss and asked, "Can I go to the movies?"

Her mother wasn't sure how to answer—was this appropriate for a ten-year-old, she wondered—and then she said, "You can go to the movies if the Green Vale School allows you to . . . is that all right?"

"Oh yes it is," the child assured her, and added, as if instructing her mother, "because I have been to the movies."

The film little Gloria wanted to see, *One Night of Love*, starring the beautiful blond singer Grace Moore, was playing at the recently built Radio City Music Hall. Gloria agreed to take her; she loved movies herself and spent a great deal of time at them—movies had always helped her escape when the world seemed too much for her. Grace Moore was special, too, because Reggie Vanderbilt had taken her to see this star in *The Music Box Revue* the night he proposed.

At lunch, little Gloria sat next to her mother. Directly opposite sat the omnipresent nurse Keislich, who enjoyed the privileged-servant status of a nanny: she was permitted to eat in the dining room when accompanied by her charge, otherwise a tray was provided for her in the child's bedroom. Nurse Keislich was fond of saying that she had been with little Gloria "always"; she'd taken the three-week-old infant directly from the hospital and even now she insisted on sleeping in the same room with her. When Gloria asked her daughter questions, the child would often glance across the table at her nurse as if seeking permission and reassurance before answering. Little Gloria called her nurse Dodo and obviously adored her, but Gloria didn't share her daughter's enthusiasm. She found nurse Keislich to be truculent, meddlesome, and extravagant—but a necessary convenience.

It was Mamma Morgan who had actually hired the nurse, and the two women seemed to agree on everything, particularly that Gloria's daughter was the exalted Vanderbilt heiress and had to be indulged and protected within an inch of her life. Gloria chose to stay out of such things. She wasn't even sure if "Miss" or "Mrs." was the nurse's proper form of address, although Keislich had mentioned something about having been married and having had a little boy who had died—Gloria couldn't remember the details. In any case, until recently she had always acquiesced to Mamma's wishes, unable to resist her manipulative, domineering personality and her uncontrollable rage. Besides, she loved Mamma, supporting her from her own small income. She'd even let Mamma live with her until the situation became impossible. Lately Gloria was hurt and bewildered by Mamma's conduct; she could hardly believe that her own mother had turned against her and was siding with Gertrude Whitney.

The rest of the Morgan family was on Gloria's side. There were four Morgan children—the eldest was Harry, then Consuelo and then the twins, Gloria and Thelma. Gloria sensed that all their lives Mamma had tried to pit her children against each other in order to maintain her power, but her strategy hadn't worked: her four children were close, like the survivors of a disaster. Indeed, Gloria and Thelma shared a mystical twinship, they were almost one person, not two, and Consuelo had completely cut herself off from Mamma's influence; she hadn't seen or spoken to her for years. In fact, all the Morgan children agreed that Mamma was crazy and hysterical. She looked eccentric too, like a circus clown, this tiny wren of a woman with her face powdered flour-white, her eyebrows plucked away and replaced by two exaggerated penciled half-moons, her hair dyed ginger-blond. Gloria was convinced that money was her mother's god, that she was "money mad" and obsessed with the idea of being little Gloria's grandmother. She paid hardly any attention to her other grandchildren, but then they weren't Vanderbilts.

Gloria glanced across the table to where her sister was sitting. Two years Gloria's senior, Consuelo was handsome rather than beautiful; it was Gloria and her twin Thelma who were acknowledged to be the beauties of the family. Before Gloria had become a Vanderbilt and Thelma had become Lady Furness, Maury Paul in his Cholly Knickerbocker column had named them "The Magnificent Morgans." But Consuelo was clearly the most self-possessed and efficient of the three sisters; she'd left her husband, Benjamin Thaw, in Oslo and had spent the entire summer with Gloria, trying to help her regain her health and her child. When Gloria had come to Consuelo for help she'd been so upset that she couldn't sleep or eat or keep a thought in her head. Now that they had a plan she felt better, although she still had trouble retaining her food. Glancing significantly at Consuelo, Gloria announced that they would go to the two-thirty movie, but that first she must visit her lawyer.

"Oh Mummy, don't go away, because I'll miss half the picture," wailed little Gloria.

"No, Gloria," her mother replied. "I promise you won't. You can go there first, and I'll join you as soon as I can."

Since Theodore Beesley, the chauffeur of the Pierce-Arrow she kept exclusively for her daughter's use, was off for the day, Gloria arranged for little Gloria to use the Rolls-Royce. Then Charles Zaug, the portly, middle-aged Vanderbilt butler, was sent out into Seventy-second Street to hail a cab for Mrs. Vanderbilt. Not for the first time, Gloria reflected on how her child's priorities always came before her own.

The most logical route to Radio City Music Hall would take little Gloria down Fifth Avenue, a thoroughfare containing much history pertinent to her past. Four blocks down the avenue, at Sixty-eighth Street, the child could not fail to notice 871 Fifth Avenue, Gertrude Vanderbilt Whitney's palatial mansard-roofed château. Even now, Aunt Ger, who had told the child that she planned to spend the week in the city, might be there. One block farther down, at Sixty-seventh Street, stood the fifty-room Gothic limestone mansion that for the seven years before her death had been occupied by Alice Gwynne Vanderbilt, little Gloria's grandmother. The shades in the windows were drawn now, as if the mansion, too, were dead. Little Gloria had one painful memory of her paternal grandmother: two summers previously she'd been in Newport and had gone to play with her cousins at The Breakers. Her grandmother descended her marble staircase, stopped and stared at the children. They stared back silently. Then she said, "Who are these children?" Little Gloria had "wanted to cry. I thought, she's my grandmother! Why doesn't she know me?"

Still farther down the avenue, the sidewalks became crowded with shoppers and strollers. The two-way traffic moved slowly past the windows of Bergdorf Goodman which were featuring newly arrived copies from the leading Paris couturiers. Bergdorf's occupied the site of what had once been the block-long mansion of little Gloria Vanderbilt's grandparents, Alice and Cornelius II, who had lived there for forty-seven years in the largest private city residence in the world. In 1893, *The New York Times* called it "the marvel of America" and noted that the entrance hall alone was "conspicuously larger than the Supreme Court of the United States." Little Gloria's father, Reginald Vanderbilt, and her aunt, Gertrude Vanderbilt Whitney, and their brothers and sister had grown up in this house, princes and princesses in a family of American royalty, their house marking the uptown boundary of Society in a time when seven Vanderbilt mansions dominated the avenue from Fifty-first to Fifty-eighth Street. One of these Vanderbilt mansions, 640 Fifth Avenue, though only half the original structure, remained the largest private residence in the city. It had belonged to the child's great-grandfather, William Henry Vanderbilt, son of the Commodore, Cornelius Vanderbilt, the founder of the clan. Although he'd been a generous father and philanthropist, William Henry was remembered for one unfortunate remark: "The public be damned!" Little Gloria Vanderbilt's uncle, Cornelius III, and his wife Grace, the present owners of this edifice, were not now in residence; no doubt they were escaping the incredible noise of the blasting of bedrock taking place across the street, where the entire block from Fiftieth to Fifty-first Street and from Fifth to Sixth Avenue was cordoned off by an eight-foot-high wooden fence behind which the construction of the Rockefeller Center complex was providing thousands of desperately needed jobs.

The Vanderbilt Rolls-Royce turned the corner onto Sixth Avenue and pulled up in front of Radio City Music Hall, a shining gem dominating the dingy latticework of the Sixth Avenue elevated. Little

Gloria, her nurse, and her aunt entered the Music Hall's block-long foyer, ablaze with mirrors and chandeliers, and proceeded up the sweeping staircase into the mezzanine of the theater, where they sat facing a gold curtain set into a series of golden arches evoking a sixty-foot-high stylized sunset. Organ music swelled, and as the strains of "Don't Blame Me" filled the theater, the curtain was suffused with red light which faded into a warm purple and deepened almost imperceptibly into a piercing blue that shimmered gradually into a sea of green and then amber. . . .

While little Gloria waited for the movie to begin, Gloria Vanderbilt was seeing Nathan Burkan in his law offices, which occupied the entire twenty-fifth floor of 1450 Broadway. Burkan's offices were plain in the extreme—a rabbit warren of tiny partitioned cubicles in the center of the floor, and small offices clustered around them under the windows. The atmosphere here was one of homey chaos, which was not unlike the personality of Burkan himself, he being short, plump, pugnacious, and brilliant, a man with a prickly outside and a custard-cream center. Burkan was the most famous of the so-called show-business lawyers. A founder of the American Society of Composers, Authors and Publishers, he represented giant film companies, theater and film stars, private businessmen, and Café Society celebrities in trouble.

Burkan had felt protective toward Gloria Vanderbilt since that first day when his friend and client A. C. (Blumie) Blumenthal had literally brought her in by the hand to see him. She'd been tearful and overwrought and he'd had to figure things out for himself, but finally he'd realized that although Gloria saw the situation in emotional terms, there were two practical issues here—the child's money and her custody—and they were interwined. This poor creature was caught in a circular trap: her daughter's guardians wouldn't give her enough to live on because the child wasn't with her—over a two-year period her income had been cut from $48,000 a year to only $9,000—but they refused to allow the child to return to her. In gradual stages they were easing her out of both financial support and the custody of her own daughter. "Oh, Mr. Burkan, I'm so confused. I don't know what's happening to me," she'd cried out plaintively that first day.

Burkan had been astounded by Gloria Vanderbilt's naïveté and bewilderment. She was not at all the way he had imagined her from the newspapers: they said she was an international beauty, and she *was* lovely, but in a quiet, well-groomed, natural way. "She's just a little slip of a thing with a big name," Burkan told an associate. "She's wet behind the ears." For all his famous clientele, Burkan was a conservative family man who lived a quiet domestic life. He knew very little about Gloria Vanderbilt, but he sized her up as "a sweet, innocent kid." Burkan felt he was good at sizing people up. And he had a way of giving his heart to his clients; he carried their troubles with him.

Even though Burkan knew she couldn't pay him, he'd given her good advice, and once she came into that legacy from Alice Gwynne Vanderbilt, they had the money to get going legally. Burkan was convinced that there had been a real injustice done here. After consulting with his associates, he decided that the only solution was for Gloria to file a petition in the Surrogates' Court to become sole guardian of her child's person and co-guardian of her child's property. In that way, she could both regain her daughter and obtain a voice in her own financial affairs. Unexpectedly, Gloria's own mother, Laura Kilpatrick Morgan, and Gertrude Vanderbilt Whitney formed an alliance to oppose the petition. Finally, a tentative agreement was reached, but now it was clear that Mrs. Whitney intended to break it. What she'd said on the telephone to Gloria was a bold-faced lie, a call for action on their part.

That afternoon Burkan instructed Gloria to rent a house in Old Westbury near little Gloria's school, without asking the child's guardians for the money, so they'd know nothing of the plan. If everyone insisted that country life was so healthy for her daughter, it would be provided, but she would take the child. Then Gloria would be the one holding the trump card.

Gloria Vanderbilt slipped into a seat next to her little girl. Before their eyes, Grace Moore, as an innocent American abroad who becomes an opera diva, was transformed into Madame Butterfly and Carmen. Then, when the film was over, the stage show began. From the orchestra pit a huge stage, on which twelve baby-grand pianos were massed, mysteriously levitated. After a moment, the curtain drew back to reveal a full orchestra. "Oh Mummy, look, look. Isn't this marvelous. Isn't this beautiful!" the child murmured. After the orchestral performance came a dance act, a glee club of 150, and some daring acrobats. Then out strutted the Rockettes dressed as Quaker girls, and at last the forty-six beautiful girls began their high-kicking routine, legs moving with piston precision. It was ten minutes to five when the vast stage darkened and two exaggerated cigarette embers began to glow in "Two Cigarettes in the Dark," a sensual dance routine involving intertwined lovers. The nurse shifted uncomfortably in her seat and after a few moments leaned over and whispered to little Gloria that it was time to go. "Mummy, do say I can stay a few minutes longer," begged the child. Consuelo Thaw was pleased to note that her sister said little Gloria might stay. Nurse Keislich was such a prude and spoilsport!

The grand finale was worth staying for. The cast of hundreds gathered on the immense stage, with the Rockettes dancing on top of the pianos. Then the gold curtains swooped closed and the organ console ushered them out onto an oddly deserted Sixth Avenue where shops were bolted shut as the eve of Yom Kippur, the Jewish Day of Atonement, approached with the sunset.

The moment they returned home nurse Keislich ordered the child upstairs to bed, but little Gloria paused to kiss her mother and ask, "Will you come and kiss me good night again when I go to bed?"

"Yes, of course, dear," replied Gloria.

Wann brought little Gloria her dinner on a tray. When she entered the room the child was sitting up in bed and the nurse was standing in front of the fireplace frowning into the flames; she turned to Wann and complained that the grate was too low, so that the fire wasn't burning properly. Wann promptly found a higher grate, but instead of thanking her, the nurse remarked that the room was damp. Wann recalled how Mrs. Thaw had lived in this lovely room all summer without complaint and how she'd given it up and taken a small back bedroom for the child's sake. But with this nurse there was always something wrong. On leaving the room, Wann passed Mrs. Vanderbilt, shook her head in disapproval, and being outspoken, remarked how unusual it was that such a healthy child, so full of vitality, should be put to bed at six o'clock and have both dinner and breakfast on a tray. That nurse acted as if she were dealing with an invalid, always hanging over the child as if she were made of crystal. Wann thought it foolish to treat a child that way; foolish and strange. When Gloria went in to kiss her daughter good night, she asked the nurse if it really was necessary for the child to spend so many hours in bed. Nurse Keislich replied that she was simply carrying out the orders of the child's doctor, William St. Lawrence.

Wednesday morning the child ate a light breakfast in bed, and since the day was sunny and warm, nurse Keislich decided to take her to Central Park. Instead of walking the short distance, the nurse asked that Theodore Beesley, little Gloria's own chauffeur, drive them. At Seventy-ninth Street and Fifth Avenue she instructed Beesley to park the car and then meet them at the base of Cleopatra's Needle, a nickname given the 69½-foot, 3,500-year-old granite shaft located in Central Park at Eighty-fourth Street. (It is doubtful that either the child or her nurse knew that in 1861 this monument had been presented to the city by the child's great-grandfather, William Henry Vanderbilt.) Beesley, a thin young man who bore a striking resemblance to the dapper former mayor, Jimmy Walker, did as he was told; spotting little Gloria, he watched from a discreet distance as she began roller-skating. He noticed how isolated the child seemed—she didn't speak to any of the other children playing around her.

When they returned from the park the child came dashing into her mother's bedroom. Gloria had just washed her hair and was seated at her dressing table, a brush in her hand. "Mummy, I have a new game. Come on and play it," said her daughter.

"Just as soon as I put my hair up," replied her mother, parting her hair in the middle and deftly squeezing waves down the right side of her head and securing them with thin metal clips. She always wore her hair classically waved and drawn back in a chignon secured with hairpins at the nape of her neck. Gloria and her twin, Thelma, had worn their hair this way since they were teenagers. Now it was more fashionable than ever.

Consuelo, who was sitting nearby, volunteered, "I'll play the game with you," so little Gloria spread it out on the rug—it was a game with brightly colored tiny wooden horses that raced down a board—and the child and her aunt played until lunch was announced. After eating, little Gloria asked if she could rest in the library because she wanted to be close to her mother. Then after her rest she asked if Dodo could take her to see her cousin Nancy, one of Aunt Ger's grandchildren, who was in Doctors Hospital recovering from a tonsil operation. Over the years Gloria had become so used to acquiescing in her child's wishes that she replied almost automatically, "Oh, yes, of course you can go there."

It was late afternoon when the child and her nurse returned, and as they walked past the library door Gloria called them in. Soon the butler, Charles Zaug, brought in a pitcher of orange juice and a bucket of ice. Gloria, whose favorite cocktail was an orange blossom, poured orange juice and gin into a shiny silver shaker, wound a key at its base, and then touched a button on the shaker's side. The contents whirled around, churned by a metal propeller. Little Gloria begged, "Oh, Mummy, may I push the button?"

"Why, yes, of course."

Gloria poured the drink into a cocktail glass and asked her daughter to hand it to her aunt Consuelo. Then Gloria reached for another glass and asked her daughter, "Would you like a little orange juice?"

Instead of replying, little Gloria looked at her nurse, who shook her head. Then the child said, "No. I don't like orange juice."

"I thought you had it every morning," remarked her mother in surprise, but before she could pursue the subject the phone rang, and soon Gloria was speaking excitedly: "Yes, Mrs. Thaw is here. And we are going to fight!" When the phone conversation came to an end, Gloria took her daughter into a small adjoining sitting room to have a private moment with her—it was important for them to get back to being the way they used to be. "When was the last time you saw Naney?" Gloria asked, using the child's pet name for Mamma Morgan.

The child seemed to be searching for the answer before she replied, "I can't remember."

How odd! thought Gloria, and after the child went upstairs she asked nurse Keislich, "Has little Gloria seen her grandmother recently?"

"Yes," replied the nurse, calculating that it was only two days since Mrs. Morgan had visited the child.

And Gloria mused aloud, not really as a question requiring an answer, but more as a statement of surprise, "Why did she lie to me."

Gloria was determined to rent a house in Old Westbury as soon as possible. She spent all day Thursday with Sidney Ripley, a real estate agent and friend of her late husband, and when they returned from Long Island late in the afternoon, little Gloria and her nurse joined them in the library. Mr. Ripley smiled at the little girl. "My goodness, how she looks like Reggie. And how big she's grown." He held his two palms out facing each other, about a foot apart. "I haven't seen you since you were a little tot about that big." His voice dropped to the pseudoconfidential tone people tend to use with children. "And you don't know what we've been doing all afternoon. We've gone down to Long Island and picked out the loveliest house. And you're going to be so happy with your mother."

Little Gloria tilted her head and said, "Oh." Nothing more.

Friday, September 21, 10:30 a.m. Nurse Keislich was alone in the child's bedroom when Mrs. Vanderbilt came in and told her that she'd just received word that she could take possession of the Long Island house immediately. They would move tomorrow or the next day. The child was not going back to Mrs. Whitney.

Gloria could see the disapproval on Keislich's face—this complaining, difficult woman. Well, it was just a matter of time until she would no longer be needed; soon it would be time for a governess to take over. Gloria looked around the spacious room and saw that the floor was literally covered with Shredded Wheat and fragments of toast for the puppy. In the center of the debris lay a single white sock. This simply would not do; since the child was going to live with her, the nurse had better learn a thing or two about neatness. "This is like a pigpen," Gloria said, paying the nurse back for that sour face.

"I will sweep it up," Keislich snapped back.

"No, the maid will do it," said Mrs. Vanderbilt.

Keislich disregarded her completely; she turned and left the room abruptly, returning a moment later with a carpet sweeper. While Mrs. Vanderbilt stood there, the nurse furiously ran the sweeper back and forth across the carpet.

Following what was now an established routine, Beesley drove the nurse and the child to Central Park, parked the limousine, and then watched the child while she romped with her jump rope and roller-skated under Cleopatra's Needle. When they returned to the house little Gloria played a game of Slap Jack with her mother. Wann, walking past the library door, observed with satisfaction how happy little Gloria seemed to be. And at lunch, when Charles passed the silver platter, Gloria noticed that the child's appetite was excellent: she ate three French lamb chops and several helpings of rice. When dessert arrived Gloria mentioned that on Sunday they would all be moving down to the house in Old Westbury.

After lunch the child went upstairs for her rest as usual. Gloria told Charles Zaug to prepare for the move on Sunday. Then she went to her bedroom and began to pay her monthly bills. Finding themselves alone, Zaug whispered agitatedly into Beesley's ear. Beesley decided to risk it; he moved quickly to the phone and placed a brief call.

At about three o'clock little Gloria dropped into her mother's bedroom dressed in her English tweed coat and carrying her roller skates under her arm. Looking at the papers spread out in front of her mother, she asked, "What are you doing?"

"I'm writing out checks."

"How do you do it?"

Gloria showed her how you subtract the check from the number and write the balance.

"Oh, I don't like arithmetic," little Gloria said.

"Arithmetic is a very useful thing," replied her mother, saying what she thought was best for the child to hear and not revealing that she didn't like arithmetic either.

The little girl asked if she might ask Charles for some bread crumbs to feed the pigeons in the park and of course Gloria said yes.

Little Gloria hugged her. "Goodbye, Mummy," she said, "I'll see you later."

Just before four, Gloria finished the last of the checks. Then she remembered that she had to get some sheets for the servants to use at the Long Island house. She was expecting some friends to stop by in half an hour, but there was no controlling her sudden urge, she had to get those sheets right away, so she dashed off with Consuelo to Bloomingdale's. They were back in three-quarters of an hour—fifteen minutes late for the friends, but luckily they didn't show up. Consuelo suggested they settle down to a game of bezique that was interrupted only once, when Tom Gilchrist—one of little Gloria's guardians—phoned to discuss the question of registering little Gloria at the Chapin School sometime in the future. Gloria no longer trusted Tom, not since that day a year ago when he'd told her that he thought of himself solely as the guardian of the child's property and that "if there is any controversy, why, you mustn't consider that you can rely on me. . . ." Gloria deliberately kept the conversation vague, telling him nothing of her plans.

Gloria was once again absorbed in their game when she glanced at her watch and exclaimed, "Why, it's twenty minutes past six. I haven't heard Gloria. Maybe she's in her room."

She went to the child's bedroom. The puppy was gone, but everything else was still there. A rumpled blue bathrobe lay on the floor, a pair of fleece-lined brown bedroom moccasins peeking out from beneath its folds. On top of the dresser stood a small statuette of Jesus. And in front of the dresser, rummaging through the drawers, stood Charles Zaug.

"What are you doing here?" demanded Mrs. Vanderbilt.

"The chauffeur is downstairs, madam. They have sent for Miss Gloria's watch," replied Zaug.

Gloria rushed downstairs and confronted Theodore Beesley. "What have you done with Miss Gloria?"

Beesley muttered something about the child being very sick and that he'd taken her to Mrs. Whitney's. Gloria ordered him to leave at once and bring little Gloria back to Seventy-second Street. Then she rushed to the phone, called Gertrude Whitney, and demanded, "What has happened? Where is Gloria?" Gertrude explained that the child was ill, crying and hysterical. "*Where* is she?" Gloria asked again: her child might be in any number of places—at Gertrude's studio, at her town house, in the country at Wheatley Hills.

"She is here at my house," came the reply.

Gloria slammed down the phone and called out to Consuelo, "Put on your coat, we're going to Gertrude Whitney's." They rushed out

Gloria Morgan Vanderbilt

Gertrude Vanderbilt Whitney

Little Gloria

into the street, hailed a taxi, and drove the few blocks to 871 Fifth Avenue. When a liveried footman opened the door they rushed up the wide white marble staircase into the enormous reception hall where Gertrude Whitney waited. Seeing this austere, imposing woman, who was old enough to be her mother, Gloria felt terror flood over her and her lips began to tremble. Consuelo spoke to her sister in Spanish. "Don't be afraid," she said. Gloria steadied herself, noticing that Gertrude was also upset, and the thought flashed through her mind that Gertrude had not planned things this way. Gloria again asked Gertrude what had happened, and Gertrude answered that she really didn't know; the child had been brought to her in a hysterical condition and she could think of nothing else but to call a doctor.

Gloria asked to see her child and Gertrude led them into a bathroom where little Gloria stood with nurse Keislich at her side. The child seemed all right, but it was obvious from her blotched red face that she'd been crying. Gloria turned to that dreadful nurse who had spirited her child away and said, "I will never forgive you for what you did . . . get out of this room." The nurse obeyed her order and once she'd gone Gloria turned to her daughter and asked, "What is the matter?"

The child looked up at her mother, then with a sudden movement she thrust her arms around Gertrude Whitney's waist and hung on for dear life, shrieking, "Take her away. Don't let her hurt me. I'm frightened. . . . Oh, don't let her take me. . . . Don't let her come near me. She's going to kill me!"

"Gloria, what are you frightened about? What has happened?" Gloria asked. She was stunned. In response, little Gloria started screaming—long, eerie, piercing screams—and she shrank from her mother as if she expected to be hit. Gertrude eased the child into an adjoining bedroom, but little Gloria wouldn't let go of her aunt and they sat on the bed joined together by the child's hysterical embrace. Gloria, afraid that if she came near she'd frighten little Gloria even more, pulled a chair up to the foot of the bed and sat utterly still as her daughter went on screaming and screaming, and between the screams sobbing out, "I hate her. I hate her. Don't let her come near me. Don't let her take me."

Gloria couldn't bear it. It broke her heart to see her own child shrinking at the very sight of her. Her baby had never acted this way toward her, never been frightened, never said she hated her. What had they done to her?

Dr. Stuart Craig came into the room, followed by a white-uniformed nurse. Gloria thought Craig an odd choice for a moment like this—he wasn't a pediatrician but an eminent eye, ear, nose, and throat specialist who had removed the child's tonsils and adenoids and had treated Gloria herself for a throat abscess. Dr. Craig firmly suggested that everyone leave the room so that he and his nurse could quiet the desperate child.

Gertrude, Gloria, and Consuelo went into an adjoining sitting room and Gloria asked to see the nurse. Keislich entered the room and sat on the very edge of the sofa.

"Nurse, what happened?" demanded Gloria.

The nurse sprang to her feet, her fat body quivering with emotion. "No wonder the child is in this condition in that hole you've put her in."

"What hole are you referring to?" Gloria asked, incredulous.

Keislich replied with a torrent of accusations and invective. The house Mrs. Vanderbilt lived in was not fit for pigs and she herself was a hypocrite; maybe she wore white gloves, but underneath! . . . No wonder the child was in hysterics, since her mother objected to her having dogs and complained because there were a few pieces of Shredded Wheat in the room. . . .

Gloria cut in. "It was not a few pieces, the whole room was littered with Shredded Wheat and pieces of bread. It looked like a pigsty. I am not going to have my daughter brought up in a place that looks like that. You should be neater."

Keislich muttered. "Ah, what I could say. And what I am going to say!"

"You can say the rest in court," Gloria told her, and dismissed Emma Sullivan Keislich on the spot. After the nurse left the room, Gloria turned to Gertrude and said, "Gertrude, what do you think of that?"

And Gertrude answered, "I have never heard anything so rude in my life."

"You see I have to fire the woman?"

"You are quite right, Gloria. You cannot possibly keep her," agreed Gertrude, in a tone Gloria took to be extremely sympathetic.

After a time Dr. Craig came in and said that the child was calm enough to see her mother now, but as Gloria reentered the bedroom little Gloria, pale as a bedsheet, whispered a warning, "Don't come near me."

"Why?" asked her mother, in a voice of forced calm.

The child hesitated, and then answered pitifully, "You've got a cold. You mustn't kiss me."

"You're quite right. I have a sore throat. Good night, darling.

God bless you and sleep well," said her mother—anything to avoid another hysterical fit. She knew it was useless to try to force the child to come home with her that night. But the next morning, following Nathan Burkan's instructions, she arrived back at Gertrude's with Consuelo and Dr. Frederick Hunt, a child specialist, in tow. Dr. Craig was already there, but Gloria insisted that Dr. Hunt examine the child as well, and told Gertrude, "If she is well enough to come back to me . . . I certainly am going to take my baby back."

At that moment little Gloria entered the room. She seemed normal and she put her arms around her mother and kissed her and said, "Hello, Mummy." Then she began to play with her puppy, but she was extremely fidgety and after a few minutes said to her mother in a low stammering voice that resembled Gloria's own, "I think I'd like to go now," and her mother gave her permission to leave.

Drs. Craig and Hunt both examined little Gloria and later Dr. Hunt told Gloria that it would take some time to win the child back. And Gloria understood from what he said that little Gloria's mind had been poisoned against her. How foolish she'd been to listen to all those people who'd said that she should leave her child with Gertrude! In that household they'd twisted little Gloria's emotions until she imagined her own mother to be a monster.

Gloria turned to Gertrude and said with furious resolve, "All your money, all your position, all the power of your influence—use it. You will find it is not strong enough to kidnap a child from its mother." An hour later Gloria burst into Nathan Burkan's office and told him what had happened. "Get me that child," she demanded. "They're poisoning her against me. They're doing terrible things to my baby!"

Burkan explained that the only measure open to them was to secure a writ of habeas corpus. "That's a legal demand, it says in effect, you bring the child to court and we'll discuss it. I don't want to take that legal action if I can avoid it. I'd prefer to talk to Frank Crocker informally when he gets back to town on Monday."

"Oh, no," exclaimed Gloria, "I won't wait any longer. I want her now. God only knows what they're doing to my child!"

Burkan argued that since it was Saturday he doubted if a writ could be signed, but Gloria was so insistent that he finally located Justice Alfred Frankenthaler of the New York Supreme Court, who signed the writ.

Later Gloria would create a fantasy about what happened next; perhaps she may have even convinced herself that her fantasy was true. Gloria would imagine that she'd rushed home and initiated a series of international phone calls: first to Prince Friedel and his wife, the former Princess Margarita of Greece and Denmark, who promised to take the next boat. Then to her brother Harry Morgan and his wife Edith, who also promised to come as soon as possible. Finally, in this version of reality, Gloria reached her twin sister Thelma at Claridge's in London, where she was with Aly Khan, attending a ball he was giving for his father, the Aga Khan. Gloria begged Thelma to catch the *Empress of Britain*, which was sailing the next morning.

"Do you realize it's three o'clock in the morning in England and if the boat sails at eight it gives me but a few hours . . ." said Thelma.

"Yes, darling, I realize it. Catch that steamer," replied her twin.

In a silver lamé evening dress and dancing slippers Thelma arrived in Southampton and caught the *Empress*.

All of this was pure invention—the way it might have been, but wasn't. In fact, it was two weeks later, on October 6, that Thelma, Lady Furness, and Harry Morgan sailed on the *Empress of Britain*. Prince and Princess Hohenlohe embarked on the *Bremen* October 9. On Saturday afternoon, September 22, Gloria had no need of their aid. She already had obtained the affidavits from Hohenlohe denying the accusations her mother had made against her, and Nathan Burkan had told her that there was nothing in the law that warranted depriving her of her child in favor of Gertrude Whitney; only in cases of the most extreme unfitness could a mother be refused this natural right. It was not until October 2 that Nathan Burkan inadvertently elicited from Gloria's French maid, Maria Caillot, an accusation against Gloria so shocking that it would reverberate around the world and strike at the very core of the British royal family.

Now, ten days before that, Gloria was optimistic, more determined than ever to do whatever was necessary to get her child back. She would not stand by while the imperious Gertrude Whitney violated the Surrogate's agreement. The child was being detained at her aunt's unlawfully. A mother had a right to her own child.

She would not let them kidnap little Gloria.

The Visit: Gertrude Vanderbilt Whitney's Version

I hate my mother.

LITTLE GLORIA VANDERBILT

SATURDAY, SEPTEMBER 15, 1934, 5:15 P.M.; the day of Gloria Vanderbilt's arrival on the *Europa*, the time that Gloria telephoned Gertrude Whitney to ask for little Gloria. But this version of what happened is filtered through the intelligence of Gertrude Vanderbilt Whitney and those around her. And that makes all the difference.

Gertrude sat quietly holding the telephone to her ear while her right hand moved rhythmically to and from her mouth as she puffed on her cigarette. At fifty-nine, her years had at last caught up with her. Her five-foot-eight-inch figure, once willowy and lithe, now seemed painfully thin and sinewy. Her skin had a grayish cast, attesting to her chain-smoking and poor circulation. Her face in repose looked rough-hewn, with the rather coarse features that made the Vanderbilt men so handsome. At nineteen, Gertrude's intense green eyes had looked at her own image in a mirror and concluded, ". . . you are shy and foolish, your waist is big, your hands and arms badly formed, your features out of proportion, your face red . . ." With cool determination she had transformed herself into an exotic beauty. Just as, with extreme objectivity, she had come to accept the fact that she was a great heiress, using her vast fortune to move beyond the constraints of her social kingdom into a heady bohemian world of art and the sensual pleasures of many lovers. But this side of her life was known to only a few trusted intimates since, above all, Gertrude Vanderbilt Whitney prized the privacy which protected her from censure. Her upbringing had given her the tools with which to conceal both her bohemian life and her feelings: to avoid confrontation, to remain always in control—these were the marks of good breeding. Carefully hidden was the Gertrude who saw herself as "restless . . . a lonely, selfish, weak person with violent desires and wild dreams of impossible things." All that most people were permitted to see was the formidable dowager: mother of three, grandmother of eight, chatelaine of vast estates, sculptor, patron saint of American artists, creator of the Whitney Museum of American Art.

Gertrude sat listening to Gloria's silky, stammering voice coming through the telephone, full of pretended naïveté. It had been blessedly quiet the last three weeks with Gloria in Europe, but here she was, popping up again like the proverbial bad penny, explaining breathlessly that she'd just landed and asking, "What has happened to little Gloria? Everyone is out of town. It's Saturday, and I can't get any news."

What in the world did Gloria think had happened? Nothing had changed. Gertrude answered her patiently. "Our agreement stands exactly as it did before you went away . . . I am to have the child for the next year . . . you are to see the child any time you want to . . . you are to have the child for one month during the child's vacation. . . . After that, the question of the child's future will be reopened before Surrogate Foley." Then, like a small child reciting a lesson, Gloria began repeating the agreement back to Gertrude, and the terms were all the same. Except for one—the crucial one: Gloria was insisting that the child was to be handed over to her in a year's time, no matter what! Immediately Gertrude was on guard. This was a blatant lie, and an absolute violation of their agreement, and Gloria followed it up by demanding that the child be sent to her for lunch on the following day. Twice before Gloria had tried to snatch little Gloria from Gertrude; perhaps this was another trick. But if Gertrude refused to let the child visit her mother, Gloria could claim it was Gertrude who had broken their agreement and use this as a legal means to take the child. A wary Gertrude agreed to send little Gloria to town on Sunday but as soon as she hung up she called her lawyer to make sure she'd done the correct thing.

The following morning, Gertrude awoke to a Sunday headline in the New York *American* that read:

MRS. REGGIE VANDERBILT
WILL FIGHT FOR HER CHILD

> . . . This is the calm before the storm . . . when the fight is carried to open court—as it surely will be unless Mrs. "Reggie" Vanderbilt has her daughter returned to her—the "dirt" that will be "dished" will cause more than one Park Avenue face to turn an ash-can hue. Mrs. Vanderbilt is determined to have her child—no matter whose reputation suffers. And every mother in the U.S.A. will sympathize with her and say she is right . . .

So Gloria was preparing to wage an "open court" battle, and how like this silly woman to carry her fight into the newspapers. This article had been written by Gloria's friend Maury Paul under his pen name of Cholly Knickerbocker, so of course it was totally sympathetic to her. What a maddening and demeaning way for Gertrude to learn such vital information—by reading it in the newspapers. Well, she shouldn't be surprised; that's how she'd found out about Gloria's adulterous relationship with that Café Society promoter they called Blumie. Gertrude loathed publicity, but Gloria seemed to live her entire life in print, with absolutely no regard for dignity. Indeed, her face appeared yet again in this same Sunday paper in a full-page advertisement for Pond's Cold Cream. To make a few dollars, Gloria was posing like a common model, trading on the Vanderbilt name. This woman would do almost anything for money. Gertrude's late husband, Harry Payne Whitney, had pegged Gloria Morgan Vanderbilt years ago. In 1924, the year of little Gloria's birth, he'd written to Gertrude, "Regi was drunk and apparently is most of the time . . . Gloria is no good . . ."

Gertrude's dark-haired little niece came into her bedroom, sat down very close to her, and asked, "Do I have to go and have lunch with my mother?"

"Yes, you do," Gertrude answered. She didn't explain to the child that she couldn't violate the terms of a legal agreement; instead, she said, "Your mother has been away and she wants to see you."

"I don't want to see my mother. I don't want to go. I'm afraid of my mother."

"There's nothing to be afraid about," Gertrude reassured her. "Your mother wants you to go to lunch and you will be coming back in the afternoon."

"Well, I'll go," little Gloria answered, "but I don't want to."

Sunday afternoon, not two hours after Gertrude had sent the child to town, the rumblings of trouble began. The phone rang and Gloria, with some lame excuse about their all having fun, asked Gertrude's permission to keep the child. Did Gloria really think for an instant that Gertrude would be taken in so easily? She replied with no display of emotion that she'd given her promise to her niece that she would be coming back that very afternoon. Then Gloria asked if little Gloria could be sent back to town the following week, and Gertrude had no choice but to agree. However, she cautioned Gloria that little Gloria must return to Wheatley Hills the following Sunday in order to get ready for the opening of the Green Vale School.

Gertrude was caught in a personal and legal vise that was slowly but inexorably tightening; the last thing she wanted was a legal action, but she had no choice. Because of the terrible truths she had learned about Gloria, and knowing how little Gloria felt about her mother, for over a year she'd been consulting a battery of lawyers to find means to protect her niece. Frank Crocker was the captain of her legal Praetorian guard; he'd been her husband's legal and business adviser until Harry's death in 1930, and Gertrude relied on him in all matters. Then there was Thomas Gilchrist, the guardian of little Gloria's property, who had proved himself to be Gertrude's most valuable ally, and Walter Dunnington, who'd been engaged to represent Mrs. Morgan when she'd volunteered to legally oppose her daughter's petition to take custody of little Gloria and control of the child's money.

After a series of meetings, it was agreed that unless it was absolutely necessary, the Whitney lawyers would try "to keep out any mention of immorality, but base everything on neglect and indifference. . . ." In the eventuality that anything of a scandalous nature concerning Gloria had to be said, her own mother would be the one to say it. Gertrude would remove herself from this mudslinging. If called upon, she'd only say exactly what she'd said to Gloria all along: that little Gloria was doing so well at Wheatley Hills; she'd made friends; she was progressing nicely at the Green Vale School; she was in good health; that all Gertrude wanted was to keep her niece in this healthy country atmosphere as long as possible.

The Whitney lawyers had assured Gertrude that there would be no problem in effectively squelching Gloria's petition, and Mrs. Morgan added her assurances that her daughter could never stand up to a court battle—not with everything they knew about her. They'd engaged the right people to gather the facts about Gloria Vanderbilt's past life and conduct, and they'd begun obtaining affidavits to oppose her. This seemed the most logical way to proceed, but somehow things weren't going according to logic; that irrational woman didn't seem to realize what was at stake. To everyone's amazement, Gloria refused to withdraw her petition. Just six weeks ago, Surrogate James A. Foley had been able to effect an agreement—a shaky truce that was the only thing that now stood between them and a court case. It had finally dawned on Gertrude that if she didn't want to face a court fight, she'd have to consider sending little Gloria back to her mother. That is, *if* little Gloria was willing to return.

On Monday, at Gertrude's request, Mrs. Morgan came to Wheatley Hills to ask her granddaughter once again if she wanted to go back to her mother. Little Gloria said she didn't want to go back, and she wouldn't go back, and "I hate my mother." So Gertrude would just have to find some other way out. She couldn't in all good conscience *force* her dear dead brother's child back to the life she'd once led with people who clearly did not have her best interests at heart.

Tuesday morning's newspaper headlines proclaimed that Gertrude's first cousin, Harold Stirling Vanderbilt, skipper of the *Rainbow*, had lost the first of the America's Cup races in Newport. Gertrude's brother Neily and many of her friends were in Newport, but she felt she must stay put at Wheatley Hills to deal with this unpleasant matter. Gertrude waited until late in the morning to tell little Gloria that she was going back to town because she didn't want to upset her. When she finally told her, little Gloria protested, "Oh, I can't go and stay with my mother. I don't want to go. I don't want to see her. I don't feel *happy* with her." Again, Gertrude didn't explain that legally she had no other choice; instead, she tried gentle persuasion. "Your mother wants to see you. Your mother's very fond of you. I'm sure you will have a very nice time." And she promised, "Gloria, you *will* be back by the end of the week."

"Are you sure?" asked little Gloria, and she repeated the question several times.

"Yes, I am sure," replied Gertrude.

Nurse Keislich rang the doorbell and Charles Zaug answered her ring. Little Gloria disappeared up the stairs carrying her puppy. Keislich went up to the bedroom they had been assigned, with the elaborate flowered-chintz-covered Louis XVI bed and the second bed, which had been put in the room for her. She opened the child's suitcase and placed a small statuette of Jesus on the bureau. Lord knows they needed a protector in this terrible place. They'd sent the child here without her bodyguards. At Wheatley Hills there was an "inside man" and an "outside man," but here there was no one, even though the child's life had been threatened more than once. "They're responsible for her life, not me," Keislich said bitterly to herself. But she didn't mean it. Little Gloria *was* her life.

Her consuming fear was for little Gloria's safety. All summer long because of "that woman" it had been in the newspapers how wealthy little Gloria was. Keislich thought, "Never in my whole life will I understand the kind of woman she is!" Mrs. Morgan had often told Keislich that the child was an "obstacle" in Mrs. Vanderbilt's life and that one way or another she was going to get rid of her. Mrs. Morgan said that when little Gloria died, Mrs. Vanderbilt would weep like a Magdalen, but the child's millions would be hers. And Mrs. Morgan was Mrs. Vanderbilt's own mother!

To Keislich these accusations seemed completely logical: little Gloria was "a wealthy child, and wealth brings greed. . . . They are avid for that money. . . . Even from a baby lamb, an innocent child. It would make no difference to them." Keislich knew that there were many ways a child could die. Neglect was one—she knew about that full well. Not protecting a wealthy child from kidnappers was another. She moved to the bedroom window and looked down the two stories to the street. In Hopewell, New Jersey, the kidnapper had put the ladder to the second-story window and had taken the baby. His nurse, Betty Gow, had not been with him. The Lindberghs were wealthy people, prominent people. Keislich had told Mrs. Whitney that the child ought not to go to this house, that it was a terrible place, but it was not Keislich's decision and it would only be four days.

At lunch Mrs. Vanderbilt informed them that they were going to a movie that afternoon. With absolutely no regard for little Gloria's routine, they stayed past dinner time and when nurse Keislich put little Gloria to bed as Dr. St. Lawrence had ordered and served her dinner on a tray, Mrs. Vanderbilt came into the room and questioned Keislich's authority. She and that maid Wann actually looked at her as if she were cuckoo for trying to take proper care of little Gloria.

All that night Keislich would not leave the bedroom; she could feel the anxiety flowing through her body, and she thought, "It is a terrible thing to have a little child in a life that she can't be seen to and guarded—there must be a way of taking care of her and guarding her."

Laura Kilpatrick Morgan

Nurse Emma Keislich (Dodo)

Finally, Keislich fell into a fitful sleep. Just before dawn she heard a terrible scraping noise outside; she bolted upright in bed, trembling, then realized it was the sound of ash cans being dragged to the refuse trucks on Seventy-second Street.

Wide awake in that limbo just before dawn, nurse Keislich lay in her narrow bed. From the time little Gloria was three weeks old, Keislich had nurtured her and loved her. In the ten and a half years of little Gloria's life she had never taken a single day off and had never slept anywhere but in the child's room. She would never leave this child. Nurse Keislich had a sacred mission, she knew what she must do: "Watch her, guard her—every move she makes—her money, her life!"

Wednesday, September 19, 1934. While little Gloria was sitting up in bed in her mother's house eating her breakfast, in the Bronx a thin, nondescript man left his tan stucco two-story house and tramped through a ragged plot of goldenrod and weeds to the garage he himself had built. The man got into his black Dodge and backed it out. When he stopped for a red light at Tremont and Park Avenues, his car was surrounded by policemen. They ordered him to get out. When they found the twenty-dollar gold certificate in his trouser pocket, Bruno Richard Hauptmann was arrested. Then policemen literally ripped apart Hauptmann's garage. By Thursday night, $13,750 from the Lindbergh ransom had been found. A crowd of more than six hundred spectators joyously carried away souvenir pieces of wood and the diapers of Hauptmann's ten-month-old son, Manfred, which had been strung on a clothesline behind the house.

Keislich tried to fill the days to make them pass quickly, and she devised means to remind Mrs. Whitney of their existence. Wednesday morning was spent in Central Park where chauffeur Beesley was ordered to stand guard, while Wednesday afternoon Keislich instructed him to drive them to Doctors Hospital where Mrs. Whitney's granddaughter, Mary Anne (called Nancy) Whitney, was having her tonsils removed. (Both little Gloria and nurse Keislich were so happy to see Gertrude Whitney there.) Then Keislich had Beesley drive them to the Museum of the City of New York, on upper Fifth Avenue, where they spent two hours looking at exhibits that were sure to please a child: in case after case were exquisite life-size female mannequins in beautiful period dresses. It was almost five o'clock when they left the museum, but instead of returning home, Keislich took little Gloria back to Central Park. She was deliberately trying to stay out as late as possible because in the daylight, under Beesley's watchful eye, she felt safe. But by six o'clock, the child's dinner hour, she felt she could delay no longer and reluctantly returned to the house.

As they walked past the library door the child's mother summoned them in. She was up to her usual afternoon occupation of mixing cocktails, and she said to little Gloria, "Come on and I'll show you how to mix them," and proceeded to teach the innocent child to mix a cocktail, as if training her for what was to come later. Then Mrs. Vanderbilt tried to force little Gloria to drink some orange juice and Keislich had to intervene, telling her firmly that "all liquids are forbidden by Dr. St. Lawrence."

Just then the phone rang and Mrs. Vanderbilt picked it up. Pretty soon she was saying excitedly, "We are going to have a fight!" And Keislich, looking at little Gloria, saw the color drain from her face until she became pale . . . ghastly. Then Mrs. Vanderbilt hung up and took little Gloria into the next room and shut the door so Keislich wouldn't hear what was going on. When they came out, that mother sent the child upstairs and in her stammering voice asked Keislich, "Has Gloria seen her grandmother recently?" "Yes," said the nurse without thinking. Mrs. Morgan had visited the child only two days previously. Then Mrs. Vanderbilt mused aloud, not really as a question requiring an answer, but more as a criticism of her daughter: "Why did she lie to me?"

As soon as she could break away, Keislich went upstairs and asked little Gloria about the private conversation. "I told her I couldn't remember when I had last seen Naney," explained little Gloria. "I had forgotten, Dodo." Little Gloria had not lied to her mother, thought Keislich. She had forgotten. This child was not a liar!

In a pitiful voice little Gloria asked, "When am I going to go home? When will I get out of here?" Keislich answered, "Well, you were told four days. We're going back on Saturday." But in her heart, nurse Keislich began to fear that perhaps they would never get away. And the child asked, "What is the fight? Is it going to be about me?" This sweet baby knew nothing about the legal controversy, but she could recognize an atmosphere of strife. She had been brought up in such an atmosphere, with her grandmother trying to protect her, trying to be kind to her, standing up for her against that woman who was her mother. Keislich had told the mother to be more lenient with the child, and once when the mother asked her when little Gloria would be well, Keislich had told her the truth. "When you do right by her," she'd answered.

Keislich took the child on her lap and opened a picture book and tried to soothe her. "Calm down, Gloria, they don't mean a fight over you. Everybody can have an argument. It sounds worse than it is."

And as she comforted the child, she comforted herself with the thought that if there was to be a legal fight, then afterward the law would step in and protect little Gloria. "And I will see that they do," Keislich swore to herself.

Even in this dreadful place nurse Keislich tried to follow the routine that was essential to the child's well-being. Thursday morning, little Gloria again ate her breakfast in bed, and after she dressed, Keislich had Beesley drive them to Abercrombie & Fitch, where they browsed around looking for a gift for Mrs. Whitney. Little Gloria finally selected a glass matchbox and enclosed a note, signing it with the pet name she'd adopted after seeing the film *Little Women*.

> *Dearest Aunty Ger,*
> *I hope you will like this little match box. I miss you a lot. I hope to see you soon. I will be very glad to get back to Westbury and you.*
> *lovingly*
> *XX Jo OO*

Keislich instructed that the gift be hand-delivered to Mrs. Whitney at 871 Fifth Avenue, a reminder to the child that her Aunt Ger was nearby. Then they headed to Central Park, where little Gloria played and roller-skated, then back to the house for lunch, and after the child's rest, back to the park again. When they returned at about five-thirty, Mrs. Vanderbilt, her sister Mrs. Thaw, and an older gentleman were in the library. The gentleman was introduced as a friend of the late Mr. Vanderbilt, and soon he blurted out, "We've gone down to Long Island and picked out the loveliest house. And you're going to be so happy with your mother."

The child was startled, and exclaimed, "Oh!" Keislich looked at Mrs. Vanderbilt and observed bitterly to herself, "She didn't go gradually to coax the child, but frightened her all of a sudden to throw it at her."

Little Gloria ran upstairs and into the bedroom. She raced across the room to the window and looked down to see how far it was. "If I can't get away, I'll jump out the window, Dodo," she swore. Then she began to cry.

"God help this child," thought Dodo. Her precious innocent, whose every mood she knew, was desperate.

Friday morning the child ate nothing. She looked at Keislich and asked in her pitiful voice, "When am I going home? I'm afraid she'll keep me here, and I'm not going back."

"You will only be here a little while," the nurse assured her. "You *are* going back to Long Island."

Little Gloria dressed and went downstairs. Shortly thereafter, Mrs. Vanderbilt appeared at the bedroom door and began to reproach Keislich because a little of the puppy's Shredded Wheat had spilled onto the carpet. She lashed out at the nurse. "This is like a pigpen," and then she told Keislich, "You'll have to learn a thing or two about neatness, because starting tomorrow you'll be living with me. . . . Little Gloria is not going back to Mrs. Whitney's!" The moment she left the room, little Gloria came running in and said she'd heard the same news. She began to scream and cry and again ran to the window and threatened to jump out. And Keislich, loving her, cried out, "Gloria, darling, don't say that!"

"When am I going to see Auntie Ger?" little Gloria pleaded.

Keislich replied with one word: "Soon."

The week's routine continued as before—the park, lunch, a rest. At three-fifteen little Gloria, carrying her roller skates under her arm, said goodbye to her mother and got into the Pierce-Arrow. Beesley was at the wheel, Keislich was in the back seat; she had taken little Gloria's puppy. Keislich told Beesley to drive them to Larrimore's drugstore, where she placed a phone call. Then she got back in the car and ordered Beesley to drive them downtown to Mrs. Whitney's studio.

At two-thirty, Gertrude Whitney was working in her MacDougal Alley studio behind her museum when the telephone rang. It was the child's guardian, Thomas Gilchrist, and he sounded upset. The Vanderbilt chauffeur, Beesley, had just called him to report that tomorrow Mrs. Vanderbilt was going to take the child and move her to a rented house on Long Island. Gertrude Whitney asked Mr. Gilchrist to come to her Eighth Street apartment above the museum to discuss exactly what to do, but Gilchrist replied that it wouldn't be a good idea for him to come because he didn't wish to be thought partisan.

Then Gertrude phoned Frank Crocker: there was no answer either at his house or his office. Then she phoned Walter Dunnington who, because he represented Mrs. Morgan, was completely informed on this matter, and she asked him if he'd be in his office the rest of the afternoon as there was something she might want to talk to him about. He said he'd be there for her.

It was one of the rare times in her life when Gertrude Whitney was not sure what to do next. She remembered that when little Gloria had come to live with her in the summer of 1932, she'd been desperately ill, in a state of nervous collapse. It had been a time of screaming night terrors and excruciating stomach pain and little Gloria had cried out, "Don't let me die!" At that time, Gertrude hardly knew her niece or what had reduced her to this pathetic state. Gradually she'd begun to find out. Nurse Keislich told her horror stories of their life abroad and warned her that if she permitted the child to return to her mother, "it would be her downfall." The nurse's damning assertions were soon substantiated by more objective sources—doctors whom Gertrude respected; Thomas Gilchrist, who told her what he had learned from Beesley and Zaug; her own lawyers, who had engaged the proper people to investigate Gloria's past as well as her present relationship with Blumie. It was Gloria's own mother, however, who provided the strongest reasons for little Gloria's remaining at Wheatley Hills. Gertrude found Mrs. Morgan to be excitable and overwrought, her words, marked by a pronounced Spanish accent, tumbling out in a rush, but Mrs. Morgan adored her granddaughter; and what—just what—if her accusations were true? The accusations of neglect, immorality, and decadent associations were appalling, but the other accusations, that her own daughter might . . . No, it was too terrible. The strictures of polite society precluded an accusation as outré as MURDER. Yet, there it was.

Gertrude reluctantly admitted that little Gloria's pathetic condition when she'd arrived at Wheatley Hills provided mute evidence to substantiate at least some of Mrs. Morgan's accusations. And the child herself seemed sure that something terrible was going to happen to her; that she was going to die. Mrs. Morgan accused her daughter of wanting to murder little Gloria, and the child acted as if she knew she *was* going to be murdered. It had been hard work to put this child on her feet, and Gertrude was justly proud of the fact that little Gloria, in her nurse's words, had "become for the first time in her life . . . a normal child."

At about three-thirty Gertrude's phone rang again. The nurse and the child had escaped and were on their way to her. About fifteen minutes later, little Gloria came clambering up the narrow stairway of the Eighth Street house, ran across the room crying, threw her arms around Gertrude and pleaded, "Don't make me go back to my mother. I don't want to go back. I'm afraid of her. I would rather die than go back to her."

The child's body was racked with sobs. Gertrude tried to comfort her, asking softly, "Gloria, what is the trouble?"

"My mother told me that she's taken a house in Long Island . . . I don't want to go. I'm not happy with her. I'm afraid of her."

Gertrude did her best to quiet the child and sent her into the bedroom. Then she moved quickly to the telephone, dialed Thomas Gilchrist and asked, "Won't you please come up? I don't know what to do. I can't find Frank Crocker." Gilchrist could not refuse her. Next she phoned Walter Dunnington, who also agreed to come right away.

Both lawyers arrived within half an hour and Mrs. Whitney led them into her living room where nurse Keislich told them that she was taking the child for a ride in the park when little Gloria became hysterical. Not knowing what else to do, she'd brought her to Mrs. Whitney.

Once Keislich had left the room, Gertrude Whitney said, "I want some advice as to what I should do under these circumstances. . . . I don't want to do anything which is not in accordance with the agreements arrived at between counsel with the Surrogate. I want you to tell me what I ought to do."

Walter Dunnington did not hesitate. "I think under no circumstances should you keep the child. I think you should send the child back to the mother immediately. Otherwise, it will look as though you're trying to shorten the child's stay with Mrs. Vanderbilt."

"I want to do exactly what is right," replied Gertrude.

"Well, that is my advice. Send the child back right now to the mother."

Gertrude Whitney turned and asked, "What do you think, Mr. Gilchrist?"

Gilchrist was trying to gather his thoughts; after his initial conversation with Mrs. Whitney, he'd dialed Gloria Vanderbilt at Butterfield 8-8730 and under the pretext of discussing the child's education, had given her every opportunity to reveal her plans. But she had told him nothing. After all Gilchrist had done for her, Gloria was simply acting as if he did not exist; she had taken matters into her own hands. Also, Gilchrist and Mrs. Whitney knew what Dunnington did not—that if they returned little Gloria to Mrs. Vanderbilt she might never send her back.

"I do not wish to express an opinion until I have talked to the child alone," he said. He walked upstairs, entered the bedroom, and asked nurse Keislich to leave the room. Little Gloria was semireclining on a couch, a blanket tossed across her legs. Her face was tearstained, her eyes red, and she caught her breath as though she'd been sobbing. Gilchrist sat on the couch beside her, his long legs stretched out awkwardly in front of him. He put his arm around her and said, "Now everyone here is trying to do what is best for you. Won't you be a good girl and go back to your mother until Sunday?"

"No. No. If you send me back there I'll kill myself." Little Gloria clutched at Gilchrist. "I hate her. I hate her. I never want to see her again."

Gilchrist began patting her back. "You mustn't talk that way, Gloria. You just be calm and go back to your mother. Everything is all right, don't get excited."

"No. No. No," she wailed, and then she began to scream.

Sitting downstairs, Gertrude could hear little Gloria screaming. She sat rigid in her chair, thinking, "This is terrible!"

Gilchrist came downstairs and announced, "Mrs. Whitney, I haven't any doubts about what should be done."

"What do you think?"

"Since I've talked with the child, I believe it would be very wrong to send her back to her mother at this time in her present hysterical condition. Harm might result to her." Gilchrist realized that they must stall for time until they could take steps to prevent Mrs. Vanderbilt from taking little Gloria. "My advice to you is to take the child up to your house, get a doctor who knows the child . . . call up Mrs. Vanderbilt at once and tell her to come over, and tell her everything that's happened. Then you can't be accused of doing anything underhanded."

"I think that is good advice," replied Gertrude, who was also fully aware of the situation. "What doctor should we get?"

"Get St. Lawrence if you can—because he's the one in control of her now."

"Dr. St. Lawrence is in Southampton. We can't get him."

"Dr. Hartwell?" suggested Gilchrist. Although John Hartwell was not a pediatrician, Gilchrist knew that Gertrude Whitney trusted him. He did *not* know that Hartwell was her lover.

"Hartwell is out of town."

"Dr. Schloss?"

"Schloss is ill . . ."

"How about Craig?"

Walter Dunnington phoned Dr. Stuart L. Craig. "Craig will come," he said.

Gilchrist said, "Then the thing for you to do is to go immediately to your house."

Gertrude, the child, and the nurse were driven uptown by Beesley; as they got out of the car, Gertrude directed the chauffeur, "Go immediately to Mrs. Vanderbilt's house and tell her that the child is not feeling well and that she is here with me, and that I will telephone her in a few minutes." Then just as they were about to enter the house, Dr. Craig arrived with his trained nurse.

Craig thought that perhaps he had been called because little Gloria had an acute ear infection. He didn't know what to make of this little girl whose face was distorted from crying. He asked her why she'd been crying, and she replied, "Because my mother wants to take me."

"That is nothing to cry for," said Craig.

"Well, I don't want to be taken . . . I hate my mother."

"No, you don't hate your mother, Gloria. You're just excited. Nobody hates their mother."

"I hate my mother," little Gloria cried over and over again, growing increasingly hysterical until Craig assured her that she could stay at Mrs. Whitney's for the night. Then he suggested that she be given a bath and be put to bed.

While this was being done, Gloria Vanderbilt and Consuelo Thaw came storming into the house—Consuelo snapping out orders to her sister in Spanish. They demanded to see the child then and there, so Gertrude led them into the bathroom where little Gloria was with nurse Keislich and the trained nurse. Gloria Vanderbilt burst through the door like a madwoman, screeching at nurse Keislich, "Get out of this room," but when the nurse obeyed, her departure triggered another hysterical fit in the child, the worst one of all. Little Gloria grabbed hold of Gertrude for protection as if her mother were going to hit her or kill her. "Don't let her come near me . . . don't let her kill me! . . . I hate her," she shouted, and then began screaming like a wounded animal. The screams went on and on. Gertrude Whitney had never in her entire life witnessed such a display; she was at a loss to know what to do. She eased her niece into an adjoining bedroom and tried to put her to bed, but little Gloria wouldn't let go of her. Then Dr. Craig, attracted by the screams, came in and said that if everybody left the room, perhaps he could quiet the child. Gertrude, Gloria, and Consuelo went into the sitting room where Gloria insisted on calling nurse Keislich in and firing her on the spot. This woman obviously didn't give a rap about her daughter, who adored the nurse, and then she tried to justify herself to Gertrude by saying, "You see I have to fire that woman?" Gertrude would have none of this; nurse Keislich was, to her mind, the most devoted of persons, and except for her quick action, little Gloria would have been taken away from her. She replied icily, "You are quite right in discharging the nurse, because she's prevented you from carrying out your plan."

It took Dr. Craig a long time to persuade little Gloria to say good night to her mother, but finally she did and at last Gloria Vanderbilt and her sister left for the night. Gertrude Whitney went back into little Gloria's bedroom and sat with her, quieting her and comforting her until her sobs ceased and she fell asleep.

By noon the next day these women were back with their own

doctor in tow, demanding that little Gloria come with them, but after examining her, even their own doctor told them that the child must remain quietly where she was. Gloria didn't listen, she kept demanding the child and saying such irrational things to Gertrude as, "You bring her to me yourself." Gertrude remained calm and unyielding and finally Gloria just gave up and left.

Gertrude went in to see her niece. Little Gloria asked in a tiny voice, "Oh, I don't have to go back to my mother, do I?"

"No," replied Gertrude Whitney. Although she rarely showed emotion, Gertrude was deeply touched by this pitiful, frightened child. The last two days had exhausted Gertrude completely. Now that she had the child, she wasn't quite sure what to do with her, and the intensity of the child's fear mystified and disquieted her. "When the child showed hysteria and began to shriek or scream when her mother came into the room, that was not just because she didn't want to go down and live with her in the country," thought Gertrude. "When the child said, 'If I have to go back, I would rather die,' that was not simply a fear of going back." It was something more.

That afternoon at two-thirty, Louis D. Frohlich, an associate of Nathan Burkan's, arrived at the Whitney house accompanied by a process server. Mrs. Whitney refused to come downstairs to accept the legal papers, but sent a message that her lawyer, Frank Crocker, would accept on her behalf. The men refused the offer and departed.

About half an hour later, the process server returned alone, carrying a pot of paste. When the footman opened the door, he delivered the following message from the Burkan office, "Tell Mrs. Whitney that unless she accepts in person, I will plaster the whole front of 871 Fifth Avenue with these court papers."

Gertrude Whitney then descended her white marble stairs, walked past the footman, and accepted the papers. The writ of habeas corpus began:

> To Mrs. Harry Payne Whitney
>
> Greeting:
>
> We command you that you have the body of Gloria Laura Morgan Vanderbilt by you imprisoned and detained, as it is said, together with the time and cause of such imprisonment and detention by whatsoever name the said Gloria Laura Morgan Vanderbilt is called or charged, before Honorable John F. Carew...

The writ was returnable the following Tuesday, September 25, 1934, at 10 a.m.

Well, Gertrude was more determined than ever to keep the child.

When little Gloria had begged not to be sent to her mother, Gertrude had given her word that the visit would last only a few days, and she considered her promise sacred. How dare this common adventuress threaten her? Gloria didn't want little Gloria, she wanted money to support her depraved life. It was out of the question to let the child return to that environment. So Gloria and her Broadway-type lawyer thought they could strong-arm Gertrude, did they? They knew how she hated publicity and were counting on that to force her to settle out of court. But they were wrong, and Gertrude was about to show them just how wrong. By her own assessment, Gertrude Whitney was a woman who almost always got what she wanted. She had the means to hire the best legal minds in the nation and whatever other services she needed—money was no object.

No, she would not let this ridiculous woman ride roughshod over her and violate the Surrogate's agreement. She would not let this dear child be torn away from her surreptitiously, against her will.

She would not let them kidnap little Gloria.

Glorious Gloria

Society is not made by society, but by its reporters . . .

ELSA MAXWELL

When she thought about it later, and she did, she still could not comprehend how it had happened. It seemed to her that fate had woven a dark, inexorable web from which she was powerless to escape. It was all beyond her control. She was a victim of cruel circumstance. There was no choice she could make on her own. Not where to live. Not whom to love.

Hadn't she always done what was expected of her? And more. She'd kept her beauty unmarred by debilitating sports. Mamma had warned her that exercise made large, knotty muscles, and told her, "Dainty hands are a woman's greatest asset." When she was little, Gloria's hands were creamed every night and she was put to bed in white cotton gloves. Her complexion, sun free, was compared to a magnolia. She ate little. Her body was a fragile instrument. She dressed beautifully, romantically . . . seductively. She became what she had always been trained to become—a prize for a rich, socially impeccable man; a bijou that he could own and display like his mansions and his horses. She had given Mamma exactly what she'd wanted.

As children, Gloria and her twin sister, Thelma, would sit for hours under a portrait of Mamma, gazing up with admiration. Mamma was everything to them, all-knowing. Magic. Her fierce tempers, her violent all-encompassing love, marked the boundaries of their world. "I worshipped my mother," recalled Gloria. "When I was a young girl, the only thing that really mattered was my mother. I simpled adored her. I thought about her all the time." Later, Gloria was to observe in this tempestuous woman a streak close to madness. "For some unknown reason, the Latin and American blood did not fuse in my mother. . . . She was caught up in some overwhelming restless air pocket of acutely changing emotions. . . . We never knew her in any other spirit." Laura Kilpatrick Morgan was totally unpredictable, loving one moment, lashing out the next. Still Mamma's domineering love was the only constant element in the lives of the four Morgan children. They journeyed from country to country, school to school, language to language, propelled by their father's diplomatic career and their mother's penchant for restless wandering.

To Mamma, appearances were all-important. Her children were sent to the best schools, but there were cruel, hidden economies. When the time came for their first communion, Mrs. Morgan screamed at her three daughters: "I've told you a thousand times money doesn't grow on trees. Why should I spend money on dresses you will never be able to wear again?" Instead of flowing gowns, the girls wore remade short-skirted white tulle dresses that made them look "like horrid little ballerinas." One week they would dine with royalty, the next they would find themselves on a train in third class or in a hotel so inexpensive and filthy that Gloria would wake up to find cockroaches crawling on her body.

Laura Morgan held tight to the family's thin purse strings, while her easygoing, charming husband spent freely and was often heard to remark, "The party's on me." The frugality of this woman and the constant emphasis she placed on money could not fail to impress themselves on her children.

And Mamma never let them forget who they were—or who she imagined them to be. She had what Gloria termed "an obsessive pride" in her ancestry. Laura Morgan's father was Hugh Judson Kilpatrick, who had entered the Union cavalry at age twenty-five, had fought at Gettysburg and was twice wounded. He'd led the cavalry in Sherman's march to the sea. (It was reported that Kilpatrick's men were among the worst offenders in pillaging the countryside.) Kilpatrick had been dubbed with the dubious nickname "Kill-Cavalry" for his recklessness in attacking the enemy. General William T. Sherman pronounced him "a hell of a damned fool," but just the type of man to command the cavalry. By the time of the Confederate surrender in April of 1865, Kilpatrick had risen to the rank of major general.

At thirty-one, this stormy, impetuous officer became United States minister to Chile, where he met and married a local aristocrat, Louisa Valdivieso. As a tiny child, Gloria had been told by Mamma that she would be taken to place flowers on the graves of Ferdinand III, "King of Castile and León and Ponce de León, Lord of Villagareia." She told her daughter that these men were her ancestors, as was the Empress Eugénie of France. Only as an adult did Gloria realize this to be fantasy. It was ironic that at the custody trial of 1934, Laura Kilpatrick Morgan was to excoriate her daughter Gloria for her "mania for titles."

Laura Kilpatrick was married at seventeen to a minor American career diplomat, Harry Hays Morgan. It would have been nice if he had had the wherewithal of the great American John Pierpont Morgan family, but the name turned out to be mere coincidence. Harry Morgan was the son of Philip Hickey Morgan, a Louisiana Supreme Court justice who had served as American minister to Mexico and as a justice of the International Court in Egypt. Harry Morgan had been married before and had one daughter, which, although Mamma was a Catholic, apparently presented no obstacle. His first marriage was annulled on the ground that he had married his cousin, and he converted to Catholicism. His daughter, Gladys, who was six at the time of his second marriage, was placed in a convent near Geneva and eventually shipped off to a destitute aunt in New York City. Her father sent her no money.

Through Mamma's entreaties, President William McKinley gave Papa an appointment as American consul to Berne, Switzerland, at a salary of $2,000 a year. The President told Papa, "This is your bride's wedding gift." From the first, it was Mamma's explosive personality that dominated the marriage.

In 1898, Harry Judson Kilpatrick was born. Consuelo was born in 1902, but later her mother would tell her that she was born in 1903. Gloria and Thelma were born August 23, 1904, at the Hotel Nationale in Lucerne, where their father was serving as American consul, but Mamma would tell the twins that they were born in 1905, possibly because she was to discover that seventeen-year-old girls were even fresher on the marriage market than eighteen-year-olds.

As if waiting for her daughters to emerge from the chrysalis of childhood, in 1916 Mamma Morgan dropped fourteen-year-old Consuelo at the home of Edith and George J. Gould in Lakewood, New

Jersey. Edith Kingdon Gould was a former actress who had met her husband when he'd flung his calling card across the footlights of the stage on which she was performing. At first, Edith Gould bitterly resented the fact that Laura Morgan, a casual social acquaintance, had used Edith's vague invitation as an excuse to dump this child on her doorstep. Later she confided to Consuelo, "I was furious the day I had to meet you." Soon, however, she was taken by Consuelo's charm and treated her like a daughter, providing her with an expensive wardrobe and introducing her to Society. George Gould was seldom home, spending most of his time with his mistress, who had borne him three illegitimate children.

Mamma tucked Gloria and Thelma away at the Convent of the Sacred Heart, Manhattanville, a school she herself had attended as a girl. The atmosphere at the convent was intense and repressive. Gloria worshipped several times a day, acknowledging her imperfection and her guilt; her every movement was supervised and she developed a fervent attachment to the righteous mother superior, whose "pale strong hand wiped away my tears."

The first Mass was at 6:30 a.m., but Gloria was found to be sickly and was permitted the luxury of remaining in bed until nine o'clock Mass. This may have marked the start of a pattern that was to remain with her all her life—sickness provided both an excuse not to do what she didn't care to do and a retreat from the world.

This European child of twelve felt herself a complete "misfit . . . a bewildered, rather morbid young girl much given to reading Edgar Allan Poe and Oscar Wilde." She had been christened Mercedes Gloria, but at the convent they began calling her Mercy, which she hated, so then and there she dropped her first name. Her sister Thelma pronounced her name in the European fashion, Tell-mah, and they nicknamed her Tamar. Gloria was far behind the other students in Latin, algebra, geometry, and American history. She could speak five languages—English, French, Dutch, Spanish, Portuguese—but had no idea how to write them. Both she and her twin stammered. Gloria declared, "We speak French like Spanish and Spanish like French, and English like—well, like something I can't mention."

At the convent Gloria and Thelma were an inseparable unit. Gloria thought of Thelma as her other self, her mirror image. Sometimes they even assumed each other's identities. They shared a psychic rapport so strong that it enabled them to read each other's thoughts. Gloria claimed that even when an ocean separated them, sometimes she could actually feel the physical sensations her twin was experiencing. Gloria felt that Thelma was stronger than she was—physically stronger—and although Thelma's stammer was even more pronounced than her own, somehow more in command. "Thelma always leads and I follow," said Gloria, who seemed constantly to be waiting for someone to show her which path to travel.

Although most people felt them to be physically indistinguishable except for a tiny scar on Thelma's chin, their expressions were quite different. Gloria was possessed of a dark-eyed melancholy, a poignant fragility. Her expression was that of a fairy-tale princess who awakes bewildered, unsure of her environment; perhaps she has been asleep for a hundred years. Thelma's expression was harder, crisper, more in vogue with the times. The twins were to remain at the convent from the ages of twelve to fifteen, three formative years during which they were totally cut off from their parents by World War I.

In March of 1920, Mamma and Papa finally came to the United States to fetch Consuelo to Brussels, where, since the armistice, Papa had been serving as American consul general to Belgium. Within three months Mamma had arranged seventeen-year-old Consuelo's marriage to thirty-three-year-old Count Jean Marie Emmanuel de Maupas du Juglart, a man she hardly knew. The count, however, came from a wealthy French family and possessed a title dating back to the eleventh century.

Gloria and Thelma sailed on the S.S. *France* to attend the wedding. When they arrived in Paris Gloria found Consuelo, usually so animated, to be pale and drawn. Her eyes were lifeless as she stood motionless in the center of her room at the Ritz Hotel that hot July day, while helping hands draped her body in a Worth wedding gown and affixed a massive tulle bridal veil decorated with valuable specimens of *point d'Alençon* lace which had been used in de Maupas weddings since the time of Louis XIV.

Consuelo and the count were married by the archbishop of Laodice, and the wedding was considered *the* event of the Parisian summer social season. Mamma gloated over the match. Gloria listened while Mamma explained her view that "arranged marriages tend to maintain a pure line of ancestry, and besides, they are the only way to control fortunes and keep them in the hands of the aristocrats where they belong." Yes, Consuelo had contracted "a brilliant marriage," a phrase Mamma and her set—and the newspapers—were fond of using. In this highly structured era, a show girl or actress could barter her beauty and talent to marry well, but this was exceptional. When a gentleman of Society married out of his class, it was so unusual an occurrence that one could count on newspaper headlines like SON OF SOCIALITE ELOPES WITH DAUGHTER OF LAUNDRESS.

Mamma Morgan,
Harry H. Morgan,
and Consuelo

Gloria and Thelma

Gloria,
Harry J. K. Morgan,
and Thelma

Thelma and Gloria

Beauty, charm, virginity, and the added credential of being of the *right* class became commodities to be traded for wealth and social prominence. Women who struck this bargain rarely acknowledged that the exchange might also include alcoholism, abuse, and unfaithfulness, nor did it take into account the repressed rage of these women, which often they themselves did not recognize, but which expressed itself in cupidity, indifference, and a desperate gaiety. In today's world, where beauty and sexuality are plentiful commodities, where Society itself is of little importance, where the symbols of affluence have become a burden, where self-discovery is a prized possession, it is difficult to remember what the conditions of life were less than sixty years ago.

Within a year of her marriage, Consuelo's soft face became angular, her dark eyes outlined with kohl. The new Countess de Maupas attended parties with her husband, but refused to speak to him in public. In November of 1922, after two years of marriage, they were divorced, the count alleging "light conduct" on the part of the countess. Her demand for alimony was denied. Among the papers produced in court were letters written by Consuelo and her husband. "I am wrong to be so gentle," he wrote. "You cannot understand me and in reality I have the profoundest contempt for you." To which Consuelo replied, ". . . You disgust me, and for nothing in the world would I consent to return." Soon it would be time for the twins to contract brilliant marriages of their own. In 1921, the twins were seventeen, although they still believed themselves to be a year younger, and the United States should provide a fertile field of millionaire gentlemen to whom a fresh face was welcome relief. (It was the all-powerful Vanderbilts, in fact, who had started a vogue for young Catholic wives to refresh their tired society.) With school behind them, Gloria and Thelma went to live in New York City, unchaperoned—a highly unusual occurrence. Mamma elected to remain in Brussels. Papa promised to send the girls two hundred dollars a month for their expenses which was all he could afford on his slim salary.

On their own in New York, Gloria and Thelma experienced an exquisite sense of newfound freedom. They rented a tiny floor-through apartment consisting of two rooms and a kitchenette in Greenwich Village, in the private brownstone of Dr. Travell at 40 Fifth Avenue. Mrs. Travell had serious doubts when the two young girls presented themselves, and she insisted on a confirming letter from Mamma before she would let her husband rent them the apartment. The rent was $135 a month, which left only sixty-five dollars to pay for everything else. However, the day they moved in, the twins' first act was to crowd the apartment with masses of flowers and to name it Chez Nous. They were filled with the romantic expectation that something wonderful was about to happen.

For the first time in her life Gloria felt that she was completely her own mistress. Free at last, she set out to do exactly what Mamma had programmed her to do. Gloria and Thelma used Mamma's and Papa's contacts to plunge into their first social season. Always together, they visited the Montmartre nightclub where they danced to Emil Coleman's orchestra. They mastered a frantic Charleston and waltzed to "Mexicali Rose." At *thés dansants* at the Plaza Hotel across the street from the block-long Vanderbilt mansion, they watched smartly turned-out college lads in white flannel trousers and blazers pin gold Greek-letter fraternity pins above the seemingly tiny breasts of debutantes in flatboy brassieres. They smoked cigarettes in ivory holders (they had smoked since they were thirteen) and, for the first time, drank bootlegged cocktails (previously they drank only wine). They went to parties where Gloria watched as other teenaged girls marched into the powder room, removed their corsets, rolled down their silk stockings and, naked from waist to knee under clinging chemises, rejoined their partners on the dance floor.

Millicent Hearst, undaunted by the public knowledge that her husband, publishing czar William Randolph Hearst, preferred the company of Marion Davies to her own, had established herself as the doyenne of the Junior Set. She gave parties and dinners for these privileged teenagers and set them to work for her pet charity, the Milk Fund. On a borrowed police motorbike, Gloria wove in and out of Fifth Avenue traffic, stopping cars and pleading prettily for donations. Gentlemen in boater hats and women with bejeweled hands reached through rolled-down car windows to hand her money. Gloria was amazed to find that a man in a Rolls-Royce gave her a mere fifty cents and a sour look, while another man leaned down through the window of a trolley car to hand her a ten-dollar bill.

Gloria and Thelma both loved to do needlework. When they wanted new dresses they bought fabrics and created their own chic wardrobe for pennies. At Christmas they saved a great deal of money by making hand-embroidered sachets and pincushions and huge puffed-out DuBarry dolls with voluminous skirts of taffeta and lace that fitted over the ten-inch-high telephones of the day.

One day a friend dropped by Chez Nous with a copy of the New York *American* in which a columnist named Cholly Knickerbocker had written about Gloria, referring to her as "Glorious Gloria" of "the Magnificent Morgans." Gloria thought the reference "sweet" and wondered who Cholly Knickerbocker could be. She soon found out, when she attended her first fancy-dress ball, given by the glamorous Cobina Wright. Gloria and Thelma arrived in identical medieval pageboy costumes they had made themselves, their long dark brown hair tucked up under smooth jet-black wigs. Gloria was introduced to an impeccably groomed, immensely fat little man who reeked of cologne ("I smell to heaven," he said of himself) and who sported a red carnation in his lapel. His name was Maury Paul and he was "Cholly Knickerbocker." Gloria, terribly impressed, explained, "He was *the* social arbiter par excellence. He knew all and everything about anybody who was anybody." They quickly became friends.

"Society is not made by society, but by its reporters," said Elsa Maxwell, who added that "New York society was what it was because of Maury Paul." It had started with his desperate need to belong. Maury Henry Biddle Paul was born in Philadelphia in 1890. He was no relation to the Philadelphia Pauls, but claimed that his mother was a distant cousin of *the* Biddles. *The* Biddles denied the relationship. Eventually giving full vent to his florid fantasy, Paul devised a chronology in which he traced his family through thirty-two generations, claiming to be a descendant of Rolf, the Norseman Conqueror.

This blue-eyed, decaying cherub moved through the Society world making friends and confidantes of the women. Society women felt at ease with Maury, who chatted like one of the girls and seemed instinctively to understand their innermost thoughts. He even told his special favorites what to wear, and instructed them on which resort to appear at, and when. Society photographer Jerome Zerbe said of him, "He understood those women because they were exactly what he wanted to be."

Paul became Society's most powerful reporter in an era when copious Society news appeared daily and occupied voluminous Sunday newspaper sections. His good fortune had come as a direct result of an accusation of blackmail. He'd been writing for four New York newspapers; in the *Evening Journal* he appeared as Billy Benedick; in the *Evening Mail* he was Dolly Madison; in the *American*, Cholly Knickerbocker; and the *Evening Post* carried his "Social Notes" column. In addition, he was syndicated across the country as Polly Stuyvesant. Then it all fell apart. Arthur Brisbane, editor of the *Evening Journal*, fired him for the poison-pen tone of his writing, and shortly thereafter a story appeared in the *World* (a paper with which Maury Paul had no connection) stating that a wealthy woman had gone to the district attorney to ask protection against a Society editor "on one morning newspaper and two evening newspapers" who was, she said, attempting to blackmail her. The *Evening Post* promptly dropped Maury's column.

William Randolph Hearst sized up the situation and reacted by offering Paul a salary of $250 a week if he would work only for the *American*, writing his Cholly Knickerbocker column. Hearst had been watching Paul ever since the day in 1919 when he had returned home to San Simeon to find Marion Davies's curly blond head buried in Paul's Dolly Madison column. He reasoned that if Marion cared about a writer, millions of others would care too, so he hired Paul exclusively and Paul, in turn, consolidated his platform and power.

No one ever again accused Maury Paul of blackmail, although it was common knowledge that he received lavish gifts from grateful Society figures. Eve Brown, who was employed by Paul for twenty-five years, remembers his walking into the office one Wednesday evening at seven, after a visit to a Society lady whose name frequently appeared in his column. Paul drew an enormous roll of thousand-dollar bills from his pocket, looked at Eve, and said, "I think my assistant Society editor should have a mink coat." With that, he peeled off a bill and handed it to her.

Paul's booty also included a rare Aubusson rug, a station wagon that had appeared wrapped in cellophane in the driveway of his country home, and the $5,000 mortgage on the house itself, which had been canceled by Mrs. Christian Holmes, a name one often read in the Cholly Knickerbocker column.

When the Morgan twins arrived on the social scene, radio was in its infancy, talking films had not yet arrived: a voracious public found its idols in royalty, theatrical stars, and Society. "Ordinary" people consumed news of Society figures, living vicariously through their peccadilloes and exuberant luxury. Maury Paul knew instinctively that Gloria and Thelma were real news. Seeing double—two beautiful young women all alone on the loose in New York City—was a social novelty, and Paul kept writing about their activities and praising them as extraordinary beauties. It was he who created them as the quintessential debutantes of 1922. Personally, he found Gloria both flighty and fickle, but he transformed this handsome teenager of no fortune, good family, and sketchy education, into a star. He dubbed her Glorious Gloria, inventing her in order to write about her in the same way he had invented the phrases Glamor Girl, Old Guard, and Café Society, inserting into each category the names with which his column sparkled.

Maury Paul was the first to recognize in the Morgan twins those traits that, in full bloom, would attract what were considered to be the most desirable men in the world. Gloria's and Thelma's dark good looks hinted at something foreign, exotic—sensual. Even their speech impediments worked for them, making them seem achingly vulnerable and feminine. Their speech intonations sounded aristocratic, continental, conjuring up visions of South American grandees, of ancient French nobility. Thelma's accent was more pronounced than Gloria's, but in both sisters the *s*'s were sibilant and sputtered like firecrackers, and the *r*'s rolled into the letter that followed, crowding the end of the word. Tallulah Bankhead, who became known for the deep timbre of her own voice, was jealous of the twins. She remarked to director George Cukor, "They are sweet, Thelma and Gloria, but those boring accents!" With the passage of years, Gloria's accent was to become more British, Thelma's more guttural; but when Gloria was with her twin, after a few moments they spoke almost identically. Thelma was always the stronger.

Cecil Beaton photographed Gloria and Thelma in the late 1920s, at their zenith, and said of them:

> They are as alike as two magnolias and with their marble complexions, raven tresses and flowing dresses, with their slight lisps and foreign accents, they diffuse an Ouida atmosphere of hothouse elegance and lacy femininity. They are of infinite delicacy and refinement and with slender necks and waists and long coiled, silky hair, they are gracefully statuesque. Their noses are like begonias, with full-blown nostrils, their lips richly carved, and they should have been painted by Sargent, with arrogant heads and affected hands, in white satin with a bowl of white peonies near by.

Gloria would remember that early time in New York as one of gay young escapades. One day Agnes Horter, Gloria's friend from the convent—the only school friend with whom she remained intimate—told the twins that Cosmopolitan Studios was casting extras for a film, *The Young Diana*. Gloria and Thelma presented themselves at the casting director's office (they used the alias Rochelle because they were afraid of what Mamma and Papa might say if they found out about it). They were given identical tights and pieces of chiffon the size of handkerchiefs, which constituted their entire costumes. When they inquired what role they were to play, the wardrobe lady snapped, "Northern Lights," and called out, "Next." The girls proceeded to a brightly lit stage, where they stood barefoot, ankle deep in rough salt made to represent snow. After a time Gloria's feet began to hurt, then to bleed.

Several hours later the star appeared—Marion Davies, wearing a white chiffon ball gown covered with pearls and diamonds. A voluminous train of wispy white marabou fell behind her. Her three-foot-

Thelma and Gloria, "The Magnificent Morgans," by Cecil Beaton

high headdress was composed of white marabou and diamonds. Thelma whispered to Gloria that Marion Davies resembled a jewel-studded powder puff. Marion had the makings of a delightful light comedienne, but her protector, William Randolph Hearst, liked to see her decked out in these elaborate costumes. W. R. had purchased Cosmopolitan Studios to make Marion a star, and seemed unable to accept the fact that he was drowning her spark of talent in a torrent of chiffon.

The twins left the set at dusk—they had each been paid $12.50 for the day's work—and that night they went to Sherry's for dinner with Junior Converse. Junior's given name was James Vail Converse; he was the grandson of Theodore N. Vail, a founder of the Bell Telephone Company and a relative of *the* J. P. Morgan. Well accepted in Society, Junior had been married and divorced. While the newspapers had announced that he was "heir to the thirty-odd-million-dollar estate of his late father, Edmund C. Converse," in reality, Junior had very little money, a fact that Mamma Morgan with her vast knowledge of such matters knew full well and could have told Thelma.

During dinner Thelma's eyes began to swell and hurt. Soon she couldn't open them. Junior escorted the twins back to their apartment and telephoned his own doctor, who arrived and diagnosed a case of klieg eyes, caused by excessively hot lights used on the set. For days Gloria dripped castor oil into Thelma's swollen eyes. Junior came every day to be with Thelma, and when she recovered she promptly eloped with him to Rockville, Maryland. Gloria was her only attendant, and neither twin knew the denomination of the officiating minister.

With this marriage Thelma broke into Society. When she made her initial appearance in Palm Beach, dressed in a frock of periwinkle-blue chiffon, she was surrounded by Society well-wishers. Thelma felt that the first days of her marriage were "golden," describing herself as "wined, dined, feted. I felt thoroughly possessed and I enjoyed the possession." Junior told his friends, "Thelma and I just tangoed into marriage."

For the first time in her life, Gloria was truly alone and lonely. But as soon as the young Converses returned from their honeymoon, they planned a small, exclusive dinner party in the private dining room of the Café des Beaux Arts. Junior took care of the bootlegger. Thelma consulted with the maître d'hôtel, chef, and florist. And, in what was to become an established family pattern, one sister was about to help the other scramble up the social ladder.

The night of the party, Gloria had been at a *thé dansant* at the

Plaza. When she left, it was snowing and she couldn't find a cab, so she walked to the Beaux Arts, which took the better part of an hour. She thought her sister would be angry at her lateness but Thelma greeted her lovingly and directed her to a table, where she saw Angie Duke talking to a thin, flat-chested girl. Gloria noticed that the girl had a band of silk pulled tightly across her breasts and hooked in back. The girl also affected the debutante slouch, her stomach pushed forward, back well arched, one hand perched on her hip, while the other manipulated an almost foot-long cigarette holder. It was Irene Castle, Gloria thought, who was responsible for this pose becoming the rage, but it really didn't look good on anyone else. "I'm glad Thelma and I let our bosoms and waists remain where God placed them," she said to herself.

Gloria sat down. A man she later described as "rather heavy set . . . with dark brown hair slightly touched with gray at the sides" looked at her casually. "I'm Reggie Vanderbilt," he announced.

Of course Gloria knew who he was. The Vanderbilts, as Lucius Beebe observed, constituted "the nearest thing to a royal family that has ever appeared on the American scene. . . . Their palaces and summer palaces, their balls and banquetings, their royal alliances and their vendettas, their armies of servitors, partisans, and sycophants, their love affairs, scandals, and shortcomings, all were the stuff of an imperial routine."

Since his divorce three years before, Reggie Vanderbilt had been considered *the* catch of the social world. He was a famous gentleman-rake whose gambling exploits, all-night parties, love affairs, carriage and later auto races all made colorful newspaper copy. He'd given a party in this very room and had led in a hansom cab horse, declaring that the animal was his guest of honor. Reginald Vanderbilt was surrounded by an aura of glamour that totally concealed the man he had become.

Gloria's first impression of Reggie was that he looked rather bored, but he complimented her on her gray dress, which he took to be an auspicious sign since his racing colors were gray and white—the colors of King Louis XVI. (Gloria's dress was, in fact, green. She put the mistake down to the dim light.)

Reggie began talking at length about his horses, especially his champion stallion, Fortitude. Gloria knew nothing about horses and cared even less, yet she pretended to be enormously interested. Warming to his subject, Reggie said, "Promise me you'll let me take you out to see Fortitude one day. Then you'll see why I'm so proud."

"I'd love to see Fortitude," replied Gloria.

"Bully," he exclaimed.

Gloria was delighted. "Bully" was an expression she associated exclusively with Papa. Her own father, however, had always been an elusive presence, and in this man who was a quarter of a century her senior, she may have been seeking another father. (Twice during the Vanderbilt custody trial she would inadvertently refer to Reginald as her *father*, only to be gently corrected by her lawyer.) In fact, Gloria freely acknowledged that she was attracted to mature men: "All my life my imagination had been captured by men older than myself—they bring with them a tone and a manner . . . the years have polished them and . . . they come out with some heightened quality that has always been extremely fascinating to me—a casual, effortless treatment of things in life which cushion the seats for one."

Later that evening the immensely rich Cuban, Hannibal de Mesa, asked Gloria to dance, and as he whirled her around he said with admiration, "I see you have charmed the most eligible bachelor in town."

The party ended just before dawn. In front of the Beaux Arts seven inches of new-fallen snow covered the ground. The wind swirled snow around Gloria, who hugged her worn winter coat tight about her. She heard the tinkle of bells and the clip-clop of horses' feet; a sleigh appeared and glided gracefully past. Gloria clapped her hands in delight. "Oh look, a troika. We are in Russia," she exclaimed. Then she turned and looked up to see Reginald Vanderbilt. She felt like such a fool. All night she had pretended to be a woman of the world, and now, caught off guard, she knew she had ruined the carefully created illusion. Here she was, clapping her hands like a schoolgirl.

And on that snowy night the world-weary Reginald Claypoole Vanderbilt, a dissipated Society prince, saturated with affluence and alcohol, saw before him youth and exuberance in the person of this fresh, spontaneous, impossibly young child-woman.

Reginald Claypoole Vanderbilt

. . . Reggie was full of flaming enthusiasm and indomitable willfulness, both behind the wheel and before the cocktail bar.

EDWIN P. HOYT

REGINALD VANDERBILT was a dying man the night he first laid eyes on Gloria Morgan. Inside his body, lethal flakes of fat were coagulating into balls, choking the healthy cells of his liver. Every minute one and one-half quarts of blood fought to enter this purification chamber, only to find it necrotic, inflexible. His liver had enlarged in its futile attempt to handle this flow of blood which backed up into the portal vein and then, desperately seeking other pathways, forced itself into the lower veins of his stomach and those at the base of his esophagus.

As the pressure mounted higher, blood and plasma separated, the latter seeping through the hardened surface of the liver and collecting in the abdominal cavity below. The visible signs of Reggie's alcoholism were his bloated appearance and his distended abdomen. In this, he looked no different from many other Society gentlemen of his time.

Reggie told Gloria that he had been suffering from sclerosis of the liver since he was an undergraduate at Yale. Sclerosis, a term no longer in use, was used then to describe the hardening stage of liver disease. Reginald would have had to have been drinking heavily since he was approximately fifteen to develop this condition in college. It is possible that, in her mind, Gloria confused the words sclerosis and cirrhosis, or perhaps the doctors had used the more acceptable word to mask the truth. Sclerosis might have a benign connotation; cirrhosis, never. In any case, Gloria placed little significance on what Reggie had revealed to her or on his steady consumption of alcohol. Reginald himself had been repeatedly warned by his physicians that he must stop drinking. He would not. Or could not.

From birth, Reginald Claypoole Vanderbilt, the youngest son of Alice Gwynne and Cornelius Vanderbilt II, had been subjected to a set of mixed signals. His parents were religious, puritanical, hard-working, abstemious, yet they existed in an atmosphere of magnificent waste, surrounding themselves with luxury greater than that of Oriental potentates. Their 137-room mansion on Fifth Avenue, their palatial seventy-room "cottage," The Breakers, in Newport, Rhode Island, became settings for a life hemmed in by arcane, inflexible rules. Once, as a young man, Reggie's face had flushed with embarrassment as he'd entered a Newport party only to discover that he had forgotten his gloves—an unpardonable error. An obliging butler opened a drawer and let him choose a pair from the dozens reserved for the household staff.

Reginald shared with his sister Gertrude, who was five years his senior, a loathing for formality and the hollow forms of Society. Gertrude's way was to observe these conventions on the outside while secretly rebelling; in effect, she led a double life. Reggie's way was to throw himself into the frantic pursuit of pleasure; to become the family jester.

Reggie's three older brothers, William Henry (Bill), Cornelius III (Neily), and Alfred Gwynne, all possessed the Vanderbilt good looks and dash. Reginald, with his plain homely face, resembled the Gwynne side of the family. He was always the kid brother tagalong. At eighteen, he was still the smallest of the Vanderbilt boys; his chest measurement when inflated was under 39 inches, his hips just over 35. He wore a size 6 shoe and a 6¾ hat.

In 1898, Reginald followed his brothers to Yale, arriving with dozens of trunks and portmanteaus full of English clothes, a manservant, a great deal of massive furniture, a horse and trap. The servant, forbidden by college law, was promptly sent home.

Reggie moved into a suite of rooms reserved for members of his family over the archway at Vanderbilt Hall. Six years earlier, in 1892,

Reggie's brother Bill had died of typhoid fever while in his junior year at Yale, and their father had built Vanderbilt Hall as a memorial to him. In 1895, three years before Reggie's arrival at Yale, his brother Neily had graduated with honors. Alfred Gwynne, however, was still a senior when Reggie arrived and he worshipped this older brother and aped everything Alfred did: playing polo, driving horses, and fencing. Reggie performed all these sports competently but much less spectacularly than Alfred. The other Vanderbilt boys had been good students, but Reggie attended classes only sporadically and was tutored the entire time he was at Yale. Alfred had been chosen for the senior society, Skull and Bones, and Neily for Scroll and Key. When Reggie's turn came, he was asked to join the less desirable Wolf's Head, and only after one of the fifteen men originally chosen had dropped out.

What Reggie seemed to have learned early on was not to compete. He reserved for himself one area in which he excelled: he lost with consummate grace. All his life he seemed to seek situations in which he could demonstrate this quality. By the time he reached Yale, he was already gambling heavily and had a reputation for being a good loser.

Of his years at Yale, the New York *Evening Journal* observed, "He has no prestige or influence. He has made few friends and no enemies. . . . He will be remembered chiefly as a colorless young man who lived much alone, had few associates, entered little into the life of the undergraduates and was inclined to bet heavily at times on college sporting events. It is a matter of college gossip that he dropped $3,500 on the Yale-Harvard football match."

On his twenty-first birthday, December 19, 1901, two years after his father's death, the vast wave of Vanderbilt wealth engulfed this unprepossessing young man. Reginald Claypoole Vanderbilt inherited $7.5 million outright, which yielded him an income of approximately $375,000 annually. He also received various legacies from his grandfather and several aunts, estimated at $3 million, yielding an approximate additional income of $150,000 annually. He received another $5 million in trust: he could spend the annual income of this trust, about $250,000, but was not permitted to invade the capital. Upon his death, this $5 million was to go to his children to be distributed when they reached twenty-one. (It was this inviolable trust that was to figure so significantly in little Gloria's future.)

On the night of his twenty-first birthday, Reginald celebrated the acquisition of $15.5 million with its yearly income of $775,000 by heading straight for Richard Canfield's elegant, illegal gambling house on Forty-fourth Street. He ordered a fine meal from Delmonico's, which was next door, then, under the watchful eye of the fastidious, soft-spoken Richard Canfield, Reggie lost $70,000.

It was the beginning of a pattern that was to endure throughout his lifetime. Canfield was said to have taken well over $1 million from Reginald Vanderbilt, while the rest of his fortune was spun away on roulette wheels in Cannes, Monte Carlo, and Deauville. Reginald Vanderbilt became known to gamblers as "the perfect sucker." He played leisurely, lost amiably. During one two-week trip abroad, the Deauville Casino paid $48,000 in commissions to those responsible for delivering Reggie to the casino each evening. The casino was hardly the loser—Reggie's first night's losses alone were $60,000.

On one night in early 1902, Reggie, accompanied by a few Yale classmates, lost $120,000 at Canfield's roulette table. An observer said, "He wrote out a check for all he had lost, yawned slightly, put on his hat and went home." That spring, police smashed the windows of Canfield's town house and with axes destroyed the intricate wall paneling behind which were concealed the roulette wheels and faro layouts. The officers also found $300,000 worth of IOU's from Reggie Vanderbilt in Canfield's safe. There was a barrage of newspaper publicity as the New York District Attorney, William Travers Jerome, tried unsuccessfully to subpoena Reggie to testify against Canfield. He simply refused to appear, and the charges were dropped. A grateful Canfield agreed to settle Reggie's IOU's for $130,000.

On June 24, 1902, Reginald showed up for his Yale graduation only to discover to his astonishment that his name had been withheld from the commencement list because he had failed an examination. He returned the following November for a month and was granted his B.A. degree.

At twenty-two, Reginald became engaged to Cathleen Neilson, a twenty-year-old Catholic heiress. *The New York Times* engagement announcement included a character analysis of Reginald far kinder than any he had previously received:

> So far it is very difficult to decide as to what the young man will do in the future. He is very fond of outdoor sports, is a good polo player, has a fondness for horses, is a capital whip and has proved himself quite an adept chauffeur. He did not distinguish himself at Yale last year and missed his examination. But he was very much in love, and made frequent visits to town, and was besides a part of the time in ill health. Those who know him say that there is much good material in him, and that he will settle down and make

a very practical business man. He has not expressed as yet any aptitude for following the pursuits of his father or his uncles.

In applying for a marriage license, Reginald stated that his father's occupation had been "capitalist" and his own was "gentleman." He married Cathleen Neilson in an opulent Newport ceremony. His wedding gift to his bride was $1 million. The next year a daughter, Mary Cathleen (called Cathleen) was born.

Reggie worked hard at his chosen occupation of gentleman—in the company of his brother Alfred he devoted much of his time to Thoroughbred horses and harness racing; together they owned seventy-five racehorses. Soon after his marriage, Reggie purchased Sandy Point Farm in Portsmouth, a 280-acre farm adjoining Alfred's Oakland Farm. In his stables he kept sixty horses, the name of each inscribed on a solid gold plate over the entrance to his stall. Reggie also stocked twenty types of carriages, with appropriate harnesses trimmed in sterling silver and gold. He developed a reputation as an expert at four-in-hand, driving his perfectly matched pairs of Thoroughbreds at fashionable European and American tracks where his gray-and-white colors became famous. He was the prime force behind the Newport Horse Show, and became president of the American Hackney Horse Society.

At Sandy Point Farm, Reggie's particular pride was The Ring, a building that housed an indoor oval ring 300 feet long, 150 feet wide, with a roof 40 feet above the tanbark and a glassed-in living room at one end. The walls of this room were lined with glass cabinets which held Reggie's ribbons and trophies. He took to raising many breeds of dogs in kennels that occupied nearly an acre of land; his prizewinners were registered with the American Kennel Club, the Dalmatian Club, the Russian Wolfhound Club, the American Fox Terrier Club, and the Old English Sheepdog Club.

Motorcars also caught his fancy. The pudgy Reggie Vanderbilt was a startling sight speeding down country roads in his roadster, a bull terrier seated at his side on the open front seat. The dog wore leather leggings, a leather coat, and driving goggles that matched Reggie's own.

The first "bubbles," as the new motorcars were called in Society slang, had arrived in Newport in the summer of 1897, imported by Reggie's Aunt Alva. Alva, who had divorced Reggie's uncle William K. Vanderbilt in 1895 and had promptly married Oliver H. P. Belmont, had to be the first with everything. In 1899, Alva held the first motorcar rally in America on the lawn of her Newport mansion. An obstacle race was run through a course peppered with dummy policemen, nursemaids, and babies in carriages. The driver who "killed" the fewest people won the race. Once Alva had pointed the way, motorcars became a favorite play toy of the super-rich. William K. Vanderbilt eventually built a hundred-car garage in which he kept his motorcars—his De Dion Bouton, his Stevens-Duryea, his Hispano-Suiza, his Mercedes, his Bugatti, his Bentley, his Isotta-Fraschini, his Duesenberg, his Rolls-Royce, and so forth. He employed twenty chauffeurs and repairmen to attend his vehicles.

Harry Payne Whitney, Gertrude's husband, acquired a stable of thirty motorcars, and Alfred and Reggie each had approximately the same number, but Reginald held the dubious distinction of being the most reckless driver. Eventually, the Newport townspeople took to pelting him with rocks as he careened along country roads in clouds of dust. In 1902, Reggie was arrested for driving twelve miles an hour in an eight-mile zone; he was fined ten dollars plus two dollars and eight cents for court costs. By 1913, he was being arrested for doing thirty in a twelve-mile zone. Vanderbilt biographer Edwin P. Hoyt described Reggie as "full of flaming enthusiasm and indomitable willfulness, both behind the wheel and before the cocktail bar."

Unfortunately, Reggie and his chauffeur were involved in a series of automobile accidents involving pedestrians. On four separate occasions, two men were killed and two others seriously injured. Also, a small boy of seven was struck by Reginald's car; *The New York Times* provided the handy excuse that the child had been playing when he "slipped on a banana peel" and fell "directly in front of the automobile."

In 1907, when Reggie's sister Gladys became twenty-one, he received an additional distribution of $2.5 million from his father's estate. It was noted at this time that although the fortunes of the other Vanderbilt children had appreciated in value, Reginald's had severely diminished. It was said he lavished jewels and fortunes on a series of spectacular women. In September of 1910, all Newport was aflutter with the gossip that Reginald had been waylaid on the road to Sandy Point Farm and thoroughly thrashed by the husband of a Newport Society lady. The beating evidently did not get the point across, and rumor had it that the irate husband had returned several weeks later and shot Reggie. From Sandy Point Farm, Reginald's doctor telegraphed major newspapers: "There is absolutely no truth in the statement regarding Mr. Reginald Vanderbilt. He is suffering from a plain case of typhoid. . . . His fever is his only ailment." However, not even Reggie's most intimate acquaintances were permitted to visit him.

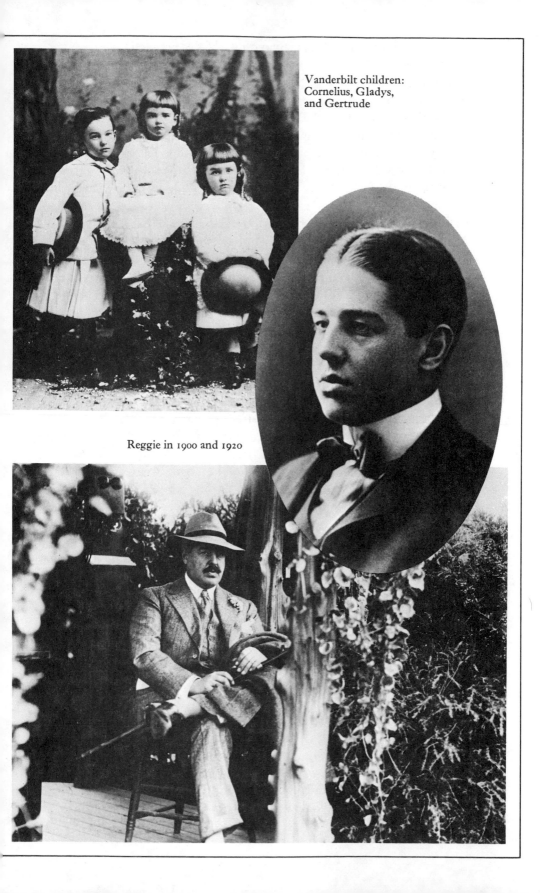

Vanderbilt children: Cornelius, Gladys, and Gertrude

Reggie in 1900 and 1920

In 1912, Reginald Vanderbilt sailed home from a trip to Paris. It seems he had forgotten something—stranded there without funds were his wife and daughter and the child's governess. Cathleen Vanderbilt appealed to her husband's Parisian agent for the money to return to America; the agent sent a wireless to Reggie on shipboard, who radioed back instructions for him to provide them with the money for passage. When they returned to New York no one met them. From that time on, Reggie ignored his wife.

He took as his "fast friend" and "favourite dancing partner" (both phrases were Maury Paul's euphemisms for mistress) the flame-haired actress Charlotte Carter Flather, known as "the most beautiful girl in Greenwich Village." Charlotte hoped to marry Reggie, but at first he was still married to Cathleen and later, when he was free, he had tired of her. In desperation she took an overdose of opium and Veronal in a suite at the Plaza Hotel paid for by Reggie. A few minutes later, a bellboy heard her screaming and ran for the Plaza's physician, who arrived in time to save her life. In 1922, when Reggie found himself drawn to Gloria Morgan, his lawyers paid Charlotte $10,000 on condition that she sign a paper releasing him from any further responsibility for her. She signed. Later on, however, she tried to get more money. She was refused, and repeated her earlier suicide attempt. This time no one came. Charlotte was found by her maid, sprawled across the pink satin spread of her bed. An empty bottle of silver-slipper polish lay on its side on the carpet. Eight suicide notes rested on her desk—none to Reginald Vanderbilt.

On May 1, 1915, Alfred Gwynne Vanderbilt had boarded the *Lusitania*—he went down with the torpedoed liner. Reginald received a bequest of $500,000, as well as a release from a debt of $44,000 owed his brother. That year he was accused by the federal government of falsifying his income tax returns and of failing to report this legacy. During the investigation, it was established that except for Alfred's bequest, all Reggie had left of his fortune was a gross annual income of $217,000 from his inviolable $5 million trust. In fourteen years almost $25 million in income and capital had vanished.

In 1919, Cathleen Neilson Vanderbilt finally got around to suing Reggie for divorce and her suit went unopposed. *The New York Times*, in reporting the divorce, noted that Reginald Vanderbilt "has never been interested in society or business, giving up much of his time to the breeding and exhibition of show horses." At thirty-nine, Reginald was free to become a gay bachelor. Somewhere along the line he'd had a kidney operation, and his doctors would answer reporters' queries by saying that Reggie's periodic confinement to bed was due to rheumatism or an infection. But these doctors told Reggie the truth: that if he didn't stop drinking, he would soon die. When Reginald Vanderbilt met Gloria Morgan, he was living on credit; both physically and financially, he had overdrawn his account. Only no one understood that. Not the merchants who were delighted to extend credit to a Vanderbilt, not the public who equated the name Vanderbilt with limitless wealth, not Miss Gloria Morgan.

Your Only Chance of Financial Security

Good Lord, a Mrs. Vanderbilt without any money!

REGINALD VANDERBILT

GLORIA PERCEIVED LIFE through an emotional haze that made her the heroine of her own fairy tale. She was a damsel in distress who was beset, then rescued, only to be beset again. For Gloria, there would always be the rosy tones of romance, the white paper doily and red crayon sentiment of a child's Valentine. If what actually took place was not romantic or even pretty, but rather in the nature of a bargain, she would never see it that way. She would remember it quite differently.

The slim, dark-haired girl sat alone in a suite at the Waldorf-Astoria, her head bent close to the aquamarine satin dress, her hand moving rhythmically, making small, precise stitches. Gloria was good at sewing and she enjoyed it; it was not just an economy measure. She glanced up at the clock and felt a rush of anxiety. It was getting terribly late, and she was due at Reggie's house for dinner. No time for the hem, she thought, and began rapidly pulling the threads from the bottom of the dress, creating a deep fringe. She repeated this procedure on the ruff at the low-cut neck. The February night was bitter cold and she could see snow swirling outside the window, but she draped a delicate, brightly embroidered Spanish shawl over her shoulders; her evening coat was too shabby to wear. This was a special night and she wanted to look beautiful—for him. Tonight was the night Gloria Morgan would be asked, in the presence of that famous Society columnist Maury Paul, to become Mrs. Reginald Claypoole Vanderbilt.

Gloria's fantasy of her courtship by Reginald Vanderbilt was a highly sentimental one. Over the years she would repeat it to reporters and would write of it in two books. Perhaps she even came to believe it. Here is that fantasy which existed only in her mind and in the press: Gloria would maintain that a few weeks after the Beaux Arts dinner, Thelma's marriage to Junior Converse had broken up and Mamma Morgan had come to New York to help Thelma settle her financial affairs. She'd taken a suite at the Waldorf-Astoria and both Thelma and Gloria moved in with her. Finally, Mamma decided to take Thelma back to Brussels with her, while Gloria was to be sent to visit family friends in Cuba.

Thelma and Mamma were packing to leave for Brussels when the phone rang. It was Helen Beadleston inviting Gloria to dinner that evening. Happy to escape the mess and confusion, Gloria gladly accepted. When she arrived at Mrs. Beadleston's, Reginald Vanderbilt was waiting in the living room. "Oh, the troika girl. Hello, Gloria," he said. For the first time Gloria noticed that Reggie's eyes were blue and his lids turned up at the corners, in Oriental fashion.

They went to the theater, where Reggie insisted on sitting next to her and afterward he begged, "Don't go home, please don't go home. Let's go out somewhere, I have so much I want to say to you."

"I'm sorry, I can't, I have to get up very early. Thelma and my mother sail for Europe tomorrow," Gloria answered.

Reggie then said he'd come to the *Lapland* at noon to see them off. He didn't show up.

Gloria was disappointed, but on returning to the empty suite at the Waldorf, she found it full of flowers—orchids and every available flower of the season crowded every surface and even filled the bathroom sink. A moment later Reggie phoned to explain that his butler, Norton, had forgotten to wake him; then he invited Gloria to lunch.

Lunch was the start of what Gloria and her set called a "rush." They lunched again the next day, and that evening Reggie took Gloria to see *Glory*, playing at the Vanderbilt Theater. He smiled as he told Gloria he'd chosen that theater because of its name. Gloria was "thrilled and flattered, the world seemed full and beautiful. . . . But to what was all this leading?"

Two days later they went to *The Music Box Revue*. In one of the scenes, Grace Moore and John Steele were singing in a California orange grove. In the middle of the song, small valves opened under each seat and the theater was drenched with the smell of orange blossoms. Gloria would never forget that moment.

After the theater, at supper at the Colony, Reginald Vanderbilt asked Gloria Morgan to marry him, and she accepted. She noted, "I had known him but four days."

A beautiful whirlwind courtship—and utterly untrue.

Here is what actually happened: Gloria did indeed do all the things she remembered, but over the period of a year—not four days. Thelma had provided the initial access to Reginald Vanderbilt, but it was his daughter, Cathleen, who unsuspectingly furthered the relationship. Cathleen was Gloria's age, both young women were Catholics, and in their first social season. In the winter of 1922, Cathleen was the guest of honor at a series of debutante entertainments culminating in a dinner dance given by her grandmother, Alice Gwynne Vanderbilt. For the first time in more than a decade, Alice threw open her filigreed wrought-iron gates at 2 West Fifty-eighth Street and used the entrance she reserved for royalty and state occasions.

For all her pedigree, Cathleen longed for a father. Her resemblance to Reggie was striking—the same slanted eyes, the same round face. Cathleen had been eight when Reggie had walked out on the family, and since then she'd rarely seen her father. In 1922, two pleasant things happened to this sensitive girl: Gloria Morgan suddenly began paying attention to her and soon became her closest chum, and her father suddenly began paying attention to her, seeing her frequently. Over the next few months Gloria and Cathleen were often together in the company of Cathleen's father. On several occasions the girls were observed eating ice cream at the Colony, while Reggie drank stingers laced with absinthe, his favorite aperitif as well as after-dinner drink.

Shortly after the Beaux Arts dinner, Thelma had begged Gloria to move in with her, she'd become frightened of being alone with her new husband. Junior borrowed money, never paid his bills, and drank constantly and heavily. When he drank he became abusive to Thelma, cursing at her and beating her. At one dinner party in their home, Junior threw a glass jar at Thelma. On another occasion, while dining in a restaurant, he stood up, walked around the table, and ripped the dress off her body. (Converse was to marry five times. All of his wives would charge that they had been subjected to physical abuse; his fourth wife, a former Ziegfeld Follies girl, charged that he had beaten her into unconsciousness.)

Thelma might have left Junior, only she discovered that she was pregnant. One day in August, when the temperature was in the high nineties, Thelma put on her hat and walked out the door of her house on to the stoop. Dazed by the bright sunlight, she missed a step and tumbled headlong to the pavement. She lost the baby.

Rumors began to circulate that the chic young Converses' marriage was in trouble. Thelma vehemently denied them, and Maury Paul wrote in his Cholly Knickerbocker column: "It is pleasant, decidedly pleasant, to brand as false, tales about the Converse matrimonial debacle. 'Junior' Converse and his pretty bride are supremely happy. . . ."

By January of 1923 Gloria had been seeing Reggie for almost a year but he had not proposed to her. Thelma's marriage was a shambles of debt, abuse, and alcohol. That's when Mamma Morgan decided to take her twins in hand; she arrived in New York, retrieved her daughters from the Converse flat, and took them to live with her in a suite at the Waldorf, an action that represented an uncharacteristic extravagance on the part of this frugal woman. But Mamma had plans. Thelma was promptly dispatched to Brussels to obtain a divorce; then Mamma turned her full attention to Gloria.

Mamma had been in New York only ten days when Reggie Vanderbilt marched into Tiffany & Co. and purchased a $75,000, 16¼-carat, heart-shaped diamond ring mounted in platinum and set off by two ¾-carat baguette diamonds. That same week, Mrs. Morgan placed an order for Gloria at dressmaker Sonia Rosenberg's for a wedding gown of light gray faille, made with a wide skirt and a tight-fitting bodice, a shape that was copied from the coronation gown of Alexandra of Russia.

On the night of January 20, Mamma helped put the finishing touches on a costume Gloria was to wear to a debutante ball being given by Reggie in honor of Cathleen. Gloria went as Marie Antoinette, in a flowered brocade dress and tiny shepherdess hat. She was one of the most admired of the young dancers. Reggie had given Gloria the Tiffany ring, but she did not wear it and no one suspected that she and the host considered themselves engaged.

As the dancers moved across the floor, Reggie drew his daughter aside and told her that he had important news for her and would like her to drop by for lunch the following day. When Reggie told her of his engagement, Cathleen Vanderbilt burst into tears. She felt she had been used by Gloria and, worse, by her own father.

Much later, when Gloria announced to the press that Cathleen would be her bridesmaid, Cathleen fled New York and went to stay with her mother in Palm Beach. Then Gloria told the press that Cathleen was expected back momentarily, and that a bridesmaid's gown was being made for her. But Cathleen didn't show up at the wedding rehearsal and, in spite of her father's pleas, refused to return for the wedding. The day after the wedding the *Daily News* reported: "Cathleen Vanderbilt failed to arrive . . . a gray gown had been made for her to match one that the Countess de Maupas intended wearing. When it became clear that Miss Vanderbilt would not appear at the wedding, the countess changed to a dress of Alice blue moire silk. . . ."

The following June, Cathleen married Harry C. Cushing III. Her father and his bride did not attend the ceremony. Three months after her marriage, Cathleen suffered a complete nervous breakdown. The New York *Herald* reported that her collapse was brought on by "a shock she suffered during a thunderstorm. . . ."

At the end of January 1923, when all the arrangements for Gloria's wedding had been completed, Mamma sailed back to Belgium, leaving her daughter alone in the Waldorf suite. Both Gloria and Reggie knew that the newspapers could have a field day with the May-September engagement of a forty-three-year-old Vanderbilt to a teenaged girl. They understood that they were public personalities and wished to be presented in the most sympathetic manner possible. In his Cholly Knickerbocker column, Maury Paul could make or break a Society figure—he seemed to delight in doing both. And so, even though everything was already arranged, they decided to stage a small drama for the benefit of that very special columnist.

On the morning of February 8, 1923, Reginald Vanderbilt telephoned Maury Paul and said, "Gloria Morgan is coming to dinner tonight. I'm going to ask her to become my wife, and if I have the good fortune to secure her 'yes,' I want you to announce our engagement for us."

Paul, unaware that he was to play a role in a prearranged drama, was pleased. This would certainly be a big Society story, and that was what he lived for. He left his office that snowy February evening and went home to find everything in perfect order. His custom-made London dinner jacket and shirt were carefully laid out on the bed. His trademark, a fresh red carnation, reposed in a glass vase on the dresser. His mother was responsible for that. He adored her. She was sixty-four years old and her son thirty-two, but he still selected every dress she wore and supervised her every activity. She returned his affection in kind.

That night, after he left, his mother applied creams and unguents to her face and body, put on her hairnet, and strapped on the chin strap Maury insisted she wear. "After all," she said of herself, "I must look my best for Maury. . . . I'm his best girl."

Maury Paul arrived at the five-story Vanderbilt brownstone at 12 East Seventy-seventh Street where Norton, the Vanderbilt butler, escorted him down in the elevator to the basement. The elevator door opened into one corner of a large room with a brick floor, dark oak walls, and double doors opening on to a garden. Easy chairs and comfortable couches were massed in groups about the room, interspersed with little tavern tables covered with bright red-and-white checked cloths; a grand piano stood in one corner. The dominant feature of this room, however, was a massive mahogany bar (a replica of the one in the William the Conqueror Tavern in Deauville) behind which Reggie was standing. Maury Paul noted that this was where he spent most of his time.

Maury felt that Reggie was a fool for not obeying his doctor's orders, but he understood that alcohol was the background color in the fabric of Reggie's life. Prohibition had been in force for three years and never was the consumption of alcohol greater or more encouraged. On his nightly rounds, Maury Paul watched as debutantes took gold, jewel-studded flasks to parties and passed out cold on the dance floor. Most of his friends had their treasured bootleggers whom they treated with deference. This was the era of postwar affluence, the Joe-sent-me culture, the speakeasy life. Alcohol was not tolerated, it was glorified. Maury himself drank little; his obsession was work, not alcohol. He carried his own special brand of tea in a silver snuffbox and asked that it be served to him in nightclubs. Maury had observed a steady decline in Reggie's health and he was intolerant of the lack of discipline that would allow a man to throw his life away. When Reggie asked him what he wanted to drink, he asked for ice water.

A few minutes later Gloria Morgan arrived. Seeing Maury, she smiled at him, feeling that he was her dear friend, "not alone a connoisseur in social civilization . . . but a man of the greatest capacity for human understanding I know." Paul, on the other hand, whose self-proclaimed nickname was Mr. Bitch, responded to her smile with the thought that Gloria's flimsy Spanish shawl was worn for reasons of economy, not fashion. Paul also recalled that a few months earlier Gloria's twin Thelma had posed for a series of photographs wearing that same shawl—and nothing else.

After dinner Gloria perched next to Reginald, who was, Paul observed, "For the first and only time in his life deadly serious."

"Gloria," Reggie said, looking at her like a puppy dog, "I want you

Maury Paul
(Cholly Knickerbocker)

Gloria in the movies

Such Matrimonial Prizes!

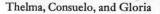

Thelma, Consuelo, and Gloria

to marry me. But I want our mutual friend here to hear what I feel I must tell you. As my wife, you'll have a big name but little money to live up to it. I've spent every cent of my personal fortune and I live on the income of a $5 million trust fund established by my father. As long as I live, you will be taken care of. But I am an ill man. Should I die, the $5 million goes to my daughter Cathleen."

Reginald paused, then, concentrating on Gloria's face, continued, "Your only chance of financial security in the future would be to have a child who would then share the trust fund with Cathleen. Your chance of having a child by me is one of those hundred-to-one shots, for my doctor doubts that I can become a father again."

Paul, always the objective observer, sipped his ice water. Although he did not know that Gloria had already accepted Reginald's proposal, he had no doubt of the outcome. Reggie went on: "Now that I have told you the truth, if you still want to marry me and eventually be the poor widow Vanderbilt, I'll be the happiest man in the whole world, and our friend here can report for his paper at once the news of our engagement."

The scene was almost played out: Gloria reached over and squeezed Reggie's puffy hand. "Reggie dear, it's you I love—not your name or the Vanderbilt money. I don't care about being poor or about the future as long as I have you now." Then the vibrant young girl reached up and kissed her short, stout, ill, forty-three-year-old Vanderbilt.

Reginald turned to Maury and exclaimed, "I'm the proudest and happiest man in the world. What this angel sees in me I will never know." And shaking his head he added, "But I still don't believe Gloria realizes what she might be up against. Good Lord, a Mrs. Vanderbilt without any money!"

In response, Maury and Gloria both laughed, and Reggie, smiling too, said, "I haven't talked this seriously in years. I need a drink."

Maury Paul beamed benevolently on the couple, wished them well, and, as soon as he could, excused himself. He went immediately to the Salmon Building on Forty-second Street, rode up to the ninth floor, and unlocked the door to office 908. The small anteroom was papered at random with dollar bills; the idea had occurred to Maury and Berwyn Hughes one day and—just like that—they did it. Berwyn said his boss was making so much money they might as well. Eve Brown thought Berwyn resembled Adonis; he served as Maury's valet, butler, comforter, and companion. The office rent was paid for by a friend who was to remain forever anonymous. It gave Paul privacy, and through the doors of the inner office paraded a stream of young men whom Eve Brown described as "fragile, slim youths with high complexions and curly hair, boys with an airy manner, trailing clouds of perfume. . . ." Society women also visited Paul, and Eve commented on their good looks, but Paul responded with the pronouncement, "No *woman* is beautiful!"

Maury walked through the anteroom into his office. He removed the flower from his lapel and put it in the bud vase on the desk. He draped his dinner jacket over the back of the scarred dark wood chair, unfastened his jeweled cuff links, and rolled up his shirt sleeves. He removed his heavy platinum ring set with a pigeon's blood ruby and his wristwatch with the gold-link strap and placed them on the far corner of the desk.

Maury Paul was ready. He eased his bulk behind the desk and pressed the chair back against the wall. He unfastened his belt buckle, opened his fly, and expelled the pent-up air in his vast stomach. He inserted a sheet of yellow copy paper in the typewriter and with two fleshy fingers he began hammering at the keys. Cholly Knickerbocker was about to produce another extraordinary Society Scoop.

Alice Claypoole Gwynne Vanderbilt

She usurped the simplicity of being known merely as *the* Mrs. Vanderbilt. First names were superfluous, as are last names in the royal houses of Europe.

LUCIUS BEEBE

ALICE CLAYPOOLE GWYNNE VANDERBILT was in her seventy-ninth year when her youngest son, her beloved Reggie, telephoned to request an audience. She knew exactly what it was about: Reggie wished to marry young Gloria Morgan and it would certainly be awkward if he did so without her consent. Once, years before, her eldest living son, Cornelius III, had done just that, and he'd become a family outcast. The breach had not been healed when her dear husband, Cornelius II, died. In his will her husband passed over this disobedient son, who thereby forfeited over $40 million and the title, Head of the House of Vanderbilt. The lesson had been learned.

Alice understood full well the immense power and control her fortune provided. She'd told Reggie that if their relationship remained warm and affectionate, upon her death her Fifth Avenue mansion, valued at approximately $7.5 million, would be his, as well as $1.25 million, which represented a one-third share of a trust created by her husband.

Although Alice was a woman known for her icy reserve, a woman who deemed overt displays of affection unseemly, Reggie was her dear love. Once she'd had four fine sons. Now, with two of them dead and the third an outcast, Reggie represented her only hope that one of her sons would be Head of the House of Vanderbilt. For Alice this was no mere title—it represented the control of a business empire and the continuance of a dynasty.

Reggie strongly resembled his mother's side of the family. Years of the high life had bloated his appearance, but when she looked at her youngest son, Alice could distinguish clearly the countenance of her own father who had died long ago. Abraham had been his name, and like the biblical father, he had been just and stern and steeped in tradition. It was Alice's fervent desire that if Reggie married again, he would at last settle down and take up the royal mantle that was his. But in this expectation she was an old woman indulging herself in a double delusion: Reginald's entire life had been a testament to his inability and unwillingness to assume responsibility, and the tradition which meant so much to Alice no longer existed—it had been washed away in a tidal wave of Vanderbilt wealth.

Alice herself had helped create this wave. Her vanity and pride had led her to an unparalleled display of riches. She had set for her family an example of conspicuous consumption of the most profligate kind, while staunchly espousing the values of discipline, religion, charity, and honor. She had become known as "Alice of The Breakers," which was the name of her $7 million summer "cottage" in Newport. (After visiting The Breakers, Grand Duke Boris of Imperial Russia exclaimed, "I have never dreamed of such luxury. Such an outpouring of riches. It is like walking on gold.") The Breakers had been erected as a tangible demonstration to Alice's competitive sister-in-law Alva (Mrs. William Kissam Vanderbilt) that Alice was *the* Mrs. Vanderbilt, and her husband, Cornelius II, Head of the House. Yet over the white marble fireplace that had been ripped intact from the Château d'Arnay-le-Duc at a cost of $75,000, was an inscription in archaic French: "Little do I care for riches, and do not miss them, since only cleverness prevails in the end." Alice saw neither humor nor irony in this.

Had they been born in an era of more solid values, Alice and Cornelius Vanderbilt II, these two stern moralists, undoubtedly would have led quiet, contemplative lives. Instead, they devoted themselves to becoming supreme Vanderbilts—the most visibly wealthy family in America. Amid the splendor and style they created, they neglected to produce a concomitant sense of family purpose or responsibility. Wealth was merely a commodity to be squandered, and a time was to come when Alice would find that she had squandered her future.

For Alice, history had suffered a terrible compression. In the span of only twenty years, Alice Gwynne Vanderbilt had watched four generations of Heads of the House of Vanderbilt flourish and die. Commodore Cornelius Vanderbilt, founder of the fortune, had died in 1877, at eighty-three. Her father-in-law, William Henry, had died eight years later, at sixty-three. Then her own husband, Cornelius II, died in 1899 at fifty-six. Most bitter of all was the death of her son William Henry, who had died his terrible writhing death from typhoid fever when he was twenty-one. Alice had watched the Vanderbilt family in its four-generational meteoric arc, from the force of the rapacious Commodore, who thought he was founding a dynasty for the centuries, to Reginald, the hedonistic sportsman, aimlessly seeking diversion.

In June of 1863 Gloria Morgan's grandfather, General Hugh Judson Kilpatrick, moved his troops to Gettysburg in a desperate attempt to crush the Confederate forces; Alice Claypoole Gwynne, a dainty girl of nineteen who stood scarcely five feet tall, with a wistful heart-shaped face surrounded by masses of dark brown hair, attended the funeral of her father, a Cincinnati lawyer of impeccable reputation; and sixty-nine-year-old Commodore Vanderbilt bought his first share of railroad stock. The Commodore was a man who, through single-mindedness and physical and financial courage, had risen from a penniless, barefoot Staten Island farmboy to the owner of a vast shipping empire.

Of all the titans in the game of fortune, Alice Gwynne's future grandfather-in-law, Commodore Vanderbilt, loomed the largest. "Law! What do I care about law? Hain't I got the power!" he had bellowed. And to Charles Morgan, who had speculated against his interests, he wrote, "I won't sue you, for the law is too slow. I will ruin you."

The Commodore's conversion to railroads had come late in life when he observed that his fat, phlegmatic, eldest son, William Henry, had, in five years, taken the defunct stock of the Staten Island Railroad and run it up to $175 a share. The Commodore had considered William Henry a "sucker" and a "blatherskite," and for twenty years had consigned him and his large family of eight children (including Alice's future husband, Cornelius II) to a farm in Staten Island which yielded an annual income of $12,000.

But as William Henry began to demonstrate his business acumen, the Commodore perked up. Goaded on by his son's example and a sense of competition from which even his flesh and blood were not exempt, the Commodore bought heavily into the Erie, Hudson, and

Harlem Railroads. In 1864 he removed William Henry from the purgatory of his Staten Island farm and brought him and his family to New York City, where William Henry was appointed vice-president of the Harlem Railroad.

Alice's future husband, Cornelius II, then twenty-one, was put to work by his grandfather, first as a clerk in New York's Glove and Leather Bank, and shortly thereafter as an accountant in the treasurer's office of the Harlem Railroad. The Commodore, who believed in working your way up, had a soft spot for this particular grandson, his namesake, whose tall, slim figure and piercing blue-gray eyes bore a startling resemblance to the Commodore's own.

Cornelius II was studious and serious. His salary was fifty dollars a month, and he lived on it. Acquaintances who knew him for decades said they had never seen him smile. He was deeply religious, attended church daily, and soon began to teach Sunday School at St. Bartholomew's Episcopal Church.

The year after her father's death, Alice Claypoole Gwynne also began to teach Sunday School at St. Bartholomew's. It was here that she met Cornelius, and she was immediately attracted to this handsome young man who was as righteous, stern, and humorless as Alice herself. Cornelius II worked diligently at his menial railroad job, and when the Commodore volunteered to take him on a European vacation, he inquired if that would mean giving up his salary.

"Well, I don't suppose it would go on while you're away," answered his grandfather.

"Then I'd better stay here," he replied.

Cornelius's fortunes were to change, but never his puritan ethics. Years later, when Cornelius and Alice lived in a Fifth Avenue mansion larger than the original Grand Central Terminal, a statue of a nude bather was placed in the Plaza Fountain of Abundance at Fifty-eighth Street and Fifth Avenue. Her bare back faced Cornelius's bedroom windows, a sight that so offended his sensibilities that he complained to the town fathers, requesting that the statue be removed. When they would not comply, he moved his bedroom one full city block away, to the Fifty-seventh Street side of his residence.

Alice and Cornelius were married in 1867, the year the Commodore, then a vigorous seventy-three, gained control of the New York Central. In the first decade of their marriage they lived quietly in a brownstone on the southwest corner of Forty-ninth Street and Fifth Avenue, and Alice gave birth to her first four children: William Henry, Alice (who died at seven), Cornelius III, and Gertrude. In that time the Commodore doubled his fortune to $100 million, but despite all their money, the Vanderbilts were not accepted into the kingdom of New York Society, ruled by the imperious Mrs. William Backhouse Astor. The only real difference between the Vanderbilts and the Astors was one generation. William Astor's grandfather, John Jacob, had been known to eat his peas and ice cream off his knife blade, and at the Albert Gallatins' dinner table, he had committed the social error of wiping his greasy fingers on the white dress of the daughter of the house. Still, to Mrs. Astor, the Commodore was totally unacceptable. In his headlong drive for fortune, Commodore Vanderbilt had no time or inclination for the constraints of Society. His speech was crude, his profanity spectacular; he could not write an intelligible letter and had never read a book until he was in his seventies. He chewed tobacco and was known to expectorate it onto his hostesses' Persian carpets. Perhaps his least acceptable practice, however, was his fanatic exploration of what Alice termed "the world beyond." After his mother's death, the Commodore spent countless hours in darkened rooms trying to communicate with her. Soon he was reporting their conversations to the family as well as repeating business advice given him by dead business associates. Thousands of dollars were spent consulting spiritualists, hypnotists, phrenologists, crystal-ball gazers, and faith healers. Upward of $75,000 was paid to a Staten Island seer who advised him to put saltcellars under the legs of his bed to ward off evil spirits, more to the flamboyant sisters Victoria Woodhull and Tennie C. (Tennessee) Claflin, who'd been run out of Urbana, Illinois, on charges of faith healing and prostitution. Tennessee, a beautiful redhead of twenty, took up residence with the Commodore as his official "healer" while Victoria gave him messages from his mother. Soon these sisters opened a Wall Street office where they made a fortune on tips supplied by the Commodore.

At seventy-five, the year after his wife of fifty-three years died, the Commodore took as his bride thirty-five-year-old Miss Frank A. Crawford, the great-granddaughter of his mother's brother. When people suggested that he might have been wiser to wed her mother, he responded, "If I married her, Frank would have gone off and married someone else. Now I have them both."

In the winter of 1876 the Commodore became terminally ill and called in his assorted faith healers to bring him relief from his constant abdominal pain. His physician recommended champagne to soothe his stomach. "Oh no, Doctor, I can't afford champagne. Won't sody-water do?" he asked.

At ten o'clock on the morning of January 4, 1877, thirty relatives gathered in the Commodore's bedroom. In his turn, Cornelius II stepped forward and whispered a brief farewell in his grandfather's ear. Then William Henry approached his father, who croaked out in a hoarse whisper, "Keep the money together, hey. Keep the Central our road." Finally, the Commodore requested a hymn session. It ended with Frank's soprano solo of "Come Ye Sinners Poor and Needy," followed by a reading of the Lord's Prayer. "That was a good prayer," the Commodore whispered. His eyes were like glass. One physician whispered to another that he was now sightless. The Commodore overheard them, raised his hand, and with his own fingers pushed his eyelids shut. Ten minutes later he died.

The Commodore's estate was valued at $110 million—$5 million more than the entire Federal Reserve had in its treasury at the time. He was survived by ten children—to his eight daughters, of whom he'd said, "They're nice children, but they're not Vanderbilts," the Commodore left modest bequests, the largest being a trust fund of $500,000. To his flawed son, Cornelius Jeremiah, an epileptic and a wastrel, he left only the income of a trust fund of $200,000.

William Henry's three younger sons each received $2 million worth of railroad stock. Alice's husband, the eldest son, received $1.5 million outright and $5.5 million in railroad stocks as well as the family portraits and statuary in the Commodore's Washington Place residence. With these bequests, the Commodore marked Cornelius II as a crown prince. Then in one bold stroke the Commodore left all the remainder of his estate—over $90 million—to his son William Henry. Through his bequest the Commodore created a cohesive empire and made William Henry ruler of a dynasty—the House of Vanderbilt.

With the social encumbrance of the Commodore's presence permanently removed, the Vanderbilts decided the time had come to enter Society, but the Commodore's crusty specter reached from the grave to stifle their plans. Cornelius Jeremiah and his sister Mary Alicia LaBau brought suit to have the Commodore's will declared invalid. Throughout the year of 1878 the newspapers daily dished up the latest salacious accusations in what was referred to as "The Great Vanderbilt Will Trial." Cornelius Jeremiah contended that William Henry had unduly influenced the Commodore, allowing him to commit their mother to an insane asylum when she had objected both to his plans to move to Manhattan and to his lust for the children's governess; that when the governess left, William Henry had secured a buxom young girl to satisfy his father's rather florid taste, saying, "The old man is bound to have his way, and it is useless to oppose him."

The trial dragged on for months while the public devoured every

Alice Gwynne Vanderbilt

Cornelius Vanderbilt II

Commodore Cornelius Vanderbilt

detail of the scandal. The Boston *Herald* righteously observed, "The haughty house of the Vanderbilt railway king . . . is, for a parvenu race, possessed of quite a respectable collection of family skeletons." Of all the accusations, the newspaper's allegation that the Vanderbilts were parvenu must have wounded Alice Gwynne the most. *She* was descended from a fine old family who had come to America in 1683. The Gwynne men had fought in every American war and the Gwynne women were members of the National Society of Colonial Dames.

Finally, after much pleading on the part of his wife and daughters-in-law, William Henry settled the contest by giving each of his sisters $500,000 outright, and presenting Cornelius Jeremiah with the income of $1 million in trust and paying off his gambling debts. Cornelius Jeremiah was free to start a new life, but within the year he put his pearl-handled Smith & Wesson revolver in his mouth and blew off the top of his head.

The trial scarred Alice Gwynne Vanderbilt for life, leaving her with an insatiable need to prove her respectability as well as an almost pathological aversion to the press. Her demand for privacy became an obsession. She was never to set foot in a shop. Muslin dressmakers' dummies of her form stood in the workrooms of Worth and Paquin. Worldly goods in profusion were brought to her doorstep. She refused to be photographed, and on more than one occasion, when a photographer took her picture, she directed her footman to overpower him and smash his camera.

The scandal drove her into an icy shell from which she was never to emerge. "We cannot always control other people's desires," she remarked. "Most certainly we can control our own." She became the most imperious and austere of the Vanderbilt women, "the family snob," her sister-in-law Alva called her. Her own sister, Cettie Shepherd, had a different opinion. Alice, she observed, "is frightfully shy."

To Alice, the glorification of the Vanderbilt name became a religion. She engaged experts to research the Vanderbilt family in hopes of finding an ancestor worthy of standing beside the progenitors of the Livingstons, Roosevelts, Stuyvesants, and Schuylers. Failing in this, she had her own ancestry traced back to William the Conqueror (who was at that time the most fashionable ancestor in the world of Society); Alice designed a family coat of arms, an acorn surrounded by oak leaves, a symbol that was to appear in profusion on the walls, upholstery, and fretwork of her mansions. And she waited for Society to open its doors to her. Which it did not.

Alice's sister-in-law Alva was not a woman to wait. In this plump, pugnacious woman of twenty-five burned the white-hot flame of social ambition. Alva never tired of telling people that her mother's family were the socially prominent Deshas of Kentucky and her father's the Smiths of Alabama. What she neglected to mention was that the Smiths had lost everything during the Civil War, after which her father moved his family to Paris. Four years later Mrs. Smith, without Alva's father, came to New York with her four daughters. Here, she ran a boardinghouse to make ends meet. Alva was determined to remove herself forever from the bitter memory of those days.

With the will contest behind them, the Vanderbilts decided to move to Fifth Avenue. At that time, Thirty-ninth Street was considered the uptown border of Society and millionaires discreetly concealed their fortunes behind what Edith Wharton described as "a universal chocolate coating of the most hideous stone ever quarried." The Vanderbilts shattered New York's brownstone façade: between Fifty-first and Fifty-second Street on Fifth Avenue William Henry commissioned twin palaces for himself and two of his daughters, and he assumed all expenses for Alva and Willie K.'s mansion at 660 Fifth Avenue and Alice and Cornelius II's mansion at 1 West Fifty-seventh Street.

The daring Alva moved quickly, commissioning architect Richard Morris Hunt to design a sixteenth-century French Renaissance château that might have been snatched intact from the Loire Valley. Alva's château was completed first and she announced that she would inaugurate it by giving a ball not for four hundred guests (the maximum number that could be accommodated in Mrs. Astor's ballroom) but for a thousand. It was to be a costume ball in honor of Alva's dear friend (and the woman for whom Alva had named her first child) Consuelo, Lady Mandeville, whose husband just happened to be heir to the title of Duke of Manchester. The clever Alva understood the appeal of European titles to American Society, and she'd discovered Mrs. Astor's Achilles' heel as well.

For months, New York Society spoke of nothing but "the Ball." Costumes designed by famous French couturiers were ordered from Paris, and the guests arranged to perform a series of entertainments. In the ballroom of the Astor brownstone mansion, Carrie Astor, the daughter of the house, and a group of her friends practiced a quadrille. The ladies, arrayed in gray tulle and diamonds, represented stars. The gentlemen wore the gray satin court dress of Louis XV. Mrs. William Astor, looking on, acknowledged that the effect was charming. But as the time for the ball neared, neither Mrs. Astor nor her daughter Carrie had received their invitations. Mrs. Astor commandeered her boon companion, Society majordomo Ward McAllister, to rectify this obvious oversight.

Dutifully, McAllister presented himself before Alva. They conversed amiably and McAllister mentioned Miss Caroline Astor's beautiful quadrille. Alva looked startled. "I'm so sorry," she drawled in a low, sweet Southern voice. "It's too bad Miss Astor has gone to all that trouble and the quadrille should be wasted."

"W—wasted?" stammered McAllister.

"But how can I invite her?" asked Alva in mock distress. "Neither Miss Astor nor Mrs. Astor has ever called on me."

The following afternoon Mrs. Astor drove up to the door of 660 Fifth Avenue. Her footman climbed down from her carriage, walked to the door, and presented a calling card which read "Mrs. Astor" (the lack of a prefix connoting that this was the card of *the* Mrs. Astor). Within half an hour Mrs. Astor's invitations were delivered to her. "I think that the time has come for the Vanderbilts," pronounced Mrs. Astor. The bastion of Society had fallen.

And so, in 1883, the Vanderbilts entered the world of Society, a world ruled by women in a time when there were few other acceptable outlets for their intelligence and energy. Rich women invented the game of Society as a salve to their egos and to feel that they belonged to a superior race. Their men shared this feeling, but when the strict conventions of Society palled, they could find release in business, gambling, drinking, and discreet love nests. Soon these outlets came to be regarded as precious symbols of affluence in themselves, along with mansions, yachts, private railroad cars, Thoroughbred horses, and the plunder of European palaces. The trouble was that the women, who had invented the game, had no escape. They were forced to keep playing it for higher and higher stakes until they were constricted and crushed by their own creation.

Alice Gwynne Vanderbilt was to become one of Society's most magnificent victims. Watching Alva's initial social success, Alice felt the first twinge of a jealousy that was to bloom into the most bitter social rivalry of the century. But Alice succumbed to splendor joylessly and in stages, as if her puritanical nature was resisting only to be overwhelmed by her need to prove herself *the* Mrs. Vanderbilt.

If Alva had a French château, Alice must have one too, and she commissioned George Browne Post to design it for her. He received permission from the French government to copy the Château de Blois and it was erected on Fifty-seventh Street and Fifth Avenue at a cost of $375,000 for the land and $3 million for construction. In spite of Alice's efforts, it was Alva's château that was praised and called "a marvel of beauty and harmony," and nine years later when Alva boasted to the press that she was the only innovator in the family ("I always do everything first"), and the first woman of "breeding" to marry a Vanderbilt, Alice retaliated by instructing Post to double the size of her mansion so that it would occupy the entire block-front on Fifth Avenue from Fifty-seventh to Fifty-eighth Street. If Alice couldn't do it better, she could—and did—do it bigger. Cornelius II solemnly stated his intention: "I want to dominate the Plaza." In this pursuit, he paid $604,000 for additional land and demolished every building standing between his mansion and Fifty-eighth Street.

Because of her mania for privacy, Alice insisted that a twenty-five-foot wall be erected around the construction site as her $3 million mansion became a gutted shell. For two years 700 workmen and artisans toiled in shifts around the clock. When the wall was finally removed, the Château de Blois had vanished, to be replaced by a garish fairy-tale castle stretching 200 feet along Fifth Avenue, 125 feet into Fifty-seventh Street, and 135 feet into Fifty-eighth Street—a full block of peaks, gables, and dormer windows. This mansion looked like an enormous palace from an operetta by Franz Lehar—part Fontainebleau, part Victorian, part pure gingerbread. Cornelius and Alice refused to say how much it had all cost, but the *World* noted that "Money has been expended without stint . . . and all Europe has been ransacked for the choicest statuary and bric-a-brac." Alice's palace contained 137 rooms—the largest private city residence ever erected in America.

It was Alice who brought the phrase "red carpet treatment" into the American vernacular. She employed sixteen footmen who, decked out in a livery of narrow black britches, white lace shirts, maroon jackets, and powdered wigs, rolled maroon Vanderbilt carpeting from Alice's two château entrances to the door of each carriage as it arrived. Years later, when the Vanderbilts wished to mark the 20th Century Limited as the ultimate luxury train, they decided to carpet it in Alice Vanderbilt's maroon carpeting.

Alice arranged matters so that one entered a white-marble-floored vestibule facing Fifth Avenue where her leather-bound book on the Gwynne lineage was shrewdly displayed on a table. To the left was a white marble staircase with an elaborately carved balustrade in a design of interlocking V's, to the right an art gallery with walls of crimson velvet and a ten-foot-round velvet seat topped dead center by a palm tree. In this room Alice displayed hundreds of landscapes and still lifes which, she was informed by art experts, were the most fashionable paintings of the day. Her immense Louis XIV white-and-gold ballroom with a raised musicians' gallery measured seventy-five by fifty feet. Her dining room seated two hundred guests who often consumed elaborate ten-course banquets served on Alice's acorn-crested solid gold service; she needed no extra servants to accommodate this group.

The Cornelius Vanderbilt II residence, Fifth Avenue from 57th to 58th Street

The decoration of the Vanderbilt palace was wildly eclectic: the dining room was an incredible melange of wood, ivory, marble, silver, bronze, and mother-of-pearl. There was a Moorish smoking room with tile walls reproducing those of the Alhambra, and a stained-glass dome, executed by Louis Comfort Tiffany from a John La Farge design. There was an Oriental room full of priceless Chinese scrolls, rugs, and porcelain. A Louis XV salon featured a chandelier made for Cardinal Mazarin of France. A second-floor billiards room had walls and ceiling swathed in striped satin fabric held aloft by crossed scimitars; here one reclined on red satin pillows. In her Colonial Room, Alice displayed Early American furniture and family memorabilia dating back to the American Revolution.

On the third floor, above the fantasy rooms and the state rooms, one could see how the family actually lived when they weren't showing off. Here cozy Victorian clutter filled rooms decorated with lace and flowered fabrics. On the walls were family portraits and peaceful pastorals. The bathrooms were tiny and the bathtubs were tin encased in wood. Reggie's bedroom had soft green velvet walls, dark green and gold upholstered furniture, a hardwood floor, and a Turkish rug in bright, warm colors. Gertrude's room was virginal white. "Six windows are draped with silky white bolting cloth; over these come magnificent white lace curtains, and the third curtain is of heavy white silk looped back with curious chains of gold . . . the carpet is rich white velvet . . . a fire crackles on the white tiled hearth." In Gertrude's dressing room her ball gowns, too heavy to hang, reposed on twelve-foot-long cedar shelves.

Because of Alice's puritanical nature, the Vanderbilt family rose earlier than most New York Society people. Thirty-three servants cleaned the first two floors of the mansion between 6:00 and 9:00 a.m. so that the routine of the day would not be marred by their presence. The parlor maids then disappeared to change from their calico uniforms into their black afternoon uniforms. Occasionally, Alice Vanderbilt donned a white glove and ran it over the surfaces of paintings and furniture. If one speck of dust appeared, the offending servant was promptly dismissed. Alice never spoke to her servants save through her majordomo. *The New York Times* printed the story, though it sounds apocryphal, that Alice was once hours late for a party because even though she knew the way to her hosts' home, she refused to speak to her chauffeur to give him directions when he became lost.

With the Commodore's death, William Henry had elevated Cornelius II to be first vice-president of the New York Central and vice-president of the Harlem Railroad. William Henry, who had spent fifty-five years of his life standing discreetly in his father's shadow, had emerged as an obsessed businessman. His reputation became that of a business tyrant who squeezed his workers dry. During the depression following the Panic of 1873, he instituted a 10 percent cut in the salaries of employees who made over a dollar a day. Alice, however, found her father-in-law to be gentle, generous, and charitable. He contributed to hospitals, universities, St. Bartholomew's Church, the erection of Cleopatra's Needle in Central Park. He gave Ulysses S. Grant $150,000 to save him from financial ruin. In 1885, William Henry contributed $500,000 for a new medical school for the College of Physicians and Surgeons to be constructed at Fifty-ninth Street and Amsterdam Avenue.

December 8, 1885: William Henry and Robert Garrett of the Baltimore and Ohio system sat in the Vanderbilt library discussing the feasibility of a railroad terminal on Staten Island. In the middle of the afternoon a servant lit the fire in the grate, and Garrett noted William Henry's strangely ruddy countenance, but ascribed it to the reflection of the flames from the hearth. Then William Henry began to slur his speech, his color turned purple, and he toppled to the floor—dead.

In the eight years since his father's death, William Henry had quietly doubled his patrimony. His estate was valued at a staggering $200 million, in a time when President Grover Cleveland vetoed as excessive a bill to give each Union veteran a pension of twelve dollars a month. The stock market, thrown into confusion by William Henry's death, was forced to close down for three days. It was calculated that this Midas's annual income had been $20 million, and that, converted into gold, his fortune would weigh 500 tons.

The family gathered at William Henry's mansion for the reading of his will. He bequeathed to his widow 640 Fifth Avenue and a yearly income of $200,000. To each of his four daughters, he gave the house in which she lived, and he established a trust fund of $40 million to be divided outright among his four sons and four daughters. Another fund of $40 million was left them in trust. All the rest of his estate William Henry divided between his two eldest sons, Cornelius II and William Kissam. Alice Gwynne Vanderbilt cast Alva a triumphant glance when she heard the portion of the will that specifically named Cornelius II Head of the House of Vanderbilt. Willie K. inherited $65 million, Cornelius II $67 million.

And so the cornucopia poured forth a shower of overripe golden fruit which swelled and burst and lay rotting in a display of wanton waste unparalleled in American history. In the final decade of the nineteenth century, the indulgences of the rich careened out of control as fierce social competition goaded women on to ever greater extravagances and removed them forever from human scale and values. Society women of the decade, observed Thomas Beer, lived "in a state of domestic prudery and rampant rapacity."

"I know of no profession, art or trade that women are working in today as taxing on mental resource as being a leader of Society," said Alva Vanderbilt wearily. And Mrs. John R. Drexel commented that the social pace was enough to make one "drop down in harness."

In those virtually tax-free days, Society women were given access to the fortunes of their husbands so that they might enter the competition. Ward McAllister observed in 1890, "For one to be worth a million dollars was to be rated as a man of fortune, but now . . . at least fifty million is required."

The most prized summer resort of Society became Newport, Rhode Island. To be accepted here was to pass Society's severest test. Henry James saw this bleached New England seaside town as a lovely woman's "little bare, white, open hand with slightly parted fingers," into which, with the arrival of Society, suddenly and dreadfully gold was heaped up "to an amount so oddly out of proportion to the scale of nature and of space." Millionaires flocked to Newport to erect a hodgepodge of immense Florentine palazzos, French châteaux, Roman villas, and Tudor castles. Oliver Hazard Perry Belmont stabled his horses on the ground floor of his Belcourt mansion; at night they slept on crested white linen sheets. William Fahnestock, like Midas, hung from his trees artificial fruits of solid gold. While her husband was away, one titaness, on a whim, demolished their $5 million mansion—it bored her.

Society hostesses spent $200,000 for a single ball, and favors worth thousands of dollars were commonplace. One dinner featured unset rubies, sapphires, emeralds, and diamonds hidden under sand in the center of the table. At each place was a silver pail and shovel. At a given signal, the guests began frantically to dig for the treasure. And leading this grandiose parade were two women—Alice and Alva Vanderbilt—who had more of everything than anyone else. "When other and later magnificoes wanted schooling in spending money, they turned to the Vanderbilts," said Lucius Beebe. "This was as high as education could go."

At the start of the decade Alva Vanderbilt had commissioned Richard Hunt to design her a Newport summer "cottage," a replica of the Petit Trianon. Marble House, named for its abundant use of that material (500,000 cubic feet installed at a cost of $7 million), contained so much European marble, statuary, and furniture that the Willie K. Vanderbilts constructed their own wharf and warehouse and purchased a ten-ton derrick. Newport townspeople joked that the Italian accents they heard in the streets belonged either to Alva's marble cutters or to fortune-hunting counts seeking to marry her daughter Consuelo. Marble House was adorned with the trappings of royalty—Louis XIV sunbursts and portraits of French kings were rampant. A marble medallion of Richard Morris Hunt was hung next to one of Louis XIV's architect, Jules Hardouin-Mansart—to emphasize that both owners were royal.

As Alva's Marble House was nearing completion, Alice went to Alva's architect, Richard Hunt, and commissioned him to design her a larger and even more spectacular residence. The Cornelius Vanderbilts had lived in Pierre Lorillard's "cottage" at Ochre Point and Ruggles Avenue, but it had burned to the ground in 1892. Now on this site rose Alice's seventy-room, thirty-bathroom "cottage," a gargantuan Italian Renaissance palace set high on a promontory, fighting to overpower the sea below. It was originally to have had three stories but Hunt added a fourth, to accommodate thirty-odd servants.

"The Breakers," observed a reporter, "was the Marble House story all over again, but intensified—more imported marble, more imported stonecutters and iron workers and parquet fitters, more gilt, damask and cut velvet, more tapestries, more allegorical frescoes." Entire shiploads of material and workmen were consigned to this vast palace. Alice Vanderbilt, following the fashion of the day, surrounded herself with ornate European furnishings; there was nothing American about The Breakers, and every surface that could be gilded, was.

At The Breakers, Alice's vast wealth provided a tangible expression of her fears and eccentricities. Since their previous "cottage" had been destroyed by fire, Alice stipulated that no wood was to be used in the construction. The kitchen was housed in a separate wing and the furnace room was placed underground hundreds of feet away from the residence; it was connected to the main house by a tunnel large enough to drive a team of horses through. Like Queen Victoria, Alice mistrusted electricity and so the entire mansion was equipped with both gas and electric light. The bathrooms offered a choice of salt water or fresh, and above each bathtub was a series of servant call buttons. In all, Alice's call board registered fifty-four positions from which she could summon her servants. This was supplemented by two intercom systems.

Alice's and Alva's Newport palaces were built to last centuries—Richard Hunt told Alice that the construction of The Breakers was such that it could stand a thousand years. Yet unbelievably, the competitive function for which these palaces had been built would be limited to one season—only ten weeks of furious dueling for social supremacy—after which the battle over who was *the* Mrs. Vanderbilt would be resolved in a manner that afforded the winner a hollow, bitter victory.

The season was 1895, and guests were invited for the first time to The Breakers for the coming out ball of the Vanderbilts' eldest daughter Gertrude, called Gertie by her friends. At twenty, Gertrude was tall, thin, gawky, quiet, and immensely intelligent. A cousin observed that Gertrude "could not be called pretty, nor even very feminine . . ." and Alice was concerned about her social future.

The competitive Alva also had a nineteen-year-old daughter, Consuelo, whom she had raised simply as an extension of her own ambition. Consuelo was a fragile, dark beauty, polished by her mother to possess the quality of a rare porcelain. Unlike Gertrude, Consuelo was not allowed to indulge in sports. She spoke fluent French and was required to address her parents in that language only. As a child she had been forced by her mother to sit with a steel rod strapped to her spine while she spent many hours at her arduous lessons. When she misbehaved, Alva personally administered punishment by whipping her on the legs with a riding crop.

Gertrude and her first cousin Consuelo were good friends. In the mornings they could often be seen, their white-gloved hands holding parasols aloft as they walked to the Newport Casino to hear the orchestra, or sitting side by side at Bailey's Beach. In the evenings they appeared at the same dinner parties and fancy-dress balls. Both were keenly aware, as the newspapers frequently noted, that they were "great heiresses."

The night of Gertrude's ball, Alva entertained her guests in her Marble House dining room where they sat on rose-velvet upholstered chairs of cast bronze so heavy they could not be moved without the assistance of a footman. Alva, who had broken Society tradition by always serving quick dinners, tonight presented endless course after course, deliberately making her guests late for Gertrude's ball. Toward the end of dinner she declared, "I have something to tell you later on." At that her daughter Consuelo paled, knowing what was coming. Consuelo was in love with Winthrop Rutherfurd, but Alva had other plans for her docile daughter. Alva's guests waited through dessert and fruit, coffee and liqueurs. Then Alva made her announcement: Consuelo was to marry His Grace, the Duke of Marlborough! "And now we must all go down to The Breakers," she added casually. Once again, Alva had upstaged Alice.

At The Breakers, the petite Alice Vanderbilt stood in front of the massive white marble fireplace in the Gold Room (which Alice referred to as the Grand Salon because there *was* a Gold Room at Marble House). Alice's gown was red satin with a voluminous skirt. Ropes of pearls hung to her waist in front of a massive diamond stomacher; her dark pompadour was decorated with ostrich plumes. Standing at her side was Gertrude, who was draped in white chiffon and towered over her mother by eight inches. The room was decorated with bubbling fountains and thousands of American beauty roses, for which Alice had paid two dollars apiece. Rare potted palms and orchids from her greenhouses were massed against the walls.

During the dancing, twenty-two-year-old Neily Vanderbilt could not take his eyes off the beautiful Grace Wilson. The dashing Alfred danced every dance, while fifteen-year-old Reggie and his nine-year-old sister Gladys sat side by side on two of the hundreds of golden chairs placed around the periphery of the salon and connected with gay French ribbons. That night the Cornelius Vanderbilt II family was described as "America's royal family."

But while Alice devoted herself to Society, its endless entertainments and conventions, her husband grew increasingly nervous and discontent. He had little interest in social life; like his father he was an obsessive businessman. He never took more than twenty minutes for lunch, owned no yacht, did not smoke or gamble, and was known to drink only one glass of claret or champagne at dinner. He spent much of his leisure time studying the problems of foreign Episcopal missions. Known as the most charitable Vanderbilt, he donated millions of dollars to various institutions. Alice's frantic social pace tore at the seams of their marriage. Finally, Cornelius simply refused to attend any further functions. He moved out of The Breakers and retreated to nearby Oakland Farm in Portsmouth, a 185-acre working farm that he'd purchased in 1886. Here he improved the livestock, built new barns, took long solitary walks, and communed with nature.

Like their father, all the Vanderbilt children—Neily, Alfred, Gertrude, Reggie, Gladys—seemed oddly torn in the atmosphere their mother created for them. Alice surrounded her family with the most self-indulgent atmosphere imaginable, while behaving as strictly as the Sunday School teacher she once had been. Like most climbers, she was snobbish about her children's associates, but none of the Vanderbilt children cared for Society—like royalty, they were bored by their inherited rank. In a moment of rare clarity, their Uncle Willie K. observed, "Inherited wealth is a real handicap to happiness. It is as certain death to ambition as cocaine is to morality."

Alice as the
Electric Light
at a ball in 1883

THE BREAKERS

Alva as a
Venetian princess
at the same ball

MARBLE HOUSE

While Alice sacrificed her family to her social battle, her opponent, the restless Alva, grew bored with the rivalry. In August of 1895, Alva decided to leave her husband—Cornelius tried to effect a reconciliation, but failed. Then in November Alva's daughter Consuelo (who had a guard posted outside her bedroom door so she could not escape) became the ninth Duchess of Marlborough. No Vanderbilts except her father and brothers were asked to the wedding. The moment the ceremony was completed, Willie K. signed over to "the Most Noble Charles Richard John Spencer-Churchill of Blenheim Palace in the County of Oxford, England" 50,000 shares of capital stock in the Beech Creek Railroad, valued at $2.5 million, on which an annual dividend of 4 percent was guaranteed by the New York Central. Consuelo had purchased a husband who delighted in ridiculing her—the marriage was considered to be the most *brilliant* ever contracted by an American heiress. Shortly thereafter, Alva divorced Willie K., thus making divorce acceptable—another Society first—and promptly married the equally wealthy Oliver H. P. Belmont. Then Alva deserted Marble House, although she continued to have her washing and ironing done there.

At last Alice had won the title of *the* Mrs. Vanderbilt. But this could not have been the victory she'd envisioned. Alva had tossed the title away as if it were a soiled dance slipper, and by then Cornelius II was dying—mortally wounded in the social strife his wife had created.

The final blow to this nervous, reclusive man came unexpectedly in June of 1896. The month had started with Cornelius II's joyous announcement of the engagement of his daughter Gertrude to Harry Payne Whitney. Harry's social background was considered to be superior to Gertrude's own and he was known as "the handsomest man in New York." Gertrude's parents were delighted with the match. But on the very day Cornelius issued Gertrude's engagement announcement to the press, Neily told reporters that he too intended to be married—to Grace Wilson. For over a year he'd been pursuing Grace in the face of his parents' disapproval. Grace was of Society, but her family were known as "climbers," she was twenty-eight, which was considered "long in the tooth," and she had several broken engagements behind her. Also, as far as Alice was concerned, she'd committed the unpardonable social sin of being known as the "pet" of Edward, Prince of Wales. Alice Vanderbilt's stern social morality manifested itself—Grace was not fit to be a Vanderbilt, Gertrude wrote in her diary, "This is her last chance—no one else would marry her. . . . That woman will do anything."

Cornelius Vanderbilt summoned reporters to say that Neily's engagement plans had been canceled—the official reason given was that

Neily was suffering from an attack of rheumatism. Within a week of his announcement, however, newspapers reported that Neily had been seen in a carriage with Grace. Cornelius read the news at Oakland Farm and immediately boarded his private railroad car to New York to fetch back his disobedient son. That night Alice learned that her husband had suffered a stroke.

She rushed to New York, where her first dictum was that her husband's illness must be kept secret; no one outside the immediate family was to know of this catastrophe. Then at one o'clock in the morning, a crew of thirty laborers, working by moonlight, began to spread a thick layer of tanbark over the asphalt of Fifth Avenue for three blocks, from the middle of Fifty-sixth Street to the middle of the Grand Army Plaza, and halfway down Fifty-seventh Street toward Sixth Avenue. The morning light revealed a thick brown cushioning layer in front of the Vanderbilt palace. A reporter found out that a permit had been obtained from the department of public works, and that a Dr. McLane had stated that Cornelius II was "desperately ill . . . he cannot endure the noise of vehicles on the pavements." The next day's newspapers printed the story that Cornelius II and his son had quarreled violently, and that at the height of the argument young Neily had struck his father, thus causing the stroke.

Wednesday night the temperature soared to ninety-eight degrees, followed by violent cloudbursts. By Thursday morning the rain-soaked tanbark had hardened and was proving ineffective. Cornelius's sister, Mrs. Elliott F. Shepard, owner of the Fifth Avenue Stage line, commanded all her coaches to turn off Fifth Avenue from Fifty-sixth to Fifty-eighth Street and the police rerouted the rest of the traffic to Madison Avenue. At 10:00 a.m. the driver of a heavy wagon almost came to blows with a policeman. "I know my rights," screamed the driver, "I'll not let a sick rich man interfere with my business." When threatened with arrest, however, the driver moved on.

By midday a crowd had gathered in front of the Vanderbilt mansion. There was a carnival atmosphere as vendors sold lemonade from their handcarts, bicyclists rested their machines against the tall wrought-iron fence, and children climbed the fence bars. At one o'clock Harry Payne Whitney and his father, William Collins Whitney, left their residence and proceeded directly across Fifty-seventh Street to the Vanderbilt mansion. "Is he gone yet?" called out a young man. William Whitney stopped and addressed the crowd. "We know that Mr. Vanderbilt's condition is serious—dangerous—but we do not expect that it will end fatally," he said, and then disappeared into the mansion.

As with the mortal illness of a great monarch, official bulletins were issued to the crowd approximately every three hours. They were informed that Mr. Vanderbilt's stroke had completely paralyzed his right side. He could not speak. At seven-thirty that night, Gertrude, Alfred, Reggie, and Gladys arrived from Newport. At 10:15 p.m. the crowd still remained, awaiting the final bulletin, which read: "Mr. Vanderbilt's condition shows no material change."

For three days traffic was rerouted. On the fourth day, Harry Payne Whitney and Gertrude were seen walking in nearby Central Park. Shortly thereafter, a bulletin was issued by the doctors saying that Cornelius II could speak and had taken solid food. At midnight on July 26 he was transferred by an ambulance with special rubber-coated wheels to the *Conqueror*, the steam yacht of his brother Frederick W. Vanderbilt, which was anchored in the East River; he was then taken to Newport. The tanbark that had coated Fifth Avenue was swept up, moved to Newport, and spread over the gravel paths of The Breakers.

While her father lay in his sickbed, Gertrude wrote her cousin Adele Burden about the situation: "Neily is to [be] married. He *knows* it is his behaviour (that of course is private) that gave Papa the stroke. . . . He is inhuman, crazy. . . . I don't believe he will ever come in the house again. He won't come without her and that is out of the question." Less than two weeks later Neily married Grace Wilson. No Vanderbilt attended the wedding. In contrast, Gertrude and Harry were married at The Breakers on August 25, 1896, the ceremony taking place in the Grand Salon. *The New York Times* described the event:

> The ushers led the way down the magnificent staircase, closely followed by the bridesmaids, and then came Alfred Vanderbilt, with the bride resting on his arm. He was taking the place of Mr. Vanderbilt, his father, who was watching the charming picture from the gold room, where he sat in good range of the great doorway and in full view of the great marble and onyx hall. . . . Alfred Vanderbilt conducted his sister to the alcove in the gold room, where the wedding was to take place, then he delivered her over to her father.
>
> . . . Cornelius Vanderbilt gave his daughter away in due form, the sight being a rather affecting one for the family. He did not stand, though he might have done so with assistance, but reached up from his plush-covered chair, and, placing his daughter's hand in that of the groom, he assented to the union. . . . He seemed not unhappy at the formal departure of his daughter from his household, but appeared, though looking ill, to be well pleased with the situation. . . .

In fact, Cornelius II was the empty shell of the man he had been. He could not stand or walk and could hardly speak. Soon rumors began to circulate that his illness was mental in origin, brought on by the intense pressures of Society and his aggravation over his son Neily's conduct. His physicians could do nothing to help him. Alice did not return to The Breakers the following summer; instead she began an endless round of European spas and physicians, who also could do nothing. In despair, she turned to Dr. Charcot, the French hypnotist, who gave Cornelius some relief from his nervous disorder.

In 1899, after a summer spent with Dr. Charcot in Paris, the Vanderbilts returned to New York, where Cornelius was confined to bed. On the morning of September 12 he called Alice into his bedroom, took her hand in his, and announced simply, "I am dying." He never spoke again. When he died, Alice suffered a temporary collapse. She chose to wear black for the rest of her life.

Cornelius Vanderbilt II's will was read in the Circassian walnut-paneled library of The Breakers. It was dated June 18, 1896, the day that Neily first planned to marry Grace Wilson. Cornelius II's estate was valued at $72.5 million. He virtually disowned Neily, bequeathing him a mere $1 million outright and $500,000 in trust. To his next son, Alfred Gwynne, he bequeathed $42,575,000, Oakland Farm, and the title, Head of the House of Vanderbilt.

Alice received the Fifty-seventh Street mansion and a trust fund of $7 million. To his youngest son Reginald and to each of his daughters, Gertrude and Gladys, Cornelius II left $7.5 million outright and $5 million in trust; the beneficiary could use the income during his lifetime but could never invade the principal. At the time of Cornelius II's death, Reginald was nineteen and Gladys thirteen so they did not immediately come into their inheritance.

Neily, like his great-uncle, Cornelius Jeremiah, was unwilling to accept his father's financial rejection. He consulted his lawyers and decided to contest the will, but Alice, having suffered through "The Great Vanderbilt Will Trial," persuaded Alfred to give his older brother $6 million to settle the affair. Neily remained a family outcast.

Alice now turned her attention to the new Head of the House, her third son, Alfred, who resembled both the Commodore and his own father. In 1900, Alfred married Ellen (called Elsie) Tuck French. Eight years later Elsie sued for divorce and Alfred's valet, Howard Kempster, who had formerly attended Alice's husband, testified that Alfred had been guilty of misconduct in his private railroad car with one Mary Agnes O'Brien Ruiz, wife of the Cuban attaché in London. Elsie received her divorce, $10 million, and custody of their son, William Henry III. Mrs. Ruiz committed suicide in a London apartment for which Alfred paid the rent. In 1911, Alfred married Margaret Emerson

McKim, the daughter of the Bromo-Seltzer magnate, Captain Isaac E. Emerson. They had two sons, Alfred Gwynne II and George Washington III.

On May 1, 1915, nine months after Germany invaded Belgium, Alfred Gwynne Vanderbilt, Head of the House of Vanderbilt, boarded the Cunard liner *Lusitania*, stating that he wished to offer his services to the British Red Cross. Standing on the deck of the 45,000-ton liner, Alfred, the consummate gentleman, assured reporters, "The Germans would not dare attack this ship. They have disgraced themselves and never in our time will they be looked upon by any human being valuing his honor save with feelings of contempt. How can Germany, after what she has done, even think of being classed as a country of sportsmen and men of honor on a par with America, England and France?"

At 2:12 p.m. on May 7, two torpedoes struck the *Lusitania* midship. At 2:15 the Queenstown station received the *Lusitania*'s wireless for assistance. At 2:33 the ship disappeared from the surface of the ocean ten miles off the Old Head of Kinsale.

At 1 West Fifty-seventh Street, Alice, Gertrude, and Alfred's wife Margaret began receiving hourly bulletins from Ireland. It was not until the following Tuesday that the family admitted to themselves that Alfred might be dead. This was an era in which war was still considered a glorious game and Gertrude reflected this attitude when she wrote to her daughter Flora, "If he gave his life one must at least try to remember that it was a splendid death."

Some of the first survivors described Alfred's conduct when the torpedoes struck. "Find all the kiddies you can, boy," Vanderbilt directed his valet. Together they conducted women and children to the lifeboats. Alfred, who, oddly enough, could not swim, gave his lifebelt to an elderly lady. A few minutes later he joined theatrical producer Charles Frohman and three others on the ship's deck. "Why fear death?" Frohman declared with ardor. "It is the most beautiful adventure life gives us." The five men joined hands. "We'd better get set," Frohman commented as the steamship lurched forward. Alfred Vanderbilt stood erect and unperturbed, the personification of sportsmanlike coolness. He looked like a gentleman waiting patiently for a train.

Reginald was now the only son left on whom Alice could pin her hopes for the continuance of the Vanderbilt dynasty, but it was clear that he preferred racetracks and gambling houses to business and charitable enterprises. When Reggie was in his twenties, his mother had worried that he might have inherited the gambling mania displayed by Cornelius Jeremiah, the epileptic ne'er-do-well son of the Commodore. She'd sought the advice of her friend, New York Central Vice-President

Chauncy Depew, who had reassured her by recalling that the Commodore himself had liked a lively game of whist and by saying, "Don't worry, my dear lady. Young men sow wild oats. All of them do."

But Reggie was no longer young, and he seemed constantly to be in hot water—gambling scandals, the suicide of a former mistress, automobile accidents. His fortune had been dissipated and lately Alice had given him large sums of money. Still she closed her eyes to the truth about her youngest son and imagined him as Head of the House of Vanderbilt.

Cholly Knickerbocker's announcement of the engagement of Reggie and Gloria was front page news in the *American*, but there were no congratulations from the dowager Vanderbilt. In the haste with which the engagement had been arranged, perhaps the most important element had been overlooked. With an instinct for self-preservation, Gloria realized that without Alice Gwynne Vanderbilt's approval there would be no more generous gifts and probably no wedding at all, and she told Reggie, ". . . I will not marry you unless your mother gives her consent."

Reginald arranged to call on his mother with Gloria, who wore one of Mamma Morgan's dresses, a discreet green taffeta with a mink collar designed by the House of Lucille. Reginald picked Gloria up in his limousine and they proceeded to the Vanderbilt mansion. On entering, they passed through the vast white marble reception room and into one of the smaller drawing rooms where Alice Vanderbilt stood like a queen. Gloria observed that the grande dame was tiny, her hair snow white. She wore a black velvet floor-length dress—her habitual costume. A *sautoir* of magnificent pearls hung to her waist, a four-inch dog collar of pearls and diamonds imprisoned her neck. Alice poured tea and led the polite conversation through many subjects, from life abroad to the price of eggs, but she spoke not a word on the subject Gloria was longing to discuss—her engagement. When they left, Gloria complained plaintively to Reggie that she still had no idea where she stood. Reggie, however, had read a warning in their meeting and his marriage plans crumbled. That afternoon, Norton issued a statement from Reginald Vanderbilt to the newspapers. "I have read the story about my reported engagement and planned marriage to Miss Morgan and I know nothing about it."

Gloria had no idea why the dowager Vanderbilt was withholding her approval, but at card tables, lunches, and *thés dansants* the Society gossip of the week was that "Glorious Gloria," who was so high-spirited and had lived unchaperoned, had obviously "been around." Eventually the rumors reached Gloria herself, and she recalled the reasons why, years ago, Alice Vanderbilt had objected to Neily's marrying Grace Wilson.

One afternoon Gloria arrived alone and uninvited at the Vanderbilt mansion. She requested an audience with Alice Vanderbilt. When the dowager appeared, Gloria demanded the name of her personal physician, and as soon as Alice gave it, Gloria promptly departed, leaving the tiny matriarch astounded.

Within ten days Alice Vanderbilt received a report from her personal physician—Gloria Morgan was a virgin!

Maury Paul then published this report in his column. As his assistant observed, the only drawback to Cholly Knickerbocker's friendship was that "you lived your life in Macy's window."

Gloria's daring act completely captivated the dowager Vanderbilt. Within the week, a letter arrived from Alice. "Dear Gloria, You will be at my house tomorrow afternoon at four o'clock to meet your future relatives . . ."

Reginald promptly called in the press: "I wish to confirm my engagement to Miss Gloria Morgan," he told them, and explained that his previous denial had been prompted by the fact that "we did not receive the consent of Miss Morgan's parents until today."

For the remainder of her life, Alice Vanderbilt would defend and protect Gloria and would turn away criticism with the phrase, "She makes Reggie very happy." At a luncheon at The Breakers, Alice told Gloria, "When I am gone, my dear Gloria, you will be *the* Mrs. Vanderbilt." But, even at nineteen, Gloria understood the futility of Alice Vanderbilt's dream. She explained, "One must understand Reggie . . . was not just a rich man's son, but a very, very rich man's son. . . . By virtue of his inheritance and the distinction of the social class in which he was born, he should have taken on its responsibilities. But he was too self-indulgent, too indolent to surrender any of his time to what it asked of him."

Alice Vanderbilt went out of her way to demonstrate her approval of Gloria. One day while the three were lunching at the Ambassador Hotel, she inquired of Reggie, "Has Gloria received her pearls yet?"

"Now, Mother," Reginald replied, "you know I would love to give Gloria pearls, but I do not intend buying her a cheap necklace, and I can't afford the kind I would like."

"Bring me a pair of scissors," the dowager imperiously commanded the maître d'hôtel. She then removed the rope of pearls that wrapped twice around her neck and fell below her waist, cut off about one third, or $70,000 worth, and handed them to Gloria. "There you are, Gloria," she said. "All Vanderbilt women have pearls."

Mr. and Mrs. Reginald Claypoole Vanderbilt

A Brilliant Marriage

Reginald Vanderbilt died—drank himself to death!

FROM THE DIARIES OF ABBY A. SHERMAN

GLORIA WAS ABOUT to contract "a brilliant marriage." She had become the exquisite toy woman she was groomed to be, and in doing so had captured Reggie Vanderbilt, "the most eligible bachelor in town." The life upon which she was about to embark would be by her own description "extraordinary."

On the morning of March 6, 1923, Gloria awoke feeling that she was "living in some burning world that would never cool again—ever." She took her temperature—the thermometer registered 103. But she had overcome so many obstacles that she was not going to change her plans; nothing was going to prevent her from marrying Reginald Vanderbilt that very day. Already Gloria had received several spectacular wedding gifts: an enormous pear-shaped diamond from Reggie, which she found to be "a wonderful symbol of Reggie's love!"; a diamond tiara from Alice; a gold vanity embellished with a thirteen-carat carved sapphire from Gertrude and Harry Payne Whitney; and an emerald and platinum ring from Reggie's other sister, Countess Gladys Széchényi.

Because Alice Vanderbilt loathed publicity, Reggie had devised a plan to avoid the press. He announced that the wedding would take place at noon at the Marguery Hotel apartment of Gloria's godmother, Mrs. Glenn Stewart. While a crowd of reporters waited outside, shivering in an unexpected March snowstorm, Gloria donned her gray faille wedding gown and sent her luggage out the front door to the Vanderbilt limousine which was stationed there as a decoy. Then Gloria and the Stewarts sneaked out a rear entrance and climbed into a second limousine which took them to the East Ninety-second Street house of Reggie's friends the Edward von der Horst Kochs, where the wedding was really to take place.

The wedding was small, only fifty guests: the Vanderbilt family was represented solely by Reggie's mother. His sister Gertrude and her husband Harry were unable to attend because they were in Paris where, on the previous day, their son Cornelius Vanderbilt Whitney (called Sonny) had married Marie Norton (Sonny's bride was two years older than his uncle Reggie's bride). When Gloria had cabled Mamma Morgan of her engagement, Mamma answered that she would be over on the next ship to make all the necessary arrangements. Gloria, unable to "bear the thought of the chaos she would create if she were there," cabled back asking her not to come. Mamma acquiesced and sent the capable, low-keyed Consuelo in her place. Papa did not consider coming and Thelma was unable to come because she was trying to obtain her divorce decree and was not permitted to leave Belgium.

Gloria remembered little of the wedding ceremony which, at Reggie's request, was performed by an Episcopal minister, and she endured the luncheon that followed in a flushed haze. Finally, she and Reggie departed, only to run the gauntlet of reporters and photographers who had caught on to their ruse. More reporters were massed at Grand Central Terminal, where the newlyweds boarded the private Vanderbilt railroad car, which consisted of four mahogany-paneled staterooms, a library, dining compartment, pantry, kitchen, bar room with built-in wine cabinets, and a main salon upholstered in deep blue velvet, containing a piano and a harp.

When they descended from the train at the Portsmouth station, a March gale engulfed them. Reggie's chauffeur managed to get them to Sandy Point Farm. As Gloria stepped from the limousine her bridegroom held out his hand to her. She could hear the roar of the wind off Narragansett Bay. Later she was to remember falling, then Reggie picking her up and carrying her into the house—nothing more. She had contracted diphtheria.

She was ill for six weeks, and the disease left her with what she described as "heart attacks of such virulence that they would cut off my breath on the slightest pretext." Thelma, unable to obtain her divorce, came to Sandy Point Farm to be with her. As soon as Gloria felt better, she delighted in showing her twin her new digs. Trailed by dozens of Reggie's dogs, they would walk about the 280-acre estate which was dotted with small rustic cottages—thirteen in all. (Gloria was quite sure that the manager lived in one and "presumed" that Reggie's enormous staff of stablemen and gardeners lived in the others.) Reginald and Gloria were residing in the largest of these cottages while what Reggie referred to as "the Big House" was being renovated. The Big House was a large, white-pillared colonial building set on a gently sloping lawn with an elaborate Italian garden at its foot. From it, one could see in the distance a windmill tower, The Ring, and the stables. Reggie, who had previously shown no interest in decoration, had filled this house with shabby but comfortable furniture and had allowed it to deteriorate.

When Thelma returned to New York she told reporters that her sister had almost recovered. "I watched Gloria flitting about the rooms of the great mansion patting Reggie's cheeks as though he were a little boy," she enthused. As for herself, she said that she had given up Society. "What do I care? Society is insincere. Society is in a rut. Everybody is afraid to do what they wish. . . . They have good minds, and could do things, but they're afraid and self-conscious. Why isn't marriage satisfactory today? Because there is nothing for the woman in Society to do." In her post-Society condition, Thelma told reporters that she was going to open her own film company—Thelma Morgan Pictures—with $100,000 capital, but she refused to say who had supplied her with the money.

By the middle of May, Gloria felt well enough to sail for Europe to attend Consuelo's wedding to Benjamin Thaw, Jr. Consuelo's first marriage had been for Mamma; this time she married for herself, and did very well indeed. Benny Thaw was first secretary at the American Embassy in Brussels. His grandfather had built up a vast fortune in shipping, railroads, coke, and coal. The Thaws were considered *the* family of Pittsburgh, despite the fact that in June of 1906, Benny's uncle, Harry Kendall Thaw, had shot and killed the famous architect, Stanford White, in a jealous rage over Thaw's wife, show girl Evelyn Nesbit. There was a slight problem for Consuelo and Benny in that two Episcopal ministers refused to marry them, but one was finally found who was willing to oblige.

With one of the Morgan sisters a Vanderbilt and one a Thaw, the

American newspapers went wild. "A magical Morgan has done it again!" declared the *World*. "The eldest sister is but twenty-one, each has won glittering social position and great wealth. What can their secret be?" To find the answer, handwriting experts analyzed their handwriting, phrenologists their heads. "Look at the forehead of Gloria Morgan. It is about twice as broad as it is high. That means discretion, good judgement, social instinct, and a wide interest in many things. The proportions of all the Morgan sisters' foreheads are ideal for success in the social careers they have chosen." An article in the *American* inadvertently touched on the psychological reason why the Morgan sisters generated such excitement—their lives were not far removed from the fantasies of every shop girl. The article directed, "If you are young, feminine and unmarried, you too can look in the mirror . . . for your chance of realization of marble halls and a wandering Prince on a white charger."

One morning in Paris, Gloria awoke feeling dizzy and nauseated, and subsequently she discovered to her delight that she was pregnant. At the end of the summer, Gloria and Reggie returned to America for the Newport Horse Show, an event of great importance to Reginald, who was now president of the Association of American Horse Shows. Since the renovation of Sandy Point was not completed, they stayed with Alice Vanderbilt at The Breakers. To Gloria, the overpowering stone château was dismally medieval in feeling. She was introduced by the dowager Vanderbilt to the rigid Newport social life where *the* Mrs. Vanderbilt calling card opened every door, but she found Newport "magnificently dreary and elegantly dull." Gloria and the dowager would arrive at Bailey's Beach promptly at eleven o'clock, dressed as if for tea, with hats, white gloves, and parasols. Swimming was forbidden unless one wore stockings: Rose Nano, a diplomat's wife, unaware of the taboo, had shocked Newport society by appearing in an Annette Kellerman one-piece tank suit. One day on the way to the beach Gloria experienced an attack of nausea and confided to the dowager that she was pregnant. It was the only time she was ever to see a display of emotion from this woman. Alice Vanderbilt leaned over and kissed her.

In the fall, Gloria and Reggie returned to his town house on Seventy-seventh Street, where Gloria discovered that she had moved into a way of life that had existed for a quarter of a century. "Previous to our marriage it had been understood quite definitely that I was to be given no hand in the running of Reggie's establishments. 'After all,' Reggie had informed her, 'you have never managed a large household. Mine has been running on greased wheels for over twenty years in

Behind the Curtains With the "400

The Dowager Mrs. Cornelius Vanderbilt, Queen Regent of the Vanderbilt Clan. © U. & U.

And from what I saw of them during those few days—and from what I know of their romance since its inception—I am here to tell society that it simply doesn't know what it is talking about when it whispers, "Will it last?"

Their courtship, for example, wasn't the swift whirlwind affair so many people seem to suppose. It has been more than a year since they first met one another at the series of teas I held after my marriage to "Junior" Converse.

Gloria used to help me preside at the teas, and together we spent as much eager thought and pains on these little "at homes" as two children giving a party to their paper dolls. The teas were very popular, too. Of those who nearly always came, including Countess Zichy (the former Charlotte Demarest), Mary Terry (Mrs. James Taylor Terry), Mrs. Miller Graves, "Angie" Duke, Julian Little and others—none was more constant than Reggie Vanderbilt.

"Junior" and I lived on East Fifty-first street. Reggie's town house isn't far from there. After his separation from his first wife, who was Cathleen Neilson, and is now Mrs. Sidney J. Colford, Jr., Reggie kept bachelor hall in a mansion on East Seventy-seventh street, just off Fifth avenue.

I suppose there was no bachelor in New York with a greater reputation for hospitality. The "cock-tail hour" always found a stream of cars parked outside his door.

By THELMA MORGAN CONVERSE,

Twin Sister of Mrs. Reginald C. Vanderbilt.

CHAPTER III.

THE world knows Reginald C. Vanderbilt chiefly through his social interests as a man of wealth and through his activities in the realm of sportsmanship, the latter evidenced by his success year after year at the National Horse Shows as a prize running exhibitor of fine horses bred at his famous Sandy Point farm.

The real Reggie Vanderbilt is a big, good-natured boy without a streak of snob in him. He does love horses. He does love pretty women. He plays bridge more cleverly than he plays Beethoven. He can shake a cocktail better than he can swing an axe, and his library, I am afraid, runs rather to Rabelais than to Shakespeare.

But if Reggie Vanderbilt has his weaknesses, including too many hangers-on and parasites sponging on his generosity, he is by no means the waster and philanderer whom the public regards as the archtype of society man. I like Reggie Vanderbilt. I am glad he has married my twin sister, Gloria, and I believe they will be very happy.

These few remarks are called forth because of the spoken and written insinuations, none too thinly veiled, by society chatterers and gossip journals, to the effect that marriage between Seventeen and Forty-three is foredoomed to failure, especially when the bridegroom is a fickle fellow.

Well, I have just returned to New York from a week-end with Gloria and Reggie at Sandy Point Farm, Reggie's Newport place, and if you tell me America holds a pair of honeymooners more ardently devoted than these two I simply can't believe you.

I watched Gloria, trailed by a dozen adoring Vanderbilt dogs, flitting about the rooms of the great mansion that is anything but a "farmhouse"; telling me, as excitedly as a little girl with a doll's house, her plans for playing Vanderbilt hostess; patting Reggie's cheek as though she were the woman of forty and he only a little boy.

I watched Reggie, constantly at her heels like a faithful angel himself, anxious for her every minute of the time, afraid she would overdo herself after the attack of diptheria that overtook her on her honeymoon, cherishing her with more care than he would lavish on some priceless family heirloom.

Reggie's bar was famous. It was modelled after a bar in the tavern of "William the Conqueror," near Deauville, in France, and from four to seven every afternoon in the old days it was the Mecca for many thirsty souls. It was on the ground floor of the house, a five-story affair.

You walked up a flight of steps entering the house and then took a lift to the lower floor. The lift opened in one corner of a big room paved with brick flagging. Easy chairs, cozy corners, settees, piano, victrola, sporting prints on the walls, silver cups, horse show trophies—this is a thumb-nail picture of the scene, plus the chattering groups of people.

The bar itself was in one corner of the room opposite the lift. It had a little gate and a counter, just as I imagine "regular" bars have. Behind it were stacks and stacks of glasses, fruit, fizz water and—bottles.

Reggie always did the shaking and serving himself. He prided himself on being as expert as any bartender, and though he had for butler and valet old "Norton," who has been in the Vanderbilt family longer than Reggie has, he carried out the role of genial host in person to the very squeezing of the limes.

You could have anything you wanted, from champagne to beer. Reggie's specialty was a drink he called the "stinger." I don't know what the ingredients were, except that it tasted strongly of absinthe. In fact, there was a dash of absinthe in nearly all his cocktails.

(I am neither a prevaricator nor a prude, by the way, when I say that I don't drink. Oh, I've had more than one cocktail, but I honestly don't like alcohol. Later on I will have an interesting story to tell of how society gossip gave an abstainer the reputation of a "lush.")

I will always keep a fond mental picture of Reggie behind his bar. He was—and is—such a thoroughly affable, jovial chap, a "good fellow" with everybody, never more delightful than when he was entertaining a group of friends. It made no difference to him that more than one of them flattered him and kowtowed to him only because he was a Vanderbilt. I really believe he was innocent enough to think every one liked him just as he liked them—because, simply, they were "good fellows."

Women are fond of Reggie. He has charm. In repose his features seem heavy, but when he smiles his jolly brown eyes and his gleaming white teeth—he has splendid white teeth!—make his whole face light up. He becomes a handsome fellow. I don't wonder Gloria fell in love with him!

It wasn't one of your "love-at-first-sight" cases, however. Though they saw each other frequently at teas the acquaintance extended no further. The society journals at that time were printing rumors

of a romance between Reggie and Peg
Watson, a popular debutante. Regg
in fact, was an eternal subject for t
match predicters. Always, it appeare
he had some "only one." But no o
suspected a romance between him a
Gloria then. There seemed to be sm
mutual attraction.

About a month before I sailed f
Europe, after a final quarrel with "Ju
ior," I gave a party at the Beaux Ar
The guests were Mary Terry, Count
Zichy, Reggie, Angier Duke, and,
course, Julian Little. Gloria promised
join us after the theatre, and she did.
noticed that night for the first time th
Reggie Vanderbilt seemed smitten w
my twin. And she glowed under his
dent eyes.

Chance added fuel to the flame th
began to burn between them. I have t
my readers how, on the day I saile
Reggie arrived at the dock just as t
Lapland was towed out. I thought
glimpsed him in the crowd at Glori
back, but not until weeks later did
learn what important events hinged
my departure that blustery January d

"I was crying when Reggie came
all out of breath," Gloria tells me. "
told me to cheer up, and said, 'Let's
to lunch.' So I went to lunch with hi
and—well, that's really when we fell
love, Thelma!"

Gloria was on the eve of sailing f
Havana with Mrs. Sailing Baruch. Re
gie begged her to marry him. She w
stopping at the Waldorf with our Au
Mrs. William Rafferty. She told Reg
she would have to have time in which
make up her mind—the month in t
tropics. But he was too impetuous f
her. Three days later they were e
gaged, and within a month the weddi
took place.

I can add little to what the wo
knows already about that, for the ne
leaked out that Reggie had cabled
father in Brussels for his consent, a
from that time on we were all harass
by the newspapers.

Reporters besieged Reggie for news
the wedding plans. They camped on t
steps of the Park avenue house of M
Glen Stewart, to whom Gloria had g
from the Waldorf. Gloria fled to
friend, Margaret Power, who lives w
her aunt, Mrs. Peter Larson, on Fi

Thelma Morgan Converse (Sister of Mrs. Reginald Vanderbilt)

Amazingly Intimate Revelations of the Loves, Feuds, Pranks and Personalities of Society's "Circus Set" in New York, Europe and Newport, by the Young Heiress Who Was "One of Them" Until She Rebelled

A Striking Studio Pose of Mrs. Converse, Made Especially to Illustrate This Chatty Chapter of Her Story, in which She Tells the Details of the Romance of Her Sister Gloria and Reginald Vanderbilt.

"I watched Gloria, trailed by a dozen adoring Vanderbilt dogs, gliding about the rooms of the great mansion, patting Reggie's cheeks as though he were a little boy."—Mrs. Converse, in a Description of Her Sister at Sandy Point Farm.

d His Bride, Gloria Morgan.
© Hess.

avenue. The publicity and the hounding of the reporters was making her ill, so every effort was made to "camouflage" proceedings on the day of the wedding.

It was no good, though. The Vonderhorst Kochs offered their home. Reggie planted his car in front of the Stewarts' house as a blind. He, Gloria, the attendants and friends motored secretly to the Kochs. But the newspaper boys trailed them. Reporters and photographers stood out in the snow, and when the ceremony was over and the bride's health toasted, Mr. and Mrs. Vanderbilt ran into a battery of questions and cameras as they rushed out of the house.

I heard all the exciting details from Gloria's own lips when it was a matter of social history and she and Reggie were honeymooning at Newport. Poor little kid! She looked very frail and wan from the diphtheria that she really was suffering from on the very day of the wedding, but she brightened with enthusiasm as she showed me over Sandy Point Farm and told me her plans when she returns from Europe and takes her place in New York society as Mrs. Reginald C. Vanderbilt.

Sandy Point Farm is a wonderful, rambling old estate, six miles from Newport—two hundred and thirty acres of green pasture land, stables, porticoed houses, gardens, hedges and tenants' cottages. The farm fronts the blue sea. It is a real farm, too. Reggie, or rather his tenants, raise all kinds of garden truck, fruits, and so on by the latest agricultural methods.

Reggie's particular pride is the stables. More than sixty horses are kept on the place—all of them thoroughbreds—and their quarters are larger than those of the master of the farm. The kennels, too, occupy nearly an acre. Reggie has many breeds of dogs, with shepherds (police dogs) predominating.

(Continued on Page 19)

charge of Norton. He knows my needs, he knows my wants, he understands me—and if it's the same to you, I would like the conditions to remain unchanged.' "

William Norton had been with Reggie for twenty-one years and in all that time Norton was said never to have drawn a sober breath. In the wee hours of the morning, when Reginald finally retired, Norton brought a tray of sandwiches and a Thermos bottle to his bedside. When Reggie awoke, he brought him his tea, toast, and hash or poached eggs. Every morning Reggie would spend an hour or so on the telephone talking to his broker, his clubs, his friends, and several railroad offices. He received $10,000 a year from each of a dozen subsidiaries of the New York Central where he was listed as a vice-president, but he never went near any of them. His real day never began until lunchtime and he rarely retired before the night was out. Reggie had difficulty sleeping, and his taproom was open all night to friends who dropped in as one would to an after-hours club. Behind the bar Reggie stood smiling, skillfully mixing cocktails, always the affable host.

On the rare occasions when there were no guests, Gloria and Reggie would play solitaire until dawn, when Gloria would excuse herself and fall into bed exhausted. Reggie taught her to reverse the pattern of day and night. He also introduced her to other new experiences—Thelma observed that Reggie's taste in literature "ran more to Rabelais than to Shakespeare," and remembered seeing the entire ten unexpurgated volumes of Sir Richard Francis Burton's translation of *The Thousand Nights and a Night* (The Arabian Nights) on Reggie's bookshelf. This work featured erotic tales of heterosexual copulation, homosexuality, bestiality, and obscenity. The sensational footnotes attested to Burton's copious knowledge of bizarre sexual customs and curiosities, particularly of the Orient and Africa, running the gamut from descriptions of incest, hermaphroditism, and sapphism in harems, to the rape of women by gorillas in Africa.

In many ways, Reggie reminded Gloria of Papa. Her husband spent money with abandon, denying himself and his bride nothing. In the first year of their marriage he lavished jewelry on her and he bought her her own car—a gray Marmon with white stripes (his racing colors for his most beautiful possession). This father-teacher taught her his ways: drinking, sensation, profligacy, ignoring the future. And Gloria, the pupil, lived the life Reginald had chosen for her.

Gloria had always been a clean slate upon which each person wrote his own tale, seeming to possess no identity save that which others thrust upon her. In becoming Mrs. Reginald Vanderbilt, she had fulfilled Mamma's greatest expectations for her. Now she began to fulfill

Reggie's expectations as well—she became his fantasy wife, but even the fantasy was not of her own making. Certainly she felt powerless to alter the pattern of Reggie's life. "I was subjected to criticism for leading the life he wanted me to, but it is to be remembered that one does not expect to marry a man of Reggie's age and change his manner of living." She came to believe that everything that happened to her was inevitable; her role was that of the innocent victim. The course of her marriage was clearly marked with the signposts of disaster, but she failed to recognize them—behavior on her part all too consistent with everything that was to follow.

In the summer of 1923, when Gloria and Reggie returned from Europe, she met Reginald's sister Gertrude Vanderbilt Whitney for the first time. "It was not surprising to me that Reggie was so fond of Gertrude. In many ways they were much alike. Both disliked any form of ostentation, any show or ceremony. Each went his merry way, disregarding formalities, ignoring the pressure of convention and the sniffings of gossip. Each was a strong, highly individualistic, self-contained person." Later, Gloria was to change her mind about Gertrude.

As the time approached for Gloria to give birth, Mrs. Morgan left her husband in Brussels and moved to New York to be near her daughter. Mrs. Morgan's relationship with her husband had grown increasingly strained; she was bitter about his infidelities and no longer wished to live with him. Her considerable energies were turned toward the prospect of a Vanderbilt grandchild. On February 20, 1924, at the Lying-In Hospital in Stuyvesant Square, Gloria gave birth to a seven and three-quarter-pound baby girl by Cesarean section. As at a royal birth, her mother insisted on being present in the operating room. Five doctors attended. Reggie was so delighted with his new daughter that he slipped a diamond and emerald bracelet into the folds of the baby's blanket when she was presented to her mother. Maury Paul observed that there was great rejoicing among Reggie's friends because this birth meant that Gloria would be financially secure for life.

Nursing the infant was so painful for Gloria that she wept, and the baby was placed on formula. Mamma Morgan took command. From the moment of the child's birth, Gloria assumed a secondary position. Mamma interviewed prospective nurses, but refused to let Gloria meet the applicants, one of whom was a thirty-three-year-old woman, Emma Sullivan Keislich. At first, Mrs. Morgan found this plain, pudgy woman to be "very hard and narrow lipped," but Keislich came with excellent references from top Society families and she was unusually well qualified. Her grandfather had been a doctor at Presbyterian Hospital and

Emma herself had been trained in Switzerland, had raised the children of Mrs. McIlvane Luquere, the former Anne Pierpont, and had spent two years with Mrs. William Stanley Dell, the daughter of President Grover Cleveland. When Mamma told Gloria she was undecided about Keislich, her daughter remarked casually that they could always replace her. And so Emma Sullivan Keislich was engaged at a salary of $125 a month.

Gloria remained in the hospital for thirteen days, during which she was kept virtually immobile. She developed phlebitis in her right leg and was sent home from the hospital in an ambulance. Nurse Keislich, assisted by Mamma, took over the care of the new Vanderbilt heiress.

Reggie wanted the baby to be christened in his own Episcopal faith. (His first daughter, Cathleen, had been christened a Catholic against his wishes.) Although Gloria was a Catholic, she acquiesced in her husband's wish. At the same time, Alice Gwynne Vanderbilt left St. Bartholomew's—which was referred to as "The Vanderbilt Church" because of Alice's and Cornelius's generosity over half a century—and quietly switched her allegiance to St. Thomas's. She would not say why, but Gloria told Maury Paul that the dowager had changed churches because Dr. Leighton Parks, pastor of St. Bartholomew's, disapproved of Gloria and refused to baptize the baby. Bishop Herbert Shipman was selected in his place. Gertrude Vanderbilt Whitney was chosen as godmother, but she was in Paris arranging the installation of a cast of her sculpture of Buffalo Bill Cody at the Grand Palais of the Paris Salon, so her own mother stood in for her. Alice Gwynne Vanderbilt's soft, liver-spotted, blue-veined hands held the baby in the magnificent white christening gown. Maury Paul, standing beside "Glorious Gloria," saw Norton indicate to the bishop that an enormous silver bowl, a horse show trophy, was to serve as the font. "Water," murmured Bishop Shipman—a discreet reminder that someone had forgotten to fill the vessel. Norton picked up the silver bowl, dashed across the hall that separated the drawing room from the dining room, snatched up a bottle of White Rock from the dining room buffet, poured the contents into the font and quickly returned to the drawing room. Maury observed that Bishop Shipman's face flushed when he saw this fizzy brew in place of holy water, but he proceeded with the ceremony, and the baby was duly christened with White Rock—Gloria Laura Madeleine Sophie Vanderbilt.

From the first, little Gloria was tangential to the lives of her parents. The care of the child was entrusted to Mamma Morgan, who became a permanent fixture in the Vanderbilt household, and to nurse

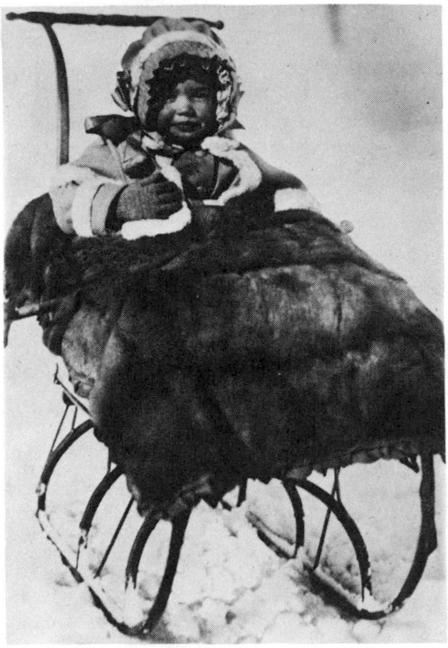

Little Gloria and her parents

Little
Gloria

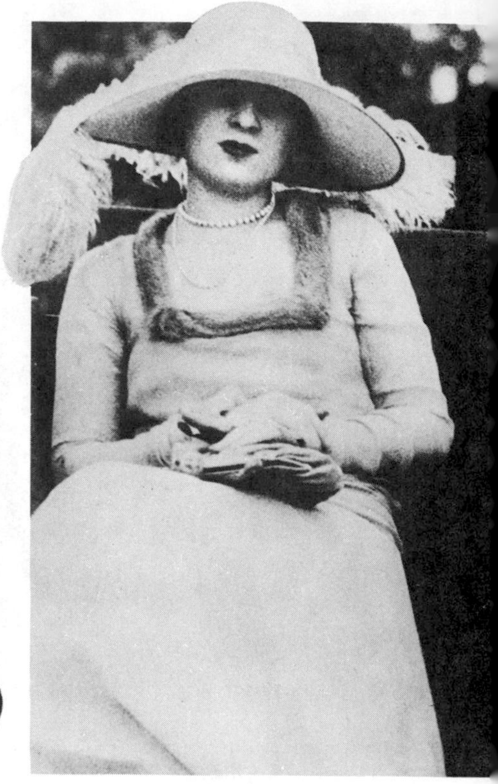

Gloria and Mamma Morgan

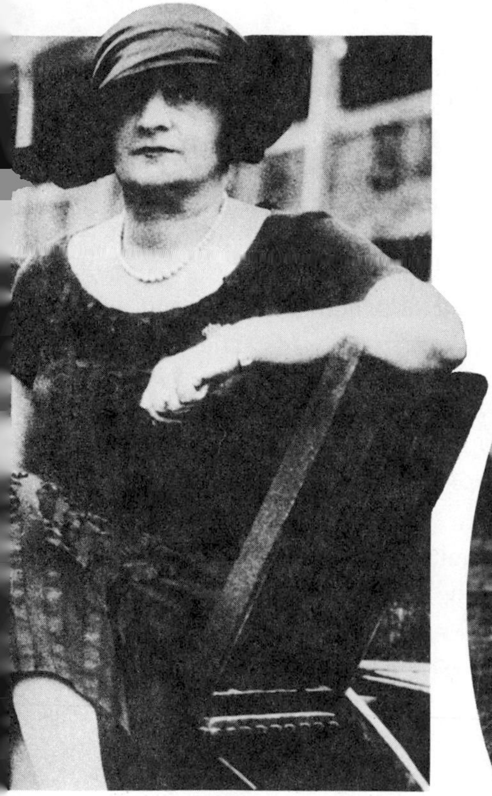

Reggie and
Gloria

Sandy Point Farm

Keislich. Both parents, however, were enormously fond of the baby and Reggie, after staying up all night, would enter the nursery at six in the morning and stand over the crib admiring little Gloria.

Although it was common knowledge that Reggie was desperately ill—and he himself had told Gloria of his condition—it was only after they'd been married for over a year that Gloria actually noticed that her husband was not looking at all well. When she asked him if he'd seen a doctor, Reggie replied that he had and had been advised that he'd be all right if he curtailed his drinking for a while and confined himself to light wines and champagne.

In the spring of 1924 the baby, in the care of Mamma and nurse Keislich, was sent to Sandy Point Farm, while Gloria and Reggie went to Europe. They returned three months later in time for the Newport Horse Show and moved into their newly renovated house. The summer of 1924 was filled with the endless entertainments of Society—lunches, brunches, teas, dinners. Reggie bypassed the teas, spending time instead at the Reading Room, an exclusive men's club which offered something stronger. The Reading Room, which was established in 1854, was the oldest club in Newport and boasted the first flush toilets in existence. In its seventy-year history no woman had been permitted inside this small yellow and white frame house, and if any female, even a member's wife, walked past the club, the men on the porch ignored her presence.

For Gloria, the highlight of what she found to be a sweet summer was the costume ball she arranged for five hundred guests to be given on her birthday, August 23. Gloria adored fancy-dress balls—she felt an enchantment about them, a freedom that came from being able to transform oneself into someone else. Paradoxically, she also felt that in disguise her real self might be set free, "all personal elements extinguished by change of dress—like masks suddenly taken off."

Gloria designed her own costume for the ball, a copy of the coronation gown worn by Marie Leczinska, queen consort of Louis XV of France. The gown had a white taffeta skirt draped over immense hoops, and decorated with hundreds of yards of gold lace secured by white satin roses—an amethyst taffeta train trailed four feet behind her. Alice Gwynne Vanderbilt did Gloria the extreme honor of receiving with her, but declined to wear a costume. Reginald also refused to wear a costume, but indulged his wife to the extent of donning his Yale blazer, class of 1902.

On the night of the ball, the road to Sandy Point Farm was ablaze with colored lights and Japanese lanterns. Great baskets of flowers decorated the ballroom, where a sunburst of roses formed a frame around the Meyer Davis orchestra. The rooms filled with lavish costumes and brilliant jewels. Kings, queens, harlequins, harem girls, appeared: Fernanda Goelet as a Polish princess, Millicent Hearst as Mary Queen of Scots, Hannibal de Mesa as a matador, Mrs. Drexel Biddle, Jr., as Helen of Troy. Princess Miguel de Braganza came as Marie Antoinette, and everyone applauded as she danced a minuet with Hamilton Fish, costumed as Louis XVI, to the strains of "Jardinier du Roi," said to have been written by the real Marie Antoinette for the real Louis XVI.

Norton, Reginald's ever-present butler, became very drunk. Thinking that Bishop Herbert Shipman's clerical habit was a costume, he remarked, "It's all right, Bishop, but you won't feel like a bishop in the morning, I can tell you."

Only one thing threatened to mar Gloria's perfect evening. Someone brought a Prince Michael Romanoff to the party, but Gloria's instinct immediately told her that this man was an impostor, and she asked him exactly who his father was. In reply Romanoff hemmed, dodged, and stuttered. Gloria cut him off: "The truth of the matter is that you are no more Prince Michael Romanoff than I am—because he does not exist."

Romanoff was ejected from the party. In a parting shot, Gloria told him, "You shouldn't have tried it, you know. You couldn't have possibly gotten away with it—not in Newport."

"I'm here, am I not?" he replied.

Gloria was astounded. "He was an East Side Jew, and where he picked up his cultured speech or his air which enabled him to impersonate successfully a Prince of the blood so as to convince a Newport hostess, is a mystery known only to himself." In any event, the party was a triumph for Gloria. As her mother-in law remarked, "*Everybody* was here."

At the end of the summer, Gloria and Reggie were off again to Europe on the *Mauretania*, along with a dozen other celebrities to inaugurate a new five-day express service that docked in Plymouth in the morning and delivered passengers to London the same night. Mamma Morgan, the nurse, and the baby moved back to East Seventy-seventh Street. Papa Morgan had been appointed U.S. consul general to Buenos Aires, but Mamma showed no inclination to rejoin him and was "bitterly hostile" toward him. Through her granddaughter, Laura Morgan had become a necessary adjunct to the Vanderbilts' lives. When Gloria and Reggie returned to New York in November, Gloria began spending many afternoons with her mother, shopping, going to the movies, and visiting other Society matrons to play bridge. (The following year Reggie's cousin, Harold Stirling Vanderbilt, would invent contract bridge, but for now auction bridge was all the rage.) Mamma and Gloria would often stay so long at the bridge table that Reggie would telephone to summon Gloria home.

By the winter of 1925 Gloria found that Reggie's nights had become one continuous nightmare. He couldn't sleep—he drank constantly. Finally, in the spring, on the doctors' advice, it was decided that they would go to Europe where Reggie would undergo a cure. Gloria felt her twin sister Thelma needed a helping hand and so she was asked to come along.

The previous spring, Thelma, having failed to secure her divorce in Belgium, had gone to Hollywood to establish California residence in order to divorce Junior Converse there and to pursue her film career. The financing for her own film company evaporated, but she met Samuel Goldwyn, who arranged a small part for her in the film *Cytherea*, which starred another nineteen-year-old making her film debut, Constance Bennett.

Thelma and Connie Bennett became great chums, and after meeting Charlie Chaplin at a Goldwyn party, Thelma became a part of Hollywood's inner circle. At this time Chaplin was attempting to seduce Lita Grey, a fifteen-year-old whom he had cast as a dance hall girl in his film, *The Gold Rush*. To cover his actions, he told Lita's parents that Thelma was his fiancée, and assured them that she would act as chaperone if Lita were permitted to accompany them. Knowing the power of the Vanderbilt name, Charlie explained, "My fiancée, Thelma VANDERBILT, will always be with us." Lita's parents, properly impressed, gave their consent.

One night while Thelma waited impatiently inside the Santa Monica Swimming Club, Charlie took Lita for a walk on the beach, undressed her, and tried unsuccessfully to have sex with her. Lita cried and told him his "thing" was too big. A week later they tried again, with more success.

Chaplin's lie about his relationship with Thelma became so well known that newspaper headlines announced their impending marriage. In New York, Gloria read the headlines and wired Thelma, ARE YOU OUT OF YOUR MIND? Mamma's wire commanded, COME HOME AT ONCE.

Thelma didn't. Instead, she began an affair with Connie Bennett's father, stage actor Richard Bennett. Thelma, like Gloria, was attracted to older men, who in turn were drawn to alcohol. Bennett danced attendance on Thelma and although Thelma was not yet divorced, he gave her an immense solitaire diamond engagement ring. In the fall they were both in New York as he began rehearsals for Sidney Howard's play *They Knew What They Wanted*, which opened in November to rave reviews, but Bennett's daughter Joan observed that her father was drinking "more than usual . . . and for the first time his performances began to suffer. It was the beginning of his diminishing powers." Then Richard Bennett deserted the play for an unscheduled trip to Montreal for what Joan termed a "little merriment which combined the consumption of large amounts of alcohol with more athletic pursuits." On his return he was fired, and went into a New Jersey sanitarium to dry out.

It seemed an auspicious time for the Vanderbilts to take Thelma under their wing, and so Gloria, Thelma, little Gloria, nurse Keislich, Mrs. Morgan, a maid, and a valet all embarked for Paris. Reggie, avoiding this huge entourage, decided to travel a week later and join them at the Ritz.

Gloria now took care of Thelma in the same way Thelma had helped her: she gave Thelma money for living expenses and to keep up with her own splendid shopping. Then two days after Reggie's arrival in Paris, Gloria arranged a dinner party at which Thelma was seated to the right of Marmaduke (nicknamed Duke), Lord Furness, Britain's great shipping tycoon. Duke Furness was forty-two, almost Reggie's age—a redheaded, steely-eyed, hard-swearing, high-living peer who had about him an air of scandal transmuted to glamour by virtue of his $40 million fortune, his family seat at Grantley in Yorkshire, three other country residences, and London's famous Sunderland House, which he had purchased in 1919 from Reggie's first cousin Consuelo, Duchess of Marlborough.

In 1921, Duke's wife of seventeen years, Daisy Hogg Furness, mother of his two children, Averill and Christopher, had died suddenly under mysterious circumstances aboard Duke's yacht, the *Sapphire*, and had been buried at sea. At the time, there was much talk about why a man with the most powerful steam yacht in Great Britain, one equipped with refrigeration apparatus, could not have managed to have his wife buried in her native soil.

Marmaduke Furness's title was only one generation old—his father had begun life as a stevedore on the docks at Hartlepool. Upon his father's death in 1912, Marmaduke inherited his title, and in 1918 was granted the title of Viscount Furness of Grantley. He was a shrewd businessman of little patience who usually managed to get exactly what he wanted. It was not long after meeting her that he decided what he wanted was Thelma Morgan Converse. One evening at the Embassy Club in London, Duke Furness demanded of Thelma, "When will you get that bloody divorce?" Thelma explained that Junior was still hoping for a reconciliation. Duke suggested that detectives follow Junior and offered to pay for them; within the month, Junior Converse had consented to a divorce.

In New York, Richard Bennett heard the news of Thelma's divorce and announced that as soon as she returned from Europe, he intended to marry her. Thelma rushed to a Paris cable office to telegraph her denial and told reporters that she was returning Bennett's ring to him. Bennett insisted there must be some mistake; he told reporters that Thelma had asked him to make a film career for her and he'd told her he could only do so if she married him. "When I assured her I meant it, she said her first big act after her divorce became final would be to marry me." Mamma Morgan put an end to the matter by holding a press conference in which she announced Thelma's engagement to Duke Furness.

Certain patterns were becoming an established part of Gloria's life. Her entire family was growing used to living in luxury, courtesy of Reggie Vanderbilt. Only Consuelo, at present in Buenos Aires with her husband, was not the recipient of Gloria's largess. Gloria's brother, Harry Morgan, and his wife, the former Ivor Trezvant, had moved into the Ritz as Reggie's guests. Harry's emotional balance was precarious—he'd served in the Argonne campaign where he'd been "slightly gassed," and returned to Paris in a highly emotional state. After the war he'd fallen in love with a young Parisian actress, but when she failed to return his affection he tried to commit suicide by shooting himself. A year later he married Ivor. Gloria thought Ivor was fun, but certainly not dignified. At a beer-drinking contest in Paris's Harry's Bar, she drank every man under the table. And there was talk that Ivor's indulgences extended to drugs, that she had a penchant for morphine. Gloria looked upon the marriage with some skepticism and predicted that Ivor would come to a tragic end.

While the rest of their entourage remained at the Ritz, Reggie, Gloria, and Thelma decided to motor to Bad Kissingen for Reggie's cure, but he loathed the strict atmosphere of this German spa and found the people hostile. At a dinner party in a local restaurant, he requested that the orchestra play "The Star-Spangled Banner." As the first strains wafted over the room, the German patrons began to boo. Then they left their tables and moved menacingly toward the Vanderbilts. The music was halted abruptly, which ended the incident, but Reggie refused to stay in this oppressive atmosphere and they returned to Paris.

Gloria looked on the bright side of things, noting that Reggie could still manage to walk. For her this was a happy, exhilarating time: she and Reggie were entertained by what she considered to be all the best people. But suddenly Gloria's delightful Paris days came to an end. One morning she entered Reggie's bedroom to find him pressing a blood-soaked handkerchief to his mouth. Inside his esophagus the fatal eruptions had begun. Reggie told her he was having a nosebleed, but she could see the blood pouring from his mouth. This time the cure took them to Vichy. There, Reggie drank the required gallons of water while complaining that it was only fit to rot your boots and that the food was foul. But he stopped drinking alcohol and Gloria could see him improving daily.

At last, Gloria, who had blocked all awareness of Reginald's self-destructive pull toward death, was forced to understand the seriousness of the situation. Dr. Binet, the attending physician in Vichy, insisted on seeing her privately; then he informed her bluntly that if her husband wished to prolong his life he would have to give up alcohol totally. As Gloria walked back to the hotel, she asked herself how she could possibly get Reggie to stop this habit. How could she keep tabs on Reggie? How could she know what he ordered at the Reading Room, Brook, Metropolitan, Knickerbocker, or at any of his other clubs? She feared what would happen when he returned to his old life and friends, and longed to keep him in Europe for another year. She knew he would never agree. In a flash of comprehension, Gloria realized that Dr. Binet had pronounced a death sentence on her husband.

In August Reginald insisted that they return to America for the Newport Horse Show. They gathered up Mamma, nurse, and baby, and embarked on the *Leviathan* from Cherbourg. On boarding the ship, the Vanderbilts posed patiently for photographers, Gloria holding little Gloria, a winsome, seventeen-month-old baby with a sweet face and a soft corona of brown hair. As soon as they disembarked in New York, Gloria rushed to the telephone to tell the dowager Vanderbilt how successful Reggie's cure had been. His mother was elated and suggested they stop at The Breakers for dinner on their way to Sandy Point Farm the following day. As their motorcar neared Newport, Reggie insisted that he be dropped at the Reading Room; he told Gloria he would meet her at The Breakers later on. It was eight at night when he arrived, his face "ruddy with an alcoholic glow."

Two weeks later, Mamma Laura Morgan received a cable from Santiago, saying that her own mother was dying, and she begged Gloria to come with her to Chile. Gloria was later to remember that the day she left for New York, Reggie was complaining of a slight sore throat, but he said he would come to New York the following day to see them off. Reggie kissed Gloria goodbye, saying, "I'll see you tomorrow." In fact, Reginald Vanderbilt had been ill all week. On Tuesday, September 1, he'd been treated for a throat inflammation. When it did not respond to treatment, two other doctors had been called in for a consultation and they'd decided he was suffering from an intestinal disorder. They then summoned Dr. Edward A. Locke, a Boston specialist. Just as Gloria was departing for New York, Dr. Locke was on his way to Sandy Point with a registered nurse and a man ready to supply blood for a transfusion, if necessary.

As soon as Gloria was settled in at the Marguery Hotel, she phoned the farm and was told by Norton that her husband was resting. Later that evening she went to dinner at Jack and Charlie's, known as "21," and then to the theater with a family friend, Forest O. March. After the second act, she phoned Reginald once again. A strange woman answered the phone and said that she was a nurse and that Mr. Vanderbilt had suffered a slight hemorrhage and was sleeping. Gloria gave instructions to have a car meet the midnight train from New York to Providence, then she rushed to the station. She arrived at Sandy Point Farm at 4:30 a.m.—Alice Gwynne Vanderbilt's limousine was parked outside the house. Norton opened the front door. "Mr. Vanderbilt died two minutes ago," he said. Alice Vanderbilt came out of Reggie's bedroom. She showed no emotion, but she refused to allow Gloria to enter her husband's room, as she wished to spare her—Reggie's death had been a violent one.

He had begun to hemorrhage slightly at 9:00 p.m.; Dr. Locke had started a blood transfusion at 9:30 p.m. (Doctors had not yet learned that a blood transfusion might prove fatal in such cases; it raises the pressure of the blood and accelerates the bleeding. Today, an accepted treatment, which is still only effective in about 10 percent of these cases, is to insert a balloonlike device down the patient's throat which, when inflated, presses against the ruptured blood vessels and stanches the bleeding. In 1925, this technique had not yet been discovered.) By 2:00 a.m. the pressure was so great that Reggie's esophageal varicose veins began to rupture in a series of violent explosions. Reggie spewed and vomited out the blood which could find no haven within his body—until life itself burst from him.

Reginald Vanderbilt's death was reported by *The New York Times* as "sudden and unexpected . . . a severe shock not only to his relatives but to members of the summer colony at Newport." The last stage of his illness, however, cost $5,512 in doctors' bills, a figure that indicates his death was hardly as sudden as reported. The death was duly recorded in the Newport *Town Record*, which stated the cause as "cirrhosis of the liver, acute internal hemorrhage." A prominent local resident, Abby A. Sherman, who kept copious diaries, made her own entry: "Reginald Vanderbilt died—drank himself to death!"

At Sandy Point Farm Reggie's body was placed in a bronze casket silvered to the shade of his horse show gray. It was placed on display in a drawing room banked with American beauty roses and lilies. All social events, including the annual luncheon and shoot at the Clambake Club, were canceled. The flag at the Newport Casino was lowered to half-mast. The house overflowed with visitors who revealed hidden wells of feeling. Cathleen Vanderbilt Cushing arrived, barely recovered from her nervous breakdown. She stayed only a moment, exchanged angry words with Gloria, and stormed out of the house. Harry Payne Whitney arrived and wrote out a check for $12,000 to cover the funeral expenses. He went upstairs to see Gloria and perched on the edge of her bed while they discussed the funeral. Gloria had thrown a bed jacket over her nightgown. Mamma walked into the room and, noting the scene, spoke angrily to Gloria, calling her indecent and her behavior shameless. Harry rose, looked at Laura Morgan with contempt, and said, "You are a meddlesome old woman, and what's more you're a horrible one."

Early Monday morning, September 7, Reginald Claypoole Vanderbilt's funeral cortege moved from Sandy Point Farm to South Portsmouth. Norton insisted on walking behind the hearse the entire seven miles. Reggie's two favorite horses, Fortitude and Onward, were led from the stables to stand by the road as the procession passed.

St. Mary's Episcopal Church in South Portsmouth overflowed with flowers, the surplus obscuring the steps outside. After the funeral service, family and friends were driven to Bristol ferry, where they boarded a private train for New York City, stopping at New Haven, where members of the Yale faculty placed a wreath of blue and white flowers on the coffin—the white flowers formed Reggie's class numerals, 1902.

The funeral procession proceeded from Grand Central Terminal down Fifth Avenue, past the spot where Commodore Vanderbilt had tied up his first passenger ferry. At the Battery a private ferry waited, its decks swathed in black bunting anchored in place with masses of black plumes according to Vanderbilt tradition. When they reached Staten Island, Reginald's body was taken to the Vanderbilt mausoleum (a replica of the Romanesque Chapel of Saint-Giles at Arles) at the Moravian Cemetery in New Dorp. According to the Commodore's wish, no person except those who at death bore the name of Vanderbilt could be interred here. Every fifteen minutes, day and night, a watchman clocked in to prevent body snatchers from violating this tomb.

For Gloria, death was a devastating new experience. For Alice Gwynne Vanderbilt, it had become part of a pattern: this vault contained so many who were dear to her. Among the Vanderbilts were her grandfather-in-law the Commodore; her father-in-law William Henry; her husband Cornelius II; her daughter Alice; her son William Henry; and a memorial niche to her son Alfred Gwynne, lost at sea.

Gloria watched as Reggie's coffin was placed in a chiseled marble recess. When she turned to leave the tomb, her last thought was that Reggie, who had refused to be alone for one moment during his lifetime, was now to be left forever in his marble loneliness. The party reboarded the ferry where deferential waiters from Sherry's appeared with cups of steaming bouillon, platters of turkey galantine, lobster à la Newburg, and champagne.

Forty miles north of Inverness, Scotland, Viscount Furness and Thelma Morgan Converse were returning at teatime to his hunting lodge. They were in high spirits because Duke had bagged a record royal stag he had been stalking for days. While Thelma went upstairs to change her dress, Duke studied a just-delivered telegram and wondered the best way to tell his fiancée of her brother-in-law's death.

Gloria's brother, Harry Morgan, was behind the wheel of his race car at Monza when an English mechanic handed him a copy of the *Continental Daily Mail* containing the news of Reginald's death. He cabled his condolences to his sister and rushed off to his race at San Sebastián.

The World's Most Beautiful Widow

She's really in mourning. She threw her legs up, when she sat down on the sofa, and she was wearing black underwear!

THOMAS B. GILCHRIST

OVERNIGHT Gloria found herself transformed from the glamorous Mrs. Vanderbilt into a penniless widow. Reporters and irate bill collectors converged on 12 East Seventy-seventh Street, making it impossible for Gloria to return to her home. She dispatched her baby daughter to Alice Vanderbilt at The Breakers and sought refuge in a suite her mother rented at the Marguery Hotel.

Instead of sailing for Chile, Mamma assumed command of the situation as usual, suggesting that they immediately seek the legal advice of George Wickersham of the firm of Cadwalader, Wickersham & Taft. Uncle George, as Gloria called him, was an old family friend. Gloria thought the tiny, spry, sixty-seven-year-old man, with his huge, drooping white mustache, resembled Clemenceau. One of the most conservative and august lawyers in America, George Woodward Wickersham had served as Attorney General of the United States from 1909 to 1913. He'd met the Morgan family when he'd been sent to Cuba in 1918 on a secret mission for President Woodrow Wilson to divert

South American supplies, headed for Germany, to allied countries. At that time Harry Hays Morgan represented the United States Food and Fuel Administration in Cuba and worked closely with Wickersham. Then, with the signing of the armistice, both men were sent to Belgium to negotiate the reconstruction of that country. When Gloria and her mother sought his help, Uncle George was out of town, but on hearing of their plight, said that he would immediately send a representative of his firm to assist them.

Thomas Byron Gilchrist arrived the following morning, a tall, athletically built man of thirty-nine with light-brown wavy hair who looked as if he'd be more comfortable on the deck of a yacht than in the suite at the Marguery. Gilchrist had obtained a copy of Reginald's will and explained to Mrs. Morgan and to Gloria that apparently Reginald had been insolvent at the time of his death; the only true asset in the estate was the $5 million trust created by Cornelius II in 1899, which would now pass in equal shares to Reggie's two daughters, Cathleen and Gloria's own eighteen-month-old baby. Gilchrist advised the ladies that it was imperative a guardian be selected to protect the property of little Gloria, who was about to become an heiress. Laura Morgan explained to Gilchrist that her own daughter was only twenty, which made her ineligible to serve as her child's legal guardian; besides, Gloria herself admitted that she was totally inexperienced in financial matters. George Wickersham was mentioned as a suitable guardian, and Mrs. Morgan and Gloria agreed that he would be ideal. Gloria also requested that he serve as her own guardian until she became twenty-one the following August.

On paper Reginald appeared to have been a wealthy man and Gloria the recipient of his generosity. His will specified that Gloria was to receive both 12 East Seventy-seventh Street and Sandy Point Farm, "and all appurtenances thereto," as well as his residuary estate. Had Alice Vanderbilt's death preceded his own, Reggie would have inherited 1 West Fifty-seventh Street (valued at $7.5 million) and he bequeathed $500,000 to Gloria from the sale of this mansion. But since Alice Vanderbilt was still alive, this provision was void.

The newspapers also had obtained copies of Reginald's will and on reading its generous provisions assumed that he was as rich as any other Vanderbilt. Headlines tell the story of the gradual awareness of the situation. R.C. VANDERBILT LEFT $7,000,000 TO YOUNG WIDOW $5,000,000 TO TWO CHILDREN—WILL GIVES HER TOWN HOUSE AND FARM, said the *Sun* on September 25. R. VANDERBILT'S PERSONALTY UNDER $100,000, reported the *Times* less than three weeks later. And finally: VANDERBILT DEBTS EXCEED ESTATE and REGGIE DIED BROKE.

Reggie Vanderbilt had spent it all. And more. He was indebted to scores of people. Merchants had taken pride in extending credit to a Vanderbilt, a name synonymous with wealth and prestige. Doussourd & Filsen claimed $5,344 for fruits and groceries. Michael F. Naughton, a butcher who was owed $8,372.60, said that he had considered himself "lucky" to have a Vanderbilt as a customer. How long must the newsstand Trinin & Solodkin, on Madison Avenue, whose papers cost pennies, have extended credit for Reggie to run up a bill of $269.30? Consider the time taken to accumulate a bill of $236 for cigarettes, or $463 for ice, $1,562 for hardware, $712 owed a Newport laundress.

Reggie's creditors provided a clear picture of the Vanderbilts' lifestyle. Two thousand one hundred dollars went to Sonia Rosenberg for gowns, $3,069 to the 79th Street Garage, $8,358 to Tiffany & Co., $3,900 to B. Altman & Co., $225 to Dabney's Syncopated Orchestra, $424 to L. P. Hollander for little Gloria's baby clothes. In all, Reginald's creditors in Rhode Island, New York, and abroad collected $116,671.86. The United States Treasury Department collected $106,930 in unpaid taxes. The wages of most of Reggie's employees had been far in arrears at the time of his death, making his bequest of a year's salary to each employee who had been with him at least five years a macabre joke.

Thomas Gilchrist, knowing that it would be futile for Gloria to pursue her bequests, suggested that her only chance to obtain any money would be by exercising her dower rights. In so doing, as Reginald's widow, she would then have claim, before any other creditor, to a one-third share of the revenues yielded on the sale of the New York town house and Sandy Point Farm. But until she could exercise these rights, Gloria was destitute. Alice Vanderbilt gave her the money on which to live.

The only asset no creditor could touch was the trust fund created by Cornelius Vanderbilt II. Gloria's infant daughter received $2.5 million to be held in trust until she reached twenty-one, at which time she was to receive the principal. This trust generated an income of $112,448 annually. And so it came about that there was an enormously rich Vanderbilt baby with a penniless Vanderbilt mother.

Little Gloria's trust came under the jurisdiction of the New York Surrogates' Court, to be administered by Justice James Aloysius Foley. George Wickersham and Thomas Gilchrist consulted with Gloria and together they drew up a rough budget of her expenses. Then the following petition was submitted to Judge Foley. It read in part:

> . . . the father of said infant is dead . . . the mother of said infant has no property, excepting the property to which she will be entitled as her share of the estate of her husband . . . the said Gloria Morgan

Vanderbilt is at present receiving no income from said estate and is not likely to receive any income from said estate until the administration thereof is completed and the real estate left by said decedent has been sold.

Your petitioner has been informed by the said Gloria Morgan Vanderbilt, the mother of said infant, that she is maintaining a home for said infant at No. 12 East Seventy-seventh Street, in the Borough of Manhattan, City and State of New York, and that her average monthly expenses necessarily incurred for the maintenance and support of said infant and the maintenance of the home in which said infant resides, are as follows:

Servants	$ 925.00
Food for servants	250.00
Food for infant and mother	400.00
Coal	100.00
Gas	20.00
Laundry	80.00
Garage and automobile accessories	300.00
Physician	50.00
Clothing for infant and mother	1,500.00
Telephones and telegrams	40.00
Incidental	500.00
	$4,165.00

. . . WHEREFORE petitioner prays that an order be made herein permitting your petitioner, as Guardian of the estate of said infant, to withdraw from the income which your petitioner may receive from time to time belonging to said infant's estate, the sum of Four thousand dollars ($4,000) in each and every month . . . to be applied to the support and education of said infant. . . .

GEORGE W. WICKERSHAM,
Petitioner

With the submission of this petition, Gloria Vanderbilt met Surrogate Foley for the first time. Foley was one of the two surrogates of the New York County Surrogates' Court, an immensely powerful man whose court dealt annually with half a billion dollars relating to estates. On seeing him for the first time, with his glittering steel glasses and magisterial air, one might not understand that here was a man who loved the law and considered himself to be its servant; a man who thought first of humanity, and only later of form and procedure.

Foley was born in 1882, and had worked his way through New

York University Law School. By 1919, he'd served five years as an assemblyman and seven as a state senator and was the minority leader of the state senate. That same year he married Mabel Graham Murphy, the stepdaughter of Tammany Hall leader Charles F. Murphy. It was tantamount to marrying a crown princess of politics. One month after his wedding, he was nominated for the Surrogates' Court on the Tammany ticket and won the post in the November election. When Murphy died of a heart attack, New York State Governor Alfred E. Smith moved to have Foley elected leader of Tammany Hall. On May 14, 1924, this political dream was achieved by the forty-two-year-old Foley. It lasted exactly one day. On May 15, Foley's doctor announced that he had suffered "a complete nervous collapse." Foley abandoned high-pressure politics. Three months before Reginald Vanderbilt's death he'd turned down an offer to run on the Tammany ticket for mayor of New York City against John Hyland. James Joseph (Jimmy) Walker was selected in his place. He was then asked to run for the United States Senate. Again, he refused and the bid went to Robert F. Wagner.

Because he was a practical man, Surrogate Foley immediately granted Gloria Vanderbilt's petition for $4,000 a month, knowing that this was the only way she could receive funds. He regarded this young widow with a combination of emotions—pity for her, and anger at the law which was about to force her to live a lie. Her petition stated that the money she requested was for the "support and education" of her daughter, when, in fact, this money represented her *only* means of financial support over and above what she could glean from her right of dower—a right Foley considered outmoded and barbarous. Since he'd come to the Surrogates' bench in 1919, Foley had handled estate after estate in which women had exercised this tenuous right of dower to secure a one-third share of the sale of any real property connected with their husbands' estates. (Often, a widow's only income would derive from the sale of the house in which she'd lived and the property that had formed the foundation of her life.) Foley felt the law left such women degraded and unprotected, and he was determined to effect a change that would provide substantial security for widows.

At his meeting with Gloria Vanderbilt, Foley had a fleeting thought that perhaps George Wickersham might have found a way to deal honestly with this situation. If Foley had written the petition, he would have considered granting Gloria a modest allowance from the child's trust that would be all her own and acknowledged to be for her personal use. However, he had not been consulted in this matter; he had only been asked to rule on the petition—and he did.

In this manner, $4,000 a month was hit upon as a temporary stopgap allowance to enable Gloria Vanderbilt to support herself and her child. No provision had been made for rent, since Gloria and the child were again occupying Reggie's town house, or for travel. Over the next seven years circumstances would change, but this sum would continue to be the amount Gloria Vanderbilt would receive each month. If, at the close of a year, she had not used up the entire $48,000, she would be given the remainder to spend as she saw fit.

This unusual arrangement had one unforeseen consequence—it projected Gloria's infant daughter into the media spotlight. Although by no means the most wealthy child in the world, little Gloria soon appeared to be so in print. Newspapers began referring to her as THE WORLD'S MOST EXPENSIVE TOT and at regular intervals ran stories about the FOUR THOUSAND A MONTH BABY VANDERBILT HEIRESS. Little Gloria had joined her mother as a media personality—"the tiny Heiress" and the woman Cholly Knickerbocker now dubbed "the world's most beautiful widow" both began living their lives "in Macy's window."

In the spring of 1926 Reginald's town house was sold for $150,000; Gloria received $39,892. Then Sandy Point Farm was sold to Moses Taylor, who owned the adjoining property, for $165,000: Gloria received $45,655. Taylor declared that the Vanderbilt house was so ramshackle that he planned to tear it down and only use the property itself. Then the contents of Sandy Point Farm were auctioned off in a manner that Gloria found particularly brutal. She arrived alone at Sandy Point Farm on a clear May day to find a macabre carnival—the farm was overrun with thousands of people, lured there by the magic of the Vanderbilt name. Hundreds of cars from flivver trucks to Rolls-Royces were parked at random on the lawn while families sat munching on hot dogs, sandwiches, and bakers' pies sold to them from concession stands with bright umbrellas.

Guards whisked Gloria into the almost empty house. From the bay windows of her bedroom she watched as crowds swarmed over her front porch and pressed their faces against her downstairs windows. Most of the furniture from the house had been moved to The Ring. There, massed on the tanbark, were beds, bureaus, tables, kitchen supplies, her own bed linen. People strolled around the perimeter of The Ring as if they were circus-goers inspecting freaks in a sideshow. They were prevented from touching the objects by the wooden railing that ran all around The Ring: Gloria herself had often stood behind this railing watching Reggie drive his famous hackney horses.

Gloria left the house and walked to The Ring for the first day of the three-day auction that was to dispose of the Vanderbilts' possessions. The auctioneer climbed a ladder to an improvised platform held up by scaffolding, and the bidding began. The prices paid had little to do with the objects; these people wanted to possess something that had belonged to a Vanderbilt, to carry away a souvenir of a magical high life. One man bid $20.00 for a gallon jug inscribed with a *V*; a dozen badly chipped kitchen plates brought $2.50; a dilapidated wastebasket netted $8.00; a white kitchen spoon went for $4.00; a meat grinder (which one could buy new for $1.00) went for $2.50; a mahogany cask which bore the inscription, "What will you have?" went for $25.00.

Gloria watched as her possessions were sold off. Late in the day there was a particularly pitiful consignment: a child's toy gas range, followed by a stuffed elephant, four feet high, and, finally, a gray English baby carriage, in splendid condition, complete with cushions. There was a silence as little Gloria's baby carriage came before the block. No bid was made. Finally a matron broke the silence with the giggling offer of $1.50. There were no further bids and the carriage went at that price.

Gloria left the auction and retreated to the house. The last cars did not depart until dawn, leaving Sandy Point a litter of garbage. A newspaper headline the next day read: KITCHENWARE SOARS AT SANDY POINT AUCTION. In the morning Gloria gave orders that all articles bearing the Vanderbilt initials were to be withdrawn from the auction. She also insisted that Reginald's bed be removed from the sale. Then she returned to New York.

Alice Vanderbilt sent an agent to purchase all Reggie's horse show trophies, as well as rugs, linen, silver, and tapestries. She also paid his estate $5,500 for two family portraits—one of Commodore Vanderbilt and one of Reginald's grandfather William Henry—which had been willed by Cornelius II to the Head of the House of Vanderbilt. Reginald's first wife, Cathleen (now Mrs. Sydney Colford, Jr.), agreed to relinquish her claim to $30,000 a year alimony for the remainder of her life. The matter of the estate of Reginald Claypoole Vanderbilt was finally resolved.

From the first, it was Thomas Gilchrist who was assigned the day-to-day administration of little Gloria's guardianship, George Wickersham being busy with a multitude of legal and governmental duties. Gilchrist had gone with Gloria to submit Wickersham's petition to Surrogate Foley and because of his good advice she finally received $130,000 from Reggie's estate.

From their first meeting, Thomas Gilchrist had liked Gloria and felt that she had great charm. He was pleased when she began calling him Tom. Yet there was something disconcerting about this woman, a sensuous quality that kept him off balance and sparked his fantasies. He imagined how her sexuality had attracted a Vanderbilt—he imagined other things about her as well. His attitude, perhaps unconsciously, was expressed to his family one night when he laughingly remarked of Gloria, "She's really in mourning. She threw her legs up, when she sat down on the sofa, and she was wearing black underwear!"

From the start, a sexual tension colored their relationship. Gilchrist treated Gloria as a force of nature, trying desperately to hold her in check. He quickly came to regard her as a woman who would pursue her own desires without regard for the practicalities of a situation. Two weeks after Reginald's death, she came to Gilchrist and asked him for $15,000 from the estate; he told her it would be impossible to arrange. That same week she took off for Paris, even though there were business details still to be resolved. In the next six months Gloria made three trips abroad. On the last one she wrote Gilchrist from Paris announcing her intention to live there permanently. Gilchrist began to realize that he'd have a job controlling this willful, impetuous woman, but he had one powerful weapon with which to fight—the child's trust. He answered Gloria's letter by saying that Surrogate Foley had expressed his "strong desire" that her infant daughter be raised as an American; if Foley's wishes were not respected, he might substantially reduce Gloria's trust income. It seemed to Thomas Gilchrist that he had performed an important service in protecting the child's welfare.

If Gilchrist had seen the situation from Gloria's point of view perhaps he would have acted differently. From the moment of Reginald's death, Gloria's life had been thrown into confusion and Mamma Morgan ruled supreme. Two weeks after Reggie's death, Mamma told Gloria that Papa had written a letter from Argentina demanding $15,000 and threatening that if Gloria did not send him this money, he would take action against another member of the family. That was when Gloria had gone to Tom Gilchrist and, without telling him why, asked for the money she needed. When he refused her, Gloria pawned her 16¼-carat engagement ring and gave her mother the $15,000 to send to her father. (Eight months were to pass before she was able to redeem her ring.) That same week reporters discovered that Gloria was at the Marguery Hotel and besieged her there, demanding to know how it was that a Vanderbilt had managed to die leaving no money. She referred her inquisitors to Gilchrist and, in a state of partial nervous collapse, sailed for Europe, where she spent a week with Thelma buying proper mourning frocks and a long crepe veil.

When Gloria returned to New York the excitement had subsided and she was able to return to the Vanderbilt town house—Mamma came too. Mrs. Morgan became the self-appointed arbiter of her daughter's conduct, constantly reminding her of what was proper. Gloria obeyed Mamma but her life was oppressive. She felt ill and suffered from insomnia; she began a sculpture of Reggie's head; she did jigsaw puzzles far into the night; she went to the movies, where she could lose herself in fantasy. With Reggie dead, Gloria felt that New York Society slammed its doors on her. No invitations were forthcoming. (It did not occur to her that members of this group presumed her to be in deep mourning.) After three months she felt the atmosphere was too bleak to bear and she sailed back to France. Thelma met the night train from Cherbourg and on the way to the Ritz suggested that Duke take them to Prunier's for dinner. Gloria felt relief—for a time she would be able to escape the strictures of her mourning. But when she returned to New York, Mamma was there with new rules and demands. In the spring Mamma Morgan insisted that they bundle the baby into the Vanderbilt limousine and drive her to the Convent of the Sacred Heart where the Reverend Moorhouse F. X. Millar baptized little Gloria a Catholic. Before they left, the Reverend Millar gave Mamma and Gloria a tiny statuette of Christ so they might always remember this day. Gloria didn't tell Alice Vanderbilt of the Catholic christening. She didn't want to offend the formidable matriarch who was so generous to her.

In late spring Gloria again escaped her dreary life and returned to Paris; she was so much happier there that she decided to make Paris her home. But no sooner had she written Tom Gilchrist of her decision than he wrote back telling her that her allowance would be reduced if she didn't return to New York. For the first time, Gloria began to realize the potentially punitive nature of the financial arrangement that had been made for her. She sailed back to New York expressly to plead her cause to Tom Gilchrist, but he refused to help her so she insisted on speaking to Surrogate Foley herself. Once she was permitted to state her case directly to him, the situation improved: Gloria explained that she had no home of her own and that her entire family lived abroad. She said she would like to live in Europe until her daughter was of school age; that it would be valuable for little Gloria to learn French while she was young; and she promised, "When she is old enough to go to school then I will bring her up in America." Foley was touched by Gloria's personal appeal and approved her plan. But this was the beginning of a pattern that Gloria was eventually to find intolerable. "From this moment on I had a sword of Damocles hanging over my head. . . . I was never to make a move that entailed the expenditure of money in which I could act as a free agent."

Living at a Pretty Extravagant Rate

I never squandered my money, but if anybody in my family asked me for help . . . I was only too glad and willing to do it.

GLORIA MORGAN VANDERBILT

At the end of May 1926, Gloria, Mamma, little Gloria, and nurse Keislich embarked for Cherbourg on the *Leviathan.* Gloria felt that Mamma was much in awe of the Vanderbilt money and power and was thrilled that her granddaughter bore the Vanderbilt name. She seemed "hysterically . . . unnaturally fond of the child." When Gloria wished to carry the child on deck with her, Mamma turned on her, declaring that the sea was too rough and accusing her, in a rage, of deliberately trying to harm her own baby. Mamma asserted that she would "see to it that 'the little one' was protected."

At that moment Gloria realized that "by a strange twist of her disoriented mind," Mamma might be fantasizing that Gloria was capable of killing her own child. Her supposed motive: if little Gloria died before reaching twenty-one years of age, Gloria would inherit the child's money.

It was too patently absurd. If there were the slightest truth in the thought that she might harm her own child, surely she wouldn't allow both her mother and a nurse to be with the child every moment of every day of her life! Mamma's behavior was obviously pathological but Gloria felt she couldn't call her to account, and she allowed her mother's wishes to prevail. Little Gloria remained in her cabin.

Nurse Keislich was also giving Gloria "trouble: She had adopted toward little Gloria—and in some respects toward me—an attitude that seemed patterned on my mother's; to Keislich, Gloria was an especially delicate child whose fragile nature was not properly respected by me. She was, moreover, an heiress whose privileged status was not adequately acknowledged by those whose duty it was to serve her." On shipboard, the chief dining room steward reported that no matter what the chef prepared, Keislich returned it to the kitchen as unfit for the child. In Paris, when the three women and the baby moved into the Ritz, Gloria observed that the nurse insisted on cooking the child's food herself on a hot plate resting on the toilet seat. The food at the Ritz, Keislich explained, was not fit for anyone to eat, much less a "sick child."

Gloria conceded whatever parental authority that might have been hers to these two authoritarian older women. Indeed, the child was the main concern of their lives, and their justification for being in Gloria's household. Emma Sullivan Keislich had never expected to live abroad—now she found herself totally alone with her charge, whose every movement she supervised. Laura Morgan was glorying in her exalted position as grandmother to the Vanderbilt heiress. And Gloria—a twenty-one-year-old widow—was anxious to get on with her own life.

Gloria's behavior was not unusual for a Society woman of her day. It was a mark of status to remove oneself from the upbringing of one's children, to place them in the hands of a nanny, and later a governess. These middle- and lower-class mother surrogates of English, Swiss, German, and Scottish origin were entrusted with the health and morals of the children of the privileged. Often these women were superstitious and uneducated, often they were unmarried and sexually repressed. They devoted their lives to their charges, lavishing on them the fervor of their own stifled lives, giving these children their own stern morality and sometimes, their love.

This was the pattern set by the British royal family, an example to Society the world over. Edward, Prince of Wales (who was to play a pivotal role in Gloria's life), spent his early years, while his parents were still the Duke and Duchess of York, in the gloom of York Cottage, Sandringham, where the rooms were tiny, the bathrooms scarce. The nursery accommodation consisted of two small rooms; Prince Edward, Prince Albert (who became King George VI), Princess Mary, and their nanny shared one small room by day and slept in the other at night.

The nanny, who never left Prince Edward's side, was sadistic and deranged. She loved him with a strange perverted passion so compelling that when she took him to visit his parents at teatime, she would stand on the threshold of the room and twist the fragile child's arm and viciously pinch him. Prince Edward would enter the room crying and screaming, which so disconcerted his parents that he was speedily sent back to her. This was her gift of love. This nanny finally called attention to herself by having a nervous breakdown, and was dismissed. For generations, Vanderbilt children, the American equivalent of princes and princesses, had been reared by armies of nurses, governesses, and tutors.

In Paris, Gloria set about practicing the lessons her husband and mentor had taught her: she lavished every luxury on herself, and her family and friends gathered round to enjoy her largess. Gloria remarked that "$48,000 a year didn't go as far as a quarter of a million" had, but refused to let this impinge on her life-style. Her brother Harry, who had separated from his wife Ivor and was permanently unemployed, came to stay at the Ritz as Gloria's guest. He needed spending money—she gave it to him. In the past, Gloria had given Thelma money too, but there was no need for that now—Thelma arrived in Paris gorgeously gowned and bejeweled, courtesy of Duke Furness. In June, Gloria and Mamma went to London for Thelma's wedding. Because Reggie had been dead only nine months, the wedding was small, attended by relatives and a few intimate friends, and Mamma insisted that Gloria wear a black dress.

Papa Morgan did not come to the wedding; indeed he seemed to have totally lost touch with his family. Ten days after Thelma's wedding he arrived in New York from Buenos Aires on the liner *Southern Cross* and was met by reporters asking if he was on his way to visit his new son-in-law.

"What son-in-law?" asked Harry Hays Morgan.

"Lord Furness," replied a reporter.

"Did Thelma marry Lord Furness? Well, that's the first I ever heard of it!" exclaimed Mr. Morgan. Then, realizing his predicament, he added: "I'm sure he'll make an excellent husband for her and I'll gladly give my blessing to them both."

The rigid social schedule followed by the International Society set prescribed Biarritz or Cannes in July. (Gloria said that "the hoi polloi" arrived in August.) This invisible social calendar was known to all members of this select group, so that wherever they went, they saw the same faces, as if there were only a few hundred people in the entire world. In July of 1926, Gloria rented the opulent Villa Ourida in Biarritz, and Mamma—still living with Gloria—enjoyed a lavish vacation paid for by the child's trust stipend of $4,000 a month and supplemented by Gloria's $130,000. (Mamma told her children that she had no money of her own.) Harry was also staying at the villa, as was his friend, a Mr. Brown, who was affiliated with the O'Cedar Mop Company. Papa turned up unexpectedly and lived with them for several weeks. Gloria insisted on giving Papa spending money too.

Gloria awoke daily at about eleven-fifteen when her personal maid, Olga Wright, stepped into her bedroom and pulled back the drapes to reveal the Pyrenees looming in the background. Then Olga presented her with a tray holding the glass of water or cup of coffee that constituted her breakfast. At noon, she went down to the Grand Plages near the Hotel de Palais, where she had rented a bathhouse, and she and her guests would change into bathing suits. At about one-fifteen, they would have lunch and then go back to the beach and lie around in bathing suits until about five. Neither Gloria nor her brother played golf, but sometimes they motored down to the South Club, where they would have tea and watch the golfers. Dinner was served at 8:45, after which they had coffee and liqueurs, and would sit and talk, or play bridge, or go to movies, or the theater, or nightclubs, or gambling—Mamma was particularly fond of the casino and went there frequently.

In the fall, Gloria rented an enormous, newly renovated triplex apartment in Paris at the fashionable address of 37 Avenue Charles Floquet, for which she paid 60,000 francs ($12,000) rent a year. She bought approximately $40,000 worth of furniture for this apartment and, from the United States, Alice Vanderbilt shipped to her as a gift all Reggie's belongings that had been purchased at the auction. On the main floor was a marble-floored entrance hall, a dining room, a formal drawing room, and an entire room devoted to Reggie's trophies. On the second floor were five bedrooms, and on the top floor were the servants' rooms—Gloria was unsure of how many there were. She thought her staff consisted of eight live-in servants, although Mamma put the number closer to fifteen.

In October, Gloria booked first-class passage for herself and her brother on the *Leviathan* to New York. This was to be a special voyage, one that the newspapers had been writing about for months. Queen Marie of Rumania was to be on board the *Leviathan*, to begin an official tour of the United States. In 1926, America was at the height of a personality craze in which those few who distinguished themselves from the masses were showered with frantic, if temporary, adulation. It was a mere two months after the spectacle of Rudolph Valentino's funeral and seven months before Charles Augustus Lindbergh's dramatic transatlantic flight. Queen Marie was another perfect candidate for deification. At fifty-one she resembled a glamorous blond movie queen, but she was *real* royalty—the granddaughter of Queen Victoria on one side and the Empress Marie of Russia on the other. She distinguished between her grandmothers by referring to them as "Grandmamma Empress and Grandmamma Queen." Sir John Foster Fraser in London's *Evening Standard* described the reaction to Queen Marie's impending visit as a "royal spasm" on the part of "the richest and least responsible people in the world," and suggested that "the United States should buy a king. . . . They will never be happy until they do."

The frenzy of anticipation generated in the United States was due largely to the increasing power of the press. The *World* acclaimed the visit "because it brings together the world's first ultra-modern publicity machine and the world's first ultra-modern queen." This queen was to become the perfect media personality: she would ride in an open car in a rainstorm up Fifth Avenue while being showered with wet paper; she would kneel on a white buffalo robe with a Sioux war bonnet on her head and Catherine the Great's pearls about her neck, extending her right hand to Tomahawk, the aging Sioux chief who became a celebrity himself by murdering Sitting Bull. She saw reporters any hour of the day or night, and would even conduct interviews in the bathtub while reporters stood in front of a screen which had been placed around it.

Queen Marie received free passage for herself and her retinue of twenty. The *Leviathan* was not the loser—342 passengers booked first-class passage solely to catch a glimpse of her and newspapers throughout the world booked similar space so their reporters might observe her every activity. These reporters, hard put to supply news to a voracious public, noted such trivia as the fact that the queen walked on deck daily in the company of her nephew, Gottfried, Hereditary Prince of Hohenlohe-Langenburg, and that they both swam in the pool after lunch, except one day when Marie was said to have a sniffle. At one luncheon the queen was served fried chicken, corn fritters, fried bananas, biscuits, and honey. While a band serenaded her with renditions of "Old Black Joe," "My Old Kentucky Home," and "Dixie," "Queen Marie enthusiastically clapped her hands in time to the music." Her nephew Prince Gottfried Hohenlohe-Langenburg was observed eating a chicken leg with his fingers.

The name Mrs. Reginald Vanderbilt also appeared in newspaper dispatches. One day "the world's most beautiful widow" was a guest at lunch at the captain's table. Seated at the table were Captain Herbert

Hartley, Queen Marie and her son and daughter, Mrs. Woodrow Wilson, and the twenty-nine-year-old Prince Gottfried, called Friedel by his intimates. The prince shared his aunt's impressive royal lineage. His mother was Queen Marie's sister Alexandra (called Sandra); his father was a first cousin of the Empress of Germany.

Since feudal times the Hohenlohes had owned Bavarian estates of farmland and timber forest, and two castles, one at Langenburg—which since the thirteenth century had been occupied without interruption by twenty-one generations of the House of Hohenlohe—and a medieval castle at Weikersheim, in the valley of the River Tauber. When his father died, Friedel would inherit these properties. In the meantime, he was penniless. He was on the *Leviathan* in the capacity of secretary to Baron Thyssen of the German industrial family.

Gloria was seated to the left of Prince Hohenlohe. Her first impression of him was that "he had one of those ugly feudal faces which, however plain, shows great race." Reporters who watched their every move noted that the captain's guests dined on plover eggs and trout and that Queen Marie kept the party "dry." Prohibition was in force, and the *Leviathan* was a United States liner, but almost everybody flouted the law. What the reporters did not know was that Queen Marie had not consumed alcohol or danced since 1916 when her three-year-old son, Mircea, had died in a typhoid epidemic during the Great War. They also were unaware that Queen Marie slept every night with the child's last pair of shoes in an embroidered case under her pillow. The luncheon was described as "the ultimate in chic." Gloria saved her luncheon card. Friedel saved his.

The *Leviathan* dropped anchor in New York harbor on the morning of Monday, October 18. One hundred and fifty reporters rushed on board, led by Mrs. Vincent Astor and Mayor Jimmy Walker in top hat and morning coat. While fireboats shot gushers of white water into the air, planes buzzed overhead, and guns bellowed a twenty-one-gun salute from Governors Island, Queen Marie, dressed in a sable-trimmed maroon velvet coat and twinkling gold turban and carrying an armload of American beauty roses, greeted her welcomers. For once in her life, Gloria Vanderbilt, in the company of Friedel Hohenlohe, slipped away unnoticed. But one week later, they were photographed together in a box at the National Horse Show, and in December they both sailed back to Europe on the *Majestic*. Hohenlohe accompanied Gloria to Paris and, for the first time, they discussed the possibility of marriage.

At the luxurious Paris triplex little Gloria's income supported a household that now included Gloria, Harry Morgan, Mamma, nurse

Keislich and many other servants, and Prince Hohenlohe as an increasingly frequent guest. The $130,000 from Reginald's estate was almost gone, yet several afternoons a week Gloria would go to the couturiers Jean Patou or Paul Poiret, or to Mr. Bunting to have shoes made, or to Chenille, the hat shop.

When Gloria first hinted to Mamma that she might become Her Serene Highness, Princess of Hohenlohe-Langenburg, her mother reacted violently. Mamma was hostile toward men and she "was obsessed with the belief that women had to use their wiles to manipulate men to get what they wanted." As far as Mamma was concerned, Prince Hohenlohe had nothing she wanted—he was penniless, he might take her precious granddaughter away from her and carry her off to Germany. Mamma grew increasingly hysterical on the subject of Friedel, swearing that she would do everything in her power to stop this marriage. Gloria considered this to be an idle threat.

The day before Friedel's thirtieth birthday, in March 1927, he secured his parents' consent to the marriage and the engagement was officially announced. Gloria and Friedel told reporters that they intended to live three months a year in Germany, the rest of the time they would reside in New York, Palm Beach, and Paris. Unbeknownst to her daughter, however, Laura Morgan had written a lengthy, impassioned letter to George Wickersham and Thomas Gilchrist, requesting that they present it to Surrogate Foley. In this letter, she outlined a series of complaints concerning her daughter's way of life and companions and accused Gloria of neglecting her child. She wrote that if her daughter married Prince Hohenlohe, he would live off the child's money and abuse her. She believed that the child would be whipped.

Mamma Morgan's obsession with the death of her granddaughter had found a new object in the person of His Serene Highness, Prince Gottfried Hohenlohe-Langenburg—she came to believe that once Friedel was married to her daughter, he would murder little Gloria so that his wife would inherit the child's millions.

Not only did Mrs. Morgan make this accusation of murder with alarming frequency, but she did so in front of her daughter, the prince, and even the three-year-old little Gloria. In the name of love and protection Laura Morgan exposed her granddaughter to an accusation that touched upon the deepest, most primitive of childhood fears. One morning Gloria noticed that little Gloria, dressed to go to the Bois, was wearing new white kid gloves. She instructed nurse Keislich to change them, but little Gloria began to cry, insisting that she wanted to wear them. At that point, Mamma rushed in and told the child that she could wear whatever she wanted, at any time. "Your mother would be in the streets were it not for you, my darling, my poor little orphan, but I will protect you. As long as I live no one will take a penny of yours." Then, turning to her daughter, white with rage, she yelled, "I know what you and that Boche are trying to do. You are trying to kill this poor, unfortunate child. Oh, yes! I know! It will be an accident. A little push down the stairs—seeing that she is left in a draft—a million ways! And you, Gloria, will weep like a Magdalen, but just the same, the Vanderbilt millions will be yours!"

In this atmosphere little Gloria became nervous and hyperactive and began a retreat into fantasy. Her mother was a remote and inaccessible figure to her; one of little Gloria's first memories was of Gloria "wearing a crystal-spangled white gown, looking more fragile and pale than any moonflower, disappearing down an endless hotel corridor." On the other hand, Mamma Morgan, whom she called Naney, and nurse Keislich, whom she called Dodo, hovered over her as if expecting disaster at any moment. In April of 1927, nurse Keislich learned that her mother was dying in New York. She was upset, but insisted that she would not leave little Gloria even for the short time it would take to go to her mother's side. Although the child appeared quite healthy to her mother, both Mamma Morgan and nurse Keislich frequently summoned her doctor who finally took a complete set of tests and reported that little Gloria had a slightly positive Mantoux test for tuberculosis. He suggested that she be treated with mountain air, sunbaths, ultraviolet rays, and a compound of arsenic and iodine.

Mamma Morgan used the child's so-called delicate health as a weapon to try to destroy Gloria's relationship with Friedel Hohenlohe. That spring, Gloria took a trip to Biarritz with him. No sooner had she arrived than Mamma called to say little Gloria was desperately ill with tuberculosis. Gloria rushed back to Paris, traveling all night. She arrived at her apartment to find that the child was not sick at all, she was not even there, but out playing in the Bois. After that, Gloria began to feel that every time she went away her child would contract some disease, real or imagined, to bedevil her. Also, she began to feel that it was little Gloria who prevented her from leading her own life. Gloria wanted desperately to marry Friedel but Tom Gilchrist kept writing her letters indicating that Surrogate Foley might not look kindly on a foreign alliance—little Gloria was an American heiress and should return to her native land. Furthermore—and here was the threat—Foley found her present allowance to be unusually generous. Should she remarry, her husband would be responsible for her support. Her child's funds could not be used "to finance a second marriage."

There was one ally who could help her—the formidable dowager

Vanderbilt. Gloria took her child and sailed for New York. Alice Vanderbilt had moved to the fifty-room Gould mansion on the southeast corner of Fifth Avenue and Sixty-seventh Street, having sold her Fifty-ninth Street palace—the area had become increasingly commercial and the noise from the construction of the Sherry-Netherland Hotel across Fifth Avenue had disturbed her immeasurably. With pride, Alice Vanderbilt showed Gloria around her new residence. Gloria was surprised to see the childlike delight this austere woman displayed as she pointed out the solid gold faucets and fixtures in the bathrooms. While Gloria went to a hotel, the child and her nurse remained at Mrs. Vanderbilt's. Although Alice was delighted with her granddaughter and sympathetic and kind to Gloria, she refused to take a position concerning Gloria's marriage plans, telling her that she made it a point never to interfere in her children's lives and that Gloria must make her own decision.

Gloria then went to see Uncle George Wickersham and Tom Gilchrist. Not aware of her mother's intervention, she was surprised to find these men so knowledgeable about the details of her life and of Hohenlohe's financial position. Uncle George and Tom warned her that Surrogate Foley would never approve of this marriage. Once again, Gloria insisted on seeing the Surrogate, but this time Tom went with her and Foley told her exactly what to expect: whenever she remarried, she would receive only an amount of money commensurate with the actual expenses incurred for her child's support and education within her husband's household. Gloria returned to Paris. What she had heard from Surrogate Foley was not what she had wanted to hear and so she behaved as if the trip had not happened, continuing her relationship with Hohenlohe. Mrs. Morgan, who had expected that financial pressure would compel Gloria to break her engagement, was furious. She boarded the next ship to New York and, still without her daughter's knowledge, went to see Wickersham and Gilchrist, and then Surrogate Foley himself. She repeated her written accusations to them and told Foley about "the unfortunate plight of my granddaughter who has a calvary on earth." Then she returned to Europe and moved in with Gloria for their summer vacation at the villa in Biarritz.

Prince Hohenlohe resigned from his job and arrived at the Villa Ourida on August 22, in time for the twins' birthday party the following night at the Cassanova nightclub. The party abounded with titles—only half a dozen Americans were present.

That summer Gloria lived under the cloud of her mother's displeasure. At the dinner table Friedel Hohenlohe was exposed to Mamma's sharp tongue—he found her to be hysterical and incoherent: "She objected to my marrying Mrs. Vanderbilt on the ground that I had no fortune to speak of, and she accused me of all sorts of things, wanting to murder the child and such ridiculous things as that." On this subject, she accused Hohenlohe "a hundred times." It was "her theme song," he declared wearily. Meanwhile, the three-year-old child who was the object of these accusations moved quietly about the house following her own strict routine. On sunny days she and Dodo would go to the beach at St. Jean de Luz where she built sand castles and splashed in the calm waters.

At summer's end the family returned to Paris and Gloria went to visit Friedel's parents to explain the delay in their nuptial plans. She also prevailed upon Consuelo, whom she considered sensible and persuasive, to go to New York and do whatever was necessary to talk Uncle George, Tom, and Surrogate Foley into granting her permission to remarry. Gloria's trip to Germany was a fairy-tale experience for her. She visited the castle at Weikersheim, considered to be one of the most perfect examples of medieval architecture in the world, and was caught up by the romance of the throne room where ancient tattered banners still hung from their stanchions. But it was the castle at Langenburg that made her catch her breath—she found it as large and impressive as Buckingham Palace. From the enormous stone archway that bore the Hohenlohe coat of arms it was a twenty-minute drive up a mountain to reach the castle. Five hundred people lived and worked on the estate. Behind Gloria's chair at dinner stood both a man and a woman servant; a third servant handed the food to one of these two, who then served the guest. Friedel explained that this custom had originated in his family in feudal times when the third servant was required to taste the food to see if it was poisoned. This trip strengthened her resolve to become Princess Gloria.

Upon her return to Paris, however, the following letter awaited her:

My dear Mrs. Vanderbilt,

Your sister, Mrs. Thaw, called upon me today in connection with your grandmother's estate. During our conversation something that she said caused me to doubt whether you correctly understand the attitude of the Surrogate with respect to the continuance of the allowance which he has made for the maintenance and education of little Gloria, in the event of your re-marriage. Although nothing that Mrs. Thaw said to me has given me the impression that the subject has progressed any further than it had when you talked with me last Spring, nevertheless the fact that the matter appears to be still within the realm of contemplation impels me to remind you of the conditions imposed by the Surrogate when he made the allowance . . . the allowance was extremely generous and . . . would be drastically reduced if at any time he should receive credible information that any part of the infant's income was being used, as he put it, to "finance a second marriage." . . . and if he found that you did contemplate matrimony he would be likely to materially reduce the allowance.

You may rest assured that anything that you said to me on the subject will be treated as absolutely confidential and that under no circumstances would I, without your permission, repeat to the Surrogate what you have told me or anything that you may hereafter tell me on the subject; but if he should raise the question, you will perceive the embarrassing position in which I would be placed, for I would not wish to deceive him regarding a matter in which he originally acted upon my representations. . . .

Very sincerely yours,
Thomas B. Gilchrist

Gloria and Friedel discussed this letter; then they called in the press to say that their engagement had been postponed. Gloria gave as a reason, "I do not speak one word of German; furthermore, I love Paris and the good old United States too much to live in Germany. The Prince also adores Paris and America. But so far we have been unable to win his parents to our viewpoint." The prince turned to Gloria and added, "I am sure, Gloria, if anyone could win over anybody else, it would be you."

But she couldn't. Gilchrist's letter was followed by one from Uncle George demanding that she immediately submit an accounting of her expenses for the past year demonstrating that her income had been used solely for the child's benefit. Since all parties concerned knew that she had no income of her own, this demand was part of a terrible charade. Gloria well understood the lip service and subterfuge necessary to play the game. And she hated it. (On many of her trips she took her little daughter along. Often the child would be sent to stay at a different place from her mother, but the expense report would read, "trip with Miss V.") Now she submitted the requested list of expenses and wrote:

Dear Mr. Wickersham,

Enclosed please find statement duly signed by me.

I wish to assure you that every cent of the $48,000 given to me from Gloria's estate has been spent on herself as you will see by said statement, not only that but whatever moneys I inherited from my *late husband's estate has gone in making Gloria as comfortable as I could. You will realize that I had no house, no furniture to speak of, no linen, or car for her. All this I have provided for her.*

Dear Mr. Wickersham, I want you to know that everything I can do for Gloria has been done and as you know will always be. I think I told you when I was in N.Y. that I will do just as the Surrogate thinks best in all things, only please remember that the last four years of my life have been very hard, and that I hope things will go well from now on.

Please thank the Surrogate for all he has done for me in the past, for his kindness to me and Gloria.

As ever,
Gloria

Wickersham's response was immediate and cold:

My dear Gloria:

I have showed your letter of March 30th to the Surrogate, who, after looking over it, remarked that you were living at a pretty extravagant rate, and that he thought you would be much better off, if you were living in this country.

These, of course, were only impressions, but it showed a disposition on his part to scrutinize with some care the reports as to your scale of living.

Faithfully yours,
George W. Wickersham

Gloria, not knowing what to do, did nothing. As long as there was no marriage, the financial arrangement continued as before. Then Gloria received a hand-delivered document from her father, who was visiting in Paris. It was a draft of a petition written in a semi-legal manner, undated, unsigned, and with certain pertinent dates left blank since Mr. Morgan could not recall Gloria's birth date, marriage date, or little Gloria's birth date. The petition accused her of leading a dissolute life and of squandering her money so that she was deeply in debt. Accompanying it was a letter from Papa stating that if Gloria didn't change her manner of living, he would send this petition to Surrogate Foley requesting that she be removed as general guardian of her child.

Gloria was enraged. The petition was ridiculous in that she had never *been* general guardian of the child. But what it showed her was that even Papa had turned against her, and Gloria knew that Mamma had put him up to it. Papa's accusation was infuriating to Gloria for another reason: Gloria declared, "I never squandered my money, but if anybody in my family asked me for help . . . I was only too glad and willing to do it." And Papa had asked, and had received. Gloria and Thelma confronted Papa at his suite (which Duke Furness had paid for) at the Hotel Lotti. He admitted that Mamma had nagged him into writing the petition and told Gloria to forget all about it. Then he took the twins for cocktails and lunch at Prunier's. When Gloria returned home she had an argument with Mamma, who screamed that the petition was accurate and that if anyone asked her, she would "tell the truth."

And so Gloria and Prince Hohenlohe, who remained unemployed, drifted into yet another summer of pre-marital limbo. Gloria rented another villa in Biarritz. Long lazy days were spent on the beach and in the water at St. Jean de Luz, but behind the bright days were Mrs. Morgan's continuing hostility toward Friedel Hohenlohe and the increasing frequency of the letters from Wickersham and Gilchrist, urging Gloria to return to the United States to live, and to justify her expenses.

At summer's end Gloria's personal maid left her employ, and she engaged in her place a pleasant, rather pretty young Frenchwoman named Maria Caillot. Uncle George Wickersham arrived in Paris and Gloria introduced him to Friedel Hohenlohe; his response to the introduction was to reiterate to her that the Surrogate felt she was spending too much money.

In November of 1928, Gloria decided to make one final try to marry Friedel. Taking her child, the nurse, and Maria Caillot with her, she went to New York and moved into the Sherry-Netherland Hotel. Little Gloria was sent to stay with her grandmother. The dowager Vanderbilt was becoming fonder of the child daily; perhaps the child might provide a means to effect her purpose. In January Gloria returned to Paris, but she left little Gloria with Alice Vanderbilt. The first week in February of 1929, several newspapers carried a curious report. The New York *American* article read:

CASH SMOOTHS BRIDAL PATH
OF MRS. VANDERBILT

. . . A sudden turn in their romance was revealed at a midweek dinner at the fashionable La Poularde, given by Mrs. Vanderbilt, with Prince Hohenlohe as the guest of honor. . . . While the guests came believing that financial obstacles made the marriage out of the question, all left convinced that everything is arranged . . .

The impression is that Mrs. Cornelius Vanderbilt, who is Gloria's mother-in-law, has effected an arrangement by which her daughter-in-law will be guaranteed an adequate income in her own right after marriage. . . . Meanwhile Gloria's little daughter is making her home with Grandmother Vanderbilt, and it is understood she will continue to live there after her mother's marriage.

It looked surprisingly as if a trade was about to be effected, but once again Gloria had overlooked the power of her controlling mother. Laura Morgan had come to New York in December and when her daughter returned to Paris she became a frequent visitor at Alice Vanderbilt's mansion. It was not long before she was confiding to Alice just what kind of man Prince Hohenlohe was, and warning her what the disastrous consequences to little Gloria might be if Gloria was permitted to marry him. Alice Vanderbilt was eighty-five years old and in failing health and she knew that the time in which she could protect her granddaughter was limited. In order to ensure little Gloria's future she withdrew her support of the marriage. Gloria had no idea what had happened. She came to New York and after several futile attempts to repair the situation she removed her daughter from the Vanderbilt mansion.

Instinctively, Gloria began to realize that her mother had defeated her and she went to see Tom Gilchrist, demanding that he draw up a new will for her. In the event of her death, Gloria had designated her mother to be little Gloria's guardian; now she gave joint custody to Thelma and Consuelo. From her purse she produced her father's petition and letter and held them out to Tom Gilchrist, explaining, "I'm afraid my mother has completely lost her mind. She has instigated my father into doing this." Then she told Tom that she wanted him to have this document so that there would be no question later about why she had changed her will. With that she burst into tears, saying through her sobs that she knew now that she could never marry the man she loved.

Tom Gilchrist was thrown off balance; although he found Gloria to be improvident and immature, she was so beautiful and charming and touching. Seeing how distressed she was, Tom explained once again that she could marry whomever she wanted and he told her that he would do his utmost to work out the details of where they might live. However, her husband *must* provide for her. Gloria tearfully replied that the prince wanted to marry her even if her allowance were curtailed, but she was the one who'd decided that she couldn't take it upon herself to have the child's income reduced and as a result she'd broken off her relationship with Hohenlohe completely. That afternoon Gloria collected her daughter and sailed back to France.

Mamma Morgan had won—she moved back into Gloria's triplex—but this time Gloria fought her authority. She had a confrontation with

Mamma in which Gloria told her that since the Surrogate thought her expenses too great, she would now be forced to rent a smaller place. Unfortunately, there would be no room for Mamma! When her mother protested that she had no money to rent her own apartment, Gloria arranged that she and Thelma would each give her $250 monthly. Then Gloria rented a small house on the rue Alfred Roll for 30,000 francs ($6,000) a year, only half of her old rent. Although she had promised that the child was to be back in America when she reached school age, she signed a six-year lease on this house—a lease that would not expire until January 15, 1935, when little Gloria would be eleven.

Gloria did not sever her relationship with her mother even though Mamma disapproved so violently of her plans and her way of life. Later Gloria explained why she hadn't discontinued the relationship. It was simple: "She was my mother." Mamma had been banished, but she moved into a hotel only ten blocks from Gloria's house. That's when the real trouble began.

Fast Friend and Favourite Dancing Partner

The world must have its heroes, and where today are they? What's left? Wales! Just a nice boy but . . . a dash of gold and crimson in a drab world.

Daily News, SEPTEMBER 1, 1924

THERE WAS NO DEFINITIVE MOMENT, no clear instant when the course of Gloria's life could be seen to veer away from a magazine ideal of love, marriage, a child. In April of 1929 Gloria, free of Mamma's constant surveillance, moved into the house at 14 rue Alfred Roll, situated near the old fortifications of Paris, but whenever Mamma visited there were constant arguments. Both Mamma and nurse Keislich were concerned that the house was so isolated; they felt little Gloria's life was in a constant danger and wanted Gloria to hire bodyguards for her. Gloria told them that this was ridiculous and an unnecessary expense; she had friends who were far richer and more famous than she and they didn't hire detectives to guard their children. Mamma also voiced endless complaints about little Gloria's "delicate health", and if it wasn't Mamma, it was Keislich who was distressed by little Gloria's throat or glands. By this time, Gloria was thoroughly convinced that all this talk was invented to torture her and that in reality her child's health would be fine, if only Mamma would leave her alone.

Little Gloria was frequently exposed to what she later described as her grandmother's "sudden moods of volatile hysteria which erupted unexpectedly," and she experienced these moods "as ominous tremors of thunder, as though something terrible were about to happen." Gloria observed that at these times little Gloria "would become like a vibrating tension gadget—rocked back and forth by my mother's uncontrolled emotions." Most of little Gloria's ailments seemed farfetched to her mother: one day the child complained that she could not stoop down to pick up a toy. "I'm getting just like Dodo," five-year-old little Gloria declared, taking on the characteristics of her arthritic nurse.

Naturally, Gloria considered this situation abnormal, but she put it out of her mind and removed herself from it. That summer she sent the child and nurse Keislich to live in an apartment in Biarritz while, for the first time, she went to Cannes. She found this place to be one of the most "spectacular spots . . . on earth" with its "inflammable combination of beautiful women and expertly fascinating men." Until 1926 Cannes had been considered a winter resort, but in the last three years it had been discovered by the International set—the richest, most colorful, most spoiled people in the world, who decided that July was *the* month for Cannes and flocked there to play in a setting where every indulgence was available to them without risk of censure. Every eccentricity was tolerated as long as it was done stylishly: Cannes was a place tailored to those who lived for sensation. Sex permeated the atmosphere—the mammary shapes of the twin cupolas of the Carlton Hotel were said to be inspired by the shape of a royal mistress. The tone of Cannes had been set by the winter vacationers, royal, rich, powerful men who had built sumptuous villas for their mistresses and illegitimate children—the Aga Khan for a former Italian ballet dancer, Ginetta Magliano, and her son Aly Salomone Khan; King Leopold II of Belgium for Caroline Dubois, an eighteen-year-old waitress to whom he granted the title Baroness Vaughan; and by women such as the Grand Duchess Anastasia Michaelowna, who was said to exhaust scores of young lovers. The most beautiful courtesans in the world flocked to the Côte d'Azur to parade along the beach promenades hoping to achieve the same success as others of their number.

A decade earlier, Gloria Vanderbilt had been in a convent; five years earlier she had been a virgin bride; during the summer of 1929 she was to progress to the next phase of her life and become a full-fledged member of the International set. That summer in Cannes, Gloria met the glamorous Nadeja, Lady Milford Haven at a party given by Nadeja's cousin, Grand Duke Boris. Nada, as she was called by her friends, was thirty-three, dark, and severely handsome. She was married to George Milford Haven, a brilliant, quirky, great-grandson of

Queen Victoria. The Milford Havens, an exotic and intriguing couple, were leaders of the International set. Nada was at the heart of the fun—that summer she and Prince George (later Duke of Kent) won the Charleston contest at the Cannes Sporting Casino. It was Nada's idea to order a tub of champagne to soothe her dance-tired feet. Her hostess received a whopping bill which read, "Champagne for Marchioness of Milford Haven's feet." In Nada, Gloria found the attraction of opposites. She thought herself shy and inarticulate because of her stammer—Nada was outgoing, full of life and verve. Gloria thought that she was "brilliant," her face "startlingly alive." Gloria found Nada to be "entirely Russian in thought and in action" but knew nothing of her exotic background. Nada's mother, Sophie Merenberg (who upon her marriage was granted the title Countess Torby), was a granddaughter of Russia's most famous poet, Alexander Pushkin. In 1891, Sophie had contracted a morganatic marriage with Nada's father, Grand Duke Michael Mikailovich. For three years they had sought Czar Alexander III's approval of the marriage, and in 1894 renewed their efforts with Czar Nicholas II, who had just ascended the throne. Their appeal was backed by Edward, Prince of Wales, but still the new emperor withheld his approval, so Grand Duke Michael left Russia to establish residence in England, thereby forfeiting everything but his private fortune, which he removed from the country in his private train in bags of gold. Grand Duke Michael's deposit of gold was described by the governor of the Bank of England as the largest ever received by the bank from a private individual. This grand duke became prototypical of those Russian aristocrats who spoke French, owned private yachts and railroad coaches, resided in England, and vacationed on the Riviera. He owned a lavish villa in Cannes as well as Kenwood, a mansion on Hampstead Heath designed by architect Robert Adam. His dead-white face soon became familiar at Wimbledon and at horse shows throughout Europe.

Nada's maternal heritage was as violent as her paternal heritage was royal. The earliest known Pushkin ancestor was a soldier who in A.D. 1146 was recorded as "taking the city" of Kiev. Four Pushkins signed the Romanov election charter. In 1725, Petrovich Pushkin, Alexander Pushkin's great-grandfather, in a fit of rage, slit his pregnant wife's throat; he died in prison that same year. Alexander Pushkin wrote that in the next generation, his grandfather's first wife "died on a straw pallet, locked by her husband in a dungeon on the estate for having an affair, real or imagined, with his son's French tutor, who was hanged in the courtyard by his order." The poet himself died from an injury incurred in a duel with a persistent, though platonic, admirer of his beautiful young wife.

Nadeja's name was an anglicized version of that of Alexander

Pushkin's mother, Nadezhda, who was the granddaughter of Ibrahim (called Abraham) Hannibal, known as "the Abyssinian Negro" and "the favorite of Peter the Great." During Peter's reign, little blackamoors had become the rage at every court in Europe. The emperor instructed his Turkish ambassador to procure one for him. In 1705, the child, then eight—the son of an Abyssinian princeling, taken as a hostage to Constantinople—was abducted from the sultan's seraglio and brought to Russia, where he served first as Peter's pet, then as valet, personal secretary, and finally general in charge of the Russian engineer corps.

Deciding to rid himself of his first wife, Eudoxia, in order to wed his mistress Christina Scherberg, Hannibal locked her in a room and tortured her to persuade her to confirm his accusations of her infidelity. While she hung by her hands at a height which kept her feet from touching the ground, he beat her with a whip. Nadeja Milford Haven was a sixth generation descendant of Abraham Hannibal and Christina. The genes of this Abyssinian were such that for generations to come his descendants, including Nadeja, would possess tightly curled black hair and enormous dark eyes.

In November 1916, Countess Nadeja Torby married Prince George of Battenberg in a ceremony attended by King George V, Queen Mary, and Dowager Queen Alexandra. George's mother, born Victoria of Hesse, had been the favorite granddaughter of Queen Victoria and one of her sisters was Alexandra, Czarina of Russia. George's father, Prince Louis of Battenberg, had been the First Sea Lord of the Royal Navy at the start of World War I, but had been forced to resign as a result of anti-German sentiment. The year after George and Nada's marriage, at the height of this anti-German feeling, the British royal family abandoned its German titles and assumed the dynastic name of Windsor (causing Kaiser Wilhelm II to scoff, "Fine, next time we play Shakespeare we'll call it 'The Merry Wives of Saxe-Coburg-Gotha' "). By royal decree, the name Battenberg was anglicized to Mountbatten and George's father and mother were granted the titles First Marquis and Marchioness of Milford Haven. There were four children in this family, two sons and two daughters: George was named Earl of Medina and his brother Prince Louis of Battenberg became Lord Louis Mountbatten. The latter was visiting aboard a British naval cruiser when he was informed of his new title; he wrote in the guest log, "Arrived Prince Hyde, departed Lord Jekyll." Princess Louise became Lady Louise Mountbatten. The eldest sister, Princess Alice, was married to Prince Andrew of

Greece, but they had been branded "the German Greeks" and forced to flee to Switzerland, where they lived a hand-to-mouth existence.

By 1929, all had gone well for George, who'd inherited his father's title, and for his brother Lord Louis, who had married the beautiful heiress Edwina Ashley. Louise had married Crown Prince Gustav of Sweden and would be queen, but Alice was enduring a second period of exile and was living in France with her five children, who ranged in age from Margarita, who was twenty-four, to Philip, who was eight. Alice had led a terrifying and difficult life, and it had taken its toll on her emotions. That summer Nada and George had succeeded in persuading Alice to allow Prince Philip to come to England the following year to be educated.

Gloria and her newfound friend Nadeja Milford Haven were often together and Gloria soon became a frequent visitor at Lynden Manor, the Milford Haven estate near Maidenhead. A sixteenth-century barn near the manor house housed George Milford Haven's favorite project, a miniature railroad. There was a train house equipped with tiny trains that ran over two miles of track and through tunnels cut into the five-foot Tudor walls. George Milford Haven worked on this railroad for years and had spent over $60,000 on it. Nada had wealth, but for George money was a problem; he'd just decided to go on half-pay from the Royal Navy while trying to pursue a business career, hoping to generate some additional income of his own.

Besides, there was another hobby—a secret, expensive one—the amassing of a collection of pornography. In the Milford Haven set there was an active trade among bluebloods in blue books. Charles Reginald Dawes, a contemporary of Lord Milford Haven, possessed a vast collection of erotic works characterized by beautiful paper, magnificent bindings, and florid endpapers. George Milford Haven's collection was of a different nature—a collection of pornographic books supplemented by a series of seven privately assembled scrapbook albums. Albums one through six were said to contain erotic photographs. Album seven is a dark blue leatherette scrapbook containing eighty-one meticulously hand-mounted items augmented by a precisely executed, hand-written, two-page index and a master list of each item. Among these items are detailed prospectuses from pornography publishers written both in French and English and covering a wide range of sexual activities. One catalog is devoted exclusively to listings of sadomasochistic books, another is of photographs depicting incestuous situations—entire family orgies, mother and son, and sister and sister engaged in sexual relations; others specialize in homosexuality and bestiality. Certain catalogs contain advertisements for artificial genitalia and aphrodisiacs; the catalog of a rubber goods manufacturer offers such items as condoms with knobs and ticklers of several varieties.

Throughout album seven, neat blue crosses are penciled next to many of the offerings as though the reader intended to buy them. Several of the catalogs in George Milford Haven's collection list titles dealing with flagellation. A typical selection includes *Lady Gay: Sparkling Tales of Fun and Flagellation*, *A Tale of the Birch*, *The Convent School or Early Experiences of a Flagellant*, *A Treatise on the Use of Flogging in Venereal Affairs*, *The Spirit of Flagellation*, *Raped on the Railway*, described as "a true story of a lady who was first ravished and then flagellated on the Scotch express"; *Les Callipyges*, "the whole philosophy and secret mystery of luxurious flagellation by former English aristocratic ladies." Two other titles, *Memoirs of a Russian Ballet Girl*, described as "the slave perversion in all its beauty, rigor, cold-bloodedness and ignominy . . . where naked young girls are horsewhipped," and *La Flagellation des Femmes en Amerique*, were similar to books that four years later would be shockingly introduced into the testimony at the Vanderbilt custody trial.

George Milford Haven's pornography was a secret within his own household. In 1930, in addition to their thirteen-year-old daughter Elizabeth Tatiana and eleven-year-old son David, George's nine-year-old nephew Prince Philip of Greece and Denmark had become like a member of the family. Philip had arrived in England that winter and had moved in with his sixty-seven-year-old grandmother, the Dowager Marchioness of Milford Haven, at Kensington Palace. Philip, like his cousin Edward, Prince of Wales, enjoyed playing a jazzy saxophone, which disturbed his Great-Aunt Princess Beatrice, who was seventy-three and who felt that the palace was not the right place for "the younger generation." That's when Nada and George took Philip in. They assumed financial responsibility for sending him to school at Cheam, along with their own son David. It was Aunt Nada and Uncle George who appeared on parents' day and at sports day and who sent their car for Philip to bring him to Lynden Manor to spend his vacations. They treated Philip as their own son.

Philip and David became best friends—at school they were known as the Mountbatten boys. George Milford Haven converted his garden barn into a badminton court so that the boys could make all the noise they wanted. Philip lost half a tooth playing hockey with David. (His royal smile was repaired.) On one adventure the two boys bicycled from Lynden Manor to Dover and then hitched a ride back on a grain barge up the Thames. For two days and nights they slept on sacks of grain in the ship's hold.

Neither George Milford Haven, nor Nada, nor Gloria Vanderbilt, who visited frequently at Lynden Manor, could know that this rambunctious towheaded boy would, in 1947, marry the heir apparent to the throne of Great Britain, with David as his best man. And that in 1952, upon the death of her father, Elizabeth II would ascend the throne with Philip at her side bearing the title of Duke of Edinburgh.

While Gloria was cementing relationships that led her into the heart of the British royal family, her identical twin Thelma was moving in a similar direction. At the end of the summer of 1929, Gloria received a phone call from Thelma urging her to come to London immediately—she desperately needed her sister's help. It seems that Thelma had become (in Maury Paul's words) the "fast friend" and "favourite dancing partner" of the most spectacular social catch in the world.

Edward Albert Christian George Andrew Patrick David—half a century ago women reeled off this string of names like a litany. Edward, Prince of Wales, called David by his intimates, was the object of a fantasy so strong that he was publicly called Prince Charming. Perhaps it was his somewhat antiseptic, asexual, curiously androgynous quality that made women feel safe in admiring him so. He was born in 1894 when his great-grandmother, Queen Victoria, then in the fifty-seventh year of her reign, was still ruling over the most powerful and largest empire in the world and her children and grandchildren sat upon the thrones of Europe. Edward, Prince of Wales, who so briefly was to be King Edward VIII, and then lived out his life as the exiled Duke of Windsor, wrote, "Mine is the story of the life of a man brought up in a special way, as a prince trained in the manners and maxims of the nineteenth century for a life that had all but disappeared by the end of his youth." By the end of World War I the great Romanov, Hapsburg, and Hohenzollern monarchies had toppled. In the future a British monarch might reign, but never again would he rule.

Prince Edward's mother, Queen Mary, was a reserved woman who resisted overt affection and was revolted by the process of pregnancy. As a young mother, she was so shy and remote that she could not deal with her staff or correct the people who served her. But she was strong in her conviction that her husband's needs came first and she gave him her absolute loyalty, saying of her children, "I have always to remember that their father is also their King."

Their stern king-father, George V, possessed a great sense of majesty and was given to unexpected bursts of rage. He believed that his children should be reared to fear their father and saw to it that his sons were indifferently educated, both out of an upper-class suspicion of intellectual pursuits and a desire to keep them in their place. In an empire of rich intellectual tradition, they grew up ignorant of literature, art, the theater, and music, save for the blaring of bagpipes. Their first tutor effectively stunted their intellectual growth with his dreary, empty curriculum. King George V did not allow Prince Edward instruction even in the sports he himself enjoyed—shooting and golf—nor, more significantly, a knowledge of politics or the requirements of sovereignty.

This high-strung young prince lived in terror of his father's remonstrances, yet possessed a subtle streak of rebellion. In manhood, he remained tiny in stature, with bones fragile as crystal, his nervousness manifesting itself in chain-smoking and a constant touching of his tie. As he became a public personage, his life was directed by two forces: the will of his father, and that of the people. His classic features, topped by a shock of straw-colored hair, were known around the globe. He became the most photographed man in the world. His smile was radiant. In repose, his face bore the look of a wistful boy.

At twenty-one he returned from World War I to be sent out by Prime Minister Lloyd George on a series of world tours, to thank Britain's allies for their participation in the Great War. "Primarily my job was to make myself pleasant . . . and in various ways remind my father's subjects of the kindly benefits attending to ties of Empire." Everywhere he went he was greeted by tumultuous crowds, parades, delegations, honors, hero worship. Edward, Prince of Wales, became his country's most valuable export. He was called "Britain's Greatest Ambassador," her "Best Salesman." In trying to analyze his incredible appeal, a newspaper editorial explained, "The world must have its heroes, and where today are they? The war dashed to earth regal idols to which millions raised awed eyes. There fell the gilded princes and potentates who shed glamor on a workaday existence. . . . What's left? Wales! Just a nice boy but panoplied with the remembrance of the pomp and picturesqueness once the mark of kings . . . a dash of gold and crimson in a drab world."

By 1925, Prince Edward had traveled the equivalent of six times around the globe and had shaken over twenty-five thousand hands, so many that his bruised and swollen right hand ended up in a sling while he smiled and gamely continued to shake hands with his left. His duties were totally of a token and ceremonial nature. Indeed, his father, King George V, who was steeped in tradition, shored up his world with these symbolic duties which could still be executed without exactly acknowledging that the sovereign's power had become merely the power of suggestion, or that the entire political and economic condition of the world had changed. "You must always remember your position and who you are," he frequently cautioned the heir apparent.

"But exactly who was I?" his son mused. "The idea that my birth and title should somehow or other set me apart from and above other people struck me as wrong . . . my capacity was somehow not appreciably above the standards demanded by the fiercely competitive world outside palace walls. . . . I suppose that, without quite understanding why, I was in unconscious rebellion against my position."

As the years passed he was given no greater responsibilities. His speeches were carefully gone over to make certain they suggested no political position: the royal family must be above politics. In England he continued his endless round of ceremony—inspections, cornerstones to be laid, trees planted, hospitals toured. Sent abroad again, he wrote in his diary: "What rot and waste of time, money and energy all these state visits are!!" Eventually he became less anxious to please, less punctual, frequently peevish, often subject to unexplained periods of melancholy. There was talk of beautiful women, nightclubs, drinking too much, and dancing till dawn. After a day crowded with official engagements, the high jinks would begin. An irreverent American newspaper speculated that the motto of the Prince of Wales, *Ich dien* (I serve), might apply to the hours spent behind the bar preparing drinks for his friends. His private life became the antithesis of that of his father who "disapproved of Soviet Russia, painted fingernails, women who smoked in public, cocktails, frivolous hats, American jazz, and the growing habit of going away for weekends," the very things, with the exception of communism, that his eldest son embraced.

To most of the British upper class, the word *American* had a pejorative connotation. Like the products that were eroding Britain's export trade, things American were thought to be gaudy, cheap, and improper. To the Prince of Wales, *American* meant a respite from tedious formality. He doted on American jazz, which he played on the saxophone; American slang—he'd taken to saying "I guess" and "Whoa baby!" as his golf ball rolled toward the cup; American cigarettes—although he directed that they were to be rewrapped in British paper in order not to incur the ire of local manufacturers and the public. He also admired American women; he called them "snappy."

In 1925, King George V and Queen Mary had commissioned the refurbishing of Marlborough House, at the cost of £50,000, to receive the Prince of Wales and his bride when he married. Although his name was linked with that of scores of young ladies, nothing ever came of it; the Prince of Wales sat on his gilded throne at garden receptions watching the most eligible debutantes curtsy before him, head to knee, his face wearing an expression of exquisite boredom. His first love was said to be Lady Coke, a married lady twelve years his senior. For the past decade his "fast friend" and "favourite dancing partner" had been Freda Dudley Ward, a married woman with two children who seemed to provide the strong maternal love he needed.

Prince Edward's frustration and inner tension found release in a passion for horsemanship. At twenty-seven he began to devote himself to fox hunting. Although he had always enjoyed physical exercise, this sport became something more. Here he could completely forget his round of duties; he could excel as a man and "show that, at least in matters where physical boldness and endurance counted, I could hold my own."

After his first three seasons, he selected as his headquarters rooms at Craven Lodge, a hunting club in Melton Mowbray, Leicestershire, and began to assemble a string of hunters. On the hunt field he found the cosmopolitan society he enjoyed: English nobility mixed freely with local gentry, farmers, American sportsmen, and American ladies "whose pursuit of the fox was only a phase of an even more intense pursuit of romance." He began riding in steeplechases and point-to-point races where he displayed great courage and recklessness. He took many spills and, because he was the Prince of Wales, each one was minutely recorded in newspapers at home and abroad where he was described as an inept horseman. In 1924 at an army point-to-point, the prince's horse, Little Favorite, thundered toward a jump with a front height of three feet and a sloping drop of six feet to ground hard as a paved road. The horse sprung forward too soon and collapsed in a heap on the far side of the jump. A flailing hoof struck the prince in the face; blood spurted from his nose and mouth, drenching his turtleneck sweater. Three men ran forward and carried him out of the path of the charging horses.

An ambulance arrived and a Red Cross nurse began wiping the blood from his face. "What happened?" the dazed prince asked.

"You fell off, Sir," replied the nurse.

"I fell off? I did not!" he protested, knowing of his reputation. "No! The horse *must* have fallen with me."

The prince had suffered a brain concussion that confined him to bed for nearly a month. His father expressed disapproval of his son's participation in so dangerous a sport and asked him to stop. In an unexpected move, the prince's riding was brought before the House of Commons. A Member of Parliament made an impassioned speech, noting that the throne was the sole political link of an empire of more than 450 million people, and that the safety of the heir apparent could be presumed to be a high affair of state. This was followed by a letter from the Prime Minister, Ramsay MacDonald, begging the prince, on behalf of his country, to refrain from endangering the royal person. Never before had the personal habits of a member of the royal family come under scrutiny in this manner. But the prince continued to ride and by 1928 he had taken dozens of spills, broken his collarbone twice, sprained his wrist, and seen two of his hunters drop dead under him.

In December of that year the prince was summoned back from East Africa to his father's bedside for what the family thought to be King George's terminal illness. Within the week the stricken king turned over his power to a crown council on which Prince Edward served. Up to that time, the prince declared, "I actually possessed no prescribed State duties or responsibilities." It seemed that, at last, he might have access to the traditional red leather boxes containing the official ministerial documents and diplomatic reports that were delivered each morning to the king. As the people began to turn to the Prince of Wales for leadership, two gestures immediately endeared him to them: he toured the coal fields where jobless, poverty-stricken men were suffering through the coldest winter in European history, reporting with disarming sincerity that the unemployment situation was "a ghastly mess! Worse than I would ever have believed." And he agreed to sell his horses. The auction was scheduled for February 23, 1929, at the Leicestershire House Repository. The night before the auction, the prince, dressed in evening clothes, appeared unexpectedly at the stable. To the astonishment of the stable hands, he walked from stall to stall patting each glossy coat and whispering words of farewell into his horses' ears. "And so I reluctantly abandoned the one pursuit that gave outlet to my competitive spirit," the prince noted.

That same month King George V was moved to Bognor on the Sussex coast. He was placed in an ambulance, the rear of which was composed completely of glass so that he might be seen by his subjects en route. The glass box resembled a coffin and he lay in it still as a corpse, eyes shut, two pillows propping up his emaciated head at a forty-five-degree angle, a rumpled sheet pulled up loosely under his chin, one hand protruding from a dark jacket sleeve rimmed by a shirt cuff. Miraculously, the king began to recover. By early summer he returned to Buckingham Palace. It became clear that Edward, Prince of Wales, would be returned to his former token duties. The public still found him to be a most charming boy. He was thirty-five.

That summer he attended the Leicester Fair, set in the heart of his once precious riding country. He had yet another official duty to perform. He stood in the center of a ring in front of six sleek, plump cows, his right hand holding a pleated blue satin pinwheel from which two long streamers descended. He glanced out at the crowd and saw a face he recognized—the dark, handsome American, Thelma, Lady Furness. At once, the radiant smile that had become his trademark burst across his face as he raised his hand to pin the rosette on the collar of the winner of the class.

Toodles and the Teddy Bears

The Lord saved Daniel from the lions' den,
but who will save David from the fiery Furness?

GERTRUDE VANDERBILT WHITNEY, SUMMER, 1932

THELMA WAS BORED. Her son William Anthony (Tony) had been born in March 1929, and had promptly been turned over to a nanny. Thelma knew about nannies. "From the moment you put your baby in their arms they nobly allow you to adore him, but nothing more, all other privileges are theirs."

In the winter season when guests gathered for fox hunting, shooting, and parties at neighboring estates, Burrough Court at Melton Mowbray could be fun. But now it was summer, and while her twin was off in Cannes, Thelma was stuck in this lonely place recuperating from childbirth, with only her stepdaughter, Averill, for company. Averill was only three years younger than Thelma and although they were complete opposites, they'd become good friends. Averill was a tomboy who loved riding and shooting (she'd shot her first stag at age six) and disliked Society, spending much of her time alone on the moors. She was plain and gangly, with a large nose and the same steely eyes as her father, but she had one lovely feature, a mass of curly auburn hair.

Thelma and Averill did not discuss Averill's father, who was off leading what he euphemistically referred to as "my own life." Duke's repeated infidelities angered Thelma. In a way, they had been her own fault. One night they'd been dining at the Embassy Club when Peggy Hopkins Joyce came in. Blond, fragile, aristocratic-looking Peggy was known as the original gold digger; it was said she'd collected $3 million in alimony from five husbands. Thelma knew her only too well: the detectives who'd followed her first husband, Junior Converse, had found him whiling away the nights in Peggy's apartment. This information had enabled Thelma to force him to consent to a divorce. Also, Peggy had been the flame of Thelma's intimate acquaintance, Charlie Chaplin, having captured his attention by inquiring of him, "Is it true what all the girls say . . . that you're hung like a horse?"

When Peggy entered the Embassy Club, Duke looked at her but had no idea who she was. Thelma told him, and on an impulse, bet him ten pounds that Peggy wouldn't dance with him. Thelma lost the bet. Duke followed this liaison with another affair. He began spending more and more time away from his wife.

Averill, sensing Thelma's loneliness, asked her to come with her to the Leicester Fair where she was showing her favorite hunter. Thelma wandered through the flower show and came upon a crowd jampacked around a ring. She sauntered over to see what the attraction was. There in the center of the ring stood the blond, handsome Prince of Wales. He glanced out at the crowd and stared straight at Thelma. Then, smiling the smile she had seen in so many photographs, he raised his right hand to pin a rosette of blue satin on one of the six cows lined up in front of him.

The prince walked over to Thelma and said, "Congratulations on the birth of your son." Then he asked casually, "Are you at Burrough for the summer or do you plan to come up to London at all?"

Thelma made a quick decision. "As a matter of fact, I plan to be there next week."

"Eight o'clock Wednesday night at St. James's Palace? We'll have cocktails and then go out for dinner and some dancing," announced the prince.

With this invitation, Thelma Furness began a love affair that lasted five years. The prince received Thelma in his private study at York House, St. James's Palace. They sat side by side on a quilted-chintz sofa in front of a fireplace over which hung a portrait of his mother, Queen Mary, at her most imperious. These two had much in common: neither was interested in the theater, books, or art. As the prince chain-smoked, they gossiped about people: what fun he'd had at her sister Consuelo's house in Buenos Aires; they spoke of Gloria—four years previously he'd been introduced to her in a restaurant and had asked her to dance, but she'd replied that she was in "half-mourning," and they'd had a nice chat instead.

Thelma seemed almost a natural choice for the prince. In her dark beauty there was a hint of the exotic—her Latin blood made her appear smoldering, with a suggestion of *vicieuse* sexuality. She was married. She was American. For all her sophistication, however, at twenty-four she still seemed like a child dressing up to play a part. Elsa Schiaparelli caught her quality: "She was very beautiful but she was heavy to talk to. She was gay and friendly and chattering, always chattering. But she had no sense of wit or repartee. She was what the French call *flou*—vague." The prince, at thirty-five, shared this hothouse immaturity. The love name he chose for Thelma was Toodles, and the symbol of their love—teddy bears. One evening Thelma was late for cocktails with the prince because she'd been shopping at Harrod's and had forgotten the time. As she dashed for the door she saw a table piled high with tiny pink and green teddy bears scarcely three inches high—two for a shilling. She bought four of them and, on entering the prince's study, held them out to him as a peace offering. David was delighted and immediately declared that each of them should keep one pink and one green bear. When they were separated, they would trade bears. "I'll give you my green one and you give me your pink one and we'll always have something of each other," he said with the delight of a child inventing a new game.

Shortly before he began his affair with Thelma, the Prince of Wales, in search of a country retreat where he could lead a private life, found Fort Belvedere, a grace-and-favor residence (which is a crown property usually assigned to a loyal courtier upon his retirement, or to members of the royal family) located on the edge of Windsor Great Park. It had fallen vacant and he asked his father for it. King George growled, "What could you possibly want that queer old place for? Those damn weekends, I suppose." But then he smiled. "Well, if you want it, you can have it."

Fort Belvedere was half-house, half-fort, and incredibly ugly. When the Prince of Wales was granted Fort Belvedere, he referred to it as a "pseudo-Gothic hodgepodge. . . . An intrusion of yew trees kept one side of the house in perpetual shadow, staining the walls with green acidulous mold. The garden was untended; the surrounding undergrowth was wild and untidy. But the half-buried beauty of the place leaped to my eye."

The Prince of Wales promptly took his new love, Thelma Furness, to see the Fort (he never called it Fort Belvedere). She couldn't conceal her disappointment. "You're not very impressed, are you, darling? But wait and see what I'm going to do with it," he told her.

Thelma wanted to spend every minute she could with David, but she was "hoping to keep up appearances." Her husband, Viscount Furness, was a powerful and vastly wealthy man who'd just completed the sale of only one of his interests, the Furness-Withy Shipping Line, for $30 million—the contract had been drawn up on the back of a menu. He was not a man to be publicly cuckolded. If Thelma were to carry off her affair she needed help, and she turned to Gloria.

At the end of the summer of 1929, Thelma summoned her twin to London. Gloria had planned to go to New York City that fall for an extended visit, but after meeting with her sister, she abruptly changed her plans. She still maintained her fully staffed house in Paris and she had been rebuked for being too extravagant, but nevertheless she decided to rent a secluded country estate. She informed George Wickersham that little Gloria had an intestinal disturbance and that the doctor had recommended that she take her daughter to the country. Wickersham then approved the added expense of another residence, and Gloria was able to rent Three Gables in Sunningdale, approximately twenty-five miles west of London. This house happened to be located directly opposite Fort Belvedere.

Gloria moved into Three Gables with her daughter and nurse Keislich, providing an absolutely private place for Thelma and David to meet. Then Thelma's other sister, Consuelo, was called into action; she and her husband were recalled from Buenos Aires and Benjamin Thaw was awarded the prestigious post of diplomatic attaché to the Court of St. James. The Thaws acquired a tiny town house in London at number 10 Farm Street. Immediately, the Prince of Wales became a constant visitor at Gloria's country and Consuelo's city residence while Thelma, Gloria, and Consuelo became the most sought-after guests of London Society. As Thelma's successor Wallis Simpson was to observe, the prince's favor cast "a glowing radiance. . . . I became aware of a rising curiosity concerning me, of new doors opening and a heightened interest even in my casual remarks. I was stimulated; I was excited. . . . Now I began to savor the true brilliance and sophistication of life in London."

For Gloria this was a time of "acute happiness . . . filled with everything the world has to offer." New York Society had spurned her, but now a far more exclusive and exalted circle was open to her. And Thelma was Gloria's exact duplicate, even Mamma had not always been able to tell them apart. When one of them entered a room people were never sure—was it the favorite of the Prince of Wales? Was it Gloria Vanderbilt?

Gloria stayed in one place for the longest period of time since Reggie's death. Mamma Morgan, thrilled with Thelma's new status, arrived at Three Gables in November of 1929 for a visit. She brought with her the news that in the recent American stock-market crash, she'd "lost thousands." Both Gloria and Thelma were astounded by this declaration since Mamma had always told them she had no money of her own. Gloria wrote Uncle George inquiring about little Gloria's income, and was relieved to hear that the child's trust had not been appreciably affected by the crash and would continue to yield approximately $112,000 annually. However, George Wickersham took this opportunity to remind Gloria yet again of her promise to return the child to America.

Three Gables provided a comfortable retreat as Gloria watched the renovations on the Fort begin. David's plans were years ahead of their time. The interior of the main building was gutted and rebuilt to include central heating, built-in cupboards, and private baths for almost every one of the twenty-seven bedrooms. There was to be a ballroom, a gymnasium containing a practice golf tee and net, and a steam bath in the basement. Plans were made for a tennis court and a rectangular swimming pool to replace the ancient, muddy lily pond at the foot of the battlements.

The prince began taking flying lessons. This rapid and completely private means of transportation delighted him. King George V, hearing of the lessons, expressly forbade the issuance of a pilot's license to his son. The prince overcame the problem by flying without one, and purchased his own De Havilland Gypsy Moth. A new road was built from the front door of the Fort to Smith's Lawn in Windsor Great Park where he supervised the construction of a private royal aerodrome.

His sudden enthusiasm for domestic alterations extended to York House in London where bedrooms were hacked away to create a ballroom and new dining room to accommodate a hundred guests. For the first time in his life, the prince's quarters were cut off from the rest of the rooms, ensuring him absolute privacy. These renovations and his refusal to occupy Marlborough House created press speculation that "definitely his Royal Highness is preparing for infinite bachelorhood."

The York House renovation was celebrated with a ball. As soon as Gloria entered the ballroom, the Prince of Wales rushed over to her and brought her to the table of Elizabeth, Duchess of York. The two women sat stiffly side by side; the duchess seemed shy, but when Gloria mentioned little Gloria, her intense cornflower-blue eyes lit up. Soon they were discussing their children—five-year-old little Gloria and three-year-old Lilibet (Elizabeth)—and the differences between American and English training.

Edward, Prince of Wales, with Thelma, at Fort Belvedere, 1929

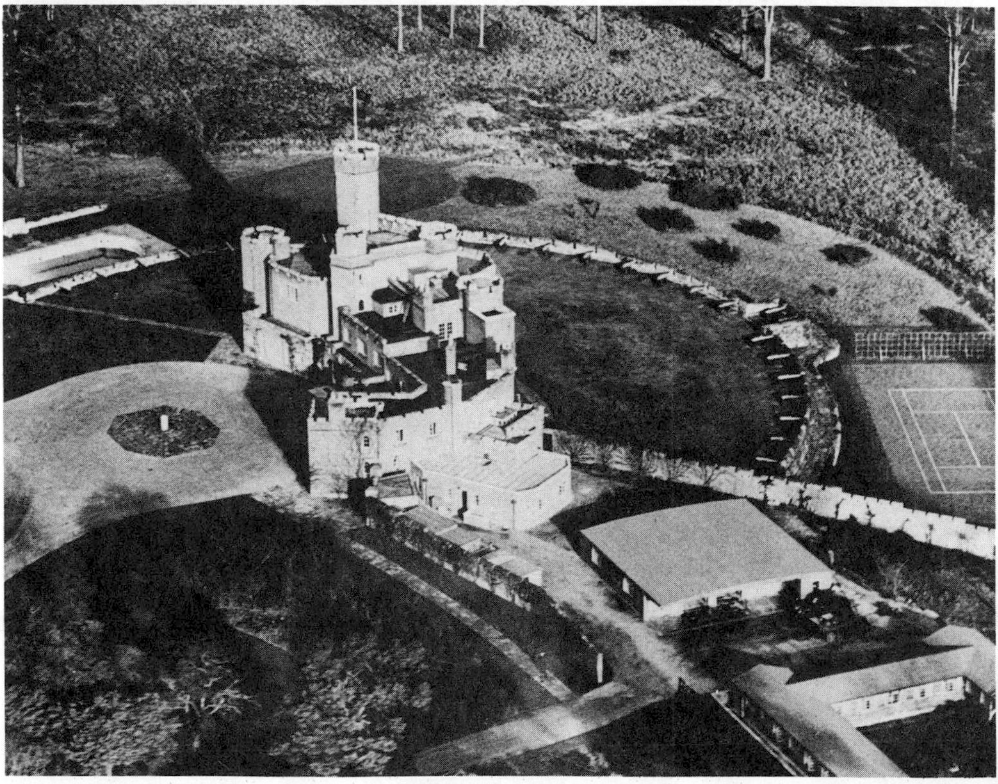

Nadeja and George, Second Marquis and Marchioness of Milford Haven

Marmaduke (Duke) Furness

Thelma and the Hon. Averill Furness

In January the prince left for a four-month hunting trip in Africa. Thelma and Duke went on safari soon after and Thelma contrived to join David at his camp in Nairobi. At night they would sit by the embers of the prince's campfire, where, Thelma said rapturously, "No one could remain insensitive to the vastness of the starry sky, the teeming, fecund sense of nature at its most prodigal. As the Prince and I would feel enveloped in all this, we would instinctively draw closer as if we were the only two people on Earth. . . . This was our Eden. . . . His arms about me were the only reality; his words of love my only bridge to life."

The high point of Thelma's "enchanted time" was a lion hunt which both she and the prince photographed. As the natives closed in on the lions, Thelma, aiming her Bell & Howell, got "a wonderful though rather harrowing" shot of the prince photographing a native boy at the instant he was clawed by one of the lions.

After seven days their idyll ended and David decided to drive Thelma in an open car across the wilderness to rejoin Duke at the railroad at Voi. As they drove he was flushed and silent. Finally he said, "Darling, I've got to stop for a bit, I feel frightfully seedy." He slumped over the wheel and it was some time before he could drive again. At the station he told his physician, Dr. Breckenridge, "I feel terribly ill, Doctor." His temperature was 105 degrees. However, when Duke's train arrived, the prince had a drink with him and chatted amiably until Duke left with Thelma for Mombasa.

On shipboard heading home a week later, Thelma received a coded cablegram from her prince telling her that he had contracted malaria and was recuperating in Nairobi. The deciphered message went on to say: "Missing you and wanting you more than I can say. . . . So don't worry. But I do for you as I guess voyage will be hell and I think of you all the time. But we feel happy, too, don't we, my darling?"

At the end of April the prince sped home from his eighth tour abroad in ten years. At Three Gables, Thelma and Gloria were waiting for him. The interior renovations at the Fort were nearing completion. For his bedroom the prince chose a color scheme of maroon and blue. At the foot of his bed he had a miniature stairway erected, to enable his favorite cairn terrier Cora to sleep on his bed. In the family tradition, David doted on dogs (at her death, Queen Victoria had owned eighty-three).

The room that Thelma occupied was decorated for the most delicate feminine taste. The walls were hung in pale pink satin. An enormous fourposter bed, draped in the same satin, dominated the room. At each post the gleaming fabric was drawn back and fastened with pink ostrich feathers. The bedroom had a large terrace that overlooked the gardens and swimming pool.

For the Prince of Wales, the Fort was his "get-away-from-people-house," and he lived there precisely as he pleased, free from the duties that plagued him at York House. Because of Gloria's presence nearby, his relationship with Thelma remained known only to his friends. Mrs. Dudley Ward was still thought to be his favourite dancing partner. (The truth was that he'd instructed his secretary that her calls were no longer to be put through to him.) In public, Thelma maintained the façade of a happy marriage, attending charity affairs, garden parties, and balls in the company of her husband. Eventually, however, the Prince of Wales was faced with the problem of explaining Thelma's constant presence at the Fort. He solved this by issuing an ingenious edict worthy of a Restoration comedy. In order to escape criticism for indiscreet behavior, he explained, it was his intention to impose severe restrictions upon himself: no *unmarried* woman would be entertained at Fort Belvedere! Unbelievably, the press accepted this declaration without question. In Britain he was warmly applauded for his behavior: "For obvious reasons the Prince does not wish to become the host to his unmarried girl friends, whose number is legion." In America *Time* magazine noted: "Times have changed, the new Edward is discretion itself in applying his married-woman rule."

The Prince of Wales, however, could not disguise certain changes in his social pattern. He began to refuse most private dinner dances and weekend invitations in order to spend time with Thelma at the Fort. Along with his newly private life came a spate of rumors concerning his sexuality. A German nightclub featured a skit in which an English tourist boasts of how his homegrown wonders excel those he is being shown. Upon seeing the Matterhorn, he says, "The Tower of London is even more impressive." When the guide conducts him through Venice and refers to "the fairylike Venetian night," the tourist boasts, "Our Prince of Wales is even more so!"

American newspapers, having none of the reticence of the home press, speculated that the reason for the prince's quiet life might be accounted for in the unexpected announcement by Mrs. Dudley Ward that she was seeking a divorce. However, guests at the Fort knew the real reason—David appointed Thelma to act in the capacity of hostess, a most unusual procedure in bachelor households, and an acknowledgment of her status. At Fort Belvedere, Thelma Furness reigned.

Thelma saw to it that her sisters were included in life at the Fort. "We entertained a great deal," Thelma explained, "but our guests were always people we liked to have around—There were no dignitaries, no representatives of state and empire." Lunch was a pick-up meal at best—David and Gloria were both known to settle for an apple. An elaborate tea was served at six-thirty, which was late by English standards (some of the guests mistakenly took this to be an American custom), cocktails began at eight-thirty, dinner was served at ten. David often wore kilts, and after dinner would walk ceremoniously around the table playing his bagpipes. After dinner, guests gathered to talk, play cards or backgammon, or watch a film.

Thelma, who did excellent petit point, worked night after night on an elaborate fire screen for the prince. It took her a year and a half to complete, and David, watching, became intrigued and asked her to teach him how to do it. (As a child, he'd learned to knit and was excellent at it.) It distressed Thelma that David frequently drank late into the evening and she welcomed this request, remarking to a friend, "The hand that holds the needle cannot hold the brandy snifter!"

The elusive Papa Morgan, who had seen so little of his children, was now retired; he visited frequently at the Fort and at night would read aloud from Dickens and Scott. Mamma arrived to stay with Gloria once again. She had taken to boasting of Thelma's amorous conquest everywhere. When someone ventured to ask her, "You surely don't expect her to become Queen?" Mamma Morgan shot back, "Stranger things than that have happened!"

With the renovations completed and the Fort secured for privacy, Gloria gave up Three Gables—it had served its purpose. Little Gloria and nurse Keislich were sent off to the Paris house while she remained in England, weekending with the Milford Havens or Thelma and David, and spending the week in London, where she enjoyed the company of such people as Emerald, Lady Cunard, Winston Churchill, Sir Arthur Balfour, Sir Thomas Beecham, Lady Ludlow, and the Prince of Wales's sister, Mary, Viscountess Lascelles. Also, there was a new Society in Great Britain itself. For generations, British Society had been static, with royalty at the top of the pecking order, and this group stuck with its own kind, in exclusive private residences and clubs. After World War I, however, certain aristocrats began to seek pleasure in public places. Maury Paul observed, "Society has decided to dine out." Some of these aristocrats were no longer able to entertain in the grand manner, and public nightclubs began to replace their dining rooms. Others, like the Prince of Wales, sought new, exhilarating company. In public places aristocrats now mingled freely with the nouveau riche, the famous, the foreign, the eccentric.

On their first date Thelma and the prince had set off to the Hotel Splendide for dinner and dancing, a pastime the prince dearly loved.

The great ballerina, Anna Pavlova, had called him the greatest ballroom dancer in the world. As the weeks passed, David and Thelma were seen together at Ciro's, the Kit Kat Club, the Café de Paris, and at Malmaison, where one night Thelma wore a sheath of silver sequins as they waltzed to "The Blue Danube." The prince's favorite nightclub was the Embassy Club, which he called "the Buckingham Palace of nightclubs." Thursday was the Prince of Wales's regular night at the Embassy, and Society hostesses knew better than to throw a party on Thursdays. The Embassy was an underground restaurant with couches and tables around the periphery of the room and a tiny square of parquet in the center for dancing. The walls were lined with mirrors which, as the evening progressed, became clouded with cigarette smoke. Often on Thursdays the Prince of Wales would appear with Gloria on one arm and Thelma on the other. The sisters wore chiffon dresses, their hair was pulled back into sleek chignons. On their wrists were row upon row of narrow diamond bracelets jokingly referred to as "service stripes."

For over a decade David's social circle had included celebrated entertainers, sports figures, the American Embassy group, and at its very heart what the Fleet Street newspapers indulgently referred to as "The Palace Gang." Nada and George were part of this group of British royalty, as was Nada's sister Lady Anastasia (called Zia) Wernher and her husband Harold. David's closest friends were George Milford Haven's brother Dickie (Lord Louis) Mountbatten and his wife Edwina, said to be the richest, most beautiful, most headstrong woman in England. The press portrayed Dickie Mountbatten only as a polo-playing playboy, but he was also an obsessive worker dedicated to his naval career. His wife Edwina, however, had no outlet for her immense energies—she smoked incessantly, threw party after party, spent more money on clothes than any woman in Great Britain. Then one day Edwina simply left her husband and baby daughter and, with only one suitcase, traveled across Siberia to China and to the South Seas. Dickie had no word from her and feared she might be dead until she suddenly reappeared four months later and resumed her frenetic life.

One person who understood Edwina's wanderlust and need for escape was Nada Milford Haven. Both women had exotic backgrounds, both were endowed with wealth and restlessness. These sisters-in-law would escape on trips together and return to take their places as pacesetters for "The Palace Gang."

The Depression was now in force on both sides of the Atlantic, but Gloria, deeply involved in her glamorous existence, didn't notice. After a night on the town both Gloria and Thelma would frequently remain in bed until two the following afternoon. Benny Thaw would compensate for watching the sun rise by arriving at the American Embassy, opening his morning's mail, and then taking a snooze on the couch in his office. The newspapers duly reported their every coming and going, but for the first time, the British public began to look askance at the company the Prince of Wales was keeping. Britain's economic slump grew steadily worse—in 1930 over a million men were out of work—and dancing till dawn in frivolous company no longer seemed merely high jinks. "Now—or so it seemed," said an observer, "the Prince's set began to move over the invisible border that distinguishes gay from *fast*. There is no reason to believe that Lady Furness, her sister Mrs. Thaw, her brother-in-law Benjamin Thaw or his other close acquaintances of this period were any more *fast* than Edward's previous company. But they were more sophisticated, and what was to be important later, they were American—alien."

Queen Mary and King George V considered the ceremony of being presented at court to be sacrosanct; no divorcée or bankrupt could be presented because they felt that this represented a broken promise. Somehow an exception was made for Thelma Morgan Converse Furness. Then, without warning, one afternoon at five Consuelo informed Gloria that a candidate was ill and that the American Embassy had substituted Gloria's name—that evening she too was to be presented at the Court of St. James. Thelma rushed over to the Thaws' house with the required three white plumes, known as the Prince of Wales feathers, her own train and long tulle veil. Consuelo donated her pearls. Nada loaned Gloria a magnificent pearl and diamond tiara, fashioned in the form of a Russian peasant headdress, which she had inherited from her mother. As Gloria's limousine joined the line on the mall outside of Buckingham Palace, a woman broke free of the crowd, peered in the window of the car, and exclaimed: "Gor' blime . . . it's the Queen of Sheba herself."

Gloria walked up the broad marble staircase lined on both sides with the Beefeaters of England dressed in Elizabethan uniform, an immense white ruff pinwheeling about the neck. She entered a waiting room. When the court chamberlain called out her name, she proceeded to the throne room where fifty gentlemen-at-arms in gold and crimson uniforms with tall hats adorned with white plumes formed two lines flanking a dais on which sat King George V and Queen Mary on massive thrones. Both wore the star and broad blue ribbon of the Order of the Garter. Gloria curtsied first to the king and then to the queen. At this moment she felt "a heightened sense of mightiness." She rose and saw that her friend Edward, Prince of Wales, was standing behind the thrones. Seated to the left of the monarchs were Elizabeth, Duchess of York, and then, to Gloria's astonishment and delight, the Marchioness of Milford Haven. Nada's mouth twitched slightly with amusement. She looked straight at Gloria and winked.

> *Dear Momey,*
> *Please send me a bear boy. With a case and clothes, also a book, Robin Hood.*
> *All love,*
> *Gloria*

> *Dear Momey,*
> *Please send me a jumping lion. Please also baby animals like the ones you gave me when ill. I have a small lion that you gave me also a pussy cat, horse, calf and a bull. Certainly I need a pig chickens and a cow.*
> *love*
> *from*
> *Gloria*

Little Gloria had been sent off to the Paris house. For the first time, at six, she began to express herself in writing. Her mother was an elusive presence in her life; when she was away little Gloria missed her but did not question her absence or seem to resent it. Her nurse, Dodo, and her grandmother, Naney, marked the boundaries of her world. Her mother was a luxury, someone she could write to for things she wanted, and who usually sent them. "I really have so few memories of her from those days. I saw very little of her. . . . She was beautiful and exquisite . . . she was mysterious, remote and unattainable to me. The ropes of pearls against the soft velvet of her yellow dress. How could I ever reach her or be a part of her?"

In the summer of 1930, little Gloria and Dodo went to Evian while Gloria again went to Cannes. She visited with her daughter for one afternoon. Then the child returned to Paris while her mother went to London. Gloria had enjoyed the time with her daughter at Three Gables where there had been "no Mamma to hook onto her days apprehensive fears of constant sickness, no Mamma to connive with the nurse about imaginary illnesses . . ." but now on the occasions when Gloria tried to include her daughter in her life she felt there were always obstacles put in her path. In the fall she arrived in Paris and after three days decided to take little Gloria to visit the Milford Havens at Lynden

Manor. Nurse Keislich objected violently, referring to Lynden Manor as "that damp place" and protesting that little Gloria had "glands."

"When will she get over them?" asked Gloria.

"When you do right by her," Keislich snapped.

Gloria sighed. "Perhaps you had better go," she declared.

Keislich did not answer her, knowing that if she spoke another word Mrs. Vanderbilt might actually discharge her. That day they left for Maidenhead, and Gloria stayed with Lord and Lady Milford Haven, while the child and nurse were sent to a hotel. When the visit was over they were dispatched to Burrough Court, in Melton Mowbray, and Gloria went to visit Thelma in London.

After the run-in with Mrs. Vanderbilt, nurse Keislich realized that if she made her negative feelings known she would be dismissed, and she felt she must stay on for the child's good. Keislich found it difficult to get money for the child's living expenses, or for anything else, but by using her wits she was able to make a life for the child. At Burrough Court Lady Furness gave them some nursery furniture—they painted it bright red. Keislich arranged a visit to Gaddesby Hall, the estate of the Deprett family, which was about a twenty-minute drive away. While they were there she managed to see that little Gloria attended school and was given the riding lessons she wanted so much. The nurse's letters to her employer were tactful, and she kept her rage to herself as she justified every tiny expense—2 shillings 6 pence for a game, 1 shilling 9 pence for toys, 1 shilling for a book. She wrote her employer, "I keep account for you what ever money you send. . . . I shall have to tip the man who teaches Gloria riding and the other servants." When they returned to Burrough Court, Keislich requested two pounds a week to pay for little Gloria's continued schooling at Gaddesby Hall and she explained that by using her own name instead of the name Vanderbilt, she'd been able to arrange transportation at a reasonable cost.

The previous winter, when little Gloria's clothes had become too shabby to wear, Mr. Morgan had told Keislich to buy new ones and he'd pay for them. Now the child had outgrown these, and Keislich purchased others. When she sent Mrs. Vanderbilt the bill, she was upbraided, and there was no money forthcoming for the child's schooling. Keislich wrote to Mrs. Vanderbilt hoping to persuade her to change her mind.

> . . . *I am very sorry about the bill, the coat and skirt Gloria can wear for two years as she does always, also her first waist. She has been going out visiting here and I am sure you want her to look smart. I shall be very careful of everything. I shall want you to see*

everything I bought. There are only plain things. The Jaeger Jerseys were winter things.

Please let me know if you want her to continue school here. I can teach the same and then there will be no expense. The estimate of the car I am sending you. What ever you decide will work out for the best. Saturdays we are invited for the day. It is a little athletic class and the teacher only charges girls 4 shillings. Lady Blandford's little daughters and sons are in the class. . . .

Gloria wrote back that she was coming to Burrough for a visit and these matters could be settled then. Thelma had planned a hunting weekend with the Prince of Wales at Burrough. Duke was off on safari, but to maintain appearances, Consuelo and Benny Thaw were to act as token chaperones. At the last minute, Benny's mother was taken ill in Paris and asked Consuelo to come to her. Gloria, being unmarried, was not considered a suitable chaperone, so Consuelo suggested that the perfect couple to play this mock role would be her dear American friend, Wallis Warfield Simpson, and her husband, Ernest. Thelma thought the idea splendid. Consuelo had introduced Wallis to Thelma, saying, "Mrs. Simpson is fun. You will like her." Thelma did indeed like Wallis, and she, in turn, found Thelma to be "strikingly attractive." The two women were the same general type: Wallis, at thirty-three, was eight years Thelma's senior, but both women were immaculately groomed and wore their dark hair in the same style; both had experienced unfortunate first marriages to heavy drinking "sportsmen." In 1916 Wallis had married a naval lieutenant, Earl Winfield Spencer, Jr., but she'd discovered "before our brief honeymoon was finished, that the bottle was seldom far from my husband's thoughts or his hand." During the next four years the marriage deteriorated—her husband took to locking Wallis in a room when he went out and to disappearing for days at a time—finally they divorced. Wallis was now more comfortably married to Ernest Simpson, whose family was in the shipping business.

Thelma recalled introducing Wallis to the Prince of Wales at a cocktail party at the Furness house on Grosvenor Square. Wallis remembered it differently. The weekend at Burrough Court was to be the first time she had ever seen the Prince of Wales. On the train to Melton Mowbray, Benny Thaw gave Wallis, who had never had occasion to meet royalty, a lesson in the curtsy. "The trick," he told her, "is, or appears to be, to put your left leg well back and behind the right one."

At Burrough Court there was much excitement—little Gloria and Dodo were moved in with Tony Furness and his nanny to make more room for the guests. Averill changed from her habitual riding habit into a becoming tailored dress. The Simpsons and Benny Thaw arrived at five o'clock. Averill greeted them, led them into the drawing room for tea, and explained that the rest of the party had been delayed by the foggy weather. About seven o'clock Thelma arrived with Prince George and the Prince of Wales, who wore very loud checked tweeds. ". . . how much like his pictures he really was," thought Wallis. "The slightly wind-rumpled golden hair, the turned-up nose and a strange wistful, almost sad look about the eyes when his expression was in repose. But I was surprised on seeing him for the first time to discover how small he was."

Wallis had been briefed on the strict protocol regarding the prince: she must curtsy, address him as Sir, never initiate a conversation but always follow his lead. Instinctively, she seemed to understand that these rules were made to be broken, and that a willful, opinionated approach might breach the fortress of his isolation.

The Prince of Wales recalled that in his first conversation with Mrs. Simpson, having been informed that she was American, he observed that she must miss central heating.

"A mocking look came into her eyes. 'I am sorry, Sir,' she said, 'but you have disappointed me.'

" 'In what way?'

" 'Every American woman who comes to your country is always asked the same question. I had hoped for something more original from the Prince of Wales.' "

Later on the prince would become impressed with Wallis's knowledge of politics and her wit, but it was her boldness that first captured his attention. "Most of all I admired her forthrightness. . . . She never failed to advance her own views with vigor and spirit. That side of her enchanted me. A man in my position seldom encountered that trait in other people. . . . I always welcomed a chance to argue. . . ." It would be months before he would see her again.

In the morning the Prince of Wales, in high spirits, decided to follow the Quorn hounds for the first time since he'd sold his hunters. Little Gloria was allowed to go in a small pony cart to watch the meet assemble. The ladies were dressed in black riding habits and wore no make-up as it was considered bad taste to do so; the men wore the pink coats with sky blue lapels that marked them as members of the Quorn. Little Gloria watched until the last gleaming horse and barking hound disappeared from view. The Prince of Wales rode with daredevil abandon, placing his head low on the neck of his hunter, jockey style. His brother, Prince George, was close behind him as they guided their mounts over difficult hedges, fences, and ditches. When the fox crossed a river most of the other riders followed along the river bank and finally crossed at a bridge, but the royal brothers plunged into the river after the fox. As Prince George galloped across a field, his hunter tripped in a ditch and Prince George flew through the air and crashed down on his left shoulder. The Prince of Wales galloped to his brother's assistance, but he said his injury was slight. The Prince of Wales then resumed the hunt while Prince George went to the Melton Mowbray War Memorial Hospital where an anesthetic was administered and his dislocated shoulder set. Gloria went to fetch him and they returned to the Furness estate in time for tea.

In South America the British export trade had fallen off drastically due to the encroachment of German and American goods and the onset of the world Depression. David was to be sent out again as his empire's salesman to try to recapture this market. At Burrough and the Fort, Thelma and Gloria made it a point to speak to the Prince of Wales in Spanish. The climax of the trip was to be the opening of the $20 million British Empire Trade Exposition in Buenos Aires in March of 1931, at which time he was to deliver a speech in Spanish. Thelma wrote the speech for him. The prince's official language teacher, Dr. Antonio Pastor, unaware of the extra help he was receiving, found his progress astounding—he told the press, "The Prince is extraordinarily gifted for language." Thelma and David spent Christmas together, and then went to Paris. In January she bade him farewell as he and Prince George embarked on their South American tour with ninety-six pieces of luggage and a special satchel crammed full of American cigarettes.

From South America the prince wrote Thelma, damning fate for separating them. The letter ended: "I can't write much more tonight except to say that I love you and that it is wonderful to think that every day is bringing us nearer together. That is a wonderful thought, my darling, and about the only thought that keeps me alive and doing what I have to on this trip. All my bears and my love to you and yours, my precious Toodles." Sometimes his letters contained long passages in Spanish which Thelma felt was a language especially suited to endearments. In one letter he wrote: "Pardon my breaking into Castillano, my sweet, but I want to warn you that you'll have to talk a lot to me in that language when I get back."

In another letter he rhapsodized: "I'm so happy you love me still, my Toodles, because I have not changed at all, *at all*. I do love you more than ever . . . I want you so terribly I don't know how to say it or how I'll get through these months away from you. But time passes quicker when one is travelling as we are. It is worse to be left behind in England."

Duke Furness cabled Thelma from Nassan, Africa, begging her to join him and she took the eighteen-day boat trip to Mombasa. At first, Duke was solicitous and attentive, but after two weeks he "resumed his habitual shouting and swearing." It was then that Thelma belatedly concluded, with monumental understatement, that they "had drifted too far apart."

When they returned from Africa, they brought with them two zebras captured by Duke's famous white hunter, Andrew Rattray. Duke thought it might be amusing to harness these animals to a pony cart and drive them to hunt meets, so Rattray was brought along to train them. Although of Scottish origin, Rattray said, "Kenya is my country. It is a part of myself." His home was a shack in Isiolo, one of the loneliest spots in Kenya. At Burrough Court his status in the household was confusing. Was he a guest or a servant? "Let's have him eat with us," decided Duke, ". . . he is an interesting man."

Averill Furness was fascinated with the zebras. The day of their arrival she went to the stable to see them and asked Rattray if they were Grevy zebras. Rattray's weathered face broke into a smile and he answered in his thick Scottish burr, "No, they are Grants. Grevys can't be trained. In captivity they refuse food like suffragettes, but unlike suffragettes they die." Averill pleaded with Rattray to let her help break them in. Day after day Rattray held the long leather lead line while Averill rode the zebras. The training went well until one day one of the zebras turned on Averill and bit her on the leg. The wound festered, and gave her considerable pain. Several eminent British specialists were called in but they could do nothing. Then Rattray produced a salve he'd used on injured animals in Africa; he rubbed the salve on Averill's leg, and it healed.

At the end of April the Prince of Wales and Prince George returned from their 18,000-mile tour of South America. After a rough flight from Paris, they landed at Smith's Lawn. At the window of the plane the Prince of Wales smiled and waved to the Duke and Duchess of York, who stood waiting with their five-year-old daughter Princess Elizabeth. As the Prince of Wales climbed out of the plane, little Princess Lilibet ran forward on sturdy legs, her ringlets bobbing, threw her arms about his neck, and gave him a loud kiss. The heir apparent's favorite cairn terrier, Cora, jumped from a waiting car and bounded across the grass to lick the feet of her master.

Gloria, who had not been to the United States in over a year, decided to take little Gloria to spend Christmas with her grandmother, Alice Gwynne Vanderbilt, in New York. She wanted to talk to Tom Gilchrist, George Wickersham, and Surrogate Foley to persuade them to let her continue her life abroad, a life she was determined not to abandon for the sake of their whims concerning her child's education. Gloria checked into the Sherry-Netherland with her daughter, the nurse, and her personal maid, Maria Caillot. Alice Vanderbilt was delighted to see little Gloria and gave Gloria a generous Christmas check.

In a game of deception that she had learned to play with some skill, Gloria spoke with Gilchrist and Wickersham. She knew these men had a paternalistic attitude toward her. Tom, in particular, persisted in treating her like an unruly child, but she was also aware that he was attracted to her. Vagueness was her ally. Gloria explained that the lease on her Paris house had four years to run, and that when little Gloria, who was seven, was of proper school age Gloria would return to New York to live. Tom then assured Gloria that it was not necessary to speak to Surrogate Foley, and Gloria took this as a sign that she had placated these gentlemen and had successfully postponed her return to the United States.

The Milford Havens arrived in New York; George had agreed to represent the Sperry Gyroscopic Company in the United States and wished to pursue the possibility of working on Wall Street as well. He had definitely decided that economic pressures meant he must give up his naval career. While he remained in New York, Gloria and Nada went to California. It was the first time Gloria had ever been there. In Los Angeles they stayed at the Beverly Wilshire Hotel. At the polo matches in Santa Barbara they "thrilled Society with their chic and beauty."

Edwina Mountbatten had arranged for Gloria and Nada to meet her friends Fred Astaire, Mary Pickford, and Douglas Fairbanks. They stayed at San Simeon as the guests of William Randolph Hearst and Marion Davies. At the time they visited, forty guests—movie stars, writers, politicians—were in residence. Each was assigned a personal maid or valet on arrival; Hearst forbade his guests to bring their own. Drinks were served just before dinner and then only in the Great Hall, though Marion and Gloria sneaked a few in Marion's bedroom. Nada was amused at the idea that bottles of Heinz Ketchup and jars of Gulden's Mustard were placed on the unadorned wood refectory table at meals and that paper napkins were used. This was Hearst's way of stressing that this was just an informal ranch, after all.

Bison, zebras, llamas, gazelles, and kangaroos roamed the 240,000-acre estate. Each guest was provided with a catalog of the art objects to be found at the main house called, appropriately enough, Casa Grande. Gloria felt that San Simeon was an Aladdin's lamp: you had but to express your desire, and swimming, tennis, horses, cars, a private train to Los Angeles, promptly appeared.

In March Gloria retrieved her child, maid, and nurse and embarked on the *Majestic* with the Milford Havens. Gloria arrived at Lynden Manor the same week that her former fiancé, His Serene Highness Prince Gottfried Hohenlohe-Langenburg, was to be married. His intended bride was Princess Margarita of Greece and Denmark. It was ironic that after Gloria had parted with Friedel over finances he had chosen to marry someone else with almost no money. Margarita was twenty-six, exactly Gloria's age, suitably royal but a poor exile, plain and a bit plump, and it was her brother, Prince Philip, who was so frequently at Lynden Manor. Gloria knew a great deal about Margarita—they'd met through Nada. Margarita was the Milford Havens' niece.

Three days before Friedel and Margarita's wedding, Gloria received a letter from George Wickersham informing her that he was making arrangements for little Gloria to go to school in New York that very fall. Evidently what she had said to him in New York had meant nothing. The anger welled up in her—she was furious at the inconvenience little Gloria was causing her—but it was more than that. She felt manipulated by forces she could not identify. Gloria answered Wickersham's letter with an unprecedented outburst of rage.

The Bridle and the Bit

The bridle and the bit were constantly in evidence . . . everything was under constant surveillance. I was never able to do anything on my own initiative when it came to expenditures without first consulting my child's guardians.

GLORIA MORGAN VANDERBILT

My dear Gloria:

I have today your letter . . . written from Lynden Manor. I assume it is written in answer to mine of April 6th, although I cannot, for the life of me see what it is in that letter which has provoked your outburst. All I said there was that I thought it was important little Gloria should be in this country next Winter, and that if you had not been able to make arrangements with Miss Chapin to take her into school next Fall, there was the Spence School which was equally good, and that I thought I might arrange to have her admitted . . .

I know Judge Foley has felt it was important that little Gloria should be educated in this country. Of course, you are the guardian of the child's person and can decide that, as well as all other questions concerning her education, except that the Surrogate has the last word to say on the matter of allowance. Knowing his views, I have felt that unless you had arranged to bring the child to this country, to be educated, we would have difficulty in getting the allowance continued for next year at anything like the same sum which is now being granted. You say that if the Surrogate insists, you will move back to New York . . .

I have no doubt whatever that unless you are prepared to give assurances of that, you would have difficulty in getting a continued allowance of the present sum for next year . . .

Faithfully yours,
George W. Wickersham

THE THREAT was barely concealed by Wickersham's polite prose. Gloria immediately saw that "somewhere under his bland and friendly phrases lay a peremptory tone coupled with a cold finality." Gloria balked at the restraints that were being imposed upon her. "The bridle and the bit were constantly in evidence . . . everything was under constant surveillance. I was never able to do anything on my own initiative when it came to expenditures without first consulting my child's guardians." In her frustration she turned on her daughter. It was all little Gloria's fault! Somehow the child had come between her and the marriage she so desperately wanted. Now it was because of little Gloria that she would have to give up her glorious life abroad. Also, Gloria was suffering from a severe misconception—she considered that little Gloria's money was rightfully her own. The child's birth had been meant to ensure her own financial security. Hadn't Reggie planned it that way? She had given birth; she had done her part, but still "the threatening calamity he thought obviated by the baby's coming was not avoided."

Once again Gloria stalled for time. Controlling her feelings of anger, she wrote a carefully thought out letter asking for a compromise: if she could have one more year abroad, she would faithfully return to America and put little Gloria in Miss Chapin's school. Wickersham consulted Foley and then acquiesced in her request, writing, ". . . If you will make all your plans to bring the child here for the Autumn of 1932, and allow nothing to interfere with that, it will be all right." His letter went on to say that Tom Gilchrist was sailing for Europe that week and would see Gloria in Paris to settle some outstanding questions. Gloria had successfully postponed her return for at least one more year.

In June, at Thelma's request, another exception was made to the rule forbidding a divorcée's presentation at court, and Thelma lent her train, veil, and feathers to her best friend, Wallis Simpson. Gloria and Thelma were taller than Wallis, so Consuelo lent her her dress. After the presentation, Edward, Prince of Wales, walked past Wallis with his great-uncle, the Duke of Connaught. She heard him mutter, "Uncle Arthur, something ought to be done about the lights. They make all the women look ghastly."

Later that day Thelma gave an informal party to celebrate her friend's presentation. Over a glass of champagne the prince complimented Wallis on her gown. "But Sir," she responded, "I understood that you thought we all looked ghastly."

"I had no idea my voice carried so far," he replied. Then he smiled at her.

Thelma and David spent part of July in Biarritz and visited Cannes, where there were so many high-spirited companions: in residence at the Miramar Hotel were four—Gloria shared a room with Nada Milford Haven, and next door Consuelo Thaw shared hers with Wallis Simpson. Each lady brought only her personal maid. Maria Caillot saw to Gloria Vanderbilt's wants.

As for little Gloria, her year had been full of travel, of being shunted out of her mother's life. In January she had been taken to the Sherry-Netherland in New York and remained there while her mother and the Marchioness of Milford Haven went to California. In March she had been sent back to Paris while her mother went to England. In April she had been brought to England and stayed first at the Hotel Braycourt in Maidenhead, and then at Burrough Court, Melton Mowbray. In late April and May she had visited at nearby Gaddesby Hall. In June she had been sent back to Paris where she contracted scarlatina. In July and August she had been sent to the Hotel Victoria in Glion. Her mother was slipping away from her, becoming more and more remote. Years later little Gloria would say of this time, "I lived from hotel to hotel until I was eight and a half years old, Paris, Monte Carlo, England where my mother's twin, Thelma Furness, was having *that thing* with the Prince of Wales," but at the time the child's letters expressed no resentment. They were sweet and filled with longing, with dozens of XX's and OO's, the signs for kisses and hugs, scrawled in the margins.

> *Dear Momey*
>
> *I have lost a tooth. We went up a mountain Friday I bought two little bears. I will give you one . . .*

> *Dear Mamy*
>
> *I hope you are very well. I long to see you back again . . .*

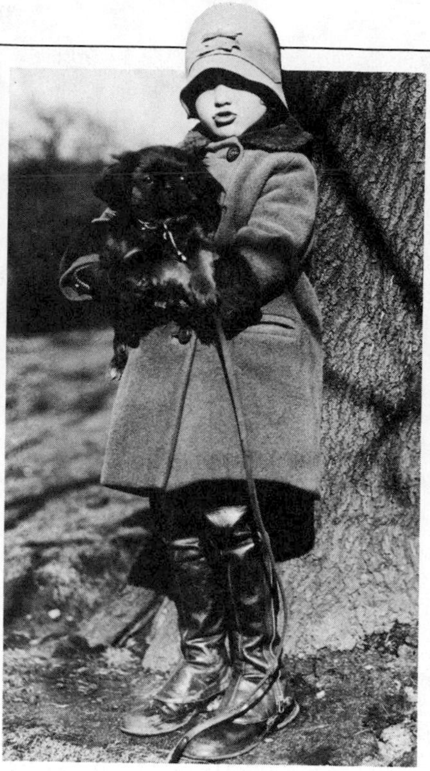

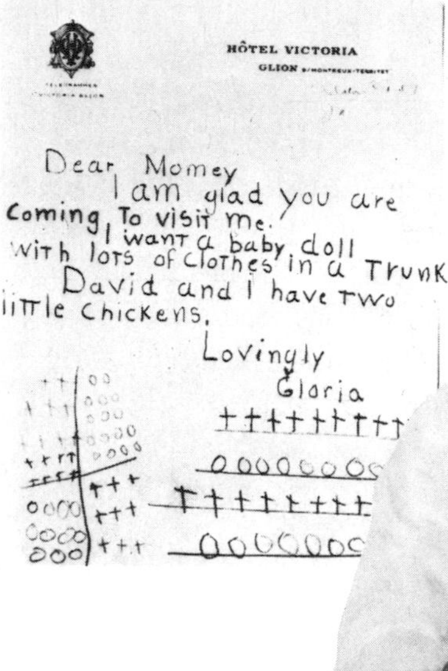
HÔTEL VICTORIA
GLION s/MONTREUX-TERRITET

Dear Momey
I am glad you are
coming to visit me.
I want a baby doll
with lots of clothes in a Trunk
David and I have two
little chickens.
Lovingly
Gloria

Little Gloria with Dodo
and with her mother

Dear Momey
I am glad you are coming to visit me. I want a baby doll with lots of clothes in a trunk . . .

In late August Gloria spent two weeks with her daughter in Monte Carlo. Tom Gilchrist tracked her down on the Riviera and came in person to deliver a reminder—she was expected back in the United States in 1932, and that was that! In response, Gloria drew from her purse a packet of bills which she insisted he pay, over and above the $4,000 a month allotted to her.

Money troubles seemed to plague everybody—even her friend, the Prince of Wales. The Bank of England was threatened with bankruptcy; the deficit for 1932 was projected at £170 million. The British government had turned to J. P. Morgan and Company in the United States to borrow £75 million. Morgan had replied that Britain must first tighten her budget. In a magnanimous gesture, the king gave up £50,000 out of his yearly income, and the Prince of Wales sacrificed £10,000, but the Socialists pointed out that the king would still retain £420,000 a year, and the prince £70,000 as the Duke of Cornwall.

It was during this period that Thelma told the Prince of Wales what she considered to be really momentous news—she had decided to leave her husband. David took her to his arms and said, "Oh, my darling, I am sure you have made the right decision. I am so very very happy."

Duke Furness left for another winter in Africa. Averill begged to go with him. She confided to Thelma that once there, she intended to marry Andrew Rattray. "I want to live free," Averill explained to her stepmother. Thelma warned Duke of this conversation, but while her father was out hunting in the lion country of Tanganyika with his native boys, Averill eloped with Rattray—her maid and her father's typist acted as witnesses. They had intended to keep the marriage a secret, but within two days it seemed to Averill that all of Nairobi had congratulated them. She then wrote her father a note telling him the news and asking for his blessing and sent a plane into the jungle to deliver it. She cabled Thelma at Melton Mowbray, and Thelma wired back her wishes for every happiness.

The pilot located Duke Furness, who read the note, let forth a string of curses, and stalked into his tent. One hour later he reappeared, and when the pilot asked for his answer to the note, he bellowed, "There is no answer!" That same week, Duke placed an advertisement in the *East African Standard*, stating: "Mr. Andrew Rattray has ceased to be the white hunter to my safari . . ." Then he cut his daughter off without a penny. Within the year Rattray died mysteriously and Averill returned to England. Thelma found her to be in a pitiful condition, "disheveled, unkempt," and persuaded Duke to settle £500 a year on her. But Averill refused to stay in England and returned to Rattray's shack in Africa: her nearest white neighbor lived eighty-five miles away. Six years later, just before her thirtieth birthday, Averill died alone in this isolated place.

Gloria was making the most of the time she had left abroad. There was a constant round of parties and weekends at the Fort and at Lynden Manor. Maury Paul came to visit, and Gloria confided in him about Thelma's conquest. Paul discreetly reported:

> Mrs. Vanderbilt, for the past five or six months, has spent most of her time on the "Golden Arrow," the de luxe train which plies between Paris and the Channel boat for England. While she still maintains her home in the French capital, Mrs. Vanderbilt now has so many close friends in English society she passes many weeks with Lady Furness in Grosvenor Square.
>
> H.R.H., the Prince of Wales, frequently is the honored dinner guest at Lord and Lady Furness' London home, and the future King of England makes many informal visits to "Duke" Furness and the former Thelma Morgan at their Melton Mowbray place.
>
> For some time past Lord Furness has been in Africa, where he has acquired a place in the famed Kenya colony . . . Lady Furness does not like the African climate, and while Lord Furness has been hunting big game, she has kept the Furness social banner flying in the smartest of London breezes.

Maury Paul rode the Golden Arrow with Gloria, little Gloria, and nurse Keislich. He remembered the trip because they were one compartment short and he generously sat up all night so that the child and her nurse could get some sleep. Gloria remembered the trip too, her memory colored with bitterness. Gloria said that it was she who had been forced to sit up all night. "Nothing in my household ever moved but they did so first on the foundations of Gloria's desires or necessities. . . . Whatever the demand of hers, she was given it by prior right—nothing belonged to me but the governing of her time and her years."

Once again the child's health had become an issue. Little Gloria was being taken to London because nurse Keislich insisted that she see a throat specialist. Gloria put the nurse and child in the Dorchester Hotel and went to stay with the Thaws on Farm Street. Because of her impending divorce, Thelma had left the Furness town house and was also living with the Thaws. The specialist saw little Gloria and recommended that her tonsils be removed. From the United States the incessant reminders continued:

My dear Gloria,

It just occurs to me that if you have not already done so, you ought to enter Gloria's name for Miss Chapin's school in the fall of next year, 1932. If you desire, I could drop a note to Miss Chapin, whom I know very well, which might be helpful in connection with it; but you ought to make the entry without delay.

I am,

Faithfully yours,
George W. Wickersham

Tom Gilchrist also wrote a letter, another reminder of her promise to return to New York. From her reply it is clear that Gloria had decided that when she was forced to bring little Gloria to New York City (and she would manage to postpone this another five months) she would then leave her daughter and return to Europe. She wrote:

My dear Mr. Gilchrist,

I have received your letter of Oct. 26, 1931, you must have misunderstood me when I last saw you in the south of France. I did not think of going to New York until the first week in April of 1932, but now I find that I will have to come over the first week of Feb. I came to London with Gloria a week ago and went to see a doctor about her throat. He tells me that she should have her tonsils out. As I do not want to have this done in France or London, and I want her to see her own doctor about this, I think it is best for me to come back home. I am sure that both you and Mr. Wickersham will think that I am right in this.

I hope to leave Gloria in New York when I come back to close the house in Paris. She could stay with Mrs. Vanderbilt or with Mrs. W. H. Vanderbilt. They would be very happy to have her I am sure.

I have I think rented my house for the next five months, it is yet not sure, but if I have I will then stay in London with Mrs. Thaw my sister and Gloria can go to my other sister at Melton until we sail. . . .

Gloria did not rent her Paris house but she did send little Gloria and nurse Keislich to Burrough Court at Melton Mowbray anyway. Christmas week she arrived for a visit with her sisters and Benny Thaw. Later Gloria was to remember this as a particularly lovely time. On

Christmas Day everyone gathered in front of the yule fire to sing carols. There were so many gifts that Thelma told little Gloria that they'd surely keep her busy long past her birthday on February 20.

It never occurred to Gloria that nurse Keislich thought it a terrible Christmas. She hated Burrough Court and felt that they'd been sent there solely for Mrs. Vanderbilt's convenience, to get them out of the way while she was off living her gay life. When Gloria Vanderbilt finally did arrive for Christmas, she and her sisters brought so many guests that little Gloria and the nurse were moved out of their own room and stuck into the nursery with Tony Furness and his nanny. Tony's nanny, who ruled the roost, clearly favored her own charge. Then, as nurse Keislich understood it, Lady Furness cruelly told little Gloria that since her birthday was so near Christmas, she was not to have any birthday presents.

Even worse, from Keislich's point of view, was the fact that little Gloria was sick so much of the time. Dr. Gavin, the London specialist, and Dr. Helie, the Paris doctor, had repeatedly recommended a warm, dry climate, but Burrough Court had no central heating; it was cold and damp—a terrible climate for the child's health. Nurse Keislich had come to rely on Mrs. Morgan to persuade Mrs. Vanderbilt to take care of the child but now Mrs. Morgan's power seemed to have waned. When they were sent to Burrough Court for the second winter in a row, Mrs. Morgan had gone to New York vowing to do everything in her power to see that they returned to the United States, where little Gloria could receive proper medical care. Mrs. Morgan wrote to them from New York and little Gloria answered her letters.

In the last bleak months of 1931, seven-year-old little Gloria began to express in writing a different view of her mother. No longer was she just a sweet luxury, a gift giver, someone beautiful whom she saw infrequently. At Burrough Court, with only her nurse for company, the child seemed for the first time to develop the bitter feeling that she had been abandoned. She began to learn bad things about her mother—when she was sick in bed and in pain she was told of her mother's gay life in Paris. Somehow, in childish terms, little Gloria's letters began to duplicate exactly the view of her mother held by Dodo and Naney. In New York, Mrs. Morgan received these letters and promptly took them to the offices of Cadwalader, Wickersham & Taft. Little Gloria wrote:

> *Dear Naney*
>
> *I love you so much and I am longing to see you. I am very unhappy in England. Toney's*

mother said that I cant have any birthday presents because it is so near Christmas. I do want to learn to dance and ride as all children can

I am making you a hankerchief case. Dodo sends her love

Love from Gloria

Momey promised me that she would take me to a pantomime and never did so Dodo took me to see Dick Whittington and his cat. . . .

Dear Naney

Toneys mother is puting me in to another room every week. My mother is so bad to me I wish that I could run away to a New York to you. I am very unlucky girl . . .

Dear Naney

I love the cards that you send me. dear Naney this is not ritten very well because I am in bed ill and . . . the doctor says that I have a bad sore throat and a bad gland and my neck feels if a dagger stic through it . . .

Dear Naney

I love you so much and I love the cards that you sent me my mother was in Paris enjoying herself while poor me was unhappy in Englan. My cold is better and my temp as gone to normal and the docot lets me get up for a little while. good by Naney dear

Love Gloria

Dear Naney

I received your letter and your cable. I am writing this letter in bed to you as I have a bad throat. I hope that you will excuse my letter. i do want to go to New York. Toney's nurse is treating me very badly and some times I cry

Love From Gloria

After Christmas Gloria had returned with her sisters to London, where they were working on a benefit for the League of Mercy, the favorite charity of the Prince of Wales, who served as its president. This was a time when Thelma and David were inseparable. The last weekend in January, Thelma suggested that her friends, the Simpsons, be invited to the Fort for the first time. They eagerly accepted the invitation. Wallis had found herself following the newspaper articles of the prince's South American tour with "more than a casual interest," and she'd become attentive to personal information and gossip concerning him. She'd "studied" photographs of the prince and "found myself wondering about the strange, sad expression that fleetingly manifested itself in the otherwise unmarred gallery of smiling or laughing vignettes. For all the surface spontaneity, he must be, I decided, a withdrawn and solitary spirit, importuned and harassed by too many to have confidence in more than a very few."

The Simpsons arrived at the Fort at dusk. Seated side by side on the sofa, the Prince of Wales and Thelma bent their heads over their needlepoint. "This is my secret vice," the prince explained to Wallis, with a smile. "The only one, in any case, I am at pains to conceal." At his feet, his cairn terriers, Cora and Jaggs, romped playfully. Cora snarled at Ernest Simpson and dashed up to snap at his ankle. The prince snatched her up. "Cora is always this way when anybody new appears. Now Jaggs has a much more hospitable temperament." Wallis extended her hand to Jaggs, but the dog stalked away.

After dinner, the prince taught Wallis how to play a card game called Red Dog. After she'd had several excellent hands, the prince said playfully, "I don't think you need any more instruction from me. I'd better look after myself."

Thelma stood before the mahogany-cased gramophone sorting through some records. "I feel like dancing," she announced. The Prince of Wales looked up and moved toward Thelma with outstretched arms. As Wallis watched, they began to whirl across the floor, David sweeping Thelma out of the room and onto the octagonal black-and-white marble-floored hallway, where they moved together slowly and gracefully. The moment was to stay forever in Wallis's mind: "I have a poignant memory of the melody. It just happened to be 'Tea for Two' . . ."

Thelma's and David's relationship was now quite open, and everywhere were the appraising, approving stares that marked Thelma and Gloria as celebrities. Although Gloria had promised to return to New York in February, she wrote postponing her trip until March. The response was an ultimatum—return, or your allowance will be drastically reduced! Gloria knew she could delay no longer, but she comforted herself with the thought that there were many reasons to return to Europe. Surely little Gloria's guardians would understand that almost seven years of her life could not be terminated without giving her some leeway: there was the Paris house to be closed, friends to see—she did not intend to sever her valuable relationships.

Gloria suspected that her mother had played a role in forcing her to return to the United States. When she visited Burrough Court in February, although she knew nothing of little Gloria's letters, with a flash of angry instinct she belatedly forbade her daughter to contact Mamma Morgan.

Little Gloria disobeyed.

> *Dear Naney*
>
> *My mother said not to write to you but I will not pay any attention to her. She is a rare bease. Well I will be in dear old New York soon. Lote of Love and lote of kiss to you Naney dear*
>
> *Gloria*

> *Naney dear*
>
> *We are moving again oh what a life. Well I shall soon be in my own country in 20 days and I am so thrilled about it . . .*

> *Dear Naney*
>
> *Did you like the bookmark that I made you. I am making you a scarf that I am knitting and I am making you a tray cloth for your breakfast. I am so pleased that I am going to New York City in March*
>
> *Could you come to meet me. I dreamt about you and you would not speak to me*
>
> *Well good by*
> *Naney dear*
> *Love*
> *Gloria*

Of course Gloria had been right about her mother. Mrs. Morgan had used little Gloria's letters to bolster her position, taking them to Tom Gilchrist and George Wickersham and telling these men of the privations her sick and neglected granddaughter was being forced to endure. After many visits she insisted on seeing Surrogate Foley himself and she stressed to him the urgency of making her daughter honor her pledge. For two years little Gloria's guardians had been trying unsuccessfully to secure her return. Now Foley must act! Money was the key—if he was really prepared to cut off Gloria's allowance she would be forced to return to New York, where these sensible men could control her and see to it that little Gloria led a decent, healthy life. For five months Laura Morgan did not stop talking, begging, cajoling; until, to her relief and delight, she was informed that her daughter and granddaughter were finally coming home.

At the end of February, little Gloria and Dodo were summoned to London where they stayed two nights at the Dorchester Hotel. On the last night before they were to sail, the child was so tense that she had severe stomach pains. As long as little Gloria could remember, she'd been moving from place to place—now she was going home to live.

By an ironic twist of fate, this high-strung child's return to her native land was to coincide with an event unique in its horror—"The Crime of the Century" it would be called—a crime that held a special significance for a generation of children. On March 2, 1932, little Gloria boarded the *Majestic* for New York City. As her sturdy brown leather shoes clomped up the covered gangway of the ship, world headlines blared out the news that the previous night the infant son of the American hero, the Lone Eagle, Charles Augustus Lindbergh, had been snatched from his crib in Hopewell, New Jersey.

Don't Let Me Die

Don't let me die. . . . Don't let me die.

LITTLE GLORIA VANDERBILT

FOR DECADES she would not speak of it at all, and when at last she did, she would accept the description of herself as a pawn in the custody trial and would maintain that her grandmother was crazy and hysterical and that both her mother and her aunt were indifferent and inaccessible.

Yet neglected, manipulated, coerced, violated as little Gloria had been, it was the child's own actions that made this trial inevitable.

To the world, the Vanderbilt trial was about the custody of a child. To the child herself, it would be a trial for her very life. The accusation on each side would be that the other sought to kidnap little Gloria. KIDNAP. In the apprehensive atmosphere of the 1930s, children felt that word in the gut. KIDnap it was—and that meant *kids*!

In March of 1932 little Gloria returned to a country in desperate trouble. In New York City alone, one million of the 3.2 million working force was unemployed. For the lucky ones who had jobs, wages had dropped 60 percent since the crash of 1929—the average annual family income was $1,600. In 1932 alone, American business had lost between five and six billion dollars. A new Ford V-8 automobile sold for $460; their slogan was "Buy a Car Now—Help Bring Back Prosperity," but their sales were the lowest in the company's history. A quart of milk cost ten cents, and a loaf of bread five cents, but there were eighty-six bread lines in New York City.

As the Vanderbilt limousine drove across town from the West Eighteenth Street pier, children at noon recess in the St. Ambrose's school play yard on West Fifty-fourth Street saw a man jump to his death from the roof of an adjoining building. In front of Tiffany & Co., a policeman prevented a man from bleeding to death by fashioning a tourniquet out of his nightstick and a piece of rope and binding it around the man's slashed wrist, while he protested, "I spent my last fifty cents to buy that razor to kill myself." Over 20,000 people had committed suicide that year.

People felt bewildered and betrayed. They had lost faith in their moral standards, their efforts had proved futile, they were frightened. In this atmosphere of desperation and frustration kidnapping became a viable way to make a buck. The day that little Gloria arrived in this country, *The New York Times* announced: "Abduction for ransom has become a big money crime, taking its place beside the liquor, vice and drug traffic among the prominent rackets of this country." It had begun with the onset of the Depression—since 1929 more than two thousand people had been kidnapped for ransom in the United States, and millions of dollars had been extorted from victims or their relatives and friends. But of all the kidnappings, the taking of the Lindbergh baby was the most shocking. The Lindbergh kidnapping was symbolically perfect for the Depression, for it demonstrated that an individual—no matter who he was—could not control his own destiny.

By coincidence, little Gloria arrived in New York just seven days after the Lindbergh kidnapping. The hysteria was mounting—a committee of six hundred mothers was hastily organized and they demanded that plainclothes policemen mingle with their children in Central Park. At Columbia University, football players were recruited for a volunteer "Kidnap Patrol" and sent out to guard children who might be potential kidnap victims. The Pinkerton and Benjamin Kerin detective agencies both quadrupled their personnel in one week. In the next ten days the Lindberghs received 38,000 letters—New Jersey state troopers grouped them according to category—12,000 were dreams, 11,500 were sympathy, 9,500 were suggestions, 5,000 were the work of cranks. Anne Morrow Lindbergh was optimistic about the return of her son. She noted in her journal that "in a survey of 400 cities, 2,000 kidnaped children returned" and "Never in the history of crime has there been a case of a gang bargaining over a dead person."

Gloria Vanderbilt paid little attention to the constant barrage of Lindbergh publicity; she was anxious to dispose of the bothersome details required of her so that she might return to Europe. She settled her daughter and the nurse at the Sherry-Netherland Hotel and began looking for a suitable house. Reggie's Seventy-seventh Street town house was available, and she would have liked to live there again, but the rent was too high. Instead, she rented a town house at 49 East Seventy-second Street. The rent was $6,000 a year and as an inducement to sign a long lease she was given six months rent free. She signed a four-year lease.

Little Gloria was taken to see Dr. Oscar Schloss, the well-known pediatrician who had been her doctor in America since birth. Schloss was an expert in child nutrition and a gifted diagnostician, often pinpointing exactly what was wrong in cases that had eluded other physicians. This skill made him a favorite choice of many physicians who sent him their own children and grandchildren. After almost a quarter of a century Schloss had decided to give up his private practice to become the Pediatrician-in-Chief of the Children's Hospital at the New York Medical Center. He was only waiting for the construction of the new building to be completed. Schloss confirmed that little Gloria needed her tonsils and adenoids removed and suggested Dr. Stuart L. Craig, a specialist. Gloria told Dr. Craig that late July would be a convenient time for the operation since she intended to return to Europe and she'd arranged for little Gloria to spend June and July with the William H. Vanderbilts at Oakland Farm in Portsmouth.

While Gloria concentrated on completing her arrangements, both nurse Keislich and Mamma Morgan followed every detail of the Lindbergh case—day after day the newspapers had page after page of news—and it seemed that the baby was about to be recovered. On April 2, in St. Raymond's Cemetery in the Bronx, a $50,000 ransom in bills and gold certificates was delivered to the Lindbergh extortioner in return for the information that the infant could be found on the "boad Nelly" near Buzzards Bay. Colonel Lindbergh set out in an airplane to rescue his son while special church services were held across the nation and millions prayed for the baby's safe return. After a two-day airplane search of the Long Island Sound, Lindbergh gave up.

Whenever Gloria was at the Sherry-Netherland, nurse Keislich would not stop plaguing her, pointing out that it had been a month since the Lindbergh kidnapping and that she feared for little Gloria's life. Little Gloria and her mother both existed in a glare of publicity:

their return to the United States and their residence at the Sherry-Netherland Hotel was mentioned again and again in newspaper articles, which often also included the information that the child was the richest in the United States—worth millions. Nurse Keislich begged Gloria to hire bodyguards for the child, but Gloria refused to fall victim to what she considered hysterical behavior and she told Keislich to stop talking that way. One morning the nurse came to her carrying an anonymous letter containing a threat to kidnap little Gloria. Then Mamma Morgan arrived at the Sherry-Netherland and told Gloria that because of the letter she must call Wickersham's office immediately to hire detectives. Gloria called Tom Gilchrist, who sent up some Pinkertons to guard the child and suggested that Gloria should wait until August before returning to Paris to close her house. But August was four months away—no one could really expect her to spend the heat of the summer in New York City! Gloria booked passage on the *Ile de France* and waited until the day of her departure to mail the following letter:

April 29, 1932

My dear Mr. Gilchrist,

This is just a line to tell you that I am sailing today for Paris. The Dr. tells me that Gloria can not have her operation until late in July, so she will go to Mrs. W. H. Vanderbilt in Newport until then. I will be back for it.

You understand that if I have to close my house in Paris and I do not sail until the first week in Aug. I can not do it.

I will be at 14 Rue Alfred Roll if you need me.

Please forgive this letter as I am in great haste.

Sincerely,
Gloria M. Vanderbilt

Tom Gilchrist was surprised by Gloria's departure, and telephoned Mrs. Morgan to tell her that he would write to Gloria to inquire if the detectives' services should be continued. Mrs. Morgan's response verged on hysteria—she insisted that they *must* be continued. This child was far richer than the Lindbergh baby. Her life had been threatened. And did he know the shocking condition her granddaughter was in? "She is looking like a skeleton!" Mrs. Morgan exclaimed, and told Gilchrist that the child's face twitched and she couldn't speak without stammering. She implored him to come up to the Sherry-Netherland to see for himself. Although Tom Gilchrist was deeply involved in what he considered to be little Gloria's health and welfare, actually he had not seen the eight-year-old child since she was two.

When Gilchrist finished speaking with Mrs. Morgan, he did write to Gloria asking if she wished the detectives to remain on in her absence. Gilchrist himself was convinced that it was just a matter of time before the Lindbergh infant would be safe at home; as soon as the publicity died down and there was a modicum of privacy, the kidnappers would return the child. Gilchrist posted his letter to Gloria Vanderbilt and decided to go and see the child. When he arrived, Mrs. Morgan led him into a bedroom—little Gloria was in bed and nurse Keislich sat by her side. Gilchrist observed that Mrs. Morgan had told him the truth: the child was pale and drawn, she did stammer, and her face twitched. Then the two women led him into the living room for a conference. Nurse Keislich told Gilchrist that the total responsibility for the child's health, for the child's safety, was too much for her. Mrs. Morgan interrupted to explain that her daughter had run off, leaving them with this sick child and only the vaguest of instructions. Although Dr. Craig had said that the child should be operated on as soon as possible, she had ignored him. Both women seemed so upset that Gilchrist assured them that he would continue the detective service and that he and Mr. Wickersham would have a talk with the doctors.

Tom Gilchrist was not surprised to discover that these women had been accurate. Dr. Schloss did not know that Mrs. Vanderbilt had left the country. He was disturbed by this news and said that both he and Dr. Craig felt it would be detrimental to the child's health to postpone the operation until July. As soon as little Gloria was well enough, Craig would operate.

Tom Gilchrist felt a familiar frustration at this situation and wrote Gloria another letter informing her that he had decided, on his own initiative, to continue the detective service, and that "the nurse seemed to be relieved when I told her that I had reached this conclusion, as she evidently feels her responsibility for the safety of the child rather keenly" and "your mother . . . shared the same view." In the matter of the operation, however, Gilchrist asked George Wickersham to take over. As the legal guardian of the child's money, Wickersham's wish was tantamount to a command. On May 9, 1932, Wickersham wrote to Gloria that Schloss

> *will keep in touch with me regarding the child's condition, and let me know just as soon as he thinks she has reached the point where she should be operated on, and I will send you a cable telling you the date beyond which he thinks the operation should not be delayed.*
>
> *It is leaving a very heavy burden of responsibility upon the nurse and the doctor to leave them with the child in her present con-*

dition and without the mother at hand to make decisions which should be made in the child's interest, and I feel confident that you will promptly respond and return directly you receive the cable from me with regard to the time when the operation should be had. . . .

May 12, 3:15 p.m.: Charles Augustus Lindbergh, Jr., was found. Anne Morrow Lindbergh wrote to her mother-in-law that evening:

Dear M.,

. . . The baby's body was found in the woods near the road from Hopewell to Princeton. It was identified by the homemade shirt Betty and I put on it. Also the teeth and hair. There seems to be no possible doubt. The child was evidently killed by a blow on the head—killed instantly undoubtedly, and, from the state of the body and from its being so near here, a long time ago, perhaps in panic during the first blast of publicity.

On May 23 George Wickersham cabled Gloria to return for her child's operation, which was scheduled within ten days. She booked round-trip passage on the *Bremen*, which left June 1 and was to return to Europe June 18. Gloria arrived just in time to take little Gloria to the hospital and stay with her until she went under the anesthetic. Six days later the child returned to the Sherry-Netherland to begin her convalescence. On the night of June 17, Gloria told her daughter that she was leaving again for Europe the next day. Then she went out to dinner with some friends. All through dinner it kept bothering Gloria that she couldn't recall the name of the famous hat shop in Paris that had come up in conversation. Then she remembered that the label was sewn into one of her hats. At about eleven-thirty she telephoned nurse Keislich and asked her to look in the hat and tell her the name. Keislich complied. She told Gloria that all was well.

Shortly after midnight Dr. Oscar Schloss groped for his bedside telephone. It was Mrs. Morgan, who explained that her granddaughter was having a terrible attack and that she had rushed over to the Sherry but didn't know what to do. Schloss said he would come immediately. Twenty minutes later he walked into little Gloria's bedroom and saw the frail child writhing on the bed, her grandmother and the nurse hovering nearby. Schloss stood over the child and asked in his soothing firm voice what the matter was. Little Gloria said that her stomach hurt, then she looked up at him and pleaded, "Don't let me die!"

Schloss gently examined the child. He felt her abdomen. His experienced hands immediately told him there was nothing seriously wrong.

"Don't let me die!" the child wailed. Schloss could see that she was in mortal terror. Her fear was so great that two years later, after his records had been burned, after examining hundreds of other children, the details of this visit would still remain vivid in his memory. Dr. Schloss stayed with little Gloria until her terror subsided.

As Dr. Schloss walked out into the cool black night, the clock high up in its black stanchion in front of the Sherry-Netherland read 3:00 a.m. Little Gloria's condition troubled him greatly: there was no "adequate reason" of a physical nature to account for her hysterical behavior. Schloss was sure her trouble was "mostly psychological" and he decided that nurse Keislich's attitude must be at the root of little Gloria's unnatural fear. He thought that she must have instilled her own concern over the child's health in the child herself. Schloss was later to say, "The nurse was constantly on the alert for symptoms . . . The child was surrounded with an atmosphere of apprehensiveness." Little Gloria was convinced that she was going to die. "She was agitated and apprehensive and fearful" just like the nurse. But also there was something more: "She was fearful she was going to be hurt. That something was going to be done to her." And for this Schloss had no explanation. It puzzled him because no matter how long he thought about it he could think of "no concrete thing that she was fearful of." This sensitive physician had picked up on the atmosphere of terror but he did not realize that little Gloria knew about the Lindbergh kidnapping or that she herself had been threatened with kidnapping.

The Lindbergh kidnapping had a tremendous impact on the lives of many children of the thirties. All around them they saw adult fear and they quietly assimilated it as their own. Two months after the Lindbergh baby was kidnapped, he was found in a shallow grave in a densely wooded area. Even though his daddy had paid the kidnapper $50,000 he'd done something to him—his skull had been bashed in. Some children would remember that the baby had been so pretty, like a real Dy Dee Doll in his yellow sleep suit, and some children noticed that he had a pushed-out place in his chin exactly like his father's. He'd had his father's name too, but he didn't have it anymore because he'd been taken away and they'd done something to him. Murdered him. For money. And when they found him, he was decomposed. The Lindbergh baby would never grow up, never ride a pony, never have a dog. He was gone forever. IT had happened!

Special phrases became part of the kidnap vocabulary that children of the thirties understood like a secret language. The victim's body was often found in a *shallow grave* in a *densely wooded area—decomposed.* When you're kidnapped they *take you away.* Then they *do something to you. Murder* you. For *money.* IT has happened. (In the Supreme Court of New York State little Gloria would explain her fears in a language that many other children could understand.)

We can never know exactly what little Gloria was thinking on the night of June 17 as she lay writhing in pain, and perhaps her terror could never be put into words, but the genesis of her fears seems obvious: to this child the words *money* and *murder* were not new. Before she was old enough to understand, her Grandmother Morgan, her dear Naney, told her that she had a lot of *money.* Before she was old enough to understand, her dear Naney said that her Momey would *murder* her for *money.* When her mother spent time with Prince Hohenlohe, Naney got very angry and said that Momey and "that Boche" would *murder* her for *money.* Naney said this many, many, many times. A child knows that *murder* is a bad word, but it is an abstraction.

It becomes reality. The week of the Lindbergh kidnapping little Gloria arrived home for the first time since she was a baby and was taken to the Sherry-Netherland Hotel. Dodo, who created her very atmosphere, was afraid. Dodo told her that she "needed more protection than any child in the world." Naney came to see her and she was afraid too.

Then a terrible thing happens—Dodo gets a letter saying that you're going to be taken just like the Lindbergh baby. KIDNAPPED. Strange men in dark suits appear: one is with you and Dodo all day. Another sits on a chair outside your bedroom door all night. They never leave you, but Momey does and you experience a "sense of loss . . . at never seeing enough of her . . . or feeling that she belonged to me." You miss her and you miss your cocker spaniel, and you write:

Dear Momey
I hope that you are very well
and having a happy time.
I miss you so much.
When are you going to
send Amber?
Much
Love
from Gloria

And while your mother is gone, while that strange man sits outside your bedroom door, they find the body of the decomposed Lindbergh baby in a shallow grave in a densely wooded area. And now you know exactly what MURDER is.

The next three weeks are filled with pain—they take you to the hospital and put you to sleep and when you wake up your throat aches from what they've done to you. Then they take you back to the hotel and your Momey tells you she's leaving again the next day. Then you're put to bed. The Lindbergh kidnapper came at night after the baby had been put to bed. He took him away and did something to him. Someone wants to take you away. You've been told again and again that you'll be murdered for money. The terror mounts. The pain begins and grows worse and worse. And you know you are going to die!

Gertrude

It seemed to me that there were two of me. One figure the sensible middle-aged woman with a family, with ties of the most ordinary and pleasurable kind, a family whom she loved, longed to make happy; a person well dressed, normal, healthy. But someone else was in the background, a restless person, a lonely, selfish, weak person with violent desires and wild dreams of impossible things.

GERTRUDE VANDERBILT WHITNEY

DRESSED IN BILLOWING Turkish harem pants with a tightly wrapped magenta silk top, Gertrude Vanderbilt Whitney, resembling a Delacroix odalisque, reclined on a stack of patterned pillows as she wrote in longhand on a pad. Her six-year-old granddaughter Gerta (Gertrude Whitney Henry) sat on the floor nearby, watching her grandmother's large, strong hands with the long blood-red nails move across the paper. "The coroner established the fact that Mabel Thompson had committed suicide by drinking—" Gertrude hadn't yet decided what the poison was to be. Later she would choose "hydrocyanic of prussic acid salts, an ingredient of silver polish," and would change Mabel's last name to Randolph.

Gerta admired her grandmother, who never treated her as a child. It was to Gertrude that Gerta confided her own secret ambition to be a writer. Gerta found scraps of paper covered with handwriting scattered about her grandmother's house, and whenever she saw the name Mabel she knew they were notes for her grandmother's book.

"No one will ever know I wrote this," Gertrude solemnly informed Gerta.

"But why?"

Gertrude shrugged. "I'd rather be remembered as a first-rate artist than as a third-rate writer."

Walking the Dusk was published under the pseudonym L. J. Webb in the fall of 1932. It was not "third rate," but it was shocking—a bizarre tale of a dark beauty named Mabel Randolph, an opportunistic Society girl who is said to have committed suicide. Her friend Diana suspects that Mabel has been murdered. Diana is proven right, but the solution to the crime is so scandalous that she lets the murderer go free rather than bring public exposure to his motive.

In reviewing this novel, *The New York Times* Sunday book supplement seemed more involved with the morality of the situation than with the novel's literary merit.

> It is evident that there had been some secret in Mabel's life and that this secret is the key to the mystery. . . . When Diana eventually does learn Mabel's secret and the truth about her death, she decides to let sleeping dogs lie, and it's perhaps just as well that she does. This is not so much a detective story as a study in morbid sex psychology.

The element in the mystery which seemed so shocking at the time was the revelation that Mabel's lover was the fabulously wealthy, well-connected Katharine Osmund. No doubt this lesbian theme was a major reason for Gertrude's use of a pseudonym.

Gertrude's family and intimate friends, however, were not surprised by *Walking the Dusk*—and several agreed that it was highly autobiographical. The world of this novel was Gertrude's own. The estate Katharine Osmund and her husband live on could be a duplicate of Gertrude's own Wheatley Hills. The Osmunds' "camp" in the Adirondacks also could be Gertrude's. To get there people travel in a private railroad car, then proceed to a private dock and complete the twenty-minute trip in a private launch—just as Gertrude did.

This is Gertrude's world of tennis courts and swimming pools, of bridge, jigsaw puzzles, backgammon, and boredom. In the heat of the summer "we played ping-pong instead of tennis and foolish games instead of bridge, we bathed by the hour, and seldom wore any clothes except bathing suits." On "a delicious day" personal maids pack clothes, liveried footmen carry heavy silver trays laden with tea and scones, and Benson announces dinner. There is a Fourth of July annual summer dance where beautiful couples tango, smoke "butts" and grow "tizy wizy" on champagne. On August 4, there occurs the seasonal exodus to Southampton, Bar Harbor, Newport, and abroad.

The characters spend much time "sitting in the piazza" complaining that "amusing places are so crowded" and philosophizing. "Strange about Mabel, wasn't it? Usually in our crowd when a girl gets hard hit she either takes to dissipation or else has a nervous breakdown and goes in for interior decoration as an after-cure." Almost everyone finds the whole affair "ghastly" and "a beastly shake up."

The characters too are people Gertrude knows well. When Diana describes her relationship with her husband, it duplicates that of Gertrude with Harry Payne Whitney.

> We had always looked at life from the opposite ends of an opera glass. The violence of our coming together was so entirely physical that its duration was barely six months. After that I was just bored or miserable. Horace was constantly out doing something athletic or preparing to do it, or else feeling badly because he had not done it. . . .

And Mabel Randolph could be only one person—Gloria Morgan Vanderbilt.

> By force of circumstances I had come to know Mabel well and to have a very real affection for her. The more I knew her the more I was surprised by something pathetic about her. She had so few illusions and found her happiness—such as it was—in excitement and activity.
>
> But you had to know her to guess this. Casually she presented an altogether charming façade, and though she was not exactly popular, she was liked and greatly admired for her unusual type of beauty. Her small head was like a challenge, she held it high. Straight black hair combed tight back from a white forehead and drawn into two sleek points in front of small, bare ears.
>
> Her mouth in repose drooped at the corners, but when she laughed it was reckless. Her eyes had consorted with perplexity and trouble and never quite lost the contamination.

Mabel's mother, Mrs. Randolph, an uncanny re-creation of Laura Morgan, is talkative and emotional as she says of her daughter: "She's always been used to luxury and couldn't get on without it. . . . I told my husband she'd come to a bad end—running around with people like— Oh!—I beg your pardon!—no offense meant, but I never thought it would end like this."

Of course, no one outside Gertrude's intimate circle knew that she was the author of *Walking the Dusk*. And no one at all asked why the themes of lesbianism and murder so occupied her mind at this time.

Gertrude Whitney had been introduced to Prince Hohenlohe in 1929 when Gloria brought him to her Paris studio, hoping that Gertrude would use her influence to persuade Alice Vanderbilt to help them financially. Gertrude refused to interfere. By summer Gertrude began hearing scandalous things about Gloria from her friend the sculptor Jo Davidson, who owned a villa on the Riviera. She was not shocked by what she heard, but she was dismayed at Gloria's lack of discretion and she remembered Harry's judgment—"Gloria is no good. . . ."

In the spring of 1932, when Gloria Vanderbilt and the child had returned to the United States, Gertrude hardly knew her little niece; she calculated that she had seen the child no more than eight times in her entire life. But at Mrs. Morgan's behest, she invited little Gloria and her nurse to dinner. Gloria was in Europe at the time. Gertrude was disturbed to see how thin and pale and nervous her niece was. It was then that Mrs. Morgan confided to Gertrude her terrible tale of neglect and deprivation amid luxury, and begged Gertrude to help her. With her gift for efficiency Gertrude did what she could: she visited little Gloria several times and spoke to Dr. Schloss, who took care of several of her grandchildren. She went to see Dr. Craig, who had performed a tonsillectomy on one of her granddaughters and arranged the details of her niece's operation. After the operation, at Mrs. Morgan's request, she volunteered to see Gloria and ask her if little Gloria might come to Wheatley Hills until she regained her health.

Mrs. Morgan said that Gertrude Whitney was "a saint" to take little Gloria in and nurse Keislich declared she was "a great lady." What these women saw was Gertrude Whitney's public persona, that of wealthy society matron, sculptor, and art patron. With consummate organization, Gertrude attended to her estates, her art activities, her children, and her grandchildren. She was devoted to her mother, who was ill, spending a great deal of the week at Alice Gwynne Vanderbilt's bedside. Above all she appeared to be a woman with an overpowering sense of duty—austere, unapproachable, lofty, cold.

But the woman who wrote *Walking the Dusk* was a bohemian, a hedonist, a sophisticate who accepted bizarre behavior without judging it. She was a woman who took lover after lover and gloried in the pleasure they gave her; a woman of immense vanity, who created herself as a seductive, exotic, unique personality. Said her granddaughter Flora Irving, "She was a true Bohemian. She believed that passion was the guiding nourishing force of life."

Gertrude Vanderbilt Whitney

"Uptown she was very regal. Downtown she was entirely different," observed her friend Jo Davidson. The uptown Society matron felt guilty about the conduct and wanton needs of the downtown bohemian. Gertrude's life became a struggle between these two people—the perfect lady in the House of Worth ball gown and the $600,000 Payne pearls, and the passionate bohemian in an exotic costume dancing barefoot in the moonlight.

Passionate feelings were considered unseemly in the world of Society. Gertrude's mother was the most controlled of women, and living under her strict, puritanical domination, Gertrude learned early to suppress her desires and to hide her emotions. She wrote of herself, "I was always reserved, too much so, they said, and I froze people up if I did not want to be intimate with them until they actually became afraid of me. I had a way of hiding my feelings so completely that even my best friends, those who knew me best, could not tell what was passing within me. . . ."

As Gertrude matured and her feelings became intense and different from the norm, she kept herself in tight check, afraid that if she did not, her emotions might overpower her: "I think that in the end I will do some perfectly mad thing," she wrote. "Then I will give myself away and the world will know as I know myself that I am mad."

What she did was to encase her emotions in ice. "I have become hard inside and that hardness is spreading so that now only a little softness covers it which is inside—beware lest the outside harden also. That curse of manners which has come to hide all things is getting [to be] a menace to me."

Eventually, Gertrude removed herself so far from her guilty longings that she achieved a perfect glacial state; she was never to display anger or to confront an unpleasant situation with a hard truth. When her husband's infidelities wounded her beyond endurance, she poured out all her feelings in a letter to him and then hid it away. He was never to see it. Wild sexual fantasies, love letters, letters of anger, all were written and passionately felt and hidden away, as Gertrude hid away the feeling part of her nature.

An understanding of her removal from her own emotions is essential in comprehending why the tragedy of the Vanderbilt custody trial would come to pass. She was never to say what she thought because her thoughts were too bizarre and terrible to be acceptable; these gothic thoughts would be relegated to a book that would never be associated with her. She avoided confrontation at all costs, and when she had to fight, as at the trial, she had others do her dirty work, convinced that she could remain remote and pristine. Her wealth enabled her to interpose between herself and Gloria Vanderbilt a Praetorian guard of doctors and lawyers who shielded her from the ugly realities of the matter, but who also served to cut her off from grasping what a custody trial might mean to her, both publicly and personally. She had spent a lifetime removing herself from this kind of understanding.

First there was the world of her birth, a gilded universe created to confirm her superiority. She was born on January 9, 1875, at the inception of the most opulent era in American history, a princess in America's royal family, waited on by an army of servitors in palaces filled with the plunder of royal Europe—Gobelin and Boucher tapestries; Old Masters; rooms ripped from castles in England, Italy, France; boiserie, malachite, gold; great works and fashionable grotesque kitsch heaped high from floor to soaring ceilings.

Gertrude grew up aware of her potential power. She wrote of herself: "My ways are deep and I cover my tracks with discretion but none the less when I want something it often happens." The sculptor John Gregory, who became one of her lovers, took a less charitable view. He wrote, "Your whole life you have imposed your will on everyone but your equals. . . ."

When, as an adult, Gertrude espoused the unpopular cause of American art, she was thought to be a woman of immense courage. John Sloan observed that when she arrived on the American art scene in the first decade of the twentieth century, "to buy such unfashionable pictures was as revolutionary as painting them." But those who understood the world of her childhood knew that she gave criticism not a thought. It was the world, not Gertrude, that would have to adjust. It always had for the Vanderbilts.

In childhood, Gertrude had a strong desire to be a boy. She was educated at home and at the Brearley School in an atmosphere where her relationships with boys were chaperoned but those with girls were allowed to develop freely. She passionately adored her teacher, Miss Windsor, and wrote her letters which were never sent, explaining, perhaps without fully understanding the implications of what she was saying, "I am not exactly the same as all the other girls."

Her lifelong habit of separating her Society life from her passionate emotional life which she kept hidden lest the "mad" Gertrude with the "wild and ungovernable desires" be discovered, blossomed with her first love experience. Her attachment, shocking even by today's standards but unthinkable then, was to Esther Hunt, daughter of "the Vanderbilt architect," Richard Morris Hunt. Gertrude's astute biographer, B. H. Friedman, noted that by Gertrude's eighteenth year, "Esther is in love with her [Gertrude], really in love, so passionately and completely that it will make Gertrude's relationships with other girls seem like the 'crushes' they are and those with boys—to date and even until marriage—seem by comparison, like child's play."

For the next three years, until Gertrude was twenty-one, this lesbian relationship seemed to increase in intensity. Esther wrote Gertrude love letters filled with specific physical details: "Come to me and lie beside me and let my arms enfold you. . . . Your mouth—Gertrude—your mouth someday will drive me crazy, I kiss it softly at first, perhaps shortly too, then for longer, then somehow I want you all, entirely, and almost I care not if I hurt you . . . so I love, even worship you."

As Gertrude acquired male suitors, she became conflicted, writing that she felt "extreme blueness. It is Esther perhaps. I loved her more yesterday afternoon than I have ever done before. I felt more thrill at her touch, more happiness in her kiss."

Alice Gwynne Vanderbilt suspected the nature of her daughter's relationship to Esther. When Gertrude returned home late from a Newport carriage ride with Esther, with the excuse that they had taken a wrong turn in the road, her mother forbade her to go to Esther's for a month. Gertrude asked why, and her mother answered, "Because I don't like the way you act—with her." Without confronting her daughter, Alice Vanderbilt went on doing her utmost to discourage the relationship. She saw to it that suitable young men were invited to the Vanderbilt mansion: in the winter season of 1894 Gertrude attended ninety-two dinner parties, dances, evenings at the opera.

Gertrude was nineteen, five feet eight inches tall, rawboned. Her Oriental Vanderbilt eyes were an intense green, but her chin receded and her face was unusually long, surrounded by a mass of tightly waved brown hair. Gertrude was aware of her own awkwardness and was the first to see the ruddiness of her complexion and the hugeness of her hands. "She was not beautiful, but she *made* herself beautiful," observed Flora Irving. But for now, Alice Vanderbilt seemed to have a problem on her hands. In an effort to attract proper suitors for her daughter, she deliberately violated her sacred rule of privacy and allowed the press into her Fifth Avenue mansion. The result sounded like an advertisement for marriage.

> HOW THE PRETTY HEIRESS ENJOYS LIFE
>
> Miss Gertrude Vanderbilt, the richest prospective heiress in America, is still a girl in skirts to her shoe tops. Her father's fabulous wealth is estimated at $150,000,000 . . . her portion of the estate will hardly be less than $20,000,000. . . .

> It must be a pleasant sensation to live in a $7,000,000 house and to have most of the good things of life without even the trouble of wishing for them. This is the goodly heritage of Miss Gertrude Vanderbilt. . . . The richest debutante in America is as sweet as a May blossom, this fortune-favored young girl, and as modest and unassuming as any little country maid. She is of medium height, slender and graceful, with beautiful brown hair, gray-blue eyes and fresh, healthy coloring. . . . Unlike most rich girls, she has never been abroad to school, but has been thoroughly drilled by the best masters in music, the languages and all of the lore which the modern woman is expected to be up in. . . . She opens her eyes on the prettiest room in all New York. It is on the corner of Fifth Avenue and Fifty-seventh street. . . . The wall is hung with white silk and so is the ceiling, where the rich material is drawn up in the centre in canopy fashion. The little single bed, the dainty dressing-table, the dressing-stool, desk and some of the easy chairs are of white mahogany, inlaid with quaint wreaths and garlands of mother-of-pearl. The canopy and curtains for the snowy bed are of the filmy bolting cloth, embroidered in pink roses and blue forget-me-nots. All the brushes, mirrors, combs and toilet bottles on the dressing-table are of Dresden china, covered with roses and forget-me-nots, and with the monogram "G.V." in gold. . . .
>
> When Miss Vanderbilt has been to a great reception the night before she does not rise until 10 o'clock. Then she has her breakfast served in her room and does not make her appearance downstairs much before luncheon. Ordinarily she rises at 8 o'clock and slips into a bathrobe of rose-colored silk, lined with fur and dainty enough for an opera wrap. There are rose-colored shoes lined with fur by the side of her bed, all ready just to slip her pretty feet into.
>
> She walks across the room and enters her own little bathroom, where her maid has left the bath in readiness. It is all pure white and silver. The walls, ceiling and floors are of white marble and all of the fittings are of exquisite porcelain and solid silver.
>
> After her cold plunge she exercises with a pair of dumb-bells for 10 minutes and then she is ready to make her toilet. Every article she wears is rich and fine enough for any princess, and her house gowns are much more beautiful and elaborate than the simple ones her mother chooses for her to wear to the ball and opera.

That season Gertrude was seeing several suitors, including Moses Taylor, Jim Barnes, and Harry Payne Whitney, who caught her interest by his honesty when he told her, "You will always have a good time because when your looks give out you will still be a great heiress." Gertrude had known Harry casually for years; he lived just across Fifth Avenue at 2 West Fifty-seventh Street and his sister Pauline was one of her closest friends. Harry had been a friend and classmate of Gertrude's brother Bill and, four years previously, had visited at Bill's bedside when he was dying of typhoid fever.

In the winter of 1895, Alice whisked her daughter off to Europe to meet eligible men. Before she left, Gertrude paid a farewell visit to Esther: ". . . we fixed ourselves comfortably on the sofa for a nice long stay. I don't say talk because sometimes we hardly speak at all. Esther puts her arms about my waist and I put my head on her shoulder and we are happy."

Alice saw to it that there were many suitors in Europe and more when Gertrude returned to the United States. Although Esther's passion did not wane, Gertrude's did. In February of 1896, Alice Vanderbilt arranged a trip on the private Vanderbilt railroad car to Palm Beach, Florida. Among the guests she invited was the dashing Harry Payne Whitney. On this trip Harry proposed to Gertrude and she accepted. Alice Vanderbilt was thrilled and no doubt, quite relieved.

Harry was considered a great catch; his father, William Collins Whitney, came from a fine old New England family (Harry once declared on a questionnaire that he could trace his ancestry "out of sight"), was a brilliant lawyer, and had served in Grover Cleveland's cabinet as Secretary of the Navy, where he created the first modern U.S. Navy by replacing obsolete wooden ships with steel battleships. His mother, Flora Payne Whitney, was a high-spirited, elegant maverick who was reputed to be "America's richest woman"—her fortune derived from the generosity of her father, Harry Payne, a railroad tycoon and Ohio senator, and from her bachelor brother Oliver Hazard Payne, the treasurer and a major stockholder of Standard Oil. Oliver worshipped his sister and lavished on her family extravagant residences and possessions. Will Whitney seemed to take a back seat to Oliver in regard to his own family; he wanted Harry to go to Harvard but Oliver decreed Yale and his wish prevailed. Flora died in 1893, leaving her entire fortune to her husband. Somehow this impelled Will Whitney to seek a fortune of his own and for the first time he began to establish a close relationship with Harry, who was then twenty-one. They went into business together; within five years they had assembled a vast network of street railway companies. When Harry became engaged to Gertrude in 1896 he was already on his way to being a successful businessman. He was also an outstanding athlete—a daring polo player, a yachtsman, a crack shot. He was known to wager $10,000 on a set of tennis, $25,000 on a polo match, and $50,000 on a horse. He lost a bet of $125,000 to his friend Charlie Clark one morning and paid him that afternoon. Harry was a man who all his life would take the small, protected world of Society to be *the* world.

Gertrude and Harry's marriage was considered to be *the* event of the Newport social season and neither guests nor reporters dwelt on the fact that Gertrude's father was partially paralyzed and unable to speak, as a result of the stroke he'd suffered during the conflict with his son Cornelius. The Vanderbilt-Whitney nuptials were hailed as "the union of two great American families" and Gertrude was referred to as "Our American Princess." At the wedding reception Nathan Franco, leader of the forty-seven-piece Metropolitan Opera Orchestra, broke into a spontaneous rendition of "The Star-Spangled Banner," explaining, "It is so rarely that an American girl of fortune marries one of her own contemporaries that I thought the selection decidedly in keeping with the occasion."

From the beginning of their marriage certain patterns became evident: Harry had chosen as his wife a woman much like his mother—intelligent, high-spirited, independent, and splendidly spoiled. Harry himself allowed nothing to interfere with his desires and pleasures. The young Harry Payne Whitneys started married life awash with possessions—estates, servants, yachts, polo ponies, racehorses. Their set was composed of the children of the ultrarich who had been given everything and who sought nothing more than to relieve the boredom of their privileged lives. The Whitneys moved from their city mansion to "cottages" in Lenox, Bar Harbor, and Newport, to "camps" in the Adirondacks. They were transported in a private railroad car staffed with a French chef, a butler, and a personal maid.

During the winter of 1896, Harry's father had been courting Edith S. Randolph, the beautiful widow of a British army officer. His former brother-in-law Oliver Payne objected, telling Will Whitney that a remarriage would be an insult to Flora's sacred memory. He then prevailed on the Whitney children to intercede. Harry wrote his father: "The house is so much Mamma's that it is hard enough to think of somebody living in it in her place." William Whitney solved that problem by giving the Fifty-seventh Street residence (originally a gift from Oliver Payne) to Harry and Gertrude as a wedding present. On the day they sailed on their honeymoon trip to Japan, Will Whitney married Edith Randolph. He then purchased a mansion at 871 Fifth Avenue, on the corner of Sixty-eighth Street, and commissioned Stanford White to remodel it at a cost of $2 million.

Oliver Payne never forgave William Whitney. The great and consuming love of his life had been for his sister Flora. Of the Whitney children, William Payne and Pauline sided with their immensely rich uncle, while Harry and his sister Dorothy (who was only nine at the time of her father's remarriage) stuck steadfastly by William Whitney. The two children who denounced their father were rewarded with an immense fortune. When Oliver Payne died he left the bulk of his estate to them. William Payne dropped his first name—his father's name—and became known as Payne Whitney, and when he died in the spring of 1927 he left a fortune of $178,893,655, the largest ever recorded in the United States.

William Collins Whitney died in 1904, leaving the bulk of his $21,243,101 estate to Harry and Dorothy. Harry received $10 million and his father's vast array of estates, which included:

The $2 million Renaissance palace at 871 Fifth Avenue.

An 85,000-acre game preserve in the Adirondacks, with three "camps" and seven private lakes.

A Venetian palace at Wheatley Hills in Old Westbury, Roslyn, Long Island, with 5,000 acres of land.

An Aiken, South Carolina, estate, comprised of a mansion, a racecourse, and 2,000 acres of hunting land.

A Lexington, Kentucky, stock farm of 3,000 acres, with 100 brood mares and 10 stallions, each valued at $60,000.

Stony Ford Farm, in Goshen, New York, used as an auxiliary to the Kentucky stock farm.

A Sheepshead Bay house, with a private racetrack and 300 acres of land.

A Berkshire Hills mansion at Lenox, Massachusetts, with 700 acres of land.

A house at October Mountain, with an 11,000-acre game preserve.

A lodge at Blue Mountain Lake, with its own 18-hole golf course.

In addition to these real estate holdings, Harry inherited many of his father's directorates, but he was already serving as director of two dozen companies, including banks, transportation, and utility companies. He also inherited his father's stable, but he already owned his own racehorses and had won more purses and stakes in ten days with his Irish Lad than his father had in a lifetime of racing. Harry, inundated with possessions and responsibilities, gave Gertrude little time or attention as he simplified and consolidated his holdings and used his energies to establish himself as America's top polo player, a ten-goal player and captain of the Meadow Brook polo team. Called the Big Four, Harry and his teammates—Devereux Milburn, the Waterbury brothers, J. Montgomery and Lawrence, and Louis E. Stoddard as reserve—won three consecutive times the American Challenge Cup which had been held by the British since 1886.

Gertrude dutifully attended her husband's polo matches and the horseraces which his entries invariably won; the yachting events, the hunting parties. She watched them all with a slightly bored expression. In the first decade of her marriage, she managed her numerous households and had three children: Flora Payne, Cornelius Vanderbilt (called Sonny), and Barbara. In the fashion of the day, she entrusted their care largely to servants, leaving them for months at a time. She felt she had little in common with Harry, and the discovery of his repeated infidelities hurt her and angered her. In her Society world, there were few outlets for her energy: to climb in Society was the most common activity, but by virtue of her birth she already held a preeminent position. Her art work was considered an eccentricity: "Mrs. Whitney is one of Our Set who does things and does them well," said a New York *Press* Society column. "She is as devoted to her art as her sister Gladys is to baking pies." Gertrude's wealth provided a solution to her problem available to few women. She did not desert her husband or the world of her birth. She simply bought herself another world.

The year was 1908. Jo Davidson, a dedicated young sculptor, arrived in the city of his dreams—Paris. He was twenty-five and working long hours on clay portraits that no one purchased; he drank absinthe in Montmartre cafés with fellow artists, he argued philosophy, he was practically penniless—his normal meal was a loaf of bread, cheese, and wine. Davidson's dog fared better. Sultan, a Great Dane he had found on a walking trip through Switzerland, begged food at local restaurants.

One evening Davidson found Sultan in the Café d'Harcourt "being fed sugar by a group of well-dressed swells." Davidson claimed his dog, and one of the men, a sculptor whom he knew slightly, invited him to join them. Davidson looked the group over—they seemed too rich and made him uneasy—so he declined the invitation. One member of the group, a woman, was wearing a large hat and pearls. Davidson was intrigued by her and found her "striking . . . dark and distinguished." She looked up at him and said, "Oh, do sit down. I have heard so much about you from our mutual friend, John Gregory."

Davidson sat down at the table and was introduced to "Mrs. Harry Payne Whitney." Gertrude told him how she too was a sculptor, had studied with Andrew O'Connor and Hendrik Christian Andersen, and kept a studio in Paris. According to Gertrude's account of the meeting, she indiscreetly mentioned that John Gregory had given her the book of Musset poetry she was carrying and Davidson instinctively understood that Gregory was her lover. He drew a picture of John Gregory in his sketchbook, tore it out, and gave it to Gertrude. She flirtatiously told Davidson that the next time he wrote to Gregory, "tell him you met me and we had an amusing night at Montmartre."

After a gay hour the group went on to Monico's where Davidson feasted on lobster and champagne. While he was eating dinner a beautiful redheaded Swiss girl he knew appeared by coincidence at the café. Davidson gave her the key to his studio. When the group teased him, he explained that he was sculpting a head of the girl. Amid jeers of merriment, Gertrude said that she would come to his studio the next day to see the result.

Davidson did indeed make a hasty portrait of the girl that night and, while she slept, he cast it in bronze. The concierge had barely finished scrubbing the floor of his studio when Gertrude Whitney arrived. She looked at the head and said, "I must have it." Davidson had made his first Parisian sale. It was the beginning of an enduring friendship.

The previous spirng in New York, Gertrude, who wished to be near "real artists" and in particular her teacher, James Earle Fraser, had purchased a twenty-five-foot-wide ivy-covered stable at 19 MacDougal Alley. The Alley was full of impoverished artists who lived and worked in what had once been the stables and servants' quarters of the fashionable houses on Washington Square. She converted her stable into a studio—more luxurious than any in the city—one huge room, in which the north wall was fitted out with glass panes that reached two stories high. From two tall, narrow south windows Gertrude could look past maple trees to the Washington Square Arch, erected the year of her birth, and beyond to the tall spire of the Judson Memorial Church which rose like a Moorish fantasy, its thin green-bronze cross dominating the sky.

Gertrude covered the walls of her studio in red velvet, massed potted palms on either side of the fireplace, and went to work. She seemed unsure of her talent and her identity. She used a pseudonym, producing a variety of pieces which were decorative and without character. She was not accepted by Village artists or intellectuals. *Tribune* art critic Forbes Watson, who later came to admire Gertrude and to be the editor of *The Arts* magazine which she supported, spoke of her arrival in the Alley with disdain, noting that her studio floor was littered with reproductions of Old Masters and her first exhibitions were of "second-rate foreign artists" whose work was purchased by Gertrude's social friends whom Watson referred to as "uptown swillage."

The raggle-taggle infant American art was struggling for its very existence there in MacDougal Alley. In this place of intellectual ferment the poverty-stricken renegades who depicted the life they saw about them—the people, the urban landscape—found no market for their work. (Those who wanted to eat copied Old Masters or painted mundane landscapes and still lifes that were accepted for exhibition at the National Academy of Art.) Gertrude soon recognized the talent of the young American artists who, in their isolated way, were moving in the same direction as the radical European artists she admired in Paris. She learned quickly. The reproductions vanished. With absolute conviction, she championed the cause of American art.

Gertrude Vanderbilt Whitney stepped into a vacuum; she became a bountiful godmother. The Eight, a group of these new artists led by Robert Henri, held an exhibition at the Macbeth Galleries. Only seven paintings were sold; Gertrude bought four. John Sloan, who had never sold a painting, was not among the lucky ones, a fact that must have influenced his diary entry of February 20, 1908: "All sales in the exhibition, seven, went to three buyers—Mrs. Harry Payne Whitney, the rich sculpturess—at least she has a fine studio for the purpose—bought four."

Word spread quickly that one of the wealthiest women in America had come to the Alley—a Vanderbilt, a Whitney—and soon Gertrude found herself without the privacy that she required to render her bohemian world invisible. She purchased a house at 8 West Eighth Street, situated directly behind her studio, and connected it to her studio with a steep cathedral-ceilinged stairway. At a time when artists lived in their studios only when poverty forced them to do so, Gertrude created a pied-à-terre upstairs in the Eighth Street house. Downstairs, in two identical rooms, she created galleries where avant-garde American art could be exhibited.

The Village artists flocked to her. Stuart Davis, Robert Henri, George Luks, John Sloan, and scores of others had their first exhibitions in her Eighth Street galleries. Gertrude encouraged her uptown friends to view the work and to buy what they saw, and she herself purchased at least one painting from every exhibition, usually more. Her purchases often coincided with the artists' rent payments. When doctors' bills came due, money was known to appear from an anonymous donor. Gertrude was sensitive to the plight of the artists. In bitterest winter Edward Hopper walked down the four flights of stairs from his studio at number three Washington Square to purchase the one scuttleful of coal he could afford, carried it back upstairs, and continued working. John Sloan had no suit or overcoat. On certain days Everett Shinn was too hungry to work at all. Stuart Davis lived in a room on Fourteenth Street that measured eight feet by eleven feet. It contained a bed, a sink, a stove, and three hundred of his unsold canvases—eventually Gertrude bought dozens.

In this atmosphere of poverty, the power of Gertrude's money was magnified. She confided to Jo Davidson that she felt her wealth a great handicap. She wanted desperately to be accepted as an artist among artists. She never was. It was Gertrude Vanderbilt Whitney's money, not her own work, that was to secure for her an important place in American art.

In return for her beneficences, Gertrude began to play a vital role in the lives of the artists. In her MacDougal Alley studio the secret sensual quality of her personality found expression. One artist who was of her own social set was Robert Winthrop Chanler—a strapping six-foot-six-inch man of wealth, related to the Delanos, Rutherfurds, Winthrops, Livingstons, and Stuyvesants. His mother had been adopted by her grandparents, Society leaders Mr. and Mrs. William B. Astor.

Chanler was totally dissolute. His sister-in-law, Mrs. Winthrop Chanler, said of him, "He lived for sensation and excitement, for pleasure rather than happiness, had taken the good things of life as they came, without thought or scruple." In 1893 he married Julia Chamberlain. They lived for a decade in Paris until their divorce, when he returned to the United States and bought a farm in Dutchess County, near Rokeby, the Astor estate in Barrytown that his mother had inherited. He spent $20,000 on a political campaign and was duly elected sheriff of Dutchess County. For the rest of his life he was known as Sheriff Bob.

In New York City Chanler purchased two adjoining houses on East Nineteenth Street. He decorated them with his own works, creating what he called his House of Fantasy. This residence became the center of the Village artists' play world—Chanler's front door had a trick lock so that his friends could enter any time of the day or night. "The parties at the House of Fantasy were apt to last through the next day and into the morning after, during which interval a great deal of whiskey was consumed and almost anything or everything might and often did happen," observed his sister-in-law.

Gertrude found in Chanler a kindred spirit from her own social world. She wrote of him, "Put aside the fact of his being a fraud and a flirt, and he is inspiring. . . . He says live—live—get all you can out of life and he wishes the best of all things. 'I would like to see you go to the Devil' were his words and instead of being shocked or reproving him I merely smile and I suppose my Puritan ancestors would turn in their graves were they to hear our conversations."

Chanler was the ideal choice to decorate Gertrude's studio. She purchased 17 MacDougal Alley, next to the building she already owned, and in these buildings Chanler created an environment for Gertrude worthy of a pagan goddess dedicated to the pleasures of the senses. He flanked her studio fireplace with sculptured flames of plaster over steel which shot up in an irregular pattern forty feet into the air and fanned out around the perimeter of the ceiling. The focal point of this ceiling was an enormous sunburst whose rays impaled nude maidens, dragons, griffons, and an immense octopus. The flames and sunburst were coated with gold leaf and the figures were lacquered deep red.

In the small bathroom, fantasy was tinged with kitsch; this room resembled a library: wooden trompe l'oeil books, fronts only, scarcely one-half-inch deep, were packed together on mahogany shelves. A mahogany toilet tank hung on the wall, its pipe gold plated, a heavy gold pull chain ended in a massive gold and red tassel.

At Wheatley Hills in Old Westbury, Long Island, Gertrude had commissioned a second and much more elaborate studio—a vast Roman palace with a glass roof. A lush tropical mural by Howard Cushing spiraled up the wall behind a curving staircase, ending at a landing which held a portrait of an exotic Gertrude in a black and white tunic, orange harem pants, and upturned brocade slippers. On the second floor, Sheriff Bob Chanler created a bedroom with murals depicting a medieval court scene in black and white set off against a black and white marble checkerboard floor. An adjoining bathroom had a sunken tub turned into a grotto full of Chanler's imaginary sea creatures that swam up gold and coral walls through a dark green ceiling of shells and seaweed.

Scattered about outside the studio were broken fragments from ancient villas in Pompeii and Florence. Gertrude surrounded her studio with gardens of trimmed topiary and five thousand flowers set into formal beds, at the center of which was a circular blue and gray marble fountain. In back of her studio, broad steps led down to a sylvan setting of a freshly created woodland glade and a newly dredged lake. Exotic birds—peacocks, parrots, macaws—moved freely about the studio's interior and the gardens. It was a setting of fairy-tale splendor, of fantasy run rampant. Painter Arthur Lee, who visited the Wheatley Hills studio, wrote to Gertrude that this was a place where "your spirit could play untrammeled," and went on to say, "O what a god-like place or shall I say goddess? The studio as splendid as a temple and the garden O glorious! . . . As soon as I saw the strangely dull blue pool I ran back to the enchanted house and stript and I dove in. . . ."

Gertrude began spending a great deal of time in her fantasy clothes in her fantasy environments at work and with lovers. She came to value the seductive power of her body and her wealth and to savor sensation and excitement. When she participated in the social world she wrote a lover, "I hate this life of pretense and ridiculous ideas. Dear love, I want to run to you to leave the absurdity of this world." In truth, she had no intention of deserting the world of her birth where she lived tormented by her fury at Harry's promiscuity that seemed undiminished by her own increasing assortment of lovers. Then Harry added to his conquests a member of their own social set, a cousin of Gertrude's who was accepted freely in the Whitney household so that Gertrude was forced to see her frequently. She wrote her husband of her frustration and disillusionment.

It seems very obvious that we are drifting further and further apart and that the chances of our coming together are growing remote. . . . Every one of your pleasures (I don't think I exaggerate when I say this, just think it over) is disconnected from me. Most of mine from you. You are dependent on me for nothing. Our occupations are separate, our pleasures are not the same, all the things I think essential you look down on, I look down on you because you have thrown away most all the things I admired you for. I don't trust you, you talk to your friends of the things I don't want talked of. You are a hypocrite, which I don't admire. . . .

. . . There is one very important phase of it all that I have not yet spoken of: that is, women in your life and men in mine. I suppose that is the hardest thing of all to be honest about or to understand. You have several times behaved pretty rottenly, but I think, at least you have not been terribly open about these matters, so that they were very much discussed. But you are now behaving differently. I object to this. There is no use, I suppose, my objecting to your caring for someone else, it would simply be ludicrous, but I do object to several things which I will state. I have never been seen

> *around all the time with* one *person. I have never been talked about with* one *person. . . . Even in Paris where it would have taken so little to give one a bad name I have not been maligned. All this probably seems unimportant to you. I don't blame you for the things you don't give me and that I want because it must be my own fault not to inspire them, but just the same it's hard not to get these simple things that everyone craves and almost has a right to. . . .*

When Gertrude finished writing this letter she sealed it, put her initials and the date on the envelope and hid it away. It was discovered thirty years after her death. She avenged herself on this man, who she felt had betrayed her, by freezing him out and by allowing him to find the love letters she had received from his trusted friend William Stackpole; Harry, who practiced a double standard, was deeply hurt. In the winter of 1913, she became a part of the wild nighttime life of bohemian Paris where every form of pleasure was available to her. Lesbian, male homosexual, and outré sexual combinations were not frowned upon; drugs were in evidence at artists' parties—morphine was the most popular—and at mock Oriental feasts guests reclined as the hookah and pipe made its rounds of the room. Alcohol was consumed in gargantuan quantities—in later life Gertrude complained of her penchant for alcohol and seemed to fight fiercely to control it. After that winter both Gertrude and Harry seemed to abandon all efforts to integrate their lives, their distant relationship crystallized—Gertrude was to lead a dual existence for the rest of her life.

On the night of February 17, 1913, for the first time, Gertrude's two worlds came together. At the 69th Infantry Regiment Armory on Twenty-fifth Street and Lexington Avenue, Society people and downtown artists rubbed elbows at the opening of the International Exhibition of Modern Art sponsored by the Association of American Painters and Sculptors. Approximately three thousand works of art by the most radical European and American artists of the day were displayed. While a regimental band played military marches, the American public was exposed to the new art of Europe and America. They found it scandalous, or humorous, or hateful. No one left the Armory unaffected.

Soon Gertrude's uptown friends were clamoring to go with her to the Armory Show. It became fashionable to attend elaborate dinner parties and then head down to Twenty-fifth Street. Arthur B. Davies guided Teddy Roosevelt through the exhibition. He waved his arms as he stomped past the works of Picasso, Braque, Renoir, Gauguin, van Gogh, Cézanne, Sloan, Glackens, Prendergast, and scores of others, proclaiming loudly, "That's not art. That's not art!" Stopping in front of Marcel Duchamp's *Nude Descending a Staircase, No. 2*, he turned to Davies and demanded: "Where is that woman?" A critic called this painting "an explosion in a shingle factory." The canvases of Matisse were reviled as "childish scrawling." Constantin Brancusi's *Mlle. Pogany* was described as "a hard-boiled egg mounted on a cube of sugar."

The Europeans came in for the greatest share of the criticism and the limelight, but the new American art, one thousand works strong, showed the public alternatives to the stifling tradition and complacency of the Academy. The *Globe* prophesied, "American art will never be the same again." In a welter of publicity, modern art burst upon America. Galleries began to open their doors to sell the new art and collectors began to buy it. Society, not Gertrude, had begun to change its opinion.

At no time was the duality of Gertrude's life more evident than during the years of the Great War. In October of 1914, she twirled and undulated on the gleaming ballroom floor of Clarence Mackay's Harbor Hill estate. She wore an Oriental costume of silk and gauze pants entwined with emeralds and gold. Her hair was tucked up into a tiny gold and pearl cap, and a veil covered the lower portion of her face. As she danced, nine trained macaws flew about her head and perched on her extended arms and on her shoulders, their brilliant plumage matching her own. After the dance she sat at the side of the ballroom and listened to a rendition of "Under the Juniper Tree" by Louise Cox and a recitation of "My Love Is Like a Red, Red Rose" by Mary C. Canfield—colorless, pedestrian fare compared to the sensuality of Gertrude's performance.

That same month she completed her forty-first and final figure for the El Dorado frieze to be installed the following year at the Panama-Pacific International Exposition in San Francisco. She organized a Committee of Mercy "Fashion Fete" at the Ritz Carlton, had thirty-two guests for tea to meet Anna Pavlova and then attended another event—the bloodiest holocaust the world had known.

In July of 1914, Austria declared war on Serbia. In August, Germany declared war on Russia and France, Great Britain declared war on Germany. But in the United States the war seemed remote. Elsa Maxwell said that to most Society women the Great War was "simply a beastly inconvenience that interfered with their annual trips abroad," but Gertrude spent $250,000 of her own money and personally organized a group of four surgeons and fifteen nurses headed by Dr. Hugh Auchincloss of New York's Presbyterian Hospital. She supplied ten motor ambulances, one thousand blankets, clothing, bales of lint, dressings, and other medical supplies, and sailed for France to establish her own 225-bed hospital in the ancient Collège de Juilly, near Soissons. Gertrude declared her hospital neutral, saying, "Germans will receive as much attention as the French or English wounded," then was surprised to find that it was dark-skinned Algerians and Moroccans who provided the initial cannon fodder. A doctor at her hospital predicted that "the greater speed of the bullets, as compared to former ones, will cauterize wounds and prevent infection." He was wrong. Gangrenous limbs were commonplace and the smell of rancid flesh assailed Gertrude's nostrils.

In April of 1915 Gertrude returned to America on the *Lusitania* because her daughter Flora was suddenly taken ill. Within the week, her brother Alfred boarded the same ship on what was to be its final voyage. The day after the *Lusitania*'s sinking, Harry's chestnut Thoroughbred Regret tore across the finish line of the Kentucky Derby two lengths in front of the next horse to become the only filly to win the Derby. Then in deference to Gertrude's loss, Harry removed the Eton blue and brown Whitney colors from the racing circuit for a year, thus sacrificing a potential $100,000 in winnings.

After a week with Harry and her children, Gertrude boarded the White Star liner *Adriatic* to return to her hospital. In her absence, the Germans had begun using chlorine gas. Now, in addition to battle wounds, there were scalded eyes, lungs, and stomach linings to be treated. A great typhus epidemic swept the troops. Lights out was set at eight-thirty to avoid the attack of zeppelins. Gertrude dwelt amid the constant din of war and the human debris it created. She expanded her hospital to accommodate five hundred men and dispatched teams of doctors and nurses into the field with tents to establish first-aid stations —*Postes Secours*—to stanch the first blood and remove the largest fragments of shrapnel.

In June she crossed the Atlantic once more to an America whose daily life was scarcely touched by the war. In the last half of 1915 Gertrude became chairman of a benefit for French War Relief (for the occasion Society women wore black evening gowns and no jewelry). She had an appendectomy, worked on a fountain for the Colony Club, arranged two art exhibitions, took a cross-country trip in Harry's private railroad car, the *Wanderer*, rode in Harry's new hydroplane, and went sailing on Harry's new 175-foot, $250,000 yacht, the *Whileaway*.

Gertrude could never have kept up with this schedule and continued her active participation in the art world had it not been for Juliana: Juliana Rieser Force was the daughter of a Doylestown, Pennsylvania, grocer. She opened a stenography business in Manhattan in 1908 and began working for Helen Hay Whitney, transcribing her poetry and keeping her social calendar. One day she was commandeered by Helen's sister-in-law Gertrude to type a manuscript, and in 1914 she was summoned to 8 West Eighth Street for an interview concerning full-time employment to organize Gertrude's art activities. Juliana reported to Eighth Street, opened the small wooden door, ascended the steep stairway, and walked into what was to become her life.

Gertrude's selection of Juliana Force had been instinctive and unerringly correct. Juliana was no meek underling—she was vital, straightforward, possessed of an artistic sensitivity and a quicksilver mind. Within a short time she was acting as a buffer between Gertrude and the constant demands of the artists, and she was guarding Gertrude's privacy with the ferocity of a Cerberus.

These two women were a contrast in types: Gertrude was dark, thin, aristocratic, reserved; Juliana, a year older than Gertrude, was amber-haired, blue-eyed, and extroverted. The artist Peggy Bacon characterized Juliana Force as "dependably indiscreet, brutally witty; she talks effectively, constantly, sparing no feelings, letting people know exactly where they stand. . . ." Gertrude spoke in measured phrases in a low, melodic, drawling voice which was never raised.

Lloyd Goodrich, the first director of the Whitney Museum, said of Gertrude, "Some people took Mrs. Whitney to be shy. Not I. She was reserved, which is quite a different thing. She had the supreme assurance that makes it unnecessary to throw your weight around. Mrs. Force was perfect for her, she liked nothing better than a good fight. She was quick on the trigger, volatile, opinionated, and absolutely loyal. Force was the right name for her."

Juliana had known little about art, but she gobbled up knowledge with a voracious energy. She befriended Village artists as well as the misanthropic art critic Forbes Watson, who became her mentor, guiding her in her choices among the artists who sought patronage and exhibitions. Watson said of Gertrude and Juliana:

> Americans love success stories and I think they like them most when they do not follow the rules and supply no aphorisms. The only aphorisms that I could suggest after years of seeing Mrs. Force and Mrs. Whitney together are, first and foremost: never bore the boss, and secondly: be there when the boss wants something done. These rules Juliana Force obeyed by instinct. If Juliana Force had bored Gertrude Whitney there would be no Whitney Museum of American Art. . . . There was nothing goody-goody about either of them.

At first, Gertrude regarded Juliana as on a level with her uptown secretary who handled the Whitney social life, but soon this remarkable woman became Gertrude's indispensable friend and confidante, and, after a time, director of the Whitney art endeavors. Juliana Force understood the aesthetics of art and, perhaps more important, she recognized the nourishment and release the bohemian world provided for Gertrude. The parties Juliana arranged were always lively and uninhibited. At one particularly uproarious party, Juliana and artist Gerald Kelly sat in a bathtub drinking champagne while the guests cavorted about them. At another party, after a great deal of drinking, a sculptor picked Gertrude Whitney up by the waist and spun her around and around. A shocked John Sloan stepped forward to stop the man but Juliana held him back and told him not to interfere.

A high point of this period was "The Works of Indigenous Sculptors and Painters" exhibition, organized as a Red Cross benefit. In two rooms of the Eighth Street house blank canvases were hung on the walls and the painters drew lots for them. (Eugene Higgins, who specialized in miniatures, drew the largest canvas.) In the next three days the artists were required to complete a painting. The center of the room held a long wooden table on which reposed an endless supply of paint, brushes, bottles of Scotch and rye, and food: artists ate, drank, and painted, around the clock. George Luks, unused to such plenty, became quite drunk. With a sweep of his brush, he sloshed paint over Goldbeck's canvas, saying, "You ought to round up the head." When Gertrude entered the room, Luks staggered up to her, breathing his whiskey breath in her face. He stayed at her side until she demanded, "Mr. Luks—why do you keep following me?"

"Mrs. Whitney—because you are so God damn rich," he replied.

Even Gertrude's children loved the free spirit of Eighth Street. Her daughter Flora said, "It was the gayest place that ever was. When we were kids it was very exciting to be invited there. Mother would pack a big metal hamper and we'd drive down from our house on Sixty-eighth Street for a picnic lunch."

Juliana was put in charge of renovating a house at 147 West Fourth Street to house the Whitney Studio Club. This club provided more space for the exhibition of American art, as well as a social atmosphere in which ideas could be exchanged. There were supposed to be club dues—there never were. The founding members of the club included: George Bellows, Thomas Hart Benton, Alexander Brook, Jo Davidson, Stuart Davis, William Glackens, Edward Hopper, Rockwell Kent, Yasuo Kuniyoshi, Jules Pascin, Guy Pène du Bois, Charles Sheeler, Everett Shinn, John Sloan, Eugene Speicher, and William Zorach—a list

The many facets of Gertrude's life: top left, with Harry Payne Whitney

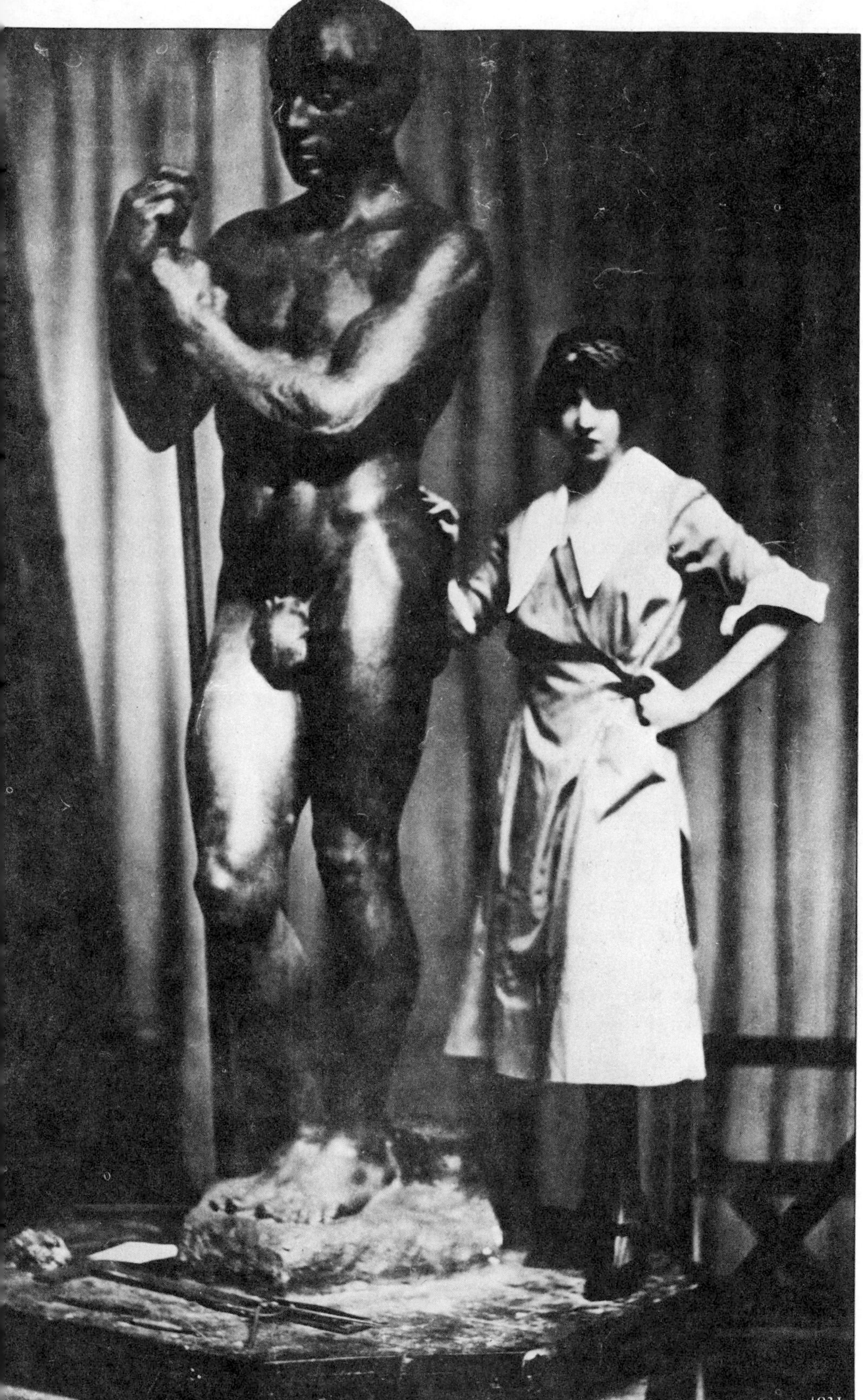
1921

that later would read like a *Who's Who in American Art.* There were life classes on the top floor. Sometimes twenty cents was collected from each artist to help defray the cost of the model. Sheriff Bob Chanler's fiancée of the moment, Lily Lagler, posed as their nude model. Gertrude took this class with other artists.

Many exhibitions at the Studio Club opened with a tea where uptown caterers provided fancy cakes and tiny crustless white-bread sandwiches which the impoverished artists, many of whom were literally starving, would grab and cram into their mouths. Sometimes special artists were invited to Gertrude's mansion at 871 Fifth Avenue. Niles Spencer, who went to such a party feeling self-conscious and out of place, looked across the room and was relieved to see a man who, like himself, seemed uncomfortable. He approached this man and remarked, "I suppose you come from below Fourteenth Street, too." The man was so taken aback by this remark that he backed away from Spencer and inadvertently sat down on an immense chocolate cake placed on the table behind him. He was Gertrude's brother Reggie Vanderbilt.

Gertrude remained in America for the duration of the war; the U-boat menace made it too dangerous to risk another crossing. In 1917 mustard gas was added to the vocabulary of war. Men whose skin had been burned off their faces and bodies were carried into her hospital. In the spring of 1917, Soissons was selected as the center of the major French campaign to repel the enemy forces. Spies discovered the battle plan and the German troops were pulled back some twenty-five miles. As they retreated they pursued a scorched-earth policy—they poisoned the wells, booby traps and field mines were sowed deep in the charred earth. In their pursuit of the Germans, French soldiers died by the thousands—120,000 on one April day. Gertrude's hospital was in the center of the destruction. What had started as an abstract concept of private philanthropy became, in that place of pain and death, a desperately inadequate repository for the dead and dying.

After the war Gertrude recorded her experiences in such sculptures as *Gassed*, *In the Trenches*, *The Spirit of the Red Cross Nurse*, *Doughboy*, *Refugees*, *Private in the 15th*, *Orders*, *Honorably Discharged.* Her figures became more massive and muscular (clearly showing the influence of Auguste Rodin, who in later years was credited with being her teacher, but who in fact had merely commented on her work). She created large memorials: two panels for the Victory Arch to be temporarily erected at Madison Square; the Washington Heights Memorial at 168th Street and Broadway, the Harbor Memorial at St. Nazaire, France, commemorating the landing of the first American Expeditionary Forces on June 26, 1917, the Columbus Monument, a monolithic statue 114 feet tall, dominating the port of Palos, Spain.

In the harsh crucible of war, Gertrude's decorative work might well have been transmuted into art, but it seemed lifeless. Even her most ardent admirers saw her as an adequate but not gifted artist. Art critics questioned how much of her own labor went into her larger memorials; her long, blood-red fingernails which were professionally manicured daily, hardly marked her as a committed sculptor. Critics further noted the lack of emotional content in her work: the fact that Gertrude had cut herself off from her feelings could no more be disguised in her sculpture than it could in her life.

Although in the abstract she had dearly loved her brother Reggie, in actuality she had little contact with him. During the summer of 1924, Harry wrote to Gertrude in Paris saying that he had visited Alice Vanderbilt at The Breakers and that "Regi had been upsetting her. . . . Regi was drunk & apparently is most of the time." Gertrude's sister Gladys (Countess Széchényi) had asked Harry "to take him to task" but Harry felt that was "impossible." Within the year, Reggie was dead.

In the next few years Reggie's child assumed little importance in Gertrude's life. She began spending increasingly long periods of time in Paris working on commissions; in the United States she continued her bountiful support of American art. In 1928, Gertrude Whitney had decided to disband the Whitney Studio Club whose unpaid membership had swelled to an unwieldy four hundred, with a long waiting list. In a final statement, Gertrude and Juliana Force noted that "artists for whom twelve years ago it was necessary to fight are now in high favor. More than this a general liberal movement in art is in high favor. The primary work for which the Club was organized has been done . . . the liberal artists have won the battle which they fought so valiantly."

Not quite—the following year Gertrude sent Juliana to the Metropolitan Museum of Art to offer them her entire collection of more than six hundred contemporary American works, with enough money to build and maintain a wing of the museum to house the collection. Juliana carried the offer to the Metropolitan's director, Dr. Edward Robinson, who told her, "We don't want any more Americans. We have a cellar full of that kind of painting."

Juliana stalked out of his office and returned to Eighth Street to Gertrude and Forbes Watson. Over lunch at the Brevoort Hotel the idea of keeping the collection intact until it was appreciated was born and, by the time lunch ended, the concept of the Whitney Museum of American Art had become a fait accompli.

On October 29, 1929, the stock market crashed; Harry Payne Whitney found himself in possession of nearly 400,000 shares of worthless stock. However, the demand for gold escalated the value of his holdings in the Hudson Bay Mining Company and his other mine stocks held fast. He lost a few million, gained a few, and came out ahead of the game. He boasted to his family, "One day you can tell your children that I'm one of the few who made money during the Crash and the Depression."

As the years progressed, Harry's steady consumption of alcohol affected his liver, and he complained about his health with such regularity that many of his relatives and friends assumed he was a hypochondriac. He seemed a lonely man and when Gertrude was away he was known to lock himself in his darkened bedroom at Wheatley Hills and drink.

On the night of October 21, 1930, Harry returned to 871 Fifth Avenue after a business day. He had a cold and a fever and stayed in bed the next day, calling his physician, Dr. John Augustus Hartwell. For years, Josh Hartwell had been friend as well as physician to the Whitneys. Harry and Josh belonged to many of the same clubs and they'd gone fishing together in Canada and shooting together in Scotland. Recently Hartwell had helped Gertrude over a bout of phlebitis. Within the year he would become her lover.

Hartwell was not alarmed by Harry's condition, and told him to remain quiet and drink plenty of fluids. On Thursday, Hartwell came again and said the cold had turned to pneumonia, but that it was not severe and there was no need for concern. But Harry's liver was damaged and he suffered from hardening of the arteries; he seemed to grow weaker and weaker. Other physicians were called in but could do nothing. His temperature rose, he did not respond to oxygen. Finally, the family was called; first Gertrude, then, one by one, his children gathered in his bedroom—Flora Miller, Sonny Whitney, and Barbara Henry accompanied by her husband, Barklie. Gertrude watched Harry gasping for breath, scarcely believing what she was seeing. At 9:35, Saturday evening, Harry Payne Whitney died. He was fifty-eight.

Gertrude performed one final act in connection with her husband. She called for a craftsman, who coated Harry Payne Whitney's face with tincture of green soap, then carefully mixed and applied the plaster. The white mass hardened and dried. It was then removed. Gertrude packed the brittle shell away and later that year dispatched it with

Flora to Paris, with instructions to give it to Jo Davidson to execute a sculpture from this mask of death.

Harry left an estate of $72 million, mainly in trust for his children and grandchildren. He left Gertrude his personal effects, Wheatley Hills, and 871 Fifth Avenue (with the stipulation that the residence be razed upon her death). He made no gifts to charity, but asked that Gertrude and his children "continue the support I have given during my life to public institutions and charities."

November 18, 1931: The Whitney Museum of American Art opened its doors to the public. On a national radio hook-up, the soft, measured voice of Gertrude Vanderbilt Whitney announced how "terribly pleased" she was on this occasion. The museum had the distinct personal touch of a family enterprise: Gertrude had purchased four Eighth Street houses, and Flora's husband G. Macculloch Miller's architectural firm of Noel & Miller had designed the renovation. The façade was pink stucco with large glass doors through which was visible a half-round staircase encircling a fountain designed by Gertrude. There were eleven galleries of American art. In the first hung Arthur B. Davies's *Crescendo*, where posturing nudes stood with arms extended in an enchanted mountain valley. This canvas was valued at $25,000 (Gertrude had been considered extravagant when she'd purchased it for $1,000). George Bellows's seething canvas of the Dempsey-Firpo fight hung near George Luks's portrait of Mrs. Gamley clutching a white rooster. Across the way was Eugene Speicher's portrait of Fira Barchak. At the top of the stairs Jo Davidson's serious, thoughtful head and shoulders of Gertrude was enshrined on a pier of speckled granite. Three years later Nathan Burkan, Gloria Vanderbilt's lawyer, would try to prove that the work exhibited at the Whitney Museum of American Art—the work of Sloan, George Luks, Guy Pène du Bois, and of Gertrude Vanderbilt Whitney herself—was pornographic.

But within a decade, the time when Gertrude had been young and sensual and the artists she had helped had been starving and unrecognized would be forgotten. Fame, wealth, and age would lend these vivid personalities the patina of respectability. Renegade artists would become the Old Masters of American art—serene, successful. Gertrude Vanderbilt Whitney, within her own lifetime, would be transmuted into something not quite human—an oracle, a patron, an institution in herself, far removed from the surge of life.

A Nightmare Only Money Could Buy

Little Gloria slept in the room next to me, and she used to waken at night screaming with nightmares. I went in and tried to comfort and quiet her . . . she looked and acted so ill.

GERTRUDE VANDERBILT WHITNEY, SUMMER, 1932

ON THE NIGHT of June 17, 1932, Gloria returned to the Sherry-Netherland at 4:00 a.m. The living room was a blaze of light and her mother and nurse Keislich were waiting there to tell her that little Gloria had had a dreadful stomach attack and that Dr. Schloss had left about an hour earlier. Gloria told her mother to go home and the nurse to go to bed; then she went in and sat at her sleeping daughter's bedside, remaining there throughout the night and into the next day, thereby missing the *Leviathan* which sailed without her—she booked passage a week later on the *Mauretania*. On her last afternoon in New York, Gertrude Vanderbilt Whitney dropped by for a visit and told Gloria that she had spoken to both Dr. Schloss and Dr. Craig and that they thought little Gloria was not yet up to going to Oakland Farm. Then Gertrude asked casually, "Why not let me take her into the country at Old Westbury?"

Gloria replied, "That is very kind of you, Gertrude."

And it was settled.

. . .

The day after Gloria sailed, nurse Keislich packed their belongings and Gertrude sent her limousine to bring them to Wheatley Hills in Old Westbury. In the limousine Dodo sat on one side of little Gloria and a bodyguard sat on the other side. The cityscape soon gave way to green, and from miles away the windmill tower, which stood at the highest point on the Whitney property, seemed to beckon them. At the fieldstone gate house on Whitney Lane the limousine turned and entered the Whitney estate, moving past green fields marked off geometrically with white split-rail fences. Over the next two years little Gloria would become familiar with this estate. There was Gertrude Whitney's own Venetian-style mansion, the former William C. Whitney house, and three other residences for her children—Sonny and his second wife, Gwladys (nicknamed Gee); Flora and her second husband, G. Macculloch (Cully) Miller; and Barbara and her husband, Barklie (Buz) Henry. Also on the estate was the residence of Harry's sister Dorothy (Mrs. Leonard Elmhirst). There was a gymnasium with an indoor tennis court and swimming pool. The famous Whitney stable had sixty-three stalls, each opening onto the green lawn; there was an indoor riding ring and the outdoor polo field where Harry Whitney's Big Four polo team had practiced.

In the piazza at the front of her house, Gertrude Whitney was waiting for them. In winter this enormous area was glassed in, but on this late June day it was swathed in a diaphanous veil of mosquito netting. Gertrude had prepared for little Gloria's arrival by hiring extra detectives: "Since the kidnaping and murder of the Lindbergh baby, no child seems safe, especially no one with the name *Vanderbilt*," observed Gertrude's biographer, and besides, her niece had received a direct kidnap threat. Little Gloria was put in a room next to Gertrude's own, with a bathroom and small corridor separating them. Nurse Keislich's room was across the hall, but she refused it, insisting that she *always* slept in the same room with the child.

Little Gloria had come straight from her bed at the Sherry-Netherland to this isolated country estate peopled with strangers. The child looked around the room with its fireplace, mahogany chiffonier, tall windows—then she clutched her stomach in pain. She was promptly put to bed. Gertrude Whitney knew almost nothing about the child or her nurse—she had no idea that the nurse might be overprotective, or that the child might be aware of the kidnapping threat and was in fear for her life. But Gertrude wished to be scrupulously careful of the responsibility she had assumed; as a result, little Gloria was forced to endure a medical nightmare only money could buy.

Within an hour of the child's arrival, Gertrude herself telephoned to Dr. Everett C. Jessup and asked him to come immediately since her niece was quite ill. Jessup lived nearby in Roslyn, and was director of medical services at the North Country Community Hospital in Glen Cove. Dr. Schloss had recommended him as the local physician—"the man on the spot"—in case they needed a pediatrician for little Gloria. Jessup examined the child, who seemed exhausted; her stomach was distended and had gas in it. The next day he came twice—little Gloria seemed better.

Four days later nurse Keislich phoned Dr. Jessup to say that little Gloria had experienced half an hour of dizziness, followed by severe pain on her right side. Jessup made three separate visits that day and located a mass in the lower right side of the child's abdomen. He thought that she might be having an appendix attack. To see if her white blood count was elevated, he asked the child to extend her finger, and pricked it. Jessup then asked Mrs. Whitney to come into the room and, in front of little Gloria, requested that she telegraph the child's mother for permission in case an immediate operation was needed.

Gertrude sent the cable and then, concerned about her niece's illness, decided to telephone Dr. John Hartwell, who in the past two years had become her ardent lover and trusted friend. Josh Hartwell bore a strong resemblance to Franklin Delano Roosevelt, down to the long, thin cigarette holder that he clamped between his teeth at the same jaunty forty-five-degree angle. In his youth he'd been a great athlete and was still in excellent physical condition. Because he was a physician and moved in Gertrude's own social circle their affair flourished unnoticed. Josh spent every moment he could with Gertrude, secretly meeting her at her studios in Old Westbury and in New York City, and even posing for her to secure an extra few minutes of her time. His devotion to Gertrude was so obvious that once, after he had treated her granddaughter Gerta Henry for a leg infection, the seven-year-old child asked, "Are you going to marry Dr. Hartwell?"

Taken aback for one of the few times in her life, Gertrude replied, "Certainly not, he's too young for me." Hartwell, at sixty-five was, in fact, eight years older than Gertrude, but he'd been married for twenty-two years.

Josh Hartwell came immediately when summoned; he spoke to Dr. Jessup, who told him that he was not sure of his own diagnosis. It was then arranged that the following morning Hartwell, Jessup, and Schloss would all see the child. Although Schloss was no longer seeing private patients, he felt an obligation to this little girl whom he'd been treating since her infancy. The other doctors didn't know her at all, and Schloss thought he should explain the psychological factors he was convinced were involved in her illness.

The child had been at Wheatley Hills less than a week when these three eminent physicians congregated at her bedside. Again the child's finger was pricked for a blood count. Keislich produced a stool specimen. Little Gloria no longer complained of stomach pain but had developed a cough. After examining the child, the three doctors went with Mrs. Whitney and nurse Keislich into the library. In such formidable company, Jessup was tentative in his diagnosis, saying that the symptoms might indicate appendicitis, but an infected gland or a kidney condition were also possibilities. Hartwell made no diagnosis but told Gertrude reassuringly that he doubted it was appendicitis. Dr. Schloss was convinced that the source of the child's illness was fear and the person responsible for that was sitting not five feet from him—nurse Keislich. He didn't confront the nurse but said pointedly that he was sure little Gloria's symptoms "were due to a considerable degree to mental and emotional upset." The child suffered from "a nervous condition that caused her to magnify any discomfort she felt or perhaps even to complain of more discomfort than she actually felt." After the nurse left the room he explained to Jessup and Hartwell that the problem was due to the attitude of the nurse and the mother's frequent absences. He was sure there was no pathological reason for the child's illness.

Jessup disagreed. He had suggested three possible areas of physical impairment and he was not going to have them dismissed by Schloss. Determined to justify his position, the following morning he suggested to Mrs. Whitney that he and Dr. Craig examine the child to make sure that the trouble did not come from her nose or throat. Little Gloria was sitting up in Gertrude Whitney's own bed when Craig arrived. After examining her he concluded that her nose and throat were perfectly normal. Jessup found that her stomach was also normal, so Gertrude Whitney cabled Gloria Vanderbilt that the child would not need the appendectomy.

During the next four days Dr. Jessup visited every day looking for a pathological reason for little Gloria's illness. On the second day he noted that her oral temperature was 99.6 degrees. In his opinion, 99 degrees was normal, and anything above that indicated a fever, especially in so delicate and special a child. Jessup took another blood count which proved normal and by the end of the week little Gloria was able to be up for part of the day and to go out and sit in the sun. Gertrude, thinking the child on her way to recovery, left for The Breakers to visit her sick mother. Keislich was left in charge.

At last nurse Keislich had at her command all the medical help she felt she needed. The day after Gertrude Whitney left for Newport, Drs. Schloss, Craig, Jessup, and his assistant Dr. Carman all were summoned by nurse Keislich. Little Gloria's only symptoms were a slight cough and the 99.6 temperature—Craig and Schloss agreed that the child had nothing more than a common cold.

The next day Schloss was called yet again to the Whitney residence, where a worried nurse Keislich explained that the child was constipated and had complained of stomach pain, but Schloss could find nothing of a serious nature wrong with her and recommended mild measures—a bland diet to cause as little intestinal irritation as possible; prune juice and bran cereal to get her bowels moving. After Schloss left, nurse Keislich called Dr. Jessup who, unaware of Schloss's visit, suggested that the child receive enemas and mineral oil and that acid milk be substituted for sweet milk in her diet. Keislich zealously administered all the remedies suggested.

Schloss in turn knew nothing of Jessup's visit, but in a phone conversation the following day Schloss told him that the child's atmosphere was what needed altering. Jessup ignored this advice and ordered that little Gloria be given a Mantoux test for tuberculosis, thinking that the origin of her cough might lie in this area (Schloss had performed the same test in March). The result showed a slight redness, but no active infection.

On the following Monday, Gertrude returned to Wheatley Hills, exhausted by the double burden of her mother's illness and that of her niece. Earlier that month, she had planned a short trip to Europe to take a cure at the Châtel-Guyon spa, followed by a love tryst with Josh Hartwell in Orléans, but she felt that in all good conscience she could not leave until her niece's health improved. Gertrude had been totally unprepared for the sick, nervous child who'd arrived at Wheatley Hills. Little Gloria couldn't speak without stammering and her face twitched. Her room was next to Gertrude's own, and in the night the child would wake screaming; that piercing animal sound would jolt Gertrude from her bed and she'd throw on a robe and join the nurse in trying to comfort her niece. Josh told her that Dr. Schloss was sure that the nurse's apprehensiveness caused little Gloria's fear, but Gertrude disagreed. On those awful nights it was nurse Keislich who was a calming presence, who did everything in her power to soothe this strange child. The child loved her, and she loved the child as her own. Gertrude was sure that without the constancy of nurse Keislich, little Gloria would be lost.

Little Gloria was absolutely convinced that something terrible was going to be done to her; that she was going to die. Gertrude began searching for the reason why she felt this way. Both the nurse and Mrs. Morgan had told her of the privations little Gloria had been forced to endure, but now Gertrude listened to these women with a new, firsthand awareness of her niece's pathetic condition. Laura Morgan's most shocking accusation was that her own daughter would bring about her granddaughter's death: neglect was one possible way, not protecting her from kidnappers was another, direct murder was a third! Mrs. Morgan said that there were many ways little Gloria might die, but die she would, so that Gloria could inherit her millions—Gertrude's brother's money, Vanderbilt money.

Mrs. Morgan might be unstable, a hysteric about the extremes to which her daughter would go for money, but in little Gloria's desperation Gertrude found mute evidence to substantiate this accusation. Laura Morgan accused her daughter of wanting to murder little Gloria, and the child acted as if she knew she *was* going to be murdered. Night after night, Gertrude heard little Gloria's screams coming from the next room, and the passionate bohemian, the other Gertrude, put the final touches on *Walking the Dusk*, her gothic tale of depravity in the midst of luxury, of sexual perversion, and of murder. She wrote, "I felt myself to be two people, one a woman moving peaceably in an ordinary, rather gay life, the other a sleuth, terror-stricken at moments, eagerly catching at threads of information, acutely aware of things up to now unnoticed."

When both Schloss and Jessup agreed that little Gloria was on the road to recovery, a relieved Gertrude made the final arrangements for her niece to go to Oakland Farm and embarked for France. Nurse Keislich was again left in charge and she began to worry that her "baby lamb" might not be as well protected at Oakland Farm as she was at Wheatley Hills where they were well guarded with an "outside man" and an "inside man." It was then that she decided, on her own initiative, that little Gloria was still too sick to travel and told her that she must stay in bed.

By morning little Gloria was again complaining of stomach pain. Keislich called Dr. Jessup, who examined her; again he felt a definite mass in her lower abdomen, but two days later the pain and the mass had disappeared. Jessup planned his own vacation within the week; he had little time left to find the cause of the child's illness. On Sunday he arrived at Wheatley Hills with his assistant, Dr. Carman. Jessup left the child with Dr. Carman, who pierced her finger for a blood count.

On Monday, at Keislich's insistence, Jessup examined little Gloria twice. On Tuesday morning he returned with a radiologist, Dr. Williams, from North Country Community Hospital. The child was told to drink barium, and a complete X-ray series was taken of her intestinal tract. Her head, sinus, and chest were also X-rayed.

In studying the X-rays and Williams's accompanying report, Jessup finally found what he had been seeking: there was a congenital narrowing in the child's cecum, the first part of her colon, and above that a widening two or three times the normal diameter. In the transverse colon to the right were two U-shaped loops of gut. Jessup felt that when these U-shaped loops constricted, a blockade was caused, trapping fecal matter in the dilated portion of the child's colon. When this area filled with excrement, you could feel the mass, and the child experienced pain.

Jessup called Schloss to explain his discovery. Schloss was skeptical; he'd seen these changes very frequently in the gastrointestinal tracts of perfectly normal individuals.

To Schloss, the X-rays did not adequately account for the child's symptoms. Unless the abdomen was cut open and looked into, you could never be sure. Despairing of ever convincing Jessup to consider psychological areas, Schloss said that he was on vacation and suggested that if the trouble persisted, Jessup should contact Dr. Hutton in New York City. The next day Jessup called Hutton, who, over the telephone, prescribed tincture of belladonna, five minims three times a day, a favorite remedy for spasms of the gastrointestinal tract. Nurse Keislich added this remedy to all the others.

NOT GOING NEWPORT REMAINING
WESTBURY BY DOCTORS ORDERS
GLORIA SENDS LOVE
E KEISLICH

The nurse took it upon herself to send this cable to Gloria at Nada Milford Haven's villa in Cannes. Then she picked up the telephone and called George Wickersham, explaining that both Mrs. Whitney and Mrs. Vanderbilt were in Europe and that the latter had left her with only $150. She'd received no wages since May and had no money. She mentioned that the doctors had said the child was too ill to be moved.

Wickersham sent the nurse $200 and then telephoned Dr. Schloss to say that he was distressed to hear that the child was not well enough to travel. Schloss said that in his opinion the child *was* well enough and added "a change of atmosphere can only do the child good." He recommended a Newport physician who he was sure could handle the case.

Wickersham was confused by the differing stories and so he went to Wheatley Hills to see for himself. When he arrived, little Gloria seemed "cheerful and bright," but Wickersham did not want to take it upon himself to make the final decision. He requested that both Schloss and Craig see her again to make sure she was well enough to make the trip. During the next week, little Gloria was examined every day; then

Dr. Schloss firmly told nurse Keislich that the child *must* be taken to Oakland Farm.

Over a six-week period little Gloria had been attended by eight physicians. They had examined her more than fifty times at a cost of thousands of dollars. They had found nothing.

The day that Gloria arrived in Paris she had been alarmed to receive a cable from Gertrude asking permission to perform an appendectomy on little Gloria. Gloria cabled her permission, saying that if an operation were to take place she would return to New York immediately. A few days later a second cable came from Gertrude rescinding the first. This was followed by a cable from the nurse saying that little Gloria was too ill to go to Oakland Farm, but within three weeks Gloria received a letter from her daughter from the farm, and it certainly did not sound as if she was desperately ill. Little Gloria wrote:

> *Dear Momey,*
>
> *I am having a very nice time. Cousin Ann bought a donkey when she was in Italy and we have lots of fun with him.*
>
> *Will you bye me a fancy beaded bag because Emily has one. I hope that you are having a nice time . . .*
>
> *Love from Gloria*

Gloria concluded that all the cables were part of a continuing plot to harass her by making her unnecessarily apprehensive about her child's health. For the month of August she'd decided to join Nada in Cannes where she'd rented the spectacular Villa Domaine de la Croix des Gardes. July was the fashionable month in Cannes—Gloria had never been there in August—she thought the experience great fun. Consuelo was staying at the Carlton and, in a welter of publicity, Thelma and the Prince of Wales came from Biarritz to visit. At summer's end Gloria went to Paris with her personal maid and instructed Maria to begin closing the house. Moving was expensive and twice Gloria was forced to cable for the money to pay the movers. She found it humiliating.

As soon as possible, she went to Lynden Manor to say goodbye to Nada and Edwina Mountbatten, who were about to leave on a trip from the Black Sea to the Persian Gulf across the deserts of Persia. Edwina, in particular, had had quite enough of Society for a while. Earlier that year a London magazine, the *People*, had printed an item referring to ". . . one of the leading hostesses in the country, a woman highly connected and immensely wealthy. Her associations with a coloured man became so marked that they were the talk of the West End. Then one day the couple were caught in compromising circumstances." The item concluded by stating that the lady in question had been exiled to Malta on orders "from a quarter which cannot be ignored." Edwina's husband, Lord Louis Mountbatten, was presently stationed in Malta. There could be no doubt that the woman in question was Edwina. A rumor began that the man was a popular black crooner, Leslie Hutchinson, nicknamed Hutch. Another rumor was that Mrs. Paul Robeson would sue for divorce and name Lady Louis Mountbatten as corespondent. Edwina stepped forward and sued the *People* for libel. In July she won her case, magnanimously refusing a cash settlement. The solicitor for the defense was Theobald Mathew of the firm of Charles Russell & Company. Although he lost the case, Edwina was impressed with him.

As soon as Edwina won her lawsuit, Queen Mary and King George invited the Mountbattens and the Dowager Marchioness of Milford Haven to lunch at Buckingham Palace. The gesture was duly observed by the world press as a sign of support and social acceptance "from a quarter which cannot be ignored."

Edwina, who had taken fifty-six trunks for one month's stay in Mexico, now set off with Nada, who told reporters, "We will take only the clothes we stand up in and one change as well as a light tent and two sleeping bags." She said that there were to be no maids, secretaries, companions, or motion-picture cameras. "If you don't hear from us after three months you'll know the bandits got us," added Nada, laughing.

Constantinople and Palestine were their first two stops. In the Kingdom of Iraq, they dined with King Feisal, who, on hearing their plans to travel through wild country full of bandits, warned them that three weeks previously the U.S. consul had been ambushed and killed by Kurdish tribesmen. They disregarded his warning, purchased an ancient motorcar, and set out over six hundred miles of open desert and mountain ranges never before transversed by a woman. Within three months they had covered approximately 10,000 miles—6,000 by airplane, 4,000 by automobile—crossing both the Great Salt Desert and the Great Sand Desert. "Our only mishap was one puncture and that the chauffeur easily repaired," Nada told reporters, as if they had been for a drive on the Grand Corniche.

On September 5, 1932, another cable arrived for Gloria.

GLORIA MUCH IMPROVED BUT DOCTORS ADVISE
WOULD BE MOST BENEFICIAL FOR HER TO REMAIN
OUT OF TOWN TILL DECEMBER IF I CAN ENTER HER

GREENVALE SCHOOL LONG ISLAND WHICH PREPARES
FOR CHAPIN MAY SHE STAY WITH ME UNTIL THEN
PLEASE ANSWER THE BREAKERS

GERTRUDE WHITNEY

Gloria cabled her assent and on receiving it Gertrude began making plans for her niece, taking her to the Green Vale School, which was located directly opposite Whitney Lane. The school, housed in a Georgian mansion, had the air of a home away from home; the staff was strict but warm. Green Vale's student roster read like the membership list of the Meadow Brook Club; children of minority groups or the nouveau riche need not apply. The pupils lived in the great estates of this area, arriving in the morning in chauffeur-driven limousines or station wagons accompanied by Nanny or Mademoiselle.

Gertrude found little Gloria to be "frightfully backward"—her niece told her that she'd never been to a regular school—so Gertrude spoke to the teachers at Green Vale and arranged that her niece go into a grade a year below her age group and be tutored two or three afternoons a week.

Then Gertrude began to look for a pediatrician to replace Dr. Schloss, who had retired from private practice. She decided on Dr. William P. St. Lawrence. Personable and self-assured, St. Lawrence was as welcome a presence at a dinner party as he was in a child's sickroom. He had a large Society practice which included the children of both Flora and Sonny who "swore by him." Gertrude spoke to Dr. St. Lawrence and made an appointment for him to examine her niece on September 29. When Gloria returned to New York that same week, Gertrude suggested that she go along to meet the new pediatrician. Dr. St. Lawrence greeted Mrs. Vanderbilt and the nurse and spoke briefly to little Gloria before his nurse took her into the examining room. St. Lawrence turned to the two women seated in front of him; he withdrew a printed physician's form from his desk drawer, filled in the child's name and age and skipped the first three categories listed, reasoning that in so famous a family there could be no syphilis, insanity, or alcoholism. As he began inquiring about little Gloria's medical history, he noticed that the nurse did almost all the talking while the mother sat quietly, contributing little. Before long, the nurse began to grate on Dr. St. Lawrence's nerves. She wouldn't stop talking, flitting rapidly from one subject to another before exhausting the first, and weaving back and forth through a series of ideas without any logical progression. What was most irritating to Dr. St. Lawrence was that this garrulous woman fancied she knew more about the proper care of the child than he did.

Nevertheless, he recorded nurse Keislich's observations: the child had enlarged glands; she'd been constipated all her life—she was unable to evacuate her lower bowel—passed gas, and burped. The child was high-strung and would easily grow hysterical. Her tears were "near the surface," she would cry on the slightest provocation; she was incessantly active; she had temper tantrums; she was terrified of the dark and suffered from nightmares and night terrors. The nurse was so insistent in detailing the child's episodes of nocturnal screaming that Dr. St. Lawrence wrote, "Dreams + + Night terrors +."

From little Gloria's mother, Dr. St. Lawrence learned the child was naturally left-handed, and when she'd been forced to use her right hand a stammer had resulted. The mother told him that she too stammered and had been left-handed. St. Lawrence asked what had been given to alleviate the child's constipation? The nurse cited a jumble of medications—cascara, milk of magnesia, bran cereal, prune juice—but failed to mention the mineral oil or the enemas she had administered.

St. Lawrence tried to sort out the information. He asked about the child's diet, and was told that for dinner the child was fed soup, fish, and two vegetables. He noted that she was not getting any starch with dinner, which displeased him. She drank a pint of milk and a pint of water per day. St. Lawrence thought a pint of milk was all right, but soup was not necessary and the child was being given too much water.

As the nurse rambled on, St. Lawrence concluded that there was much here to be changed. The child was not being given proper nourishment, her rest was improper, her activities improper, her background of travel bad—and this nurse! He looked across at her moon face and wrote on his chart: "God awful nurse." As she continued to speak, he wrote: "Lack of proper care." And as she babbled on and on, he put an equal sign next to "God awful nurse" and wrote: "A terrible person for Gloria! She hovers over her like a hen and makes the child self-centered, introspective and a neurasthenic." Then St. Lawrence drew a line up from this observation to the margin and scribbled: "She suffers from a flight of words and ideas."

Finally St. Lawrence excused himself and went into the examining room to see little Gloria. She sat on a white metal table covered with a white linen sheet. Her feet dangled over the side. Her dress, underclothes, coat, and leggings were folded on a chair in the corner. The little girl was quiet and solemn. Dr. St. Lawrence felt that she regarded him with apprehension, but did not cry as he approached her. He noticed that she was unusually pale and tired looking, with dark circles under her eyes.

He helped her down from the table. She was weighed and measured. He observed that the child was thin for her height, age, and sex, being 52¼ inches tall and weighing only 56¾ pounds. Her ribs stood out. Obviously she was poorly nourished which in itself could cause anxiety, he thought, and anxiety could cause constipation.

Little Gloria remounted the three black rubber-coated steps to the examining table, and St. Lawrence began to go over her. When he felt her neck he noted that the child's glands were not enlarged and in his opinion never had been enlarged. The nurse had certainly gotten that wrong, too. As the examination drew to a close, St. Lawrence prepared to take a blood count. Suddenly little Gloria's face began to twitch—she seemed to know exactly what was coming. In a small, terrified voice, she pleaded with him not to prick her, and seemed so upset that St. Lawrence decided to forgo the test. He could tell just from her coloration and behavior that she suffered from secondary anemia.

After St. Lawrence finished examining little Gloria he returned to his office and told Gloria that he thought the child should remain at Wheatley Hills for the time being; that the country life would certainly be good for her health. Gloria offered no objection and left with the nurse and child. It was then that St. Lawrence settled down behind his desk and thought about his new patient: little Gloria had had a great deal of attention devoted to her; many well-known doctors had attended her, but still she was unfit. St. Lawrence was convinced he could succeed in helping this child where the other famous physicians had failed. He asked his secretary to get Dr. Schloss on the line—St. Lawrence discussed the case with Schloss, who reiterated his opinion that there was nothing wrong with the child, insisting that the child's condition was due to her relationship with the nurse and the situation with her mother. St. Lawrence hung up. He was sure Schloss was wrong; this child might be organically normal, but functionally she was abnormal. St. Lawrence was convinced that her night terrors were caused by two factors—"one, chronic constipation; and two, her undernourished state with its consequent instability." He would change all this. However, with that nurse he'd have a hard time getting his way. He agreed with Schloss about one thing, the child needed a completely new atmosphere. At the bottom of the third page of his medical record, he wrote, "See Mrs. Whitney about chucking nurse. . . . Needs new start."

St. Lawrence went to see Gertrude Whitney the next day. The dark woodwork in the library of her Fifth Avenue mansion had, centuries before, been part of an Italian chapel. Along the walls grotesque figures writhed in poses of penance. The white marble fireplace was flanked by two great swirling pilasters. St. Lawrence, somewhat subdued in this awesome atmosphere, explained to an attentive Gertrude Whitney the child's need for a new person to look after her. Mrs. Whitney politely but firmly disagreed with him. Nurse Keislich was devoted to little Gloria, she had seen the nurse try to comfort and protect the child and give her mother love. No, the nurse would stay. However, she assured him of nurse Keislich's full cooperation.

Gertrude Whitney asked to see nurse Keislich; she explained that Dr. St. Lawrence had just been to see her and that he wished to be in complete charge and would insist that the nurse follow his orders. Keislich understood the warning behind Gertrude's tactful words. Miraculously, St. Lawrence found that his apprehensions had been needless. Nurse Keislich was on the telephone that very day asking him for his orders, telling him how much they needed him. St. Lawrence altered the child's diet from the one Schloss had given her, adding pudding and potatoes and strictly limiting her water. He prescribed vitamins, iron, minerals, cod-liver oil, malt in oil, and a special kind of cereal meal available at the food-specialty store Charles and Co. In dealing with the child's constipation, he ordered that no help was to be given her before forty-eight hours had elapsed. He laid down stringent rules under which the child was to be in bed sixteen out of every twenty-four hours. She was to attend Green Vale for half a day only. She was to receive absolutely no physical exercise.

Only six days later Keislich brought little Gloria back to his office. She reported that she had carried out his orders to the letter and that the child had improved beyond all expectations. Dr. St. Lawrence began to change his opinion of this woman; "in spite of her drawbacks, she had a very intense and good interest in the child." Soon St. Lawrence and nurse Keislich became a team, both deriving great satisfaction from the care of little Gloria. Keislich scrupulously followed St. Lawrence's intricate, time-consuming rituals, which made her feel indispensable. She, in turn, praised the results of each new suggestion, which gave the doctor great ego gratification. St. Lawrence was so pleased with the "beautiful result" he was achieving that he repeatedly recommended that little Gloria remain at Wheatley Hills.

Little Gloria stood alone—the forgotten person. No one inquired what she was thinking or feeling, assuming that she thought nothing and felt nothing. The gap in communication, between the adults around her and the child herself, yawned wide. Only Dr. Schloss considered psychological factors, but it didn't occur to him that little Gloria might fear kidnapping; kidnapping was so prevalent that many intelligent adults overlooked the obvious. As a result, eight doctors had subjected little Gloria to a prolonged period of medical torture which in itself could easily drive an "introspective and neurasthenic" child to the brink of a nervous collapse.

We can imagine the situation as little Gloria experienced it. The day after your mother leaves for Europe you are brought to Wheatley Hills, a vast place peopled with strangers—even Aunt Ger is really a stranger. In the night, the terror comes and engulfs you and you wake screaming from the demons in your head. The doctors come—so many—all strangers, except for Dr. Schloss. When your stomach hurts the most, they call Aunt Ger into the room and ask her to get Mummy's permission for an operation. Are they going to do that to you again, put you to sleep and do something to you? The stomach pain disappears and you begin to cough. The doctors keep coming—they prick you and prick you and Dodo saves what should go in the toilet and gives it to them. And they keep undressing you and pricking you. They stick four prongs into your arm, and Dodo keeps looking at the spot to see if it gets red. You can't go to the bathroom—Dodo gives you slippery oil and bran cereal and some kind of drops that turn the water milky, and milk that has turned sour. And the enemas—the water flows into you until you're too full to hold it, and everything comes out into the toilet.

A new doctor makes you drink a thick white liquid, heavier than cream, and then covers you with a heavy silver-colored apron, and puts you in front of a machine that buzzes. And at night you scream and scream while Dodo holds you and tells you there's nothing to fear. After Aunt Ger goes to Europe, Dodo says it's best for you to stay in bed at Wheatley Hills. Finally, after a long time, she says it's all right to get up and go to Oakland Farm. At the farm the terror begins to go away. Dodo finds out that cousin Bill (William H. Vanderbilt) is an important man, a state senator. When she tells him how you've been threatened, he arranges bodyguards for you and for his own daughter Emily, who is only a year younger than you are, and for his baby twin girls. In the fall you're taken back to Wheatley Hills and for the first time in your life they let you go to a real school. Both Dodo and Naney are happy and have stopped worrying about you because as long as you stay where you are you won't be kidnapped. You'll be safe.

When Will I Get My Baby Back?

Your prolonged absence from this country, coupled with your daughter's continued residence with Mrs. Whitney . . . creates a troublesome situation. . . . It is possible the Surrogate may require Mr. Wickersham to discontinue payments to you. . . .

THOMAS B. GILCHRIST, MARCH 1, 1933

ALTHOUGH LITTLE GLORIA was living at Wheatley Hills, Gloria decided to move into her rented Seventy-second Street town house. Her friend from convent days, Agnes Horter, moved in to help her organize the household. Tom Gilchrist also proved most helpful, recommending a butler, Charles Zaug, who had worked for friends of his. Gilchrist also arranged the purchase of a Pierce-Arrow automobile; a chauffeur, Theodore Beesley, came with the car. Consuelo, on a visit to New York, sat next to George Wickersham at a dinner party and couldn't resist complimenting him on the efficiency of the employment agency he was running down at Cadwalader, Wickersham & Taft.

Little Gloria's trust stipend of $4,000 arrived every month; Gloria used these funds to pay her bills until the morning that a two-page bill for $607.15 arrived from DePinna. Without a by-your-leave, nurse Keislich had waltzed herself into the store and purchased twenty-one sweaters for little Gloria, not to mention six dresses, leggings, bloomers, knickers, blouses, hose, and hose stretchers. An irate Gloria complained to Tom that the nurse was running wild at Mrs. Whitney's, and she wouldn't be responsible for this outrageous bill. Furthermore, she announced her intention of closing her charge accounts so it could not happen again. Tom answered that he would try to work out a plan whereby the child's bills might be paid direct from his office. He arranged for extra money to be given Gloria for this bill and for the child's extraordinary medical expenses incurred over the previous summer. Gloria was granted $7,500 in additional monies, which pleased her. She did not realize that control of the $4,000 monthly trust stipend was being wrested from her.

Fall drifted into winter: almost daily newspaper columns mentioned Gloria Vanderbilt's gay presence at the Central Park Casino, the Colony, Jack and Charlie's "21," the Cotton Club in Harlem, El Morocco. In mid-December she spent an evening on the town in the company of her frequent escort, Society gentleman William Rhinelander Stewart. Will Stewart had divorced Laura Biddle (of *the* Philadelphia Biddles) in 1928, and since then he'd established himself as New York's most eligible bachelor, a man who knew just which wines to order, flowers to present, places to go. He was on the board of governors of the Central Park Casino and was a director of the Skouras Theaters; through these two affiliations, he'd become a close friend of a millionaire promoter named Alfred Cleveland (Blumie) Blumenthal. Around midnight, Gloria and Will Stewart went to a party in Blumie's office-apartment which occupied the entire third floor of the Ambassador Hotel.

Blumie greeted Gloria warmly, paying special attention to her. She had two qualities that he considered to be of great value: she was a beautiful woman, and she possessed that magic name, Vanderbilt. At thirty-eight, this five-foot, two-inch dynamo retained the look of a fresh-faced schoolboy. He was a new kind of celebrity, one who had emerged with the Depression. Blumie became instantly famous, said writer Alva Johnston, because he convinced people that he had "ready money" and "a black speck looks big on a pool of red ink."

Five months previously, when Florenz Ziegfeld had died, Blumie had taken over his interests, keeping *Show Boat* out of receivership by paying ten cents on the dollar to Ziegfeld's creditors, reorganizing the company, and announcing that he would produce a new *Ziegfeld Follies*. He'd become so close to Ziegfeld's widow, Billie Burke, that she turned to him for advice on all matters, including what to feed her daughter Patricia's dogs.

Blumie's formula for success was this: dazzle the businessmen with celebrities and the most beautiful show girls in New York; dazzle the politicians and show-business folk with the gleam of the entrepreneur's gold. At Blumie's "the visitor is sometimes uncertain whether he is the guest of honor or the party of the second part," wrote Alva Johnston. "Blumie's parties break up into conferences and his conferences break up into parties. Contracts are served with the liqueurs."

Blumie's opulent, flamboyant image was his own clever creation. He was the son of a San Rafael, California, kosher butcher. (He'd decided to adopt Cleveland as his middle name because "you can't get classier than a president.") While still in his twenties he'd made a fortune buying and selling movie theaters but was wiped out in the Los Angeles panic of 1924 and was carried off to a sanitarium to recuperate. Later that year, he came to New York in the company of his close friend and business associate, United Artists president Joseph Schenck.

During the next five years Blumenthal hit upon the idea of convincing movie studios that they must own their own movie houses: he prodded Warner Brothers and Paramount into frantic competitive bidding for theaters, and forced prices up to three times their former value, taking hefty commissions on the sales. Blumie bought and sold hundreds of theaters and properties in transactions that he boasted totaled "somewhere between $300 and $500 million." The boom climaxed in March of 1929 when Blumie arranged for William Fox to purchase control of Loews, Inc., the corporation that owned Metro-Goldwyn-Mayer and a nationwide chain of film theaters. Blumie negotiated the sale with his friend Loews president Nicholas J. Schenck, and 400,000 shares of Loews, Inc., stock were sold to Fox for $50 million. Blumie's commission was $1,230,000. Then, sensing that the economy had peaked, Blumie promptly converted his own assets into cash and government bonds. When the stock market crashed that fall, Fox's movie empire collapsed with it, and Loews stock fell from 90 to 2. Blumie then sold Fox out for another hefty commission. "God will strike you dead for what you did to me," swore Fox.

In 1927 Blumie had married Ziegfeld show girl Peggy Fears—Charlie Chaplin had introduced them. When they married, Peggy was well known, but the public had never heard of A. C. Blumenthal. "My family wouldn't speak to me for two years after I married him," Peggy recalls. "The day we married he was flat broke, but within the year he'd made $7 million. We both went crazy. Blumie bought four Rolls-Royces. I opened a charge account at Cartier's. One ring cost $250,000. I bought a $65,000 chinchilla coat. We began to give fabulous parties." In addition to the Ambassador office-apartment, Blumenthal bought a twenty-two-room Georgian-style mansion in Larchmont. Here, guests sunned themselves around an immense swimming pool where they talked business, had suntan oil applied by show girls, were rubbed down by masseurs, and exercised in a private gymnasium. In the winter a commodious living room replaced the pool. Music wafted from a concealed $25,000 pipe organ which Blumie played with skill. Movies were previewed in a special building, constructed for that purpose, which also contained an indoor swimming pool.

After the stock-market crash, Blumie made a calculated decision. He was convinced that if he appeared to be famous, he would become so. Also, he'd decided to sue for $2 million in commissions, and wanted public opinion on his side, so he hired the famous press agent Harry Reichenbach to tell the world what a modest genius he was. Newspaper stories began appearing about Blumie; one headline read, WIZARD OF $500,000,000 DEALS HAS KEPT SHYLY OUT OF PAPERS. Blumie confided to reporters that he had closed a $50 million deal in exactly one minute of negotiations in a taxicab. He boasted that by his thirtieth birthday he had sold over one thousand movie theaters. He modestly admitted that he was "worth more than any businessman in America." He said he was surrounded by detectives because he and his wife were such likely kidnap targets.

Soon Blumie, intoxicated by his own publicity, began demanding that Reichenbach get his name in the newspapers daily. When the *Evening Graphic* wanted to run a series on the former loves of his wife, Peggy Fears, Reichenbach vetoed the idea as too tasteless to print, saying that it would be "bad publicity." Blumie shot back—"Any publicity is publicity!"

In the fall of 1930 Blumie found a shortcut to stardom in the person of New York's Mayor Jimmy Walker. The mayor began to show up at Blumie's parties where he would marry show business couples with scores of reporters present. Blumie became a celebrity by the simple expedient of reaching high up and clutching Walker's arm at numerous press conferences. He became known as Walker's "benefactor," although the exact nature of his "benefices," other than party invitations and the company of beautiful show girls, was not made clear. He was dubbed "Premier of Walker's nocturnal cabinet" and was the only person admitted into the mayor's presence day or night without being announced. Before meeting Blumie, Walker had said that he liked to talk politics in "the back room" of a saloon, but by 1930 it was acknowledged that the third floor of the Ambassador was the place where matters in the city of New York were decided, and that Blumie had become the undisputed master of Walker's three-ring circus of business, celebrity, and personal profit.

Dapper and devil-may-care, Jimmy Walker had been the perfect mayor for the high-stepping, freewheeling twenties, but with the onset of the Depression New Yorkers began to take a hard look at their mayor. In his Tin Pan Alley days Walker had written the lyrics, "Will you love me in December as you do in May?" New Yorkers now answered this question in the negative as a series of investigations into city-wide corruption began under the aegis of the incorruptible Judge Samuel Seabury. On September 8, 1931, Seabury subpoenaed Blumie to appear before his legislative committee. His lawyer, Nathan Burkan, advised him to skip the country; Blumie went to Mexico and Burkan told the committee that he did not know his client's whereabouts. Eleven months later, Mayor Walker was called before Governor Franklin Delano Roosevelt for removal hearings. Blumie rode up to Albany with him. At 1:40 p.m. a hush fell over the chamber as Roosevelt appeared in the doorway; he looked around the room and then, his hand resting heavily on the arm of his secretary, began to move forward, his braces creaking as he inched toward his desk. When he reached his destination, he gripped the sides of the desk, then transferred his hands to the arms of the chair, trying to lower himself smoothly into the seat. Unable to do so, he dropped into the chair with a thud. The hearings began. Roosevelt was courteous and in complete control. In question after question, he ascertained that Walker had little explanation for his actions and those of his officials.

On Friday afternoon, August 26, 1932, the hearings were adjourned for the weekend. Walker left the Hall of Governors on Blumie's arm. On Sunday Walker's younger brother George died and the hearings were postponed a week. When Walker attended his brother's funeral, James A. Farley, Roosevelt's presidential campaign manager, was heard to remark, "Jim looks worse than George." That night Walker resigned "effective immediately." As Walker's star fell, Blumie moved on.

After Harry Reichenbach's death in July of 1931, Blumie took over his own promotion, issuing daily announcements of the dramatic shows and musicals he planned to produce, of opening his own grand opera company, of lawsuits against Fox Theaters Corporation and Paramount-Publix Corporation. *The New York Times*'s drama department vowed to keep Blumie's announcements out of the newspaper for one day; they failed when he turned up on the financial page, suing to have the Fox Theaters Corporation removed from receivership so he could obtain the $520,000 in commissions owed him.

Not unlike Count Dracula, Blumie was constantly on the lookout for suitable people to supply his craving: "His ever changing collection of sensational people are the lifeblood of the chatter columns," said Alva Johnston. Gloria Vanderbilt was to become the newest source to feed his insatiable appetite for self-aggrandizement.

Mayor Jimmy Walker
and A. C. Blumenthal
(Blumie)

Gloria with Blumie
at a Repeal party at the
Central Park Casino

As the year of 1933 began, the nation's fortunes hit rock bottom. Twelve and a half million were unemployed; industry was operating at half its 1929 volume; 31,922 businesses and 1,456 banks had failed in the year just ended. One million Americans hit the road, hoping that work existed somewhere. It didn't. In January, Gloria received a cable from Thelma that Papa was desperately ill at Thelma's house in London. Gloria left immediately, and when she arrived it became clear to her that Papa was dying. She settled in to await the end. However, no one at Wheatley Hills knew of this; all they knew was that Gloria was once again in Europe and that there was no word from her. The second semester at Green Vale was about to begin, and not knowing when Gloria would return, Gertrude allowed her niece to continue there. Gertrude was proud of little Gloria's progress—she was gaining weight and was now attending school for the entire day. At first her cousins had teased her because she dressed so differently, but her nurse had gone to DePinna and bought her a suitable wardrobe, and within a short time little Gloria and Gertrude's granddaughter Gerta Henry had become inseparable. However, as time passed, Gertrude began to grow resentful—there was still no word from Gloria, and Gertrude envisioned her trotting around Europe living luxuriously on the child's money with no thought of her daughter. As a matter of principle, Reginald's trust should not be squandered by an outsider, but should be preserved for little Gloria.

When, after three months, there was still no word when Gloria would return, Gertrude discussed the matter with Frank Crocker, who was more than just her lawyer: eleven years previously he'd left his own practice to become Harry's personal business and financial adviser. Frank looked enough like Gertrude's late husband to have been his brother and his social background was equally impressive (he was a descendant of the poet Henry Wadsworth Longfellow). Gertrude and Frank moved in the same social circles, belonged to the same clubs, and both attended St. Bartholomew's Episcopal Church. In the two years since Harry's death, he'd served as an executor of Harry's estate, as a founding trustee of the Whitney Museum of American Art, and had been invaluable in organizing Gertrude's personal finances. Frank Crocker spoke to Thomas Gilchrist about the unfairness of the situation and impressed upon him that Mrs. Whitney hoped he might do something to help and that she was most anxious to meet him personally. Tom Gilchrist was flattered by this assignment and set about showing that he was indeed capable of fulfilling it.

In London Gloria spent her days by her father's bedside, unaware of what was happening in the United States. On Saturday, March 4,

1933, Franklin Delano Roosevelt was inaugurated President of the United States. The following Monday, Americans woke up to a cashless society, as their new President declared a national bank holiday. Within the week, the first piece of Roosevelt legislation, the Emergency Banking Act, which in effect took the country off the gold standard, had been enacted. Monday, March 13, the banks reopened, the tide had begun to turn. The New Deal had arrived.

Five days later, just before dawn, Gloria's father died. His last words to her were that his only regret was that he had written that document denouncing her. Mamma cabled her condolences but would not come to the funeral. Two years previously, after thirty-four years of marriage, she had divorced Harry Morgan in Baltimore, using the method of posting a notice in the local newspaper that he had deserted her. When her daughters expressed their chagrin, Mrs. Morgan said that Papa had been "gallivanting about" with other women for years.

Gloria saw no reason to rush back to New York. The Prince of Wales visited the house almost daily, taking both Thelma and Gloria on his nightly rounds of parties and nightclubs. His public speeches concerned his avowed "war" on England's slums. He described the situation as "truly pathetic" and advocated the immediate demolition of these areas—this being as far as his thinking on the matter had progressed. He was taking magic lessons and had learned the sleight of hand necessary to turn a handkerchief into a Union Jack and was trying to master a trick whereby an egg placed in a paper bag was made to disappear forever.

At the end of March Gloria left for the Milford Havens' Lynden Manor. Gilchrist, not sure where to reach her, had written to her there weeks before. Gloria opened the letter and was shocked by its contents:

Vanderbilt Guardianship

Dear Mrs. Vanderbilt:

. . . Your prolonged absence from this country, coupled with your daughter's continued residence with Mrs. Whitney, who appears to be bearing a substantial portion of the cost of her current maintenance, creates a troublesome situation, regarding which the Surrogate has already spoken to me. You should furnish Mr. Wickersham with an itemized statement showing the manner in which the moneys which Mr. Wickersham has paid to you since your last statement have been expended by you for the benefit of your daughter. It is possible the Surrogate may require Mr. Wickersham to discontinue payments to you under his order and require Mr.

Wickersham himself to apply the moneys directly for your daughter's maintenance.

Please let me know when you expect to return to New York.

Yours very sincerely,
Thomas B. Gilchrist

Gloria, with Thelma as her ally, caught the next ship to New York to see Gilchrist. He repeated that Surrogate Foley was not disposed to continue paying Gloria $4,000 a month when her child was living with Mrs. Whitney. Gloria would be allowed to keep the house, but starting in June she was to receive only $750 a month for her personal expenses; the rent would be paid direct by Mr. Wickersham, as would the wages of nurse Keislich, butler Zaug, and chauffeur Beesley; all her household bills and the garage bills for her Pierce-Arrow would also be paid by Wickersham, the inference being that if Gloria were given the money she could not be trusted to pay these bills.

There were to be other changes: Wickersham was to see a list of the child's medical and personal expenses, drawn up by nurse Keislich. Either Gloria herself or Gertrude Vanderbilt Whitney could approve these expenses and they too would be paid direct.

Gloria was completely bewildered. How could she get by under such reduced circumstances? She explained to Gilchrist that she and Thelma each gave Mamma $250 a month on which to live, and he agreed either to raise her personal allowance to $1,000 a month to cover her mother's maintenance or to pay her mother $250 from his office.

Gloria sat very still. Finally she asked, "Oh, Mr. Gilchrist, when will I get my baby back?"

"Little Gloria seems very happy in the country," Tom Gilchrist replied.

There was another moment of silence, then Gloria began to weep. Looking at Tom, she asked plaintively, "Can't something be done for me to get my baby? Whatever I do is wrong."

Gloria was caught in a circular trap: she could not get $4,000 each month unless little Gloria lived with her. However, Tom Gilchrist was insisting that little Gloria was better off with her aunt, and would not return the child to her.

Thomas Gilchrist drove out to Wheatley Hills to see Gertrude Vanderbilt Whitney. He explained the steps he had taken to protect little Gloria's financial future and assured her that Mrs. Vanderbilt's spending had been brought under careful control. No longer would Mrs. Whitney pay the child's bills while Gloria spent the monies allocated for that purpose on herself. Gertrude then told him that both she and all the doctors involved felt that little Gloria had gained a great deal from being at Wheatley Hills and she would hate to see these gains lost. Gilchrist replied that, although he liked Gloria personally, he had grave reservations about the atmosphere at the Seventy-second Street house. The dangers the child might be exposed to could be of a moral nature, and this awareness had prompted him to place "a trustworthy chauffeur," Theodore Beesley, and a butler, Charles Zaug, in the Vanderbilt household. These servants were to be paid by him and already they had mentioned certain irregularities to him that they considered detrimental to the child's welfare. He had spoken to Mrs. Vanderbilt about these irregularities. He certainly agreed that little Gloria should not live in that house.

Frank Crocker advised Gertrude that legally she could not deny Gloria free access to her daughter, so the following day, Gertrude sent her niece into the city for a visit. Little Gloria arrived at Gloria's house with nurse Keislich and Emily Vanderbilt—it was the first time she'd seen her mother in five months. Gloria let the girls play dress-up in some of her old dresses. They paraded up and down the stairs playing "ladies." Little Gloria said she felt "grand," and "wasn't it swell?" She stroked and hugged her mother's old dress and asked if she could keep it. Nurse Keislich kept looking at her watch and staring out the window. Gloria felt that she couldn't wait to take little Gloria away.

When they arrived back at Wheatley Hills the nurse told Mrs. Whitney that she "was glad that they had not been compelled to spend the night." Everything in that house was very bad for the child. "Everything . . . in every way." Laura Morgan was even more vociferous: she continued to assert that if little Gloria returned to her mother she would surely die. Gertrude began a protracted series of meetings with Crocker, Wickersham, and Gilchrist to discuss "the protection of little Gloria and her inheritance."

Added to all the deleterious information Gertrude heard concerning Gloria was the fact that she continued to lead her life in headlines. Throughout April of 1933 Gloria and Blumie were the objects of intense press speculation. "Rumor Hints Romance," read the caption of a *Daily Mirror* photograph of them. At the Baer-Schmeling fight they were photographed at ringside, Blumie's left arm casually encircling Gloria's back.

News of Blumie's and his wife Peggy's tiffs began filling the columns, mentioning Gloria Vanderbilt as the source of the trouble. Peggy called *World-Telegram* staff writer Helen Worden and informed her that, in spite of Mrs. Vanderbilt, she was still very much married to Mr.

Blumenthal. The *Mirror* printed a triangle of photographs, Peggy and Gloria at the base, Blumie at the apex. Blumie made the most of the situation, calling frequent press conferences to protest the rumors of his romance with a VANDERBILT. On the tenth of June, Blumie, followed by a pack of reporters, left his Ambassador apartment and checked into suite 28H at the Waldorf. Reporters noted that "he paused in the act of signing the register and then picked the name 'Mr. Morgan' out of the air."

Peggy hired lawyer Max Steuer, who decided to serve Blumie with separation papers. Blumie's own lawyer, Nathan Burkan, advised him to secretly engage the services of detective Benjamin Kerin, Broadway Benny, proprietor of the Kerin Detective Agency, to find out exactly what Peggy was planning. Kerin, a small man with thinning sandy hair and a missing front tooth, was the detective Burkan used again and again in his divorce actions. In New York State, adultery was the only admissible ground for divorce, and Benny kept a list of young ladies willing to be caught with a gentleman for a price. He staged "love nest" raids and then supplied photographs of the couples caught in flagrante delicto. Kerin informed Blumie that Steuer's process servers would soon be on their way to the Waldorf. In the past year Blumie had been involved in four lawsuits; presently he was fighting a receivership proceeding and had been subpoenaed to appear in the New York Supreme Court on June 21. Nathan Burkan advised him not to take the stand; Blumie had recently settled his Paramount-Publix suit for an undisclosed amount and the records of the case had been removed from the court files. There had been a great deal of curiosity among the other bondholders of Paramount-Publix as to the terms of Blumenthal's settlement. On the stand Blumie could be questioned on this matter as well as on issues dealing with his association with former Mayor Jimmy Walker.

On Thursday, June 15, various members of the press were tipped off by an anonymous female caller that Gloria Vanderbilt and A. C. Blumenthal were planning to leave the country on the S.S. *Europa* the following night.

At approximately 11:00 p.m. on Friday, a gangway was lowered from the *Europa* and Gloria Vanderbilt, her maid Maria Caillot, A. C. Blumenthal, Broadway Benny, and four of his men were whisked aboard the ship.

Some minutes later Benny Kerin and his men were spotted patrolling the decks which were crowded with newspaper reporters, photographers, and process servers armed with separation papers from Peggy and a Supreme Court subpoena for the receivership proceedings.

Pandemonium reigned as "a swift little game of Blumey, Blumey, who's got the Blumenthal, was played up and down the decks." Neither Gloria Vanderbilt's nor A. C. Blumenthal's name appeared on the passenger list, but reporters found three separate Morgans ("the name reported to be used by Blumenthal at smart hotels since his marital troubles") on the ship's register. They dashed into one suite but were greeted by an angry woman who was sailing with her children; two other staterooms turned up two more Morgans, but no Mr. Blumenthal and no Mrs. Vanderbilt.

Dejected reporters clustered around Broadway Benny, grilling him as to why he was there. Benny gave his gap-toothed grin and replied, "Keeping an eye out for Mr. Blumenthal—one way or another." When Benny couldn't shake the reporters, he intimated that he was in Peggy Fears Blumenthal's employ and confided to them that he'd discovered Blumie and Gloria weren't really on the ship but planned to sail the next day on the *Ile de France.*

The following day an irate Peggy Fears Blumenthal walked into the Ambassador and found forty reporters waiting for her. She was told that only two days previously Gloria Morgan Vanderbilt had denied any romantic involvement with Blumie but had spoken of her high regard for him "and for his charming wife too."

"Well, it certainly was lovely of Mrs. Vanderbilt to say that about me. Just darling! I wish I could say the same for her," Peggy snapped, adding that the whole affair was in "bad taste" and "just cheap publicity."

As the *Europa* moved across the Atlantic, the odor of scandal drifted out to Wheatley Hills:

BLUMENTHAL-VANDERBILT BOARD SHIP SECRETLY

Denials of the yarn linking the very old name of Vanderbilt with the very new one of Blumenthal have been plentiful, but gossip is raging furiously as Blumey and the fair widow sailed at midnight on the same ship.

Unseen by a posse of process servers for Peggy Fears, eagle-eyed reporters and over attentive room stewards. . . . The super-realtor, politician and de luxe entrepreneur A. C. Blumenthal basked aboard the S.S. *Europa*. . . . With him, west flying sea terns report, is Gloria Morgan Vanderbilt, social register headliner. . . .

Gertrude found out that Gloria had left the country by reading about it in the newspapers. The Vanderbilt name, her family name, was being sullied by Gloria's association with a married man, an accused criminal, a publicity seeker, a Jew.

When little Gloria was told her mother was gone again she wrote to her,

Dear Momey . . .
if you love me
as I love you
no knife can cut
our love in two
from
Gloria

She drew a bird carrying a letter in his beak on the upper right-hand corner of the paper.

At the Vanderbilt custody trial the child would be shown this poem and would say that she had lied when she'd written it, that she'd never loved her mother. Her mother, in a state of shock, would exclaim, "Why is she lying? She has no reason." But she had a reason.

Possession Is Nine-tenths of the Law

The Vanderbilt women lived according to a set of social rules, prohibitions and taboos as complicated and inexorable as the laws of the Medes and the Persians. The highest cultivation of manners, they believed, enabled one to conceal from the world one's true feelings.

CORNELIUS VANDERBILT IV

SHALL BE IN TOWN THURSDAY WILL YOU STOP IN TO SEE ME EIGHT SEVENTY ONE FIFTH AVENUE TWELVE O'CLOCK WOULD LIKE TO TALK OVER WINTER PLANS FOR GLORIA SCHOOL AT ROSLYN STARTS TWENTY EIGHTH ST LAWRENCE SEEMS VERY ANXIOUS SHE SHOULD HAVE THIS WINTER IN COUNTRY WOULD BE DELIGHTED TO HAVE HER STAY ON WITH ME PLEASE ANSWER THE BREAKERS IF YOU CAN SEE ME THURSDAY.

GERTRUDE

GERTRUDE'S TELEGRAM arrived on Wednesday, September 13, 1933, the day that Gloria returned to New York after three months abroad. In the past few months Blumie had become her guide and counsel—he had a talent for involving himself in the lives of those around him until he became indispensable. In Blumie, Gloria had found a sympathetic ear. He "is a fixer . . . a born ambassador," wrote Alva Johnston. "He has an ingrained love of wire-pulling, interceding, arbitrating, reconciling. . . . His counsel in affairs of the heart is considered of the highest quality. He is the Beatrice Fairfax or Dorothy Dix of lovelorn headliners, and a general impresario of the love pageants of sensational people. If you want good advice about love or money, get your name in the lights and consult Blumey."

Gloria was unsure of the implications of this wire. Tom had cut her down to an allowance of only $750 a month and she didn't know how long he would continue to pay for her house and servants in New York City if her daughter remained at Gertrude's. She went immediately to Blumie's office where he studied the telegram and told her that of course she must see Gertrude, but warned her that she must not let this powerful woman "push her around." Then Blumie leaned forward, pressed the button on his intercom and spoke into the brown cloth-covered box, instructing his private secretary to take a wire on behalf of Mrs. Vanderbilt. Blumie himself dictated an answer to Gertrude's telegram. The message captured the exact tone he felt Gloria should assume. It was short, affirmative, but noncommittal.

The telegram lay on Gertrude Whitney's desk.

WILL BE VERY HAPPY TO SEE YOU
THURSDAY NOON LOVE
BLUMIE

Blumie—that name—that person who lived his life in the tabloids! This telegram proved that Blumie was masterminding Gloria's actions.

At noon, Thursday, a gracious Gertrude received Gloria in her library at 871 Fifth Avenue. Neither woman would speak of her true concerns. Gloria would say nothing of what she felt to be the punitive financial measures that were being enacted against her because of the child's absence. Gertrude would not speak of her apprehension regarding the atmosphere which she had come to consider both morally and physically dangerous to her niece. There existed between these two women an exquisite noncommunication that avoided all the ugly realities of their relationship.

Gloria, faced with Gertrude's gemlike intelligence, was at a decided disadvantage. In soothing tones, Gertrude told Gloria of her daughter's progress: the child had gained weight, her color was better, she caught cold less easily. Dr. St. Lawrence was so proud of himself at having achieved this "beautiful result" and thought it would be harmful to send little Gloria to Miss Chapin's in the city. Little Gloria was doing so well at Green Vale; she had made her little friends. "The country is so good for her," she concluded enthusiastically.

Gertrude was surprised at Gloria's response. Instead of simply thanking her as she had previously done, Gloria answered that if the country was so beneficial, "then perhaps I should get a house in Old Westbury and Gloria can live with me."

Gertrude had no intention of telling Gloria that it was the atmosphere Gloria created *wherever* she lived that was injurious to the child. She thought for a moment, then made light of the suggestion. "Oh, that is silly and an unnecessary expense for you as I have plenty of room and would be pleased to have you visit any time for as long as you like."

Then Gloria replied, "All right, I'll leave Gloria with you"—or so Gertrude recalled the conversation. Gloria was to maintain that she'd said nothing.

Gloria left the Whitney mansion and reported the conversation to Blumie, who literally took her by the hand and led her to the offices of his lawyer and friend Nathan Burkan. Gloria had met Burkan and his wife, Marienne, at Blumie's Larchmont house and liked them both. She immediately trusted this short, rotund, older man who seemed both authoritative and paternal. Burkan was born on November 8, 1878, in Rumania and came to America in steerage at age four. His parents were Orthodox Jews whose dream it was to have their Nathan climb out of New York's Lower East Side ghetto through education. Burkan rapidly worked his way through public school, the College of the City of New York, and New York University. He was admitted to the bar in July of 1900, four months before his twenty-third birthday, and he went to work for lawyer Julius Lehman, among whose clients was the prominent composer-conductor Victor Herbert. After Lehman's death Herbert became Burkan's client and in 1913 Burkan and two associates enlisted Herbert's aid in founding the American Society of Composers, Authors and Publishers, an organization to protect the rights of artists whose works were being performed without their permission. Once ASCAP existed it faced the problem of providing a way to police the unauthorized use of material. Burkan single-handedly solved the problem, traveling across the country, and in each territory, hiring a legal representative who, in turn, hired spotters. These men worked on a percentage basis and since there was no radio yet and no talking movies, their job was relatively simple. Burkan, at a yearly retainer of $25,000, became the general counsel for ASCAP.

With enormous energy and drive, Nathan Burkan became a business go-getter; he represented United Artists, the Academy of Motion

Picture Arts and Sciences, Columbia Pictures Corporation, Metro-Goldwyn-Mayer, Paramount Pictures. His client list read like a smorgasbord of theatrical, musical, and international celebrity types: Al Jolson, Mae West, Charlie Chaplin, Florenz Ziegfeld, Gloria Swanson, Corinne Griffiths, Ernst Lubitsch, Constance Bennett. He was the lawyer for financier Otto Kahn, tea merchant Sir Thomas Lipton, and the estate of gambler Arnold Rothstein, who was said to have controlled the cocaine and heroin markets until he was gunned down in November of 1928.

Burkan's clients had a way of becoming his friends, and he lived vicariously through their exploits. In 1927, when Charlie Chaplin faced divorce proceedings instituted by his wife, Lita Grey, he fled California and found refuge in Burkan's Great Neck, Long Island, home. Chaplin suffered a nervous breakdown and Burkan engaged Dr. Gustav Tiek, an eminent nerve specialist, to treat Chaplin, who remained at Burkan's house until he recovered. Burkan then defended Chaplin against Lita Grey's charges, which included the allegation that he'd insisted on reading aloud to her such immoral literature as *Lady Chatterley's Lover*, and that he'd suggested she perform fellatio on him, saying, "Relax dear—all married people do those kind of things."

Herman Finkelstein, the youngest of Burkan's associates, had a standing joke with his wife that whenever he raised his fork to take the first bite of dinner, the phone would ring; it would be Burkan calling to discuss a client's problem. Frequently, Burkan worked far into the night. The first thing in the morning he would call his associates into his office, one by one, to discuss with them the advance sheets of judges' decisions and the transcripts of cases in progress. This material sprawled in untidy profusion across his plain wood desk. Shreds of toilet paper served as markers for the relevant passages.

Burkan had no partners and the men he hired for his firm were, like himself, self-made men, men of diamond-in-the-rough charm, smart Jews who were unacceptable in the conservative, social, predominantly Episcopalian downtown law firms. The style of operation at the Burkan office was light-years removed from the propriety of a Wall Street firm like Cadwalader, Wickersham & Taft, which functioned in dark-paneled serenity. Burkan's establishment was a seat-of-the-pants operation, full of élan, excitement, and disorganization. Doors were almost always left open and if a lawyer had a bright idea, he simply dashed round to see an associate. One lawyer who worked for Nathan Burkan remembers finding the key to winning a multimillion-dollar suit while conversing with an associate in front of the men's room urinals. When Elmer Rice wrote his famous comedy, *Counsellor-at-Law*, Burkan's associates said the madhouse depicted was a re-creation of their firm.

Burkan surrounded himself with men who supported and complemented him. The ones who were to become involved with Gloria Vanderbilt included Louis Frohlich, who specialized in research and amassing the facts for affidavits; his engaging personality made him the ideal liaison to deal with potential witnesses and the press. There was James A. (Jim) Murray, who had the polish other Burkan associates lacked and the political and social connections to open many doors; he was the son of Hugh Murray, a Hearst relative who helped manage their publishing empire and was a partner in Moses Annenberg's *Racing Form*. Burkan referred to Jim as "the house goy." And there was the brilliant Herman Finkelstein, who was considered an expert in the technical aspects of copyright law and the most adept man in the entire firm at writing a brief.

Nathan Burkan was an ideal lawyer for Blumie; neither had any reticence about bringing a lawsuit. To Burkan, a suit was simply a tool to effect his purpose. Blumie loved the publicity and the game of it. Most important, both men understood how to manipulate public opinion. Once a lawyer had screamed at Burkan in court, "Your tactics are a disgrace to the profession. When the papers were filed in this action, the first thing you did was to show them to the reporters. It is the press who tries all of your cases." When Burkan successfully defended Mae West against an obscenity charge in connection with her performance in *Pleasure Man*, he had ordered her to wear shapeless, demure black dresses in the courtroom. One newspaper noted that Burkan was an expert in knowing exactly "when to require a damsel in distress to pull out her handkerchief, face the jury and cry."

At first, Nathan Burkan could not make head or tail of Gloria Vanderbilt's problem; she seemed totally fragmented and unaware of the facts of the matter. By gently asking question after question, he began to see what was involved here. In her halting, stammering way, Gloria told Burkan about how her allowance from her daughter's $2.5 million trust had been reduced from $4,000 a month to $750 while her daughter was not living with her, and how she seemed unable to secure her daughter's return. Nathan Burkan was surprised by the beautiful young woman who sat before him. She reminded him of his wife, Marienne, who was twenty years his junior and looked enough like Gloria to be her sister. Immediately he felt protective toward her.

Blumie took over the conversation, telling Burkan that Mrs. Whitney wanted Gloria to be on the dole. "They want her to come begging for every penny and to be beholden to them." Mrs. Whitney was a woman who was worth $78 million, Blumie said, and she was so powerful that she felt she could exercise her whim and no one could stop her.

She was surrounded by lawyers who would follow her every command.

"I'm not afraid of Mrs. Whitney's money or her lawyers," said Burkan with vehemence. To Burkan, Gertrude Vanderbilt Whitney was a member of a group which had always excluded him; simply because he was a Jew they'd locked him out of their world, they felt that their social background made them superior to him; they would never allow a Nathan Burkan past the front door of their clubs or their homes. He was filled with anger at the arrogance of this woman. "She thinks she is above the laws of man and of nature," he said. This child belonged with her mother. Burkan mentioned how much he loved his own two-year-old son, Nathan, Jr., and said gently, "I know how hard this must be for you."

If only little Gloria was with her mother instead of her aunt, Gloria might have some say in the situation, but this way she was relegated to the position of beggar. The child was soon to return home from her summer vacation. Burkan advised Gloria exactly what to do. He ended their discussion by quoting an old legal maxim to her: "Possession is nine-tenths of the law!"

Two days later, on Sunday, September 17, 1933, little Gloria and Dodo arrived at Grand Central Terminal on their way home from the Whitney camp in the Adirondacks. Little Gloria held tight to her nurse's hand as they pushed through the crowd of people moving rapidly in all directions; then she looked up to see her mother walking toward them. Gloria bent down and hugged little Gloria, and as she straightened up, Dodo said pointedly that Mrs. Whitney's car and chauffeur were waiting outside. "We are going to Mrs. Whitney's."

As if anticipating this, Gloria contradicted her. "No. Certainly not," she snapped. "You are going home with me." There was nothing Dodo and little Gloria could do but follow Mrs. Vanderbilt, who briskly led them out of the terminal and into her limousine. The moment they arrived at Seventy-second Street, Dodo excused herself, dashed to the telephone, and called Mrs. Whitney telling her that Gloria Vanderbilt had KIDNAPPED little Gloria and was holding them at her house against their will. Gertrude immediately got in touch with Frank Crocker and all day Monday arrangements were made to secure little Gloria's safe return to Wheatley Hills. It was arranged that on the following day Tom Gilchrist and Laura Morgan would have lunch with Gloria to persuade her to let her daughter return to Long Island. The lunch masqueraded as a social occasion with little Gloria sitting at the table while Tom Gilchrist asked her about her summer. After lunch little Gloria and the nurse went upstairs and Gilchrist, Mamma Morgan, and Gloria went into the library. Gloria began the conversation by saying that she'd heard there were objections to her maintaining a house without her child in it; then she asked Tom, once again, when she could have her daughter back. Tom replied that he had nothing to do with this decision, but that Dr. St. Lawrence had told him that little Gloria must remain at Wheatley Hills.

Gloria shot back, "I don't care what Mrs. Whitney, the Vanderbilts, the doctors, or the lawyers say. I am going to take my child back." Then, for the first time, she threatened legal action.

Gilchrist sprang to his feet and said, "Of course if there is ever any controversy between you and the Vanderbilt family about this child, its custody or anything of that sort, you must remember that I am not your attorney, any more than I am an attorney for the other side. I can't be partisan in this matter . . . I represent the interests of the child . . . my position is always merely as attorney for Mr. Wickersham, as guardian of the child's property. . . . I just want to make it clear to you that if there is any controversy, why you mustn't consider that you can rely on me as your attorney."

Before Gloria had time to absorb the implications of what Gilchrist had just said, her mother broke into the conversation, telling her that little Gloria was well and happy with Gertrude Whitney and that she had a great many "financial advantages" with Mrs. Whitney. Gloria was being "very foolish"; if she would simply agree to allow her child to remain there, she could be assured that, in appreciation, Mrs. Whitney would take care of Gloria, financially, for life.

Later, Gloria charged that her mother had said, "You don't want her anyway," and had mentioned a figure of $50,000 annually for life, to which Gloria had replied, "Mamma, my child is not for sale!" Later, Gilchrist, when pressed, said that this conversation did indeed take place, but that he could not recall "an exact sum" of money being mentioned. In any event, Nathan Burkan had warned Gloria against just this type of offer, telling her that there was no guarantee that this kind of promise would be fulfilled, and adding, "How would it look if it came out in a court of law that you'd made such an arrangement?"

Gilchrist began subtle negotiations, saying that he'd hoped Gloria would agree to let her daughter remain at Wheatley Hills, and he wished to remind her that she owed 57,000 francs outstanding rent on her Paris house. In addition, her former butler Charles Fernand was preparing to sue her, claiming that he had spent 45,000 francs out of his own pocket to feed the child and the nurse when she'd visited Prince Hohenlohe in Germany and had left him totally without funds. Gilchrist then intimated that if the child were allowed to return to Long Island he would settle all these bills.

Gloria knew it would be impossible for her to pay these debts, which amounted to over $7,000, on her monthly stipend of $750, but she felt that Surrogate Foley was not aware of her true situation and suspected that Tom was lying about St. Lawrence's recommendation. "I'm being put in a very awkward position," Gloria told him, and asked him to go to St. Lawrence's office with her and "in my presence hear what Dr. St. Lawrence has to say. . . ." They left immediately for St. Lawrence's office where the doctor confirmed that his recommendation was that little Gloria be allowed to remain in the country. At this, Gloria began to cry. St. Lawrence said, "Just a few more months there, little mother, and I know your heart is breaking." Then Gloria fainted. Dr. St. Lawrence's nurse, Miss Philbrick, revived her with spirits of ammonia. St. Lawrence was solicitous, but he did not change his mind.

When they returned to the Vanderbilt town house, Gloria told Tom, "If I acquiesce this time, it will be the last time. If the question comes up again, I will insist on having my child." Following Burkan's advice, she demanded that George Wickersham put in writing that if she allowed her child to return to Mrs. Whitney, the child's guardians would still pay the expenses of her New York town house and her allowance would not be further reduced, and she added, "I insist on having a letter which exonerates me of these insinuations that have been going on that I am doing this for my own pleasures and my own sake."

Tom assured Gloria that he was prepared to give her this guarantee. George Wickersham was out of town, having gone to Washington to address the Senate, hoping to persuade them to invalidate President Roosevelt's National Recovery Act which he considered "close to a criminal conspiracy." Gloria refused to accept Tom's word and suggested that he contact Wickersham in Washington. Then she played her trump card: little Gloria and nurse Keislich would simply have to remain with her until this matter was settled to her satisfaction.

The following morning a letter arrived by messenger.

My dear Gloria:

Mr. Gilchrist has told me of the interview which you and he had yesterday with Dr. St. Lawrence, at which the doctor expressed the opinion that little Gloria should not live in New York this coming winter, but ought to be sent to Long Island, as she was last year. This being the advice of a competent physician, I think you are thoroughly justified in acting upon it, and that the interest of the child very properly leads you to decide to send her to Long Island for the coming season. I understand that there is an excellent school there, to which she can be sent, and thus her education will not suffer. I understand that Mrs. Whitney has offered to take the child for the winter, without adding to her living expenses. This, of course, will relieve you of any criticism in that regard.

Faithfully yours,

George W. Wickersham

Gloria studied the letter carefully. She spoke with Blumie, then with Nathan Burkan, then she told nurse Keislich that little Gloria was to remain where she was until matters were settled. She wrote:

Sept. 20, 1933

Dear Mr. Wickersham,

I appreciate your expression of justification in sending Gloria to Long Island, and that I will be relieved of any criticism in accordance with the very generous offer of Mrs. Whitney of having Gloria with one added exception, my position in regard to the court as to the upkeep we have incurred on this house. I should like to know definitively how we are going to deal with this question. Will I be subject to criticism keeping up this house, since Gloria is not here.

It is very essential for my peace of mind that you should clear up this situation, so that I may know how I should act.

I again stress the point, will her enforced absence, both financially and morally not fall as a criticism from the court on me.

Hoping to hear from you at once on this subject.

I am as ever,

Gloria

That evening Blumie called for Gloria and they set out for a night on the town, ending up at the Casino in the Park, Blumie's favorite night spot, where they joined some friends and drank champagne. (Because Prohibition was in force, the champagne was carried in, one bottle at a time, from a refrigerated truck parked behind the casino.) Gloria's mood was bleak, and Emil Coleman's sweet music did little to lift her spirits. When the floor show began at midnight, a restless Gloria asked everyone back to her house. At about two o'clock in the morning, one of their group, Countess Voronzoff, decided it was time for her special egg concoction and everyone trooped gaily into the kitchen while the countess turned on the oven. They chatted for a while. Then she held a match to the oven. The stove exploded. Countess Voronzoff leaped back, her eyebrows and eyelashes were singed, her face burned. Gloria ran upstairs and pounded on little Gloria's and Keislich's door. When the nurse opened the door, Gloria hurriedly told her what had happened. "Have you got anything for a burn?" she asked. The nurse hurried downstairs with some cream to soothe the burns until the doctor arrived.

In the morning Tom Gilchrist called on Gloria once again. This time he promised her that George Wickersham would do exactly as she requested if she agreed to allow little Gloria to return to Old Westbury immediately. Gloria agreed and Wickersham subsequently wrote: ". . . on the question of your right to keep up the house in town while little Gloria is in the country. I now can assure you that there will be no criticism from the court during the coming months."

Nurse Keislich was almost hysterical when she and little Gloria arrived back at Wheatley Hills. She told Mrs. Whitney, "That house is not a fit place for a child." Things had gone on that "were not fit for a child to see"; in the dead of the night little Gloria had been jolted out of bed by a tremendous explosion and was now "a nervous wreck." Gertrude Whitney checked the nurse's story with Gilchrist, who confirmed that it was true. This was the first time that little Gloria had stayed overnight at her mother's house and if this were any indication of what went on, Gertrude felt absolutely justified in keeping her niece with her. Furthermore, nurse Keislich said that in that place anything could happen to little Gloria, "she was not protected."

During the summer of 1933, the kidnapping epidemic in the United States had hit fever pitch, setting a record never to be equaled. The victims of kidnap threats were not just strangers but often people Gertrude or Gloria knew: Joseph Schenck, Peggy Fears Blumenthal, the grandchildren of George Wickersham's partner Henry W. Taft, who went to the Green Vale School with little Gloria. On July 1, *The New York Times* instituted a new information service, resembling the weather report, called "The Kidnapping Situation," to give readers up-to-the-minute facts on the latest abductions: who had been kidnapped, who had been released, how much ransom had been paid, if the kidnappers had been apprehended. Lloyd's of London began issuing kidnap insurance policies with a maximum coverage of $100,000 for an adult and $50,000 for a child. On July 21, a *Times* headline read: ROOSEVELT ORDERS WAR ON KIDNAPPING BY FEDERAL FORCES. One week later a new division of the Department of Justice was formed, the Federal Bureau of Investigation, with J. Edgar Hoover as its director; its purpose was "to conduct nationwide warfare against racketeers, kidnappers and other criminals."

While little Gloria had summered at Oakland Farm and at the Whitney camp in the Adirondacks, both places had been heavily guarded. To protect against kidnappers, in addition to private bodyguards William H. Vanderbilt had donated part of Oakland Farm to the state police and the Rhode Island state police barracks was being constructed right on his property. The Whitney camp in the Adirondacks was inaccessible—the only way to reach it was by boat. But at the end of the summer, when little Gloria unexpectedly had been taken to her mother's town house, Dodo had been afraid and she'd said that they'd been KIDNAPPED. For the first time that dreaded word had been spoken in connection with little Gloria's mother. Little Gloria knew that KIDNAP was when they took you away and murdered you for money. Naney had said all along that Mummy was the one who wanted to murder her for her money.

Psychoanalyst Dorothy Bloch points out that a small child has an "almost built-in" fear of infanticide, a belief that a parent can and will kill him, and "that the intensity of that fear depends on the incidence of traumatic events and on the degree of violence and of love they have experienced. . . . Where the parent of the same sex is frequently or permanently absent . . . the child may develop a distorted concept of . . . his relationship to the world." In little Gloria's case, the fear of infanticide must have been greatly magnified by her grandmother's repeated accusations. Little Gloria had begun to exhibit the classic symptoms of the child who fears infanticide: a strong reliance on fantasy, representing "the child's attempt to defend himself against the early terror of being killed," and a conviction that "his 'badness' causes his mother to leave him." "I am so bad," little Gloria wrote to her grandmother shortly after this time.

During the enforced visit to her mother in September of 1933, little Gloria had added another vital piece to the puzzle of how she was going to die. She lived in fear that someone was going to KIDNAP her. Now she knew exactly who that someone was—her MOTHER!

Unfit

> In the last analysis, the allegation of unfit guardianship really means a person is unmoral and immoral and a prostitute.
>
> NATHAN BURKAN

DECEMBER 5, 1933: the Twenty-first Amendment was ratified by thirty-six states, and repeal went into immediate effect. George Wickersham had been the chairman of the committee that had compiled a several-thousand-page opus on Crime and Prohibition and although his committee had found "the noble experiment" of Prohibition to be a failure, Wickersham personally supported its continuance. Will Rogers commented on the fate of this weighty tome. "I was down in Texas last week and they're feeding goats *The Wickersham Report*. . . . Anyhow, him and his gang wasn't loafin'." Wickersham was now seventy-four years old and this defeat, coupled with his unsuccessful battle against President Roosevelt, whom he considered to be a dictator and a traitor to his class, made him ill and unable to work. Surrogate Foley suggested that Tom Gilchrist be appointed co-guardian to serve with Wickersham, which really meant that from now on Gilchrist would be in sole charge of the administration of little Gloria's trust.

The night of December 5, Gloria had attended a repeal party at the Casino in the Park. She was photographed wearing a low-cut, white satin skintight gown; two triangular diamond clips shone on her slender shoulder straps, a diamond tiara (the gift of the dowager Vanderbilt) gleamed in her dark hair. Blumie stared at Gloria admiringly as she leaned forward, a cigarette in her right hand. Ten glasses, two liquor bottles, and a small pot of coffee littered the surface of their rectangular table. Late in the evening Gloria developed a toothache and the following day had two wisdom teeth extracted. She developed a painful throat abscess and a trained nurse was hired to look after her while Dr. Craig treated the abscess. She'd been in bed for about a week when Tom Gilchrist presented himself at her bedroom door, briefcase in hand. He explained that he had a legal document for her and he indicated where she should sign. An instinct told Gloria that something was amiss; she insisted on reading the document before she signed it. One passage said that Gilchrist was to act as co-guardian of the *person* as well as the property of her child. Gloria asked about this wording.

"Oh, Mrs. Vanderbilt, that was never intended," Tom Gilchrist replied. "That's just a slight error on the part of the secretary. I will cross it out." He then crossed out the word *person.* A notary public who had been waiting downstairs was ushered into the room by butler Zaug. Gloria signed the papers. When she told Nathan Burkan the following week, he was furious that she had signed the application without consulting him. Her position was weak enough without this. Burkan had discussed the situation with his associates Jim Murray, Louis Frohlich, and Herman Finkelstein and all of them agreed that actually Gloria Vanderbilt had *no* legal standing in regard to her daughter. She'd been a minor at the time of her husband's death and could not then serve as guardian. She'd taken no subsequent legal action to *become* guardian. Therefore, they concluded that little Gloria had no general guardian, either by will or deed. Frohlich and Finkelstein both strongly recommended that Burkan should petition to have Mrs. Vanderbilt made sole guardian of her child's person and co-guardian of her child's property. This action would give her a direct means of communication with Surrogate James A. Foley—at present, she had no voice before the Surrogate and therefore no way to present her side of the matter. On the other hand, as guardians of the property, Wickersham and Gilchrist were in constant contact with Surrogate Foley. Burkan agreed, saying, "If we don't do something, they'll simply push her right out of the picture."

This guardianship petition appealed strongly to Burkan both as the proper legal measure and because he'd become Surrogate Foley's close friend through a political alliance at Tammany Hall. Burkan also knew that Foley was kindly disposed toward women in regard to the monies they received from their husbands' estates. In 1930, largely because of Foley's efforts, the punitive and outmoded right of dower had been abolished. In its place Foley helped structure a new law, one which stipulated that a widow with one child was entitled to one-half of her husband's estate outright. If Burkan could take Gloria's case to his friend Surrogate Foley, he felt certain that his natural disposition toward fairness would stand them in good stead.

Nathan Burkan told Gloria that since she was now of age, the logical move would be to apply for guardianship, which he assured her was a routine matter. In order to strengthen their application, he advised her to keep in touch with the child, and whenever she was traveling to insist on letters or cables advising her of the child's condition.

Gloria hesitated to apply for guardianship. For the last two years Alice Gwynne Vanderbilt had been confined to bed, and it was clear that she did not have long to live. If Gloria took legal action, she might incur the enmity of the dowager, whose economic power was still intact. In the past, *the* Mrs. Vanderbilt had generously given Gloria money, but if she wished, she could stop these payments as well as cut Gloria and little Gloria out of her will.

Also, at the moment Gloria had only $750 a month, not enough to initiate a legal action that might prove costly. Blumie, for all his generosity of advice, had a reputation for being tight with a dollar, explaining grandly, that his "moral sense was offended at the idea of disturbing another man's destiny by giving him money." And Nathan Burkan always worked on a fee, never on a commission basis, which he said might tempt him "to be more eager to win than to seek the truth," and he substantiated this by quoting the maxim: "A lawyer who represents himself has a fool for a client."

The pressure of the situation was making Gloria nervous. She couldn't sleep or concentrate; she seemed incapable of making a decision. Following a pattern established over many years, she reacted to the pressure by deciding to take a trip, this time to California. She wrote to Thelma in London asking her to come along.

Thelma decided to broach the subject to David the last weekend in January when she was at Fort Belvedere. On Saturday afternoon the Prince of Wales returned from golf looking relaxed. Thelma spoke casually. "I've just had a letter from Gloria asking me to come over for a short visit. I would very much like to go. Would you mind very much?"

"Oh, darling, how long will you be gone?"

"Just five or six weeks," Thelma replied, trying to make *weeks* sound as insignificant as *days*.

Thelma saw David's face take on a look of resignation. "Of course, dear. Do what you want. But I will miss you. I will miss you very much."

Four days before Thelma was to sail for New York she lunched with Wallis Simpson at the Ritz. Thelma volunteered to bring Wallis back whatever it was she wanted from America. Wallis thanked her. There was a moment's silence, and then Wallis blurted out, "Oh, Thelma, the little man is going to be so lonely."

"Well, dear, you look after him for me while I'm away," Thelma told her friend. "See that he doesn't get into any mischief."

The high point of Gloria's and Thelma's California trip was a visit with their friend Constance Bennett on the set of *The Affairs of Cellini.* Constance Bennett was at the height of her career—a sophisticated woman, sleek, worldly, her metallic voice oozing culture—she was every shop girl's idol. In darkened theaters, these women imagined the plots of her films, set in Gay Paree or Wicked Hollywood, to be stories from her own life. Their instincts were correct.

At sixteen, straight from a French finishing school, Connie had married on a dare. It had lasted two months. At nineteen, she was married again, this time to Philip Morgan Plant, a multimillionaire playboy with a drinking problem. When she divorced him three years later, he gave her a million-dollar settlement. Constance Bennett swore she'd never touch the money but would earn her own to match it. She became known for her business acumen and toughness.

In 1929 Connie met the dapper Henri Le Bailly, the Marquis de la Falaise de la Coudraye (who claimed that his title had been granted in 1707 by Queen Maria Casimira of Poland). A title was then a prestigious symbol, more valued than a Rolls-Royce or a sable coat. The marquis, who called himself Hank, was married to Bennett's arch rival, Gloria Swanson. Hank, who represented the Joseph P. Kennedy interests abroad, was sent to Paris to persuade Connie to sign a five-year Pathé film contract. She signed. In 1931, after first acquiring Swanson's masseur, then her secretary, she acquired Hank as her third husband.

Constance Bennett demanded a closed set on her films, but she made an exception for her friends, the Vanderbilt widow and the English peeress. Gloria and Thelma sat side by side in canvas directors chairs. Under the intensely hot klieg lights, Constance Bennett reclined on a gold lamé couch, an overstuffed gold lamé pillow behind her back. She wore a gold lamé dress that clung to her figure and rippled as she moved. Her blond hair was massed in tight ringlets and sprinkled with diamonds. At lunch break the three friends headed for the studio commissary. A waiter came over to their table and whispered to Lady Furness that there was an overseas call for her. As Thelma rose, he added, in a stage whisper, "It's from Buckingham Palace!" Watching Thelma walk to the phone, Gloria noted with triumph that in a commissary full of stars everyone was looking at her twin with envy, whispering the identity of the mysterious caller.

Gloria and Thelma returned from California in late March 1934. Little Tony Furness and his nanny, who were staying at the Seventy-second Street house, went with them to Old Westbury to visit little Gloria. When they arrived, the door was opened by a liveried footman, but there was no one else to greet them. At last a maid appeared and escorted them into the living room where eight or ten children of various ages were gathered with their nannies. Gloria could see that they had been acting in a play; costumes littered the floor. Thelma greeted nurse Keislich, who was picking up costumes. Nurse Keislich ignored Lady Furness and she continued to pick up the costumes. Finally, she straightened up, walked over to Thelma, and stiffly extended her hand.

Brown-haired, doe-eyed, seven-year-old Gerta Henry stopped playing and, pointing a finger at Tony, asked, "Who is that little boy?"

It was then that little Gloria stepped forward. "Why, hello, Tony," she said, and helped her cousin off with his coat and tam. Then she sat them all down while the children put on their costumes and once again performed the play, which was based on *Little Women*. Little Gloria played the wicked aunt who bossed Jo around and made her shine the banister and was mean and snippy. Gerta Henry played Jo. After the play was over, little Gloria took Tony by the hand and led him off. All the other children followed until Gloria and Thelma found themselves alone. Thelma summoned the maid, and commanded, "Bring Miss Gloria to us at once."

A few minutes later little Gloria came back into the room with Tony. She told her mother how she'd read in the newspapers about their trip, and she wanted to know all about it. "Tell me about Hollywood," she pleaded. She'd seen Katharine Hepburn as Jo in the film of *Little Women*, and it had made her want to be an actress. She told her mother and aunt that she'd really wanted to be Jo in the play, not the wicked aunt. Actually, her identification with Jo was even stronger than she revealed. She'd read all the Alcott books and had begun to call herself Jo, and to sign her letters Jo. But she never signed her letters to her mother that way. Aunt Ger was becoming the object of little Gloria's affection and she wrote:

Dear Aunty Ger,
I am going to miss you a lot. I will call you up tonight.
Please try and be here for the horse show
I love you
love from
Jo

Dearest Aunt Gertrude
I hope you will like these Roses
lovingly
Jo

Dearest Aunty Ger—
I do so hope your cold is better. I have gone to school. I will see you at lunch.
lovingly
Jo

On the drive back to New York Thelma remarked that little Gloria had seemed quite distant, but soon she turned her attention to deciphering a complicated coded cable from the Prince of Wales. Thelma spent many frustrating hours deciphering these long cables and speaking with David on the telephone. It was now eight weeks since she'd left England and she confided to Maury Paul that her life was at a standstill: she and David had been together for over four years, and Thelma saw no future in it. She had no desire to become Queen of England and said sensibly that even if she had, it would be "out of the question," a twice-divorced commoner would never be acceptable.

At a dinner party, Thelma was seated next to the handsome, twenty-three-year-old Prince Aly Khan, a man who admired fast cars, racehorses, and beautiful women. Aly knew that Thelma belonged to the Prince of Wales, and this sparked his competitive urge. As for Thelma, she could never become a queen but she could, by marrying Aly Khan, become a princess. Gossip columns began to pair the names of Lady Furness and Prince Aly Khan, and everywhere he went Maury Paul heard the bigoted society quip, "Thelma Furness has captured both the white and the black prince."

When Thelma finally embarked for London, she walked into her cabin on the *Bremen* to find it crammed full of hundreds of red roses. The arrangements covered every conceivable surface: the dresser, the table, the floor. Thelma read the notes one after another: "See you in London, Aly." "Love, Aly." "You left too soon, Aly." The following morning Thelma was having breakfast in bed when her telephone rang. A voice said, "This is Aly. Will you have lunch with me today?" He'd sailed on the same ship. They lunched and dined together every night; they made arrangements to motor to London together. Thelma had confided to several people that "the Prince of Wales was a most unsatisfactory sexual partner," and that "his primary problem was premature ejaculation." A close friend of the prince, who had often gone swimming naked with him, added the information that, "to put it bluntly, he had the smallest pecker I have ever seen." Aly, on the other hand, was considered to be an extraordinarily gifted lover. As a young man he'd been sent to Cairo by his father the Aga Khan to learn the love technique and philosophy of *Imsák*. Thelma tactfully and obliquely referred to this when she said that Aly possessed a quality "of romantic largesse . . . and conjures up the splendid images whose forms are sketched in the books notably translated by Sir Richard Burton." In his final essay in *The Thousand Nights and a Night*, Burton explains that the essence of *Imsák* (which in Arabic means "holding" or "retaining") "is to avoid overtension of the muscles and to preoccupy the brain." Aly's biographer notes that he "learned to carry *Imsák* to its extreme. He could control himself indefinitely. . . . In the precise and complex art of love Aly had no peer. He could make love by the hour . . . the woman's satisfaction came first with Aly."

On the last day of the voyage, Thelma was called to the phone. It was the Prince of Wales, asking her to stop by the Fort for dinner on her way to London. Thelma, feeling ill at ease, replied, "No, darling, I can't stop. I've promised a lift to a friend."

"Oh, very well," answered the prince. "Then shall we dine at your house."

He arrived that night. Thelma found him unusually stiff; when coffee was served, he looked at her oddly and said, "I hear Aly Khan has been very attentive to you."

During this crisis, Thelma turned to her friend Wallis Simpson for guidance. She visited Wallis's Bryanston Court flat and told her of the prince's behavior. Wallis assured her, "Darling, you know the little man loves you very much. The little man was just lost without you." At that moment, Wallis's maid came into the room to say that the Prince of Wales was on the phone—for Wallis. Thelma heard Wallis say, "Thelma is here," and expected Wallis to call her to the phone, but she did not, and when Wallis hung up she made no reference to the conversation.

Easter weekend Thelma arrived at the Fort. Among the guests were Wallis and Ernest Simpson. At dinner Saturday night Thelma saw the prince pick up a piece of the salad with his fingers. Wallis reached out and playfully slapped his hand. Thelma caught Wallis's eye and shook her head no. "She knew as well as everybody else that the prince could be very friendly, but, no matter how friendly, he never permitted familiarity."

Wallis stared straight back at Thelma. Suddenly, Thelma understood.

Later that night when the prince came to Thelma's bedroom she confronted him. "Darling, is it Wallis?"

The prince's features froze. "Don't be silly," he replied.

Thelma knew better. She left the Fort the following morning. She was never to return.

Wallis Simpson, too, recalled the end of the affair. Differently.

> Thelma returned in the early spring. Something had happened between her and the Prince. She was back at the Fort once, but the former warmth and easiness of their relationship was plainly gone. One afternoon she came to Bryanston Court. It was an unhappy call. She told me that the Prince was obviously avoiding her—she couldn't understand why. He would not speak to her himself on the telephone. No more invitations to the Fort were forthcoming. Finally, she asked me point-blank if the Prince was interested in me—"keen" was the word she used.
>
> This was a question I had expected and I was glad to be able to give her a straight answer. "Thelma," I said, "I think he likes me. He may be fond of me. But, if you mean by keen that he is in love with me, the answer is definitely no."

In an interview in January of 1937, Thelma Furness was asked, "If you had your life to live over, what would you have done differently?" She replied, "I would not have introduced Wallis Simpson to the Prince of Wales." And Elsa Maxwell wrote, "Edward VIII might still be on the throne of England today, if not for Aly."

Gloria Vanderbilt's name and photograph continued to appear in the newspapers and in Pond's Cold Cream ads from which she derived income; most frequently her name was tied to those of Blumie and his wife Peggy who were now engaged in open warfare. Although their Larchmont house was owned by Blumie's Planet Holding Corporation, Peggy claimed that she could prove Blumie had given it to her as a gift. For a time Blumie barred Peggy from the house; then, on the instructions of Max Steuer, Peggy forced her way into the house, changed the locks, and hired guards to keep Blumie out.

At four in the morning on April 12, 1934, the twenty-two-room Blumenthal mansion burned to the ground. The caretaker was the only occupant at the time. Two firemen were slightly injured by the flames. Peggy Fears drove to Larchmont the next morning. All her possessions had been destroyed. As she was about to leave, the caretaker pulled her aside. "I'm not a religious man," he said, "but when I knew what Mr. Blumenthal was going to do, I had to get this." From his pocket he withdrew Peggy's gold St. Christopher's medal which had hung on the frame of her bedroom mirror and handed it to her. Peggy said nothing about this incident, and subsequently Blumie collected the insurance money.

In April Gloria visited her daughter at Wheatley Hills and told her that she was sailing at midnight for Europe. She'd rented her town house for $1,000 a month as another means of supplementing her income. Gloria arrived in Oslo, Norway, to visit Consuelo, whose husband was serving as consul to the American legation. When Consuelo saw Gloria she was alarmed by her condition. There was nothing in particular Consuelo could pinpoint but she felt her sister was having a "general nervous breakdown." Consuelo decided to keep Gloria with her and nurse her back to health.

In New York City an event was about to take place that would have a profound effect on Gloria, Gertrude, and little Gloria. For the past month Gertrude had spent the better part of her days at Alice Gwynne Vanderbilt's bedside as her eighty-nine-year-old mother grew steadily weaker. On Sunday, April 22, she stood in her mother's bedroom—outside the windows there was a glorious view of the sun sinking over the reborn trees of Central Park. Alice's breathing was a harsh cackle. At five o'clock her pulse jumped to 160. At 7:00 p.m. she had a stroke and the room went silent.

Gloria had been with Consuelo for only three weeks when she received a cable informing her of her mother-in-law's death. In her will, Alice Gwynne Vanderbilt bequeathed over $7 million from the sale of her Fifty-seventh Street palace—money that was to have been Reggie's had he lived—to Gertrude. She assigned the $1.25 million trust created by her husband, Cornelius II, in equal shares to Reggie's two daughters, Cathleen (now Mrs. Lawrence W. Lowman) and little Gloria. Little Gloria's inheritance now stood at $2,876,017.45. Gloria was to receive what by Alice's standards was a token bequest of $100,000 outright. For Gloria, the protector who had kept criticism of her at bay was now gone, leaving her enough money to pay for legal action against Gertrude. For Gertrude, her mother's death released her from any obligation she might have felt to protect Gloria's reputation. And for little Gloria, newspaper accounts of her grandmother's death were to run side by side with a dreadful kidnap tale about another little girl—June Robles.

Gloria sailed back to New York with Consuelo, who was so concerned about her sister's precarious mental state that she left her husband to stay close to her and help her. No sooner had the ship docked than Gloria called Tom Gilchrist from a public telephone. "Remember when you told me last September that you wouldn't be my attorney?" she asked. "Well, I have arranged for another attorney. I've retained Nathan Burkan."

After all her vacillating and indecision, Gloria now moved swiftly: on the strength of Alice Vanderbilt's bequest, she borrowed $20,000 for legal fees. Burkan prepared the guardianship application and submitted it to Surrogate Foley on June 18; a hearing was set for July 3. Burkan assured Gloria that this hearing was a mere formality; there was no doubt that Foley would approve their application.

Thomas Gilchrist, as property guardian, received legal notice of the guardianship application. Although he considered himself nonpartisan, he immediately alerted Frank Crocker and Mrs. Whitney. In the past few months, Tom Gilchrist had gathered enough information to convince himself that the welfare of the child depended on her remaining where she was. By this time Gertrude also was determined that little Gloria must remain with her until she was more mature; and clearly the child wanted to stay—as long as little Gloria remained at Wheatley Hills, Gertrude observed that she seemed indifferent toward her mother, but at any suggestion that she might be returned to her, little Gloria became frightened. Of late this possibility seemed to worry the child a great deal and she said things like, "Oh, I hope I can always live with you!" and "I don't want to go back to New York." Gertrude grew convinced that "the child did not feel that her mother loved her. She did not love her mother herself. She did not want to be with her mother."

When Laura Morgan was told about the petition she rushed out to Wheatley Hills and asked Gertrude if Frank Crocker could represent her in opposing it. After many legal conferences, it was decided that, in fact, Laura Morgan would be the ideal choice to officially oppose her daughter's application. In this way, Gertrude Vanderbilt Whitney could be kept in the background. Since Frank Crocker was so closely associated with Gertrude, he suggested that Walter Dunnington be engaged to represent Mrs. Morgan and Gertrude agreed to pay his fees.

Crocker and Dunnington had been law partners and had functioned as a unit many times. Now they began to plan their strategy in opposing Gloria's petition. They assured Gertrude Whitney that they would take whatever steps were necessary to force Mrs. Vanderbilt to withdraw her application. Although she was unaware of it, Gertrude had set in motion a legal juggernaut that began moving inexorably forward.

At the end of June, Gloria went to Portsmouth to visit her daughter, who was staying at Oakland Farm for the third summer. The William H. Vanderbilts seemed suddenly cool toward Gloria and did not invite her to stay with them, so she booked a room at a Newport hotel. On the first day of her visit, little Gloria and her cousin, W. H. Vanderbilt's daughter Emily, arrived at the hotel at nine in the morning carrying flowers they had picked themselves. Little Emily's emotional make-up was much like little Gloria's: she'd been a year old in 1926, when her mother had left her father, remarking, "I'm tired of married life." The Vanderbilts' divorce had become final in 1928, and Emily's sole custody had been given to her father. By the summer of 1934, Emily's mother was married to her third husband, writer Raoul Whitfield; within the year, she would take a revolver in her right hand, press it to her left side, and kill herself. The night before Emily's mother died, she told a friend that she wished she could see little Emily once more. At the time, the child was in Cannes with her father.

Gloria stayed in Newport for four days, and on the last afternoon of her visit, she and nurse Keislich sat on a grassy bank at Oakland Farm watching little Gloria and Emily row a boat on the pond. Little Gloria begged her mother to come for a ride, but Gloria answered that she was too big and might upset the boat. So the girls pulled the boat ashore and little Gloria sat down next to her mother. That's when Gloria told her daughter, "This winter you'll be living with me. Won't that be nice? When you come to live with me in New York I will buy you a Rolls-Royce."

Later that afternoon, Gloria left for New York City to be sure to be in town for the hearing which was scheduled for the following day. When she arrived at the Surrogates' Court she was amazed to find the room full of spectators and members of the press. Burkan read the application before James A. Foley. His crisp presentation gave no hint of their close friendship. As soon as Burkan had concluded, a man jumped to his feet and announced: "I object to the petition."

Surrogate Foley called the gentleman forward. He was impeccably dressed in a dark blue wool suit and vest, in spite of the summer heat, and identified himself as Walter Grey Dunnington of the firm of Dunnington, Gregg and Church. "On what grounds do you object?" inquired Surrogate Foley.

"On the grounds of unfit guardianship," Dunnington replied.

Foley looked out at the crowded room. "Court adjourned," he announced. "I will hear this case in my chambers after lunch."

Burkan and Jim Murray shepherded a bewildered Gloria out of the courtroom. Over lunch at a nearby restaurant she asked, "Nathan, what does it mean to be 'unfit'?"

Burkan told her straight out: "In the last analysis, the allegation of unfit guardianship really means a person is unmoral and immoral and a prostitute." The color drained from Gloria's face, and she started to shake.

After lunch Nathan Burkan addressed Surrogate Foley. "I must refuse, Your Honor, to proceed in this case unless I am informed who is bringing the complaint objecting to the guardianship."

Dunnington asked, "Does Mrs. Vanderbilt insist on hearing?"

Gloria nodded yes.

"It is her own mother—Mrs. Morgan."

Gloria was "stupefied. . . . None of the events leading to this moment had made sense to me; there seemed to be no logic, no reason, no consistency or purpose in what I had seen happen."

In the privacy of Foley's chambers, Gloria heard Dunnington present her mother's accusations against her. Then she rushed from the Surrogates' Court to her mother's apartment to confront her, but Mrs. Morgan was not at home. Next she went to Gertrude Whitney's house and when the footman opened the door, she stumbled down the three steps into the dark vestibule. Gloria walked up the wide white marble spiral staircase into the great hall, where a maid met her and led her to Gertrude's drawing room, with its walls of yellow damask and sweeping gold taffeta curtains that cascaded into immense folds onto the floor. The cool and regal Gertrude received the hysterical Gloria and offered her a glass of sherry, which Gloria gratefully accepted. Then, in a rush of words, Gloria told Gertrude all that had transpired that day. Gertrude said, "It is a terrible thing to think that you and your mother should be opposed in this way. . . . Why should your mother want to do this to you?"

"The reason why my mother is doing this is purely money. She is money mad, her God is money, money, money, and that is what made all this trouble," replied Gloria. Then, in tears, Gloria explained how her mother had tried to do this to her once before. She told Gertrude all about the document her father had written at her mother's instigation and of the awful accusations it contained, and how she had given it to Gilchrist when she asked him to rewrite her will.

Gertrude seemed interested in everything Gloria had to say. Perhaps too interested, because Gloria stopped speaking and, with a dawning feeling of apprehension, asked, "Gertrude, have you got something to do with this?"

"Gloria, I promise you that I have nothing whatsoever to do with it. This is the first I ever heard of it," Gertrude Whitney assured her.

At that moment a maid walked in and announced that Mrs. Morgan was downstairs. Gertrude told Gloria that she did not want to see Mrs. Morgan. Gloria said, apologetically, "I am sorry, Gertrude, that you are put to all this trouble, this family mess. It really has nothing to do with you. Though, after the accusations of my mother I would rather not see her, I will go downstairs and I shall bring her home."

"Yes, I wish you would," Gertrude replied.

Gloria went downstairs and said, "Mamma, Mrs. Whitney is not at home . . . I think we'd better go. This is a very undignified thing for both of us."

Mrs. Morgan insisted that she was going to see Mrs. Whitney and tell her all that had happened.

"Really, Mamma, you shouldn't do anything like that," Gloria told her, then she drove her mother home. At the doorway of her hotel, Mrs. Morgan tried to kiss Gloria goodbye as if nothing at all had happened.

Three days later Gertrude asked to see Gloria again. She said she wanted Gloria to know that she'd engaged Frank Crocker to represent her in supporting Mrs. Morgan's opposition if Gloria did not withdraw her guardianship application. Gertrude had no objection to Gloria's becoming guardian of the child's property. "My concern is that the child would be better off if she remained with me."

Gloria tried to clarify the situation. "There is no objection to my being made co-guardian of the property of this child?" she asked.

"Not as far as I am concerned," answered Gertrude.

"Do you blame me for wanting to take my child?" asked Gloria.

The question was meant to be rhetorical, but Gertrude answered it. "Yes, I do, because you know it isn't the best thing for the child."

"Why?" demanded Gloria. Why was this woman standing in her way? Why did Gloria have to keep hearing that "welfare-of-the-child—good-of-the-child—health-of-the-child" over and over again? It reminded Gloria of a song she'd heard on the radio called "The Broken Record." Gertrude was droning on, telling Gloria that in her opinion, "it was best for the child if she played in the country air with her relatives and cousins and . . ."

Gloria could stand it no longer. "Do you have anything against me?" she asked straight out. Gertrude was completely taken aback. How could this woman ask a question like that? A woman who would use her own child as a means to obtain money, a woman whose own mother had said that she would murder her child for money, a woman who neglected her child until she was ill and frightened half to death and sick at the thought of living with her?

Gertrude looked at Gloria for a long moment and then, in her soft drawl, replied to her question. "Gloria, on the contrary, I think you are perfectly charming!" And Gloria, oblivious of Gertrude's exquisite sarcasm, took these words at face value.

CHILD CHAINED IN PIT
. . . 19 DAYS IN HOLE

On the afternoon of April 25, 1934, little June Robles, the six-year-old daughter of a wealthy Tucson, Arizona, Spanish-American family, was walking home from her kindergarten class with her cousin. A man drove up in a big black car and beckoned to little June. He told her that her daddy was fixing a radio and wanted her to come to where he was working. The child got into the front seat of the car with the strange man. She was taken away. That afternoon little June's father, Fernando Robles, received a ransom note demanding $15,000 for the safe return of his daughter. The note was signed "XYZ."

Nineteen days after little June was kidnapped, when most people had given up hope for her life, Governor B. B. Moeur of Arizona received a letter with a Chicago postmark, containing directions to the child's whereabouts.

A rescue party rushed to a spot in the desert approximately ten miles east of Tucson. There, in a pit dug into the sand, they found a crude box, six feet long, three feet wide, and less than three feet deep. Its top consisted of a sheet of tin into which jagged holes had been punched. The box had been concealed by piling cactus and brush over it. Inside, crouched little June. She was chained, with dog and car chains, to a metal bar on the side of the box. Padlocks secured the chains on her tiny ankles. Blood oozed from the lacerations caused by these shackles. The box was so small that during the nineteen days of her captivity she had been unable to stand up. She was covered with bites and a heat rash, and her forehead was burned and blistered from touching the scalding tin roof of her coffin-prison. The doctor who examined her that evening said, "It is a miracle that little June has survived."

. . .

g Show
ns Elite
rce Suit

REN HALL.

G Brothers and Bailey's circus y fair show for a fit, but the Roy-i-Steinreich di-paration extrava- really got under lyn yesterday for run, is a six-air with some- every minute.
re across the vast gal documents and

th Pease Steinreich, ng the millionaire state and insurance atron, charging he in their $200,000 sdale for another

Vanderbilt Clan Buries Its Beloved Matriarch

Brig. Gen. Cornelius Vanderbilt arriving for the funeral of the dowager Mrs. Vanderbilt at the residence at 1 East 67th St. yesterday.

And here's Mrs. James Roosevelt, mother of the President, arriving for the funeral.

Dowager Queen of 400 Laid To Rest in Staten Island.

By NANCY RANDOLPH.

THE little, old lady who was THE Mrs. Vanderbilt, nonagenarian matriarch of a clan which has become the shining symbol of social and financial success for a whole nation, was laid to rest yesterday in the family mausoleum in the beautiful Moravian Cemetery at New Dorp, I.

Under a blanket of white fleur lys and valley lilies, embossed h a six-foot cross of white and ple or- ds, the wager s Van- bilt, l w of e hus- derbilt, ned to n Is- whence h u s- d 's n d- the n a modre l Van i l t, bare fferate, emerged early in teenth Century to found a and a $100,000,000 fortune.

The late Dowager Mrs. Vanderbilt

o Ferries Chartered.

pecially chartered ferry e very vehicle of trans- with which the old Com- d the foundation of the fortune, conveyed the rtege across the noisy m Whitehall to Staten

s no mark to indicate ferries were doing any y service, none to de- e was taking the head derbilt family to her place.

costly floral cover ery inch of the rich, casket in which Mrs. e Vanderbilt rested gift of her three sur- n, Mrs. Harry Payne Countess Laszlo

on page 6, col. 1)

1,000 Guns Out In Kidnaping of Cattle Heiress, 6

(By Associated Press)

TUCSON, Ariz., April 26.—A thousand men ready to shoot it out at the bat of an eye—among them the officers to whom John Dillinger and his outlaw gang surrendered meekly here last January—went gunning today for the abductors of 6-year-old June Robles. The kidnapers of the girl suddenly reduced their ransom demand from $15,000 to $10,000.

Quick-shooting cowboys and de-scendants of frontiers grew up with the law of the joined officer son with micro determined to daughter of t Robles, descen cattle barons grant days.

While the se tum and a mutt eral hundred ga County Courth talk, the old ca second ransom abductors said $10,000 "if you

"Z" Signs

The note rea manner not mad

"Child safe. W duce ransom to $ quickly child safely as per in instructions. Z."

It was the sec abductors since th up and whisked a she was going ho The first note the girl's father, operator of an ele hours after June

It demanded $ rected that the alone along a evening at 9 o'cl until contact w

Tucson looke garrison as ra with determin shooters hang lice, sheriff's legionnaires in a house-to city. Outwa days when rustlers foug

It was the rake Tucso the hunt fo to comb the

An airpl hunt by Ca County At child. He aided gre only othe of Gordo two year

Mo

Two lieved in the though whethe identit howev woma care kept A woman living

(Continued on page 4, col. 1)

ROSLYN
OLD WESTBURY
WHEATLEY HILLS
Dear Momey
I am muc
better.
I hope that
you are very
I am having
a nice time
Love
Gloria
if you love me
as I love you
no knife can cut
our love in two
from
Gloria

Vanderbilt Heiress Most Expensive Baby

Gloria Spends $4,000 a Month.

America's most expensive baby!

Little Gloria Laura Vanderbilt, youngest heiress of that well-known family, holds undisputed claim to that title. The little girl, daughter of the late Reginald C. Vanderbilt and Mrs. Vanderbilt, the former Gloria Morgan, has a larger amount of money expended on her maintenance and comfort, court records disclose, than any other youngster in the nation.

George W. Wickersham, Gloria's guardian, was some time ago given permission by the Surrogate's Court here to withdraw from the holdings of the little heiress the sum of $4,000 per month for her upkeep.

From her late father, youngest son of the late Cornelius Vanderbilt, she inherited an undivided half interest in a trust fund of $5,000,000. It is estimated that through careful investments her estate will have increased to something like $10,000,000 by the time she attains her majority and is ready to make her debut into society.

Little Gloria, who is now in New York, usually spends much of her time in Europe and during the Winter season is domiciled in a palatial villa on the shores of the Mediterranean in the south of France. Last Summer she spent much of her time on the sands at Biarritz, near which her mother's estate, the Villa Ourida, is located. Due to repeated threats to kidnap the tiny heiress, she is at all times well guarded by detectives.

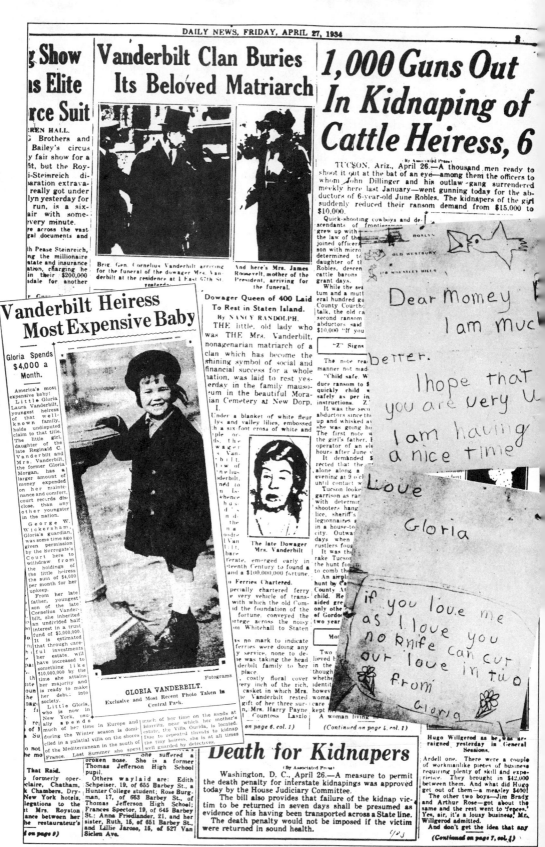

Fotograms

GLORIA VANDERBILT.
Exclusive and Most Recent Photo Taken in Central Park.

That Raid.

formerly oper- claire, Chatham, k Chambers, Dry- New York hotels, llegations to the t Mrs. Royston ance between her he restaurateur's

d on page 9)

broken nose. She suffered a is a former Thomas Jefferson High School pupil.

Others waylaid are: Edith Schpeiser, 19, of 655 Barbey St., a Hunter College student; Rose Burgman, 17, of 653 Barbey St., of Thomas Jefferson High School; Frances Spector, 19, of 645 Barbey St.; Anna Friedlander, 21, and her sister, Ruth, 15, of 651 Barbey St., and Lillie Jaroso, 15, of 527 Van Siclen Ave.

Death for Kidnapers

(By Associated Press)

Washington, D. C., April 26.—A measure to permit the death penalty for interstate kidnapings was approved today by the House Judiciary Committee.

The bill also provides that failure of the kidnap victim to be returned in seven days shall be presumed as evidence of his having been transported across a State line. The death penalty would not be imposed if the victim were returned in sound health.

Hugo Willgerod as he was arraigned yesterday in General Sessions.

Ardell one. There were a couple of workmanlike pieces of business requiring plenty of skill and experience. They brought in $42,000 between them. And what did Hugo get out of them—a measley $400!

The other two boys—Jim Brady and Arthur Rose—got about the same and the rest went to 'fences.' Yes, sir, it's a lousy business, Mr. Willgerod admitted.

And don't get the idea that any

(Continued on page 7, col. 1)

No one at Wheatley Hills realized that little Gloria read the newspapers. Later Gertrude Whitney was to state, "She wasn't interested in them." But she was. And she wrote to Mrs. Morgan, "Dear Naney. I am having a nice time looking at the funny papers." Along with Jo in *Little Women*, there was another heroine for whom little Gloria had a strong affinity—Little Orphan Annie, a plucky hoyden, all alone, who went through many trials and tribulations but wouldn't let the world get her down. Little Gloria figured out that she and Annie were exactly the same age—both were born in 1924. Annie became her mascot and remained so. Little Gloria followed Annie's adventures in the *Daily News*. Also, she read about her mother's trip to California and she knew the details of the Lindbergh kidnapping. Then, just three days after Alice Gwynne Vanderbilt's death, little June Robles was kidnapped. For the next three weeks the newspapers which were delivered to Wheatley Hills carried extensive coverage both of the kidnapping and of the Vanderbilt funeral, will, and social legacy. On April 27, the *News* ran a headline that read, VANDERBILT CLAN BURIES ITS BELOVED MATRIARCH, while the adjacent headline read, 1,000 GUNS OUT IN KIDNAPING OF CATTLE HEIRESS, 6.

Day after day news of little June's kidnapping and Alice Gwynne Vanderbilt's death appeared in the newspapers. The *News* dropped the story of the Robles kidnapping for one day only, May 11, to report on another sensational kidnapping, that of oil millionaire William Gettle. The following day the simultaneous coverage resumed with news of the Vanderbilt bequests and social legacy. "Who will inherit The Breakers and Box 31 at the Met?" inquired the *News*, while in the next column they asked, "Is little June dead?"

After June Robles was found, there were interviews with the child and pages of photographs of the coffin-box in which she'd been imprisoned, the chains and padlocks, the crowds outside the Robles home. On May 18 came the front page stories that, influenced by the worldwide publicity attendant upon the Robles and Gettle cases, President Roosevelt had signed anticrime bills amending the federal law to include the death penalty for ransom kidnapping.

Later, too late, little Gloria finally told her mother that she'd been afraid of being *kidnapped* by her, and Gloria would begin to understand and say, "My child of course reads these things and she thinks of kidnapping not simply as staying with her mother but as something horrible . . . *Kidnapping* is a monstrous word. *Kidnapping* to such a child means the Lindbergh murder and the plight of the little Robles girl left in the desert."

. . .

In June of 1934 when little Gloria's mother visited her at Oakland Farm, she told her that in the fall she was going to take her to New York. Little Gloria turned deathly white and began to shake, but only Dodo noticed. After that, little Gloria began telling people—Dodo, Naney, Aunt Ger, Tom Gilchrist—that she didn't want her mother to take her away, that she didn't want to go back to New York, that she wanted to stay with Aunt Ger always. Then the bad dreams came again and the terror in the night. And there was the mounting dread. And the words KIDNAP and MURDER and MOTHER sealed in her head.

Do You Want the Name of Vanderbilt Dragged Through the Mud?

Into whose hands are you going to confide the secrets of Mabel's life? Lawyers? Detectives? Witnesses? Uneducated people who will distort the truth? Do you want scandal? Do you want the name of Randolph dragged into court? . . . dragged in the mud?

Walking the Dusk BY L. J. WEBB, A PSEUDONYM FOR GERTRUDE VANDERBILT WHITNEY

THREE NOTED FAMILIES IN COURT
FIGHT OVER BABY GLORIA

No Agreement Reached

Despite the silence of the lawyers it was learned that Mrs. Vanderbilt will not give up her ambition to be named guardian of her daughter and the latter's estate without a legal fight. . . . Attempts will be made to postpone the case for several months.

THE NEWSPAPERS now reported on every Whitney-Morgan-Vanderbilt meeting with Surrogate Foley, although they did not know what went on in his private chambers. Gertrude Whitney's lawyers had filed a voluntary writ of intercession on her behalf supporting Mrs. Morgan's objection to the petition. Laura Morgan had assured Gertrude Whitney that once Gloria was faced with the facts, she would "never publish her disgrace." The Whitney lawyers began gathering affidavits to demonstrate Gloria Vanderbilt's unfitness. For information about her daughter's past indiscretions, Mrs. Morgan suggested they contact Gloria's godmother, Mrs. Glenn Stewart, who was Mrs. Morgan's best friend. Tom Gilchrist learned that the Whitney lawyers had hired detectives to help build up their case. He was awed by the seemingly unlimited resources the Whitney team had at its command and he told his wife and son, "They're going to great lengths to get the goods on her." Through Broadway Benny, Nathan Burkan also learned that the Whitney side had hired detectives and were securing affidavits against his client. He asked Gloria if there was anything he should know about her. She assured him there was nothing; that all the accusations against her were based on the ravings of her crazy, vindictive mother and the whims of the infinitely rich and powerful Gertrude Whitney. Burkan began to prepare for battle.

Gloria borrowed another $15,000 on the strength of her forthcoming Vanderbilt legacy and purchased a Rolls-Royce with a 1928 chassis for $4,127. Blumie arranged for the brother-in-law of his own chauffeur to drive the car. To the world, Louis appeared just as a chauffeur—but he was licensed to carry a gun, and on the first day of his employment he explained to Mrs. Vanderbilt that when the child was with her, he would function as a bodyguard to prevent kidnapping and to make sure that no one took the child back to Mrs. Whitney's before Mrs. Vanderbilt gave the order.

Theodore Beesley was still employed as chauffeur for the Pierce-Arrow. Gloria had no need of two cars, but Burkan advised her not to fire Beesley; that way, if there was a court battle, he could not testify that she had dismissed him to prevent him from knowing where she went and with whom. Also, Beesley's continued employment would prove that she expected her daughter to rejoin her. Burkan told Gloria to use the Rolls-Royce exclusively, reserving the Pierce-Arrow for little Gloria. Theodore Beesley remained on with nothing to do. Burkan also suspected butler Charles Zaug, and was relieved when Zaug assured him that he had "seen no impropriety" in the Vanderbilt household and if it came to a trial, he would testify on Mrs. Vanderbilt's behalf. The only other servant who had intimate knowledge of Gloria was Elizabeth Wann, her personal maid who had been employed in the summer of 1933 to replace Maria Caillot. In less than a year Gloria had come to rely on Wann and said that there could be no question about her loyalty.

The Whitney tactics of hiring detectives infuriated Burkan and he decided that two could play that game. Normally, he would have hired Broadway Benny Kerin to do the job, but he felt that to find out about Gertrude Vanderbilt Whitney you needed "a detective with class," someone who knew his way around the upper echelons of Society. There was only one natural choice—Valerian J. O'Farrell, the most famous and highest paid private detective in America, who lived in a twelve-room house in Jackson Heights, Queens, employed several maids, and owned a chauffeur-driven Packard.

O'Farrell, at fifty-eight, looked like a movie star, one who might be cast as a hearty, brave Irish priest. He was over six feet tall, with gray eyes and a full head of curly white hair. (His formula, which he gave to the *News*: "Give it lots of air. After putting cold water on it, comb it with an extra fine comb. Finish with a little liquid Vaseline.") O'Farrell was thirty-six when he quit the police force (after being found guilty of accepting a bribe) and decided to become a private detective. Through a blackmail case, he lucked into a lucrative specialty—rescuing the sons of ultrarich Society families from thieves and blackmailers. O'Farrell followed gin-soaked trails to retrieve young men from nightclubs and whorehouses before they could be thoroughly fleeced. " 'Sapodils'—that's what we call them in the profession," O'Farrell said of these Society playboys. "Ah, those sapodils! They ruin themselves in the white lights. I could mention offhand young men from families whose names are household words, whom I have traced through the labyrinths of Broadway night life, followed to other cities and finally lifted bodily out of dens of filth and degeneracy. They're like squirrels in the park. People feed and pamper them, they have no responsibility." O'Farrell boasted that in one year he'd rescued thirteen young men whose parents were in the multimillionaire class.

In July of 1934 Val O'Farrell was retained by Gloria Vanderbilt and given a down payment of $1,750 by A. C. Blumenthal. Laura Morgan and Gertrude Vanderbilt Whitney were both put under surveillance. Mrs. Morgan was a relatively simple subject for O'Farrell to handle; Gertrude Whitney was more difficult—there were four separate residences to be covered. O'Farrell assigned operatives to each. They watched the town house at 871 Fifth Avenue, the MacDougal Alley studio, and he also managed to place operatives at the Whitney camp at Sabattis in the Adirondacks and at the Wheatley Hills estate. O'Farrell knew that both these estates were guarded by private detectives to prevent the kidnapping of little Gloria either by professional kidnappers or by her own mother. Although O'Farrell never revealed how he had managed to place his spies at these isolated locations, it is a reasonable assumption that they were among the men hired to guard the child.

Val O'Farrell began to trail Mrs. Morgan. Her apartment, which was in a hotel at 14 East Sixtieth Street, was wired to record her conversations. It was a relatively easy matter to run a wire from the hidden microphone to a rented room nearby. Mrs. Morgan's conversations were picked up on an amplifying device and fed into a Dictaphone machine where they were recorded. The recordings were made on cylinders six inches long, thirteen-and-a-half inches in diameter, and one-half inch thick, coated with black beeswax. Each cylinder could record up to twelve minutes of conversation and two cylinders could be set up so that there would be no gaps in the conversation; the first cylinder could be replaced while the second was in use. A man was on duty at all times since the equipment was manually operated and no one could tell when a conversation would take place.

On July 21 Gloria's new chauffeur, Louis, drove Mrs. Vanderbilt to the O'Farrell offices, where Val O'Farrell carefully removed the cylinders from their fleece-lined cardboard containers. He showed Gloria how to operate the Dictaphone machine by stepping on the foot pedal. He adjusted the transparent celluloid cups of the headset over her ears. Gloria identified the voice she heard as that of her mother.

On Saturday, July 28, at 8:50 p.m., when it seemed time for O'Farrell's operatives to give up for the night, an operative heard the voice of Mrs. Morgan call out the window, "Come over a little while—perhaps I will go back with you." Another operative watching the Morgan apartment saw a woman, carrying the evening newspaper, enter the apartment. (These newspapers contained articles on the legal battle and gossip items about Gloria Vanderbilt and Blumie.) The woman spoke first. "What do you know about that! How can anyone go with that man who is married. He is the talk of Broadway. Wait until they get to Lady Furness and the Indian [Aly Khan]. They have that to talk about yet."

"They will have lots to say about her, too," Mamma Morgan said of Thelma.

"He [Blumie] has dragged her down to his level," the woman observed.

"She doesn't have much money," said Mamma Morgan.

"I suppose the child has plenty."

"Three weeks after Reggie died they gave her $4,000 a month."

"When you have lots of money, you can tell everybody to go to hell."

O'Farrell subsequently presented a transcript of this conversation to his client.

Consuelo suggested they call Thelma for help. Thelma came promptly from Europe, went to see Mamma, and tried her best to get her to stop her opposition to Gloria's guardianship petition. "Mothers don't do to their children what you are doing—blacken their characters before the world . . ." she told her mother.

Mrs. Morgan began to weep. "You have not been aware of the neglect that has been going on. This unfortunate child has been dying and Gloria has paid no attention to it."

An angry Thelma countered that little Gloria was hardly neglected, she had never been alone for a day in her life. From birth she'd been with nurse Keislich or with Mamma herself. Then Thelma tried to bring economic pressure to bear, pointing out that she and Gloria each gave Mamma $250 a month to support herself.

"If you can give me my check for August, after that I will not need money anymore," Mamma told Thelma.

"Why, Mummy, how are you going to live?" asked Thelma.

"Never mind about that . . ."

"But Mummy, you have always told me you didn't have any money and that is why we have been giving you this money."

"Darling, you need it more than I do," replied her mother off-handedly. Thelma was convinced that if her mother didn't need her money, than someone else was supporting her—Gertrude Vanderbilt Whitney.

The conference ended in confrontation. "Are you going against me, too?" Mrs. Morgan asked her daughter.

"If you ask me am I on your side or Gloria's, I have only to say I am on the right side. I don't have to tell you which that is."

"You be careful, Thelma, that I don't take *your* child away," threatened Mamma.

"Luckily, Mamma, my child has a father alive—my child has no rich aunt in England . . . if you proceed with this case, you will put a blot on this child whom you profess to love. . . ."

Mamma Morgan began fingering her rosary. "I can never face my God if I don't do this," she said.

Shortly after this, Gertrude Whitney wrote to her sister Gladys Széchényi about her progress in opposing Gloria's petition:

> *. . . there will be a hearing & if no settlement is arrived at probably a postponement until Oct. Mrs. M.'s* [*Morgan's*] *statement is excellent & I am being kept out as much as possible on the grounds that I do not wish to say anything which might hurt the child's future. If it comes up I will only have to testify as to the circumstances under which the child came to me & her condition, which will be substantiated by the doctors. Mrs. G.S.* [*Mrs. Glenn Stewart*]

fills in things in the past. We are trying to keep out any mention of immorality, but base everything on neglect and indifference. Lady F. [*Furness*] *is here trying to intimidate her mother but unsuccessfully.*

The tone of the letter was naïve—Gertrude seemed to think that if Gloria's reputation was to be discredited, as long as Gertrude personally took no part in it, she could stand aside, lily-white.

Consuelo went the next round with Mamma Morgan and proved a formidable adversary. When Mrs. Morgan argued neglect, her daughter lashed out, "You never considered it neglect when you left your children scattered over Europe. For months at a time you never went near Thelma or Gloria when they were little . . . and you left them alone in New York City and never came near them. . . . Neglect! Talk to me of money being the basis of this action, but not of neglect." Consuelo, unable to influence her mother, decided to speak directly to Gertrude, trying to determine the exact reason for her reluctance to allow little Gloria to return to her own mother. In response, Consuelo received only what she thought to be vague generalities: Gertrude said that she had no motive except "the welfare of the child"; that she had never seen Gloria "misbehaving or doing anything that wasn't quite proper," but that in her opinion, she thought that "the child would be better off with me."

Consuelo reacted with some vehemence. " 'Better off' is not sufficient reason to take a child away from its mother. Obviously, the child would have greater material advantages with you, but that is the only benefit."

"Well, that is still my opinion," replied a controlled Gertrude.

Consuelo told Gertrude that it was obvious she was basing her opinion on what Mamma Morgan or the nurse had been saying and that she felt it her duty to warn her that Mrs. Morgan was not a very reliable source of information. "She is very excitable, she exaggerates things, she imagines things. She has always . . . well, either threatened us or accused us of things, and we paid very little attention to it because she isn't a normal person, either on the subject of the child or the subject of money." Consuelo did not mince words in an effort to make this woman understand: "Unfortunately, my niece's money and your money combined must have gone to her head, because there was no reason why my mother would say that my sister was unfit to look after her own child. She lived with her for four and a half years; my sister was supporting her even then, and she was in and out of my sister's house until a few days before the third of July when this petition came up."

Then Consuelo said, "If you really care for little Gloria, you will think twice before bringing up a suit of this kind. The publicity will harm not only the child but my sister, you, and possibly me, being a member of the family. It really isn't worth doing."

"I intend going on with it, anyway," replied Gertrude Whitney.

At the end of July, Surrogate Foley held another hearing in his chambers at which the lawyers for both sides said they wanted to avoid a court battle, but neither side would change its position. The following day the *American* announced, "Fourteen lawyers are actively concerned in the litigation . . . over the guardianship of the most expensive child in the world."

The battle escalated—Mamma telephoned to threaten Gloria that if she did not drop her petition, her name would be "dragged through the mud" and her shame "broadcast for all the world to see." In a tone of voice that frightened Gloria she swore, "If you fight . . . you will live to regret it." Mamma also wrote Gloria letters pleading with her to settle the matter and leave the child with Mrs. Whitney. Consuelo received a phone call from Mamma and reported that Mamma threatened, "I will ruin the family if this case goes on." Mrs. Morgan maintained that she only had said aloud what they all knew. "The family will be ruined if this case goes on."

Nathan Burkan told Gloria that if the child were living with her instead of with Mrs. Whitney, the picture would be quite different. He reminded her that the only time she'd managed to get what she wanted had been the previous September when she'd taken the child. Then the guardians and Mrs. Whitney had treated her reasonably and with respect.

Little Gloria was then vacationing at the Whitney camp in the Adirondacks. Gloria and Consuelo took the night train to Sabattis and arrived at seven o'clock in the morning. Later, Gloria was to say that they were on their way to Canada to visit friends and just decided to stop off to see little Gloria. Louis, the Vanderbilt bodyguard-chauffeur, had been sent ahead with the Rolls-Royce and met them at the station. He drove them for about an hour until they arrived at a docking area between two lakes. It was as far as they could go. Gloria, knowing nothing of the Whitney "camp," had not realized that the only way of getting there was by boat. In fact, the so-called Whitney camp actually consisted of 85,000 acres of forest land interspersed with a series of lakes of various sizes. There were several "camps" for the Whitney family, the nearest of which was a twenty-minute boat ride from the mainland. At present, Gertrude and little Gloria were staying at Camp Deerlands, the Henrys at Camp Killoquah, and the Millers at Camp

Togus. They commuted between these camps by means of canoe, sailboat, and motorboat.

Gloria became quite upset when she realized what the geographic situation was. She felt thwarted and ill from the altitude and the emotional strain of what she was going through. Her nose began to bleed. She gasped for breath. While Gloria waited in the car, Consuelo went into a lodge located on the dock, turned the crank on the wooden box of the wall phone, and ordered that little Gloria be sent to them.

About fifteen minutes later a launch arrived, but the child was not in it, so Consuelo directed the boatman to take her to "the Whitney camp." The clear lake was a sheet of sapphire glass. The early morning air was pure and thin. Then, off in the distance, Consuelo saw another launch coming toward them. As it drew near, she saw that little Gloria was a passenger. The launch passed them, going in the opposite direction. Consuelo shouted over the sound of the motor and into the boatman's ear that he must turn around and follow the other boat. To her astonishment, the boatman refused to comply. "I have orders from Mrs. Whitney that the child is not to see her mother unless Mrs. Whitney says so," he told her.

At Camp Deerlands, Gertrude was informed that Mrs. Vanderbilt was waiting at the carry on the mainland and had demanded that little Gloria be sent to her. Since they were engaged in a legal battle, it seemed unlikely to Gertrude that this was simply a social call: she reasoned that from the Adirondacks it would be an easy matter for Gloria to kidnap little Gloria and take her across the border to Canada where she would be out of Foley's legal jurisdiction. Gertrude checked on the whereabouts of her niece and of the guards and of her own daughter Flora Miller. By the time Flora arrived at Camp Deerlands, Gertrude was prepared.

Consuelo had been waiting at Camp Deerlands for two hours. Finally Gertrude appeared and, with no excuse for her lateness, asked Consuelo where her sister was. Consuelo was so angry she did not answer; instead, she demanded, "What do you mean by giving orders to the boatman that my sister is not to see her child?"

"That must be a terrible mistake," replied Gertrude evenly. "That order was given about all the children on the place."

When Consuelo described how ill Gloria was, Gertrude went inside her lodge and emerged with a bottle of brandy and some bread. Then Gertrude, her daughter Flora, and Consuelo got into the launch and headed for the carry. Consuelo felt that Gertrude and Flora were checking to see for themselves if Gloria was really ill. When they reached the car, Gloria, who by this time had been waiting for three hours, was on the verge of fainting. After Gloria drank some brandy, Gertrude explained that little Gloria was presently at another camp and invited her to come with them to see the child. Gloria answered that she was too ill, so they volunteered to bring the child to her.

The fight was over her. They thought she knew nothing, but she knew. Her mother had told her she was going to take her and Aunt Ger was trying to stop her. News of the fight was in the newspapers and Dodo had read all about it. The Adirondacks had been little Gloria's favorite place with its woods and its freedom—she'd gone swimming and canoeing and on wild berry hunts and, for the only time during the year, she was allowed to eat with the adults. But this summer she was so worried she couldn't have any fun: she couldn't sit still, she couldn't eat much, and at night there were the terrible dreams. Dodo spoke to Dr. St. Lawrence, and after that her swimming was cut to ten minutes a day and her riding time was cut and she had to take long naps and medicine to go to the bathroom. After little Gloria's mother had come to Oakland Farm and said that she was going to take her away, she'd disappeared. Dodo thought she was in Europe, but no one knew for sure, and little Gloria was frightened that when she came back she'd be coming to get her. A sweater arrived in the mail with a note from her mother saying she'd knitted it for her. It was too small, the sleeves barely came past her elbows. She wrote her mother a thank-you note:

Dear Mumy,
I am having a nice time I hope you are allso.
I like the sweater.
love
Gloria

P.S. Where are you now?

She lied about the sweater because she was afraid.

Then that bright August morning little Gloria and Dodo climbed into a launch to go to Camp Killoquah for little Gloria's reading lesson. In the middle of the calm blue lake another launch streaked by. In it was Aunt Consuelo, who pointed toward her and then gestured to the boatman and said something to him that little Gloria couldn't hear.

About two hours later Aunt Ger and cousin Flora came to get her. They told her that Mummy had arrived unexpectedly on her way to Canada and that they were going to take her to the mainland to see her. There were four bodyguards in the launch. Little Gloria scooped up her precious Gypsy-Mitzie and climbed in. Her mouth went dry. This she knew: Her mother was going to kidnap her. She was going "to kidnap her" and "take her to Canada."

Little Gloria turned to Aunt Ger. There was so much to say, but all she said was, "My throat is so dry. I don't know what's the matter. I feel so funny."

"What is the trouble, Gloria?" asked Aunt Ger crisply.

"I don't know. My throat is dry."

When the launch pulled up to the dock, little Gloria stepped out, followed by nurse Keislich and four private detectives. The dock area was small, and it seemed to Gloria that the men loomed over her child. Gloria got out of the car and bent down and kissed her daughter. Little Gloria said, "Oh, do you think I could have a glass of water?"

Gertrude Whitney gestured toward the lodge. "Run in and get a glass there," she suggested. Little Gloria disappeared into the lodge but she didn't come out. After a time Gertrude went in after her and brought her back.

Little Gloria moved toward her mother, but after a moment backed away. Gloria sat on the running board of the car and called the child to her. The child darted up to her mother as if on a dare. A moment later she ran away. Then back. Then away. Then she ran back into the lodge. Twice more, Gertrude had to go inside and persuade her to come out. At one side of the dock was a basket of kittens. Little Gloria jumped up and ran to it and began playing with the kittens as if oblivious of her mother's presence.

Consuelo had never seen little Gloria behave so indifferently toward her mother. Gertrude spoke to the child, saying, "Gloria, since your mother has waited all this time, you might go and sit with her." Then the child came over politely, but Consuelo thought she acted stiff and unnatural. And all the time those four men were standing over her, watching.

It was now after noon and Gertrude invited Gloria and Consuelo to the main lodge for lunch. Gloria refused the invitation. Then Gertrude and Gloria both climbed into the Rolls-Royce for a private conversation. Gertrude spoke as if to a child, explaining gently over and over that little Gloria was better off remaining with her. Again she repeated the litany of friends, relatives, school, fresh air. She told Gloria, "You could come to see her whenever and as often as you liked."

"Don't you understand I want my baby," Gloria cried out in desperation. "I want my child with me. I don't want to go and visit her. I don't want to go and see her as a visitor."

"Yes, I quite understand, Gloria," Gertrude replied, "but in my opinion . . ."

"Your opinion is not the same as mine. I am the mother of the baby and I want her. I love her," Gloria protested. Gloria was so upset and exhausted by their conversation that as soon as Gertrude climbed out of the car, she ordered Louis to drive them back to the station. They took the afternoon train back to New York, abandoning all plans to go on to Canada.

Little Gloria had watched her mother and Aunt Ger as they talked, sealed together in that gray metal shell. She knew they were arguing about her. Finally, Aunt Ger climbed out of the car and her mother and Aunt Consuelo drove away. Aunt Ger had stopped Mummy from kidnapping her.

Aunt Ger and little Gloria were walking by the edge of the lake. Alone. Little Gloria moved in silence by the side of this remote woman. She felt that there was so much she wanted to say, but "there was always a wall between us." Quite suddenly there was a great roar in the sky. Startled, little Gloria threw her head back, looked up, and saw an airplane overhead—this machine that was the very symbol of the Lone Eagle, the quintessence of Charles Augustus Lindbergh. And then little Gloria said, "Aunt Ger, I am afraid I am going to be kidnapped."

At last she had spoken her fear. Gertrude Whitney heard the words. Their meaning was never understood.

Kidnap=Murder=Mother

I'm afraid of her.
Don't let her hurt me.
Oh, don't let her take me.
I'm frightened.
Then IT would happen.
She's going to kill me!

LITTLE GLORIA VANDERBILT

AND WHAT OF LITTLE GLORIA? A trial of this nature could mark her for life, that was what concerned Surrogate James A. Foley. For two months the arguments had been dragging on and on, and no agreement had been reached. Almost daily, reporters presented themselves at his chambers. He had his secretary type up noncommittal statements for them. "As a result of preliminary discussion, it is hoped that an amicable solution may be reached . . . The attorneys will be called for a subsequent conference. . . ." If the press really knew what was involved they would have a field day. Laura Morgan's accusations, coupled with Gertrude Whitney's voluntary writ of intercession alleging neglect and indifference, were just the kind of maggoty stuff the tabloids devoured. Foley was determined to protect this innocent child from public disgrace. Foley held conference after conference with the lawyers for both sides, trying to settle the matter: Frank Crocker kept insisting that Mrs. Whitney keep the child with her for a minimum of three years to ensure the child's health and education, and Walter

Dunnington was in total agreement with him. Nathan Burkan kept insisting that his client would settle for nothing less than sole guardianship of her child's person and joint guardianship of her child's property, and he demanded that the child be sent to live with her mother.

Realizing Burkan's close connections with Foley, Crocker had brought in yet another lawyer, John Godfrey Saxe, a man who was equally close to the Surrogate—or perhaps closer. Saxe was an expert in the laws pertaining to guardianship and estates and also a Tammany bigwig.

Foley, a man of vast legal experience but also a man of common sense, could see that all these lawyers were steering their clients on a suicidal course. In an unusual act of humanity, Foley asked that the lawyers invite both Mrs. Whitney and Mrs. Vanderbilt to his home on East Twelfth Street for an informal evening conference. (Also to attend were Nathan Burkan, Jim Murray, Walter Dunnington, and John Godfrey Saxe.) Foley hoped that in the informal atmosphere of his own home, these two women would put aside their grievances and work out a solution to the problem.

Gertrude Whitney sat on the sofa. Gloria sat next to her—scarcely six inches separated them. Gertrude reached out and took Gloria's hand and held it in her own. In this intimate atmosphere Foley began to explain not the legal aspects of the matter but the human considerations. He told these two women they must do everything in their power to arrive at a solution that would prevent a public display and the inevitable injury it would inflict on little Gloria.

Gloria, listening to the Surrogate, did not fully understand what he was saying. She felt that he was suggesting that she leave her child with Gertrude Whitney, but she was not sure of this.

Gertrude turned and spoke to Gloria. "I don't want to hurt you, or harm you in any way, but you will have to understand here and now that for the child's sake if you persist in going to court, I will most definitely take a stand against your control."

Then Surrogate Foley asked to speak to Gloria privately. Gertrude Whitney and the lawyers left the room. Foley closed the door behind them. His eyes peered out at Gloria from behind his steel-rimmed glasses, and he spoke with gravity. "Do you know what a trial of this caliber can do? There will be so much dirt exposed by the press that it will drag you and the child through a mire of infamy that will cling to her as long as she lives. Let me tell you what *you* face. There is a certain kind of sensational journalism in America that feeds on cases like this. . . . Remember, it is not Mrs. Whitney who will be on trial, but yourself."

Gloria could hardly absorb what Surrogate Foley was saying. She was simply following Nathan Burkan's instructions. He had told her they must do this to get her rights, and she trusted him. After a time, Foley opened the door and called Gertrude into the room. Gloria felt that she was losing ground when, suddenly, "my heart cut off my breath almost entirely." Gasping for air, she fell back on the couch. Gertrude moved swiftly and wrapped her arms around Gloria and tried to calm her. The conference was at an end.

But Foley would not give up. By this time both women were surrounded by a team of their own lawyers and there was no more direct communication between them concerning the crucial issue of little Gloria's residence and guardianship. The conferences were solely between the lawyers, and finally Foley effected a compromise. Frank Crocker informed Gertrude of the details: Gertrude understood that she was to keep the child for the next year, but that Gloria could have the child for one month. After that, the question of when the child would return to her mother and of the child's guardianship would be taken up again before the Surrogate. Gertrude seemed satisfied with this arrangement.

Nathan Burkan informed Gloria of the details: Gloria understood that Gertrude was to keep the child for the next school year, but that she could have her for one month. After that, the child would return to her for good, and Gloria would immediately be made guardian of the child's person and co-guardian of the child's property. Gloria seemed satisfied with this arrangement.

Frank Crocker advised Gertrude Whitney that the agreement was tentative and not yet in writing; because of this they should continue obtaining affidavits against Mrs. Vanderbilt. It came to Nathan Burkan's attention that, in spite of the agreement, the Whitney lawyers were still obtaining affidavits detrimental to the character of his client. Burkan told Gloria that in case Mrs. Whitney intended to violate the agreement, she should be prepared with affidavits of her own.

On August 18, 1934, following Burkan's instructions, Gloria and Consuelo sailed for Europe. Consuelo disembarked at Le Havre and went to see her husband in Oslo. Gloria went to Deauville, where Thelma had taken over Aly Khan's villa for the season while he became a guest in his own house. After a few days they proceeded to Schloss Langenburg to visit Prince Gottfried Hohenlohe and his wife, Princess Margarita. Gloria explained to Friedel that Mamma was "ready to use any means to put her hands on little Gloria." Mamma charged, among other things, that Gloria "had had immoral and improper relations" with the prince. Gloria had come to secure affidavits from Friedel and his parents refuting this charge. Prince Hohenlohe was happy to comply with her request.

Princess Margarita, aware of how close Gloria was to her aunt and uncle, George and Nadeja Milford Haven, also volunteered to help in any way she could. The Milford Havens had been—and still were—unstintingly generous to Margarita's family. At this very time they were arranging for her little brother, Prince Philip, to attend Gordonstoun, a new school on the coast of Scotland headed by Kurt Hahn, who had recently fled Germany. Once again, the Milford Havens had assumed responsibility for Philip's education and welfare.

Gloria and Thelma spent a pleasant five days at Schloss Langenburg. Only two weeks prior to their trip, President von Hindenburg died and Adolf Hitler had become head of state and commander-in-chief of the armed forces, assuming total dictatorial powers with the approval of the German cabinet. There was talk that Germany had a "messiah fixation" about Hitler. Within the week there was to be a rally at Nuremberg which half a million people were expected to attend. Prince and Princess Hohenlohe were on the most cordial terms with the Nazi government, unlike several of Friedel's cousins who had opposed Hitler. But at Schloss Langenburg the political situation was overshadowed by the news of the engagement of Marina of Greece to Prince George, Duke of Kent. Nada Milford Haven was credited with making the match. It seems that the prince had lamented to Nada, "I suppose I've got to get married one day, but all the princesses I know are so damned ugly." Nada had countered with a description of Princess Marina. The wedding was scheduled for November 29 in Westminster Abbey, the first royal wedding to take place there since that of Lady Elizabeth Bowes-Lyon to the Duke of York eleven years previously.

On their way back to the United States, Gloria and Thelma made one last stop in Paris as guests of Aly Khan, whose impending engagement to Thelma had been announced in newspapers all over the world. They had one evening only and attended the night races at Longchamps. In front of their box was a platform on which were staged performances by the corps de ballet of the Paris Opera and the Imperial Russian Ballet. At other points around the racecourse nine orchestras played. Aly rode in the last race.

Gertrude Whitney heard reports that Gloria Vanderbilt was in Europe obtaining legal affidavits. Frank Crocker and his associates speculated that soon she planned to violate the agreement. On Saturday, September 15, 1934, Gloria and Consuelo arrived back in New York. Gloria telephoned Gertrude, and during their conversation it was apparent that each woman had a radically different interpretation of the agreement. However, Gertrude, acting on her lawyers' advice that she must not be the one to violate the agreement by denying the mother access to the child, agreed to send little Gloria to her mother's New York town house for lunch the following day.

Gloria had had enough—she spoke with Nathan Burkan and began to expedite the plan to take little Gloria.

Nurse Keislich had observed little Gloria's violent reaction to her mother's announcement that she was going to take her to live with her in New York. The minute she told her that, little Gloria had turned pale—deathly white. Nurse Keislich told Mrs. Whitney that Mrs. Vanderbilt had been completely unfeeling, springing the news on her "without any preparation whatsoever." After that, little Gloria had grown increasingly nervous, so much so that nurse Keislich asked Mrs. Whitney to postpone straightening her teeth until she calmed down. The nurse telephoned Dr. St. Lawrence from the Adirondacks and he prescribed rest and laxatives over the telephone. As soon as they returned from the Adirondacks, nurse Keislich brought little Gloria to see him, but she made no mention of Mrs. Vanderbilt's visit or the legal fight over the child's guardianship. And when St. Lawrence questioned why the child was again constipated, Keislich supplied the reason that she had "difficulty in using the bathroom because of the numbers of children" at the Whitney camp. St. Lawrence did not question this reason, but wrote it on his chart. Soon an entire page was filled with critical observations concerning the child. St. Lawrence told the nurse to continue administering the mineral oil and milk of magnesia he'd prescribed over the phone (although these were the very remedies he'd scorned when the child had come to him two years previously). Once again, he insisted that the child's activities be restricted, and Keislich followed his orders so faithfully that some observers at Wheatley Hills, seeing a child of ten allowed almost no physical activity and put to bed sixteen hours out of every twenty-four, thought that both the nurse and the doctor were "cuckoo."

One week before the Green Vale School was about to start, Aunt Ger called little Gloria into her bedroom and told her that she was going to be sent to visit her mother for Sunday lunch. Little Gloria didn't want to go. She told that to Aunt Ger and said that she was afraid of her mother. Aunt Ger said that she wouldn't have to stay overnight, that she would be coming back in the afternoon. But when little Gloria and Dodo got to the house, her mother phoned Aunt Ger to try to keep her. Aunt Ger wouldn't let her, but promised to send little Gloria back another time.

She was afraid to go again. On Monday Naney came to visit and asked if she wanted to go back, and little Gloria told her she never wanted to go back. She told her grandmother that she was afraid. And she said, "I hate my mother." After Naney left, she wrote her a note:

> *Dear Naney,*
>
> *I have just had my hair washed and you have just gone away.*
>
> *I hope I do not have to go to the city.*
>
> *Please write to me.*
>
> *love Jo*

Then she filled the paper with OO's and XX's and drew a heart with an arrow through it on the paper and wrote inside the heart, "I love you."

On Tuesday Aunt Ger again called little Gloria into her bedroom. Gertrude had waited until the last moment because she knew that what she had to say would upset the child. She explained gently that little Gloria was going to her mother's to visit for a few days, but that she would be back by the end of the week, since the Green Vale School started the following Tuesday.

"Oh, I can't go and stay with my mother," little Gloria said. "I don't want to go. I don't want to see her. I don't feel *happy* with her."

Gertrude explained that her mother wanted to see her, that her mother was fond of her, that she was sure Gloria would have a nice time. Then she said, "Gloria, you *will* be back by the end of the week."

"Are you sure?" the child asked.

"Yes, I am sure."

"Are you sure?" the child asked again and again. She had her head bent and her eyes looked down at the floor. She looked at Gertrude, and then lowered her head again. Gertrude would never forget the look in the child's eyes at that moment.

Finally, when little Gloria saw there was no way out, she left a note for the kennel man:

> *Dear Walter*
>
> *Please take very good care of Gypsy. I hope you are well. . . . I am going to tell you the things you must feed puppy and at what time.*
>
> *7:30 two tablespoons of cooked cereal with half a cup of warm milk.*

12:30 two tablespoons of raw meat with half a cup of boiling water on it.
5:30 more raw meat with boiling water on it.

from your friend Gloria
P.S. Please call me up and tell me how she is.

At the last minute, little Gloria insisted that her puppy had to go with her. When they could delay no more, Dodo and little Gloria went to that house. Dodo was afraid to sleep because there was no one to guard them. Beesley watched them in the park, but at night Dodo was frightened. Little Gloria was frightened too. The second day she was there she heard her mother say into the phone that there was going to be a fight. She asked Dodo if the fight was going to be about her. But she knew it was.

Friday morning little Gloria was downstairs with Aunt Consuelo, who told her that Mummy had just rented a house in Old Westbury and that she was *never* going back to Aunt Ger's. Little Gloria rushed upstairs to tell Dodo, but she already knew, Mummy had told her the same thing.

It was then that little Gloria felt the full force of the terror—it seeped out from a tiny burning spot to become a jagged crimson explosion. It struck her with all its many elements: The Lindbergh child had been *taken away—kidnapped.* They had *done something to him.* He'd been found dead—*murdered.* The Robles girl had been *taken away—kidnapped.* She'd been starved, burned, chained in a pit in the desert. Your *mother* has *kidnapped* you and she's going to kill you. All the terrible words came together. The puzzle was complete: KIDNAP=MURDER=MOTHER.

Little Gloria was frenzied with terror. She ran to the window and screamed that she was going to jump. Dodo begged her not to and promised to help her escape. That afternoon they fled to Aunt Ger. Little Gloria cried and threw her arms around her aunt and told her she would never go back to her mother. And when her mother came, she screamed, "Take her away. . . . I'm frightened . . . she's going to kill me. . . . Oh, don't let her take me . . . I hate her!" Finally, Aunt Ger let her come back to Wheatley Hills. That week the guard was increased so her mother wouldn't try to KIDNAP her again.

A few days later Dodo told her there was going to be a "trial," and she took little Gloria to Aunt Ger's house in the city and dressed her in a party dress with a white collar. Aunt Ger came and took her to a great building that looked like a Roman palace with white marble columns. As the car stopped, a crowd swarmed around and faces pressed against the windows. The chauffeur opened the door and two men reached in and hauled little Gloria out. Other guards formed a wedge, pushing the crowd before them. Blinding flashbulbs popped in her face, and a man with a newsreel camera blocked her path.

Later she would learn to cover her face like a felon. Later, curled into a fetal position, she would be carried through the crowds by her bodyguards. But her initial response was quite different. If this child had moved rapidly past you on that balmy September morning, you would have thought that she was smiling. You would have been wrong. Photographs taken that day have impaled her expression that passed for a smile. It is feral, frightening: the lips are drawn back taut over the teeth. It is the grimace of a gargoyle, a frozen scream of pain, on the face of little Gloria Vanderbilt.

Then the child disappeared through the bronze doors of the New York State Supreme Court building. And it began.

THE TRIAL

Dirty Linen

Watch out, Gloria, all the dirty linen is going to be laundered in front of the whole nation.

MAURY PAUL

THE *Matter of Vanderbilt* exploded into headlines. All the elements of "the perfect tabloid story" were there: famous names, vast wealth, high jinks in high places, a glamorous fashion show, mother love, and the most important element of all, scandal—seamy, salacious, spellbinding scandal. In a country racked by the Great Depression, the fall from grace of the super-rich had an incredible sweetness. Little Gloria Vanderbilt, THE POOR LITTLE RICH GIRL, appealed to a disillusioned yet sentimental America. She was the perfect symbol to prove that money can't buy happiness; even the privileged had problems which, after all, made them a part of humanity, no better than the man in the street who read about them every day in the newspapers. This "gold child" was worse off than the poorest Depression child. How terrible! How marvelous! To feel sorry for a Vanderbilt was a fantasy worth pursuing.

Gertrude Whitney didn't want to bring little Gloria to court, but she had no choice. The writ of habeas corpus was a legal command to "bring up the body of Gloria Laura Morgan Vanderbilt" before Supreme Court Justice John F. Carew to answer the allegation that "the infant" had been "wrongfully restrained and detained . . . against the wishes of the Relator, Gloria Morgan Vanderbilt." The preliminary hearing was scheduled for Friday, September 28, 1934, at 10:00 a.m. in the Justice's Supreme Court chambers.

Reporters and photographers jammed the sidewalk outside the Supreme Court building. A few minutes before 10:00 a.m., Gloria Vanderbilt's black Rolls-Royce pulled up; private detectives moved forward to keep the crowd from the car. Nathan Burkan got out first and helped Gloria Vanderbilt out of the limousine. She wore a severely tailored black suit and a black felt hat with a Peter Pan brim; she carried a silver-fox fur piece. Gloria was followed by her friend Agnes Horter, who also wore a black suit. Gloria clutched Burkan's arm as they moved slowly through the crowd and up the broad steps of the Supreme Court building. A moment later, Gertrude Whitney's gray Rolls-Royce stopped at the curb. The crowd surged forward, faces were plastered against the car windows as they examined the specimen inside—little Gloria Vanderbilt. A dozen detectives appeared, forming a wedge to push the crowd back from the car as Gertrude Whitney climbed out. If fashion were to influence the judge, it would be a split decision: Mrs. Whitney was dressed identically to Gloria, down to the fox fur piece, with heads and tails intact, draped over her left arm. Two detectives reached inside the limousine and pulled the child out. Ten-and-a-half-year-old little Gloria wore a tan wool English coat and a matching hat that tied under her chin. Her ankle-length white cotton socks disappeared in wrinkles into her brown leather lace-up shoes. Her hands, which were clenched into fists, were enclosed in wrist-length brown leather gloves and she swung her arms as she trotted along at the side of the tall, thin, straight-backed Gertrude Whitney. Perhaps a foot of space separated them, but Mrs. Whitney did not reach for the child's hand. As the flashbulbs began to explode, little Gloria looked up, her lips stretched back over her teeth, and she seemed to smile a broad smile.

Reporters followed Mrs. Whitney and little Gloria into the building, up to the sixth floor, and down the narrow corridor to an anteroom outside of Justice Carew's chambers. As little Gloria walked into the room, she moved so close to her mother that Gloria stepped back to avoid bumping into her. The child turned and looked her mother full in the face, her gray eyes peering out steadily from beneath the bangs of her Buster Brown bob. Then her pale face flushed and slowly and deliberately she turned her head away. In front of the press of the nation, little Gloria had cut her mother dead.

Gertrude and little Gloria arrive at court

. . .

A few moments later, the principals in the *Matter of Vanderbilt* were summoned inside the chambers of Supreme Court Justice John Francis Carew. This custody battle was to be decided not by a jury but solely by this man. His personality and prejudices would determine, in large measure, what issues were to be considered crucial to this trial. Carew was fifty-eight—over six feet tall, heavyset, with snow-white hair, a pince-nez, and a carefully trimmed mustache and goatee. He wore a dark blue suit and old-fashioned high black shoes.

The lofty severity of the judge's appearance was matched by his views. Carew thought of himself as a man of simple language and common sense, "a practical person" not easily "buncoed." He was an ardent Catholic and felt that most of the country's problems were due to "an increasing tide of irreligion." His attitude toward women was paternalistic: he regarded them as children to be guided, patronized, and protected. He had voted against woman suffrage, and when members of the Congressional Union asked him to arrange a hearing before the judiciary committee on women's rights, he replied in surprise, "I thought woman suffrage was settled for good. I thought you were never going to take it up again."

Carew was an isolationist. "I am an American. I have no antecedents in Europe and I inherit no European tradition," he boasted of himself. He had never been to Europe, spoke no foreign language, and distrusted foreigners, whom he referred to as "aliens." In his public utterances he managed to turn both religion and chauvinism to his purpose: "Free speech on the fundamental matters of sex and morality is contrary not only to Christian principles but also to the fundamental principles of the American government."

John Francis Carew gloried in his man-of-the-people background and believed in the work ethic. He'd been born to a middle-class Brooklyn family and after graduating from Columbia Law School went to work in the office of his uncle, Thomas Francis Magner, a well-known lawyer and Tammany politician. He rose rapidly as a Tammany politician and, in 1912, was elected to the House of Representatives from New York City's Seventeenth District. As a congressman he acquired a keen appreciation of the power of public opinion and became so popular that he was reelected to office eight consecutive times over a span of eighteen years. In 1929, Carew was appointed to the New York State Supreme Court by Governor Franklin Delano Roosevelt at a salary of $22,500 a year.

At the time of the Vanderbilt trial, Justice Carew had been married for thirty-one years to Mary O'Brien and they were the parents of five children, four of whom still lived at home. Carew's home life was unusually restrictive in that when Mary was forty years old she had showed the first symptoms of rheumatoid arthritis. The doctor's treatment was to immobilize her for one full year, with sandbags weighting down her limbs. At the end of this period she emerged a hopeless cripple, permanently confined to a wheelchair and unable to perform the simplest tasks—she could not even dial a telephone. As a result, Carew assumed great responsibility in the upbringing of his children and led a cloistered life. The whole family "stuck close to home," and Mary had many visitors, especially priests, who often said Mass for her at their apartment on East Sixty-eighth Street. Mary was in constant pain, "heroic pain" her daughter Blanche called it, but she never complained. Justice Carew's only social forays away from his apartment consisted of an occasional dinner with the Friendly Sons of St. Patrick.

Justice Carew's own life pattern and beliefs would set the tone for the Vanderbilt trial. He was openly to censure Gloria Vanderbilt for her string of titled acquaintances, saying that they meant no more to him than "the Duke of Bologney." Gertrude Whitney, on the witness stand, would portray herself as an aging widow, a devoted mother and grandmother who led "a quiet country life." Little Gloria would stumble through her Hail Mary and parrot the Apostles' Creed after the judge, in an effort to prove herself a diligent Catholic.

A staunch member of one distinct class, Carew was to sit in judgment on two other classes. Gloria Vanderbilt and Nathan Burkan represented the emergent class of Café Society whose ranks were composed of show-business luminaries, titled foreigners, American businessmen—anyone different or rich enough to grab the spotlight. Carew had no respect for this group. Gertrude Whitney and her lawyers represented quiet, conservative Old Guard Society. Carew admired this group, knowing full well that he could never become part of it.

The middle 1930s marked the beginning of the breakdown of the class structure in America. There was no clearer illustration of class differences than at this custody trial. These differences could be seen in the clubs to which the principals belonged. Carew's Friendly Sons of St. Patrick was a Catholic group of Tammany politicians. Nathan Burkan was one of the Grand Street Boys, an organization of Jewish men from the Lower East Side who had spent their youth at the Grand Street Settlement House—they had risen from poverty and the streets to respected professions. The Whitney lawyers belonged to such exclusive clubs as the Piping Rock Club, Racquet and Tennis Club, the Union Club, the Metropolitan Club, the Brook Golf Club, the Meadow Brook Club, the Sons of the American Revolution.

. . .

While little Gloria sat staring out of the window, pointedly ignoring her mother's presence, the Whitney lawyers presented Justice Carew with their Return and Answer to the writ of habeas corpus to which supporting affidavits from Laura Kilpatrick Morgan, Emma Sullivan Keislich, and Drs. William P. St. Lawrence and Stuart L. Craig were attached.

Each affidavit asserted that Gloria Morgan Vanderbilt was an unfit mother and that any change in the child's custody at the present time would be detrimental to her health and welfare. Gertrude Whitney's affidavit did not impugn Gloria's character but stated that

> . . . the said infant was always a delicate child highstrung and sensitive, and required, and still requires, more than the usual amount of care and attention. At the time the child was placed in Respondent's custody by the Relator, the said infant had just undergone an operation for the removal of her tonsils and was very ill. Your Respondent loves the child as one of her own children and for the past two years and more she has been a member of the family, enjoying the companionship of her relatives and friends of her own age. Her education has been cared for by her attendance at the Greenvale School, Old Westbury, Long Island, and by instruction by private teachers, and her health has been looked after under the medical supervision of capable physicians. As a result, the little girl is in better health and physical condition than she has ever been in before, with the exception of the recent nervous attack resulting from a visit to her mother. . . .

Laura Kilpatrick Morgan did not appear at this hearing, but her lengthy affidavit was a scathing condemnation of her daughter.

> I am little Gloria's maternal grandmother, and I am making this affidavit for my grandchild's welfare as I do not believe she should be in the custody of her mother, who is my daughter.
>
> From the date of little Gloria's birth, on February 20, 1924, until she went to live with Mrs. Whitney in 1932, I was almost continually with her in order, as far as possible, to give her the motherly love and attention that my daughter withheld from her during all those years.
>
> I do not know of . . . any time in which my daughter expressed concern over the baby's welfare or showed any mark of affection for her. . . . She devoted herself exclusively to her own gay pleasures. . . . Her constant companions were people who lead a very

gay life. . . . Little Gloria was like a poor orphan. She was not wanted . . .

During all of these times Gloria never went to school and I had considerable trouble in getting somebody to give the child lessons. Although my daughter spent a great deal of money in pursuing her own pleasures she objected to this expense.

When little Gloria was brought back to America she was seriously ill with nervous disorders and terribly run-down and thin . . . and during the whole summer after the operation she was an invalid. My daughter never once inquired or communicated with me about her condition.

I have seen her [little Gloria] frequently since Mrs. Whitney has taken care of her and she has been nursed back to health. She now appears to be a splendid and happy child. . . .

Emma Sullivan Keislich substantiated Mrs. Morgan's accusations and added some of her own:

With the exception of Gloria's visit to her mother last week, the only other time that she stayed with her mother was in September of 1933 when . . . the mother saw the child but a short time during that day and Mrs. Vanderbilt entertained that evening at a large party at the house. Around three o'clock of the following morning the stove exploded in the kitchen where the guests were gathered, one of the guests was badly burned. [Little] Gloria was awakened from her sleep and became extremely nervous. . . .

[During the child's visit to her mother the week of September 18] Mrs. Vanderbilt devoted practically no time whatsoever to the child and was out every night we were at the house. . . . Mrs. Vanderbilt endeavored to show Gloria how to make a cocktail and tried to force the child to drink orange juice although all liquids are forbidden by the Doctor. . . . [Little] Gloria later . . . stated that she felt so unhappy at Mrs. Vanderbilt's that she would rather jump out of the window than stay there.

On Friday Mrs. Vanderbilt told Gloria that she was moving out to Long Island on Sunday. Gloria again cried and said to me if Mrs. Vanderbilt took her she would jump out the window. . . .

Dr. William St. Lawrence, in a short statement, said that he had been attending the infant Gloria Laura Morgan Vanderbilt for two years and had examined her on Monday, September 24, at Mrs. Whitney's house.

> As a result of this examination and of my familiarity with her case from a medical viewpoint, I am of the opinion that her health and welfare require that she remain quietly with her aunt, Mrs. Harry Payne Whitney, at the latter's home in Old Westbury, Long Island . . . and that to require her to go to her mother now might endanger her well-being.

Dr. Stuart L. Craig's affidavit supported that of Dr. St. Lawrence.

Justice Carew accepted these documents. He announced that the disposition of Mrs. Vanderbilt's guardianship petition in Surrogate Foley's court would be suspended pending the outcome of this trial. Turning directly to Gertrude Whitney, he explained that the burden of proof of these allegations of unfitness lay with her and warned her, "There is nothing in the law which warrants the exercise of the powers of *parens patriae* to deprive a mother of her child, unless that mother is so unfit that constant association of the child with the mother would prevent her from growing up a good and useful member of society. . . . Only the most unusual circumstances warrant the refusal of custody of a child in favor of any other relative, no matter how unselfish the motives of the relative might be." Carew told Mrs. Whitney that she must produce "compelling evidence" of Mrs. Vanderbilt's unfitness. In other words, he was directing her to destroy Mrs. Vanderbilt's character or lose the child.

Since this was the case, Gertrude Whitney's lawyers requested that the trial be held in private. Nathan Burkan objected. Burkan thought he had an edge in that Mrs. Whitney's hatred of publicity and concern for her niece would prevent her from going all-out to destroy the mother's reputation in open court. Burkan did not realize that Mrs. Whitney was quite willing to let others perform this service for her. As soon as the hearing ended, copies of Gertrude Whitney's Return and Answer, with the damning affidavits attached, were mysteriously delivered to every major newspaper in New York City. On Sunday morning, New Yorkers woke to the stories of the day.

KIDNAP LADDER TRACED TO HAUPTMANN: In his New Jersey jail cell Bruno Hauptmann, who had been arrested ten days earlier for the Lindbergh kidnapping-murder, was told that the wood used in the kidnap ladder had been traced to the lumberyard where he worked.

DOROTHY ANN RANSOM DEMAND: The previous week, six-year-old Dorothy Ann Distelhurst of Nashville, Tennessee, had vanished. She was last seen on her way home from school clad in a blue-and-white plaid dress and swinging a pink lunchbox as she skipped down the street. On Friday, the child's father, Alfred E. Distelhurst, Sr., received a letter postmarked Grand Central Terminal, demanding a $5,000 ransom for Dorothy Ann's return and instructing him to check into a New York City hotel and walk a specified route at specified hours until contacted. The name of the hotel was withheld.

And a new story: MOTHER OPPOSES MRS. VANDERBILT—SWEARS HER DAUGHTER NEGLECTED CHILD AND IS NOT FIT PERSON TO HAVE CUSTODY. Lengthy quotes from the affidavits appeared in the accompanying articles. Immediately, Nathan Burkan and Louis Frohlich began calling their press contacts to find out how many newspapers had received these bootlegged papers; eventually they tracked down eighteen separate copies. Burkan told Gloria, "They've played their trump by making those accusations public, there's nothing else they can do to hurt us." But Maury Paul telephoned Gloria and said that a copy of the legal papers had mysteriously appeared on his desk and he'd just finished reading them. "Watch out, Gloria," he warned her, "all the dirty linen is going to be laundered in front of the whole nation."

Monday, October 1, 1934: the trial began. The day was unusually warm, sixty-two degrees, fair and clear. The third-floor courtroom, number 355, was a square, wood-paneled room with high, narrow, unwashed windows on two sides. It seated about 150 people, but this day hundreds of spectators jammed the room. Seated in the jury box were members of the press. Photographs were not permitted inside the courtroom, so the newsreel cameramen and still photographers impatiently paced the terazzo floor of the corridor.

At 9:45 a.m. Gloria Vanderbilt walked into the courtroom, followed by Nathan Burkan and Consuelo Thaw; they moved forward and seated themselves at one of the two large rectangular counsel tables. Gertrude Whitney entered the courtroom with her daughter Flora Miller; they were ushered to a roped-off second row of spectator seats. Reporters had hoped that the real news grabber—"the tiny heiress" who "turned her little nose up at her charming mother last Friday" would be on hand. She was not.

A moment later, Gloria's mother, Mrs. Morgan, entered, a fluff of fox fur setting off her flour-white masklike face. A derby was pulled low on her forehead, tight, dyed red-blond curls corkscrewed out from beneath the hat. At her side marched the balloon shape of Emma Sullivan Keislich, a voluminous black dress and coat falling to the tops of her stolid black lace-up shoes with low wooden heels. Keislich and Mrs. Morgan seated themselves side by side in the last row of spectator seats. Gertrude Whitney turned in her seat and gestured to Mrs. Morgan, who then stood up and moved forward to take her seat next to Gertrude in a physical demonstration of their solidarity.

Justice John Francis Carew entered. The crowd fell silent and rose as he eased himself into a high-backed black leather chair under the foot-high gold letters that spelled out *In God We Trust.* Carew frowned at the packed courtroom: he disliked crowds and discouraged standees.

Whitney lawyer John Godfrey Saxe stepped to the bar and formally requested that Herbert C. Smyth "relieve me to the extent of taking charge of the examination and cross-examination of the witnesses." The Whitney side was taking no chances; to face Nathan Burkan in the courtroom, they had added to their team one of the most outstanding trial lawyers in America, Herbert Crommelin Smyth. He too was one of their own; both Smyth's maternal and paternal family had emigrated from England to the United States in the seventeenth century. His mother was a great-granddaughter of Francis Lewis, a signer of the Declaration of Independence. Smyth was born in New York City in 1870, was a graduate of New York Law School, and had been admitted to the bar in 1892. In 1912, he'd become special assistant to George Wickersham, who was then Attorney General of the United States. For many years Smyth had represented Harry Payne Whitney's street railway companies as well as such other prestigious corporations as Standard Oil of New Jersey.

One of his few forays into the tinsel of show business came in 1926 when he defended Earl Carroll in connection with the alleged champagne bath of a seventeen-year-old show girl, Joyce Hawley, which took place on the stage of the Earl Carroll Theater. Carroll persuaded Joyce to strip and climb into a tub full of the bubbly—then he passed out glasses and announced, "Gentlemen, the line forms on the right." During the inquiry into the matter, Carroll testified that the bathtub had not contained alcohol. He was found guilty of perjury and went to jail. It was one of Smyth's few failures.

Smyth, at sixty-three, had earned a reputation as a winner. He could remember testimony verbatim, his polite, elegant manner softened the witness to malleable clay. Smyth was an expert in the art of cross-examination, the first man to apply the principles of autosuggestion as set forth by a Harvard psychology professor, Hugo Munsterberg. Smyth would subtly plant a notion in the mind of a witness and then cross-examine him so skillfully that the witness would be unaware that he was saying exactly what Smyth had programmed him to say. His appearance inspired confidence; he looked Lincolnesque—tall and craggy-featured—but his intelligence was a rapier, so sharp that his executions could be bloodless.

Smyth moved forward and called as the first Whitney witness, Emma Sullivan Keislich, who lumbered up the side steps of the raised platform and plunked herself down in the witness chair. From her place in the jury box, where the press was positioned, *Daily News* reporter Julia McCarthy noted that around the nurse's neck was draped a brace of sables. As Keislich was sworn in, Smyth gave her a reassuring glance and a small smile. Then, in a low, calm voice, he began his direct examination. From the first exchange it became obvious that Keislich was ready to leap in and demolish Gloria Vanderbilt's reputation. As a matter of routine, Smyth inquired, "What is your occupation?"

"Nurse."

"Will you please tell the court what your experience has been in taking care of children?"

"My experience has been, before the ten years, that the children had loving parents instead of harsh—"

Nathan Burkan interrupted. "I move to strike that out."

"Strike it out," said Justice Carew. The nurse planted her feet squarely on the floor and glared out at her former employer. Keislich was here for one reason only—to prevent this woman from gaining custody of little Gloria—and she was prepared to say whatever was necessary to accomplish this end. For ten and a half years Keislich had kept her rage to herself, she had placated this woman because she wanted to remain with little Gloria, her "baby lamb," her love. Now the time had come when she was encouraged to speak of her grievances, and her pent-up hatred erupted in a gusher of vituperation. She began her testimony by recounting tales of Gloria Vanderbilt's decadent life abroad. In Paris, Mrs. Vanderbilt never woke until one o'clock. The child would see her mother for ten minutes while Mrs. Vanderbilt was dressing to go out to lunch. Often, she stayed out all night. "There were always cocktail parties."

In her eagerness to establish that her former employer was an unfit mother, Keislich used Smyth's questions as a springboard to launch into damning statements. When Smyth asked who had visited at the Charles Floquet apartment, Keislich replied, "There was Constance Bennett in my time."

"She is an actress, is she not?"

"Yes. And her South American lover. He was there."

A hum swept the courtroom. "I move to strike that out," said Burkan, turning toward the jury box, where the press was seated, and shaking his head.

"Yes, strike it out," agreed Carew.

"Who else?" asked Smyth.

". . . Well, of course her brother was there."

"That is Mr. Morgan?"

"Yes."

"Did he live at the Floquet?"

"Oh, yes. He was supported there."

"What?"

"That was his support there. He was supported by the child!"

"I move to strike that out," said Burkan.

"Strike it out," ruled Carew.

"He lived there?"

"He lived there. He didn't work."

"I move to strike out all the conclusions," said Burkan.

Justice Carew instructed nurse Keislich. "It is a very bad thing for a witness to volunteer too much. It discredits a witness when the witness seems to be too eager. . . . It shows a partisan spirit which discounts her testimony severely."

Seeing the effect of the nurse's testimony on the spectators, Carew began exerting every effort to control her open hostility. Again and again, he sustained Burkan's objections. When the nurse continued to speak over a sustained objection, the Justice commanded her, "Woman, woman. Stop! We have teeth in the front of our mouths, you know, to clamp down on our tongues."

Keislich's condemnation of Gloria Vanderbilt revealed a rare demonstration of class distinction. In the 1930s, wealth could still buy privacy and protection from censure, but in this courtroom there was none. With absolute moral conviction and faulty grammar, Keislich spewed out the loathing harbored by some servants for the indolent life led by certain members of the upper class. "I will never understand the type of woman Mrs. Vanderbilt is," she said. "After we went to Paris she was out all night. . . . I seen very little of her. . . . I could see her coming in at six in the morning because the room where the baby slept in was facing the street, and I could hear them talking, feeling very good . . ."

"What do you base that statement upon?" asked Smyth.

"As all the class of people that spend their nights out."

Keislich painted a vivid picture of the neglect and mistreatment of her precious charge. The Paris house "was infested with rats." One morning the butler "killed about thirty" of them. The child had no place to play except in her bedroom or in the yard which was also "full of rats." Mrs. Vanderbilt said the child could use "as a playroom . . . an attic where the rain used to come in. It was cold and damp and not any heat there. . . . I never used it."

Little Gloria was so shabbily dressed that Mr. Morgan, Mrs. Vanderbilt's father, told Keislich to buy her some decent clothes and he would pay for them, and she did. Mrs. Vanderbilt "never paid any attention to the child." When the child wanted to run to her Grandmother Morgan, Mrs. Vanderbilt twisted her arm and dug her nails into little Gloria's hand. Little Gloria cried then, and she cried when Prince Hohenlohe burned her with a cigarette.

There was another wave of sound and Justice Carew asked, "You don't know whether it was an accident or not?"

"Well, they said it was . . ." Keislich replied.

Little Gloria was a frail, delicate child, but her mother deliberately neglected her health. While Mrs. Vanderbilt was off on a trip with Prince Hohenlohe, Keislich called Dr. Helie, who X-rayed the child and discovered a potential tubercular lesion. When Mrs. Vanderbilt returned, the doctor said that the child should "go to a southern climate, she should have plenty of sunshine and a happy life." Instead, her mother "always kept her in climates where there wasn't any sun." These included a boardinghouse in Maidenhead, England, where "you had to insert a quarter in the gas stove to get it to light" and "a second-rate rooming house in Biarritz" where little Gloria never heard from her mother "once the entire summer."

Smyth now introduced the subject of Gloria Vanderbilt's liaison with Prince Hohenlohe. Keislich reported that the prince was constantly with Mrs. Vanderbilt for a period of two years. She saw him going in and out of Mrs. Vanderbilt's bedroom so frequently that she took it as a matter of course. Then she described the following scene in the villa they occupied in Biarritz during the summer of 1928. It was "two or three o'clock at night when Mrs. Morgan came to my door and called me. . . . I got up. . . . I went and looked in [Mrs. Vanderbilt's] door." Inside in the dim light "from another room" Keislich could see Prince Hohenlohe and Gloria Vanderbilt in bed together, lying side by side. Prince Hohenlohe wore pajamas, Gloria a nightgown, and "she seemed to be crying." The two women stood at the door for five or six minutes before tiptoeing away.

At the end of this recitation, the reporters scribbled furiously in their notebooks and the hum of conversation filled the courtroom. Seated at the long counsel table, Gloria shook her head in negation of the testimony. Keislich could not contain a smile of satisfaction at the reaction her testimony had elicited and, thus encouraged, she continued. Prince Hohenlohe was in the habit of reading to Gloria in her darkened Paris bedroom. She emphasized the word *reading*.

Smyth was ready to follow her lead. "Did you notice what kind of books they were . . . ?"

Keislich replied with excitement, "Yes, the books were about"—she stumbled in her eagerness—"I saw them. I saw the books." Her speech became almost incoherent in her urgency to relay her information.

Smyth tried to calm her. "What kind of books did you see? You looked at them, didn't you?"

"Yes, I looked at them and as I said, I had never seen anything like it."

Burkan was beginning to get the drift of the conversation. "I move to strike that out," he called out.

"They were vile books!" exclaimed the nurse.

"Just answer the question," said Smyth.

". . . I saw one book with . . . two women undressed, beating each other. Another day the child came in and found a picture on the table . . . of a man naked and a woman's tongue very near. It is a very embarrassing thing for me to say. . . . She saw this big red flaming thing, and the color attracted her attention."

"What did the child say?"

"The child said, 'Here is a big tongue.' "

"And that is all you remember of what the child said?"

"That is all she said."

Staring up at Keislich, Gloria Vanderbilt frowned. She removed her elbow-length black suede gloves and began twisting the enormous heart-shaped diamond ring on her wedding finger, finally turning it around so that only the platinum band was visible.

Keislich had been on the stand for almost two hours when the subject of religion was introduced. Until this custody trial, little Gloria's religious training had been minimal and rather haphazard, but Keislich had been told that it was important to Justice Carew that little Gloria be raised a good Catholic. Mrs. Whitney was a Protestant, an Episcopalian; Mrs. Vanderbilt was a Catholic, and she might use this to get this judge to give her the child. Keislich knew there was a great deal at stake here, but was confused about how to testify on a matter that up till now had been of such trivial importance. She tried her best, testifying that Mrs. Vanderbilt never said a prayer with the child. It was she who'd taught little Gloria her prayers, and she *was* a Catholic so the prayers were Catholic ones.

Carew leaned forward and interrupted the direct examination, saying that he'd been told by Nathan Burkan that the child's mother had seen to it that she "was baptized a Catholic."

Keislich shook her head in negation of this statement. "No. Not to my knowledge. I was with her at baptism, and she was baptized a Protestant."

Carew stopped the proceedings and called both Smyth and Burkan to the bench. They spoke in whispers, then Carew turned to nurse Keislich and said, "The mother is a Catholic. She has the right to make a Catholic out of her, no matter whether she was made a Protestant or not. It doesn't make much difference whether she was baptized or not, if the mother is entitled to have her, she is entitled—"

Keislich could not contain herself, she interrupted the judge mid-sentence: "She did not want to make her a Catholic!"

Burkan moved to strike out her outburst.

Through Herbert Smyth's clever questioning, Keislich was able to say that Mrs. Vanderbilt had never gone to Mass, and that she'd stayed in bed all day on Sundays. Furthermore, Mrs. Vanderbilt had told Keislich she didn't want the child raised in the religion of her own mother, who was "a fanatic!" Mrs. Whitney, on the other hand, had informed Keislich that "whatever religion she [the child] wanted to have, she could have." Trying frantically to please Justice Carew, Keislich blurted out, "Mrs. Whitney always tells me to take her to church."

At this, Carew took over the questioning. "You have taken her to your church?"

"I have—the Catholic Church. . . ."

"How often?"

"Well, whenever she can [go]. I mean if the weather is good . . ."

"You won't take offense if I tell you you should go every Sunday?"

"No, sir, because I like to go myself if I can. I have been brought up to go."

Keislich spoke of Gertrude Vanderbilt Whitney in glowing terms: in the two years they had lived with her, the child had regained her health. "She has gained weight and her glands have gone. She is out in the open air; she has had medical attention. She has had love and kindness of her family." Mrs. Whitney spent time with the child, she read to her and played games with her. Keislich declared in a firm voice, "She is happy and she is a real child." On that affirmative note, Herbert Smyth soon concluded the direct examination.

Nathan Burkan rose from the counsel table and, with a shuffling gait, moved to the front of the courtroom. He had a plain open face and wore silver-wire spectacles; his appearance was nondescript, benign—deceiving. If Smyth was a rapier, Burkan was a sledgehammer—a formidable opponent, a lawyer in the flamboyant tradition of Max Steuer and Samuel Untermyer. He believed his client could do no wrong; the opposition was the enemy and he treated them as such. In the courtroom, this affable, sympathetic man was transformed into an angel of vengeance.

Witnesses were treated mercilessly. Burkan barked out questions, asked endless variations of the same question. He confronted the witness with long lists of dates and times, asking for precise information about them. If a witness could not answer specifically, Burkan implied that he was lying. Many a witness broke down in tears under his intimidating assault. Like a terrier worrying a bone, Burkan would nip at a subject from all sides, moving in again and again from every conceivable angle. The only major flaw in his technique was that he had no instinctive sense of when to let go.

Burkan placed both hands squarely on the thick wooden rail in front of the witness box. He leaned forward until his face was close to Keislich's. She met his stare with the frightened yet righteous expression of someone warding off the devil. From her purse she removed a rosary. Would it protect her from this infidel—this Jew? Her short, swollen fingers with their unpolished fingernails began moving rapidly, fingering the beads. She looked over at Justice Carew and then resolutely back at Burkan. In marked contrast to Herbert Smyth's restraint, Burkan abruptly aimed his first question at Keislich like a fighter's punch to the solar plexus. "Have you ever had a child of your own?" he demanded.

Keislich gasped, clutched her rosary, and answered with a barely audible, "No."

"I beg your pardon?" said Burkan.

"No. Never!"

"Did you ever tell Mrs. Vanderbilt that you had had a child of your own and that it had died?"

"Never!"

"Did you ever tell Mrs. Vanderbilt that you had been a married woman at one time?"

"Never!" Keislich began to tremble, and then added the odd observation, "I can trace my life from the very beginning."

Burkan stared at the witness, who stared back. "Never. . . . Never. . . . Never!" Burkan was convinced that there was something of major importance hidden here, but he couldn't find it. Gloria could only remember that the nurse had told her about the marriage and the child and had mentioned living in Ireland, nothing more. She didn't know the name of Keislich's husband or the circumstances of the child's death. Burkan had hoped by his forceful attack to get the nurse to spill out the story, but it hadn't worked, and now he was forced to abandon this line of questioning.

Had Burkan known more, perhaps the key to this woman's psyche might have been found. There was no doubt that she was fiercely overprotective of little Gloria, constantly worrying about her health and, as Dr. Schloss observed, "apprehensive" and "on the alert for every symptom." It was as if Keislich felt that if she left little Gloria even for a day, even for a minute, the child would die. She had not even gone to her dying mother's bedside, and in that courtroom she said that she had never taken a single day off. "I have never left her!" she declared emphatically. She had been with little Gloria—"always."

Some years later, Emma Keislich would tell little Gloria crucial facts that were not known in that courtroom. She would maintain that in 1907, when she was sixteen, she had married the twenty-nine-year-old composer Ernest R. Ball. It was an arranged marriage that had not worked from the start. She would tell little Gloria that they had gone to live in Ireland and that their son was born there, but the marriage was so "untenable" that "in desperation she left her husband, leaving her son with his father's devoted sisters. . . ." The child died! Keislich became a nurse, taking care of other people's children.

But there is more: Ernest R. Ball was one of the most famous composers of his day, writing the music for such hits as "A Little Bit of Heaven," "Mother Machree," "In the Garden of My Heart," "When Irish Eyes Are Smiling," "Let the Rest of the World Go By," and scores of other songs. He was a close friend of Jimmy Walker and wrote the music to Walker's famous lyric, "Will you love me in December as you do in May?" It is doubtful that Nathan Burkan or A. C. Blumenthal would not have known of this marriage had it really occurred. Furthermore, Ball, although he wrote so many songs about Ireland, only visited that country once, after World War I, on a brief vaudeville tour. Finally, in 1907, the year that Keislich said they had married, Ernest Ball was already married to Jessie Mae Jewitt of Cleveland, Ohio. Their son Roland was born in 1905, Ruth in 1907, and Ernest in 1908; they were divorced in 1911, after which Ball subsequently remarried. He died in 1927, seven years before the Vanderbilt custody trial: records of only two marriages exist. In fact, there was no conceivable way that Keislich could have been married to Ball, and if she had a child with him it would have been an illegitimate one. And if, indeed, there were such a child, and Keislich had left him, and he had died, this stern Catholic, this moral woman, might well be plagued by a sense of sin for which she would have to expiate. Becoming a nurse would have been a logical emotional choice, and her fierce "love and dedication" as little Gloria was later to observe "was forged out of this event in her life." Whether her child had actually existed or was a fantasy, the message was clear: You deserted a child and he died. Keislich would not desert little Gloria; she felt the child's life depended on her, and this child must live!

To justify herself, nurse Keislich cast the child's mother in the role of the destroyer from whom she must protect her precious charge. Burkan pointed out that although Mrs. Vanderbilt had fired nurse Keislich for turning the child against her, this woman was still employed to care for little Gloria. "Did Mrs. Whitney ask you to stay on?" Burkan asked.

Keislich answered with vehemence. "She understood I would stay on when they said so, when it was the doctors' orders, not to kill the child."

Burkan shook his head in disbelief. He began a series of questions designed to illustrate that Mrs. Vanderbilt had been both a dutiful wife and mother. When Keislich insisted that her employer had refused to nurse her baby, Burkan established that little Gloria had been born by a Cesarean operation, that his client suffered from phlebitis, and that the doctor had forbidden her to nurse the child because of her weakened condition.

"She can get ill any time. She can play a part," was the nurse's harsh retort.

At that, Gloria Vanderbilt began to cry. Consuelo placed her arm about her sister's shoulder and drew her near. For a second, Gloria rested her head on Consuelo's shoulder, then sat erect.

In her effort to protect her precious charge, Emma Sullivan Keislich had established herself as a hostile, vindictive witness. She would not admit that Gloria Vanderbilt had even one redeeming trait; one such admission and the child's custody might go to the mother. Nathan Burkan took advantage of the nurse's extreme position, seemingly encouraging her to vent her spleen, until her assertions became such gross exaggerations that no one could believe them. She described the people who visited Gloria Vanderbilt in Paris. "They were all night life people."

"In other words, you say that no good man or woman ever crossed that threshold . . . ?"

"Not in my estimation."

"No?"

"That was my estimation. No."

Keislich said that she told Mrs. Vanderbilt that there were fleas in the Paris house, to which Mrs. Vanderbilt responded, "I haven't felt any." And she told her about the rats, but Mrs. Vanderbilt said, "Well, just get rid of them." Keislich told her employer that their room in the Charles Floquet apartment in Paris was small and noisy, but Mrs. Vanderbilt answered that she had to "make the best of it." As Keislich droned on, her complaints sounded trivial. Carew looked at his watch and declared a luncheon recess.

Nathan Burkan did not eat. He spent his lunch hour conversing with reporters in an impromptu sidewalk press conference. Burkan said that he was going to subpoena the papers in the breach of promise suit filed by Evan Burrows Fontaine against Sonny (C. V.) Whitney. "I'm going to ask Mrs. Harry Payne Whitney what kind of luck she's had bringing up her own children," snapped Burkan. "I will show she was not so hot a mother herself." Burkan was grandstanding: In 1923, *Ziegfeld Follies* dancer Fontaine had sued Sonny Whitney for $100,000, charging that he was the father of her child and had welshed on a promise to marry her. Between 1923 and 1928 her suit had been dismissed by five courts and she was then enjoined from further litigation, thus ending the matter.

At two-thirty, Carew called the court to order. Burkan was unable to shake Keislich's testimony concerning Gloria Vanderbilt's taste for obscene literature, her relationship with Prince Hohenlohe, and her dissolute life abroad. But he established that from the time of the child's birth, whenever his client traveled, the child was left in the care of two supposedly competent people—this nurse and Mrs. Morgan. With deceptive gentleness, Burkan began asking Keislich about her assertion that Mrs. Vanderbilt had forbidden her to bring the child up as a Catholic. When Keislich had gone on at length confirming this, Burkan presented his first exhibit—a certificate showing that the child had been baptized a Catholic on April 17, 1926.

Keislich looked down at the document in disbelief. Words poured from her mouth: "No . . . never . . . no. I was never told that. . . . As far as Mrs. Whitney and I know, she was a Protestant. . . ."

Taking advantage of her confusion, Burkan shot a series of questions at her forcing her to admit that little Gloria attended an Episcopal church with her cousins, as well as a Protestant Sunday school; this was a direct contradiction of her earlier testimony. Having shaken her on these points, Burkan emphasized that Keislich had complained to no one of the child's alleged neglect and maltreatment.

The nurse countered that she had frequently complained to Mrs. Whitney about the child going to the Seventy-second Street house.

Burkan took advantage of this to ask, "Everything else was all right except the house, you did not like the house?"

"It was not fit for the child; no place for her. I said the house was not fit," replied Keislich.

'Trial of the Century'

Consuelo, Gloria, and Thelma

Mamma Morgan

Begins to Take Shape

George W. Wickersham

Thomas B. Gilchrist

Gertrude, Dodo, and Frank Crocker

Burkan smiled sardonically. "The house was not fit?"

Keislich interrupted him. "I am surprised the law did not get after her, that they did not make the child go where she would be protected at night. . . ."

"You didn't know who would come in at night?"

"I had serious thoughts, where there is money, there is great anxiety sometimes, to know how they can manage to manipulate this money. . . . I had my thoughts which I will keep to myself."

"So your only objection was that this house was not sufficiently protected . . . ?"

"It was not protected. . . . She just needed more protection than any other child in the world. You realize she is a wealthy child, and wealth brings greed. Money brings greed. . . . People are avid for their greed for money, even from a baby lamb, an innocent child. . . . That was my affair!" Keislich concluded. It was as close as this woman would ever come to saying what her views really were.

Burkan steered the nurse away from the potentially dangerous subject of money and tried to demonstrate that the child and her mother had been close and affectionate. Keislich responded that the child had always "lived through fear of the mother. She was always afraid of her." When she was still a baby, little Gloria had said, "Don't tell my mother, I'm afraid of her." The reason for her fear, said the nurse, was that the child had never known "any mother love."

"So you know what mother love is?" Burkan shot back.

"Yes," she replied. "I have seen mothers with their babies, that has been my work, when their hearts would jump at anything being the matter, when they could not sleep. They were not angry with you for telling them their child was ill. I have known mothers for years and I have seen mother love. I have not seen it here."

Burkan then asked if the witness was aware that the child had completely ignored her mother the day Mrs. Whitney had brought her to court. Keislich said she was not.

"Did you ever tell that child to ignore its mother?" asked Burkan.

"Never. I told her to be happy when it went to its mother. I brought her games and toys to be happy. I did not want her to be unhappy."

"You are anxious to reconcile this child with its mother?"

"What do you mean? To love its mother?"

"Yes."

"Anyone who would love her, yes, and love all, and love God first, and be honest, and good living, and clean, lead a clean life. I wanted her to have a clean life, and I hope God will give it to her, and not have her name dragged in and known like many others."

"You want to stay with the child, don't you?"

Little Gloria was her life, but Keislich answered, "If the child is happy—it doesn't matter. Whatever is best for the child suits me. Whatever is best for her health and the law."

Burkan's plan of attack was becoming clear. "You are bringing it [the child] up, aren't you? You are the one that is raising her?"

Judge Carew, catching Burkan's drift, asked, "Do you want to suggest that she be dispensed with? Is that what you want to suggest?"

"Absolutely. Absolutely. We do not want her there for two minutes, destroying the morals of this child, absolutely destroying it in every way."

"Before we come to that—" interjected Herbert Smyth.

But Carew would not be sidetracked. "He was directing his cross-examination to developing partisanship . . . and showing by her own testimony that it was not Mrs. Whitney who had the custody of the child, but it was the witness who half of the time had the custody of the child."

"That is right," affirmed Burkan.

"And suggesting she was an influence that would destroy any possible affection the child had for its mother, obviously suggesting that the services of this lady be dispensed with."

"Immediately," said Burkan.

"He says that is what he wants?" asked Smyth.

"Immediately," repeated Burkan.

Keislich looked at Burkan with undisguised hatred. "Of course!" she exclaimed.

Carew ignored the interruption. "That is what he is trying to prove," he said.

"She is absolutely unfit to associate with this child," said Burkan.

Smyth began to speak in a reasonable, measured way. "I do not see how this question shows that. The witness is trying to protect the child all the time—"

Keislich cut him off. "Of course!" she exclaimed again. "It is very necessary for them to get rid of me."

The gray, late afternoon light filtered in through the high narrow windows. Keislich sat with her rosary resting in her lap. Her face was drawn and tired. She had testified for four and a half hours, struggling to maintain her composure under Burkan's forceful attack. The very qualities that should have been assets—the great love and protection she provided for the child, her strict morality, her direct blunt speech—had been turned against her.

"You won't take any instructions from Mrs. Vanderbilt regarding this child?" said Burkan.

"I was always pleased to take instructions. I never got any."

"Will you take instruction from Mrs. Vanderbilt regarding this child?"

"Certainly, if they are good ones—she is the mother of the child—*if* she behaves herself."

"Who are you to pass upon those things?"

"Why do you ask me then?"

"Didn't Mrs. Whitney know before you came to this room that you were going to endeavor to destroy whatever vestige of good name and good reputation and character Mrs. Vanderbilt had?"

"No, she has no good name, nor her sisters either. . . . I was dragged here. I was told to come here."

Burkan blurted out, "Nobody is safe with this woman."

Keislich was almost out of control. She spoke rapidly and at length, her words a torrent of venom, until the court stenographer dramatically threw down his pad, "I can't get half of this, Your Honor," he protested. "She starts answering before the question is asked."

"Please be patient and just answer the question," Herbert Smyth instructed her wearily.

"I know you are anxious to testify," commented Burkan bitterly.

Keislich looked at him, her fat body quivered. "I want to get away from here," she said.

Burkan turned his back on the witness and muttered, "That is all."

Herbert Smyth stepped forward to begin his redirect examination. He handed Keislich a letter which read, "Dear Naney, I have just had my hair washed and you have just gone away. I hope I do not have to go to the city. Please write me. Love, Gloria."

Keislich looked at the letter, than at Smyth. It was then that she realized the ordeal of Burkan's cross-examination was over. Suddenly, she burst into tears.

"Contain yourself," Smyth commanded.

Justice Carew inquired, "Was it written to you?"

"It was written to her grandmother," Keislich said, and began to sob uncontrollably.

Carew was annoyed. "Why are you boiled up so much over it? I thought it was written to you."

Still sobbing, Keislich identified several other letters written by little Gloria, and Smyth, sensing her weariness, quickly concluded his examination. Burkan stepped forward to begin his recross-examination. Keislich, not understanding the form of a trial, had thought this man was through with her. As he extended a piece of dark blue stationery toward her, she cringed. "Don't shrink from me," he snapped.

"Don't touch me," said Keislich; she was genuinely frightened and on the edge of hysteria. She gingerly accepted the paper—as if fearing Burkan's contamination.

Burkan pointed out that all the child's letters to her mother were signed "Love."

"It was not her real love," the nurse declared. "She has no real love for her [mother]."

Burkan intimated that the child's negative letters had been dictated by nurse Keislich. She vehemently denied this, exclaiming, "We are all not liars. We are not your sort. We are not *your* kind!"

"Not *your* kind!"—the words trembled in the air. "As the only Christian in Burkan's firm, I was better equipped to see the anti-Semitism than anyone, but an idiot child could have seen it, it was so blatant," recalls James Murray. "The whole Whitney side treated Nathan Burkan as if he were unclean, a lower form of life; it wasn't even subtle. The second day of the trial Frank Crocker came up to me and said, 'Mrs. Whitney would like to meet you. She said she would like to know who that *gentleman* is sitting at the counsel table with the people from the Burkan office.' About a year later she asked Crocker to hire me away from the Burkan firm. It was very tempting—they offered me the job of the legal work for the Whitney interests abroad. At that time, I was working on an appeal for Gloria Vanderbilt. I declined."

Nathan Burkan, Louis Frohlich, Herman Finkelstein, were all aware of the anti-Semitism. Burkan's attitude was one of hurt and anger mixed with a cool assessment of the realities of the situation. When Jimmy Walker had gone before Roosevelt for removal hearings after the Seabury investigation, Burkan had prepared all the legal papers for him. Walker wanted him to come to Albany, but Burkan told him, "I'll do the work, but you're in enough trouble already without having a Jewish lawyer."

Burkan was determined that, because of anti-Semitism, Blumie must be kept out of the case at all costs. "If we have to, we'll send him to Mexico," Burkan said. He was sure that the American public had enough anti-Semitic feeling to turn against Gloria Vanderbilt if it were proved that she was having an adulterous relationship with a married Jew. For all his assimilation into the American ethos, Nathan Burkan was not a secure man. When he read of the restrictions imposed that year on Jews in Germany—they were no longer permitted to practice law—he reacted by going out and buying a large quantity of diamonds which he placed in a bank vault. After a lifetime in America, there was still a part of him that was ready to run when the pogrom came. But now Burkan fended off Keislich's anti-Semitic remark by letting her know that they were in a place where he felt accepted and secure. "Madam, this is not Mrs. Whitney's home," he informed the nurse. "We are in a courtroom."

Carew cut the discussion short. "The stenographer says his arm is not made of cast-iron. We will adjourn until tomorrow at 10:00 a.m."

Reporters rushed from the courtroom to their typewriters. Julia McCarthy marched over to Gloria Vanderbilt. "Where did you find that woman? If you had searched the whole world over, you couldn't have found a worse biddy," she said. That afternoon Julia McCarthy was to write her first article on the Vanderbilt trial, which appeared on page one of the *Daily News*. It was to be the only article in which she did not cast herself in the role of Mrs. Vanderbilt's champion.

VANDERBILT BOUDOIR SECRETS BARED . . .
SERVANT IN SABLES . . . PEEPED ON PRINCE

. . . At Mrs. Whitney's behest a servant in sables crept up society's back stairs—to the witness stand—to tell a shocking tale. . . . Painting her former employer as a lazy, loose, erotic woman—addicted to books and pictures treating of sadism and other forms of abnormal sex-behavior—indifferent to rats and vermin that swarmed in her house and cruel to her child. . . .

For five hours Mrs. Gloria Morgan Vanderbilt . . . listened to a tight-lipped nurse denounce her with virtuous relish as a cocktail-crazed dancing mother, a devotee of sex erotica, and the mistress of a German Prince. . . . It was a blistering tale no skin lotion could soothe.

Maury Paul, who was staunchly on Gloria's side, and ever the consummate snob, came to her defense by pointing out in his Cholly Knickerbocker column, "It is just as impossible to keep rats out of an ancient Paris house as it is to keep mosquitoes from infesting a bungalow on the Jersey coast."

Tuesday morning, October 2, 10:00 a.m.: Gloria Vanderbilt approached the Supreme Court building. This morning she wore a silver fox cape composed of three horizontal rows of fur, a jaunty black hat, and elbow-length black suede gauntlets. At the deep V-neck of her black crepe dress, two triangular-shaped diamond clips flashed. Her sister Consuelo wore a burgundy-colored fluffy angora sports dress, a scarf of moleskin fur dyed to match, and a tiny cap also of the same color, made popular that year by Princess Marina.

Inside the courtroom all was orderly. Justice Carew had left strict instructions that there were to be no standees. When the benches were filled, the overflow crowd was shunted into the third floor corridor. At 10:15 a.m., nurse Keislich was called upon to continue her testimony. She seemed rested and in control of her emotions. Burkan introduced letter after letter written by the child to her mother. They were signed "Love" or "Much Love" and had rows of O's and X's to indicate hugs and kisses. Keislich said that the child signed all her letters that way as a matter of form.

"Isn't it your testimony that this child never loved and does not love her mother?" demanded Burkan.

The nurse breathed one word in answer, "Fear."

"Do you say to His Honor that this child loves its mother?"

"No. I say no. Fear!"

There was no point in continuing. Burkan dismissed the witness. Nurse Keislich rose from her chair and walked down the three steps leading from the witness stand. As she passed Gloria Vanderbilt she stopped and looked at her with hatred, then she marched out of the courtroom.

The next witness, Maria Caillot, had served as Gloria Vanderbilt's personal maid from 1929 to 1933. Burkan felt that Maria would be a weak witness for the Whitney side. He told Jim Murray, "They're basing their whole case on backstairs gossip." Maria Caillot sat in the witness chair, carefully smoothing her black skirt under her. She was twenty-three, a brunette with thin eyebrows in the Dietrich style, and dark eyes, one of which was partially obscured by the sharply angled brim of her brown felt hat. Her lips were a dark red, her clothes were tight and revealed a voluptuous figure. She seemed typecast for the personal maid in a French farce. Her accent was pronounced and it soon became clear that she had difficulty understanding some of the questions, but Justice Carew denied Smyth's motion that an interpreter be brought in, and instructed the lawyers to speak plainly and slowly.

Maria explained that she had worked for a dressmaker and "for a few weeks" as a ladies maid when, at eighteen, she was engaged as Mrs. Vanderbilt's personal maid. She began her employment at the rue Alfred Roll house, which "was a very old-fashioned house, not very comfortable." Maria lived on the second floor with the cook and the extra man. The butler, Charles Fernand, went home at night.

Maria's duties included bringing Mrs. Vanderbilt her breakfast tray when she rang. "Mrs. Vanderbilt got up every day about one o'clock, sometimes half-past twelve, one o'clock, sometimes two, sometimes three, sometimes four, and sometimes she stayed in bed all day," announced the French maid brightly.

"What time did you get up in the morning?" asked Carew.

"Half-past seven."

"What did you do between half-past seven until one o'clock?"

"I always go down and see the little girl and make a fire in the bedroom, and go down for my breakfast." Then she would go back upstairs to the sewing room and press and repair Mrs. Vanderbilt's dresses. When Mrs. Vanderbilt finally called for her breakfast, which consisted of coffee or hot water, she was always in bed.

Carew asked, "You didn't see anything in the way of a hangover from the night before, did you?"

Gloria Vanderbilt pursed her lips in disdain and looked down at the floor. Maria shrugged and lifted her hands, palms toward the ceiling, to indicate that she did not understand the question.

Herbert Smyth said, "I think we will have to put that in French."

"I can't do it," said Justice Carew. "Do you know what it is in French?"

"They don't use that word in French."

"You mean they don't have them over there?" asked the Justice, smiling.

"Not the French people. The Americans have taught them that. The American colony imported that," answered Smythe. The spectators began to laugh. Carew rephrased the question. "You never had to give her something for a headache in the morning?"

"No, I don't remember that."

Maria said that Mrs. Vanderbilt saw little of the child, days would go by when she did not see little Gloria at all.

"Was the child sick while you were there?" inquired Carew.

"It was very, very delicate," Maria replied, shaking her head mournfully. "I know she has a gland there, she has a gland there." Maria pressed her fingers to both sides of her neck, indicating the position. "She was always looking pale. She was always looking very delicate."

Maria said that during a serious illness in 1931, Mrs. Vanderbilt had paid her daughter only a brief visit. Again, on the night of June 17, 1932, the child was very sick. Mrs. Morgan and Dr. Schloss were called, but Mrs. Vanderbilt could not be located. She returned at four in the morning. The following week she left for Europe.

"We want to know why she left a sick child in New York. . . . Can you tell?" asked Carew.

Maria did not answer the question directly but seemingly went off on a tangent to explain that they had rushed back to Europe to stay with Lady Milford Haven and that Maria had accompanied Mrs. Vanderbilt and Lady Milford Haven to Cannes, where they stayed at the Miramar Hotel.

Maria then described Mrs. Vanderbilt's life-style. In Paris "Mrs. Vanderbilt always had a cocktail party in the afternoon after five o'clock" and other parties which lasted "until the morning, five or six o'clock." Once, three bands had played at a party, keeping the baby and Maria awake until dawn. Among the guests at this party were both of Mrs. Vanderbilt's sisters, her brother, Prince Hohenlohe, and a Mrs. Helen Thomas, who was "so drunk she had to be carried upstairs . . . and somebody had to help her . . . to go to the bathroom." The cocktail parties did not abate when they moved to New York City.

Maria confirmed the nurse's testimony that there were rats in the Paris house, and added that she had seen them scurrying across her bedroom floor and on a tray in the butler's pantry. She, too, had seen "six or seven very dirty books" around the house. One was titled "*La Jolie Flagellante de New York.* The Beautiful Flagellant of New York," Maria helpfully translated. It contained "dirty pictures."

Justice Carew looked bemused. "She does not mean they were dirty with dirt? That isn't what you mean?" he asked.

"No, that is not."

"They had pictures of things you are not allowed to look at, is that what you mean?"

"Yes," replied Maria, with a slight smile and a shrug.

"Sure," agreed Carew, making a clucking sound with his tongue.

Then Smyth asked what seemed a most odd question. "What kind of pictures were they. . . . I am trying to find out whether they were pictures of one sex or both sexes . . . ?"

"What difference does it make what sex they were?" asked Carew.

"Supposing they were homosexual, Your Honor?" answered Smyth in what might be considered a textbook example of Munsterberg's autosuggestive technique.

But Carew did not grasp the nuances of the question. "It wouldn't make any difference whether they were "homo-sexual or uni-sexual or bi-sexual or tri-sexual."

"That is what we call a circus," said Smyth in a professorial tone.

"I do not know what it is. That is something I learned since I got on this bench," Carew snapped back.

"I will withdraw the question."

Obviously, this line of questioning embarrassed Carew and he took over the examination and moved it immediately to an area in which he was comfortable, that of the child's religious education. Maria Caillot said the child and her nurse attended the American church on the rue de Klepper.

Nathan Burkan said, "The American church is not Catholic. It is a Protestant church. Your Honor can ascertain that very easily."

Carew seemed irritated by Burkan's assertion. "This is an American Catholic," he declared.

"Of course, but they go to Madeleine, and they go to—"

Carew turned to the maid. "This church that you saw the nurse taking her to, that was a Catholic church?"

"Yes, it was a Catholic church."

"It was not what you call an American church?"

"An American?"

"I mean what Mr. Burkan calls an American church?"

"No."

"Catholics are entitled to have a church!"

Although he was correct, Burkan knew better than to anger Carew further. He said nothing.

Maria reported that for the past two years, Mrs. Vanderbilt had been constantly in the company of Mr. A. C. Blumenthal. This was the first time Blumie's name had been mentioned in the courtroom. Herbert Smyth asked Maria questions that established that Blumie and Mrs. Vanderbilt had sailed together on the *Europa* on June 16, 1933. Maria said that, on shipboard, they were "always together." In the past two years Blumie was at the house "nearly every day." Several times Charles Zaug had served champagne to Gloria Vanderbilt and a man she presumed to be Blumie in her bedroom. During these visits Mrs. Vanderbilt wore a negligee.

Carew stopped the proceeding to inquire what a negligee was. "One might call it a continental house gown," explained Herbert Smyth. Carew became agitated. "I do not know anything about it. They don't wear them in my house—or the houses that I go to." A ripple of laughter swept the courtroom. Gloria and Consuelo also could not hide their smiles. Justice Carew said severely, "This is a pitiful case and there is no occasion to be funny about it."

Maria testified that when Mrs. Vanderbilt lived at the Sherry-Netherland, sometimes her friend Agnes Horter shared her bedroom and "many times in the morning . . . Agnes drank whiskey before breakfast." Sometimes Mrs. Vanderbilt joined Miss Horter in this early morning drinking. Maria commented that Agnes Horter "looked always very dirty."

Herbert Smyth turned the witness over to Burkan for cross-examination. Burkan prepared to counter the maid's testimony with some character assassination of his own. Burkan asked if Maria had spent time in a hospital here in America. She answered that she had spent ten days in St. Luke's Hospital. Smyth objected to the questioning as having nothing to do with the child. Burkan smiled and replied, "Don't you worry about this. It has a lot to do with it." Leaving the subject hanging in the air, he asked how Maria had gotten to the courthouse.

"I came," she replied.

"You came in a taxi?"

"Yes."

What had she said to the driver? inquired Burkan.

"To the courthouse," answered Maria.

"Nothing else but 'to the courthouse'?"

"Yes. . . ."

"Did he ask you *which* courthouse?"

"No, he did not."

Clearly, Maria was lying; she did not wish to say how she had gotten to the courtroom. Since this was the case, Burkan turned her attitude to his advantage. Invariably, witnesses were informally examined before trial; it would be foolish to put a witness on the stand without determining if she could be helpful. Some witnesses, however, were reluctant to admit that they'd been questioned. If they lied about this, then the opposing counsel could imply that *all* their testimony was a lie. This ploy worked well with a jury, but never with a judge. Judges knew the mechanics of the law, and had heard this particular line of attack used again and again—it was the oldest trick in the book—but that didn't stop Burkan from using it now, embellishing upon it and adding a flamboyant wrinkle of his own. Nathan Burkan looked out at the spectators and then let his gaze rest on a man in the fourth row, a ruddy-faced, white-haired man, dressed in a gray suit—Valerian J. O'Farrell (the detective in Gloria Vanderbilt's employ). Burkan pointed a finger at O'Farrell and asked Maria, "Did you give a statement to Val O'Farrell of the Valerian J. O'Farrell Detective Agency?"

Maria stared out at this strange man, dumbfounded. She answered truthfully that she had never seen him before.

"Who brought you to the courtroom this morning?" Burkan demanded.

"I come."

"Did Mr. O'Farrell bring you here?"

"Nobody."

"Do you know Mr. Val O'Farrell?"

"No."

"You don't!" Burkan shouted, and threw his right hand up in the air in a dramatic gesture.

"No, I don't know anybody," Maria protested.

Justice Carew had had enough of these histrionics; he refused to let this "unnecessary line of questioning" continue and declared a recess. Nathan Burkan was pleased; he was not fooling Justice Carew, but it was clear that he was impressing others who would also judge this case—the reporters who sat in the jury box.

Laura Kilpatrick Morgan, who'd been sitting alone in the last row of spectator seats, stood up and pulled her massive fox coat around her. The moment she reached the corridor she lit a cigarette, greedily drawing the smoke into her lungs. Gloria and Consuelo walked past her as if she were invisible. Helen Worden of the *World-Telegram* spoke to Consuelo, who nervously rubbed her hand across her moleskin cape and said, "These stories are so ridiculous that they are more ludicrous than lewd. It is pointed piffle maliciously arrived at."

"Do you think it will last much longer?" asked Helen Worden.

"I'm afraid so. Now they say they are going to bring witnesses from the coast."

"Do you expect to see many of your friends here?"

"No. Why should they come? It is long and tiresome."

When the elevator arrived, reporters crowded in with Gloria and Consuelo and interviewed Mrs. Vanderbilt as the elevator descended. Would she answer the charges of champagne *à deux* while dressed in a nightgown in her boudoir? Gloria tossed what a reporter noted as "her expensively-coiffed head" defiantly. "Every story they've told is a lie. There's not a word or a syllable of truth in anything they've said about me. I'll have plenty to say when I get my day in court." She spoke firmly, without stuttering.

At two o'clock, Maria Caillot continued her testimony. Burkan asked her a series of abrupt questions. As a result of the harsh questioning concerning Val O'Farrell, a man she had never seen before, Maria was now cautious. She hesitated before replying, and frequently indicated that she did not understand Burkan's questions. Finally, Smyth objected. "If you please, these questions are not fair. The woman speaks English quite imperfectly. If you rattle it off, as Mr. Burkan asks his questions, you don't get any intelligent answers. You have got to be patient with her."

But Burkan continued to hammer at the witness as if Smyth had not spoken, eliciting the admission that she had gone to the offices of

Mrs. Whitney's lawyers and had given her testimony while a stenographer wrote it down.

Maria was becoming extremely agitated and confused. She was angry at this bully who was questioning her, but she seemed unable to fight back.

"Do you remember whether anybody ever told you how much you were going to get if Mrs. Whitney got the child back?" Burkan asked.

"What do you mean?" asked Maria.

"Just what do *you* mean. How much are you going to get for testifying here?"

"I didn't ask any money."

"Was it promised?" asked Burkan.

"Yes."

"Who?"

"I didn't ask for any money."

"Who?"

"Nobody promised me money."

"Didn't you say a moment ago that money was promised?"

"I didn't say anything like that."

Burkan requested that the stenographer read Maria's testimony back to her. When he had done so, Maria protested, "I am not interested."

Smyth asked the question clearly and distinctly. "Was it promised?"

"No. There was no promise," answered Maria.

"I object to Mr. Smyth interfering with my cross-examination," said Burkan.

"Be fair," protested Smyth.

"I am very fair."

Reporters scribbled in their notebooks. Julia McCarthy wrote, "Maid admits promise of pay for her testimony."

At that moment, Gertrude Whitney entered the courtroom with her daughter Flora and sat in the last row of seats. In rapid succession, Burkan forced Maria to admit that the cocktail parties and bedroom champagne interludes were reported to her by the butler—she had not witnessed them. She had not told Mrs. Vanderbilt about the rats, although she knew that rats contaminated food, and that a rat bite was dangerous. She had not complained of the lack of heat or of the music far into the night. In fact, she had not complained at all.

When Maria asserted that she had seen Mrs. Vanderbilt drunk, Burkan nodded his head sagely and inquired, "How could you tell Mrs. Vanderbilt was drunk?"

"Because she always smiled and always, sometimes, she told me the things two or three or five times—the same things. . . . She seemed to be very happy."

"And if I should smile in this courtroom and appear happy, you might conclude I am drunk?"

"I don't know."

"You cannot say?"

Maria seemed unable to reply. She folded her hands in her lap. Her lips were set in a tight line.

"How many times in 1929 do you say that Mrs. Vanderbilt was drunk?" Burkan demanded. With that, Gloria Vanderbilt sprang to her feet. She stood glaring at her former maid, then slowly sank into her seat.

"Well, I cannot say how many times. But I saw her!" protested Maria, her face flushing with color.

Burkan began to list the guests who frequented Mrs. Vanderbilt's Paris house: Forest O. March, Mr. and Mrs. Donald Mixsell, Gloria's family, including her mother and father, her brother and sisters. Under Gloria's gaze, again and again, Maria admitted that these were indeed solid, respectable people.

Maria was now agreeing with Burkan's character assessments, she appeared cowed, and seemed almost to be defending Mrs. Vanderbilt. At the end of this list, Burkan introduced the name of Gloria's royal friend, Nadeja Milford Haven. "By the way, had you ever seen this Lady Milford Haven drunk?" inquired Burkan.

"No, I don't remember."

"You don't know?"

"I don't remember," she repeated.

"You never saw her drunk?"

"No. I never saw her drunk," answered the maid wearily. Then added, "I don't remember."

"And the lady appeared to you to be a fine decent lovely lady?"

"Yes."

"You saw nothing objectionable to the Lady Milford Haven, did you?"

"No."

Full of self-confidence, Burkan plunged on. "And Mrs. Vanderbilt was with her at that hotel?"

"Yes."

"And did you see any impropriety at that hotel or during those two months at the Miramar Hotel?"

Maria Caillot hesitated. "I do not understand."

"During those two months, did Mrs. Vanderbilt get drunk?"

"I don't know," said Maria.

"You did not see her drunk?"

"No. I did not see her drunk."

"Was she running around with people?"

"Yes."

"Who?"

"She always go out with Lady Milford Haven," said the maid in a matter-of-fact tone.

"You told us that," said Burkan. The maid was missing the point. "Were there some men, some gentlemen, or some men?"

"I always saw Mrs. Vanderbilt go out of the Miramar with Lady Milford Haven," she repeated.

Burkan sighed. He had beaten this witness into docility. He began relaxing, and smiled for the first time that day. Instead of moving on, Burkan apparently could not resist administering a final blow to this witness. He asked, "You saw nothing improper in her conduct during those entire two months, isn't that true?"

Maria Caillot shrugged her shoulders. It was the smallest of movements. "Yes, I remember something, it seems to me very funny."

"Tell us if you can the thing that you saw."

"Once, one day, Mrs. Vanderbilt called me for breakfast, like she do, for breakfast, she called me."

"She called you for breakfast?"

"Then I served breakfast, and I take her things up to my room, pressing them and a few minutes afterwards I come back in Mrs. Vanderbilt's room to bring back the clothes in the closet. Then when I came, Mrs. Vanderbilt was in bed reading a paper, and there was Lady Milford Haven beside the bed with her arm around Mrs. Vanderbilt's neck—Lady Milford's arm around Mrs. Vanderbilt's neck—and kissing her just like a lover."

The courtroom fell silent. Gloria leaned forward and buried her face in her hands. The diamond on her left hand and the square emerald on her right glittered. Then there was a roar of sound.

Burkan, trying to fight over it, continued to question Maria. He could hardly be heard. Judge Carew raised his left hand, palm vertical, and moved it forward as if to push back the sound. His face was a mask of indignation; his voice boomed out. "In view of this, the future sessions of this trial and the future testimony of this trial will be taken privately. I think I will excuse everybody now except the parties in the case."

Lies—Lies—Lies

It's all a pack of . . . malicious lies.

GLORIA VANDERBILT

. . . A set of malicious lies.

MARCHIONESS OF MILFORD HAVEN

. . . the most monstrous criminal lie I've ever heard.

PRINCE GOTTFRIED HOHENLOHE-LANGENBURG

NATHAN BURKAN'S EXAMINATION of the French maid in the *Matter of Vanderbilt* would be taught in law schools across the nation as an example of asking that one question too many. Burkan's sledgehammer had struck his own client a near-fatal blow. By morning, the nation would know that "the world's most beautiful widow" stood accused of a lesbian relationship with a member of the British royal family.

Nathan Burkan and his assistant Jim Murray flanked Gloria, as if protecting an accused felon, as they pushed out of the courtroom doors and through the seething crowd. Gloria pressed a handkerchief to her face. She lifted her head just once to cry out, "It's all so utterly false. I'm overwhelmed!"

Burkan proclaimed grandly, "In view of the maid's testimony, I will be compelled to bring Lady Milford Haven from England to deny these accusations on the witness stand."

On the ride home, Gloria would not lift her face from her handkerchief. She was half carried into her house and taken to the drawing rooms, where she collapsed on the couch. Nathan Burkan, with a dawning realization of the enormity of what had happened, said, in a choked voice, "If only you had told me she was your *special friend*."

"I told you about our friendship," Gloria replied, and began to sob. "It's all a pack of lies—malicious lies."

"Gloria," said Nathan Burkan, "if you have anything else to tell me, for God's sake, tell me now."

"Nothing. There's nothing to tell." Even now, Gloria did not say that pornographic books were a special hobby of George Milford Haven or that *La Jolie Flagellante de New York* and the "vile books" described by Keislich were exactly the type of books that appeared in the Milford Haven catalogs.

Burkan and Murray began to discuss strategy, deciding that they should move for a postponement until things had quieted down. In the meantime, they'd check with Val O'Farrell to see if he could come up with anything on Mrs. Whitney that might— Guided by his instinct, Burkan moved to the door and jerked it open. Charles Zaug almost fell into the room. Burkan's face colored. "You. You're the one who's been reporting to Crocker. What did you say? What did you tell him?"

"I refuse to say," replied Zaug.

Burkan turned to Gloria and Consuelo. "Pack your things. It is unsafe to remain here among spies." Within the hour, Wann had packed five suitcases, and she, Gloria, and Consuelo had checked into the Sherry-Netherland. The house was deserted when Charles Zaug opened the front door and admitted two dark-suited men he'd never seen before but had been told to expect. Zaug calmly stood by while they ransacked the house.

At 871 Fifth Avenue, Gertrude Whitney was involved in a meeting of her own. The scene in the courtroom had unnerved her, and she commanded her lawyers to stop the trial. Frank Crocker explained that they had not initiated the suit, Gloria Vanderbilt had started it, and only she could withdraw it. Crocker reminded Gertrude that they had based their case on neglect, as she had ordered, but that Burkan himself had clumsily blundered on to the accusation of homosexuality.

The morning's headlines were worse than either side could have imagined. FRENCH MAID BLURTS OUT SECRET . . . LADY MILFORD HAVEN KISSED MRS. VANDERBILT . . . EVIDENCE SO REVOLTING THAT COURT BARS PRESS AND PUBLIC. Newspaper articles minutely detailed both the nurse's and maid's accusations and one succinct report said, "No sooner had the testimony of an Irish nurse placed Prince Gottfried Hermann Alfred

Paul Maximilian Victor zu Hohenlohe-Langenburg in the bed of Mrs. Reginald Claypoole Vanderbilt than the testimony of a French maid put the Marchioness of Milford Haven in the same place. Said the maid, pertly: 'She put her arms around Mrs. Vanderbilt and kissed her.' "

Reporters contacted Thelma Furness at the Ritz Hotel in Paris, where she told them that she and her brother, Harry, had spoken to Nathan Burkan (her twin was too upset to speak to her) and they would take the Golden Arrow and sail as soon as possible on the *Empress of Britain.* When informed that Mrs. Morgan would be the next witness to testify against Gloria, Thelma exclaimed, "My mother must be mad!"

Julia McCarthy was the first reporter to reach Prince Hohenlohe by transatlantic telephone at Schloss Langenburg. When told of the maid's accusation, he emitted a low whistle followed by an exclamation in German. Julia asked for his comment. "I cannot comment on anything so outrageous as that," he said. Julia then told him about the nurse's testimony of his bedroom tryst with Gloria. "I have heard of this," he said. "It is the most monstrous criminal lie I've ever heard. I am flabbergasted . . . I'm not going to let people sling mud at me." He then told Julia that he and Princess Margarita would sail on the *Bremen* to testify on Mrs. Vanderbilt's behalf.

Nadeja Milford Haven was cornered by a pack of reporters when her plane landed at Croydon airport as she was returning from Paris. Her lips quivered and tears ran down her cheeks as she spoke. "What you have heard are a set of malicious lies. I am going now to see my husband and then my lawyer. I cannot say definitely whether I shall go to the United States. What I can say is that I shall stand by Mrs. Vanderbilt to the bitter end." Reporters noted that during the conference "the Marchioness was held upright by a *woman companion* who then helped her to her motor car."

On Friday, the New York *Mirror* headline read,

ROYALTY OF BRITAIN FORBID
LADY HAVEN TO TESTIFY

> King George and Queen Mary hastily summoned the Marchioness of Milford Haven to Buckingham Palace to give an account of her connection with the case. After seeing the Sovereigns, she said it was unlikely that she would testify in New York. . . . King George and Queen Mary have requested her to remain in London. The Marquis of Milford Haven is a cousin of the King and he and Lady Milford Haven are extremely popular at the palace. At the last court

levee, she sat beside the Queen and she is known to be one of Queen Mary's favorite friends.

In a telephone interview a considerably calmer Nada informed *The New York Times* that she was consulting with the firm of Charles Russell & Company about the feasibility of sending a representative to New York to protect her name. "The whole thing is disgusting and I feel just as does everyone else who knows Mrs. Vanderbilt that there is no truth in the picture drawn of her, as depicted from New York."

"The picture . . . as depicted from New York" was not the picture as depicted in Great Britain. Although a Reuters communiqué on Maria Caillot's accusation of homosexuality had been issued, British newspapers merely alluded to "lurid stories concerning Mrs. Vanderbilt," and reported that "a titled woman was mentioned in some connection with this case." London's *Daily Express* reported that "Mrs. Vanderbilt and a titled English woman were involved in a kissing incident in a Cannes hotel." No British newspaper mentioned the homosexual nature of the "kissing incident," nor was the Marchioness of Milford Haven identified as the person who had kissed Mrs. Vanderbilt.

If this accusation had appeared in the press it might possibly have led to some speculation. It was well known that the Marchioness of Milford Haven and her sister-in-law Lady Louis Mountbatten had disappeared from Mayfair for months at a time on their remote journeys, and in light of Maria Caillot's testimony, these restless wanderings might have taken on a different cast. Nada and Edwina Ashley Mountbatten nestled at the very heart of the royal family. The two great press lords, Rothermere and Beaverbrook, were unusually discreet in matters touching upon the sanctity of the British monarch's family. (They were, for instance, fully aware of the relationship between Edward, Prince of Wales, and Wallis Warfield Spencer Simpson, but it would be two years hence, and a full six months after the American press had revealed this relationship, before news of it would appear in British newspapers.)

Wednesday morning, October 3, as the *Paris* glided toward New York City, Constance Bennett and her husband, Henri, Marquis de la Falaise de la Coudraye, finished their morning coffee and croissants. At that moment, Blumie and his friend, movie tycoon Nicholas (Nick) Schenck, were aboard a government cutter speeding toward Quarantine to warn their friends of yesterday's events before the press got to them. The cutter pulled alongside the liner and both men scrambled aboard and raced for A-deck. They were too late—the ships' reporters were clustered around Constance Bennett, who stood clutching the *Daily News*, a stricken look on her face. From his position behind the reporters' backs, Blumie signaled her frantically. Connie saw him and, with a slight gesture, waved him away, as she told reporters, "I promise I'll give you an interview at the pier. You know I won't run out on you."

While reporters repaired to the cabin-class bar, Connie Bennett returned to her stateroom. Blumie, Nick, and her husband were waiting for her. Connie slammed the door and hurled the newspaper across the room. They'd caught her off guard, those damned reporters. She was right to live in Europe, where they treated you as a person, where autograph hounds didn't follow you everywhere and reporters didn't jump on every piece of gossip. Lately, Connie kept reading those disgusting divorce rumors that Louella Parsons had started by printing that "Connie Bennett and Gilbert Roland have become inseparable companions." Now Blumie filled Connie in on what the Vanderbilt nurse had said about her having a "South American lover." For Christ's sake, Gilbert was Mexican, not South American, but it was too close for comfort.

Hank was being wonderful; he and Blumie and Nick were discussing how to handle the reporters. Ships' reporters were a tough bunch and were known to crucify you if you tried to hand them a written statement or, even worse, refused to see them at all. Blumie told her that the Whitney side would undoubtedly subpoena her to testify as soon as she arrived in New York. Connie wasn't about to get up on that stand. She'd been involved in lawsuits before and she knew that on the witness stand you had no privacy left. They could work it around to asking about Gilbert—about anybody!

Three hours later, Connie left the *Paris* and was immediately surrounded by reporters. Blumie could not stand being ignored. Pushing his way to the center of the crowd, he declared in a loud voice, "I just came out to see Miss Bennett. I haven't told her a thing about the *Vanderbilt* case, and I don't want the name of *A. C. Blumenthal* dragged into this or linked with Mrs. *Vanderbilt's* in any way."

Connie told reporters, "Of course I will testify for Gloria Vanderbilt. I know her well, and I can tell you if all mothers were like her, it would be a good thing for the United States . . . Mrs. Vanderbilt is an ideal and perfect mother." When reporters mentioned the nurse's testimony concerning her lover, she turned to her husband and commented, "Why, I have a libel suit on my hands." Connie said she knew Prince Hohenlohe and that "he couldn't possibly have been Mrs. Vanderbilt's lover. . . . How could that be? Mrs. Vanderbilt lived with the baby and her own mother. Prince Hohenlohe was her fiancé at that time. His mother, too, often came to the house to be with him." Tapping a cigarette on her palm, she continued, "I've never had a drink in my life . . . I have nothing against it but I don't care for alcohol," and, "Mrs. Vanderbilt only had an occasional glass of sherry. . . . So much for her alleged wild life."

When reporters asked her why the nurse had made these accusations, Connie answered, "Because she is a liar!" Then, taking her husband's arm, she waved reporters off and stepped into Blumie's Rolls-Royce, which took them to the Waldorf-Astoria where they registered for a two-week stay.

On the following morning, the hotel manager phoned their suite to report that process servers were waiting in the lobby to make sure Miss Bennett testified at the Vanderbilt trial. At noon, the star appeared in the lobby. A process server ran up to her and tried to hand her a subpoena, but she walked past him, her hands pasted on her hips, down the steps, out the door, and locked herself in a waiting Rolls-Royce. The marquis checked out and joined her in the limousine.

Reporters caught up to them at Grand Central Terminal as they were about to board the 20th Century Limited. Connie Bennett, holding a bouquet of orchids, explained that "Hank has been ill with a fever ever since working on a film in the South Seas. . . . After all, my husband's health comes first," she cooed. "I am taking him to Arrowhead Springs. Later, I shall be glad to fly back to testify for Mrs. Vanderbilt." It would be eight months before she returned to New York City.

In Gloria Vanderbilt's Sherry-Netherland suite, Nathan Burkan called one newspaper after another, summoning reporters to a press conference. He dispensed bits of information, like jewels, to each reporter. He told Julia McCarthy of the *News* that Gloria had not been able to eat in the three days since the maid had made her unfounded accusation. He told Jane Franklin of the *Mirror* that Gloria suffered from phlebitis. He told Denis Morrison of the *World-Telegram* that "she misses her child so much that she suffers from chronic insomnia."

At the press conference, Gloria was stretched out on a gold brocade sofa, her face dead-white, her dress stark black. Nathan Burkan spoke for her. "I will insist on the fullest hearing. This woman will be vindicated. . . . So far, only Whitney witnesses—two destructive servants—have been allowed to speak. . . . Those obscene books described by Mrs. Vanderbilt's discharged servants never existed, nor is she disposed to morbid affection for women friends." At that, Gloria bit her lip and turned her head toward the wall.

NRA MEMBER U.S.
WE DO OUR PART

DAILY MIRROR

3 CENTS

Copyright, 1934, by Daily Mirror. Registered U. S. Patent Office.
Entered as second class matter Post Office, New York, N. Y.

VOL. XI. No. 88 P New York, Thursday, October 4, 1934

LADDER SKETCHED IN BRUNO'S DIARY!

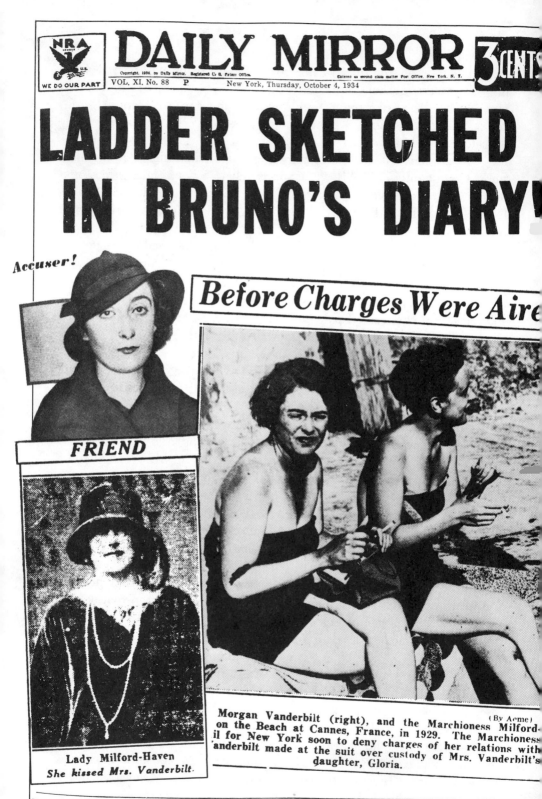

Accuser!

Before Charges Were Aire

FRIEND

Lady Milford-Haven

She kissed Mrs. Vanderbilt.

(By Acme)

Morgan Vanderbilt (right), and the Marchioness Milford-on the Beach at Cannes, France, in 1929. The Marchioness il for New York soon to deny charges of her relations with 'anderbilt made at the suit over custody of Mrs. Vanderbilt's daughter, Gloria.

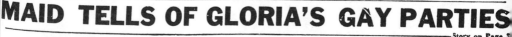

MAID TELLS OF GLORIA'S GAY PARTIES

—Story on Page 3

At the conclusion of the conference, Gloria made a short speech in a tiny, childlike, stammering voice. "I want my baby," she said. "I know Mrs. Whitney is one of the richest women in the world . . . but I'll fight to the finish for my child."

When reporters asked why her mother had taken a stand against her, Gloria's eyes widened and she seemed to be considering the question. "How curious of Mother," she answered. "Evidently, she is overawed by Mrs. Whitney."

"Overawed by what?" asked a reporter.

Gloria had evidently decided to commit herself no further. "Oh, just overawed."

At 14 East Sixtieth Street, Laura Morgan was doing some politicking of her own. She invited reporters into her tiny two-room hotel apartment and explained, "I am sure if my daughter were to win this case she would run right back to Europe and rear Gloria as a European." She said that her daughter had "a mania for titles." Mrs. Morgan admitted that each of her four children had pleaded with her, "Side with us, Mother," but she'd told them, "No . . . I feel Mrs. Whitney should have custody of little Gloria." Then, showing that she had kept up on the reportage, she harrumphed, "So Thelma thinks I'm mad, does she? It's Thelma who's the crazy one. And now you know what I think."

At three o'clock on Sunday, Val O'Farrell appeared at the Vanderbilt suite for a conference. Burkan was growing increasingly displeased with O'Farrell; even though his operatives had infiltrated every one of Gertrude Vanderbilt Whitney's residences, he'd found nothing with which they could fight. O'Farrell reported that Mrs. Whitney had been known as "the Bohemian Angel of Paris" and had had several lovers abroad, but he placed the last one in Paris in 1926—which did them no good at all. Burkan told several associates that it was a supreme irony that Gertrude Whitney was everything she accused Gloria of being: she loved to travel and had left her children for months at a time while she pursued her own life; she was extravagant, she liked to drink alcohol, she'd had many lovers and there were rumors of lesbian relationships. But there were essential differences which protected Gertrude Whitney: Gloria led her life in print while Gertrude's was shrouded in a secrecy purchased by her vast wealth. And at twenty-nine, Gloria could not disguise her sexuality while Gertrude at fifty-nine seemed the quintessential conservative, austere widow.

Burkan was beginning to regret his decision to switch from Benny Kerin, who, while not "classy," was someone who invariably "got the goods" they needed. An impatient Burkan asked O'Farrell for his latest report: Val O'Farrell began by saying that after Mrs. Vanderbilt had left her town house, two Whitney-employed detectives had searched the establishment. "Why didn't you stop them?" demanded Burkan. O'Farrell answered that this was not his job. "If that isn't your job, what is?"

At that moment it occurred to Nathan Burkan that perhaps O'Farrell was a double agent; with all his resources it was inconceivable that he'd come up empty-handed. In his frustration, Burkan began screaming at O'Farrell, demanding action, threatening him. O'Farrell took Burkan's verbal blows until this assault loosed a flood of pain in his body which fanned out across his chest and around his back. He could not answer. He gasped for air and dropped to the floor. Gloria began to scream and Burkan ran to the telephone and summoned the house doctor who arrived within minutes, examined O'Farrell, and called for an ambulance. He told Burkan to call a priest. As the ambulance sped toward Flower Hospital, the Reverend Ward J. Meehan administered the last rites. O'Farrell was pronounced D.O.A.

Little Gloria was reported to have "spent a delightful Sunday afternoon at Wheatley Hills with her prize pony, Black Beauty."

An Exceptionally Virtuous Man

A judge should not think of himself as an exceptionally virtuous man, but as merely the instrument through which the voice of principle speaks.

TELFORD TAYLOR, JUSTICE AT THE NUREMBERG TRIALS

Justice John Francis Carew had been deeply shocked by the maid's testimony. In his entire career as a judge, he'd never heard anything like it, and his decision to clear the courtroom came as an instantaneous emotional reaction. Half an hour later, he walked into his chambers to find the room full of reporters. Carew told them that there would be no session of the Vanderbilt case the following day. "I will consider the situation overnight and enter a ruling as to whether or not to admit the press to future sessions." When questioned further he only repeated, "I will have to consider."

The following morning, Carew met with the lawyers for both sides and said that, in view of the maid's testimony, he strongly recommended an immediate out-of-court settlement. Both Burkan and Crocker protested that nothing had changed—there was no basis for a settlement. Frank Crocker, however, assured Justice Carew that the Whitney side was building their case on neglect rather than character assassination and would continue to do so. After the meeting was over,

Carew, reassured by Crocker's statement, called reporters into his chambers and told them that he was again "disposed to admit the press to the hearings."

In Carew's antechamber, Nathan Burkan decided to take full advantage of the situation—neglect alone would leave the Whitney side with a weak case. Burkan boasted to reporters that he had spent the morning demanding that Carew admit them to the courtroom. "There will be no settlement unless the seditious witnesses Mrs. Whitney has placed on the stand are refuted in open court by respectable people."

Frank Crocker and Theodore Miller, Herbert Smyth's assistant, stood some distance away listening to Burkan. When Crocker had heard enough, he returned to Carew's chambers and told the Justice that, in view of Burkan's inflammatory statements to the press and Carew's own ruling that the Whitney side must produce "compelling evidence of Mrs. Vanderbilt's unfitness," he'd reconsidered and would be forced to subpoena butler Charles Zaug, chauffeur Theodore Beesley, and two of Mrs. Vanderbilt's women friends, who so far had been accused of drunkenness, Agnes Horter and Helen Marye Thomas. Tom Gilchrist had told Crocker that he'd been forced to speak reprovingly to Gloria Vanderbilt about Agnes when she was living at the Vanderbilt town house and as a result Agnes had packed up and left. The other woman, Helen Marye Thomas, who'd been accused of being "so drunk she had to be carried upstairs . . . and somebody had to help her . . . to go to the bathroom," was the socially prominent daughter of George T. Marye, who from 1914 to 1916 had served as United States ambassador to Imperial Russia. She was married to Lieutenant Commander William D. Thomas, a naval attaché at the American Embassy in Paris. That evening Agnes Horter disappeared. When a subpoena was issued to Helen Thomas, her whereabouts were also unknown.

Justice Carew could see exactly where the Whitney side was heading and he determined to keep whatever scandal might be revealed sealed within the walls of his courtroom. The Civil Practice Act empowered him to decide what testimony to reveal to the public and what to keep secret. The act provided that testimony of a scandalous or repulsive nature could be excluded without furnishing grounds for such exclusion. Once Carew had decided on this course of action, he called a press conference and announced, "I have considered the situation . . . so much scandalous gossip is being let loose from this court that it might embarrass the child's future. Therefore, I have determined to hold future sessions in private." Carew then said that he'd informed the lawyers of his decision and had asked them to tell their clients that anyone who spoke of these proceedings would be held in contempt of court. The reporters groaned and began to protest. Observing their reaction, Carew was torn—he wanted to do what was morally right, but he also wanted to please the public; having served so long as an elected official, he'd come to rely on public approval. Trying to serve two masters—the public and his own conscience—Justice Carew suggested a curious ameliorative measure. He said that he would allow the reporters back into the courtroom when Maria Caillot's examination was concluded to hear the testimony of the next witness, Dr. Stuart L. Craig, "since it will not be sensational." With this gesture, Carew inadvertently placed himself in the untenable position of prejudging the content of as yet unheard testimony.

From Nathan Burkan's point of view, Carew's ruling was the best possible turn of events, and secretly he was elated by it. The press would be permitted into the courtroom to hear bland testimony while they would be barred from hearing anything of a scandalous nature about his client. Burkan's public posture, however, was to protest Carew's so-called "gag order" and to continue pretending that he wanted a public hearing. This move was part of a carefully calculated campaign to capture public sympathy. As he had done on many occasions, Burkan intended to carry his fight to the press. By virtue of his long-standing relationship with Gloria, Maury Paul could be counted on as an ally. Burkan was also extremely close to *News* reporter Julia McCarthy.

It was said that Julia had started her career in Chicago as a cub reporter on the crime beat with Ben Hecht. In 1918, she'd come to New York to work for the *Evening Journal*, where, for a decade, she did the work of three people, appearing as herself, Margery Rex, and Julia West. She'd illustrated her own stories on the Prince of Wales, Sir Arthur Conan Doyle, and Isadora Duncan. She'd covered a series of murders—hex murders, sex murders, bludgeonings, and shootings—and she'd been present at the electric-chair execution of Ruth Snyder.

After a decade at the *Journal*, she went to the *World*, where she came to be close to Nathan Burkan when he gave her some of her best divorce stories and provided the introductions that enabled her to break into political reportage. Then the Depression hit, the paper reduced its staff—women were the first to go. Nathan Burkan came to the rescue. He managed to get her a job writing advertising copy for Gimbels at $35 a week, only Julia hated it; there were only so many ways to write about that "devastating" dress for $7.95 or "a three-piece fur-trimmed outfit that will take you anywhere" for $15.95. Julia quit, but there was no work to be had until eighteen months later, when she was hired by the *Daily News* at a salary of $50 a week. To celebrate, she bought herself a bottle of champagne, went home, and drank it all by herself. Julia had no husband and few friends. She was a strict Catholic who often attended Mass before going to the office. When she was hired by the *News*, tall, redheaded, and aristocratic-looking Julia was thirty-three; she could speak the same language as Society people and write about them in a way the shop girls and the secretaries who read her articles would enjoy. Her prose style was lively and full of minute, accurately observed detail. She had poise, total recall, and was willing to work around the clock. She also had nerve: at Alice Gwynne Vanderbilt's funeral, an event from which the press was barred, Julia marched into St. Bartholomew's and instructed the vestryman to seat her well forward as she was hard of hearing. He obligingly placed her directly behind Gertrude Whitney. A fellow reporter observed of Julia, "She prefers the front door method but also has been known to use the fire escape. She is one of the best fact-getters in the business." Julia knew the value of inside contacts and at the end of the day would often drop by the Burkan office for a chat and a drink and for the latest leads.

Burkan was convinced that once Maury Paul and Julia McCarthy came down squarely on Gloria Vanderbilt's side, the other tabloid newspapers would follow suit. The power of the tabloids to shape public opinion was formidable. In a city of approximately seven million, the circulation of the *News* in which Julia McCarthy's articles appeared numbered 1,428,908 people daily and 1,828,543 on Sundays. The Sunday circulation of the *American*, featuring Cholly Knickerbocker, was 1,013,219.

During the hiatus in courtroom sessions, Burkan carefully began to build a sympathetic image of his client. He knew that in a time when so many had lost so much, the public would not react well to the effort of a supremely wealthy woman to wrest a child from her poor widowed mother. Also, people instinctively realized that it was not according to the rules for servants to tattle on their employers, and Burkan kept insisting that if only the public could hear the testimony in this case, Gloria Vanderbilt would be "swiftly and completely vindicated."

Julia McCarthy's articles began to carry this Burkan-created image to the public, and she created the stereotypes that every tabloid newspaper would adopt. She began referring to Gloria Vanderbilt as "the harassed widow," to Gertrude Whitney as "the haughty $150 million aunt." Justice Carew was censured for "an unreasonable gag order which prevents the bereft mother from openly refuting her tattle-tale servants." Across the nation Americans began reading the tabloids and sympathy began flowing out to Gloria Vanderbilt.

On Monday morning, October 8, when the court sessions resumed, Gloria Vanderbilt arrived at the Supreme Court wearing an outfit

Nathan Burkan himself had selected. She looked like a figure in mourning in her tailored black suit and veiled black hat. To complete the stark picture, she removed her silver fox from about her shoulders and handed it to Consuelo to carry.

In answer to reporters' queries, Burkan said that his first action that morning would be to move for an open trial.

"You're not satisfied being gagged?" called out a reporter.

"Satisfied? Mrs. Vanderbilt is crushed."

Gloria looked down at the pavement and murmured, "I'm awfully sorry. I'd like to talk to you, but Justice Carew says I can't."

This morning the courtroom seemed enormous in its emptiness. Justice Carew took his seat and carefully looked around the room. His slow gaze took in the lawyers, Laura Morgan, the maid Maria Caillot, Gloria, and Consuelo. As he glanced to the right rear corner of the room, he saw several men whom he did not recognize. It was then that he announced: "Out of consideration for the interests of the infant in this case, I have excluded from attendance at this trial the representatives of the press and spectators, and nobody is to be allowed in this room during the taking of testimony except those persons who are vouchsafed for by counsel. . . . Anybody that is not here under those circumstances will leave at once and will not come back."

Carew gestured to a bailiff, who walked to the back of the room and asked the men who they were. Reporters, they admitted, and the bailiff ushered them out. Carew said, "Now, nobody in this room now is to report outside anything that occurs during the pendancy of this trial, to others than his own client."

"Except, Your Honor, if I have a witness that there may be accusations made against . . . I want the right to repeat to that person what the charge was," said Burkan.

"You can bring him here and they can deny it," answered Carew.

"But *before* I bring him here, I certainly have the right to ask him whether or not such a thing happened," said Burkan.

"I suppose that is fair," agreed Carew. "But, apart from that, I do not see any reason of anything that occurs in this room now to be reported to anybody else." Burkan nodded in agreement.

Maria Caillot was about to resume her testimony, but Herbert Smyth asked if he might place Dr. Stuart L. Craig on the stand. Dr. Craig had been waiting since the previous Wednesday to testify. He sat in the second row of spectator seats, a sour expression on his face. This trial had ruined his vacation plans. In fact, little Gloria had caused him considerable inconvenience. He was constantly being summoned by nurse Keislich to visit the child—there must have been twenty house calls in the past two years—but when he arrived, it was invariably just a sinus flare-up or a red throat and a cough. During the big blizzard of February 1933, he'd been summoned twice by the nurse and had been so annoyed that he'd spoken to Mrs. Whitney about it, saying that at $100 a visit, he felt he was making too many unnecessary house calls. Mrs. Whitney's reply was that he should come when called—whether it was necessary or not. Now Craig had been subpoenaed to testify at this trial—he was still being forced to come when called.

The disgruntled doctor sat in the witness chair. He referred to his notes, and testified that he'd first seen little Gloria in his office April 15, 1932. He emphasized that he was an ear, nose, and throat specialist, and therefore had never given the child a physical examination. "It is not customary for a specialist to go into detail of a child's general health." But little Gloria "appeared to me to be physically unfit and under par, as evidenced by the fact that she looked pale and underweight. She was nervous and excitable. In my own special field, she had a low-grade virus condition. Her tonsils and adenoids were evidently diseased, and her cervical glands were enlarged."

Craig did not think it wise to operate until the child was in better physical condition. The operation was performed on June 8 at Doctors Hospital. The child remained in the hospital six days, and then she returned to the Sherry-Netherland in the company of Emma Keislich and a trained nurse. Here, she was confined to bed for ten days more.

Carew stopped the testimony to say, "I had a child operated on, took her down to the hospital, she was operated on, and took her home the same day, and gave her some ice cream and she was running around the next morning." Craig answered carefully and tactfully, "This child, sir, was regarded by us as a case that we would handle with unusual care."

He looked down at his notes and continued his testimony. During little Gloria's convalescence she had experienced "a hysterical upset, which was disturbing." The following day he examined her and found her "upset and very nervous."

"What did you notice about her nervousness?" inquired Herbert Smyth.

Craig hesitated, "Well, nervousness in a child takes the form of apprehension as a rule. . . . She was apprehensive." When asked for an explanation for this, he said, "Following any operation . . . of a child who is not quite up to par, an attack of hysteria from what you might term the delayed shock of the operation is quite within reason." After Craig had examined the child, Mrs. Vanderbilt had asked him if it would be all right for her to go to Europe, and he'd answered, "As far as her operative condition is concerned, it is all right. If the child is sent to the country and allowed to convalesce normally, she'll be all right."

And so the child was sent to Wheatley Hills, but Craig said that her condition didn't improve and "everyone was considerably concerned about her." In the next year, however, she "steadily improved." And over the past two years the child had "so improved in general appearance that . . . it would not take a doctor to determine it." During this entire period, Dr. Craig had not seen the child's mother—the child was always with her nurse.

Smyth began to question Dr. Craig about the last time he'd seen little Gloria, the afternoon she fled to Mrs. Whitney's. Craig said, "She was quite hysterical and I asked her what she'd been crying for and she said because her mother wanted to take her away. . . . I said, 'That is nothing to cry for.' She said, 'I don't want to be taken . . . I hate my mother.' "

Carew now asked a vital question. "She had been out of the custody of her mother for two and a half years yet she said she hated her mother? Her mother had not done anything to her for two and a half years?" It was a puzzling question and Craig had not considered it before. "Not that I know of," he answered. Craig said that all his efforts had gone into calming the child; he had not probed the root of little Gloria's hatred of her mother, and all he could remember was that the child kept repeating that her mother "was going to take her away" and somchow the idea of this "seemed to make her more hysterical."

Nathan Burkan began his cross-examination by establishing that Mrs. Vanderbilt had seen Dr. Craig prior to little Gloria's operation, and that it was Craig himself who had recommended that the child go to the country to convalesce. Burkan then asked if Dr. Craig had determined the cause of the child's recurring abdominal pains. He answered that this was "not in my province. . . . Several specialists were called in with relation to these attacks." When Burkan continued to press for an opinion on why the child had experienced stomach pain, Craig grew testy; he was only "a specialist for the child's nose and throat. In other words, from the neck up. . . . If you gentlemen will leave me to my own department!" he exclaimed.

Dr. Craig freely admitted that it was "most unusual" to continue visiting a patient for two years after a tonsil and adenoid operation, as he had been called upon to do. Then Burkan made a statement in the form of a question. "The cause for this was a very wealthy child?"

"Yes, sir!" replied Craig. He certainly agreed with this assessment. It was time somebody came out and said it. "That is right," he affirmed.

Finally, Burkan's examination proceeded to the afternoon little

Gloria had run away to Mrs. Whitney's. The doctor told Burkan that, as a specialist, he felt it was very strange and unusual that he was the one who'd been called. Naturally, he'd assumed that the child's problem was her ears or throat. He was unprepared for this hysterical child who screamed out, "I hate my mother."

"You knew then it had been away from its mother some two years?" inquired Burkan, just as Carew had. "Did you ask the child why it hated its mother?"

"No, sir . . . I had no curiosity . . . it was none of my business," replied Dr. Stuart L. Craig.

Maria Caillot was recalled to the stand for further examination. Maria's photograph had appeared in newspapers across the country. She had become an instant celebrity. Today she was perfectly groomed, in a dark suit, and discreetly made-up. She seemed to have acquired a new confidence.

Burkan asked Maria to repeat the incident involving Lady Milford Haven. She described how she had entered the Miramar Hotel bedroom—Mrs. Vanderbilt, clad in a nightgown, sat on the bed. Lady Milford Haven, also in a nightgown, "was beside the bed and she . . ." At that moment, Gloria Vanderbilt rose to her feet, clutched at her throat, and collapsed onto the hard wood floor of the courtroom. She sobbed as she was carried into the corridor, through the crush of reporters and spectators, and into a small room where she was given a glass of water and a cooling cloth at her temples to revive her. The press watched through the half-open door. After a time, Gloria sat up and said, "I feel all right now," then she rose slowly and returned to the courtroom.

Maria Caillot remained calm throughout the incident and continued to testify, saying that she was aware that Lady Milford Haven was married and had two children, a daughter of seventeen and a son of fifteen.

Burkan demanded, "And did you observe Lord Milford Haven and Lady Milford Haven and these children how they behaved themselves in Paris?" When Maria hesitated, he commanded: "Don't shrug and rub your nose."

"No, I don't observe nothing. I don't pay any attention," Maria answered.

Burkan was moving in for the kill. "Did you ever visit a Dr. Thomas H. Cherry?" he inquired.

"No."

"Didn't you ever visit a doctor at 133 East Fifty-eighth Street?"

"I do not remember."

In full attack, Burkan shouted, "Didn't you have a miscarriage in the presence of the nurse and the baby in 1932?"

Smyth objected. Carew overruled his objection, then turned to Smyth, explaining why it was foolish of him to object. "You had better be careful," Carew cautioned Smyth. "If he [Burkan] proves that his client retained such a personage around her, it might bear on the client."

"Of course." Smyth smiled with relief. "I *did* have that in mind."

"You did not have that in mind when you objected," observed Carew dryly. . . . "Things do not always look the same from here as they do from there."

Burkan too must have realized that an admission of a miscarriage in front of little Gloria and, after that, the continuance of the maid in his client's employ would hardly help their side. He promptly abandoned this subject.

Burkan shot rapid-fire questions at the witness. Maria admitted that she had never actually seen Mr. Blumenthal inside Gloria Vanderbilt's bedroom but insisted that she'd heard a man's voice in the bedroom and later had removed a bottle and two glasses from the room. She held firm to her assertion that when Agnes Horter lived with Mrs. Vanderbilt, "many times in the morning" she drank whiskey and that "sometimes she sleep in the same room" as Mrs. Vanderbilt.

Burkan, wanting no more of this, said, "Now, you know at that time, that this Miss Horter was the secretary."

"At that time she was not the secretary," answered Maria. "Perhaps she was, but nobody ever told me anything."

When Burkan kept hammering away at Maria, her answers became brief. She replied with "Yes," "No," "I don't understand, I didn't pay any attention," "Perhaps." As Burkan became more and more irritated, Maria became more and more confident; she was clearly taking pleasure in Burkan's frustration, and his goads became useless. "You have got a very bad memory, haven't you, miss?"

"Perhaps."

"Don't you know whether you have or not?"

"Perhaps I have."

"You have a lot of trouble in remembering things, haven't you?"

"Perhaps," answered Maria with the smile of a victor.

Burkan dismissed the witness.

At the close of the session Carew returned to his chambers to find a group of angry reporters who accused him of reneging on his promise to let them hear Dr. Craig's testimony. Carew again tried to placate them, this time by announcing that in order to accommodate members of the press, he was prepared to provide them with his personal summaries of the testimony. He would meet with the reporters for the evening newspapers at 1:00 p.m. and the morning papers' reporters at 4:00 p.m.

From this moment on, the *Matter of Vanderbilt* would be reported not as it happened in that sealed courtroom, but as filtered through the sensibility of Justice Carew. Referring to his jurist's notes, Carew promptly supplied what the *News* termed "a brief and spotless account of the testimony of Dr. Stuart L. Craig." Carew refused to speak of Maria Caillot's testimony, except in the most sketchy terms, but he tantalizingly confirmed that the Milford Haven incident had been the cause of Mrs. Vanderbilt's collapse.

Carew also told members of the press that Burkan's cross-examination had been "very good," and provocatively said that he'd driven hard at the maid's story and had tried to learn from her the significance of an illness two years ago when she was confined for a time in St. Luke's Hospital. "In this he was unsuccessful. . . . The maid insisted she had nothing to conceal." In fact, Maria had said nothing about having "nothing to conceal." Carew was creating his own version of the proceedings.

When asked if the maid's accusation of a lesbian relationship had been disproved, Carew replied, "I am sure Mr. Burkan feels he diluted the maid's testimony somewhat, while the opposing counsel undoubtedly feels he did not. The maid stuck to her story."

Julia McCarthy's front page story the following morning was headlined.

MRS. VANDERBILT "VINDICATED"
. . . MAID RECANTS

> In a courtroom barred to the avid crowds . . . Gloria Morgan Vanderbilt's former French maid . . . admitted the promise of money for her testimony . . . she went over the incident linking her employer to Lady Milford Haven in such a fashion yesterday that Nathan Burkan felt his client had been thoroughly vindicated.
>
> Burkan himself could not say so, because of the gag imposed by Justice John F. Carew . . . But the justice, at the end of the day, revealed that Burkan felt the whole sensational affair had been put in its proper place—that of an innocent friendship. . . .

Justice Carew had set himself up as the only source of information about the trial. He was only trying to be fair and to please the public, but as a result of his actions he was beginning to find himself the ringmaster of a media circus, performing in the unrelenting glare of public scrutiny. Under this pressure, he would be transformed from a competent, fair man, sure of his abilities, into a messianic, bombastic bully who would eventually short-circuit. What was to bring this about was Carew's rigid, unrealistic conception of himself and his role. He considered himself to be a totally moral man whose obligation it was to guide others on the path of righteousness. "My proper function as based on English jurisprudence is to judge morals and conduct," he asserted. But in this case he would be faced with morals and conduct he could not even comprehend, much less control.

Within a few days, hundreds of sympathetic letters began pouring in at the Vanderbilt town house. The *Sun* reported that the majority were "from mothers who have lost children through death or failure to provide for them. . . . Many of the letters were addressed simply to Gloria Vanderbilt. Postmasters throughout the country added New York and the letters were delivered."

At the Supreme Court hundreds of other letters arrived for Justice Carew, and these were not sympathetic: he was severely criticized for preventing Mrs. Vanderbilt from saving her reputation in open court. Even Carew's children became aware that he was taking it on the chin, but he told them that he always did what he thought was "right" and as a justice he considered himself above criticism. "Pay no attention to them," he said, "they've got to write something—that's what they're paid to do." But in truth, the pressure was beginning to build. After Monday's session, Carew summoned reporters to his chambers. Letters totally obscured his desk and the overflow had been piled into stacks, tied with twine, and placed on the carpet. Carew angrily distributed copies of a stenciled message.

> I have received a number of letters in regard to the *Matter of Vanderbilt*. I have destroyed them without reading them up to this time, but for the future I will cite those who write them to show cause why they should not be punished for contempt. I do not wish to receive any more of them, and if I do I will take severe and summary means to stop them—
>
> John F. Carew

Just what did Carew intend doing?

"I want you to know that I intend to institute contempt proceedings against the writers of similar letters," he bellowed.

The reporters, looking at the mass of material, could not help smiling at the idea of hundreds or perhaps thousands of contempt proceedings. Carew looked at their smiling faces and snapped, "You are dismissed!"

The Loneliest Mother in the World

Mrs. Morgan turned her back on her children when she allied herself with the rich and social Mrs. Harry Payne Whitney in this fantastic and fanatic fight. . . . Now her children have turned their backs on her. . . . No wonder Mrs. Harry Hays Morgan is referred to today as "the loneliest mother in the world."

MAURY PAUL/CHOLLY KNICKERBOCKER

TUESDAY, OCTOBER 9, 1934: in Marseilles, France, a government automobile carrying King Alexander I of Yugoslavia and French Foreign Minister Louis Barthou was fired on by a Croatian assassin using a submachine gun, King Alexander's white tunic spouted crimson and he slumped forward—dead. Prince Gottfried Hohenlohe-Langenburg and his wife, Princess Margarita, received the news of their mutual cousin's assassination while on board the *Bremen* as they were speeding to New York City to testify for Gloria Vanderbilt. Prince Hohenlohe directed his valet to sew a black mourning band on the sleeve of one of his suit jackets.

In a courtroom in Flemington, New Jersey, Charles A. Lindbergh listened impassively to the voice of Bruno Richard Hauptmann, and then identified it as that of the man he had heard in St. Raymond's Cemetery the night the $50,000 ransom had been paid to his son's kidnapper. On the same morning, in New York City's Supreme Court, room 355, Laura Kilpatrick Morgan placed her liver-spotted hand on the worn black

Bible and repeated the oath in a high-pitched voice. Her Spanish accent was pronounced with sibilant *s*'s and a strong singsong rhythm. Today she wore no make-up, and her face looked old and wizened; her pale lips were dry and cracked. In her left hand, she clutched a large gold crucifix. Laura Morgan had never believed, not even for a minute, that this trial would actually take place, that she would be called upon to testify against her own daughter. But here she was with her entire family massed against her, and she felt that she "could not meet her Maker" unless she testified for Mrs. Whitney. All this "public humiliation" she would bear for the sake of little Gloria.

Laura Morgan was aware of the Justice's views: she had married a divorced man and subsequently had divorced him—but before Carew she would appear to be a Catholic of immense dedication. She was a woman who enjoyed her international life—luncheons, cocktails, parties, bridge, gossip—but before Carew she would present herself as a simple unworldly woman, a nursemaid-nun.

Herbert Smyth began the questioning. Laura Morgan said that she had selected nurse Keislich for little Gloria because her daughter "did not show any desires or any interest in choosing the nurse." Nurse Keislich came with "very good recommendations."

Justice Carew made his first inquiry of Mrs. Morgan. "And the mother? What contribution did she make toward the care of the child?"

Laura Morgan looked at him and replied in a conciliatory tone, "It is not my daughter's fault, but she has not been born with a maternal instinct. She was indifferent to the child. She had nothing to do with the child."

Burkan objected to Mrs. Morgan's characterization of her daughter, but Carew allowed it to stand until it was proven or disproven and began questioning Mrs. Morgan about the child's religion—was she or wasn't she a Catholic? In response Laura Morgan began to cry. She blew her nose vigorously, and then described how she had pleaded with her daughter to baptize the baby a Catholic. Finally, she was able to persuade Gloria to take the baby to the Convent of the Sacred Heart. Laura Morgan said that her daughter had made her give her sacred oath not to tell anyone—even the nurse—of the baptism, because "she did not want Mrs. [Alice] Vanderbilt to know it," which might endanger any legacy coming to her or to little Gloria.

Shortly after the Catholic baptism, the family moved to Paris, and Mrs. Morgan went along to be near her beloved granddaughter. In the fall of 1926, they settled into the triplex on the Avenue Charles Floquet.

Smyth inquired as to the routine in the Floquet house. Mrs. Morgan replied: "The same thing. My daughter always . . ."

Burkan objected. "I move to strike out 'the same thing.'" Carew agreed.

Mrs. Morgan turned to look at Burkan with disdain. "Then I will answer, Mr. Burkan, my daughter always got up late, one or two o'clock. The same life went on. . . . Do you hear me, Mr. Burkan?" Mrs. Morgan's tone cut like a knife.

"Oh, never mind that, I will take care of him," Smyth assured Mrs. Morgan.

"Now wait a minute, Mrs. Morgan, you and I are going to get along first rate . . . you and I are going to have a nice talk," Burkan cautioned.

But Burkan's warning spurred Mrs. Morgan on and she began to flagellate her daughter with her words. In Europe, her granddaughter suffered from an obstruction of the nose and pains in her side, but her own mother was indifferent to her. The child was always sick and delicate. Mrs. Morgan had spent as much time as she could with the baby because "I love that child!" In the four and a half years she had lived with her daughter she "was always helping the nurse with the baby . . . I was like a second nursery maid." When Gloria and little Gloria moved into a house on the rue Alfred Roll, Mrs. Morgan rented a room in "a little hotel nearby" so she could continue to look after her granddaughter.

Carew inquired as to why she had not moved into the Roll house with her daughter. Mrs. Morgan answered that she and Gloria had had "a very, very great difference."

Over Burkan's repeated objections, Mrs. Morgan explained that the estrangement had come about because she told her daughter she "was very worried about the conditions of things in regard to the baby and the steps that she was contemplating taking." Then one day Gloria called her mother to her bedroom and showed her a petition that her father, Harry Hays Morgan, had made to the Surrogates' Court in New York, requesting that Gloria be removed as guardian of her own child. Gloria told her mother that her father had threatened to send the document to Surrogate Foley "unless she gave up her mode of life."

"What did she say to you about that?" inquired Smyth.

"Oh, she was very angry, and she asked me what position would I take in the matter. . . . And I said I would tell the truth . . . that she neglected the child; she never looked at the child. She was never there to look after the child . . ."

"What did she reply to that? What did your daughter say?" asked Smyth.

"That she wanted to live her own life—that she was not going to sacrifice herself for anybody."

"Did you have more than one conversation at this time?"

"Oh, this has been going on for six years," replied Mrs. Morgan.

Laura Morgan presented herself as the child's protector who had tried to shield her beloved granddaughter from the horrors contemplated by her own daughter. The Alfred Roll house, from which she was excluded, was uninhabitable for a child. Her daughter told her that the baby would be moved to the attic, where both the women and men servants slept, so that she could make room for guests downstairs. They had a fight and Mrs. Morgan prevented the move. She and her daughter were at such odds that Mrs. Morgan had to arrange to meet the baby and the nurse secretly in the street or in the Bois de Boulogne. "And then in the night after my daughter and her friend—my daughter had gone out—I used to stay with the nurse to keep her company, because she was always alone." The other servants "after their duties were over, they would disappear." Of little Gloria she said, "She was utterly alone in a house . . . outside of Paris . . . and I was afraid . . ."

Smyth asked if Mrs. Morgan had something specific she feared, but Burkan objected to the question and Carew ruled, "I'm afraid I will have to sustain the objection," so no one in that courtroom was to hear what Laura Morgan might have said of her obsession—that her Vanderbilt granddaughter would be murdered for her money.

Smyth now produced a stack of over three dozen letters and cards that little Gloria had written to her grandmother over the years. Mrs. Morgan had saved every one of these and now they were introduced as evidence of the child's enduring affection for her grandmother. Mrs. Morgan said these letters were "all written from different places, from England and from Paris and from Westbury and from every place. From every place!"

After little Gloria's letters had been entered as exhibits, Herbert Smyth turned to Mrs. Morgan and asked gently, "Mrs. Morgan, will you please state, so that my position is understood, whether or not you asked me not to inquire of you with regard to matters pertaining to your daughter's morals?"

Mrs. Morgan did not answer but began to sob; dramatically, she lifted her crucifix and held it in front of her face. Gloria looked up at this woman whom she now regarded, not as her mother, but as a witness for Mrs. Whitney. She thought of how, early in life, she had worshipped this woman; how her whole world had revolved around this woman's whims. Now she saw her in another light—a woman who denounced her because she could no longer dominate her.

At the close of the court session, Laura Morgan walked past her daughters without looking at them and hurried into the ladies room. A crowd waited outside the door, but one woman barged in, grabbed

Mrs. Morgan by the shoulders, and screamed into her face, "What right do you have to do this! Your daughter has a right to her own child! You are a horrible old woman. You are evil. You do not belong to Christ!" Mrs. Morgan tried to push past her, but the woman held her firm and would not leave until the ladies room attendant came up and pulled the woman away. Mrs. Morgan, shaking, headed toward the elevator.

The following morning Nathan Burkan began his cross-examination. He was determined to destroy the picture of religious purity and grandmotherly dedication that Mrs. Morgan had created. Almost immediately, he made Mrs. Morgan admit that on one occasion she had taken $12,000 from Reginald Vanderbilt and that within two weeks of his death, Gloria pawned her jewelry and gave her mother $15,000 to give Mr. Morgan so that he would not "take action against another member of the family."

Burkan established that Gloria and Thelma had supported Mrs. Morgan right up until this trial began. Furthermore, he proved that this so-called fervent Catholic had herself divorced Mr. Morgan. At this, Laura Morgan protested, "I am a Roman Catholic, and in my religion we do not believe in divorce." She said she had gone through this "meaningless ritual" of divorce because "they told me my husband had several ladies that wanted to marry him in London and he was living a very disreputable life there and it was a shame that he was . . . and I did not wish him to live in sin."

At this, a weary Carew leaned forward to say, "I do not think it's necessary to go into that because we have enough in this case without taking in London . . ."

Burkan turned to the primary allegation of neglect: hadn't little Gloria always "had a very good doctor"?

"Yes, she had a very good doctor."

"And a very good nurse?"

"Yes."

"And a very good grandmother?"

"Well, I tried to do what I could."

The implication was clear—this certainly was not the description of a neglected child.

As Burkan continued questioning Mrs. Morgan, it became apparent that she had opposed her daughter's guardianship petition without understanding it. Burkan said, "You know, don't you, that your daughter was never appointed guardian of your granddaughter? You know that?"

"I thought she was the guardian!" replied Mrs. Morgan in astonishment. Then she turned to Herbert Smyth for help. "I do not understand what he means. She has always been considered the guardian of the baby. Nobody has disputed that!" In fact, neither Laura Morgan nor Gertrude Whitney nor Gloria herself understood the legal technicalities involved in this trial. Mrs. Morgan was convinced that Gloria had always been little Gloria's guardian. As for Gertrude Whitney, she had no objection to Gloria's being made guardian of little Gloria's property but wanted to prevent her from gaining control of the child's person. Gloria herself assumed that she was the guardian of little Gloria's person because Wickersham and Gilchrist had confirmed this by calling her "the natural guardian," and writing ". . . of course you are the guardian of the child's person." She'd only been concerned about her daughter's property until Nathan Burkan told her that she had no legal standing either in regard to person or property. Into this complicated brew of differing understandings, another element was about to be introduced. Nathan Burkan explained to Mrs. Morgan that Gloria had not been appointed guardian of little Gloria because she was a minor herself, only twenty years of age, when her husband died and therefore ineligible to be the child's guardian.

Mrs. Morgan said that this was not true. Her daughter was born on August 23, 1904, which made her twenty-one, not twenty, at the time of Reginald's death. Burkan looked at her incredulously; he walked up to Gloria, and they spoke in hurried whispers. Then he said, "The Relator states she was born in 1905."

"Her mother ought to know her age," said Smyth.

"I don't care what the mother knows!" answered Burkan. "The fact is a petition was filed in the Surrogates' Court right after the husband's death, in which it was deposed that she was born in 1905, that she was under age, and George W. Wickersham was appointed the sole guardian of the property. Furthermore, he was appointed Gloria's own guardian until the following August when she thought herself to be twenty-one. There was no guardian of the person." The irony of the situation: if Gloria had known she was no longer a minor when her husband died, she could have acted without Wickersham and this trial might never have come to pass.

Burkan forced Laura Morgan to admit that she had gone to Gertrude Whitney's lawyer, Frank Crocker, who'd found Walter Dunnington to represent her in her opposition to her daughter's petition. Hoping to catch her out in a lie, he asked, "And didn't you arrange that Mr. Crocker or Mrs. Whitney was to pay Mr. Dunnington?"

His ploy did not work. "Mr. Crocker will pay him, since I haven't got with what to pay," she answered bluntly.

Burkan examined a letter from little Gloria in which she'd written,

"I wrote this all myself without help." Then he produced several letters critical of Gloria Vanderbilt and implied that someone had helped the child to write them.

"Isn't it true that somebody helped her phrase Respondent's Exhibit D, in which she talks about her mother as being a 'rare bease'?"

Smyth cut in, "It is probably *piece*—misspelled."

Burkan persisted. Why hadn't Mrs. Morgan told her daughter that the child had called her "a rare bease"? Why hadn't she asked the child about it?

Mrs. Morgan denied that the child meant to call her mother a rare beast. "I never thought that in my heart of hearts. I never even believed anything you are believing about the baby. I haven't got evil thoughts in my mind."

"That is all," snapped Burkan, abruptly ending his cross-examination.

Herbert Smyth was just beginning his redirect examination when Carew bluntly ordered him to read aloud the nurse's testimony concerning the incident in which Gloria and Prince Hohenlohe were seen in bed together. Carew said he wished to hear Mrs. Morgan's testimony on this incident right now—if she wished to give it.

The urbane Smyth tried tactfully to elicit this information. "Mrs. Morgan," he began, "will you please search back in your memory and tell us when you commenced to say anything to your daughter by way of protest about the life that your daughter was living, or about the care of the child?"

Carew was growing impatient. "Did you complain to your daughter about her conduct?" he snapped.

Mrs. Morgan replied with a rush of words, "During the last six years, I have been all the time telling her that she ought to settle down and love her own country better than she did, to live here in this country . . . and to drop the European entanglements, and European titles and the desires for the life of pleasure and—"

Carew was not to be sidetracked. "Do you desire to tell me anything about that incident?" he asked.

Mrs. Morgan looked first at Carew and then out at the courtroom where her daughters Gloria and Consuelo sat staring up at her. She began to sob and clutched the crucifix to her chest. "Your Honor," she pleaded, "since she is my daughter, may I tell you in private chambers?"

Carew turned to the weeping woman. "I cannot listen to anything in private, but I will take you into this adjoining room," he said and indicated a door cut into the wall behind the witness stand.

"All right," sobbed Mrs. Morgan.

Carew led the way through the door into his robing room; he was followed by Smyth, who supported Mrs. Morgan on his arm. Gloria, Consuelo, Nathan Burkan, and Jim Murray entered next. Gertrude Whitney rose and walked behind them. Carew seated himself at one end of a long table in the center of the room, Mrs. Morgan sat to his right. Nathan Burkan directed Gloria, "You sit beside your mother and let her look you squarely in the eye when she tells these things."

Laura Morgan's body heaved with sobs as she told of the night in question. It was between two and three in the morning when she heard "the voice of the prince raised very high and drastic and I heard my daughter sobbing or crying." She didn't know what to do so she woke nurse Keislich and together they walked to the bedroom door, which was ajar, and peered in. Mrs. Morgan looked at the judge and said in a whisper, "We both saw them in bed."

With this, a wave of emotion flooded her body and she wept profusely. Touching Carew's arm, she said, "This is dreadful," and blew her nose vigorously in her handkerchief. "I love my daughter!" she exclaimed. "It is for the baby's sake that I do this, Your Honor. It is the sacrifice of my life that I am making, and I am going to remain alive in the world without anybody." Her sobs filling the room, she described the details of what she had seen. Her daughter was "crying and sobbing. . . . They were lying down in bed, and he was talking, vociferating there with my daughter, well, as if he was trying to say that she was helpless, that she could not—he was trying to persuade her—" she blurted it out like a cry of pain, "he was trying to persuade her to marry him!"

"Did you walk in the room and say to your daughter, 'Are you sick my child? What is the trouble with you? What is ailing you?' Did you do that?" asked Burkan.

At that moment, Gertrude Whitney's tinkling laughter filled the room.

"I did not," replied Laura Morgan.

Burkan turned on Gertrude Whitney. "You can laugh at this tragedy as much as you like, but I think it is an outrage."

Smyth interceded on Mrs. Whitney's behalf. "Who is going to walk in a room and ask her daughter if she is sick, when there is a man in bed with her?"

Burkan ignored Smyth. Why had Mrs. Morgan spied on her daughter? Why had she not gone into the room when she saw this "infamous thing"? Laura Morgan lost control and lashed out at Burkan, revealing the crux of the situation. "My daughter loved this man," she screamed. "She was completely under his domination. I knew perfectly well that he was a great danger to my granddaughter's future, and he didn't have a penny. . . . If I demonstrated at anything that she'd done that night or at any time during this infatuation with the prince, she would have shown me the door right then and there, and I would have left my poor unfortunate granddaughter all alone. I was there to protect the baby. Do you think I was there for pleasure, a woman of my age? I am an old woman, Mr. Burkan . . ."

How she hated Prince Hohenlohe. The thought of it made her gasp, and between short gulps of breath, the hatred spilled out. Prince Hohenlohe told her he wanted to adopt little Gloria, to carry her off to Germany, to bring her up as a German, to change her name, to discipline her according to his own ways, and, yes, he wanted to handle the money of the baby, and her daughter was desperate to marry this man . . . she was totally infatuated with him, in love with him in a way that she had never loved her husband.

Mrs. Morgan recalled their many arguments, how Prince Hohenlohe told her "that the baby should be whipped"; that "the curb of the bridle should be very strong, because as the tree grows, so it bends. He did not allow the baby to touch a little flower or anything over there. He said that belongs to your mother. I had very powerful reasons for trying to protect the daughter of a plebeian, as she was called. . . ." In the United States her granddaughter was a *Vanderbilt*, but in Europe—Laura Morgan repeated the bitter words—"the daughter of a plebeian!"

The prince's mother, Princess Alexandra, had come to the house in Paris and fallen on her knees and begged Gloria to marry Prince Hohenlohe. Of course she, Laura Morgan, had done everything in her power to stop this marriage, "to save my unfortunate granddaughter. . . . Wouldn't you have done it with your own granddaughter if he was trying to get her money?" she asked. "She is an innocent child, and all that stands between her money and this—"

Burkan cut her off with an objection which Carew sustained. Mrs. Morgan was now completely overwrought, hardly able to speak. Except for her intervention little Gloria might be a German, she might be dead! Her daughter Gloria had wanted only to drift about Europe with that penniless prince spending the child's money, excluding her own mother from her life, throwing an old lady out of her house, separating her from her precious granddaughter. Herbert Smyth asked Mrs. Morgan to calm herself. After a moment she explained, "My daughter and I, we were very happy together up to the time that she fell in love with this man and under his domination. I do not want to hurt my daughter."

Burkan shrugged, a look of disgust on his face. "If you don't want to hurt her—"

Laura Morgan interrupted. "If she had committed murder, I would have taken it upon my shoulders—except the baby."

"Didn't you tell Mr. Smyth and Mr. Crocker that you would corroborate the nurse's story?" asked Burkan.

"Yes . . . but I did not know that I was going to be called to go through this Calvary on earth that I am going through."

There was silence. Burkan had finished with this witness. She did not move from her chair. Gertrude Whitney moved behind her and placed her hand on Mrs. Morgan's shoulder. Laura Morgan looked up. "How has it come to this?" she asked softly.

Forbidden Fruit

At the Supreme Court building on Foley Square a game is being played . . . the name of the game—"What's Going On?"

Evening Post, OCTOBER 10, 1934

REPORTERS SPENT their days with faces pressed against the two twelve-by-eighteen-inch rectangular windows cut into the dark brown leather, brass-studded doors of the courtroom. They observed the trial as a dumb show—they could see a little, but could not hear at all. They took notes on what everyone in the courtroom was wearing and noted Mrs. Morgan's "sweeping Gallic gestures," "floods of tears," "constant fondling of her crucifix." But this was not news, and they knew it. They were under terrible pressure; the public was clamoring to know what was going on behind those courtroom doors. With the maid's accusation of homosexuality, one shoe had dropped, and now the world was waiting for the other: Was it true? Was it false? What else might this naughty widow have done? Carew's privacy ruling had made the public frantic for news, and had imbued the trial with the irresistible taste of forbidden fruit.

In Carew's chambers reporters met with more frustration. His summary of the testimony had no sensational elements: "Mrs. Morgan gave only a brief description of the environment in which little Gloria lived with her mother. Letters from little Gloria to her grandmother were read today. None of them complained of ill treatment at her mother's hands. . . ."

"What is the reason Mrs. Morgan has for turning against her daughter?" a reporter asked.

"Mrs. Morgan has not turned against her daughter. She's just telling what she knows."

"How about your telling us what she knows?"

"It wasn't very exciting. It was the dismal routine testimony usually given in such cases. It was innocent enough in its connotations. She told me that the child has been baptized a Catholic. In this, she was compelled to break a solemn oath to her daughter never to disclose this baptism."

"What about the tears we saw?"

"She didn't cry much. She just used her handkerchief a lot."

"Has Mrs. Morgan substantiated the nurse's story of the bedroom tryst between Mrs. Vanderbilt and the prince?"

"Not yet."

The reporters left Carew's chambers and went to the first-floor press room to file their stories. They were limited to descriptions of physical behavior and old quotes from the original affidavits leaked to them on the first day of the trial.

Some reporters were more enterprising. Julia McCarthy went to the Vanderbilt town house and returned to the *News* with several photographs around which she wrote an article.

October 11, 1934: Thursday morning the *Matter of Vanderbilt* was crowded off the front pages by news of two kidnappings: ALICE SPEED STOLL SNATCHED. The previous evening, a twenty-eight-year-old Louisville, Kentucky, Society matron had been taken "from the bedroom of her palatial estate." The kidnappers left a note demanding $50,000 ransom. *The New York Times*' description of Mrs. Stoll said that she wore "a negligee and blue-and-white checked coat. A brunette of sleek build, she was probably smeared on the face and shoulders with blood from the beating she received."

NEW NOTE IN KIDNAPPING: It was revealed that in response to the ransom demand for little Dorothy Ann Distelhurst, J. Edgar Hoover, director of the Department of Justice Bureau of Investigation, had sent an agent to the New Yorker Hotel who'd registered under the name of Alfred E. Distelhurst, the child's father. The agent carried $5,000 in one, five, and ten dollar bills. He'd followed the instructions in the ransom demand, but after ten days, when he had not been contacted, he'd given up. In yesterday morning's mail, a note from the kidnappers had arrived for Alfred Distelhurst saying that he had not tricked them and telling him to come to New York himself is he wanted to see Dorothy Ann alive.

To add to their frustration, reporters crowding the corridor outside of courtroom 355 found that the two small rectangular windows had been pasted over with green blotting paper, blocking their view. Inside, Theodore Beesley, the Vanderbilt chauffeur, was giving his testimony. Beesley, a man in his twenties, might easily have been taken for a young Wall Street broker, so immaculately tailored was his blue, three-piece suit. His testimony, however, was strictly limited to a chauffeur's point of view: he described his job as unusually hard, beginning at twelve noon and sometimes not ending before 5:00 a.m., when he'd put the Pierce-Arrow into the Pinehurst Garage. He'd complained to his friend, Andrew Donahue, who managed the garage, "It's not pleasant to work these hours." But at least he had a job in a time when many people had cut back by firing their chauffeurs.

Beesley's testimony consisted of a string of locations: lunch at the Colony, Fifth Avenue shopping, afternoon drives to Broadway movie theaters—the Strand, the Capitol, the Rivoli, the Rialto. At night, he drove Mrs. Vanderbilt to El Morocco, the Casino de Paris, the Casino in the Park, and up to the Cotton Club in Harlem. She was frequently accompanied by gentlemen, including Jefferson Davis Cohn, David Cowles, Prince George Matchabelli, and most frequently, A. C. Blumenthal.

Beesley reported that on occasion he would drop Mrs. Vanderbilt's escort of the evening at his residence and then drive her to the Ambassador Hotel where Mr. Blumenthal lived. She would remain there for two or two and a half hours, then he would drive her home. Frequently, Mr. Blumenthal would come to Mrs. Vanderbilt's house and Beesley would wait till 2:00 a.m. to drive him home. "On other occasions I would be dismissed." When he drove Mrs. Vanderbilt to Mr. Blumenthal's Larchmont house, he was sometimes instructed not to return until the following day. At night Mrs. Vanderbilt often visited a house located at 13 East Sixty-ninth Street. She would remain there until three in the morning. Beesley saw a man open the door to admit her to the house.

Burkan's cross-examination of Beesley did not even have the veneer of civility he reserved for those he felt were his equals. Burkan quickly established that the last day Beesley had driven for Mrs. Vanderbilt was the twenty-first of September, when he'd chauffeured little Gloria to Mrs. Whitney's studio and house. Beesley had been ordered by Mrs. Vanderbilt to bring the child back. He did not.

Burkan was peremptory in tone. "I want a prompt answer and a proper answer. Do you say that you told Mrs. Vanderbilt that instead of taking the child back to the house, you had taken it to Mrs. Whitney's?"

"Yes, sir, I did . . ."

"You did tell Mrs. Vanderbilt?"

"Yes."

"There is no doubt about it?"

"No, no doubt at all."

"Take your hands off your mouth," Burkan commanded. "Did you telephone to Mrs. Vanderbilt that you were not going to bring the child back to the home, but you were going to take it up to Mrs. Whitney's?"

"No, sir."

Burkan forced the chauffeur to admit that, although Consuelo Thaw had told him that his services were no longer required, Thomas Gilchrist was still continuing to pay him and that he had driven both the nurse and the maid to and from court. It did not occur to Burkan, however, to ask if Beesley had telephoned Gilchrist during the child's last visit to her mother. Beesley admitted that he had discussed the case with Mr. Gilchrist and had given a written statement in front of lawyers Crocker, Smyth, Miller, and Mrs. Morgan. He had limited the scope of his statement because "Mr. Gilchrist told me that the only thing he ever wanted me to tell was anything that was of any detriment to the child's welfare."

Beesley admitted that there were many cars at those Saturday night screenings at A. C. Blumenthal's Larchmont residence. Burkan interjected that the screenings were attended by such proper people as Jack Cohn, President of Columbia Pictures, Nicholas Schenck, and Mr. and Mrs. Nathan Burkan.

"Now, Mr. Witness, you told His Honor that on some occasions you drove Mrs. Vanderbilt to a house at 13 East Sixty-ninth Street?" When Beesley affirmed this, Burkan pointed out that this was the residence of Mr. and Mrs. Lawrence Copley Thaw, and that Mrs. Thaw and Mrs. Vanderbilt were friends. Beesley said he knew nothing of the occupants of the house.

The next witness posed a problem for the Vanderbilt side. Nathan Burkan had discovered that butler Charles Zaug was a Whitney spy, but the question was—what could he do about it? Since the trial had already started, Burkan decided to allow him to remain in the Vanderbilt employ at $150 a month, rather than have it appear that Zaug had been fired because of what he knew. Still, Burkan was nervous about what this man might say. Charles Zaug appeared to be the essence of Jeevesian propriety; he wore a black suit, white wing collar, and black necktie. Zaug stated that at the Seventy-second Street house he'd lived in a room "back of the pantry on the first floor . . . there is noise from the yard, from the street and the ash cans. . . . During the night times it is noisy as far as two o'clock . . . then it starts again about three or four."

He'd entered Mrs. Vanderbilt's employ in December of 1932. Agnes Horter was then living at the house. "The third day I was there [she] said to me that . . . she is giving the orders and if I don't take orders from her, I go out like that." With that, Zaug raised his left hand and snapped his fingers.

Zaug said that parties were given one to three times a week. Music played and guests drank champagne or highballs until two or three in the morning. "They were quite noisy parties." On two occasions, Zaug had seen Mr. Lawrence Copley Thaw *without* his wife.

Smyth asked if Zaug had seen A. C. Blumenthal in Mrs. Vanderbilt's house. Burkan protested that many people visited Mrs. Vanderbilt, including himself. "What crime is there in that?"

"Did Blumenthal bring you in?" countered Smyth—there was no first name or Mr. mentioned, only the last name, hurled like an epithet.

"Is that your business?" Burkan shot back. "I went to the house. Are you prepared to say I committed an act of impropriety with Mrs. Vanderbilt?"

"We didn't say that."

"The audacity of this whole thing!" said Burkan, fuming.

Smyth asked, in a matter-of-fact tone, "Do you recall an occasion, about April 1934. . . . Did you see a Helen Thomas in the library?"

"Yes, sir . . . I saw Mrs. Vanderbilt and Mrs. Thomas naked in the library about half-past six in the morning," Zaug replied, as unemotionally as if he were reciting a guest list for a party.

Burkan called out an objection but was overruled, and Smyth continued, "Where were you coming from at the time that you saw them? Just tell the court in detail how that occurred."

"I came up from the first floor, to go up and get the tray and the glasses. . . . I saw Mrs. Vanderbilt and Mrs. Thomas . . . drinking in the library. . . . Mrs. Vanderbilt was standing . . . Mrs. Thomas sitting on the couch."

"And she had a glass in her hand?" inquired Smyth.

"Yes, sir."

"Now—did they have any clothes on?" asked Smyth, although the witness had already said they were naked.

"No."

"After you saw this thing, what did you do?"

"I walked downstairs and kept on with my work . . . but I didn't know if Mrs. Vanderbilt saw me, so I turned back, and I did went up later. . . . I see Madam coming out of the library and running into her room and slammed the door. It was just across from the library."

"During the time that you were there, did you have occasion to observe certain kinds of books that were in the library and Mrs. Vanderbilt's room?" asked Smyth, getting on with it.

"Yes, sir . . . I saw one, this was shown to me by her maid, and it has pictures in it from the convent with all kinds of colored pictures in."

"What were they about?"

"Women . . . some of them got slashed by the Sisters. . . . They were Sisters and they were feeling young girls. They were all naked . . . I only saw three or four of them."

Justice Carew's voice boomed out, "Pictures of grown girls or little girls?"

"Grown-up girls, sir," replied Zaug.

Burkan began his cross-examination, quickly establishing that Zaug was a spy who had reported to the Whitney lawyers. Burkan forced Zaug to repeat the conversation they'd had in which Zaug said he had "seen no impropriety" in Mrs. Vanderbilt's house. In spite of this, the butler had given Mr. Crocker a written statement concerning Helen Thomas and the pornographic pictures he'd seen. Zaug admitted all this was true. He testified that, in July, Mr. Crocker had telephoned him, and he'd gone to see him. Since then, without Mrs. Vanderbilt's knowledge, he'd reported to Mr. Crocker. Zaug also admitted he'd let two private detectives into the Seventy-second Street house, without Mrs. Vanderbilt's authorization, and that he'd permitted them to go anywhere they wished. By freely admitting all of this, Zaug diluted Burkan's attack. Burkan now turned his anger on Thomas Gilchrist, making it clear that while Gilchrist pretended to be nonpartisan, he'd placed Zaug in Mrs. Vanderbilt's household and had paid his wages of $150 a month from little Gloria's trust fund. Every month Zaug had to come to Gilchrist to be paid.

Justice Carew was obviously still pondering earlier testimony, and he interrupted Burkan to ask, "Who was this Mrs. Thomas?"

"I do not know, sir."

"Did you ever see her there at other times?" asked Carew.

"Quite a few times, Your Honor."

Burkan broke in. "Did you know that Mrs. Thomas is a married lady?"

"Yes, sir."

"You know her husband is the United States naval attaché to the Embassy in Paris?"

"No, sir."

Burkan could not shake Zaug's story. Carew announced that because the Columbus Day holiday was coming up, there would be no session the following day, and adjourned until Monday, October 15.

As Zaug walked down the corridor outside the courtroom, Consuelo Thaw raced up to him, grabbed his shoulder, and said in a loud voice, "You are dismissed. Mrs. Vanderbilt no longer requires your services. You are to leave the house at once."

In Carew's chambers reporters complained that now even the windows had been blocked by blotting paper. "I'll see that that doesn't happen again and I'll direct that a bench be placed in the corridor for you to sit upon," Carew replied. "Now, shall we settle down for our summary?"

Carew began a list of the various locations to which Beesley had driven Mrs. Vanderbilt.

"Why did Mrs. Thaw dismiss the butler so angrily?"

"I must decline to say why his services are no longer required," the Justice said. He referred to his notes. "Zaug testified that Mrs. Vanderbilt had given a number of parties. . . . The butler stated that the guests 'were all perfect ladies and perfect gentlemen.' . . . On one occasion only, Zaug testified that Mrs. Vanderbilt had 'one drink, one morning, before breakfast.' "

"Who with?" inquired a reporter.

"A lady," replied Carew cryptically.

Reporters left Carew's chambers and did what they could with the scanty information they'd received.

BUTLER INSISTS MADAME ABOVE CRITICISM, announced the *Mirror* headline.

Denis Morrison of the *World-Telegram* took what Carew had said and concocted an article, complete with suitable imaginary dialogue.

> Unruffled under the hammering of Mr. Burkan, whose stinging forensics are noted in New York courtrooms, the impeccable Zaug said Mrs. Vanderbilt entertained numerous persons and parties in the house she occupied at 49 E. 72nd St. . . .

"Was Blumey there?"

"I know no Blumey, sir," Zaug intoned.

"A. C. Blumenthal?"

"I don't recall, sir. We had no guest lists."

"Were all the guests perfect ladies and gentlemen?"

"The guests were all . . . perfect ladies and gentlemen, yes, sir . . ."

Reporters could not vamp forever. Thursday night, Nathan Burkan received a phone call from Julia McCarthy. "Someone on the Whitney side just dropped off a summary of the butler's testimony," she told him. "Wait till you see tomorrow's paper! I just want you to know I had nothing to do with this."

"Get me the story. Read it to me over the phone," Burkan said.

"I can't," replied Julia. "It's gone down the tube. You'll have to wait for the midnight edition."

"Wait there, I'm sending someone over," he told Julia. When Burkan's messenger finally returned with the *News*, he hurriedly opened to page three where the most sensational stories appeared. Sandwiched between the news that the Stoll ransom had been paid and that 150 policemen had broken up a Columbus Day anti-Fascist rally at Yankee Stadium was an account of Zaug's testimony "concerning Mrs. Vanderbilt's nude, early morning conference with a woman chum, also unclothed. . . . Zaug testified he found both Mrs. Vanderbilt and a Mrs. Helen Thomas nude and drinking in the library of Mrs. Vanderbilt's house at 6:30 a.m. . . . Later in his testimony Zaug admitted he looked . . . at a book of erotic drawings, as many as he said he could stand, which showed women in unconventional postures, caressing one another. . . . The butler testified reluctantly."

Burkan headed for the telephone and when the *News*'s managing editor Frank Hause came on the line he yelled, "I read your story on the Vanderbilt trial and it's in contempt of court. You've published one side of it, at least in justice to Mrs. Vanderbilt you must say that under cross-examination the butler twice admitted that he told me in the presence of others that he had never seen any impropriety in that place." The 4:00 a.m. final edition of the *News* added to its earlier coverage the following: "Nevertheless, cross-examination by Nathan Burkan, counsel for Mrs. Vanderbilt, brought out that in a previous statement Zaug said he saw no impropriety in Mrs. Vanderbilt's home. In giving evidence to the court, the butler made no effort to reconcile this statement with his testimony."

Saturday morning after breakfast Burkan called the *News* again. This time he launched into a tirade against Gertrude Whitney. "That nude drinking tête-à-tête with a woman chum originated in the *nude-conscious* mind of Mrs. Harry Payne Whitney. . . . All this terrific attack on Gloria is pure fabrication coming from the mind of a lady who sculpts from the nude and views the nude constantly. . . . In her Greenwich Village studio, she often has nudes of both sexes. . . . Mrs. Whitney attributes to the mother the ideas with which she herself is most familiar."

Nathan Burkan followed this call by making dozens of photostatic copies of little Gloria's most loving letters to her mother, and Benny Kerin saw that they arrived anonymously at various newspapers.

From this point on, almost everything that happened in the courtroom would be leaked to the press, first by one side, and then by the other.

REINFORCEMENTS ARRIVE, read the *Sun* headline. As the boat train from Montreal pulled in to Grand Central Terminal, Thelma Furness could see the crowd of reporters waiting on the platform. Theobald Mathew, the British solicitor Nada had engaged on the recommendation of her sister-in-law Lady Louis Mountbatten, had sat next to Thelma long into the night and now she knew exactly what she should and should not say. She should say that the Marchioness of Milford Haven was a dear friend of both Thelma and her twin Gloria. In the eventuality that the name of Edward, Prince of Wales, entered the conversation, Thelma should say that he was a social acquaintance. She should not answer any questions she did not care to answer.

Harry Morgan removed his derby hat from the rack above the seat, and his wife Edith Arnold Morgan fluffed her boxy fox jacket before tossing it over her shoulders. Harry had come along to show that the family presented a solid front against Mamma. Gloria had been very good to him, and although this public exposure was something that made his already frayed nerves even worse, he felt he had a gentleman's debt to repay.

Thelma led the way into the crowd of reporters. Theobald Mathew sat tight, watching the scene through the train window. The reporters threw questions at Thelma, her brother, and sister-in-law. When a question seemed too personal, Thelma simply clamped her mouth shut, stared off into the middle distance, and did not answer. On the station platform, a reporter shouted out, "Your mother thinks you're crazy!" "It's all so ridiculous!" Thelma exclaimed. "As far as my mother is concerned, I have no idea *what* she is doing. . . . I'm positively amazed that my mother should side with Mrs. Whitney. To say amazed is putting it altogether too mildly. My mother taught all of us Morgans to stick together, and now she turns against her own daughter. Doesn't it seem strange that she found nothing to make her object during all these years? I, for one, can't understand it."

At this, Harry J. K. Morgan removed his hat, stroked his bald head absentmindedly, and entered the conversation for the first time. "I think so," he said.

The reporters turned back to Thelma. "Do you think Mrs. Vanderbilt should have custody of little Gloria?"

"Anyone knows that baby Gloria should remain with her mother, as every child should. I'm a mother myself, you know. I just dare anybody to try to take my baby from me. It's too outrageous to talk about."

"Will you testify to that?"

"I certainly will."

Four porters appeared, loaded with luggage, and they were followed upstairs to the cabstand. One reporter stepped in front of the cab door, trying to detain Lady Furness. She imperiously directed him to move out of the way, and with a smile he obligingly opened the cab door for her. At this point, Thelma, her eyes blazing, ended her press conference with a stunning mixed metaphor. "It is beyond my comprehension," she said, "how people in glass houses can sling mud."

At Wheatley Hills, an event more important to the participants than the Vanderbilt custody trial was taking place. A hundred and fifty gleaming hunters were assembled in front of the long gable-roofed Whitney stable under the big clock in the central tower for the formal opening of hunt season. The field of black was brightened by an occasional pink jacket worn by officers of the Meadow Brook Club. Sonny Whitney and his wife, Gwladys, had planned the day with split-second timing. There would be the hunt, followed by a hunt breakfast, after which they would dash out to the Jamaica, Long Island, track to see Sonny's famous Thoroughbred, Equipose, make his return to racing competition.

Sunday morning, after Benny Kerin had checked the Vanderbilt town house for recording devices and a twenty-four-hour armed guard had been stationed outside the front door, Gloria, her sisters, sister-in-law, and brother moved back into the house.

Laura Morgan was reported to have spent the entire day Sunday praying in church.

. . .

Justice Carew celebrated Columbus Day by taking his children to see *Our Daily Bread.*

GLORIA LAURA VANDERBILT, 10, WILL TESTIFY. "It was learned today that the child heiress herself will be called before Justice Carew and asked to choose between the bizarre whirligig world of her gay mother and the calm, comfortable estate of her rich serene aunt."

Family Skeletons

Here in the greatest metropolis of the world, this city of the purple-robed and the pauper-clad, we find this bitterest of family vendettas. And for what?—the custody of a little "golden girl" who is too young to understand what all this mud-slinging means. . . . Mrs. Vanderbilt and her sisters and brother are fighting mad. . . . Family skeletons will rattle when the now celebrated Vanderbilt-Whitney-Morgan legal battle resumes operation this morning in the Supreme Court. . . . If such a tale were pictured on the screen or staged in a Broadway theatre, the audience would shout, "Impossible!"

MAURY PAUL/CHOLLY KNICKERBOCKER

MONDAY, OCTOBER 15. As New Yorkers paid two cents for their *American* or three cents for their *Telegram*, the *Matter of Vanderbilt* shared headlines with other news of the day.

STOLL KIDNAP CAR SPOTTED: Bound and gagged, with her eyes taped shut, Mrs. Alice Speed Stoll was spotted by a truck driver when his vehicle collided at dawn with an automobile on Louisville's Shelbyville Road. A man leaped out with a pistol in hand and directed Scales to drive on. Scales, a plasterer, had helped construct the Stoll house and recognized Mrs. Stoll, who seemed to be trying to push the car door open with her shoulder.

HAUPTMANN SHOUTS DENIAL: Bruno Richard Hauptmann was put on the stand in connection with the New Jersey extradition proceedings taking place in the Bronx Supreme Court. After three hours on the witness stand, Hauptmann shouted out a dramatic denial that he was the kidnapper and murderer of the infant son of Colonel Charles A. Lindbergh.

T. B. GILCHRIST CO-GUARDIAN OF GOLDEN GIRL TO TESTIFY: This morning Thomas Byron Gilchrist was to take the stand to testify for Gertrude Vanderbilt Whitney. Herbert Smyth felt that Gilchrist would be their strongest witness. He had already proved himself invaluable—placing Zaug and Beesley in the Vanderbilt household, alerting Frank Crocker to Mrs. Vanderbilt's petition, saving the situation in the nick of time by phoning Mrs. Whitney to tell her that Mrs. Vanderbilt had kidnapped the child. So far the Whitney case had been based on the testimony of servants and of Mrs. Vanderbilt's own mother, but here was a lawyer who had observed Gloria's conduct over an eight-year period and had in his possession a wealth of documentation reprimanding her for her extravagance, neglect, and profligate life. Once these documents were introduced as evidence, Herbert Smyth had no doubt that Justice Carew would recognize that Mrs. Vanderbilt was an unfit mother.

On September 29, Gilchrist had arrived at Smyth's office carrying a leather briefcase. (Smyth could hardly wait to get his hands on the documents inside, he'd heard enough about them to know that they would make spectacular evidence.) All along Gilchrist had maintained the position that he was "not partisan," that his only concern was with little Gloria's property. His personal feelings, however, had forced him to ally himself with Mrs. Whitney. It wasn't that he didn't like Gloria Vanderbilt: from that first moment he'd seen her at the Marguery Hotel, he'd had "the friendliest feelings" toward her—perhaps more than that—he'd thought her beautiful and had felt a great pull toward her. He had tried to control her, mold her, persuade her to reform, but she had not appreciated his years of effort. Finally, she had turned on him and had hired Nathan Burkan. Gilchrist had decided that he had no choice but to protect little Gloria from this selfish, corrupt woman. Still, he was doing great battle with his conscience in order to justify these two seemingly irreconcilable positions.

Sitting opposite Herbert Smyth, Gilchrist said that legally he could find absolutely no way to make his documentation available to the Whitney side. "It is not a question of violating the confidentiality of my relationship with Mrs. Vanderbilt," he explained, "because there is none. My concern was always limited to the guardianship of the child's property. But I do not wish this question to arise." However, Gilchrist said that he'd brought along slips of paper on which he'd written the date of every document in his possession and had summarized its contents. Herbert Smyth immediately grasped the situation and a delicate game began, devised to allow Gilchrist to maintain an appearance of impartiality. Smyth said that as Mrs. Whitney's lawyer it was perfectly proper for him to inquire whether Gilchrist possessed any documents relating, year by year, month by month, day by day, to Mrs. Vanderbilt's expenditures, style of life, immorality, neglect of the child, or if he had letters urging her to return to the United States, Gilchrist brightened. "Yes, that is perfectly proper," he agreed. And volunteered, "And correspondence relating to overdue bills." Smyth slowly learned the dates and contents of each of the documents Gilchrist possessed—his plan was to obtain a subpoena *duces tecum*, a legal notice to produce these documents in the courtroom where they could then be entered against Gloria Vanderbilt.

Of one document only, Gilchrist would not speak. Smyth asked him if he had in his possession "a reprimand written by Gloria Vanderbilt's father in 1928, which Mrs. Whitney and Mrs. Morgan have both mentioned." Gilchrist's conscience would not allow him to reveal this information. Gloria Vanderbilt had given him this document when she'd asked him to draw a new will for her so that he would have an understanding of why she was changing her will. In this one instance, it would be impossible to deny, even to himself, that he had served as her lawyer. "I consider that document privileged," he told Smyth. "You must promise me not in inquire about it." Smyth promised.

After this meeting, Gilchrist's conscience also obliged him to offer Nathan Burkan the same opportunity he'd offered Herbert Smyth. The two men had never met before, but on the first day of the trial Gilchrist introduced himself, and said, "Mr. Burkan, I want you to understand my position here. Everything I have in my office you may use. Any information I have is at your disposal."

"Thank you," replied Burkan. As Gilchrist walked away, he turned to Jim Murray and said, "There goes one Greek whose gift we won't be stupid enough to accept."

As soon as Thomas Gilchrist was sworn in, Herbert Smyth set about entering his documents as exhibits. First, by specific date, he called for a petition regarding the infant's maintenance and support in 1926. Immediately Burkan leaped to his feet and called out, "Objection!" Burkan had expected that Smyth would try to enter some of Gilchrist's documents but was shocked that Smyth knew exactly what to ask for. Each time Smyth demanded a document, Burkan called out, "Objection!" contending that it would be legally improper and morally unconscionable if Gilchrist were allowed to violate the most confidential of lawyer-client relationships; ever since Reginald Vanderbilt's death, Burkan said, Gilchrist had acted as Gloria's own lawyer. After a dozen objections, Burkan told Justice Carew that he intended to object to every single one of Gilchrist's documents as well as "to Mr. Gilchrist's testifying concerning any conversations that he had with Mrs. Vanderbilt. . . . And I do not think Mr. Gilchrist has the right, acting as an attorney, to sit here in the witness box and to make disclosure of any conversations. I do not know what he is going to say, but I strenuously object upon that ground. I don't think this lawyer has the right—"

With unusual fervor, Smyth cut Burkan off; it was essential to the Whitney case that Gilchrist's documents be entered and that he be permitted to speak out against Gloria. "It is not privileged!" Smyth protested. "He was not acting as her attorney."

Justice Carew looked amused. "What was he acting as? As a doctor?"

"He was acting as the guardian or the attorney for the guardian," Smyth explained. But Carew continued smiling at this shaky argument and ruled that all conversations with Mrs. Vanderbilt were to be considered privileged, and therefore inadmissible evidence. However, he reserved judgment on the documents and said that he would consider them one by one. Smyth tried to find a rationale to introduce Gilchrist's documents as exhibits, or if he could not, to introduce them for identification only. In a jury trial this maneuver would make little difference because the judge would read the documents but would not permit the jury to do so. But here, by admitting documents for identification, Smyth knew that Carew would assimilate the information they contained. Carew accepted a stack of letters for identification and read them, each in turn, as Smyth had planned.

> October 26, 1927. I believe I told you that he [Surrogate Foley] commented that the allowance was extremely generous and . . . would be drastically reduced if at any time he should receive credible information that any part of the infant's income was being used . . . to "finance a second marriage."

> May 3, 1932. . . . was surprised at your sudden departure for Paris. . . .

> May 9, 1932. It is leaving a very heavy burden of responsibility upon the nurse and the doctor to leave them with the child in her present condition and without the mother at hand to make decisions which should be made in the child's interest.

> August 18, 1932. The nurse, Emma . . . said you had left her only $150 when you went abroad. . . . You cannot properly go to

Europe and leave your child in the custody of a maid, with no adequate money for her current needs. . . .

After Justice Carew had read all of the letters, he came down on Nathan Burkan's side. "It is my opinion that . . . though the mother was not his [Gilchrist's] client, that, nevertheless, a confidential relation existed between them. She was a quasi-client, to say the least, and so far as I am concerned, I am going to hold that that is a privileged relation." Carew turned to Smyth. "You have got plenty of evidence here . . . a volume of evidence. . . . You will have to make the case without this gentleman's testimony . . . I will construe privilege against his testimony as far as possible." Carew added that Gilchrist would be permitted to testify on matters directly relating to the child's estate. Gilchrist then estimated little Gloria's wealth at $2.9 million plus another $750,000 to $900,000 which represented her share of a trust fund left to her by Alice Vanderbilt.

Smyth inquired, "So that if little Gloria were to die before she is old enough to make a will of the personal property, it would go to her surviving heir, which would be her mother?"

Gilchrist replied, over Burkan's objection, that in his opinion the mother would inherit everything. Carew then declared a luncheon recess.

Instead of holding his one o'clock briefing with reporters as scheduled, Carew decided to join several other Supreme Court justices for lunch in the private sixth-floor dining room. At two o'clock he returned to his chambers to find two dozen reporters who had been cooling their heels for over an hour without lunch. As he seated himself behind his desk, a man's voice called out, "Instead of Ivory Soap, how about telling us what Mrs. Vanderbilt and Helen Thomas were doing when the butler caught them nude and drunk at six in the morning."

"Yeah! Was the butler the only witness?"

"Were they foolin' around?"

"Six-thirty a.m., right?"

"Will you describe those dirty pictures . . . ?"

Carew's anger boiled up in him—the austere judge disappeared. "Get out! Get out!" he screamed.

There was silence. Then a moment later, "May we ask . . . ?"

"No, not a word!" Carew banged his fist down on the desk.

Denis Morrison of the *World-Telegram* took a drag on his Pall Mall. "How about your usual summary then?" he asked.

"I tell you—get out. Get out!" Carew's face was red and he gripped the front of his desk as the reporters filed out.

Must a Woman be "Good"

And Is Mrs. Vanderbilt As "Bad" as Painted? Her Full Reply Hidden

By INEZ CALLAWAY.

MRS. REGINALD VANDERBILT'S determination to regain custody of her 10-year-old daughter, Gloria, in spite of charges that she is unfit to rear the child, keeps an interested public with ears glued to barred courtroom doors.

For the listeners are just as eager to hear what Mrs. Vanderbilt has to say tomorrow in defense of her mud-spattered character as they were to hear the unproved back-stairs gossip of tattling servants.

Like Pandora's box, the court of Justice John F. Carew was not snapped shut on the sensational case of the legal kidnaping of Mrs. Vanderbilt's daughter until after ugly charges against the morals of the beautiful widow were out. Now her sympathizers can get only the outline of the fight a mother is making to combat the attacks upon her right to her own child.

Following the habeas corpus proceedings started by the young widow herself to force her sister-in-law and little Gloria's aunt and grandmother, Mrs. Harry Payne Whitney, to give up possession of the child, the defense went to work with right bad will to ruin Mrs. Vanderbilt's reputation.

With unspoken intent Mrs. Whitney's lawyers hope to force Justice Carew to air his views on that much disputed question—whether a woman must be "good" in order to be a good mother.

Justice John F. Carew, in New York's Supreme Court, must solve the knotty problem of Gloria Vanderbilt's fitness as a mother. Justice Carew barred ... from the pro... ...hearing testi... ...t for a week.

Then Judge Carew Closed His Doors

Witness after witness—most them former servants in the Vanderbilt home—took the stand beamirth the gay young life of their former mistress... wasn't until the public knew Marie Caillot, former maid to Mrs. Vanderbilt... unproved charges... natural relations... Vanderbilt and the Marquess Milford-Haven, that Justice... closed his doors.

He probably never sto... think that his action aut... barred Mrs. Vanderbilt's defense. Even the fact... Caillot made partial retr... her charges has been... because it was warm... talked information... the Judge.

Unprejudiced... if the d... ... the... Emma... before... a chance... opponent... and af... ... le la... one en... ...

... is no... wife... ... rath... alon... der... rub...

The late Reginald Vanderbilt, at the age of 42, fell madly in love with beautiful Gloria Morgan, then 17.

... reasonable w's ruling in ting ... Mrs. ... dy and ... hitney, Mrs. ... h the the ... beauti- ... flagging ... It is not a ... e a woman ... ce and splat- ... arly when ... tattling ... ays been ... ateful to ... ant who ... the inter- ... rs it. ... Justice ... eria's ... Her

Mrs. Gloria Morgan Vanderbilt, widow of Reginald Vanderbilt maintains her right to custody her daughter in spite of the attacks on her morals.

... Jr. ... Furn... ...organ, ... of her ...ormer ... Gloria's ...court.

truly descriptive of her garden... white skin and her large, brillia... dark eyes set in a lon... face framed by dark... ly parted in the ce... knotted at the na...

Her beauty... dog and man... failed to sub... family. Aft... did not kno... At least,... from whi...

Despite ...ggie's ... to ...

lived Reg... taig... an older ...

here main... Newport, ... and Gloria ... ers. Richard ... Wilson ...

Gertrude, Mamma Morgan, and Herbert Smyth

to be a Good Mother?

Mrs. Harry Payne Whitney (left), little Gloria's paternal aunt, and Mrs. Harry Hays Morgan, the child's maternal grandmother, are allies in the fight to retain custody of the heiress to Vanderbilt millions. So bitter is the struggle that Mrs. Morgan is willing to have her daughter's morals assailed in court.

...ow ready to extend the olive...

...gie's brother, Brigadier Gen. ... Vanderbilt, accompanied ... Vanderbilt, came late to ...ceremony and left early. ...r of Reggie's sisters, Mrs. ...Payne Whitney, the former ...de Vanderbilt, nor Countess ... Szechenyi, the former ... Vanderbilt, was ... significant still ...t at the time... ...of Reginal... ...wn Vanderbilt...

...RIA hadpport that ...ts were ...o r...n ...sist... ...e ...er. ...gie immedi... ...o New...special ...pec...

Lady Furness, who is Thelma, Gloria's twin, hastened across the Atlantic to stand by her sister. She is as beautiful and as glamorous as her twin. Since divorcing Converse she has married and divorced Lord Furness, shipping magnate and one of England's richest peers. She has been one of the intimate friends of the Prince of Wales, and ... Mrs. Ernest Simpson replaced ...cently, regarded as his favor... ...een abroad. ...ttle child to lend ...ion of wealth, ...into court. The ...er life shall take ...Justice Carew's judg... ...mother's ability to behisticated and cosmo-...d lies before little ...ven into the cus-...Pomp ...ld-fash-...e ...

But probably the most crushing blow suffered by the young mother is not the defection of her own mother but the fact that her small daughter has walked past her in court without a sign of recognition, giving the cut direct.

SO MUCH for the legal angles. It is the human ones motivating this tooth-and-nail scrap that fascinates a public avidly interested in the other fellow's family row.

As far as Mrs. Whitney is concerned in this struggle for little Gloria, money is no object. Gertrude Vanderbilt Whitney is one of the richest women in America. Even the millions she inherited from her mother and father are a bagatelle compared to the $75,000,-000 estate left by her late husband.

Mrs. Whitney is not as enamored of Broadway as is most of the haut monde.

Perhaps Mrs. Whitney remembers only too vividly what Broadway did—or tried to do—to her only son, Cornelius Vanderbilt (Sonny) Whitney. The futile suit brought by Evan Burrows Fontaine, dancer, in an attempt to prove her son the child of Cornelius Vanderbilt Whitney, kept the Whitneys on the front pages for years.

Mrs. Whitney Known As Devoted Mother.

Lawyers for Mrs. Vanderbilt have intimated that they may rake over the embers of this sensational suit in question of Mrs. Whitney's fitness to rear Gloria since she could not keep her only son clear of scandal.

MRS. WHITNEY'S children adore her, and she long has been looked upon as one of society's most devoted mothers.

Of course ...00 is certain... Mrs. ...never have... in ...l. ...ut the real... ...previo... ...er do... ...osition. ...the only ...nily are ...f chan-...'s cause ...her three... ...

...e is a devou... ...gan divorced ...n 1927, a few ...Morgan sin-...ption...

Consuelo, Gloria, and Nathan Burkan

Five minutes later, he stormed back into the courtroom and commanded Burkan and Smyth to step forward. A questioning glance passed between the two lawyers. Carew's voice was choked with fury. "Somebody who was in this courtroom when the butler was on the witness stand gave a very accurate story of what he testified to the papers. . . . Somebody has betrayed my confidence. I do not know who it is. If it were not that I did not want to embarrass this case now, I would ascertain it . . ."

"If there is anything we can do in the way of an investigation, I will be glad to cooperate," Herbert Smyth said in a placating voice.

Burkan, knowing this had been a Whitney leak, was unable to bear what he felt to be Smyth's hypocrisy: "And I would suggest, Your Honor, that you get all the editions of the *News*, beginning with the first and ending with the last edition," he said. "Because . . . in Friday morning's edition of the *News*, the butler's entire direct examination was reproduced."

Carew calculated the time—"You mean *before* it was transcribed by the stenographer?" he asked incredulously. If there had not yet been a transcript, then this leak could not have come from a court clerk, typist, or stenographer who was willing to sell a bootlegged copy for money. This leak could only have come from someone who had been in this room, whose motive was to destroy Mrs. Vanderbilt's reputation. Carew had begun to see betrayal all about him. Daily, outside of this room, Burkan demanded an open trial and protested Carew's gag order, while in this room, he insisted on privacy for his client. Now someone was informing the press of the salacious accusations against Mrs. Vanderbilt in direct opposition to Carew's threat to hold anyone who said anything in contempt of court.

Burkan began explaining to Justice Carew how he'd called to request that both sides of the story be printed. Smyth spoke up. "I do not see how you could make such a request as that. It seems to me that is entirely contrary to the spirit of the court's decision. It is not fair to say that the butler did not testify to any act of impropriety. . . . I do not think counsel should have gotten in touch with the editor at all."

"You don't suppose I was going to have her crucified, without a chance!" was Burkan's retort.

"I think this is a matter for Mr. Justice Carew," replied Smyth, wishing to move on.

During the luncheon recess, Smyth had thought of a means to chip away at Carew's ruling on privilege. He asked Gilchrist to testify concerning a conversation he'd had with Mrs. Vanderbilt on September 19, 1933, in which he'd informed her: "If there is ever any controversy between you and the Vanderbilt family about this child, its custody or anything of that sort, you must remember that I am not your attorney . . . I represent the interests of the child . . ."

In view of this testimony, Carew decided to amend his ruling, and stated that he now considered the Gilchrist-Vanderbilt relationship privileged until the date of that lunch but not thereafter, and Smyth was able to enter a significant portion of the documentation he had against Gloria Vanderbilt.

As document after document was entered into evidence, the express liner *Bremen* moved swiftly past Long Beach, Rockaway, Brighton Beach, and Coney Island. At Sandy Hook, a tender pulled alongside and a pilot scrambled up a rope ladder to guide the ship into the Narrows to Rosebank and the traditional stop at Quarantine. A Sikorsky amphibian, piloted by the *Journal*'s Bill Cleveland, circled the *Bremen* like a mosquito and lighted on the water. A lifeboat was lowered over the side and headed for the plane where a crew member handed Cleveland a packet of photographs of the assassination of King Alexander, the first to reach this country, only six days after the event. Then the plane zoomed off, passing over the approaching medical boat, a U.S. mail tug, and a Coast Guard cutter packed tight with reporters. Cleveland circled low and when he saw his friend, ship's reporter Harry Acton, in the cutter he playfully dipped his wings in a salute. Acton was determined to get to Prince Hohenlohe before anyone else. As soon as a gangway was lowered from the *Bremen*'s port side, he scrambled aboard and while the other reporters headed for Hohenlohe's cabin, he took a chance and went to the ballroom. During the voyage this room had been used as a nightclub, but now United States Immigration officials sat behind a long table and a line of first-class passengers, holding their passports, stretched across the room. Acton spotted the stockily built prince, who wore a brown suit with a three-inch black cloth band sewn around the jacket sleeve. Hohenlohe stood next to a pleasant-looking plump lady, whose face was lost in a brown broad-brimmed hat, horn-rimmed glasses, and a voluminous gray-fox neck piece. Acton bolted across the room, grabbed the prince by the lapels, and practically lifted him off the floor. "You've gotta see me alone," he breathed.

Prince Hohenlohe reached up and deftly removed the reporter's hands. "I'll be glad to see *all* the members of the press after we clear Immigration." Then, with a slight gesture of his hand, he beckoned a company official, who stepped forward, aware that the prince was a man of importance, not only of royal blood but also of a family that had recently been commended by Chancellor Adolf Hitler himself. The official politely, but firmly, suggested that Harry and other press members wait for the royal couple in the Writing Room.

About fifteen minutes later, the Hohenlohes appeared in the Writing Room and sat behind a desk near the rear wall. Prince Hohenlohe reached into his trouser pocket and extracted a heavy gold cigarette case embellished with a long yellow and black tassel; he removed two gold-tipped crested cigarettes, put them both in his mouth, lit them, and handed one to Margarita. At last, he looked out at the mob of reporters, smiled, and said, "Gentlemen?"

But the reporters were uncharacteristically silent—they found it difficult to question the prince on his alleged love affair with Gloria Vanderbilt while his wife sat at his side. Not only had she chosen to accompany him on this voyage, but she'd declared that she too wanted to testify as a character witness for Gloria. The reporters were mystified by this. Why would a woman defend the virtue of her husband's former fiancée?

Americans and Europeans had little understanding of the nuances of each other's culture. Only three years earlier, the British press had reported that Buster Keaton was from "the wild crude state of Kansas." The American press had only the vaguest idea of Princess Margarita's genealogy. Since she was called Princess of Greece and Denmark, some reporters established that she was a first cousin of the greatest international celebrity of the moment, Princess Marina of Greece, who the following month was to marry Prince George, Duke of Kent, the youngest son of King George V. Several newspapers, however, referred to Margarita simply as a German woman and most contained such observations as "the Princess has mastered the English language," "speaks English with marked precision," has a "beautiful clipped English accent," as if this represented a feat of unusual skill. Not one of these reporters grasped the fact that Margarita's grandmother was Victoria Milford Haven, or that her mother had been born in Windsor Castle. Not one of them connected this "Greek" princess with the august British title of Milford Haven or knew that Margarita's aunt and uncle, Nada and George Milford Haven, were at Lynden Manor making the final preparations to send her thirteen-year-old brother, Prince Philip, to Gordonstoun, where the term was to begin in eight days. In fact, not one reporter was ever to discover the one fact that made her desire to exonerate Gloria plausible—that Nadeja, the Marchioness of Milford Haven, who stood accused of being Gloria's lesbian lover, was her aunt.

Margarita gazed out serenely at reporters, waiting for the questions to begin, but there was only a strained silence broken by an occasional cough. Prince Hohenlohe, sensing the reporters' concern, assured them, "I have come to talk frankly. You may ask any questions you please in front of the princess."

A reporter spoke up, "Why have you come?"

The prince smiled. "We are injecting ourselves into a situation out of the cinema. I have come to refute the things which have been said against me, and to do what I can for Mrs. Vanderbilt."

The questions began to flow freely; Prince Hohenlohe explained, "Gloria Vanderbilt was my fiancée. I carry with me two letters from my mother attesting to her fine character. . . . Mrs. Vanderbilt was always a good mother. Her whole life centers on Gloria. As for her being a heavy drinker, I say definitely, No! My wife can substantiate me on that, since she knew Mrs. Vanderbilt before she knew me. Occasionally a glass of champagne or sherry at her meals—that is all I know of."

Margarita promptly confirmed what her husband had just said. "I have very often been at parties with her and have never seen her drink to excess."

"How did you meet her?" asked a reporter.

Margarita hesitated. "In a nightclub—before I met my husband." But Margarita must have remembered her actual first meeting with Gloria when her aunt, Nada Milford Haven, brought Gloria to tea at the Dowager Marchioness of Milford Haven's Kensington Palace dwelling.

Throughout the press conference, Margarita frequently interrupted her husband to express her agreement with what he was saying and to emphasize how charming and what an "excellent mother" she found Gloria Vanderbilt to be. "Of course, I will appear in court," she assured reporters.

"Why does Mrs. Whitney want custody of this child?" a reporter asked the prince.

"I am mystified," he replied. "I met her several times with Mrs. Vanderbilt at the Whitney studio in Paris. I don't know the inside of Mrs. Harry Payne Whitney's effort to obtain Mrs. Vanderbilt's child. But there must be dirty work behind it."

"What do you think is Mrs. Morgan's objective?" The question came from Julia McCarthy.

Prince Hohenlohe flushed. He began rhythmically tapping his flat gold cigarette lighter against the back of his hand, which was curled into a fist on the desk. "I don't know," he said, shaking his head. "I don't know, and I don't believe she does either. She was instrumental in breaking off the engagement. She is a peculiar person. Mrs. Vanderbilt said she was apt to act queerly. Knowing her as I do, I would not be surprised if she were behind this action. . . . And the way she has spread reports about me, I would not be surprised to find myself accused of being the Lindbergh baby's kidnapper."

"What do *you* think of Mrs. Morgan?" a reporter asked the princess.

Princess Margarita raised her eyebrows slightly. "Have you ever met the lady?" she replied.

"She pestered the life out of Mrs. Vanderbilt," Hohenlohe interjected abruptly.

"And that is why the engagement was broken?"

"Yes, she pestered her," Hohenlohe sighed, "but it was finances. If I had married her, the Surrogate here would have cut off her income, and that would have made it difficult for her to come from Europe to America frequently. It was for Gloria that she broke our engagement. I felt I would be a good father to the child but Mrs. Vanderbilt feared if we married and lived abroad, Gloria's income would be cut off."

The reporters registered surprise at Hohenlohe's frankness. They scribbled notes, then looked from the prince to the princess. Would the prince care to reply to the nurse's allegation that she had seen him in Mrs. Vanderbilt's boudoir in pajamas and that Mrs. Vanderbilt was crying?

Hohenlohe answered with ease. He referred not to sleeping attire but the latest continental fashion—lounging clothes—"We all wore pajamas. In Biarritz, everyone always wears either a bathing suit or pajamas. We had dinner in our pajamas, as everyone does there. Why, even the nurse wore a bathing suit, and she wasn't a fine figure either. Also, you say that Mrs. Vanderbilt was in tears and that I was with her? Of course, she was in tears many times, her mother always pestered her."

The reporters, never having heard of lounging pajamas, were unaware that Hohenlohe had dodged the question. One reporter whispered to another, "They never got outta their pajamas. Whadda life!"

Princess Margarita added her own comment. "I have complete faith in her and in my husband." She then stood up as she had seen so many of her royal relatives do when they wished to conclude an audience. Then the pair patiently posed for photographers. "Put your arm around the princess," directed *Mirror* photographer Izzy Kaplan. At last, the reporters left the *Bremen*, which by this time was docked at its West Forty-sixth Street pier, and Prince and Princess Hohenlohe disembarked and were met by the Vanderbilt chauffeur, who drove them to the Vanderbilt house.

In the courtroom, Herbert Smyth made the request that Gilchrist's examination be suspended in order to put Dr. William St. Lawrence, "who is very busy," on the stand. St. Lawrence had flatly refused to sit around waiting to testify. He'd written out his medical schedule, informing the Whitney lawyers that he would testify when, and if, it did not interfere with this schedule. In the face of his self-assurance, the trial was reorganized so that St. Lawrence's testimony was taken in three appearances on three successive days. From the moment he settled comfortably into the leather witness chair, a brown briefcase at his feet, it became evident that this was a man convinced of his own infallibility.

St. Lawrence removed little Gloria's medical records from the briefcase and read out his initial diagnosis. The child "had been unfit all her life." He'd put her "under immediate care. . . . I think I regulated every hour of the child's life," he declared with pride. Within five days, nurse Keislich told him that little Gloria had shown "miraculous improvement."

Herbert Smyth deftly guided St. Lawrence into a description of the last time he'd seen the child, the day after she had fled to Mrs. Whitney's. St. Lawrence said that he'd insisted on seeing her alone and when he entered her room "she seemed preoccupied and discouraged emotionally."

"What has happened?" St. Lawrence asked.

Little Gloria was working on a jigsaw puzzle but, instead of looking up, she kept her eyes glued to the puzzle. "I was taken to New York. I was frightened."

"Why? What for?"

"Well, my mother wanted to keep me, and I didn't want to stay."

"Why didn't you want to stay?"

There was a pause, as if the child were not sure of the reason, then she blurted out, "Because I hate my mother."

"Why on earth should you feel that way about mother?"

There was another pause and then she replied, "Because I am afraid of her."

The child seemed so upset that St. Lawrence's only thought was to comfort her, exactly as everyone else had tried to do, and just like everyone else, he didn't ask her *why* she feared her mother or what she thought would happen if her mother took her to live with her. Instead, he put his arm around the pale child's shoulder and said, "Well, never mind, my dear, don't take life too seriously. . . ."

Burkan began his cross-examination. The day had slipped away and he had little time left to begin to build their case that little Gloria had been a perfectly normal child and had never been neglected while in her mother's care. Burkan asked that Dr. St. Lawrence's medical history of little Gloria be marked as an exhibit. After it was admitted, Burkan was permitted to look at the document for the first time. He picked up the sheets of paper and eagerly began to read them while pacing up and down in front of Justice Carew. As he turned to the third page, Burkan's eye lit upon the notation, "God awful nurse." Next to this was an equal sign and the notation "A terrible person. . . . hovers over her like a hen and makes the child self-centered, introspective and a neurasthenic." Then there was a line and the observation, "She suffers from a flight of words and ideas." Burkan smiled. But it was too late in the day to open this rich vein of testimony. Burkan asked for an adjournment, which was granted.

At 4:15 p.m., Carew, once more in control of his emotions, met with the reporters waiting in his chambers. "I think you will agree with me that I have tried to be pleasant and accommodating," he said. "These meetings are likely to give out an erroneous impression. I have made up my mind to discontinue them. . . . I have definitely decided not to admit the press to further hearings. . . . You are free to interview Lady Furness, Prince Hohenlohe, A. C. Blumenthal, or anyone else you choose, *outside* this courtroom."

There was a sigh of disappointment and a reporter said, "These interviews will not have the force of sworn testimony in open court."

"I understand that," said Carew. "They can deny and have already denied the accusations made against them, but they are not allowed to tell what happens in my courtroom. . . . I am in control of that," he said, although, in fact, he was no longer "in control of that."

The Seventy-second Street house was packed like a Christmas stocking—Thelma, Consuelo, their brother Harry Morgan and his wife were there, and Prince and Princess Hohenlohe were staying in the large front room that little Gloria had occupied. Gloria felt considerably bolstered by their presence. She began to sort her mail. Since the trial began, there had been a flood of sympathetic letters, and Gloria enjoyed reading them. Along with the letters of sympathy were letters of advice on how to get the child back, and a smattering of negative letters suggesting that she leave the child with Mrs. Whitney. Gloria picked up a long white envelope with no return address and opened it. On a plain white sheet of paper was a penciled message, written in a crude scrawl, full of misspellings. It was chilling. This writer knew a great deal about little Gloria, and he threatened to kidnap and kill her. The letter ended, "If you value the life of your child do not fail to meet me in front of the Metropolitan in Brooklyn at 10:30 p.m. Friday. I will be waiting for you. . . . Keep powdering your nose so that I will recognize you." There was no signature; in its place were two interlocking circles—a sign similar to the one that had been used in the Lindbergh ransom notes.

Lieutenant Cornelius Francis Sullivan had been in charge of the Nineteenth Precinct detective squad for only three weeks when he received Gloria Vanderbilt's frantic phone call. When he arrived at the Vanderbilt town house eight minutes later, Gloria had locked herself in her bedroom and was crying so loudly that he could hear her downstairs in the drawing room. Consuelo Thaw showed him the kidnap note and asked him what "Metropolitan" meant. Sullivan knew—it was the Loews Metropolitan Theater on Fulton Street in Brooklyn.

After reading the note, Lieutenant Sullivan telephoned the Whitney residence in Old Westbury and told them what had happened, advising them to contact the Nassau County authorities to obtain a police guard for the child. A male voice politely thanked him, and said that the child "is already under intensive private guard against kidnapping," but assured him they would follow his instructions.

After posting a police guard to supplement Benny Kerin's private guard at the Vanderbilt house, Sullivan returned to the precinct station house. The only thing to do was to follow the one lead they had. Sullivan ordered Sergeant Frank Spottke to go to the corner newsstand and buy the morning's *News* which was sure to have a photograph of Mrs. Vanderbilt. When he returned Sullivan told him to send out a call for a policewoman who resembled the photograph. "She's got to be skinny, and wear a hat with a brim and one of those fur things for your neck—and tell her not to plan on being home Friday night."

Burkan had spent the previous evening studying St. Lawrence's records and they convinced him that only when little Gloria was faced with the idea of returning to her mother did she grow sick and hysterical—sure proof that she had been influenced against her mother. He began his cross-examination of Dr. St. Lawrence by trying to establish that in the two years little Gloria had lived at Wheatley Hills, nurse Keislich and Gertrude Whitney had poisoned her mind.

St. Lawrence admitted that most of his initial information concerning the child's poor health had come from nurse Keislich, and that at first he had been doubtful about her. However, within two weeks of the child's first visit he'd written, "Have changed my mind about the nurse." In nurse Keislich, he'd found someone who "was willing to let me run the case the way I wanted to run it."

"You mean obey your suggestions?" asked Burkan.

"Obey my orders and carry them out faithfully. . . ."

Burkan looked down at the medical record. After only six days under his care, St. Lawrence had noted remarkable improvements in the child's condition. Burkan began to shake his head in disbelief. "And after only six days . . . you said her dreams were better?"

"I did."

"And terrors were none?"

"I did. . . . That is right, and I stick to it."

"She had terrors with her dreams, and then after five or six days, after you prescribed the cereal meal, the constipation was relieved, the terrors were gone. Is that true?"

"I think it is wonderful," replied St. Lawrence.

Burkan laughed. "Of course it is wonderful!" he exclaimed. "This child had a very miraculous recovery, didn't it . . . ?"

St. Lawrence shifted uncomfortably in the witness chair and he did not reply. Burkan had scored a telling point and he followed it up by proving that this information had been relayed to him by nurse Keislich—he had not observed it firsthand. Nurse Keislich had also told him of the mother's frequent absences and both she and Mrs. Morgan had come to see him on several occasions to stress the importance of little Gloria's continued residence at Wheatley Hills. St. Lawrence admitted that he had repeatedly advised Mrs. Vanderbilt both in person and by letter that little Gloria's health required that she remain in the country, and that "Mrs. Vanderbilt has been battling for her [little Gloria] for the two years I have known her. Every time I have seen Mrs. Vanderbilt there has been the question of when she is going to get the child back."

"Didn't you report to Mrs. Whitney every time the mother came to you and inquired of you about the child, and when she could have the child back? Didn't you report to Mrs. Whitney . . . ?" asked Burkan.

"I don't like the word report," St. Lawrence replied testily. "It seems as if I was subservient to Mrs. Whitney. I am not." He went on to say that he gave his reports to Mrs. Whitney because Mrs. Vanderbilt did not bother to follow the child's progress.

"She acted like any other mother wanting to know from a doctor about the condition of her child. Isn't that true? Isn't that true?" demanded Burkan.

St. Lawrence sighed. "No, that is not true. . . . No, she has not acted like an ordinary mother. You are bringing this out. I am not. It is on your soul."

Burkan again had committed the error of pushing too hard. He lashed out. ". . . I was not Mrs. Vanderbilt's attorney at that time; if I had been, I would not have brought her [little Gloria] to you. I would have brought her to somebody else." Then he asked, "Now doctor, what did you charge for a visit every time this child was brought to you?"

St. Lawrence snapped back, "For the first visit, which has not yet ended, I charged $25."

"The record shows that for the year 1934 you were paid $636. That was a considerable sum of money," said Burkan.

"Not for the work done."

"I mean in money. Not for the work done. I mean you got substantial sums of money."

"It was not so substantial to me."

Burkan noted that St. Lawrence's medical record indicated that the child had been in glowing health until the summer of 1934 when her mother visited her in Newport and told her that she was coming to live with her in New York City in September. After that, little Gloria suddenly lost weight, began to cry again, became nervous and constipated, her night terrors returned. To Burkan, this was convincing evidence that the child was then being subjected to psychological pressure.

But St. Lawrence refused to acknowledge that there could be any psychological reason for the sudden and drastic change in little Gloria's health. He testified that he'd always disagreed with Schloss that emotional factors had anything at all to do with this case. In his opinion, the child's setback was due to the exertion of swimming and riding in the Adirondacks. "I believe that swimming, which was most exhausting . . . resulted in a weight loss and when there is a weight loss . . . there is a loss of appetite which follows and there is a recurrence of emotional unstability." Also, he'd noted that the child's constipation was due to "difficulty in using the bathroom because of numbers of children."

"You mean to say that there was only one bathroom in Mrs. Whitney's huge establishment so that every bathroom in the place was occupied and this poor little rich girl had no bathroom to go into for evacuation? Is that your testimony?" Burkan demanded.

"The statement was given to me by the nurse and so recorded," replied St. Lawrence.

But, the dogged Burkan insisted, the previous summer the child had had "a free summer full of swimming and romping," and after that summer, St. Lawrence had found little Gloria to be "a happy child." St. Lawrence agreed that this was true. "And although as early as September 29, 1933, you wrote that this was 'a perfect child,' that this child was 'marvelous,' and she was 'happy, gay and wonderful,' you told her [Mrs. Vanderbilt] it was inadvisable for her to take the child to New York and better to keep her at Mrs. Whitney's?"

"The record is there. And I stand behind it."

St. Lawrence was convinced that he had produced "a happy child . . . a marvelous change . . . a beautiful result." He was pleased and proud. He knew that little Gloria's relapse was temporary and due to some obscure physical cause. No doubt of this would ever enter his head.

St. Lawrence's appearance on the stand was followed by yet another doctor—Everett C. Jessup. Burkan sized this doctor up as a man in awe of Gertrude Whitney's wealth and prestige. Jessup often visited little Gloria three times a day for ailments that proved to be no more than constipation, a slight temperature, a cold.

Burkan, in cross-examining Dr. Jessup, was determined to prove that the child had not been seriously ill when her mother left her. He established that during one period when Jessup visited three times a day, the only thing he could find wrong with little Gloria was a "continuing elevated temperature of 99.6."

"What is the normal temperature of a child . . . eight and a half?" Burkan inquired of Jessup.

"Ninety-nine by mouth."

"This slight temperature elevation . . . was not alarming?"

"Not—alarming."

"And there are thousands of children in this land of ours who suffer from constipation. Isn't that true?"

"Yes."

Nathan Burkan excused the witness.

Now it was Burkan's turn to ask if he might interrupt the proceedings in order to place Harry Wright, a former Vanderbilt butler, on the stand. Wright, he explained, was presently employed by M. Walter Blair, and if he wished to keep his job he had to leave with the Blair family for Virginia the following morning.

Smyth objected. The thought of a mere butler being taken out of turn irked him. "If he were a professional man, it would be different. But a butler . . ." Carew reacted to Smyth's snobbery. He ruled that Wright's testimony would be taken then and there.

Wright was a five-foot butterball of a man who spoke with a clipped British accent. He said he'd been with Mrs. Vanderbilt at the Hotel Ritz in Paris, at the Villa Ourida in Biarritz, and at the Avenue Charles Floquet triplex in Paris. Wright described baby Gloria as being "robust." He said that "the baby was always pleased to see its mother, always had a smile, would always run to its mother." In Paris, the child played in the Champs-de-Mars or the Tuileries or was driven to Versailles and she had "the freedom of the house."

Wright saw "no acts of impropriety . . . no rats, no pornographic books." Mrs. Vanderbilt's guests, he testified, "acted like perfect ladies and gentlemen"—a statement that might impress Carew since these were the exact words the Justice had falsely attributed to butler Zaug.

Smyth stopped Wright midsentence. "I move to strike out 'perfect ladies and gentlemen.' A butler cannot pass on that. He can give positive testimony that they swore or did not swear, but to say they were 'perfect ladies and gentlemen'—I cannot imagine how a butler should be permitted to characterize that way!"

"Mr. Wright," said Burkan, "you must tell us what they did, how they acted, how they conducted themselves, so that His Honor then can draw his own conclusion as to whether they were gentlemen or whether they were bums."

Wright said he had listened in on the conversations of the guests and family when he'd served dinner, tea, and when he'd passed the cigars to the gentlemen who had withdrawn to the library after dinner. In all that time, he had never heard anything improper, "no risqué jokes, no foul or vulgar language, no loud talking, no swearing." On this note, Burkan concluded his examination.

Smyth was unprepared to cross-examine this witness, but his natural ability as a trial lawyer came clear as he improvised his examination. He made his points swiftly and well. This man had been employed for one year only, at a time when baby Gloria was but two.

"Did she [little Gloria] talk to her mother?" inquired Smyth.

"Yes, sir, in her own baby language."

"What did she say?"

"She would say, 'Hello, Mommy.' "

Smyth moved on. "While you were at the Charles Floquet house, did you ever see Mrs. Vanderbilt drunk?"

"No, sir."

"Or under the influence of liquor?"

"Never!"

"You have seen people drunk in your life?"

"Yes, sir."

Instinctively, Smyth aimed an arrow which was to hit the bull's-eye. "You talked about how little other people drink. Did you ever drink?"

"Yes, sir."

"How much did you drink?"

"I would drink beer or whiskey and soda when I felt like one."

"How many whiskeys and sodas would you drink in a day?"

"Two or three."

"You admit to two or three. Couldn't it be four or five?"

Wright knew he was under oath. He must tell the truth. "It could be. Yes."

In his first cross-examination of the trial, it had taken Smyth less than ten minutes to demolish the credibility of this witness.

Thomas Gilchrist resumed his testimony. He was walking the shaky high wire of his conscience, balanced precariously between his avowal of nonpartisanship and his appearance on the stand as the star witness for Gertrude Whitney. As Nathan Burkan cross-examined Gilchrist, he forced him to examine both his untenable position and his morality. In hour after hour of relentless questioning, Burkan made Gilchrist admit that he had performed many legal services for Mrs. Vanderbilt, had sold securities for her, had billed her for services rendered, had written that his firm were her attorneys, had approved the lease on her Paris house. Gilchrist admitted that he had drawn two wills for Mrs. Vanderbilt. "And when you drew that will, you were acting for the child?" Burkan asked.

"No," admitted Gilchrist.

"Then for whom were you acting?"

"For Mrs. Vanderbilt," Gilchrist said.

Again and again Burkan hammered home the point that Gloria had confided in this man. She had "bared her soul" to him and Gilchrist had led her on by writing "rest assured that anything you said to me will be treated as absolutely confidential."

Gilchrist protested that this state of confidentiality had not existed, but in the event that Mrs. Vanderbilt had thought it had, he'd clearly stated his position at the lunch in September of 1933. Burkan countered, "So when an attorney wants to reveal a sacred communication all he has to do is say, 'Well, I told the client . . . I am out of the picture,' " and he pointed out that in December of 1933, a full three months after this luncheon, Gloria Vanderbilt granted Gilchrist permission to file a petition to be appointed co-guardian of little Gloria's property and at that time he still signed himself as her attorney. "He could not ask to have himself appointed co-guardian without the consent of the mother," Burkan pointed out, ". . . and the document says Cadwalader, Wickersham & Taft, attorneys for the petitioner."

When Gilchrist explained that his duties were limited only to matters pertaining to the child, Burkan said with passion, "He cannot say limited. He signed himself as her attorney and his lips were sealed . . . she had the right to go to this lawyer's office and spill her soul out to him, and he cannot take the stand and violate that oath of secrecy. . . . The law was framed for the benefit of the layman, to protect him in a sacred relationship."

As to the child over whom Gilchrist was supposedly so concerned, Burkan produced several pictures of little Gloria, but Gilchrist could not identify her, explaining, "I saw her when she was very small, before she went to Europe in 1926, and then I don't recall definitely whether I saw her again until March 1932." He admitted that although Gloria pleaded to have her child back, "I told her frequently that it would be a mistake to take the child away from Long Island," and that he had made no effort to help her solve her problem by securing a Long Island residence for her, so that her daughter might live with her. Instead, Burkan contended, Gilchrist had placed spies in her household.

This was not at all the way Gilchrist envisioned his actions and he protested that he had told the chauffeur, "Now, Beesley, I don't want you to bear any tales. . . . All I ask of you is if anything ever arises while you are in Mrs. Vanderbilt's employ that has a bearing upon the welfare of the child I would like to know about it." Gilchrist did admit that although Mrs. Vanderbilt had fired Beesley, he had continued to pay his wages of $160 a month and also, once Charles Zaug had been fired, he had placed him back with his former employers, the Charles Shattucks. "Yes, I did that," admitted Gilchrist. "Mrs. Shattuck returned from Europe after three years' absence. She asked where Charles was, and I said he has just been fired . . . 'if you want him, you can have him.' And she said, 'I certainly want him.'" During their term of employment, both Beesley and Zaug had come to his office to collect their wages, and on these occasions Gilchrist admitted that he talked to them about matters concerning little Gloria's welfare and that he'd long been "advised of the misconduct of the relator financed by the infant's estate."

Burkan was convinced that Gilchrist's testimony was that of a man with a vendetta against his client, and Gloria confirmed this, telling him that Gilchrist was responsible for her misfortunes; he had betrayed her confidence both as a lawyer and as a friend. Burkan articulated his position to Justice Carew, saying, "I am persuaded and have been from the outset that Mr. Gilchrist has been hostile . . . has shown hostility."

But Carew reminded Burkan that if his client had nothing to fear from Gilchrist's testimony and documentation as Burkan maintained, then ". . . you are shutting the mouths of men . . . who have come here under oath and sworn to tell the truth. . . . You had better take the responsibility."

Burkan replied, "Mr. Gilchrist . . . is hostile and because of this hostility I am taking the responsibility. . . . I wasn't born yesterday and

I'm not going to allow him to get on the stand with that sort of business, with a lot of letters and communications and documents."

As if to confirm Burkan's accusation of hostility, in his recross-examination Herbert Smyth could not resist probing one last forbidden area. In order to keep his promise, Smyth deferred to his assistant, Theodore Miller, who asked Tom Gilchrist the question for him. "Did Mrs. Vanderbilt come to see you bringing an affidavit and presenting to you an affidavit signed by Mr. Morgan?"

Burkan objected.

"We have a right to mark for identification such an affidavit," said Smyth.

But Gilchrist grew angry, he'd made himself clear on this point. Before the questioning could go further, Gilchrist, who all along had maintained that his relationship with Gloria Vanderbilt had never been privileged, spoke up loudly. "I decline to answer on the ground of privilege," he declared.

A few minutes later, Gilchrist was excused. In the future, he was to publicly humiliate Gloria Vanderbilt as if exorcising a malevolent presence. Perhaps he could not forgive her for causing him to look at himself.

The Whitney side had almost completed their case. Friday afternoon Gertrude Vanderbilt Whitney was scheduled to testify as the final witness, but she did not appear in the courtroom. Frank Crocker whispered to Herbert Smyth, who told Justice Carew that Mrs. Whitney was suffering from a bad cold and nervous strain and would not be able to appear until Monday. He then requested a private meeting with the Justice, but Burkan insisted on attending. In Carew's chambers, Smyth explained that Mrs. Whitney was "prepared to make unusual concessions" to avoid testifying. Perhaps they would accede to some of Burkan's demands if this would make her court appearance unnecessary. There was a problem, however, and they didn't know what to do about it. At present the child seemed so antipathetic to her mother that she would not return to her under any circumstances.

Justice Carew was sure that if Mrs. Vanderbilt were permitted to spend a few quiet, enjoyable moments with her daughter she could begin to regain the child's affection. The child's fear and hysteria were obviously without sufficient cause or reason. He said that the following morning Mrs. Vanderbilt would be allowed to go to Wheatley Hills to visit little Gloria and woo her back again. After Nathan Burkan left the meeting, Crocker stayed behind to tell Carew that he feared Mrs. Vanderbilt would use the occasion to kidnap her daughter. She had tried it twice before—once in September of 1933, and again last summer when she'd tried to take the child to Canada. The detectives had stopped her. "See that they do again," said Carew.

At 7:00 p.m., Friday, October 19, Lieutenant Cornelius F. Sullivan checked out the policewoman who stood in front of him. She was tall and slim, but the resemblance to Mrs. Vanderbilt stopped there. She'd have to do, there was no time to get someone else. Sullivan, Detective Spottke, and three other police detectives climbed into two unmarked cars and drove to Brooklyn. They parked around the corner from the Metropolitan and walked to the theater. In letters three feet high, the words on the marquee read CONSTANCE BENNETT—THE AFFAIRS OF CELLINI.

Sullivan deployed his men. One detective studied the men's clothing in the window of Weber & Heilbroner a few doors down from the theater, another strolled through the lobby toward the candy stand, still another blended in with the ticket line. From across the street, Sullivan watched the crowd form and then move into the theater, until the policewoman stood alone under the marquee; her fox neck piece obscured her chin, and the slanting brim of her felt hat hid one eye. As instructed, she withdrew a large, round gold compact from her purse and began powdering her nose with a lamb's-wool puff. She continued powdering, sometimes switching hands to relieve the strain. At midnight, when no one had appeared, Lieutenant Sullivan crumpled his third empty pack of Camels and called off the watch. There had been no contact with the alleged Vanderbilt kidnapper.

The morning's headlines carried news of two events, unrelated, except perhaps in the mind of a child. POLICE GUARD VANDERBILT-WHITNEY HOMES AFTER THREAT TO KILL GLORIA, 10, and RUMOR OF TRUCE—MOTHER TO VISIT BABY HEIRESS TODAY.

Little Gloria's Thrown the Key in the Fire

Perhaps little Gloria will be a bit upset.

GERTRUDE VANDERBILT WHITNEY

SATURDAY MORNING Gertrude Vanderbilt Whitney awoke in her huge canopied bed at 871 Fifth Avenue. She'd had a wretched, sleepless night; her throat ached and she could hardly swallow. She fumbled for the phone and dialed the number of her son-in-law Barklie Henry, who was at his house at Wheatley Hills. Barklie was married to her daughter Barbara, who'd had her share of illnesses, and over the years he'd developed a keen sense for handling family crises. Little Gloria had become very close to Barklie Henry, who was the father of her best friend, Gerta. She called him Uncle Buz and seemed to spend as much time at the Henry house as she did at her own. Yes, he would be the ideal one to handle it.

Gertrude spoke to her son-in-law, explaining that Justice Carew had arranged for Gloria Vanderbilt to visit little Gloria at ten o'clock that morning. Nurse Keislich had been sent away for the day, and her niece had been left in the care of Miss Walsh, the trained nurse they'd hired since the child's hysterical collapse. Everything was arranged except for one detail—no one had told little Gloria. "Perhaps little Gloria will be a bit upset. Would you go over and tell her the news, please?" asked Gertrude.

The child was sitting in the downstairs sitting room when Uncle Buz arrived. They chatted for a while and then, with throwaway casualness, he said, "By the way, guess who's coming to see you this morning? She's on the way right now—your mother."

The word MOTHER struck little Gloria like a bullet. She jumped to her feet and began to shake. Then the screams burst out of her. She tried to run out of the room, but Uncle Buz blocked her way and said sternly, "Now look here, Gloria, this is all right. You are going to stay here, and you must not act this way."

Uncle Buz didn't understand. Nobody understood! Little Gloria screamed and pushed past Barklie Henry and ran up the staircase and into her bedroom. Miss Walsh, who was standing in the middle of the room, watched with amazement as the child came barreling into the room, slammed the door, turned the key in the lock, pulled it out, and then frantically began scurrying around for a place to hide the key.

Barklie Henry pounded on the door. Miss Walsh saw where the child had hidden the key, picked it up, and opened the door. Uncle Buz walked in. He was more gentle as he took the child's hand and calmed her down and told her, "Your mother has just called to say that she's been delayed and will not arrive until noon. I'll tell you what," he said, "we can go riding," knowing that little Gloria would love this treat.

As the child, holding firm to her Uncle Buz's hand, walked out of the front door of Gertrude Whitney's house, she could see confirmation of her fear that her mother was coming to kidnap and kill her. She knew nothing of the new kidnap-murder threat, and it was pure coincidence that this day had come on the heels of last night's failure to apprehend her potential kidnapper. But as a result, in addition to the private guards already in service at Wheatley Hills (a force that had been increased to sixteen so that Gloria Vanderbilt would not attempt to kidnap her daughter), there were several dozen Nassau County motorcycle policemen who had been summoned to provide additional protection until the unknown person who had written the kidnap threat was apprehended. As little Gloria and Uncle Buz walked toward the stable, private detectives and motorcycle policemen with guns at their hips, standing beside their bright red Indian motorcycles, lined the road.

It was a magnificent October day. The air was cold and the sun shone brightly. It took just a few minutes to saddle up, and the horses moved out briskly, shaking their heads and snorting in the morning air. The trees had just begun to color. Uncle Buz and little Gloria rode in silence. They did not speak of the impending visit, nor did little Gloria say anything about her fear. They rode for about an hour and a half.

When little Gloria returned to the house, the fear flooded over her again and she ran up the stairs and into her room. This time, Barklie Henry and Miss Walsh stayed right behind her. Uncle Buz offered to play a card game until her mother arrived, and just as they were reaching for the cards, there was a rap on the door and a footman announced that Mrs. Vanderbilt was out in the garden and wanted the child sent down to her immediately. Barklie Henry looked over at little Gloria. It did not take a person of unusual sensitivity to see what had happened to her. She was shaking uncontrollably, her breath coming in tiny gasps. He told Miss Walsh to remain with the child and left the room.

Gloria, Thelma, and Consuelo had decided to come as a force to Wheatley Hills. They'd been delayed because Lieutenant Sullivan had arrived at the house to ask for more pictures of Gloria and insisted that she open the morning mail to see if there were any more kidnap threats. As an added precaution, Lieutenant Sullivan placed a police detective with the chauffeur, Louis, in the limousine to Wheatley Hills. Both men were armed. As their limousine turned the corner at the gatekeeper's cottage on Whitney Lane, they were greeted by a Nassau County police motorcycle escort. Gloria leaned out of the car window. "There are cordons and cordons of them," she said to her sisters. The motorcycle policemen roared ahead, guiding the car on the mile and a quarter drive to the front courtyard of the Whitney house. As Gloria stepped from the car, she turned to Thelma and asked, "Am I to see my child surrounded by dozens of motorcycle policemen and detectives?" The front courtyard of the Whitney house looked like the muster area of an army garrison. Gloria refused to enter the house; she walked around to the garden, followed by her sisters, and sent a message that her little girl was to meet her there. About five minutes later, a grave, handsome man, who introduced himself as Barklie Henry, walked up to Gloria. He explained that her child had become upset when she'd heard her mother was coming. "Perhaps it would be better not to see her just now."

The sisters hovered together like a covey of birds. Soft whispers passed between them. Gloria looked up and said one word, "Nonsense." Consuelo said, "We are here to see the child, and see her we will." Ignoring Barklie Henry, the women marched into the house. Gloria led the way up the stairs and turned the knob of little Gloria's bedroom door. The door would not open. She knocked on the door and called out, "Darling, this is Mummy."

The answer was a series of screams; and after the screams, the words blurted out. "I don't want to see you." Then more screams, and, clearly, the phrase, "Don't kill me. Don't kill me. Don't . . ."

Gloria stood outside the door listening to these words from her child. She began to cry. Suddenly her breath seemed cut off and she gasped for air. She clutched the doorknob for support and her head slumped to her chest. Consuelo, sure her sister was about to faint, moved forward and held her in her arms. Then she gently propelled her across the hall to an empty bedroom. "Come on, darling," she urged as Gloria's step faltered. Gloria barely made it to the bed and collapsed.

Thelma Furness, standing in front of the door, felt the anger rise in her. She pounded on the door and commanded, "Nurse, you must open the door. This is a court order. We are to see this little girl."

From behind the door Miss Walsh's shrill voice replied, "I know it is, but Gloria won't give me the key."

"Why did you give her the key?" Thelma demanded in exasperation.

"I didn't . . . she took it . . ."

Now there was the sound of scurrying feet, and then a gasp from Miss Walsh, followed by the child's screams, increasing in timbre. Miss Walsh yelled over them, "She's thrown the key in the fire. There's a fire and she's . . ."

Thelma, too, was screaming outside the door. "This is Aunt Toto. Open this door!" She began pounding on it with her fists.

The answer came reverberating back, "No, I won't. I don't want to see you. I hate you . . ." Then there was silence. Then the same voice, this time pleading, "I want my Uncle Buz."

"Who?" asked Thelma.

"Mr. Henry," replied Miss Walsh's voice.

Thelma moved back across the hall and stood by Consuelo's side. "Get Mr. Henry and get a carpenter," she told her. Consuelo nodded in agreement and left.

There was only the sound of the child's screams and sobs as Thelma walked back to the door and waited for Barklie Henry. He came a few minutes later with a caretaker, who held a ring of keys. One by one, the man inserted them in the door until he found one that fit, and then turned it and pushed the door open. Thelma entered the room first, followed by Consuelo and Barklie Henry.

Miss Walsh stood in embarrassed silence in the center of the room. The child was nowhere to be seen. Finally, Thelma looked down and saw two small hands encircling the nurse's hips. Little Gloria was hiding behind the nurse's skirt, clinging to Miss Walsh's back. Thelma, who had been furious a moment before, was taken aback by this sight. Her voice was gentle as she asked, "What is this all about, Gloria, darling? You are not frightened of Aunt Toto, are you?"

From behind the nurse's skirt came a tiny voice. "I am."

"Why? I haven't done anything to you."

"No."

"Then come on. Give me a kiss. Don't act like a little child."

Slowly little Gloria's dark hair peeked out, then her face followed. "All right," she whispered, and, as if walking to the guillotine, she walked up to Thelma and kissed her; and then to Consuelo and repeated the kiss. "Hello," she said, as if meeting them for the first time.

Consuelo was not nearly as sympathetic as Thelma. This child was killing her dear sister, who was nervous enough as it was. She looked down at the child. "You know," she said, "your mother is crying, and you have made her very unhappy. Won't you go in and kiss her and say you're sorry?"

"No."

Consuelo would not take no for an answer. "Look here, Gloria. Do you realize you're hurting your mommy . . . you don't really want to make her unhappy, do you?"

The child cocked her head to the side. "No," she replied.

"All right then, go and tell her you're sorry for behaving like such a silly little girl. You're grown up now and you can't behave this way."

Little Gloria looked up at Uncle Buz beseechingly. "Will you take me?" she asked. In reply, he silently grasped her hand and led her to the doorway of the bedroom where her mother lay on the bed gasping for breath. The child would go no farther than the doorway.

"Why are you frightened?" asked Thelma.

"I won't tell," answered the child.

"But why?" asked Thelma.

"I'm afraid of her," replied the child. What could she say? How could she explain?

From her place on the bed, even Gloria could not fail to realize what was happening. The child was cringing from her as if she were a vicious killer. The fear on the face of her child pierced her own distress. "Come to me," she said. Little Gloria moved three steps forward, but then ran back to the door. It was more than Gloria could bear, she felt that the pain of having her child hate her was the most agonizing thing that had ever happened to her. She clutched her throat. She would choke to death and she didn't care.

Thelma, who could read her sister's thoughts, felt her pain. She knew she must take the child away because she was only making it worse. She reached down and took little Gloria's hand and led her back to her bedroom where they both sat on the rug as if Thelma too were a child. Little Gloria's puppy, Gypsy-Mitzie, ran over and jumped into Thelma's lap and began licking her fingers. "You see," Thelma said, "this little dog is not afraid."

"Oh, that's only a dog," said little Gloria.

"Why, Gloria, dogs have brains. That is why we have them as friends."

"Yes, I suppose they have." The child seemed to grow calmer.

Barklie Henry stood in the doorway watching the scene. This visit had been an unmitigated disaster. Across the hall the mother lay prostrate, and in this room the child's blotched face looked as if she were suffering from some terrible disease. "Darling, why are you frightened of me?" Thelma was asking again. This time, the child did not reply. Barklie Henry tried to help. "Well, Gloria—has Aunt Toto ever let you down?"

The child's face went into a spasm. "Down what?" she asked, terrified. (When children were kidnapped there were lots of downs—down sewers, down holes in the desert, down wells, down in the ground.)

"Has she ever promised to do something and not done it? That's 'let you down.' "

"No."

Thelma, having had experience with her own son Tony, tried to distract the child to change her mood. She pointed to a photograph on Gloria's bureau of two little boys dressed in sailor suits. One appeared round-faced and smiling; the other, taller and grave. "Who are they?" she asked.

"Oh," said Gloria, pointing to the round face, "that is Daddy."

Thelma stood and pulled the child up by the hand and led her over to the bureau. The child reached up and took down the photograph, holding it tenderly in her hand. "This is Daddy, and this is his brother," she explained. Little Gloria reached for Thelma's hand once again and clasped it firmly as she guided her around the room, pointing out all her treasures. There were several other pictures of her father on the bureau; in one, she was a baby, and he was holding her in his arms. There was a photograph of Gerta Henry, and Kodaks of groups of her friends from the Green Vale School, and one of little Gloria on her pony Black Beauty. She reached up and lifted a blue satin rosette from a shelf and held it out to Thelma, explaining that she'd won it at a horse show in Newport. "I won a cup with it, but I left it there."

"That's a very silly thing, to bring the rosette and leave the cup," said Thelma. She was now talking to little Gloria exactly as she would her own son Tony. After a while, when everything seemed normal, Thelma said, "It's getting late and Aunt Toto is getting hungry. Shall we have lunch?"

"I'm going to a party," said the child.

Thelma was surprised. She'd thought the idea was to spend the whole day with the child, to woo her so that there could finally be a settlement. "Will you do something for me?" she asked.

"What?"

"Will you, when your mummy comes in here, kiss her?"

The child looked at Thelma. Perhaps the touch of her hand had been reassuring. Perhaps after a few minutes with a real person—not the loneliness, not the longing—things seemed different. "Yes," she said.

"Wait here, and I'll get her."

Thelma walked back across the hall. Consuelo was holding Gloria's hand as she reclined against the pillows sipping a glass of brandy. Dr. Jessup stood at the foot of the bed writing a prescription for a sedative. Thelma decided that a crisp yet loving jolt was the only way to handle the situation. "Pull yourself together, darling," she instructed Gloria, "and come along. The baby is perfectly willing and anxious to see you. Now fix your face up."

Gloria looked up at her sister trustingly; she seemed every bit as much a child as the one that Thelma had just left. Then, in a moment of recognizing the one asset that was most valuable to her, she touched her bloated face and said, "I can't let my baby see me crying like this." She got off the bed and moved to the mirror to repair her make-up; then Thelma guided her sister back across the hall.

Gloria entered the room and extended a peace offering to her little girl—two playing cards. Little Gloria saw a flash of Mickey Mouse on the back of one of the cards and reached for them. "Oh, thank you, Mummy," she said. "Would you like to see my card collection?"

"Yes, darling, I would love to."

Little Gloria pulled out a box full of trading cards and began showing them to her mother, one by one.

"I have a Mickey Mouse game in the car for you," her mother told her.

Thelma sent Miss Walsh down to the car, and she returned with the game. Little Gloria unwrapped it and examined it carefully. "I wonder how it goes?" she asked, obviously intrigued.

"When I come next time, we'll play it together," said her mother.

"That will do as well," replied little Gloria.

"Put your arms around me and kiss me," Gloria said to her daughter.

Little Gloria was later to say that at that moment she was so afraid that her mother was going to take her away that she obeyed. She gave her mother a kiss on the cheek but not "a real kiss," and she gave her a hug but she "didn't mean it." At that moment she wanted her mother to know "that I didn't love her and I was trying to say—I was too scared to say—" but those were all the words she had. And after that her mother left.

As the Vanderbilt Rolls-Royce moved toward New York, Barklie Henry was on the telephone with Gertrude Whitney, describing what had just taken place. There could be no question of a settlement. The child was in a state of mortal terror.

Saturday afternoon Nathan Burkan was called to the Vanderbilt town house to deal with this latest catastrophe. He advised Gloria to put the best possible face on the visit; the newspapers, he said, would never find out what had happened. Gloria told reporters that her visit to little Gloria had been "my happiest day since my baby was taken from me." And Jane Franklin of the *Mirror* wrote, "Mrs. Vanderbilt was so overcome by the sight of her child, who had been spirited away on September 21, that she collapsed and required a physician. At the end of the visit, little Gloria kissed her mother a fond goodbye and asked, 'Will you please come Wednesday, Mother dear, and play some games with me?' "

The *Times* ran another story—an accurate one.

> According to information obtained outside the court, there are two versions of the visit at the Whitney home in Old Westbury, Long Island . . . the opposing versions differ in that the Vanderbilt story attributes the mother's collapse to the indignity of visiting her own child "under a guard of cordons of police," whereas the Whitney story declares that the mother was overcome when the child had hysterics in fear that the mother was about to take her away from Mrs. Whitney . . .

Because of the latest turn of events, Nathan Burkan felt that the only alternative left was to try to frighten Gertrude Vanderbilt Whitney into a settlement. Benny Kerin had replaced Val O'Farrell and at last was beginning to dig up some dirt. Burkan was prepared to use whatever he could to give Gertrude Whitney a taste of her own medicine. His resentment of the Whitney side had deepened as every day in the courtroom they treated him in an increasingly cavalier manner. On Wednesday, Herbert Smyth had tried to enter a document in evidence which had berated Burkan for his conduct and tactics, and said that if he did not discontinue them, there would be a move to disbar him. Burkan had exploded. "In that document they were trying the old bluff . . . because I put up a fight . . . because this boy from the tenements said he did not care anything about the Whitneys, they told me that they were going to disbar me. If you take a case against the Whitneys, they will disbar you. . . . Well, I am not afraid to fight."

Burkan called in reporters and told them, "There is absolutely no possibility of a settlement. . . . As soon as Mrs. Whitney leaves the stand, I will begin our side by subpoenaing one Donald Hunter, a handsome young model who spent last summer at Gertrude Whitney's camp at Sabattis. . . . Also under subpoena are Frederick Soldwedell, an artist; Louis Sloden, a professional dancer; Frederick Hazeltine, a sculptor; and George Coleman—some Cody, Wyoming, cowboy." Burkan said he also intended to subpoena one Mrs. Lillian Gillman, a Los Angeles housewife who twenty years previously had been a *Ziegfeld Follies* girl under the stage name of Lily Lagler and the fiancée of Sheriff Bob (Robert Winthrop) Chanler. A. C. Blumenthal had found this witness, and when she said she'd posed in the nude for Mrs. Whitney and was prepared to tell all she knew about the wild bohemian life Gertrude led in Greenwich Village, he agreed to pay her expenses to come to New York.

Theobald Mathew read the conflicting newspaper accounts of Gloria's visit to Wheatley Hills and the list of witnesses Burkan intended to subpoena. The Vanderbilt trial continued to amaze him: only in America did they allow children to rule the roost and servants to spout off. In 1934, Theobald Mathew, then thirty-six years old, was one of Great Britain's most respected solicitors, a special favorite of the aristocracy. Two years hence, when Wallis Simpson decided to divorce her husband, it was suggested that Mathew handle the divorce for her. Wallis told Mathew that she wanted a divorce because she was "getting older but might well meet someone with whom she might happily marry," and that "it was ridiculous to imagine she had any idea of marrying the King." In the face of her lies, Mathew refused to act in her behalf.

Nadeja Milford Haven had acted discreetly in choosing Mathew to represent her interests. His closeness to the royal family made him protective of the Marchioness of Milford Haven and also of Edward, Prince of Wales, whose name could conceivably be dragged into this matter. It was Mathew's responsibility to prevent this. After only three days in New York, Mathew met secretly with Nathan Burkan and James Murray; with Frank Crocker, Herbert Smyth, and John Godfrey Saxe. He then arranged a meeting with Justice Carew and on entering his chambers, Mathew, assuming his most casual posture, strolled around the room and perused the books in the bookcases and the framed documents on the walls. One document caught his attention and he murmured, "Interesting. Most interesting." It was a photocopy of the writ of execution of Charles I for treason, given to Carew as a joke by the Friendly Sons of St. Patrick. Carew pointed out the second signature from the bottom of the list of some sixty peers of the realm who had sentenced their sovereign to the ax. "That is Lord Carew, from whom I am descended," he said in jest. Noting Carew's jovial mood, Mathew introduced the name of Edward, Prince of Wales, into the conversation, explaining how awkward it might be if that name came up at this trial, or if there were any further scandal concerning the Milford Havens. Carew assured him that he was familiar with the privileges of peers and the concept of their honor, which must be tended more carefully than that of other men. "In the past, scandal against a peer was considered *scandalum magnatum*, I believe," said Carew. "We must consider that words not actionable in a case of common persons are subject to punishment when used against a peer."

Mathew had been as pleased by this conversation as he was now distressed by the latest turn of events. He conferred with Frank Crocker and Herbert Smyth and then arranged to have dinner with Nathan Burkan, Louis Frohlich, and Herman Finkelstein in the privacy of Burkan's Great Neck, Long Island, home. The Burkan house resembled an English country estate set off by a sweeping lawn; past the south windows there was a spectacular view of Long Island Sound. Frohlich and Finkelstein arrived first, and Burkan led them into a glass-enclosed sunroom. Nathan Burkan was elated over the prospect of Mathew's visit; he told Finkelstein, "Imagine. The King's solicitor will be dining with Nathan Burkan tonight." He kept referring to Mathew as "the King's solicitor," but to Frohlich, Mathew was just another lawyer, and he wasn't sure where they stood with him. On the drive out, Frohlich told Finkelstein he was sure Mathew was "a stuffed shirt," and, hearing the reverential tone in Burkan's voice, he began actively to dislike this man whom he had never met. Burkan walked to the bar and picked up a bottle. "See what I've got?" he said like a proud child with a special toy. "A fifty-year-old brandy. That ought to impress the King's solicitor." Frohlich winced.

Mathew arrived ten minutes later, and soon Frohlich found that he was not at all as bad as expected. Mathew's appearance was formidable; Frohlich had never seen such thick, bushy eyebrows. But he was younger than Frohlich had expected and he seemed relaxed and affable.

They moved into Burkan's combination living room–library. Law books lined the walls, and Mathew walked around the perimeter of the room scanning the books before he settled himself on the sofa and opened the conversation. "I want you gentlemen to know that I'm simply here to see what's going on."

Burkan announced that their plan was to destroy Gertrude Vanderbilt Whitney's character in exactly the manner she had destroyed Mrs. Vanderbilt's. Mathew replied that he felt these tactics might prove "somewhat unwise." The Whitney side had not yet finished presenting their case. "I have reason to believe that there is more evidence of a scandalous nature against Mrs. Vanderbilt which so far has been withheld—other witnesses might still be supoenaed." Mathew then reached into his pocket, produced a paper, and reeled off the list of names it contained. Nathan Burkan shook his head in amazement. It did not take long for Mathew to convince these lawyers that their course of character assassination would backfire. Mathew said he was empowered to offer Nathan Burkan the alternative that if he would say nothing about Mrs. Whitney's friends and alleged lovers, she, in turn, would bring no further witnesses against Mrs. Vanderbilt. Naturally, Mr. Smyth would be forced to cross-examine Prince and Princess Hohenlohe, Lady Furness, and Mrs. Vanderbilt herself, but it was Mathew's wish that a certain royal party's name should never be mentioned in connection with this case. Smyth had agreed that it would serve no useful purpose to press for a name that was extraneous to these proceedings. When Burkan also agreed, Mathew said, "I'm sure you'll wish to convey these sentiments to your client." Burkan nodded in assent and to seal the bargain, walked to the bar, carried four crystal brandy snifters to the table, and ceremoniously poured the precious brandy. As Frohlich reached for his glass, he looked at Mathew and said, "Me—I prefer slivovitz—it sets a forest fire in your chest." Finkelstein smiled, while Burkan flushed with embarrassment. Frohlich had conveyed all he wished to say about himself. He was a Jew from immigrant stock, and he was a proud man.

After cigars and some social chatter, Mathew left, and Burkan, Finkelstein, and Frohlich sat back to discuss how to proceed. "That was quite a friendly chap," remarked Finkelstein. "I'm so pleased he came here only to see what was going on."

Gertrude

NATHAN BURKAN: Insofar as you observed, did [Mrs Vanderbilt] did absolutely nothing to affront or offend that child, did she?

GERTRUDE VANDERBILT WHITNEY: No, during the twice that she visited her child and myself, during 1932, and the four times during 1933, and it may have been three or four times during the next year, I never saw anything of that kind.

GERTRUDE VANDERBILT WHITNEY felt she had done everything in her power to avoid this moment. She had tried to settle with this intractable woman, this irrational Gloria Vanderbilt, who had brought this action against her. There was no avoiding today. At 9:45 a.m., Gertrude and her daughter Flora Miller walked up the steps of the Supreme Court. Both women were dressed entirely in black, as if attending a funeral.

The newspapers painted a picture of Mrs. Whitney as "the haughty matriarch of iron whim," "the magisterial dowager," a "vastly wealthy woman of stern rectitude." Not knowing what went on inside the courtroom, or why Gertrude felt she must keep little Gloria with her, people asked themselves what possessed this woman to snatch a child from her loving, if somewhat wayward, mother. They searched for reasons and the rumors spread: Harry Payne Whitney had given Gloria $12,000 for Reggie's funeral because they were lovers; the taking of little Gloria was Gertrude's revenge. Gertrude had always resented her brother's marriage to a social inferior. Mrs. Whitney had "a mania for raising children" (this suggested by Gloria herself) and was not satisfied with eight grandchildren of her own. Gertrude saw in little Gloria a replica of herself, and her narcissism demanded that she keep this little beauty at her side.

Mrs. Whitney entered the courtroom, mounted the steps to the black leather witness chair, and sat still as a statue waiting for the proceedings to begin. During the next three days she would honor her vow to say nothing against Gloria Vanderbilt's character. She would base her testimony on mild assertions of neglect, on glowing accounts of the atmosphere she provided at Wheatley Hills. To the end, she would remain a finishing school girl pouring tea at a holocaust. In all that time, Gertrude would lose control of her emotions only once, and that would be concerning a subject on which she could not contain her passion—art.

There was a deferential tone in Herbert Smyth's voice as he began his direct examination. A constant cough punctuated Gertrude's testimony and she frequently touched the white silk scarf that was wrapped twice around her neck to protect her throat. Sometimes her cough became so severe and her voice so strained and scratchy, that even Nathan Burkan asked if she wished a recess. She never did.

Her initial description of herself was that of a conservative widow. She identified herself as the mother of three children and the grandmother of eight. She said that since her husband's death in 1930, "I have led a very quiet life, mostly in the country, and I have worked, and my mother has been ill, and I have spent a great deal of time on Long Island besides, but as far as social life goes, it has been very quiet." Continuing in this vein, Gertrude described Wheatley Hills in a manner that emphasized its virtues for children. "The place at Westbury has been in my husband's family for a great, great many years. My children were brought up there, and after they married I built them houses on the place near, so that we all live in a small community, and my children and grandchildren are there, and very frequently they come up and pay me visits when their houses are closed, so that I can hardly remember any time when I haven't had some of the children and the grandchildren and other relatives staying down with me in the country. It is a little community of children."

Justice Carew, however, knew this was a woman of vast wealth. He asked, "Have you any idea how many residences there are around there?" as if perhaps there were so many that she would not know the number.

Gertrude replied, "Yes, each one of my children has a house and I have a house and there are various other buildings such as a tennis court, and I have a studio on the place and there is a farm and a stable and there are garages for all the houses."

There was no denying the luxury of her life, which again and again would be demonstrated in the testimony. "How many governesses and nurses are there around there?" Nathan Burkan asked, and Gertrude replied. "This is just governesses, not nurses?"

"We will get to the governesses first, and then the nurses afterward."

"My son has a governess for his little girl. Mrs. Miller has a governess and two nurses, and I think Mrs. Henry, besides the governess, has a nurse."

"You of course have the nurse, Miss Keislich," said Burkan sarcastically.

"Yes."

"And at your house there is a trained nurse," added Smyth, rounding out the total to eight and removing Gertrude forever from the cozy image she first presented.

The description of her domestic situation being complete, Smyth inquired, "What activities have you had in your own life?"

"Outside of my family, I have been most interested in my profession as a sculptor," replied Gertrude Whitney. For the first time she seemed to relax in the witness chair.

"How long have you been doing that?" inquired Smyth.

"For over thirty years . . ." she answered, and said that she had a studio in Old Westbury.

"Then in New York have you got a studio?"

"Yes, I have several studios in New York."

"How large?"

"Well, it is about three New York houses, but it is not all devoted to my own studio. I have always been so interested in the development of the young artists in New York—in America, I should say—that I turned part of my studios into exhibition rooms, where the artists could show their work to the public," she explained proudly.

"Is this something that you maintain yourself for the artists at your own expense?"

"Oh, yes!"

"And it is open all the time, is it?"

"Yes, sir."

"So that any artist who thinks he or she has got a work of merit can exhibit it there, so that the public can see it?"

"Yes."

"Without any expense at all?"

"Yes, sir."

"It is called the Whitney Museum?"

"Yes, after the exhibition rooms—then I turned it into the Whitney Museum of American Art."

At the counsel table, Nathan Burkan nudged Jim Murray and whispered, "This isn't a custody trial, it's an art lecture," but he noted the emotion this normally dispassionate woman displayed when speaking of art.

Gertrude explained that her niece had come to stay with her at Wheatley Hills in June of 1932, to recuperate from a tonsil operation. At that time she'd been "very pale and very thin and extremely nervous," but by early fall the child's condition had improved. Gertrude became extremely careful in telling what had happened next. That fall "Mrs. Vanderbilt returned from abroad and I asked her if she would come and see me to talk over the plans for the child." She paused, as if looking for exactly the right words. "In substance, I said I thought Gloria was getting on very well, that she had improved, but that in my opinion she would be much better off to lead a country life than she would be in New York. She wasn't strong enough to start that sort of life and I suggested to Mrs. Vanderbilt that she let Gloria go on living with me and go to the Green Vale School, which is very close to my house in Long Island . . ."

Gloria Vanderbilt agreed to allow the child to remain until Christmas. In December, Gloria and Gertrude met again. "I told her in substance that the child was doing very well in the country, that she was gaining in weight; that she was making friends down here, that she likes her school, and I hoped that Mrs. Vanderbilt would let her stay on during the winter." Gertrude remembered Gloria's reply, "I would be glad to have Gloria stay on," she had said, and had gone abroad.

Gertrude Whitney did not see Gloria Vanderbilt again all winter. Five months later she arrived at Wheatley Hills with Thelma Furness. Gertrude Whitney noticed that when little Gloria came into the room, for the first time she seemed to "display indifference toward her mother" and kissed her "in a very perfunctory way."

Burkan objected to this characterization.

"I have seen that done. I have seen two French generals kiss each other," Carew interjected, and allowed Mrs. Whitney to continue.

The pattern had been established: the child's mother left for extended periods of time, after which she reappeared for brief visits—two hours at the longest. Gertrude said that little Gloria's mother "had every privilege of seeing the child whenever or however she wanted to. I asked her to come out any time and stay with me, and just turn up when she wanted to," but Gloria seldom visited her daughter.

And so it went, until June of 1934, when Gloria lodged her guardianship petition. "Finally," Gertrude said, "a tentative agreement was reached." In order to fulfill the terms of this agreement, Gertrude forced her niece to visit with her mother. The child didn't want to go. She repeatedly said that "she was afraid of her mother." On Friday, September 21, the child arrived at her studio in "hysterical condition."

Gertrude Whitney drew a deep breath and a series of coughs racked her body. Without consulting her, Smyth asked for a recess, and when he left the courtroom he told reporters, "Mrs. Whitney is bearing up nicely." After the recess, Nathan Burkan (armed with Theobald Mathew's assurances that Mrs. Whitney would say nothing detrimental about Gloria Vanderbilt's character) began his cross-examination. "When you were playing your social part . . . you served liquor to your guests, did you not?"

"Certainly."

"And isn't it true that when Mrs. Vanderbilt came down to see you . . . that you did offer her a little sherry?"

"I offered her cocktails or sherry or anything she would like."

"Is it your recollection she took a sherry or cocktail?"

"Sometimes she took a cocktail, sometimes she took sherry."

"You never saw her under the influence of liquor?"

"No."

"During all the time you have seen her, she acted like a perfectly normal woman?"

"Absolutely."

"In all the time that you have seen her, you saw nothing objectionable about her?"

"Certainly not."

"She always, insofar as you could observe and see, demeaned herself as a perfect lady?"

"Certainly." It was ironic that in the words of Gertrude, and only Gertrude, Gloria Vanderbilt emerged as a perfect lady!

Burkan continued to question the witness, trying to demonstrate that she had taken almost no interest in her brother Reginald's family.

"Did you attend the wedding of your late, lamented brother and Mrs. Vanderbilt?" he asked.

"No, I was away at the time."

"And you knew that your brother was a very sick man?"

"I don't think he was very sick at that time."

"Well, didn't you know at one time that the doctor had said that—

I don't say this offensively—if he took one more drink that then he was a dead man?"

"No, I never knew that."

Burkan tried to show that it was Emma Sullivan Keislich who was in charge of the child and that Gertrude Whitney was away a great deal of the time.

"I was away a good deal of the time because my mother had grown iller," she explained. "I saw my mother, I think, about four or five days a week at some time during the day. . . . When I was living in New York, I would motor down to the country to see the child." On occasion Gertrude would spend the night at Wheatley Hills and see little Gloria off to school before returning to the city and she spent "about every weekend" in the country.

Burkan was determined to prove that the child's mind had been systematically poisoned against her mother, but Gertrude Whitney repeatedly denied that this was the case. "On the contrary, I always hoped that Gloria would have a closer relationship with her mother . . . Gloria spoke very little; very seldom of her mother. . . . I said everything I could, and what I thought was appropriate to arouse an affection in this child for her mother; and everything I said about her mother, I said in accordance with that idea and my desire that there should be a closer relationship . . ."

"You did not want the mother to live near the school house with her own child?"

"On the contrary, if Mrs. Vanderbilt chose to take a house on Long Island, it would have been extremely nice for the child, but I did not want the child to live with her mother at that time," Gertrude answered and then, as if to explain, added, "It was not according to our arrangement."

"When did the child first show a violent dislike to her mother?" asked Burkan.

"The first time she ever showed what I would call a violent dislike to her mother was on a Sunday, when she came to lunch with her mother, which I think was the sixteenth of September last." She had emphasized the word *violent*.

"That was the first time, to your knowledge, that this child showed any violent dislike to her mother?"

"Violent. Yes."

"Well, had she shown dislike before then, that was not violent, that was mild or moderate?"

"She showed a certain dislike, I should say, on Mrs. Vanderbilt's visit to the Adirondacks in August."

"That was August. That was the first time, to your knowledge, that she indicated a dislike to her mother?"

"Yes."

"That was after the mother had made an application to be appointed guardian of the person and co-guardian of the property of her child?"

"Yes."

"You were never curious to find out why this child violently hated its mother?"

"Why, the child has only very recently hated its mother."

"Did you, as the aunt of this child, take enough interest, did you show enough curiosity, to ask this child why she hated her own mother?"

Gertrude replied to this question in the same manner, using almost the same words as all the doctors and lawyers had. "It was not a very good moment when I became convinced that she did have that feeling of antagonism. When I found that out, the child was very upset indeed and my one idea was to comfort her and quiet her and tell her that her mother was fond of her . . ."

Gertrude Whitney said that Gloria Vanderbilt's own specialist, Dr. Hunt, had told her, "In view of the fact that she [little Gloria] has this strong antagonism for her mother, the best thing for her is to remain in the same surroundings in which she has been living. It will take some time to win her back."

"To win her back from what?" Burkan demanded.

"I gathered what he meant was to get her over this antagonism," she replied evenly.

"Insofar as you observed, she [Mrs. Vanderbilt] did absolutely nothing to affront or offend that child, did she?"

With exquisite sarcasm, Gertrude Whitney replied, "No, during the twice that she visited her child and myself, during 1932, and the four times during 1933, and it may have been three or four times during the next year, I never saw anything of that kind."

Justice Carew sought to find the root of the child's fear of her mother and he tried to clarify the situation. ". . . The child, lately at least, has displayed a fear of the mother. The mother has not done anything in two years or so to inspire such fear. She hasn't had any contact with her. Where do you think she got this fear from?"

"I think that so long as the child was living quietly with me and had no apprehension that she was going to be taken away, she was peaceful, and showed only indifference to her mother."

"You mean the fear that she now seems to have of her mother is fear that she will be taken away from where she is living? Is that the fear? Or is it the fear of something else? Or is it a fear of the mother?" Carew was puzzled.

"I think they are both mixed. I think that the child, when it first learned that her mother was going to take her away this fall, her attitude was changed. I noticed that she asked me questions frequently, as 'Will I be going to the Green Vale School next year?' 'Oh, I hope I could always live with you. . . . Are you sure that I am coming back here?' I think gradually—"

Carew cut in, "Then you think it is a fear that the mother will take her away from there?"

"I think it is."

Carew pressed on. "Not a fear of the mother, except so far as the mother might do that."

Gertrude Whitney thought for a moment. "I think at present it is actual fear of the mother which has grown out of that apprehension . . ."

"You used the word 'apprehension.' Is it an apprehension of being taken away from down there and the desire not to be taken away from down there which you call this hatred of her mother?"

"No, I think, Your Honor, that it started that way because since the child was with me, and was happy there, and there was no question of her going away, she never showed any of these symptoms which I have spoken about since. Last June, Mrs. Vanderbilt had told me that in the fall she was going to take the child away, and it was after that that I saw this—"

Carew tried to understand. In his anxiety to find an answer, he again cut Gertrude off. "Then this hatred or dislike, whatever you may want to call it, for the mother, originates in the desire not to be taken away from the place where she is enjoying herself and being happy?"

Gertrude replied thoughtfully, "No. Not entirely, Your Honor. It was a desire to remain there, yes, but also the child did not feel that her mother loved her. She did not love her mother herself. She did not want to be with her mother."

This answer infuriated Burkan and he lashed out at Gertrude. "Isn't it your testimony that the only apprehension this child had is that the mother would take her down to Long Island and keep her with her? Isn't that your testimony?"

Gertrude replied, in a measured voice, "I said that she was apprehensive about that, but I did say that she had developed a very strong antagonism for her mother, so that that was mixed. I said it was a combination."

Burkan almost shouted, "What is the other? What are you keeping it back for? Go and tell us. I am giving you every opportunity to tell us. What is the apprehension? What is this child afraid of?"

Gertrude had no intention of revealing that the child's fear was of being murdered, and she answered obliquely, "When the child showed hysterics and began to shriek or scream when her mother came into the room, that was not just because she did not want to go down and live with her in the country. When the child said, 'If I have to go back, I would rather die,' that is not simply a fear of going back—"

Burkan rudely tried to cut her off. "Are you through?"

The command in Gertrude Whitney's voice was chilling. "No, I am not. If she says, 'I am afraid of my mother, I don't want to go back to her, I don't want to be with her,' that signifies something beyond merely the fact that she did not want to go and stay in the country." There was more—but Gertrude had vowed that she would not be the one to say it.

After Saturday's visit, when little Gloria had thrown the key in the fire, Burkan had realized the impossibility of wooing the child to their side. His only course of action was to contend that Mrs. Whitney had helped turn her against her mother—so much so that she had not wanted to use her own name because it was also her mother's. "When did she [little Gloria] begin to sign her name 'Jo'?" he asked.

"I think last winter. . . . It was after I took her to the movies to see *Little Women*. . . . Jo is one of the characters she admired very much."

"Did the fact that she used the name Jo Vanderbilt have anything to do with the fact that she hates her mother and is afraid of her mother?"

"I am sure it has nothing to do with it. . . . Gerta calls herself Beth . . . Mr. William H. Vanderbilt's little girl, whose name is Emily, calls herself Paddy because she likes the name."

There were other ways to turn a child against her mother: What gifts had Gertrude given her niece? Burkan demanded.

Gertrude listed all she could remember—a pony, a Scotty dog and another puppy, a bobsled, a bracelet, books, and a rowboat called *The Half Pint*.

Hadn't the nurse marched into DePinna's and purchased twenty-one sweaters for this child? Didn't Mrs. Whitney "know of that"?

"I never knew," she replied, unable to stifle her smile.

"There is nothing to smile about, because the bill was $607."

"It seemed to me if she had twenty-one sweaters, I would have known it," she replied with authority—although she had not known.

It was Burkan's contention that when little Gloria said that she hated her mother, she had been lying so that she could stay where she was, enjoying what she had. "[Little Gloria] has been taking lessons in acting, hasn't she?" Burkan inquired.

"Just in school," Gertrude Whitney replied.

"I understand. But she has been taking lessons in acting?"

Gertrude would not give him this. "They don't give lessons. They have little plays and then they rehearse them."

"Hasn't this child told you she would like to be an actress?"

"Yes. What child has not?"

"When did she tell you she wanted to be an actress?"

"I don't remember. She told me she wanted to be a musician, she told me she wanted to be a sculptor, she told me she wanted to be a painter, she told me she wanted to be an actress. I couldn't remember when she had told me each one of those things."

"And a writer," Mr. Smyth added.

"Oh, a writer . . . yes," she agreed.

Neglect was the next allegation Burkan tried to disprove, but Gertrude held fast to her position that Gloria had indeed neglected her daughter. All the time little Gloria had been living with her, Gertrude had never seen one letter written by the mother to the child. The only picture the child had of her mother was a small six-inch photograph the child had cut out of a magazine. "It was taken of her mother advertising Pond's Cold Cream," Gertrude added.

"When the child left the Sherry-Netherland, was there in her possession, as far as you know, any picture of her mother or any little treasures that her mother gave her?" asked the Justice.

"She had a few little treasures, I don't know who had given them to her. There were no pictures that I remember seeing of her mother at that time."

Burkan's fine memory branded Gertrude Whitney a liar. During her direct examination, Carew had inquired, "Did she [little Gloria] have a picture of her mother anywhere?" Gertrude had replied, "Yes, she had a picture of her mother in her room . . . it was quite big. . . . I think her mother gave it to her," and added that she thought it was still in little Gloria's bedroom. It was a small lie, but exactly the kind of discrepancy Burkan relished. He was to take two full days and put on the stand three experts to prove that the magazine photograph of Gloria Vanderbilt, in her daughter's possession, had been published after the trial had started. The assertion that little Gloria, in order to have a photograph of her mother, had been forced to cut one out of a magazine and that it was the only photograph she had of her mother was proved without a doubt to be a lie—an attempt to elicit sympathy.

All day Tuesday the cross-examination continued as Burkan played up to Justice Carew's predilection by insisting that little Gloria must be raised a Catholic and therefore her Catholic mother must be given her custody. Gertrude said that although she was an Episcopalian, she had "always assumed [little] Gloria was a Catholic" and had let Mrs. Morgan and the nurse supervise the child's religious education. "She was going to Mass. She had her prayers, which she had been taught by her grandmother . . . and rosary beads near her bed . . . now and then she went with some of my grandchildren to an Episcopalian church, but I did nothing to interfere with the religious training which she had been given up to then."

"And yet you thought at that time the child was a Protestant child?" challenged Burkan.

Until she'd heard it in this courtroom, Gertrude said, she had no idea her niece had been baptized a Catholic. "I knew she had been christened into the Episcopalian church, and I never knew she'd been christened in any other church."

Burkan recalled the nurse's admission that little Gloria attended a Protestant Sunday School and a Protestant church and Gertrude Whitney admitted that she'd given the child her father's Bible—a Protestant Bible. Because of Carew's religious feeling, Catholicism was becoming the paramount issue of the trial.

Burkan moved into an area where he felt Gertrude Vanderbilt Whitney might prove vulnerable. One of his most successful techniques was to attack witnesses in an emotional area until they became either so angry or distraught or confused that they would say things they did not mean: the nurse's assertion that "no good man or woman ever crossed [Mrs. Vanderbilt's] threshold," or the maid's saying "Yes" to his question about the promise of payment for her testimony, had been examples of this technique in action. Witnesses had testified that Mrs. Vanderbilt surrounded herself with pornography; now Nathan Burkan made the same assertion about Gertrude Vanderbilt Whitney, saying that her sculpture and painting at the Whitney Museum of American Art was pornographic and could affect the child's morals. At this time, the art at the Whitney was still considered radical enough to give this argument some credence. It had been only five years since the Metropolitan Museum of Art had turned down the entire Whitney collection. The day Gertrude began her testimony, the *News* ran a photograph of her inside her museum under the caption, "Here is Mrs. Harry Payne Whitney and her weird art!" And a few days later, the *Mirror* ran a photograph of Thomas Hart Benton's mural, *Arts of Life*, under the headline HOW U.S. APPEARS TO FRIENDS OF MRS. WHITNEY. The text read: "Americans in the raw with sex movies, voluptuaries and gigolos, mask cacophonies of blaring jazz bands . . . as seen by . . . the famous painter who defends Mrs. Whitney's art in the 'gold child' case."

Gertrude was as calm and composed on the subject of little Gloria as a caseworker reading statistics from a mimeographed report. On the subject of her art, she was passionate. Burkan moved into this delicate area like a charging bull.

"Now you told His Honor that you maintain a studio down in Long Island, Old Westbury?" Burkan began.

"Yes."

"You have models down there?"

"Yes."

"And I don't mean this in an offensive way, Mrs. Whitney—you design from the nude, don't you?"

"Yes."

"When was the last time you had nude models down there?"

"Perhaps ten years ago." She corrected herself. "Eight years ago."

"Now, in your work in New York City, you design in the nude, don't you?"

"Yes."

"Both male and female?"

"Yes."

"Totally nude?"

"Yes."

"The breasts of women exposed?"

"Yes. Certainly."

Burkan established that little Gloria had been taken "to this museum of yours known as the Whitney Museum"; then he walked to the counsel table and picked up a paper. Handing it to Mrs. Whitney, he asked her if it accurately described the paintings and figures in her museum.

She accepted the paper and began reading. Nathan Burkan had either gone or sent someone to the Whitney Museum, and in each of her seven galleries they had selected works of nudity or works that by some stretch of the imagination might be deemed sexual. These descriptions—without the names of artists, without any mention of the media in which they had been executed, without any acknowledgment of technique or craft—might have come straight from the Milford Haven pornography catalogs. Burkan was trying to make a travesty of Gertrude Vanderbilt Whitney's life and work.

A lesser woman would have lost control. This woman transmuted her rage into ice and carefully studied the descriptions. "In the reading room on the north wall over the east window, there is a mural painting of a woman which is very suggestive. The woman is wearing a very short black slip and no panties, and black silk stockings and black shoes . . . the lack of panties and the short slip leave the thighs and the under parts exposed entirely. The slip is also cut so low in front that the breasts are exposed in a salacious manner."

Torso—"a man's torso showing the penis and testicles exposed in a very pronounced manner."

Lila—"a white sculptured model or figure, with life-sized proportions . . . a very slender cloth passes over the upper left thigh but still leaves everything exposed to view."

Gertrude continued reading this list, in which each work so crudely described meant something special to her. *Man Walking*—"penis and testicles exposed in a very pronounced manner with no covering—" Gertrude had just purchased this Gaston Lachaise sculpture the previous year. She admired its strength and heroic proportions and tried to achieve them in her own work. Another Lachaise, *Standing Nude*, was described as "a nude woman . . . the pose is slightly to the side but could be termed a frontal." *Crescendo*: "Seven nude women in various poses so that every portion of the woman's body may be noted from seven individual positions, such as front, rear, side, seated, etc." To find pornography here really required imagination: Arthur B. Davies's stylized nudes stood in a dreamlike glen, asexual in the extreme, as abstract as the notes in a scale, each figure a minute variation on a lyrical pattern of movement and grace.

Arthur Lee's six-foot-one-and-a-half-inch bronze statue, *Rhythm*, was the finest example of a recurring theme in his work, but here it was described as "a nude figure of a man with the penis and testicles exposed in a very pronounced manner." A Robert Laurent, *The Awakening*, was described as "a nude figure of a woman leaning on her hands in a sitting position, with the breasts highly developed, the legs slightly raised but apart, and heavy indentations to show the hair at the very extreme bottom of the abdomen."

How could this crude document and these ridiculous assertions be allowed in a court of law? Gertrude Whitney held herself in check as she read Burkan's description of John Sloan's *Love on the Roof, 100 Proof*. "Sketch of a woman, who had gone to the roof to hang clothes, being embraced in a corner near a chimney by a much younger man, while a small child sits at one side and plays with a clothespin and clothes basket, giving the impression of a married woman cheating in front of her child."

This was an etching, not a sketch, but Burkan wouldn't know that. And a quite typical example of the Ashcan school—but Burkan wouldn't know that, either. Here was a scene of a common, everyday happening, the tenement rooftop life in the Village during the hot summer days. Perfectly innocent, and perhaps a masterpiece.

What Burkan was trying to do here disgusted Gertrude Whitney and affected her deeply. But there would be no sign of this. She handed the paper back to Burkan. "They describe the pictures in a crude manner. Yes," she said.

Burkan had failed in his effort to shatter the composure of this witness. He moved to have these descriptions marked as an exhibit. Smyth objected, but Burkan looked up at Justice Carew. "This lady wants the custody of the child. I would like to have His Honor look at it."

Carew seemed ready to assume that these works were indeed pornographic but he pointed out one mitigating factor. "Of course, the circumstances are very different from having dirty pictures thrown around the house. . . ." Having made this pronouncement, he turned to Mrs. Whitney. "What do you mean by crude?" he asked.

"Exaggerated. Unnecessary. Exaggerated as to certain descriptions of portions of the body."

"Do you know whether the child was ever in one of those rooms?"

"She went through the museum, just as she would go to the Metropolitan Museum and see pictures of very much the same character."

"I move to strike that out," said Burkan.

"Strike it out," agreed Carew.

Gertrude was so controlled that Smyth could not help interrupting to lead the witness. "Mrs. Whitney, what you have down there, are they strictly according to the rules of art?"

"I object to that as incompetent, irrelevant and immaterial," said Burkan.

"Objection overruled. The lady seems to be an expert on the subject. She seems to have devoted her life to it," said Carew.

For the first time, Gertrude's voice rose. "They are all works of art in my opinion." She said this in a voice so loud that the reporters could hear her right through the closed courtroom doors.

"And are they any different from the same kind of works of art that are seen in the Louvre in Paris and the Metropolitan Museum of Art in New York?" Smyth was determined to establish this point.

"They are not any different." Gertrude was now looking over at Justice Carew. "These works are on public exhibition at the museum."

Burkan saw his descriptions of pornography melting away. "There are a great many more like the works I've described, are there not?" he asked.

"There are some more," answered Gertrude Whitney.

"You can buy them if you want," said Smyth.

Arthur B. Davies, *Crescendo*

ART PHOTOS SHOWN IN VANDERBILT CASE

Nudes From Whitney Museum Produced as Evidence That Aunt Hurt Girl's Morals.

BLUMENTHAL IS NAME

Heated Remarks Exchanged as Mother Is Questioned About Her Relations With Him.

Photographs of sculpture, etchings and paintings were introduced yesterday in the Supreme Court as exhibits to show that Mrs. Harry Payne Whitney is unfit to rear her niece, 10-year-old Gloria Vanderbilt, who has lived with her for t years.

The exhibits included a nude statue of Hercules, an etching of a man and a woman embracing on the roof of a tenement in the presence of a child and a mural of gay life in Greenwich Village in which nudes wearing opera hats play leapfrog.

The photographs were taken in the Whitney Museum of American Art, 10 West Eighth Street, by Nathan Burkan, counsel for Mrs. Gloria Morgan Vanderbilt, whose attempts to recover her child are being resisted by Mrs. Whitney on the ground that Mrs. Vanderbilt is not a fit mother.

While the Whitney witnesses three weeks testified concer Mrs. Vanderbilt's friendships w men, the Vanderbilt side replied yesterday with photographs of Mrs.

John Sloan, *Love on the Roof*

Gaston Lachaise, *Man Walking*

Robert Laurent, *The Awakening*

VANDERBILT EXHIBITS

Burkan, rendered helpless by Mrs. Whitney's equanimity, snapped, "I don't buy dirty pictures."

"You don't know art from dirt!" Smyth answered so loudly that again the reporters standing in the corridor clearly heard this sentence.

"When I was in Paris I didn't buy them either," said Burkan, implying that Mrs. Whitney's works had the same status as the well-known pornographic French pictures and postcards.

"Those are the ones your client had," replied Smyth.

"That is a very unfair statement and you know it isn't so."

"We proved it so."

"Oh, proved it, subject to a million contractions, 'perhaps' and 'maybe' and 'I don't remember.' "

Burkan turned back to the job at hand. "Isn't it true that you prepared a group, made for the Daughters of the American Revolution in 1928, and they were rejected because of nudity?"

"I made a single figure. And it was not rejected. And it is now erected in the D.A.R., Washington."

"Wasn't that group rejected because of nudity?"

"I think I put on one extra fold."

"One extra what?"

"When the committee first saw the sketch, they objected to its not having quite enough drapery over the breast of the woman. But when the statue was finished, it was exactly as it was in the original sketch, and it now exists in the D.A.R. in Washington."

"The breast was draped?"

"It had drapery. . . . Yes."

Gertrude said that she had worked with nude female models but her nude male models always wore a fig leaf.

"After you completed the work of designing, you tore off the fig leaf, is that it?" asked Burkan.

"On the statue I did. I did not on the model," Gertrude replied.

The following morning when Gertrude had had time to think about her cross-examination, she turned to Carew and asked his permission to clarify one thing and one thing only. Herbert Smyth explained to Carew, "She is rather anxious because it has hurt her pride, this cross-examination." Gertrude Whitney seemed to feel that Justice Carew had the impression that the art in her museum was pornographic and she wanted him to know that hers was a well-recognized museum of art, open to the public.

"To the public?" asked a surprised Carew.

"To the public, free—and except during three months of the summer we have—"

"Who goes there?" interrupted Carew.

"We have an average attendance of, for instance, on Sunday afternoon, when the museum is open from two until six, our average is eight hundred, during the afternoon . . . and on other days we average between two and three hundred people, except on special occasions when there are many more than that."

Carew wanted to make sure that Burkan had not been correct. "Did the police ever close it up?"

"Never."

"Has the Society for the Prevention of Vice or Crime ever made any complaint against it?"

"Never."

"Have there ever been any complaints made against you in a court of any kind?"

"Never, Your Honor."

"When they take their children through, do you cover any part of it?"

"No, everything is open."

"I mean, do you cover up any of the paintings?"

"No. Never. . . . There have been sixty-seven organizations of children."

"I object to that," said Burkan.

"Sixty-seven organizations," repeated Gertrude, glaring at Burkan. "Children and women's clubs, very respectable organizations. His Honor can see the list of them all." This was a matter of real importance to her.

This examination was taking longer than anyone had thought it would, and that afternoon little Gloria had been scheduled to testify secretly in Justice Carew's chambers. Nathan Burkan had tried to prevent her appearance, arguing that the child was too hysterical to testify and that it would be an incredible ordeal to drag her into a court of law. But Carew had answered that the child would have no idea that she was giving testimony; their meeting would be "disguised as a friendly chat with a kindly gentleman." She would think of it as "a conversation rather than an examination."

Gertrude Whitney glanced down at her watch and asked, "Your Honor, might I ask someone to send a message to little Gloria? I have made arrangements for Gloria to come to town, but I thought I would be able to get up and meet her myself and bring her down." Carew, wanting to make sure the child would not be upset, told Gertrude that, of course, she should go fetch her. In the last brief minutes of the examination, Smyth wished to reinforce the accusation he had secretly made to Carew that Gloria Vanderbilt had tried to kidnap her daughter. He did not make this assertion directly, but using the Munsterberg autosuggestive technique said, "One thing has not been asked you. Have you noticed anything with regard to little Gloria's attitude any time an airplane flies over the place or nearby?"

"I object to that," said Burkan. "What have airplanes got to do with this situation?"

"She will tell you," answered Smyth.

"There are airplanes in Long Island, a great many of them, and there are airplanes in New York, and airplanes all over the world. What has that got to do with this case?" Burkan insisted.

"Be patient," said Smyth.

"I think recently she has been nervous about airplanes flying over her," Gertrude Whitney answered.

"Has she said anything or indicated anything?"

"She said one day, 'I think I am going to be kidnapped,' looking at the airplane."

"Did she say who she thought was going to kidnap her?"

"No," Gertrude Whitney replied, although she undoubtedly felt she could easily supply the answer, and hoped it would be obvious to Justice Carew.

Burkan understood the inference and tried to negate it by putting the child's fear of kidnapping into the general category of the Lindbergh case. In his redirect examination he inquired, "You told His Honor that she [little Gloria] talked about kidnapping lately?"

"Yes."

"Of course *The New York Times* and the *Tribune* have carried a considerable number of stories regarding a very famous kidnapping case, haven't they? . . . You knew in the last few months the famous kidnapping story has been carried practically daily in both these two papers, in *The New York Times* and in the *Tribune*?"

"Yes."

"And she talked to you about this kidnapping case, didn't she?"

"Yes."

"That is all," said Burkan and excused the witness. There would be no further probing of the question of kidnapping.

And even now, the next witness was finishing her lunch at Gertrude Whitney's town house. What little Gloria had to say to Justice Carew that afternoon would certainly be the most important consideration in determining the outcome of the *Matter of Vanderbilt*.

I Have Always Been Afraid of My Mother

They never thought of what they were doing to me.
No child should ever be brought into court.

LITTLE GLORIA VANDERBILT

LITTLE GLORIA stood totally isolated in the eye of this fierce legal storm. Had there been communication of any kind, perhaps she would not be here on this warm Wednesday in October, called to testify before Justice Carew. There had been a time not long ago when she had loved her mother and "there was always the overwhelming longing to belong. I can remember trying to copy my mother's handwriting because I wanted desperately to merge with her and to be her. I imagined my mother and I were the twins, not my mother and her sister, Thelma."

In little Gloria's isolation, fear had replaced love. No one realized that little Gloria was fighting for her very life or even that she knew she was going to testify. "I can remember thinking I must speak very carefully because I knew I stood alone."

At eleven o'clock Wednesday morning little Gloria was in class at the Green Vale School when Dodo appeared in the doorway to take her home. When they got there, Dodo said she had to change her clothes because she was going to Aunt Ger's in New York for lunch. But after lunch, Dodo told her the truth: Aunt Ger was coming to take her to court again.

Nathan Burkan had made one final appeal to Justice Carew not to let little Gloria testify "in her present disturbed mental state." When the Justice refused, he told Gloria to go home; he was convinced that her presence would only upset the child further. When she left he explained to reporters, "Mrs. Vanderbilt suffered a heart attack on Saturday. . . . She has trouble with her heart. . . . It's no wonder after all she has gone through and the punishment she's taken. . . . She's saving her strength for her appearance on the stand."

Justice Carew wanted his examination of little Gloria to be secret. At one o'clock he told reporters, "Court is adjourned for the day. You might as well all go home." Then he put on his hat, walked down the steps of the Supreme Court and turned the corner. His ruse nearly worked, except that a reporter saw him sneaking back into the building by the Baxter Street entrance. The reporters rushed to the sixth floor and stood outside his chambers. When they refused to leave, Carew sent for a police squad to move them to the end of the corridor. He was determined to make the atmosphere as pleasant as possible for the child.

At two-thirty, Gertrude Whitney's Rolls-Royce pulled up at the rear of the Supreme Court building and little Gloria emerged with a bodyguard on either side. She wore a long woolen coat beneath which a blue linen dress peeked out. Reporters observed that she "smiled broadly and occasionally giggled as she was hustled inside." Gertrude Whitney and the child were whisked to the sixth floor in the judges' private elevator and began walking toward Carew's chambers. Policemen and court guards held the crowd at bay. From the commotion in the hall, Justice Carew, Herbert Smyth, and Nathan Burkan knew that the child was near. A moment later, little Gloria and Gertrude Whitney entered Carew's chambers. The judge looked around for Gloria Vanderbilt, and asked Burkan, "Have you anybody else coming in?"

Burkan sighed with great sadness. "Mrs. Vanderbilt had a heart attack on Saturday down in Westbury, and Dr. Jessup treated her, and this afternoon I sent her home. . . . She's in no condition to come in, but I'm asking in her place that her sister Lady Furness be permitted to come in."

"I did not expect that Mrs. Whitney was going to be here," said Carew bluntly.

"I spoke to you about it downstairs," Herbert Smyth reminded him.

"I don't recall. . . . In addition to that, though, this room is a small room, you must realize. I got the flu here one day from having a crowd in here . . . but if Mrs. Whitney remains, I think the maternal aunt of the child should be here. We've got to try to be perfectly even in this matter."

With that, Gertrude Whitney turned on her heel and left the room. Only Carew, Burkan, Smyth, and the stenographer remained, as the spindly ten-and-a-half-year-old child stood in the middle of the room clutching a packet of photographs.

The Justice beckoned the child forward and said, in the phraseology gentlemen of his generation reserved for children, "Little girl, will you come over here and sit with me for a little while?" He gestured to a large black leather swivel chair in front of a big flat-topped wood desk which held a carafe of water and several glasses.

The child examined the chair. "Shall I sit down here?" she asked.

"Yes," replied Carew.

Little Gloria sat down and placed the photographs on the desk. Her legs dangled several inches above the floor. Justice Carew beamed down at her. This father of five would put her at her ease. "I have a little girl about your age," he said.

"Have you?" answered the child.

"I was looking at her pictures last night. Are you having a good time down in the country?"

"Yes, lovely," little Gloria replied promptly. "I got a pony and a dog—everything!"

"Do you like it there?"

"Oh, I love it."

"You do not want to live in the city?"

"No. I hate the city."

". . . You don't hate the city?"

"No, I hate it. Really," protested little Gloria.

"You want to stay in the country?"

"Yes. I never want to live in the city."

"How would you like to live with your mother down in the country?"

"No. Never. I always want to live with my aunt."

"You lived a long while with your mother?"

"Yes, but I have hardly seen her"—little Gloria corrected herself—"anything of her. She has never been nice to me."

"You wrote a lot of letters to her that said you loved her."

"No, I did not. Never," the child protested. She stammered as she said, "I used to write letters to her because I was afraid of her—and when she made me a sweater I just thanked her for it—and I hardly ever—"

"Don't you think you could learn to love her?"

"No."

"Oh, you could, if you did not make up your mind not to," said the judge.

Little Gloria said nothing.

"You lived with her for six or seven years over in Paris?"

"But I hardly ever saw anything of her."

"You used to write letters to her and draw little pictures of dogs and horses?"

"Well, I had to because I was afraid that she would do something to me," the child explained.

"She never did anything to you?"

"Yes, she did."

"What did she do?"

"Well"—she paused as if searching for reasons—"she never used to let me have toys, or anything, or have children to come and see me, and sometimes in the daytime she never used to see me at all. She used to just go off with her friends."

"Why, she took you to nice places, to England, where you had little boys and girls and you had a pony over there?"

"No, I did not. Never."

"Didn't you ride a pony over there?"

"No, because I never had riding lessons. Once they got me a riding suit, and I just sat on the pony and walked around."

"I think she would get you a pony now."

"No, I never want to go back to her." The child looked at this man pleadingly. "Do I have to?" she asked, her voice trembling.

"I think you will want to."

It was then that little Gloria began to sob. Tears rolled down her face as she whispered a choked, "No."

Carew was taken aback. He looked at the tearful child and said gently, "It is not that you have to. I think you will begin to love her and want to go back."

"No, I won't," came the tearful response.

"My little girl—I used to be away a long time when I was in Washington, I used to be away all week, and I used to come home, and she used to be glad to see me."

"Yes, but probably you were nice to her."

"How was it your mother was not nice to you?"

"I don't know," answered the child truthfully—helplessly.

But Carew pressed her. "What do you mean that she was not nice to you?"

Little Gloria searched for the reasons he wanted. "Once I had a little dog and I loved him very much, and she took him away from me."

"Maybe the dog had fleas."

"No. He did not."

"Was he a bad dog? . . . A nasty dog?"

"No, he was a lovely little dog."

"Didn't Miss Keislich get a little dog for you? Wasn't she nice to you?"

"Very."

"Didn't she take you out in the park and give you a good time in the park over there?"

"She did. But my mother didn't."

"But your mother paid her for doing that. Your mother told her to do that."

"I don't think she did," little Gloria replied. Naney had told her over and over that it was her money, not her mother's, that paid for Dodo—that paid for everything.

"Your mother told her to take good care of you and take you out in the park. All the good things Miss Keislich did for you, she did it because your mother had her there."

"I don't think so," the child said.

"Is it because you have a good time in the country that you want to stay down there with your cousins?"

"No, I love Auntie Ger, and I always want to stay with her."

"Wouldn't you like to have your mother come to see you once in a while?"

"No."

The utter misery, confusion, and stubbornness of the child disconcerted Carew. The nurse had said that the child had always been afraid of her mother, but Carew had taken pains to explore this with Gertrude Whitney, who'd said that this fear was of recent origin; before that, there had only been indifference and the conviction that she was unloved. Carew tried to take the child back to those early years. "Look at all the years you lived with your mother over in Paris."

"I don't care. I don't like her," wailed the child.

"You used to like her until you went down in the country?"

"No, I did not."

Carew began sorting through a pile of postcards in front of him and removed several cards decorated with drawings of birds and flowers and signed with XX's and OO's and the word Love. "Look at all the little postal cards you sent to her. . . ."

"Well, I had to, because I was afraid of her."

"Afraid of what?" asked Carew. This was the question that disturbed them all. "You don't believe in bugaboos, do you?"

"No."

"What would you be afraid of? . . . What are you afraid of?" Instinctively, Carew knew this truth was at the heart of the case.

The question hung in the air. She had already told them the answer in so many ways, but no one had understood. "I don't know," she answered. "I am just afraid of her."

"Do you know your two aunts, Lady Furness?"

"Yes."

"And the other lady—what's her name?"

"Mrs. Thaw?"

"You like them?"

"No."

"You used to like them when they were over in France?"

"No, I did not. I used to like . . . Lord Furness. He was very nice to me."

"How were they not nice to you?"

"Well, they used to take things away from me," she began tentatively. "And in the morning she would not let me come in her room. She used to say she is busy."

"Whom do you mean by this?" asked Carew.

"My mother."

"They always bought you nice clothes, toys, dolls and fairy books, fairy tales and things like that, didn't they?"

"Sometimes." She amended that. "Hardly ever. In England, they hardly ever used to pay any attention to me. They used to go out to parties and things."

"Well, they were grown-up people, and children ought to go to bed early. 'Early to bed and early to rise makes a man healthy, wealthy and wise,' " said the Justice from his lofty perch of adulthood. "Did you ever hear that?"

"Yes."

"When you grow up you will be able to go out to parties and dances."

"She never even kissed me good night . . ." said little Gloria.

Carew was perplexed—his goal was eventually to effect a reconciliation between this child and her mother. To do that, he had to know the reasons why the child hated and feared her mother—the feeble reasons she was giving meant nothing. Carew turned his attention to safe territory, the child's religion. He was well equipped to determine if she were being brought up as a Catholic. "Do you know any prayers?" he asked.

"Yes."

"Let me hear you say some prayers."

"What shall I say?" asked little Gloria. Then, in a rush of words so fast that they ran together, she began: "Hail-Mary-full-of-Grace-the-Lord-is-with-thee—"

"Talk a little slower."

"I can't say it unless I say it fast," said the child. "Hail-Mary-full-of-Grace-the-Lord-is-with-thee-blessed-art-thou—" The child stumbled. "Oh. Gee! Blessed art thou—" She stopped. "I say that every night," she protested.

"Amongst women and—" prompted Carew.

"Amongst women and those who—" There was a long silence. "It's awfully funny. I can't remember." An agonizing silence. Then, "The Lord is with me."

"With thee."

"With thee. Blessed—"

"Blessed art thou," said Carew, leading the child.

"Amongst women. Oh gee! It is awfully funny that I can't remember." The child was silent. Every night she said this prayer for her dear dead father. She knew it well and said it at breakneck speed, which was the only way she could do it without stammering. But now there were no words.

"Do you say 'Our Father'?"

Little Gloria began in a rush, which held the stammering down. "Our-Father-who-art-in-heaven-hallowed-be-Thy-name-Thy-Kingdom come-Thy will-be-done—" She skipped the next line and plunged on. "Give-us-this-day-our-daily-bread, and-forgive-us-our trespasses, as-we-forgive-those-who-trespass-against-us, lead-us-not-into-temptation and deliver-us-from evil. Amen.

"And I know this one, this is a short one," she said helpfully. "When you want something to happen, you say, 'Little Flower at this hour show me Thy power.' "

"Who taught you that?"

"Dodo. She taught me that."

Carew wondered what this had to do with Catholicism. Was this some sort of Walt Disney jargon? This expert did not know what any European Catholic school child could have told him—the little Flower of Jesus was St. Thérèse de Lisieux, a favorite saint of children and soldiers. During World War I, thousands of French soldiers had carried her picture into battle. To them, it was the power of Thérèse, the frail girl, who thrust back the Germans from Paris, saved Verdun, and brought the United States into the war.

Carew used his precious time with the child to determine her knowledge of Catholic prayers. "Can you say the 'Apostles' Creed'?" he asked.

Little Gloria had never heard that name. Her mother called this prayer the Credo.

"Can you say, 'I believe in God, the Father Almighty'?" Carew persisted.

"I do," she stammered, "I used to know it . . . but I have forgotten."

"Let me see," prompted Carew. "I believe in God, the Father Almighty—"

"I believe in God, the Father Almighty, who has made heaven and earth—" chanted the child.

"Creator of heaven and earth," corrected Carew.

"Creator of heaven and earth," parroted the child.

"And Jesus Christ, his only son—"

"And Jesus Christ, his only son—" parroted the child.

"Our Lord, who was conceived of the Holy Ghost—"

"Our Lord, who was conceived of the Holy Ghost—" parroted the child.

"And born of the—"

"And born of the— Oh. Gee. I used to know it."

"When did you know it?"

"Quite a long time ago."

Carew frowned. "About a year ago," she tried.

"You have not been saying it lately?"

"No, and the things I say every night are 'Hail Mary' and the 'Our Father'."

"Did you ever hear of a little prayer they used to call 'An Act of Contrition'? You use it to say you were sorry for your sins?"

"No." The child was trying desperately to please. "And then at school we say one sometimes that I know, about Pretty World."

"What is that?"

"It goes in the middle, it is about sheep in the pasture—go your way unto His gates of thanksgiving."

"Is this a prayer that they read in the school?"

"No, there is a notice up, and everybody has to read it in the morning."

For Carew the most important issue had become the one in which he felt sure of his superiority and infallibility. There was no fooling him about Catholicism and it annoyed him the way little Gloria stumbled through her prayers at breakneck speed. He concluded that the child's religious education had been sadly lacking and was determined to repair this error.

The child sat frozen in the chair. Someone asked her if she wanted a glass of water. She answered yes because, "I thought they expected me to, but I didn't want the water." Then the child squirmed in her chair and someone suggested she go to the bathroom. When she'd climbed back into the chair, she tried to change the subject. "You ought to come out sometime and see my pony and everything," she said, trying to play the friendly hostess.

Carew, seeing an opportunity to begin to effect a reconciliation, suggested, "Why don't you take your mother out there with Mr. Burkan and show them all around?"

"No, I don't want to. She has seen my pony, anyway."

"The first thing you know, you will be just as fond of your mother as you are of your aunt."

"No. I won't."

Carew was getting nowhere. He turned to Herbert Smyth and asked him for help, but Smyth was reluctant to question little Gloria. Carew said, "I do not like to have the burden all put on me. You are a man of culture and experience. You should help me if you can."

"I will try," replied Smyth, and asked little Gloria, "Is it on account of the pony you want to be out there?"

"Oh, no."

"Tell me why you want to be out there."

"It is because I love Auntie Ger."

"Does Auntie Ger ever tell you to say anything?"

"No, m—m," she stammered.

"Has she ever said anything against your mother?"

"No."

"Dodo?"

"No . . ."

"Has Dodo ever told you to say—"

Before Smyth could finish the question, little Gloria cut him off, answering vehemently, "No. Nothing! Never!"

"What did you think I was going to ask you?" said Smyth.

"I thought you were going to ask me, has Dodo told me what to say . . . has Dodo ever told me to say anything."

"You say she never did."

"No. Never!"

"Why were you so frightened the other day?"

"Because I thought she was going to take me away," little Gloria answered.

"Was that the only reason?" Smyth asked—her answer seemed so inadequate.

"Yes."

". . . You feel perfectly comfortable when you don't think you are going to be taken away?"

"Yes."

"Can you recollect anything now that your mother ever did to you, used you badly? I don't mean not seeing you; did she ever take hold of you in any way or anything of that kind, if you can remember?"

"I remember quite a very long time ago, when I was four years old and I was in bed, and I was mad, she took a glass of water and she threw it at me. . . ."

"Can you remember anything else that sticks in your memory?"

"No."

"Have you ever said any bad things about your mother to anybody?" asked Smyth.

"Yes. Once I said to my grandmother, I said I did not like her."

"You said that?"

"Yes."

"Is that the worst you said?"

"And then I said I hated her. . . ."

Smyth too was getting nowhere. Carew again took over the questioning. "Do you know what it is to tell a lie?"

"Yes."

"What is it?"

"For instance, if you said—if somebody said to me, 'Do you want to live with your mother?' and I said, 'Yes,' and I really did not, or I said, 'No,' and I really did, it is a lie."

"What would happen to you if you told a lie, promising God not to?" Smyth interjected.

"I don't know."

"I don't think she heard that phrase that you inserted about promising God not to," said Carew.

"If you promise God to tell the truth and you lie, do you know then what would happen to you?"

"No."

"You would expect to be punished in some way."

"Yes."

Burkan cut in. "Mr. Smyth, I do not think that is fair. The little child says she does not know what will happen to her. Then you suggest to her that she will be punished. She said she did not know what will happen to her."

"What do you think would be the punishment?" Smyth persisted.

"Well—that IT would happen!" she blurted out. Then checked herself. "I don't know." No one inquired what IT was.

"You don't know? Do you know whether or not it is wrong to tell a lie, especially if you promise God not to?"

"Yes, it is wrong, I know that," said little Gloria.

"What other name do you call yourself beside Gloria?"

"Jo . . . from the movie of *Little Women*. . . . Everybody out there has some name from that because we liked the movie so much. Gerta is Beth and I am Jo." Then, as if to confirm the truth of her testimony, she reached into her pocket and produced a small white linen square. "You see here I have got a handkerchief with Jo on."

"But your name is Gloria?" said Carew.

"Yes, except I just took the name Jo for a pet name, I like that better."

"What is the character in *Little Women* you took that from?"

"Katharine Hepburn."

"What does Auntie Ger do with regard to reading to you? Or what has she done with regard to reading to you?" asked Carew.

But the child answered another question—as if she knew she would be asked if Aunt Ger paid any attention to her. "For instance, she goes down and rides in the pony cart with me, and goes and feeds my pony, and we talk a lot together, and she comes in at night to say good night, and I go in and see her, and we talk."

"Does she read to you sometimes?" asked Smyth, gently easing her back onto the track.

"Yes, sometimes."

"Did your mother ever read to you?"

"No. Never."

"Did she ever see you read?" asked Carew.

"No."

"Did she ever buy any books over there in Paris?"

"No."

"Has your mother written you any letters since you have been down there, since two years ago?"

"Oh, she wrote to me once and told me that she was going to Europe."

"Didn't she send you any letters?" asked a surprised Carew.

"No."

"Didn't she send you any Christmas cards, Easter cards?"

"No."

"Do you get letters down there from your friends?"

"Oh, yes, lots."

"Did you get letters from your grandmother?"

"Oh, dozens of them, and then I would get postcards, and things like 'I love you,' you know, all those postcards and things."

Smyth now asked: "Jo, in some of the letters you have written to your mother you have got lots of crosses and little circles?"

"I know," admitted the child. "Well, I had to do that, because I was afraid of her."

It remained clear that the child feared her mother and would not willingly return to her, but in this entire examination no adequate explanation had been provided. Carew declared a short recess and, while the child sat swinging her legs, he drew Burkan aside and they whispered together. Nathan Burkan sat next to little Gloria and began to take over the questioning. His voice was gentle as he asked, "Gloria, are you frightened now?"

"What?"

"Are you frightened now?"

"Yes," she replied in a tiny voice.

"Of whom are you frightened?"

"My mother."

"You don't see your mother in this room?"

"No."

"Is there anybody here of whom you are afraid?"

"No . . ."

"The judge is a kindly gentleman, isn't he?"

"Yes."

"You are not afraid of anybody here in this room?"

"No."

As if sensing Burkan's never-let-go attitude, the child asked, "How many more questions are you going to ask me?"

"I don't know, darling. I am just going to try to ask a few questions, and when you are tired you say, 'I am tired.' "

Burkan established that Gertrude Whitney, her grandmother, her nurse, Mr. Gilchrist, and Mr. Crocker all had asked her repeatedly if she liked her mother and wanted to go back to her and she had told them, no. He also asked if in her plays at school she was "taught to repeat lines and memorize speeches." And little Gloria said she did "pretty well" at it. Burkan spoke of the Grace Moore movie little Gloria had seen at Radio City Music Hall. "Did you tell your mother that you enjoyed the movie very much?"

"No, to tell the truth I really didn't like it much, because I was afraid of IT! I was afraid that she was going to do something!"

"You were afraid, with your mother?"

"Yes."

"But you did tell your mother that you enjoyed the movie very much?"

"No. I didn't say I liked it very much. I just said that I liked it."

"And you didn't really like it?"

"Yes, but the whole time I was really worrying. . . . She said, 'Did you like the picture?' And I said, 'Sure.' "

"And when you said that, did you mean it?"

"Well—"

"Did you really mean it, darling?"

"No."

"Do you often do that, little Gloria? . . . Do you often tell people things that you really don't mean?"

"No. I only tell my mother that I like things and I really don't, because I am afraid of her."

"You are afraid of your mother?" Burkan asked yet again, and yet again the child replied, "Yes."

"And you have always been afraid of your mother?"

"Yes."

"Always . . . you hated your mother?"

"Yes."

"Well, did you ever in all the letters that you wrote to your mother say, 'Mother, I hate you,' or, 'Don't like you,' or, 'I am afraid of you'?"

"No."

"Now isn't it true you said that the reason you didn't like your mother was because she had taken a dog away from you when you were four years old?"

Little Gloria leaped upon this reason: "Yes," she agreed eagerly, seemingly searching for reasons to give her dread a name. And her mother had knitted her a sweater that "was too small. It was about up to here," she said, indicating a place halfway up her chest.

"Did you write your mother that it was too small?"

"Yes. I said, 'Dear Mummy, I like the sweater and hope you are well. From Gloria.' "

"When you said that, you meant it, didn't you?"

"No."

"Do you want the kindly judge to understand that you wrote something you really in your little heart didn't mean?"

"Yes!" replied the child stubbornly.

In this ten-and-a-half-year-old, Burkan had found a worthy adversary; she would brand herself a liar before she would say what he wished her to say. Burkan's posture with this child had been a loving, gentle one, he called her "darling" and asked what she believed "in your little heart," while this child, in return, with every word she spoke, destroyed his case. Burkan searched his memory for positive things that Gloria had told him. "When you went to bed at night, four years ago, did you say a little prayer?"

"Yes."

"And wasn't it a prayer like this, 'Now I lay me down to sleep and pray the Lord my soul to keep. If I should die before I wake, I pray—' "

Little Gloria finished for him, " 'I pray the Lord my soul to take.' "

" 'My soul to take,' " repeated Burkan. " 'God bless Mommy—' "

"No!" The word shot out like a slap.

A dogged Burkan continued, "Mommy, Naney, Dodo, and everybody in the household?"

"No. I never used to say that. I used to say, 'God bless everybody in the household.' And I used to say, 'God bless Naney, God bless Daddy, and God bless Dodo.' "

"But you never said, 'God bless Mommy'?"

"Never."

"That, you never said?"

"Never."

"Never?"

"Never!"

Burkan picked up the packet of photographs little Gloria had brought to court and began to show them to her one by one.

Burkan held out a photograph of little Gloria beaming a bright smile at her mother. "You were smiling at your mommy, weren't you?" he asked.

"Yes, because when I was kneeling there, the photographer said to smile. And I did."

"And at that time you hated your mommy?"

"Yes."

Burkan presented a picture of Gloria as a tiny baby in her mother's arms. "You didn't hate her then, did you?" he asked—pointing.

"Oh, well, I was a baby then."

"How old were you when you began to hate your mother?"

"As soon as I could understand things. I mean as soon as I could talk."

"You began to talk when you were about two years and a half."

"Yes, it was about then."

"So when you were about two years and a half, you began to hate your mother?"

"Yes."

"And when you were two and half years old, you began to be afraid of your mother?"

"Yes."

This conversation seemed illogical and Carew interrupted, "What did your mother do to you that made you feel that way when you were a little bit of a tot like that?"

"Well, for one thing she was mean to me and never used to let me see anything of her. She never used to come into my room to kiss me good night."

Burkan returned to the photographs, but now little Gloria identified her father but refused to identify her mother. "I don't recognize her," she said. Again and again, Burkan presented photographs and, again and again, little Gloria refused to recognize her mother.

"The little baby in your father's arms is yourself?"

"Yes."

"And on the other side do you recognize the woman in the picture?"

"No."

"You don't recognize the woman?"

"No."

Another photograph and the question, "You say to the kindly judge that you do not recognize the woman in the picture as being your mother?"

"No."

And yet another: "Little Gloria, I show you this picture and ask you whether . . . the lady in the picture doesn't look like your mother?"

"No, that looks more like a friend of my mother's . . . Mrs. Leeds. She was Princess Xenia, or something like that, of Russia. Can I go now?" the child pleaded.

"Just a few moments. Just be patient," answered Carew.

Another picture. Then, "Don't you recognize the woman in this picture as being your mother?"

"No, it doesn't look a bit like her, I don't think."

And another. "No. I am sure. It doesn't look a bit like her."

And another. "Now, little Gloria, I show you this picture and ask you if you recognize the lady in that picture?"

"No."

"You don't recognize the woman? That does not look like your mother?"

"No."

"Just take a look at it."

"No, I don't think it is. It looks more like a painting."

"But assuming that it is a painting, doesn't the painting look like your mother? Just look at it."

"No, I don't think it does."

Burkan would not stop. He presented one photograph more. The child's mother was holding her in her arms. "Who is this lady?"

"My mother?"

Burkan smiled triumphantly. "And who is the little baby there?"

"I suppose me."

"I offer it—" Burkan began, but the child's voice cut him off. "I wouldn't know it otherwise, though."

"What do you mean that you wouldn't know it otherwise?"

"What I mean is, I don't think that my mother would have anybody else in her arms."

"And the only reason why you say that the little girl is yourself is because you wouldn't suppose that your mother would have anybody else in her arms?"

"Yes."

Burkan felt this child was making him out to be a monkey's uncle. He extended yet another photograph to the child. "Now, little Gloria, I show you this picture and I ask you whether—"

The child cut in with a rush of words, "See"—she pointed to the photograph—"there I am not smiling."

Burkan put down the photographs and reached for a pile of letters. He had begun to treat this child as if she were an adult adversary. Gone were the gentle phrases and pet names as he began questioning her about the many affectionate letters she'd written to her mother. Her answers to his questions seemed farfetched, perplexing, sometimes ludicrous. Little Gloria would not admit that her mother had ever done her a kind act, or that she had ever loved her mother. She denied the past and said that she had hated and feared her mother, "always." How could she say otherwise? If she admitted that she had ever loved her mother, then the judge might let her mother *take her away* and *do something* to her. Then IT would happen.

Burkan pointed to a letter. "Just look at this letter. I am calling your attention to Relator's Exhibit 52 . . . you asked your mother to send you a jumping lion. You also said you had a small lion that she gave you. Also a pussy cat and a bull. You asked her for those things, didn't you?"

"Yes."

"Do you say to the kindly judge that when you asked for those things that she never sent them to you?"

"No."

"What?"

"I never remember."

"Now, is it that you don't remember or that she didn't send them?"

"She didn't send them. I am sure."

"Now, you are sure?"

"Yes, positive."

"Now, little Gloria, in one of your letters from Old Westbury, you wrote, in Relator's Exhibit 13, 'If you love me as I love you, no knife can cut our love in two. From Gloria.' "

"Yes. Well, I put that there because she said, 'You are going to live in New York with me,' and that was about that time that I was most scared of her."

"So because she told you you were going to live in New York and you were scared of her, so you wrote her, 'If you love me as I love you, no knife can cut our love in two. From Gloria.' Is that right?"

"Yes."

"Now, when you wrote to your mommy, 'Dear Mommy, I hope you are very well. I long to see you back again,' you really didn't mean that, did you?"

"No."

"You then hated her and you were afraid of her?"

"Yes."

"And you did that just to fool her, didn't you?"

"I really never remember writing those letters. Never remember it!"

"Please look at that, because I don't want to fool the good judge, and tell him whether that is not in your handwriting. Is that your handwriting, Gloria?"

"Yes, I guess it is."

"When you said, 'best love and kisses from Gloria,' you didn't mean that?"

"No."

"You wanted to fool your mother?"

"Yes."

"Now in this letter, when you were at the Sherry-Netherland, you said, 'Dear Mommy, I hope that you are very well and having a happy time. I miss you so much. . . . Much love from Gloria.' . . . At that time, at the Sherry-Netherland in 1932, you hated your mother?"

"Yes! . . . Can't I go now? . . ."

Burkan sought vainly for one admission of love from the child to her mother. The child said she'd hated her mother since she was two and a half years old, yet letter after letter was bursting with love and with longing. "This is a child that craves affection," Dr. St. Lawrence had said of little Gloria, and Gertrude Whitney had testified that the child felt her mother did not love her. This was a child who had been left alone with Dodo for months at a time, not even knowing where her mother was. Every time little Gloria felt hurt or lonely, she made a wish "for a father living and a mother who loved him and loved me." Even now, she kept saying to herself, "When I grow up I'll marry and have a lot of children and I'll love them so much they'll never be lonely or unhappy."

Burkan showed little Gloria one of her letters written in April of 1934. "You signed it 'Much Love' . . . then you have five X's and three O's . . . what do the five X's and three O's stand for?"

Little Gloria pointed to the X's and said, "Kisses." Then to the O's and said, "And they are hugs."

"And at that time you hated your mother?"

"Yes."

"Nobody told you that it was a wrong thing for a little girl to write something that she really didn't mean? . . . Nobody ever taught you that?"

"No. You see, if I told her the truth, I was afraid that she will do something." The child was trying to explain.

Burkan did not ask what she meant by *do something*. He tried to show logically that since her mother was away there was nothing harmful she could do to the child. And he began badgering little Gloria as to times and dates, the way he would an adult witness. "Your mother was not down in Old Westbury in April 1934, was she?"

"No."

"What was it your mother could do to you at that time?"

"Well, when she came back she could have taken me away."

"At that time she had not in any way told you she was going to take you away from Old Westbury or from school?"

"No."

"So, you really had nothing to be afraid of."

"No—except I just was."

"You were afraid?"

"Yes."

"What was it? What was the thing that you were really afraid of?" It was an imperious demand.

And again little Gloria answered it the only way she could: "Well, I was afraid that she would take me away."

"She didn't tell you she would?"

"She said, 'When you go live in New York with me we'll go and see lots of movies and we'll have a nice time and go and see sports and everything.' "

"That was in June; so that before that you had no reason to be afraid of your mother or to hate your mother?"

"No," little Gloria admitted.

But Justice Carew joined in the inquisition. "Did you?" he asked.

"Yes."

"Before that."

"Yes."

"Why?"

And little Gloria answered yet again, as she had so many times before, "Because I was afraid that she was going to take me away."

As Burkan began leafing through the letters once again, little Gloria spoke up. "If you will ask Mrs. Morgan to show you the letters that I have written to her, you will see how it was . . ." But her reasons had not been enough for them. Burkan was reiterating them, "She took your dog away . . . she threw some water at you. What else was it your mother did to you? Tell the kindly judge what was it that she would do?"

He was demanding more reasons. "Well," began little Gloria. "For instance," she said. Then like the start of a fairy tale out came the lie. "Once it was very late at night and we were sitting in the living room, and they were smoking, and I was sitting beside her, and she had a cigarette, and she deliberately put it on me and burnt me."

"Who did that?" interrupted Smyth, suddenly coming alive.

"My mother," lied the child.

Even Emma Sullivan Keislich, who had amply demonstrated that her hatred for Gloria Vanderbilt knew no bounds, was to say that it was Prince Hohenlohe, not the mother, who had burned the child with a cigarette. Prince Hohenlohe too remembered the same incident. He had reached to hug the child, and his cigarette touched her arm. It was a small accident and he blew on her skin to make it better. But if these men demanded an example of cruelty to explain the child's fear, little Gloria had given it to them.

All Burkan's efforts to get the child to admit one moment's affection for her mother had failed. He continued his questioning for a few moments more, going over the same territory. "The only reason you were afraid of your mother, you say, is because you thought she was going to take you out of school, away from Aunt Gertie?"

"No," said little Gloria. "You see, I have always been afraid of my mother." A moment later she pleaded once more, "Can't I go now?"

"Just one half a second," said Burkan. "I won't keep you another half a second."

But Justice Carew signaled Burkan that it was enough. The examination was ended.

The child climbed down from the chair and turned to the three men. "Goodbye," she said politely.

"Goodbye, girlie," answered Carew.

Little Gloria walked out the door. She had testified for two hours and twenty-five minutes. Before this judge, she had repudiated her mother. "I hate my mother . . . I was afraid she would take me away . . . I was afraid she would do something . . . then IT will happen . . . as soon as I could understand things . . . I hated her . . . I have always hated my mother . . . always . . ." As an adult, she would say "They never thought of what they were doing to me. No child should ever be brought into court."

Justice Carew would see no deeper than the surface testimony. The moment the child walked out his door he had, in effect, decided this case. He knew it would take a great deal more time than he had anticipated to effect a reconciliation between mother and child. In all good conscience, he could not force this child to go back to her mother and an atmosphere that he felt was "in every way calculated to destroy her health and moral character." The rest of this trial—the entire Vanderbilt side of the case—would be a mere formality. From this moment on, Carew would seek ways to back up a decision that the child had made for him. Within the week, Carew would change his ruling to admit all the damaging documents against Gloria Vanderbilt, to erase the fact that privilege had ever existed between Gloria and Thomas Gilchrist.

On leaving the courtroom that night, Nathan Burkan, too, knew it was over. He went for a drink with Jim Murray and told him, "Jim, start building a record for the appeal. We want the record to be as strong as possible when we appeal Carew's decision. . . . That kid's a real Sarah Bernhardt," he told Murray. "She was coached within an inch of her life. The way she jumped in to say her nurse had never told her to say anything before Smyth even asked the question, the way she said all the good things Mrs. Whitney did for her. There I am, holding her love letters to her mother in my hand, and she swears they're hate letters. It was some performance."

In his chambers, Justice Carew was giving the press an account of the child's testimony far removed from the reality of the situation. The newspaper accounts were almost identical in content. Said the *Daily News*:

Justice Carew stated, "Little Gloria wanted it understood that she did not dislike her mother. It was simply that she hadn't seen much of her. And when she was in her mother's care they travelled all over Europe. . . ." She said she could not recall whether her mother had neglected her. Justice Carew steered back to this question several times because there had been contradictory testimony by others on the point.

Her real fun did not begin [little] Gloria said, until a couple of years ago when she began living at Old Westbury. Here she rides a pony of her own and plays with little cousins and neighbors' children. . . . The words fell naively and without rancor from the ten-year-old girl's lips.

NO ANTIPATHY TOWARD MOTHER, said the *Times*:

In the most natural setting the Supreme Court could offer . . . the child made it plain that she did not dislike her mother. She had not seen very much of her. She simply and positively did not want to be taken away from Mrs. Whitney. She did not remember much of London and Paris where she had lived. What she remembered principally was that she moved about a great deal. . . . Her good times began two years ago when she went to live with Mrs. Whitney at Old Westbury, Long Island, where she plays with a number of cousins her own age and has a pony.

If reporters had listened more carefully, which they did not, they might have understood that the case was over. "I could render a decision right now but after Mr. Burkan and Mr. Smyth get through, I might become befuddled," Carew told them and then cited several cases in which the child's wish had prevailed. "Of course, it would depend on her intelligence, and so forth," he added.

"Little Gloria is an unusually bright child," commented a reporter.

"I know nothing about children," replied Carew.

The reporters whooped with laughter. "You ought to, you have five of your own," said a voice.

"I know nothing about that. They're their mother's concern," Carew answered.

"How are you going to decide the case?" one persistent reporter asked.

"Gentlemen of the press," said Carew, "I suggest you see the D'Oyly Carte production of *Iolanthe*."

"What?" asked a reporter.

"*Iolanthe*," repeated the Justice.

"In *Iolanthe*," the *Times* pointed out, "the Lord Chancellor lets his ward make her own decision." But Louis Frohlich, an aficionado of light opera, came to another conclusion. "That's not true," he said. "What the Lord Chancellor does in *Iolanthe* is adjust the law to suit his whim. He turns the law topsy-turvy."

The Vanderbilt Side

She had the best of everything.

OLGA WRIGHT

NATHAN BURKAN was a man in a maze. Every way he turned, he found himself blocked. It was time to present his side of the case; a case he was already resigned to losing. The greatest problem was the child herself: he had to try to prove that she should be returned to her mother in spite of her own testimony.

It was his contention that the nurse and Mrs. Whitney had systematically turned the child against her mother, that little Gloria had been bribed with gifts, that she did not want to leave her friends, her school, her country life. But even to Burkan these reasons seemed inadequate to explain little Gloria's all-encompassing fear and hatred of her mother.

In mounting his case, what mitigated most strongly against Gloria Vanderbilt were the witnesses who did not appear. If the accusations were untrue, where were Nadeja Milford Haven, Agnes Horter, and Helen Marye Thomas—all of whom Burkan had said would testify for Gloria? Where were the loyal servants he had said would testify?

Where were Drs. Schloss, Hunt, Gavin, Turpin, Helie, and the others who Burkan told reporters had pronounced little Gloria in perfect health? Constance Bennett had left town. Burkan told reporters A. C. Blumenthal would testify (but privately repeated his vow to keep Blumie off the stand). He said he would call Captain Jefferson Davis Cohn and William Rhinelander Stewart—"frequent escorts of Mrs. Vanderbilt"; actor Thomas Meighan; "Rumanian oil magnate Felix Ferry"; F. L. Emory, "the night bell captain at the Sherry-Netherland"; and a dozen other character witnesses. Not one of these people ever took the stand.

Burkan had eliminated several of these witnesses in examination before trial. His discussion with Theobald Mathew had convinced him to abandon his plan to discredit Gertrude Vanderbilt Whitney's character, and therefore the witnesses ready to testify about Mrs. Whitney's wild bohemian life were not called. Lily Lagler arrived in New York ready to testify and gave Nathan Burkan her intimate letters from Sheriff Bob Chanler, as well as several books of his drawings. When Burkan said she would not be called upon to testify, she asked Blumie for the expense money he had promised her, he refused to give it to her, and she promptly hired a lawyer to sue him.

What Burkan was left with was a group of pitifully weak witnesses —Gloria's family, who stood by her no matter what; a raggle-taggle group of servants, not one of whom had been with her for longer than two years; acquaintances who had been to dinner perhaps once or twice; Prince Hohenlohe, her former fiancé, and his wife, Princess Margarita, whose presence nobody could explain. The witnesses who appeared presented a poor case. The ones who did not appear condemned Gloria by their absence.

Burkan would have to resort to picking on the smallest discrepancies in the Whitney case. He would try, and fail, to prove that the nurse and Mrs. Morgan had placed the incident where Prince Hohenlohe and Gloria were in bed together, in different villas, in different years. He would use the false allegation that the only photograph of her mother that her child had was one which had been cut from a magazine advertisement for Pond's Cold Cream, and try to use it as a prime example of how her mind had been poisoned. But this was indicative only of the paucity of his case.

With the first witness Burkan called, Lawrence Copley Thaw, it became obvious that the Vanderbilt side of the case was weak. Thaw, a tall, aristocratic, impeccably tailored member of the New York Stock Exchange, was the owner of the mysterious house at 13 East Sixty-ninth Street to which Theodore Beesley said he had delivered Gloria Vanderbilt at 2:00 a.m. and had seen the door opened by a man. Thaw testified that he was a cousin of Consuelo's husband, Benjamin Thaw, and had known Gloria Vanderbilt for several years. On every occasion when she had visited, his wife was present. He and his wife had gone to Gloria Vanderbilt's for tea, dinner, and parties.

Burkan inquired, "Not that there has been any direct charge made, but so that the record may be clear, were you ever guilty of any act of impropriety with Mrs. Vanderbilt at any time or any place?"

"Never."

Burkan began a series of questions which he would hammer out at every witness he put on the stand, sometimes repeating these questions over and over again. Thaw testified that he had seen "no acts of impropriety with respect to any person male or female, no drunkenness, no off-color books with nude men or women."

These denials on the part of witness after witness had the reverse effect desired by Burkan—they underlined the very points he was trying to disprove.

In his cross-examination, Smyth was brief, trying to prove that Thaw's wife had not always been present when this gentleman met with Gloria Vanderbilt. When he could not prove this, he excused the witness.

Thelma, Lady Furness was to be the next witness. Thelma felt this trial was "outrageous" and all these people—from Mrs. Whitney to the crowds that waited in the street, to this judge—were "monstrous." How dare they drag her sister into this courtroom? Had they no respect for the privilege of class? They were crucifying her sister as if she were no more than a common adventuress. Thelma walked up the Supreme Court steps, her cigarette held firmly between her scarlet lips. At the very last moment before entering the building, she removed it from her mouth and flicked it in the direction of the crowd.

Reporters seeing Thelma take the stand thought it was Gloria who was testifying, but the bailiff explained that it was her twin. Thelma was closer to Gloria than anyone in the world, and had shared her sister's life. From the witness stand, she described this life as a gossamer fairy tale made up of an ideal marriage between Reginald and Gloria, and a childhood for little Gloria filled with luxury and love. She began by recalling her early life with Gloria up through the time of Gloria's marriage. In 1925, she'd gone with Gloria and Reggie to Bad Kissengen and then to Vichy. Thelma said of her brother-in-law, "He was ill. He was taking a cure—a rather severe cure," but the word alcohol was never mentioned. As far as she knew, every time Reginald and Gloria went away, little Gloria was left with Mamma Morgan and Miss Keislich. "Miss Keislich was always with the baby." She said that the parents were loving and affectionate toward each other and toward the child. "Mr. and Mrs. Vanderbilt were devoted to that baby. When they used to be together, there used to be arguments as to who was to hold the baby. That sort of thing."

As Thelma described the years in Europe after Reginald's death, her testimony inadvertently revealed the tremendous distance between little Gloria and the adults who surrounded her. About once a month Thelma and Lord Furness would go to Paris, he to buy racehorses, she to buy clothes. Thelma would arrive at the Charles Floquet triplex bearing gifts for little Gloria, "dolls or little trunks with a doll in it to change their clothes. . . . The baby used to come in from the park and she used to ask the butler if Mrs. Vanderbilt was in. You could hear her from the hall. She used to rush into the room and go up to her mother and throw her arms around her and kiss her. And then she used to say, 'Hello, Aunt Toto.' She called me Aunt Toto. She used to kiss me. And then Mrs. Vanderbilt took her on her lap and asked her what she had been doing in the park. And she was picking daisies or buttercups, whatever it was that was in season."

According to Thelma, little Gloria led an ideal childhood. She "was given her own car and chauffeur. . . ." She always had "absolute freedom" to go anywhere she wanted in any of Gloria's residences. Her sister would play with the child. "She used to take her up to different pictures that were around, and she used to say, 'Who is that, Gloria? Who is this?' And she used to know. There was a picture of Mr. Vanderbilt and the baby in his arms, and there was a picture of Mme. Balsant."

"Balsant? How do you spell it?" asked Burkan, confused.

"B-A-L-S-A-N-T, I think," said Thelma.

Gertrude Whitney's face reflected the disgust she was feeling. Consuelo Vanderbilt, her dear first cousin, now Mrs. Louis Jacques Balsan and formerly the Duchess of Marlborough, was not even known to this woman. Gertrude felt Thelma had no interest in anything about the Vanderbilt family—except, of course, its money. What Thelma said next confirmed this.

"There was a picture of Mr. Vanderbilt's own father, a big picture of him."

"That was Mr. Cornelius Vanderbilt?"

"I should think so, yes. I don't know *who* his father was."

Burkan asked Thelma questions about the various places the child had lived, all of which she described in glowing terms. There were residences in England, France, Switzerland, and New York. First, there was Burrough Court, Melton Mowbray, in Leicestershire. Life here was described as an English country idyll. The mansion was set on three or four hundred acres, Thelma was not sure of the exact number. "Little Gloria occupied the nursery . . . with a room next door for the nurse. . . . In England the nurses do not sleep with the children. They sleep in another room." But Keislich refused to use this room and insisted on sleeping with the child.

"Were there any children in the neighborhood?" inquired Burkan, as if asking about an average middle-class child.

"There were lots of children—" Thelma hesitated. "There were the Blandford children—the Duke of Marlborough died six months ago and Lord Blandford became the Duke of Marlborough—they were sort of cousins of Gloria's. And then there were the Duprett children . . ." she said helpfully. "Mrs. Duprett loves hunting and she has a place about fifteen miles from where I used to be."

"During the time that little Gloria was at Melton Mowbray, at your house, at the time you are speaking of, did Gloria ever ride any horse?"

"Yes, there were ponies there . . ."

"Was she permitted to ride them at random, or did the groom lead the pony?"

"Well, she was very tiny, and the groom used to lead her with a leading rein. . . . She also had a pony cart that I gave her to go to meets for the hunting . . . it used to amuse Gloria to see the men in their pink coats, and that sort of thing."

Thelma was convinced that during the two years the child lived with Gertrude Whitney she'd been influenced against her mother. Thelma recalled that she had visited little Gloria at Wheatley Hills and had asked her, "Gloria, aren't you coming back to stay with me in England?"

"No, I don't like England."

"Why? You used to love it there," Thelma said.

"Oh, I don't like it because I don't have any horses there."

"Gloria, you did have horses—don't you remember you had a pony and a cart . . ."

"I don't remember."

Then Thelma turned to Dodo and said, "Why, Dodo, have you told her that she didn't have any horses?"

"Why, of course I haven't, Lady Furness," nurse Keislich replied.

Thelma testified that her sister had always taken excellent care of little Gloria. In fact, she said, Gloria had rented a country house, the Three Gables, because little Gloria had a stomach attack. No doubt

Thelma was aware that no one would bring up the proximity of Three Gables to Fort Belvedere, the residence of the Prince of Wales, so she blithely explained, "Dr. Gavin said she must have eaten something that must have upset her stomach. It was rather cold in London and the doctor said that after this tiny upset, he thought it would be better for the child to go and live in the country, so Mrs. Vanderbilt then took the Three Gables."

Carew interrupted—something did not make sense—the English countryside in winter was hardly less cold than London. "Her mother had her out in the country three or four months because of her poor health?" he asked.

"Because she had this tummy upset," answered Thelma, as if this were the most logical explanation in the world.

Blatantly playing to Carew's predilections, Thelma declared that both she and Gloria had had the strictest of Catholic educations. Burkan introduced as exhibits Holy Cards and Catholic prayer books belonging to the twins and even a Mass card, obviously a commercial advertisement, which was misprinted, "For the repose of the soul of MR. C. VANDERBELT."

Thelma reported that she had visited little Gloria at bedtime. "Mrs. Vanderbilt took me two or three times upstairs to the nursery when the child went to bed, and the child used to cross itself, make the sign of the cross, and say Hail Mary. She said that in French because we'd been taught to say our prayers in French."

Carew asked, "How old was she when she used to make the sign of the cross?"

"About three years old, Your Honor."

"I was talking to her yesterday. [She] didn't make any suggestion . . . that she ever knew anything whatever of making the sign of the cross."

"She made it in front of me, Your Honor," protested Thelma.

"Well, she has forgotten it. If she ever made it in front of you, she did not evidence any knowledge of it yesterday. It has disappeared, so far as I could see yesterday, entirely from her mentality," he said significantly.

"Well, she was a very young child."

"I know. She has lost it," pronounced the judge in an accusatory tone.

"We are not responsible for that, Your Honor," said Burkan, responding to the tone.

"I don't know who is responsible for it, but if it was taught to her, she certainly didn't know anything about it yesterday."

"I can't help that," said Burkan, implying the fault lay with Mrs. Whitney.

"I know you can't help it. I am not saying you can help it, but the child did not display the slightest knowledge of anything about making the sign of the cross yesterday. I watched her and gave her every opportunity." Carew would not let this point go. "Nobody ever mentioned the sign of the cross in this case until I mentioned it this morning here. There is one thing above all others that is characteristic of the Catholic. It is the making of the sign of the cross. If you go over on the river front and see a fellow jump in, he will make the sign of the cross before he jumps in, if he is a Catholic. I have seen Jewish boys make it when I jumped in the water. There was a gang of us who lived around the neighborhood . . ." His mind seemed to wander off to this childhood scene.

"I hope Your Honor is not finding fault with us," protested Burkan.

"I am not finding any fault with you, but I am saying that yesterday the child did not give the slightest knowledge of making the sign of the cross. . . . If you want me to make an announcement now, the child's spiritual and religious education has been very, very sadly neglected. I do not know who is responsible for it, or at least I am not saying who is responsible for it. But this child's religious education has been badly neglected . . ."

"But I hope Your Honor does not find fault with me because—"

Carew was well aware that Burkan was a Jew. "With you? I don't expect *you* to teach the child the sign of the cross."

Smyth began his cross-examination. It was stinging in its brevity—the antithesis of Burkan's technique. Once Smyth had explained, "Often, the most effective cross-examination is silence." His cross-examination was devoted to one point only:

"Did you marry a Catholic the first time?" Smyth asked.

"No."

"Did you marry a divorced man?"

"Yes."

"Was his wife living?"

"Yes."

"When you married him?"

"Yes."

"How many times had your first husband been divorced before he married you?"

"I object to how many times her husband had been divorced. Suppose he was divorced fourteen thousand times. What has that to do with this case here?" said Burkan.

But Carew said, "Diligent Catholics do not marry a man who has been divorced fourteen thousand times. If the lady wants to assume the character here of a diligent Catholic, she is opening herself to cross-examination on that point. If she wants to present herself to me as a diligent Catholic, I will permit her to be probed on that subject to the limit."

"I was his second wife," said Thelma.

"Wasn't he divorced altogether, including yours, four times?" asked Smyth.

"Yes, but I was his second wife."

"She certainly is not responsible for the last two," commented the judge.

"Isn't it true that Lord Furness had been married before you married him?"

"Yes, he was married, and she died. He was a widower when I married him."

Thelma ended her testimony by stating that she had divorced Lord Furness in 1932. At that time, Gloria had married once, Thelma twice, once to a divorced man. Harry J. K. Morgan had twice married divorcees and Consuelo had married twice.

This probing infuriated Thelma, who took the brief examination as a personal assault. A recess was called, and she stormed into the corridor trembling with rage. The reporters begged Thelma for a statement, and she answered with a denouncement of Gertrude Whitney. "That woman has always had what she wants. Why should she want to adopt this child when asylums are full of lovely children who would appreciate being adopted? If my sister had four or five children, I could understand her trying to do this because she was fascinated by this particular child. But why is she trying to do this when my sister has only one baby?"

Inside the courtroom the questioning continued. Olga Wright was on the stand. She had served as Gloria Vanderbilt's personal maid from July of 1926 to September of 1928. Carew commented, "This ought to be a good witness. She saw two years of the life. Tell us what you saw for two years." Olga testified that the child and her mother were always affectionate and that little Gloria led an ideal life. "She was very happy . . . sometimes she was on the beach with her mother. . . . She had the best of everything."

But Olga knew little else of what went on in the household. "My work was upstairs, so I did not know what was downstairs." In the summers in Biarritz and the winters in Paris, Olga had never seen any "drunkenness," "dirty books," or "acts of impropriety with any male or female." She also testified that although Prince Hohenlohe had lived in Mrs. Vanderbilt's villa both summers, she had never seen him: Not once!

This was more of an admission than Burkan had bargained for, and he tried to jog her memory. "I do not remember ever seeing him," Olga continued to protest. "I tried to remember, but I do not remember." In this light, Olga's testimony that the mother and baby enjoyed a most loving relationship seemed somewhat suspect.

Smyth in his cross-examination demolished Olga's credibility. Since she had never seen Prince Hohenlohe, there was no point in asking her about the incident where Mrs. Morgan and the nurse said they'd seen Gloria and the prince in bed together. "In fact, you didn't see what went on in that house, did you?"

"I was upstairs."

"Well, I mean you were the perfect maid. You didn't see anything that went on," he observed, and excused the witness.

Another servant, Monica Duffy, took the stand to testify that she had worked for Mrs. Vanderbilt at 12 East Seventy-seventh from late March, until the end of April 1926, as a temporary parlor maid. Monica said she remembered this household well because she liked Mrs. Vanderbilt very much and found her to be an affectionate mother. Monica recalled standing in the passage which led to the kitchen and looking out into the downstairs hall. "It was a very large room and there were two or three marble pillars and there was a recess which held a dressing table and a wash basin and so forth and the telephone, and that was hidden by red plush curtains. They would play hide-and-go-seek, and the little girl would always want her mother to do the hiding—she did the seeking—and there would be screams of joy when the little girl found the mother." Monica was "fascinated" by the game.

Once again Smyth speedily dispatched the witness, proving that Monica Duffy had worked for one month only, eight years ago, when the child was two years old and Reginald Vanderbilt had been dead for only six months. Smyth commented, "It is surprising that she saw or remembered anything."

Harry Judson Kilpatrick Morgan took the stand. The bearer of the name of the Civil War general had a weak face, with an underslung jaw and a dull look in his eyes. A fringe of short dark hair encircled a balding head. He was thirty-six and muscular, a man devoted to sports. He had recently taken as his second wife a woman of considerable fortune and had purchased a villa in Cannes and a ski chalet in St. Moritz. Harry Morgan was a man who found it difficult to concentrate or to stay in one place for any length of time. It had been Harry Morgan's idea to bring a film into the courtroom, taken in Paris and Biarritz in 1926, which he showed to Justice Carew, pointing out what a happy two-year-old little Gloria had been. Then, under Nathan Burkan's careful questioning, he described his sister's life. His "actual connection" with his sister, he testified, started in 1926 after Reginald's death. That summer he lived with her in Biarritz. They lived a very quiet life and at night went to movies and the theater and "on very rare occasions to a nightclub."

"Your mother stated that she was left at home at nights, and that you and your sisters would go off," said Burkan.

"I am afraid it is the other way around, Mr. Burkan. . . . As a rule, she used to go the casino herself."

"Your mother likes the casino?"

"Yes."

Justice Carew was not ready to accept this picture of the elderly rosary-fingering Mrs. Morgan. "She went out and *you* stayed home?" he asked.

"Yes, sir."

Carew provided a rationale for Mrs. Morgan's behavior. "You mean she liked to see the people and made friends there."

"Oh, I presume she did meet them," replied Harry Morgan laconically.

In September 1926, Harry Morgan returned with his sister to Paris and moved into her Charles Floquet triplex. Here, he reported, he became his sister's "constant companion."

"During the time that you lived at the Charles Floquet house, did you ever see any act of lewdness or lascivious dancing, or any wrongdoing, or any act of impropriety, or excessive drinking, or loud or boisterous talking, or any action that involved moral turpitude and involving acts of impropriety?" asked Burkan.

"I never did."

"The nurse Keislich said that . . . there were books with dirty pictures."

"There were not any."

"You had none?"

"No."

"She said in your sister's bedroom there were books with dirty pictures."

"I never saw any there."

"She says that the child had picked up a picture representing a tongue."

"A what?"

"A tongue."

"That was at the Alfred Roll house," corrected Smyth.

"In any event, at the Floquet house you say there was no lewd, lascivious, or obscene or dirty pictures?"

"No, sir."

Burkan guided Harry Morgan through a recitation of the noble and titled guests who had visited Gloria's various residences. Smyth kept interrupting to establish that the Russian titles were no longer recognized. "He's an ex . . . he's an ex . . ." Smyth kept saying. An expression of irritation clearly marked Justice Carew's face. When Burkan pressed for more names of those who had visited Mrs. Vanderbilt, Carew said in a voice which should have served as a warning, "I do not believe I ever heard their names before. I have listened to the names and they do not mean a thing to me. . . . Names like Dimitri or Dimisky, and they do not mean any more to me than Oleinski or Oskaloosky . . . they do not make a bit of impression on me."

Burkan, concentrating on his own line of questioning, apparently did not listen to Carew's tone. "Can you give us the names of some of the people that came there?" he persisted.

Harry Morgan began to list names. Captain Glenn, who had been an attaché of the British Embassy; Mr. and Mrs. Roy McWilliams, the American consul in Biarritz; the Marquis of Portago.

"Was he a Portuguese?" asked Smyth, well aware of Carew's attitude.

"No, sir, he is a Spaniard. A grandee of Spain."

"They're ex, too," said Smyth, implying that the title was just so much nonsense.

"I cannot help that," said Harry Morgan defensively.

Carew warned Burkan once again. "Do not stress too much on that exalted and aristocratic nobility, because this little girl is an American citizen."

"But, Your Honor," protested Burkan, "they tried to paint a picture that the people who came there, that visited the household, were people that were just not right, not proper people."

"They did not do it by giving their names. . . . They did it by describing specific particular details and acts," said Carew.

"They mentioned Constance Bennett . . ."

"Constance Bennett?" asked Carew.

"Yes . . ." replied Burkan.

"That did not mean anything to me, either," the Justice snapped, his voice full of barely suppressed anger. "I do not know whether I have indicated to you that some of the names do not appeal to me at all. As I indicated, this child was a little American girl. . . . Pardon me. I shouldn't give as much expression as I do to my opinions. I prefer to keep quiet." Carew stared straight ahead.

"But Your Honor must also bear this in mind," said Burkan, taking it upon himself to instruct the judge, "Mrs. Whitney herself said that one of her sisters, I believe, had married Count Széchényi—"

Carew exploded. "I do not know who he is. I never heard of him. He doesn't mean any more to me than the Duke of Bologney! I do not care if he was the king's bedfellow or bedmate. That kind of stuff does not make a bit of impression here." Carew glared at Harry Morgan as if he were an unpleasant insect. Everything Carew abhorred, this man represented. Harry Morgan was a parasite on society: weak, pleasure-seeking, jobless, worthless.

But Burkan would not, could not, let it go. He addressed the witness. "These people that came there, were they, so far as you knew and so far as you could see—I am going to follow His Honor's suggestion and I am not going to go into names now—were they decent, reputable, respectable people?"

"In my own personal opinion, they were," said Harry Morgan.

"Your opinion does not make an awful lot of difference," snapped Carew. "What did you see them do?"

"They acted like perfectly normal human beings."

Carew shook his head and made his pronouncement. "Perfectly normal human beings often do things that are disgraceful. The nature of man is such that he falls into sin, so that the fact that he is normal does not indicate that he is virtuous. He may be sinful and be normal."

Carew adjourned until the following Monday and called the lawyers into his chambers. Carew felt that Burkan was filling these proceedings with meaningless, superficial nonsense. He had given the Whitney side a leisurely three and a half weeks to present their case but now he warned, "If this case is not concluded within the week, I will institute evening sessions." Burkan protested that his side must have time to present the Relator's case, to which Carew replied, "Have time is one thing. Waste time is another."

"Mrs. Vanderbilt needs her evenings to rest. She has not enough strength to return to court then," said Burkan.

"Then let us proceed with haste," Justice Carew cautioned him. Nathan Burkan was so upset that he inadvertently put his hat on backward as he left Carew's chambers. When reporters asked him what had happened, he answered, "I'm not supposed to talk to you," and trudged wearily down the hall.

. . .

Justice Carew had said he would discontinue his press conferences—he never did. He felt that only by seeing the press could he impose a dignified version of the proceedings on the public. But, in fact, he had become a laughingstock; his bowdlerized summaries were so radically different from the testimony being leaked to the newspapers daily. Friday night, reporters filed into Carew's chambers to find him glowering at them—one foot up on the desk. He gave them the briefest account of the day's testimony and told them that he'd definitely decided that the child was to have a proper Catholic education; then he dismissed them for the weekend. Carew's behavior and the secrecy he was imposing were becoming increasingly irritating to reporters, and the weekend newspaper coverage was more critical of him than ever before.

> In a resolution introduced before the Committee of Courts and Practices of the Federal Bar Association, lawyers today denounced Supreme Court Justice John F. Carew for barring the public and press . . .

> With grievous damage already inflicted upon the plaintiff, who is asserting the most natural of rights, with every sympathy and presumption in her favor, the court saw fit to clamp the lid of secrecy on all further evidence. The plaintiff protested . . . her counsel protested . . . and yet the court has seen fit to brush aside these fundamental considerations of justice. The judge's course in this matter is wrong. . . . The judge has obviously made a mistake—and a grievous one.

> This judge is incomprehensible.

Everybody Wore Pajamas

[Mrs. Morgan's] only accusation . . . against me was that I was trying to murder the child . . . that was a theme song of hers.

PRINCE GOTTFRIED HOHENLOHE-LANGENBURG

LOUISVILLE, KENTUCKY: ten days after her kidnapping, Mrs. Alice Speed Stoll was recuperating happily at her Lime Kiln Lane estate where crowds of hundreds gathered to welcome her home. On Friday, Frances Robinson, wife of the alleged kidnapper, Thomas Robinson, Jr., had picked up the $50,000 ransom and brought it to her husband in the Indianapolis apartment where he was holding Mrs. Stoll captive. After counting the money, Robinson prepared to lock Mrs. Stoll in a closet and leave. His wife pleaded with him to go without her, for she feared Mrs. Stoll would die of suffocation. Finally, Robinson left with the ransom. Mrs. Robinson made Alice Stoll breakfast, and then both women turned themselves over to the Indianapolis police.

Flemington, New Jersey: Bruno Hauptmann was granted his wish to hold his baby son, Manfred, in his arms. A guard unlocked the jail "bullpen" and Margaret McCrane, wife of the warden, handed him the child. He stroked the child's head, kissed his eyes, and began to cry.

Long after the child's departure, Hauptmann could still be heard sobbing.

New York City: Alfred E. Distelhurst, following instructions from his daughter's kidnappers, checked into the New Yorker Hotel. He complied with the kidnappers' first demand by inserting the following ad in the *News*: "Dorothy, come home, father in New York at same place, room 1736, please write."

Monday, October 29, 1934: Dr. Oscar Schloss appeared at the Supreme Court at 9:45 a.m. He told reporters, "I have been summoned by Justice Carew, you may say that I am a dispassionate witness." Although Nathan Burkan had announced that he would call upon Dr. Schloss to testify, he did not do so, and when Carew asked why, he gave the excuse that Mrs. Whitney had paid one of his bills. Burkan did not like it that Schloss found Gloria Vanderbilt to be an inattentive mother. However, the Whitney side would not call him either; Smyth did not like it that he found the child to be more fearful and apprehensive than neglected and physically ill. Carew felt that this man had "an intimate knowledge of the case" so he sent him a note asking him if he would give testimony, and Schloss agreed.

For the past two years, Schloss had served as the first head of the Children's Hospital of New York Hospital. His had been an overwhelming and frustrating job. The enemy was not disease, with which he could deal, but poverty. Once Schloss had diagnosed the symptoms, he realized the appalling frequency of the condition—malnutrition. In the hospital he could build these children up and stress to the parents the importance of the right foods, but then he would be forced to send them back to the abject poverty that rendered his instructions and treatments useless.

In October of 1932, the New York Health Department had released statistics that more than 20 percent of New York City's school children were suffering from malnutrition. At that time, there was no federal aid program, so in addition to a Herculean load of administrative duties, treatment, teaching, and research, Schloss took it upon himself to seek money to sustain these children. He raised $350,000 but pushed himself past his limit into illness and a sense of despair. He had resigned his position in July and had only just returned to private practice when he was called upon to testify in a case where a mother and aunt struggled for custody of a child worth millions. Yet, for the child herself, Schloss felt sympathy: he remembered little Gloria as a child in desperate trouble.

Dr. Schloss said that he would have to testify from memory, explaining that when he'd resumed private practice, his secretary had gone over his records for the past twenty years, and since they had no storage space, on her own initiative, had burned the records of all his inactive cases.

He said he'd first seen little Gloria when she was an infant and her father was still alive. "At that time she was a perfectly well little girl. From that time on, I saw her very irregularly, perhaps two years might elapse without my seeing her. . . . At no time do I recall a serious or any particular illness until 1932."

In the spring of that year, Schloss referred the child to Dr. Stuart L. Craig for the removal of her tonsils and adenoids. Her convalescence from the operation was "uneventful." However, following the operation, the child was not well. "I remember one occasion, for example, and subsequent to this, a number of other occasions, she complained of abdominal pains. There was a very strong nervous element in her illness . . . she complained she was fearful of dying."

"So that in your opinion, it was nervous a great deal?" inquired Smyth.

"That was certainly a strong element in it. I cannot say that she may not have had some trivial and obscure cause for an abdominal pain, but it was nothing of sufficient gravity to make her feel as she apparently did at that time."

After her operation, the child was sent to Mrs. Whitney's estate in Old Westbury. "She was extremely apprehensive, very nervous, but I could determine no evidence of any organic condition that there was to be concerned about. . . . She was agitated and apprehensive and fearful she was going to be hurt, that something was going to be done to her." Schloss had pondered what this might be, but had come up empty-handed.

Smyth asked what the attitude of the mother had been while little Gloria was under his care. Schloss replied carefully, "I saw no definite action on the part of the mother, and heard her make no statement which I could interpret as a lack of interest. But I was impressed with the fact that her solicitude in my contact with her and her contacts with me, during the illness, was considerably less than I am accustomed to see in the mothers of my sick patients." Although over extended periods of time he visited little Gloria every day, he saw only the nurse. "I said to the nurse that I ought to be able to see Mrs. Vanderbilt, that I wanted to talk directly to her, but that was rendered possible only on very rare occasions."

Burkan inquired, "Did you tell Dr. St. Lawrence in September 1932, 'Thinks there is little physical, all psychological with nurse'?"

"Yes, yes, I very probably told him that," replied Schloss. "My feeling at the time when I left this child was . . . that her symptoms were due, to a considerable degree at any rate, to a mental and emotional upset."

"A psychological condition that was communicated by, or for which the nurse was at least in part responsible—isn't that true?"

"Yes, that is quite true," affirmed the doctor.

"So you found fault with the nurse, didn't you?"

"I found fault with the nurse, not with reference to the care that she gave the child. She was devoted to the child. She gave the child everything that she had to give. The fault with the nurse was merely the fact that this woman was terribly apprehensive about the child . . . which is always hard for a child."

"And all that influenced the mental state of that child?"

"I think so. Yes."

"Doctor, you knew there was a physical condition that affected this child's nervous condition, did you not?"

"Did I know there was a physical condition that affected her nervous system?" Schloss repeated. He knew of no such thing. He'd always disagreed with the other doctors on this point. "I cannot say that," he answered. "I only recollect there were certain changes in the X-ray plates, which I did not interpret as being of sufficient significance to explain her illness."

Burkan tried to prove that Mrs. Vanderbilt had been attentive in respect to the child's medical care, but every question he asked made his client seem less interested.

Had she visited the office?

"If she did, it was a very rare occasion."

Had she phoned when a problem came up?

"No, I would not say she did that voluntarily . . . there would be oftentimes considerable lapses of time."

Hadn't Mrs. Vanderbilt called him about one-thirty in the morning when the child was ill at the Sherry-Netherland?

"My only recollection of a night visit is that Mrs. Morgan called me up one night."

Schloss admitted that the ideal time to remove tonsils and adenoids was when the inflammation had subsided, and said he very well may have told Mrs. Vanderbilt that it was preferable to wait until summer.

Carew thanked Dr. Schloss for his testimony, saying, "I am much obliged to you," and excused the witness.

Harry Judson Kilpatrick Morgan resumed his testimony. He'd lived at his sister's Biarritz villa when Prince Hohenlohe was there, but he knew nothing of the incident in which his mother allegedly saw Prince Hohenlohe and his sister in bed together. However, "My mother did not like Prince Hohenlohe."

"She disapproved of your sister marrying a European, is that a fact?" Carew asked.

"No, sir. She disapproved of my sister marrying Prince Hohenlohe," he said, and explained that Mrs. Morgan did not object to titles or Europeans since she had approved Consuelo's marriage to Count Jean de Maupas and Thelma's marriage to Viscount Furness.

Carew addressed Harry Morgan. "Neither of your sisters who married these foreigners had an infant child with a lot of money?"

"No, sir."

It was Smyth's turn to cross-examine. Carew's apparent disdain for the witness showed Smyth which path to follow.

"What do you do for a living?" asked Smyth.

"I am chairman of the board of directors of a company known as Duraflex, Ltd., London . . ."

"I suppose you get fees at directors' meetings?"

"I do."

"Is that all you get?"

"I am the biggest shareholder in the company."

"Where did you get the money to buy the stock?" demanded Smyth.

"I object to where he got the money to buy the stock," said Burkan. "I do not see how that is competent, where he got the money to buy the stock."

"I am going to show that these people have never done anything for themselves," explained Smyth.

"Show that!" exclaimed Justice Carew.

"I am trying to. I am starting."

"Well, show it," the judge demanded impatiently. "When did you get interested in this concern?" asked Carew, taking over.

"About a year and a half ago, Your Honor."

"What is it?"

"We manufacture industrial transfers."

"What are they?"

"A transfer, Your Honor, is you print something on a piece of paper, you wet it, and then you put it on either a railroad car or window, possibly, and it is indelible and does not come off. Instead of painting it by hand, it can be applied directly."

"Oh, you mean it is what we used to call decalcomania when I was a boy . . ." said Carew.

"When did it last pay a dividend?" asked Smyth.

"It has only been in existence since 1933."

"Then it has never paid any dividends?"

"Not yet, Mr. Smyth."

"Well, what visible means of support have you outside of directors' fees?"

"I have no visible means of support. . . ."

"To be put in this family is not a very pleasant picture," commented Smyth.

Carew said patronizingly, "Well, it might not appeal to an energetic and virile, ambitious man, but, nevertheless, what of it?"

Smyth walked to the Whitney counsel table where Theodore Miller handed him a newspaper clipping—an account by C. F. Bertelli of a party Gloria had given in August of 1926, at a time when her brother testified she was in deep mourning and "hardly went out." Smyth read the headline: ROYALTY GIVEN LAVISH FETE. Knowing how Carew loathed titles, Smyth began reading from the article: "Don't you remember that 'the Count and Countess de Llovera, the Marquise de San Carlos de Pedrosco, the Countess Robilant, the Marquise de Casa Montalvo, the Duke del Arco, the Marquise Orelana, and a host of other titled guests dined heartily on the grounds'? Don't you remember that?"

"Mr. Bertelli is the man who runs the scandal sheet of the New York *American*. You know the newspapers exaggerate."

Smyth began openly sniping at Harry Morgan. When he reported that he had motored through the Pyrenees, Smyth asked, "Whom with?"

"I went with a lady and gentleman, a maid and a chauffeur."

"Were *you* the gentleman?" asked Smyth.

"No, another gentleman besides myself."

"Now, Your Honor, are we going to have these caustic comments all through, and insults," breathed Burkan with a sigh.

"What is the insult about . . . calling him a gentleman?" inquired Smyth blandly.

During his redirect examination, Harry Morgan made a stumbling attempt to justify his indolence. He explained that he had enlisted in the army in July of 1917 and had fought in the Argonne offensive. "I was slightly gassed at Vache de Veauville, near Verdun . . ." The gas "had the effect that during a certain number of years I did my best to work in the consular service. I was eventually transferred to Glasgow, where the climate for me was no good. I couldn't stand it there and I had to resign. I go to St. Moritz in the wintertime on account of the altitude."

HAUPTMANN ADMITS LIES!

PARK ROW HOST TO VANDERBILT ARISTOCRACY

Morgan Clan and Allies Dine with Business Workers in Busy East Side Thoroughfare

Prince and Princess, a titled lady and members of America's untitled aristocracy assembled as witnesses in the family feud over little Gloria Vanderbilt, rubbed shoulders with everyday business workers and dined in a Park Row restaurant yesterday.

The unconventional interlude came at recess in the proceedings before Justice Carew in the Supreme Court for the custody of the child.

Prince and Princess Hohenlohe und Lagenburg, Lady Furness and Mrs. Benjamin Thaw Jr., Mrs. Gloria Vanderbilt and Harry H. Morgan drove from court to Solomon's restaurant near Pearl st. With difficulty they obtained two tables in the crowded hour. Without difficulty, they assimilated goulash and soup and rye bread

ATTRACT INTEREST.

Other guests at the restaurant, "spotting" the party, ceased eating to study them. Solomon, proud of their distinguished patronage, yet fearful of the diminishing re-

MAYFAIRITES VISIT MR. AND MRS. EVERYDAY CITIZEN

ENJOY HARDY FARE—There was no caviar on the bill of fare, but the Morgan clan and allies enjoyed luncheon on Park Row as above photo indicates. They ar[illegible]incess Hohenlohe, (2) Nathan Burkan, (3) Mrs. Gloria Vanderbilt, (4) Harry H. Morgan, Jr., (5) Prince Hohenlohe, and (6) Lady Furness.

—N. Y. American Staff Photo.

Prince and Princess Hohenlohe-Langenburg

PRINCE HOHENLOHE DEFENDS GLORIA

Story on Page 3

"Are you able to do inside work, to work steadily in an office?" asked Burkan.

"I can for a certain time, but not for a long time."

Smyth took over to inquire sarcastically, "You didn't have any trouble about this gassing until after Mr. Vanderbilt died, is that it?"

"I was in the consular service when Mr. Vanderbilt died."

"Then you became busy as the right-hand man of your sister?"

"I wouldn't say that entirely. After Mr. Vanderbilt's death . . . I tried my best to hold my job as well as I possibly could. I had a lot of trouble doing it."

"I have no further questions." Smyth had finished with this witness.

Reggie's old friend, Forest O. March, was the next to take the stand. He knew nothing of Gloria's life abroad, but remembered that she "was constantly attentive to the child. . . . And when they were in Paris, she sent for toys for the child to be sent over from here, because she couldn't get them in Paris." In 1927, March remembered that he'd sent a tricycle and an Indian squaw suit over to Mrs. Vanderbilt by steamer.

Smyth did not bother to cross-examine this witness.

The members of the press, their faces pressed to the windows, awaited the next witness, Gottfried, Hereditary Prince of Hohenlohe-Langenburg. Before him sat two women, Princess Margarita, his wife, and Gloria Morgan Vanderbilt, his former fiancée. Reporters noted that a serene Margarita gave Gloria "a reassuring smile" as her husband began his testimony.

Hohenlohe gave his impeccable lineage—a crazy quilt of European royalty: his married sister was the Duchess of Schleswig-Holstein, his father a first cousin to the former Empress of Germany, his mother a first cousin to the former Emperor of Germany and a sister of the Queen of Rumania.

As for his occupation—Prince Hohenlohe stated that about three months previously he had been given the job of managing his father's estates at Langenburg, in the state of Württemberg, and in Weikersheim, their second residence. These estates comprised 4,000 hectares (9,884 acres), one-quarter in farmland and the larger part in forest timber.

After Carew's negativism toward Harry Morgan and his sneering at royalty in general, Nathan Burkan had warned Prince Hohenlohe to expect the worst from the judge. But instead of irking Carew, Prince Hohenlohe seemed from the outset to win the judge's sympathy and approval. Hohenlohe's frankness and forthrightness appealed to him. When asked what work he was doing from the summer of 1927 until the end of 1928, Hohenlohe replied, "From the summer of 1927 to the end of 1928 I was doing nothing."

Hohenlohe spoke perfect English and informed Justice Carew, "I have always spoken it at home as much as German." (He did not add that this was natural, since his mother was a daughter of Queen Victoria's son Alfred, Duke of Edinburgh.) Before taking over his family's estates, he'd been in the brokerage business. "I used to make . . . between $150 and $300 a month. I think I made $400 one month" (which was approximately the same amount as the combined monthly salaries of Gloria Vanderbilt's nurse and chauffeur).

Whenever Smyth tried to discredit Hohenlohe, Carew would rush to his defense. When Smyth referred to Hohenlohe's lack of money, Carew said, "This man didn't say he had any fortune. His family had just this land. He was very frank about it." And when Smyth attacked Hohenlohe for saying, "I don't know the inside of Mrs. Harry Payne Whitney's efforts to obtain Mrs. Vanderbilt's child, but there must be dirty work behind it," Carew said, "There was a dirty charge made against him . . . and I suppose that he was just man enough to say those that throw dirt at him are dirty themselves."

With Princess Margarita beaming up at him, Hohenlohe told of his love for Gloria Vanderbilt. Burkan again described the alleged incident in which Mrs. Morgan and the nurse said they had seen the prince in bed with Mrs. Vanderbilt. "I want you to tell His Honor whether at any time or any place any such scene or event took place."

"Never, Your Honor."

"Were you ever in Mrs. Vanderbilt's bedroom at any time or any place?"

"No, sir."

"Did you at any time or any place commit any act of impropriety with Mrs. Vanderbilt?"

"Never."

Prince Hohenlohe then said that the entire summer of 1927, "as long as I was there, Mrs. Thaw was in the room" with Mrs. Vanderbilt "the whole time, till we left, and we left together. . . ."

"Were there any acts of impropriety committed by anybody?"

"No."

"Excessive drinking?"

"No."

"Any lascivious action on anybody's part?"

"No."

"Any wrongdoing?"

"Nothing."

"Any drunkenness?"

"No."

"Did you meet a person known as Lady Milford Haven?"

"I have known her ever since I can remember. She is a vague relative of mine and we used to play together when we were children. She is just my age."

"Have you ever seen her commit any act of lesbianism?" Burkan inquired bluntly.

"No."

Burkan asked about the child's assertion that her mother had burned her with a cigarette. "The nurse says that the child told her it was you who had burned it with a cigarette."

"That is true." Hohenlohe described the incident. "I think it must have been the autumn of 1927, and Mrs. Vanderbilt was out, so I stayed in the sitting room to wait till she came back. And during that time the nurse and the child came in from their daily outing, and shortly afterwards the nurse walked into the room with the child and asked me, 'Is Mrs. Vanderbilt in yet?'

"I said, 'No, she is not.'

" 'Well,' she said, 'could I leave the child with you for a moment because—' I don't remember, either she was going to go out for a half an hour or she had to telephone or something.

"So I said, 'Certainly, leave her with me, and I will take care of her until Mrs. Vanderbilt comes.' And we started playing and I built a sort of house out of chairs for the child, and the child was very lively and she jumped around and was having a good time. And I was telling her some story in connection with this house and who we were and what she was and what I was; and I was sitting on the floor, and suddenly the child jumped for me, as children will do, and I was smoking when she bumped her arm—I think the upper part of her arm—against my burning cigarette and started to cry. And I took hold of her and I cuddled her in my arms, and said, 'It is nothing. Look at it, it is gone.' And I blew it, and five or ten minutes afterwards the child had forgotten it."

"Did you ever hear of any occasion that the mother burned this child?" asked Burkan.

Hohenlohe was shocked: "I have never heard of it on any occasion at all where Mrs. Vanderbilt could possibly have hurt the child."

Staring out at his wife, Hohenlohe said that when Gloria had broken off their engagement, both he and his mother had begged her to reconsider. He had pleaded with Gloria to marry him even if the child's allowance was "cut off," telling her that he would find a way to get money, but it was she who was adamant about breaking the engagement.

Hohenlohe described the opposition he'd received from Gloria's mother. "Around the month of May 1927, she started to be hostile toward me for no reason that I could detect."

"Tell His Honor what she said and what you said," instructed Burkan.

"It is difficult to say what Mrs. Morgan said because she is very incoherent: she says a lot of things and stops and begins another word. But as far as I could make out, she objected to me personally. She objected to my marrying Mrs. Vanderbilt on the ground that I had no fortune to speak of, and she accused me of all sorts of things—wanting to murder the child, and such ridiculous things as that."

"What else did she accuse you of? Did she accuse you of being intimate with her daughter?"

"No."

"Or having committed any acts of impropriety?"

"No. It had nothing to do with that. . . . The only accusation that she ever wrote—that she ever wrote up against me was that I was trying to murder the child once I got married to Mrs. Vanderbilt."

"That is, if you married Mrs. Vanderbilt, you would murder the child?"

"Yes, sir."

"What did you say to that?"

"In the beginning, I laughed. Of course, in the end, when these accusations, openly or covertly, were brought up perhaps a hundred times, I got mad."

"These accusations . . . that if you married Mrs. Vanderbilt, you would murder the child?"

"Yes. I mean that was her theme, that was a theme song of hers."

"Of complaint against you?"

"Of complaint against me."

"But during all this while, she would dine with you?"

"Oh, yes."

During his cross-examination, Smyth was to underline this theme of murder. "You have said in your direct examination that you had conversations with Mrs. Morgan in which she asserted that she was afraid that the child would be done away with in some way. Do you remember that?"

"Yes, sir."

"Did she charge you with that?"

"Of course. That was her chief argument she used against me."

"What did she say when she made these charges?"

"Well, she said in substance that she knew that the moment that Mrs. Vanderbilt and I had married, we would do away with the child."

"Did she say why she thought that?"

"No, she never said why she thought anything."

"Did she say anything about any motive she thought underlay—"

"No, never. I said Mrs. Morgan is a very incoherent person. I mean she comes forward with a thing like that, and then you ask her, 'Why do you think so?' and she says, 'Oh, I didn't say it. I didn't mean it that way.' "

Smyth handed Prince Hohenlohe a copy of the *American* which contained the interview he had given on the *Bremen* and pointed to a paragraph. "Isn't it so, that you told the reporter that really the reason that the engagement was broken was that you and Mrs. Vanderbilt feared that if you married and lived abroad, Gloria's income would be cut off?"

"No, sir, I never said such a thing. I said Mrs. Vanderbilt broke the engagement entirely for the good of the child. And then they asked me, 'Does that mean that the child's income would have been cut?' and I said, 'Yes, I understood as much at the time.' "

Smyth would accept no evasions. "I am going to find out now whether you have been misquoted or not by this *American* reporter. 'Mrs. Vanderbilt feared if we married and lived abroad, Gloria's income would be cut off.' Did you say that?"

"No. It was the other way around. I said if the child's income were cut or had been cut, it might have meant the necessity of us living abroad, which Mrs. Vanderbilt did not think was the right thing for Gloria's future welfare."

"There is nothing of that kind in the quoted interview."

"No."

"Were you told that the Surrogate objected or would object to the allowance to Gloria's mother being used to finance any foreign marriage?"

"Yes. Well, it amounts to that. It did not say any foreign marriage, to any marriage at all."

"Here is another paper that also quotes you." Smyth picked up the *Herald Tribune* and began reading from it. " 'As I understand it, there was a question of finance involved. There was a possibility if Mrs. Vanderbilt married and settled abroad, she might be cut off from the allowance she was receiving from the American court which had charge of her child's estate.' This is in quotation marks."

"Yes, that is the trend of what I said."

"So that really what you had in mind was that if you lived abroad and the child's income would be cut off, that Mrs. Vanderbilt would not be so well off?"

"No. I have said all along, sir, that Mrs. Vanderbilt said she could not take it upon herself to have the child's income reduced and, through that, perhaps not giving the child what was her due as a Vanderbilt and as heiress of the fortune she had."

Smyth again referred to the newspaper. Having visited in Biarritz, he knew exactly what Prince Hohenlohe meant when he referred to the newest mode of resort wear—lounging pajamas. (Gertrude Vanderbilt Whitney had bought a closetful of them on her last trip abroad.) But Smyth was also well aware of Carew's provincialism and took advantage of it to suggest that the life in Biarritz had been a dissolute one in which people went around day and night dressed for bed. He pointed to the *Herald Tribune*. "You said in your interview here when you arrived that in Biarritz everybody wore pajamas. Do you remember saying that?"

"Yes, sir."

"Even the nurse?"

"Well, I said that the nurse wore a bathing suit. It does not say anything about pajamas because she never did."

"Then you had in mind that the life that was led at Biarritz was rather an intimate one, so far as contours were concerned?"

"Well, everybody was bathing on the beach the whole time."

"No, but you said that even at dinner you wore pajamas?"

"Yes, very often we did not change the whole day."

"The life at this villa was such that the ladies and the men wore pajamas from morning till night, is that right?"

"Everybody does in Biarritz, sir, if the weather permits. I mean it was an exceptionally hot and fine summer, so most people—"

"You mean in these villas. Not in the hotels, though?"

"Well, in the hotels too. I mean if you went to the Hotel Miramar, for instance, there would be lots of people dining in the bar in their bathing costumes and their bathing cloaks or pajamas—beach pajamas," said Hohenlohe, as if everyone knew exactly what he meant.

Smyth, knowing that the Justice had never heard of this attire and no doubt remembering that he'd had to explain to Carew what a negligee was, continued his questions. "Pajamas and negligee was the order of the day among the ladies that Mrs. Vanderbilt had as her intimates, isn't that right?"

Prince Hohenlohe missed the nuances of this question. He answered, "Well, among everybody I saw there."

"You concentrated on Mrs. Vanderbilt's circle, didn't you?"

"Yes. I mean, after all, that was a circle within a circle. You cannot live in Biarritz without noticing practically everybody that is there. It is not such a big place as all that."

"Particularly around the American colony and the friends of the American colony. They lived a rather loose life?"

"It was not a loose life. It was a very comfortable life . . . not what I call a loose life, not with an inflection toward their morals."

To bolster the image of Prince Hohenlohe as a man of substance and breeding, in his redirect examination, Burkan entered as exhibits photographs of Hohenlohe's ancestral castles at Weikersheim and Langenburg. Smyth admired the photographs. "It is very nice to see an ancestral home," he said, lulling the witness and Burkan into security. Then, "Just think of keeping up this ancestral home by a man who perhaps earned $300 a month. Your Honor can draw an inference as to the necessity of the child's fortune." Hohenlohe's testimony was finished.

During the luncheon recess, the reporters watched Princess Margarita pat her husband's hand. "What did you think of his testimony?" one asked.

"I thought it was very good," she replied.

"Did your wife learn anything about you she didn't know before?" a reporter asked the prince.

"I don't think so," said Hohenlohe.

"Did you refute the charges made against you?"

"I certainly did," he replied excitedly. As he spoke of his testimony, he withdrew a crested cigarette from his gold case, put it in a long, ivory cigarette holder, and made several attempts to light it with his gold lighter, but his hands were trembling so badly that he could not do it. Princess Margarita took the cigarette from him, lit it, and returned it to her husband. With a broad smile, he turned to reporters and said that as soon as Princess Margarita had given her testimony they would return to Europe to attend the wedding of the Duke of Kent to Margarita's first cousin, Princess Marina of Greece, to take place on November 29 at Westminster Abbey. They planned to return home, get more clothes, and then go to London.

"What do you think of this trial?" he was asked.

"I can't say . . . I don't want to be thrown in one of your jails before I leave here. I'll write you when I get to Europe."

"What did you do while you were here?"

"I went to the movies four times, had one haircut, danced at the Casino in Central Park, saw *Personal Appearance*, and ate baked beans: A mighty fine dish!"

Gloria

If there is any justice in heaven or on earth, the judge will give me back my child!

GLORIA MORGAN VANDERBILT

NATHAN BURKAN had carefully set the stage for Gloria Vanderbilt's appearance on the stand. When the trial began, Burkan advised her to dress as if she were in mourning and to leave her jewelry at home. At first she'd dressed as he'd instructed, but she could not part with her jewelry—her armor against the world. As the accusations against her multiplied, Gloria came to see the wisdom of Burkan's advice. Burkan also had arranged for Lillian Fisher, a trained nurse they'd engaged after the traumatic visit to Wheatley Hills, to be at Gloria's side at all times. As Burkan had planned, Lillian Fisher, in her starched white uniform, provided the perfect touch as Gloria tottered into the courtroom on her arm. Gloria would have her requisite collapses in full view of the press, and nurse Fisher would administer to her in the crowded corridor. Gloria would provide floods of tears directed at newsmen. At the close of each session, reporters would observe Gloria "in a state of complete exhaustion," "comforted by her twin sister and assisted from the courtroom by nurse Fisher," "unable to move for twenty minutes after the justice left the bench."

In his effort to create a picture of a bereft, ill woman, subjected to an incredible ordeal, Burkan did not fully realize that he had produced the real thing. If her appearance of vulnerability and illness was carefully calculated to elicit public sympathy, there was also, without doubt, true suffering. It was a terrible thing for this woman to see her life smeared across the headlines. When the newspapers referred to this trial as "Gloria Vanderbilt's ordeal," they were indeed accurate. She was in a state of nervous collapse and was slowly retreating into illness. She refused to leave her bed except for court appearances and press conferences and would eat no solid food. For the first time in her life, she was not even able to communicate with her twin sister, Thelma. After her sessions on the stand, she would immediately go to bed and lie there in stony silence, unwilling or unable to speak. During the course of the trial, Gloria went from 124 pounds to 107. She developed phlebitis so painful and acute that she was forced to appear on the stand with her left leg bound from ankle to knee. The day that little Gloria had thrown the key in the fire, Dr. Jessup had prescribed a sedative for Mrs. Vanderbilt. Now nurse Fisher's brown glass bottle of sedatives was always nearby.

Because Burkan's associate Jim Murray was young, presentable, and Catholic—in other words, Gloria's social equal—he was assigned the job of escorting Gloria and nurse Fisher to court. Murray felt as if "I was walking on eggshells. There was a glazed look about Gloria. She would take forever to get ready. Then she'd walk out the front door as if we were going to a restaurant or a nightclub—except that she was shaking. There was an utter denial of the reality of the situation, and she seemed sure that eventually the Justice and the lawyers would recognize her for the charming individual she was and leave her alone. She reminded me of someone in a fairy tale who was waiting for Prince Charming to sweep all the bad dreams away. And always there was the glitter and glaze in her eyes. They looked like mirrors."

Tuesday, October 30: At 9:45 a.m. Nathan Burkan appeared on the steps of the Supreme Court to announce that Mrs. Vanderbilt would testify later that morning. In this atmosphere of anticipation, reporters paid little attention to what was going on in the courtroom. At ten o'clock promptly, Margarita, Princess Hohenlohe-Langenburg, began her testimony as a character witness for Gloria. She was dressed in a blue linen dress, oddly out of season for this cool day. Her only jewelry was a single strand of pearls.

Nathan Burkan asked Princess Margarita when and where she'd met Mrs. Vanderbilt. In her shipboard interview, Margarita had told reporters that they'd met "in a nightclub." Under oath, she told the truth. "I met her first in London in 1929 . . . with my grandmother [Victoria, Dowager Marchioness of Milford Haven], with whom I was staying in London." Margarita told of having tea with Gloria and Nada Milford Haven. "Lord Milford Haven is my mother's brother."

"So that Lady Milford Haven is your aunt?"

"Yes. . . . She is a very cheerful, gay person. She is Russian by birth. She is amusing. I like staying with her because we always have a good time." Margarita reported that her aunt's marriage to George Milford Haven was "particularly happy. They have been married seventeen years, and you might think they have been married two years."

Margarita saw Gloria several times and had visited at her Alfred Roll house. She too had never seen any "excessive drinking . . . acts of impropriety . . . drunkenness . . . lascivious or indecent acts."

Burkan concluded his examination by asking, "Are you in anywise related to the British royal family?"

"Yes," replied Margarita. "My father is first cousin of the King of England," and let it go at that, although she might have mentioned a myriad of other connections as well. Herbert Smyth declined to cross-examine the witness.

Elizabeth Wann, Gloria Vanderbilt's forty-three-year-old personal maid, testified next. The witness box was situated below and to the left of the judge's bench. Wann turned in her chair so that she faced Justice Carew, and spoke directly to him in her low, Scottish-accented voice. Burkan instructed her to "talk so the stenographer can hear you." Elizabeth Wann bristled. "How did I know I had to let him know what I was saying? I am talking to the judge. You are supposed to face whoever you are talking to, aren't you? . . . Am I supposed to sit with my back to you if I am talking to you?" she asked Carew.

Before he could answer, Burkan cut in, "Is this the first time you have ever been in a courtroom?"

"Yes, and I hope it is the last time, too!" she replied.

Carew smiled. As Wann gave her testimony, she seemed to establish a rapport with the Justice, who agreed with her canny, down-to-earth assessment of the situation. They began a conversation more intimate and revealing than any Carew had had with the lawyers or principals in this case. Carew asked Wann about the testimony that Mrs. Vanderbilt had often slept till noon. She said that that was true. "Mrs. Vanderbilt has often remarked if she had her child living with her, she would have such a different life, and she would have to get up earlier."

"I have been thinking of that myself," mused Carew.

"She has often said to me, 'If I only had my child here, I would have such a different life.' "

"I have often thought of that myself. It might be a good thing to give her something to take care of."

"She has said, 'There is nothing to interest me. What is there to get up for? If I stay in bed I can read a book.' "

"That is true. There is no doubt about that."

From this moment on, Carew himself asked most of the questions.

Elizabeth Wann said that she was called Wann by both her employer and by the child. When asked questions about Mrs. Vanderbilt's conduct and surroundings, she replied with a flat statement. "I have never seen anything wrong in Mrs. Vanderbilt's home." She did, however, reluctantly admit that A. C. Blumenthal visited Mrs. Vanderbilt, but stubbornly refused to tell Justice Carew how many times she had seen him there. "It was not my business to know that."

Smyth, in his cross-examination, cleverly concentrated on the child's last visit to her mother, when little Gloria had threatened to jump out of the window and had finally fled to Mrs. Whitney's studio. "Going back to the time that little Gloria was there last month . . . the child stayed there from Tuesday to Friday . . . whenever you saw the child there, she was perfectly happy?"

"Yes. She seemed perfectly happy."

"Extremely happy?"

"She seemed all right."

"Did you ever see any more buoyant, happier child than she was during the time she was there from Tuesday until Friday?"

"She seemed perfectly happy."

"When did you see her the last time on Friday?"

"In the morning."

"And she was tripping around?"

"Yes."

"Smiling?"

"Yes."

"And kissed her mother?"

"Yes."

"Very affectionately?"

"Yes."

"She was happy as a lark?"

"Yes. She was perfectly happy."

This witness's loyalty had been established; her veracity was another matter. Smyth asked her if her testimony had been prepared.

"I didn't know what I was going to be asked. . . . One never knows what they are going to be asked down here."

"One never knows what they are going to be asked down here," Smyth repeated, mimicking Wann's Scottish burr. "That is all."

Carew glared disapprovingly at Smyth. What a snob he was. Burkan caught the look and said in a low voice, "That is all."

At exactly 12:45 the elevator doors opened on the third floor of the Supreme Court building, and Gloria Vanderbilt emerged, "dressed all in black. She entered the courtroom leaning heavily on the arm of her nurse, Lillian Fisher." Reporters noted that she "sat immobile at the counsel table next to her twin." According to reporters, her face was "dead white and expressionless," "magnolia white with scarlet lips," "pale and drained of blood." When she began to testify, her hands trembled and she pulled at a handkerchief, knotting and unknotting it. Then, bit by bit, she tore the material to shreds.

Gloria had been on the stand only fifteen minutes when Justice Carew declared a short recess. Accompanied by her brother and trailed by Thelma and her nurse, Gloria walked out into the corridor where the press waited. She looked at the crowd, her body wilted, and she toppled forward in a faint. Her brother caught her. Nurse Fisher rushed forward and administered sedatives from the brown glass bottle. Then, leaning heavily on her brother's arm, Gloria was helped back into the courtroom.

Thelma turned to the reporters and said, "We hope for the best. We hope my sister does not collapse."

Inside the courtroom, Gloria Vanderbilt was beginning what was to become a protracted appearance on the stand. Carew wished to finish up quickly, but Nathan Burkan would not comply, he wanted the record to be as full as possible. Over a period of two weeks, Gloria Vanderbilt was to make seven separate appearances on the stand. Every aspect of her life, from her birth to the present, was to be investigated, first by a sympathetic Burkan, then by a critical Smyth. For the first time, Gloria was forced to examine her own life, and perhaps to realize that it had never been her own.

During her testimony, Gloria used the methods she had used all her life to get what she wanted and to avoid the things she did not want. But here they were to prove pitifully inadequate. First, there was illness: "I faint easily," she said of herself. Her "heart attacks" also caused her to be removed from the scene of any unpleasantness. Then there were tears. In telling of a visit to Dr. St. Lawrence to ask for the return of her child, she said, " . . . in that interview I believe I cried. I am not quite sure. I think I did. I usually do."

In preparation for her testimony, Gloria Vanderbilt had gathered together her passports, letters, photographs, and any dated material she could find and, with Consuelo's help, she'd compiled an itinerary of her travels and her life. It was a chaotic, fragmented document. Gloria clutched the itinerary in her hand as she sat on the edge of the witness chair. Burkan stood below her and to the left. She looked at him for guidance.

He began very gently, as if addressing a child. "Mrs. Vanderbilt, it is very important that you should look the judge square in the eye and speak up so he can hear you because he is very interested in hearing all you have to say."

Gloria Vanderbilt encountered Wann's problem—Justice Carew sat one level above her to her right. She twisted in the chair to look at him, then twisted back to look down at Burkan, then looked up again. She seemed bewildered and confused.

Carew interjected, "It is all right for her to look over there when she is holding a conversation with you. I'll watch her."

"When were you born?"

"August 23, 1905," Gloria whispered, supplying the date she'd been told by her mother.

"I am afraid I will have to ask you to keep your voice up."

"August 23, 1905," Gloria repeated, her voice louder.

"Where were you born?"

"In Lucerne, Switzerland."

"Will you briefly tell His Honor where you spent your early life up to the time that you married Mr. Vanderbilt?"

Gloria studied her notes. She removed her gloves and turned the white pages. "I stayed in Europe until 1916. In 1916, my twin sister, Lady Furness, and I came to America for six months. In 1917, I spent nine months in America, the rest in Europe. In 1918, I spent nine months in the United States, and went to Europe. In 1919, I spent nine months in the United States, and went to Europe. In 1920, I spent nine months in the United States. In June 1921, I went to Brussels where my father and mother were then living. In August 1921, I visited in America until the marriage of my twin sister, Lady Furness. In June 1922, I went to Brussels. In September 1922, I came to America, to the United States of America. In March 1923, I married Mr. Vanderbilt. I stayed in America from March until May in Newport. In May, I went to Europe with my late husband, Mr. Vanderbilt, until August 15 or thereabouts."

"Will you please tell us where you were educated?"

"Well, I was educated until 1916 in Europe."

"Can you give us the names of the school or schools, if you can remember?"

"No, I cannot remember them, there were so many. I was in school in Switzerland. I was in school in Spain. I was in school, I believe a very young school, in Germany. I was in school again in Switzerland, and then I went again to France." She twisted her handkerchief and began tearing at it. "It is very complicated . . ." Within a period of four years, she had attended school in four countries, conducted in four different languages.

By constantly referring to her notes, she was able to trace her life up to the time little Gloria was born, February 20, 1924. Burkan began to explore this period. Gloria denied that she had refused to nurse her baby: "I was very ill at the time. I cannot remember very much of what happened, but I can remember that it was very . . . shall I say that it hurt me tremendously. It made me frightfully nervous. I cried, and the doctor suggested that it would be better for the child to have a bottle. . . .

"My late husband was very anxious to have Gloria—that is my daughter—baptized a Protestant. His first child had been baptized a Catholic. We talked about it at length. I gave him my views, and he gave me his. I agreed that Gloria would be baptized a Protestant."

Again, in chronological order, Burkan asked the witness about her life from the time of her marriage to Reginald's death. "In June of 1924 . . . the doctor . . . told me that if my husband, my late husband, ever had within the next two months what he called hard liquor, he would be a dead man."

"Due to the injunction issued by the doctor regarding the use of hard liquor, you were constantly at the side of your husband?"

"I was constantly with him."

"And there was a time when he left you for a day?"

"Oh, certainly. He used to go to his club. I believe it was the Brook Club. He used to go to the Brook Club . . . in the afternoon, that is."

"But the life was uneventful and was one as would be expected between an ordinary man and wife?"

"Exactly," Gloria replied. She had known no other life and so she described her "uneventful . . . ordinary" life. "My husband—rather my late husband—never went to bed before six o'clock in the morning. By that, I do not mean that he was out. I don't know if he suffered from insomnia or what it was, but he never went to bed before six, and usually he used to go up to the nursery. I myself used to stay up with him until about five. I don't recall his ever going to the nursery at six in the morning because I wasn't there."

"But you say it was a habit of your husband to stay up very late at home?"

"Very late."

"And that was due to some ailment of some sort?"

"I am sure I don't know why he did. When we were out on parties we used to come home about midnight or one o'clock. My husband then would go downstairs. . . . We used to sit around, used to play solitaire . . . he couldn't sleep."

After Reginald's death, Gloria had what she described as "a partial nervous breakdown." She said that her physicians recommended a trip, so one month after Reginald's death she went to Paris.

"Can you tell us the names of the physicians?" asked Burkan.

"Oh, Lord, I have seen so many. No, I don't think I can give you any names now."

Gloria summarized the arrangements she'd made for herself after Reginald's death. She had selected "Uncle George" Wickersham to act for her because . . . "being young, I suppose, I did not know anything about finances—stocks, shares and bonds."

Burkan walked to the counsel table; in his hand he held a series of photographs of little Gloria—happy and smiling. When he presented Gloria with an elaborately framed photograph of Reginald holding little Gloria in his arms, she began to sob. She put the photograph on her lap and looked up, tears flowing down her cheeks. A photographer pressed his camera to the glass pane of the courtroom window and photographed the scene.

Carew saw the flash and looked up. He made a sweeping gesture with his hand. There was another flash. This time, Carew stood up, ran down from the bench and across the entire length of the courtroom, and pulled open the door. "Get back!" he screamed. "Get back!" Carew pointed to a small cross-corridor about fifteen feet from the courtroom doors. "That is your deadline. Anyone who comes closer to my courtroom will be held in contempt." With that, he turned, walked back to the bench, and sat down.

There was a hush in the courtroom. A moment ago they had seen this man totally lose control, now he sat regarding them with serene grandeur. Gloria clutched the wooden rail in front of her. She was shaking uncontrollably.

"Do you feel as if you want to rest for a minute or two?" asked Burkan solicitously.

"No, it is all right," she replied.

Burkan said gently, "I want you to tell His Honor what your attitude was toward the child and the child's attitude toward you during the summer of 1926."

"Mr. Burkan, the only thing I want to say is this—and you can ask me that question ten thousand times—I loved my baby then, as I love her now, and there is no use asking me that question, how much I love her, because I do love her."

Gloria identified the rest of the photographs. She stammered frequently and spoke very slowly to try to alleviate this condition. After a few minutes of this, Carew adjourned for the day.

Gloria looked over at the Justice as she would at a stern father. He nodded that it was all right for her to leave the witness stand. She began to step down the three steps, and then, for the second time that day, collapsed. Burkan rushed forward and caught her and assisted her to a chair at the counsel table. Nurse Fisher spooned out more sedatives from the brown bottle.

Carew walked to the courtroom door. "Report to my chambers," he called out to reporters. They did not budge, but watched Gloria being comforted and calmed until, some fifteen minutes later, she managed to rise shakily, supported on both sides by her sister Thelma and the nurse. The reporters followed her as she moved slowly down the corridor, her head bent. She brushed her hand across her eyes, as if to clear them of a mist, and murmured, "I'm so tired. I'm very tired."

A reporter asked her if she feared she might collapse before the end of the trial. Gloria cried out her answer. It made headlines. I WILL COLLAPSE WHEN I GET MY BABY BACK.

Justice Carew's behavior at the courtroom door was the first blatant crack in the façade of his magisterial presence. From now on, the press and the people in the courtroom would become familiar with his manic fits followed by his periods of depression. In the courtroom, again and again Carew would turn the discussion to the question of Catholicism, almost as if it were the only issue about which he felt on sure ground. The world of Society seemed to confuse him, the titles to anger him, the indolent people who testified before him seemed beyond his understanding. Outside the courtroom, with the press and the public, he had lost control also. The press leaks were becoming a flood. Again and again, he forbade the lawyers or the witnesses to speak of the trial, but daily the newspapers printed accurate summaries of the secret testimony.

After Gloria Vanderbilt left the building, the reporters assembled in Carew's chambers. He berated them for being late and said angrily, "Someone has taken advantage of the rest of you by taking photographs this afternoon. The only thing to do is to close these proceedings. I will not see you ever again anymore." But as the reporters turned to leave, Carew called them back. "I will give you a summary of today's proceedings," he announced and proceeded to do so, after which he confided, "I am unable to control the number of times Nathan Burkan and Herbert Smyth examine a witness. However, this case can't go on forever because I don't expect to live that long and I'm going to see that this is settled first." He said he would "announce a decision from the bench" as soon as the case ended.

As Carew spoke, his mood underwent a radical change; he became affable and open, encouraging questions. Asked his theory concerning the custody of children, Carew said, "In nine hundred and ninety-nine out of a thousand cases, I agree that the child should be left with its mother."

"And in this case?"

"We'll see."

Asked if he agreed with George Bernard Shaw's skeptical opinion of children, Justice Carew, now in a jocular mood, answered, "Who is that Shaw? I never heard of him; and Noel Coward must be the fellow who runs the shoe store." Carew finally dismissed the reporters and as they were leaving he called after them, "Have a nice weekend. I'll see you Monday." Julia McCarthy went straight to Nathan Burkan to report on Carew's behavior. "He's gone round the bend," she told him.

Every day Gloria testified, public sympathy for her mounted. Nathan Burkan had created a powerful image—a poor mother driven to illness and despair, given to ringing statements of bravery; a beautiful, fragile woman, with her everchanging fashion show, who appeared each morning, swaying on the arm of her nurse, to face the mudslinging, high-handed, rich, austere, stony-faced Gertrude Vanderbilt Whitney.

Gloria's own statements bolstered this image. "If there is any justice in heaven or on earth, the judge will give me back my child!" . . . "Mrs. Whitney has millions, but I will fight." . . . "I am willing to spend every penny I have to bring my baby back to my arms."

Thelma Furness also fanned the flames of public sympathy, telling reporters, "My sister still hopes that she will be able to testify in public. At present, she is under the care of a nurse. This has been a terrible ordeal for her. . . . My sister is so ill. . . . Anything might happen to her if there is an adverse verdict."

Above all, Nathan Burkan added fuel to the fire; he continued to falsely proclaim that he was fighting for an open trial. "I've asked Justice Carew again to admit the press. . . . I think it only fair to Mrs. Vanderbilt that she be given an opportunity to get her story before the public. . . . The accusations made against her were made in public and she is now completely refuting them," Burkan assured reporters while cautioning them, "She has not recovered from the heart attack she experienced when visiting her child Saturday . . . I fear for her."

Mrs. Morgan's retort, "Heart attack? Gloria could always dance all night," had the effect of making her seem a heartless mother. (In the courtroom Gloria testified, "The doctors told me I don't have a heart condition. . . ." But the public never heard this.)

Both Burkan and Gloria did their best to explain away what the public had heard about the child's testimony. When reporters asked Burkan if it was true that the child had testified that she wished to remain with Mrs. Whitney, he replied, "If the child said she did not want to go with her mother, that's the strongest reason why she should go there—to be taught the emotions of filial love and devotion." And Gloria said, "Obviously she was influenced. . . . I sincerely believe that deep down in her heart [little] Gloria loves me and needs me. If I thought otherwise I could not go through with this horrible ordeal." She said of her visit to Wheatley Hills, "We played together just as we did in the old days when there was no one trying to rob me of her custody. When I left her she begged me to come again to see her as soon as I could."

Under this newspaper blitz the crowds outside the Supreme Court swelled. They were predominantly women and children. As Gloria moved haltingly toward the courthouse, the women thrust their babies at her. One woman screamed, "God bless you, dear Mrs. Vanderbilt. We're with you all the way." Another called out, "We're praying for you and your little girl." Still another dashed forward to press a note of sympathy into Gloria's hand, and her eyes filled with tears as she murmured, "That's very nice of you. Thank you, thank you all."

In Columbus Park, behind the Supreme Court, Mrs. Edith Casse, who came daily to the playground with her child, watched Gloria Vanderbilt's pathetic entrances and exits. Edith Casse "felt her heart break." She drew up a petition and began gathering signatures from sympathetic mothers in the park and in the neighborhood.

Day after day Gloria Vanderbilt took the stand, desperately trying to justify every aspect of her life. Of course little Gloria had pets, said her mother. When they lived at Three Gables, nurse Keislich had bought an Airedale for $500. She had used little Gloria's money to pay for the dog. "Nurse Keislich said, 'I want you to take it out of my monthly checks' . . . but I didn't."

"Then you paid for the dog . . . out of the child's money . . ." corrected Carew. "That has a very different aspect from the one that it had when you said that the nurse bought a dog for $500 and charged the child for it. . . . You see, the burden of this now is on your shoulders

. . . a strong virile character probably would have said, 'Take the dog back, I don't want the dog.' "

"But, Your Honor," protested Burkan, ". . . it would have been cruel on the child."

"You have got to be cruel. I have chastised my children . . . a little spanking once in a while is a very good thing for a child," answered Carew.

As the questioning continued, Gloria confirmed that her mother, brother, and father all had lived with her in Paris.

"Who paid the bills?" asked Burkan.

"I did," replied Gloria.

"You mean the child," interrupted Herbert Smyth.

Gloria's answer revealed the basic misunderstanding that had led to so much bitterness. "Mr. Smyth . . . I do not differentiate between the child's money and my money." Before Reginald Vanderbilt's death, "I had been living at a rate which was much greater than what I had" after his death. "I found out that $48,000 a year did not go as far as a quarter of a million."

One by one, Gloria tried to refute all the accusations made against her. The infamous attic in which Mrs. Morgan insisted her daughter wanted to put little Gloria was a "light . . . bright studio, an ideal place for her to romp and play." There was never any suggestion that little Gloria sleep there. "My child slept in the room next to me. There was never any question that she should be moved. . . ."

Constance Bennett, who visited her, "was then known as Mrs. Philip Plant." As to the Argentinian who accompanied her, "Well, I can give you several names. I think probably she refers to a friend of mine whose name is Richard Moreno . . . I have known Mr. Moreno practically all my life. His father is a friend of my late father's."

Gloria denied that she had ever committed what Burkan termed "an act of impropriety . . . intimacy . . . or wrongdoing" with Prince Hohenlohe. "I never lived in any relations with Prince Hohenlohe of any immoral character, and Mrs. Morgan, my mother, never in my hearing had told me that she ever saw or thought she saw or believed that I have lived with Prince Hohenlohe."

"Did she ever tell you that you were guilty of any improper conduct?" asked Burkan.

"She never did. . . . It was a question of my marriage, not of my relations with Prince Hohenlohe."

"She was violently opposed to your marriage to the prince?" asked Burkan.

"Violently! Yes. She used to tell me that, mostly in reference to Prince Hohenlohe, that I was going to murder the baby, and Prince

Hohenlohe was going to murder the baby, and everybody was going to murder the baby, except herself, as far as I could make it out. That is the only neglect she ever has accused me of—that I wanted to murder my child."

Carew took over to summarize Maria Caillot's testimony that Gloria Vanderbilt shared a hotel room with Nadeja Milford Haven and that the maid had seen her "sitting on the side of a bed reading a paper, and the other woman was standing up beside her and had her arms around her neck and was kissing her, and you"—Carew turned to Burkan, reminding him that he brought this upon himself—"said, 'What do you mean, as a lover?' And she said, 'Yes.' "

"Mrs. Vanderbilt, did any such occurrence ever take place?" asked Burkan.

"It certainly did not."

"Were you ever guilty of any such act or similar act with any woman at any time or at any place?"

"No. Never."

"The butler, Zaug, testified that on one occasion while you were living at 49 East Seventy-second Street, at six in the morning you were in the library in a state of nudity, and a Mrs. Thomas was also nude, and both of you stood up in this library drinking. Now did any such thing ever take place?"

"Never. I have never been naked in my life walking around the room."

"The maid, Caillot, says on one occasion she observed Mrs. Thomas in a drunken state, and she was so drunk she had to be carried up to an upper floor."

"That is not true. I am sorry, that is not accurate."

"Have you ever seen her drunk?"

"No, I have never seen her drunk."

"Was Mrs. Thomas ever nude?"

"I have never seen her nude—in my life."

Gloria testified that she'd met the Marchioness of Milford Haven for the first time in the south of France in Cannes at a party given for the Grand Duke Boris. Then, catching herself mentioning a title, she looked at Carew and apologized. "I am sorry to mention names like that, but I have to."

Lady Milford Haven had come up to her and said, "Oh, you are the lady who is going to marry Prince Hohenlohe," and they'd become "very good friends." She added, "I consider Lord and Lady Milford Haven two of my dearest friends." When asked the names of her other friends, Gloria stammered as she replied, "I am sorry, it is rather difficult because most of them have titles. I cannot help it!"

Burkan inquired, "Were you ever in your own life guilty of any act of impropriety or wrongdoing or drinking to excess?"

"No, I do not drink to excess, and I do not lead a lewd life. As a matter of fact, I am rather shy and modest."

"There was some testimony given by the maid that Agnes Horter had some drinking parties with you early in the morning, that she drank whiskey and kept whiskey in her room at the Sherry-Netherland, and that she and you drank whiskey early in the morning."

"I never drink whiskey early in the morning and I very rarely drink whiskey at all."

Gloria explained that Agnes Horter was an old school friend from the Convent of the Sacred Heart. "Her father lost a great deal of money, and she has worked for her living. I think she has been a model. I think she has been in the theater. She has earned her living."

"Did you say theater?" interrupted Smyth.

"Theater, yes. She was a friend of ours, and she still is a friend of ours."

"In what capacity was she employed by you?"

"That goes into a long story. She actually was not employed by me, but she was acting as my secretary. I had at one moment in my life, before my husband's death, loaned her some money—not loaned her, I don't lend, I give it—but she took it as a loan, and when I moved into the house at 49 East Seventy-second Street, she came and acted as my secretary. . . . After about six months that she had been with me, one day she came in and she said, 'Gloria, I think that I don't owe you any more money, I am going away.'

"And I said, 'What do you mean owe me any money? You do not owe me any money.'

"She said, 'Yes, do you remember in 1925 you loaned me some money? And I think that by the work I have done in your house, it is all settled. I do not believe in money passing between friends, and it might spoil our friendship.' And she went off, and I haven't seen her. I saw her once after that. I do not know where she is now. I think in Florida somewhere, or Tennessee." Gloria was covering herself by mentioning seeing Agnes "once after that." But Smyth was unaware that it was Agnes Horter who had accompanied Gloria to court the first day of this trial, and that only after the maid's accusation had Agnes disappeared.

"While she lived in that house, did she have liquor in her rooms and was she in the habit of drinking liquor?"

"I have never seen Miss Horter drinking liquor, as you call it. I have seen her taking a cocktail, but not drinking."

"There is liquor in them," said Carew.

"What is that?" asked Burkan.

"There is liquor in these cocktails," said Carew.

"Absolutely. I think so," said Burkan.

"I think so!" confirmed Carew. He called Burkan to the bench and whispered to him.

Burkan nodded. He asked Gloria, "How many cocktails would you say you take a day?"

"I personally?"

"Yes. I will put it that way."

"I won't say I have any number a day because sometimes there are days when I do not have them at all."

"And on the days that you have them, how many do you have?"

"I take one, maybe two."

"What kind?"

"An orange blossom. That is the only cocktail I drink."

With that, Gertrude Whitney, seated in the front row of spectator seats, broke into a wide grin. Gloria registered her expression.

Burkan continued, "And at what hours do you take them?"

"Except at Mrs. Whitney's—" she blurted out. "I see Mrs. Whitney smiling over there—except at Mrs. Whitney's when I took a dry martini."

"She had served you dry martinis in her home?"

"Yes."

"And they are very good," said Smyth.

Gloria demurred. "They are too strong for me."

"Were you guilty of any impropriety—I am sorry I must put this question to you. The charge has been made, and they have to be either admitted or denied. Were you yourself guilty of any acts of impropriety with any male or female?"

"No, never."

"I am sorry to ask you some of these questions, but your child . . . when His Honor put certain questions to her in order to probe her mind and get her point of view, he asked her concerning you, and she said on one occasion you deliberately burned her with a cigarette at or about her elbow. Did you ever burn her on any part of her body?"

"I never burned her willingly or accidentally with a cigarette."

"At no time or place?"

"At any time or place."

"And she also said to His Honor . . . that you threw a glass of water at her. Did you ever throw any water on your baby, a cold glass of water?"

"I have never thrown a glass of water at my baby or at anybody else. I don't throw things."

Gloria Vanderbilt said she had never touched her daughter in anger, save once. "The child asked me for some money. In those days, she was a very little bit of a thing. . . . She used to open my bag and look through it and see what there was in it, and there was some loose change. I said, 'Gloria, you cannot have that because it has not been washed, the money. I will give it to you after it has been washed.'

"And she said, 'Oh, well, I will go and ask Naney' . . . so off she went to ask her grandmother.

"And I went after her. And I came into the room and I said, 'Gloria, Mummy says that you cannot have any money that is not washed.' And I took her by the shoulders. And I moved her around this way." Gloria gestured with a turn of her arms and shoulders. "And I did not push her, I did not ill-treat her. I just turned her around and I said, 'Off with you to nurse.' Gloria started crying because she could not get the money. . . ."

Carew took over the examination and turned it to the subject of religion. "Did you ever hear [little Gloria] say the 'Apostles' Creed'?"

"I am sorry, I do not know in English what it means."

"You do not know what the 'Apostles' Creed' means in English?"

"No. If you will start it for me—"

"Do you know the fundamental prayer of a Christian?"

"You mean the 'Credo'?"

"Yes, the 'Apostles' Creed'. . . . Did you ever hear her say that in any language?"

"Yes, in French."

"She did not say it in French or English or in any language the other day." Little Gloria did not even make the sign of the cross, he said disapprovingly.

Gloria answered, "I have seen her make the sign of the cross several times."

"You mean to say she only said her prayers *several times* in front of you?"

"Several. Numerous times," Gloria stammered. "She made the sign of the cross at her father's grave. I do not know. We always make the sign of the cross," she protested.

Carew lashed out at Gloria, berating her about the child's religious education. Finally, she asked what prayers the child had said for him.

"She said the 'Our Father' and she stumbled through the 'Hail Mary'. And that was the limit of her liturgical ability!"

Gloria said that she herself had said prayers since childhood. "I have been taught my prayers first in French, and then I lived in Spain and I was taught them in Spanish, and then I learned them again in French in Switzerland, and then I was taught them in English. I say them in French, with the exception of one prayer. . . . I have said it every night of my life, that is since my husband died. . . . It is called Prisoner of Love," she announced proudly. "That is a prayer I say every night."

Burkan's direct examination went on and on. On Wednesday afternoon Carew asked him to finish soon. Burkan replied, "I think it would be better for me tomorrow. I only need five or ten minutes."

"Finish it in five or ten minutes now. You will come back too strong tomorrow morning," directed Carew.

"I promise you on my sacred word of honor that I won't take more than five or ten minutes. There is one more subject I want to cover. I left that for the last, and then I am through."

"What do you say?" Carew asked Smyth.

"I have known Mr. Burkan's five or ten minutes to be optimistically stretched into hours," Smyth replied.

Carew adjourned and instructed the lawyers to report immediately to his chambers. In fact, Burkan was building a record for appeal and would not be rushed through his side of the case. In his own way Carew was doing the same thing; he knew that undoubtedly his decision would be reviewed by the five justices of the New York State Appellate Division and it was imperative that the record substantiate the correctness of his decision. He told the lawyers that, on further consideration, he intended to amend his ruling on the question of the privileged relationship between Mr. Gilchrist and Mrs. Vanderbilt. During Mrs. Vanderbilt's cross-examination, Mr. Smyth would be permitted to admit as evidence all of Gilchrist's documents that previously had been excluded.

"On what basis will you admit this material?" demanded Burkan.

"You will see," replied the Justice.

This would be a mortal blow to their case and Burkan could see no justification for it. He lost control of his temper and began shouting, "That spy! You're out to get me, you're all out to get me because I'm a Jew from the tenements! You're out to make me look like a horse's ass, but you won't get away with it!" Jim Murray tried to calm him down. Within seconds, Burkan caught himself and murmured, "I'm sorry. I will subside."

The following morning Carew opened the session by stating that he was amending his ruling: "Mr. Gilchrist has testified that he regarded his relation to Mrs. Vanderbilt as confidential and privileged up on to the nineteenth of September 1933. At that time he told her that from that time on she would have to deal with him at arm's length. . . .

On further reflection, I still think that the relation was confidential and privileged as against the whole world except the child and except as against the Supreme Court as *parens patriae*. . . . When Mrs. Vanderbilt retained . . . the firm of Cadwalader, Wickersham and Taft, who were the lawyers for the infant as well as its guardians, she thereby waived any privilege that she might have against the child and as against the interests of the child. For that reason, I am entirely willing to reverse my ruling on the questions that Mr. Smyth put to Mr. Gilchrist on which I sustained Mr. Burkan's objection as confidential and privileged. . . . Certain communications and letters marked for identification are governed by this ruling also."

In a final act of humiliation, Gilchrist requested and received Carew's permission to take the stand to explain how pure his conscience was. Gilchrist read aloud Burkan's accusation that he had been "hostile" and said, "This accusation of hostility is unfounded. . . . What I am going to say is not evidence, but I merely wish to state what my position has been. . . . It is a great surprise to me to have this attitude of hostility injected into this case by the Relator's counsel himself. The only hostility that exists is the hostility that he has injected into the case."

"Mr. Burkan, do you want to say anything?" asked Justice Carew.

"Yes, Your Honor," replied Burkan. "I said to Your Honor yesterday, when we were in your room discussing certain matters, that sometimes in the heat of the argument, things were said that had better not be said. But I sincerely and truly have had this feeling, and I still have it . . . and so does the Relator, and that was due to the fact that Beesley was put in there—into that household—and was asked to make reports. Mr. Gilchrist did not tell Mrs. Vanderbilt that he had somebody there to check her up, who was watching her, watching her movements. In all my thirty-four years of experience at this bar, I never heard of such a proceeding. That is not done. In connection with Zaug: Zaug was put in there through Mr. Gilchrist's influence, and the moment he was discharged, and got off the witness stand, he promptly was placed by Mr. Gilchrist . . .

"I wish to add just one thing and I am going to subside. When I made the application, Your Honor, to have her appointed, I did not ask to displace these two gentlemen. It showed my faith and confidence in them. I asked that she be appointed co-guardian with them. I did not say that they should be removed."

"Don't talk to me too much about that because I do not think that was worthwhile doing either. I do not see what possible good that would have done," said Carew.

"It might have been my fault," Burkan admitted. It was too late to think about it now.

But Carew underlined Burkan's error. "You have said that she first declined to assume that responsibility because of her inexperience, and nothing has developed to show she is any more experienced today than she was then. So I think as far as that is concerned, that was rather an unwise thing to do."

Gloria's examination was then resumed. She too wished to comment on Mr. Gilchrist's statement and asked Justice Carew, "May I say something?"

"No, you may not," Carew shot back, as if speaking to a naughty child.

Burkan did not intervene on his client's behalf. He spent the rest of Thursday morning completing his direct examination, knowing that his questions and his client's answers would be recorded and reviewed by other eyes. Burkan said, "When His Honor undertook this difficult task of talking to your child, he had made some inquiry of her regarding her attitude toward you and her reasons for the attitude. She said that she hardly saw anything of you and that you never were nice to her. Now is that an accurate statement?"

"That is not an accurate statement."

"And although she had written you lots of letters, she did not love you but wrote them merely because she was afraid of you. Now had you ever seen or noticed fear on the child's part?"

"I? Never."

"Had any doctor that had seen this child during all the years that you had her, and even during the time that she was with Dr. St. Lawrence, did he tell you, in words or substance, on examination he'd discovered the child had apprehension or fear of you?"

"No, because it did not exist."

Gloria Vanderbilt's cross-examination was about to begin but she whispered to Nathan Burkan that she was too exhausted to testify. Burkan requested a recess and the cross-examination was postponed until the following morning, Friday, November 2. In deference to Gloria's poor health the session was scheduled to begin at 11:45. At noon Friday, Gloria hobbled in the door and haltingly took the stand. Herbert Smyth, scarcely glancing at her, began his devastating cross-examination by entering document after document against her. Gloria Vanderbilt was a media creation and it was the media that Smyth skillfully utilized in her destruction: newspaper photographs, newspaper accounts of Gloria Vanderbilt's Café Society life, numerous photographs taken with Blumie, became frozen in legal tomes as Respondent's exhibits.

Smyth's first exhibit was a newspaper photograph of the twins, at fifteen, hauling their trunk down a pier in a wheelbarrow. "Doesn't that point out that you were quite healthy?" Smyth asked Gloria.

"Thelma is pushing the trunk . . ." she answered.

"During that longshoremen's strike, you and your sister, Miss Thelma, carried your own trunk . . ."

"No, not actually . . . no. They asked us to pose for it."

"You have done a good deal of posing in your life, haven't you?" Smyth shot back.

"Yes, I have," replied Gloria, either unaware or ignoring the barb. And, inadvertently, she added a disturbing truth, one that would be passed on to her daughter. "I think any child of that age would be rather impressed in being asked to pose."

Smyth produced Mrs. Morgan's large scrapbook, full of clippings about her children's activities. He read excerpts from a newspaper account of a costume party given a few months after Reginald Vanderbilt's death. Gloria grew irritated, saying that the article was inaccurate in that it said she was wearing a costume she had worn three years previously. "How could I wear the same costume?" she asked, as if *this* were the unpardonable error, not the fact that she'd given a party soon after her husband's death.

"Then you were not in mourning entirely when you said you were in mourning?" asked Smyth.

"I was in semi-mourning."

"A party of thirty people is hardly semi-mourning, is it?"

"Mrs. Graham Fair Vanderbilt gave a party three weeks after her son died, and she still was in mourning [referring to the automobile accident that had claimed the life of twenty-six-year-old William K. Vanderbilt III in 1933]. It was almost a year after my husband died."

"I know, but you said on direct examination that you were in deep mourning."

Smyth asked Gloria to give the dates of every trip she had taken from the time of Reginald's death to the present. Referring to her itinerary, she began a recitation of ceaseless travel; a trip here, a trip there, away from her child for two months, home for two days, away from her child for months again. In eight years, Gloria Vanderbilt had never stayed in one place for more than a few months, often moving on after a few days. For over an hour Gloria struggled to answer Smyth's detailed questions about her travels until at last, like an angry child, she thrust the papers she was holding at Smyth. "All right, why not read it and put it in evidence. There is my itinerary. Why make me go through this?"

But the answer was obvious—this recitation of dates provided evidence of Gloria's indifference toward her daughter that no protestation of affection could counteract. Finally, Smyth asked, "Did you spend one percent of all the days of the year with your child?"

"That is ridiculous!" Gloria snapped back, but the point had been made.

Smyth elicited admission after damaging admission. For three months, during the summer of 1929, Gloria had sent her child and nurse Keislich to an apartment in Biarritz where she never saw them. The summer of 1930, her child and the nurse were sent to Avignon; she visited them for one day. The summer of 1931, the child and the nurse were sent to Glion for six weeks, then they joined Gloria for a fortnight in Monte Carlo.

Why had she stayed in London in the summer of 1929? And subsequently, why had she made so many trips to London? Smyth asked.

There was a long silence. Gloria's eyes met those of Theobald Mathew. Mathew, who had sat unobtrusively in the courtroom day after day, stared back, his face expressionless. "For personal reasons," she answered.

Uncharacteristically, Smyth did not pursue the subject.

Again, Gloria said that when she had lived abroad she had borrowed $4,000 from a certain party to have something of "my very own, something that belonged to me and I could do with it what I liked and not have to account for it to Mr. Gilchrist or the Surrogate."

Smyth asked the name of the person who had lent her this money. She requested permission to write the name on a slip of paper and show it to Justice Carew. Taking the slip of paper, she wrote, in her spidery sprawling script, the name of Edward, Prince of Wales.

Carew looked at the slip of paper, showed it in turn to Nathan Burkan and to Herbert Smyth, then tore it into small pieces and dropped it in the wastebasket below his bench. Mathew had accomplished his mission—the name of the next King of England never appeared in the record of the *Matter of Vanderbilt.*

Smyth began entering as exhibits the reproving letters written to Gloria Vanderbilt by Thomas Gilchrist and George Wickersham. Burkan, building his case for appeal, lodged a final objection which he knew would prove fruitless. Carew, playing his part, overruled him, but then turned to Burkan and said, reassuringly, "If you continue to advise her, she will be all right: if she takes your advice."

Smyth interjected, "Yes, *if* she takes the advice."

"She will take it, Your Honor," Burkan assured Carew.

"We still have a very important thing in this case, and that is the attitude of the child and the history of eight years or ten years of neglect," Smyth reminded Carew.

"Yes. I do not hesitate to say that the lady has reversed herself—" began Carew.

"Oh, for the purposes of a situation that was confronting her. But will a leopard change its spots?" asked Smyth.

"Now, Your Honor . . . I do not think he has a right to insult her. I won't let him," said Burkan.

"That is a winged word and it would have gone through the window if you had not stopped it on its way out," commented Carew.

Smyth handed the next packet of evidence to Gloria for examination. Gloria read the letters little Gloria had written to Mrs. Morgan in 1931 and 1932, letters ringing with misery and neglect. She shook her head in disbelief. Smyth tried to continue her examination, but she asked for time to reread the letters. When she had finished, she said that she felt certain passages "did not appear to be in little Gloria's handwriting." Smyth inquired which passages and surprisingly, Gloria selected only the most innocent quotes within the letters. She pointed to the sentence: "I hope you will excuse this letter," and commented that she felt it was written by the nurse. Then she pointed to "I do want to go to New York. Toney's nurse is treating me very badly and some times I cry," and said, "That is all in her handwriting."

"I do not really myself see any change. Do you really see a change in that?" asked Smyth.

"If I didn't, I would say so. I would choose the bad parts . . ."

Gloria did not deny that all the complaints against her were in the child's own handwriting. This could be of great use to Smyth; he handed Gloria a red pencil and asked her to mark the passages in the letters that she felt had been written by another party.

As she was doing so, a man in a dark suit entered the courtroom, walked up to Smyth, and began whispering in his ear. Smyth paled. After a moment, he turned to Carew and asked, "Do you mind taking a recess now?" Burkan jumped to his feet with an objection. Smyth walked over to Burkan and whispered something in his ear. Burkan's attitude changed immediately and dramatically. He reached up and put his hand on Smyth's shoulder and patted his opponent gently. Carew announced that the court would be adjourned until the following Monday.

Outside, the newspapermen waited to interview Smyth. It had just been discovered that his three-year-old grandson, Murray S. Smyth, Jr., was dead as the result of a grotesque accident. The child had been ill, and the pediatrician had ordered a prescription for mouthwash. Through a misunderstanding, the boy was forced to swallow the medicine. It was poison.

In the corridor, Thelma Furness expressed her condolences to Herbert Smyth, but could not resist adding, "Had that happened to my sister's child, she would have been put on trial for murder."

The newspaper coverage of the *Matter of Vanderbilt* now clearly demonstrated that, through the tabloids, the nation had come to witness a simple black and white drama in which each performer had become frozen into an assigned role. Unquestionably, Gertrude Vanderbilt Whitney was cast as villain. "Why is she doing this?" asked a *Sun* editorial (and so did the public). Said the *News*, "Mrs. Whitney, elderly aunt of the child, is said to be worth something over $75,-000,000 . . . so financial odds work out to be about 750 to 1 in Mrs. Whitney's favor. If these odds were reversed it's a fairly safe bet that the aunt would have been in the jughouse or the bughouse long since."

Justice Carew, who infuriated and frustrated the press with his erratic behavior and distorted accounts of the testimony, was also by now firmly locked into the role of villain. And, of course, Gloria Vanderbilt was cast as the beautiful heroine, enduring an "incredible ordeal" to regain her beloved baby. Only there was one element in this drama that was askew—and could, in fact, destroy the entire construction. Justice Carew had stated that little Gloria said she preferred to remain with Mrs. Whitney. How could that be? There was only one possible answer—if Gloria Vanderbilt was indeed "the loving mother," then little Gloria could not understand the implications of what she was saying and had been seduced by her life of luxury with her rich aunt. And so little Gloria was assigned the only role in the drama open to her, that of "innocent pawn," "uncomprehending pawn," "happy and oblivious to the storm that swirls about her." Said the *Mirror*, "Little Gloria is blissfully unaware that her childish prattling might influence Justice Carew." From this point on, the compatible images, of Gloria Vanderbilt as the "loving mother" and little Gloria as the "blissfully unaware . . . little pawn," so essential to the basic construction of the drama, continued apace, as evidenced by the weekend news coverage.

> As Mrs. Gloria Morgan Vanderbilt . . . on the verge of a nervous breakdown . . . rested over the week-end, trying to gain strength for her battle for custody of her daughter, the little heiress . . . happiest person in the whole clan . . . amused herself with her pony, her Sealyham puppies and her guinea pigs on the Long Island estate of her aunt, Mrs. Harry Payne Whitney.

Though the 10-year-old child is said to have testified that she does not want to return to her mother, with childlike insouciance, she put her pony through his paces and enjoyed herself with no thought of the morrow. . . . In the two and a half years that Mrs. Whitney has had the care of her late brother Reggie's child, little Gloria has been showered with gifts. . . .

Mrs. Vanderbilt . . . suffering from a heart ailment attended by a nurse and physician . . . has been questioned and cross questioned . . . about little thoughtless actions throughout her widowhood . . . She has been villified by the testimony of discharged servants and at the end, smiling bravely, she faces the last issue—will her child be restored to her?

Justice Carew will conclude the ordeal of the beautiful young widow . . . in the meantime the little girl who is the bone of contention remains with her aunt at her palatial Westbury estate. A member of the household stated the child did not seem aware of the recent proceedings or if she was, she did not appear interested. . . . The little girl plays innocently with her toys and dogs while her fate is being decided by others. . . .

All but [little] Gloria fretted. The $10,000,000 Vanderbilt baby dashed into Mrs. Whitney's great farmhouse near Old Westbury, her cheeks glowing with autumn wind and her eyes dancing.

"I won the first prize!" she cried, waving a tissue-wrapped parcel. There had been a halloe'en party at school that day, and Gloria, masked and otherwise disguised, had been awarded the prize for the prettiest costume. It was a "Little Boy Blue" getup, and had been her own idea.

Give This Mother Back Her Child

If anyone else tries a petition like that, I'll make them eat it with ketchup!

JUSTICE JOHN FRANCIS CAREW

THE VANDERBILT TRIAL entered its sixth week. The pathetic image Nathan Burkan had labored to present of Gloria Vanderbilt was totally successful and unfortunately true. Jim Murray remembers: "I picked up Gloria for Monday's session. She apologized for wearing the same dress she had worn to another session, and asked, 'Do you think they'll be terribly disappointed?' She acted as if we had a social engagement at some place, but she couldn't quite recall where. She kept me waiting two hours while she did her make-up. The session was postponed until eleven-thirty. Then when we finally arrived at court, Gloria said she felt so ill that the session for the day was cancelled."

Tuesday, November 6, there was no session. This was a special day—Election Day. There was a steady light rain all day long, and the political maxim—rain is good for ducks and Democrats—proved true, although this year the Democrats needed no help from the weather. "Republicans are no longer Republicans. Democrats are no longer Democrats. The New Deal has won," announced the *Mirror*. Herbert H. Lehman was reelected to office, defeating Robert Moses by an overwhelming plurality of 400,000 votes. There were Democratic victories across the country. In New York it was Tammany's day. Wednesday morning there were two tabloid headlines:

LANDSLIDE FOR LEHMAN
and
LITTLE GLORIA TO BE RAISED A CATHOLIC.

For the first time since the trial began, Nathan Burkan, John Godfrey Saxe, and Justice John F. Carew felt united by the Democratic victory. Everyone met the morning with smiles. Smyth began by saying, "I hope this aftermath of democracy finds us all in good humor." And Burkan replied, "I am satisfied with the results." Then they turned themselves to the business of the day, Burkan offering as exhibits photographs of the nude paintings and sculpture in the Whitney Museum of Art as evidence that an association with Gertrude Whitney might corrupt little Gloria's morals. When he was finished, Smyth produced a batch of photographs of his own. "Here are some you neglected," he said, "in the Metropolitan." Smyth then offered these photographs in evidence to show that the Metropolitan Museum of Art displayed nudes of an almost identical character to the ones that Burkan had submitted.

Over the weekend, Burkan, in conference with Louis Frohlich, had decided that Gloria's best defense against her daughter's complaining letters was to take the position that the child had been forced to write them by the nurse. Smyth turned to these letters and read out the sentence, "My mother was in Paris enjoying herself while poor me was unhappy in England."

"Do you admit your daughter wrote that?" Smyth asked Gloria.

"I do not say it was written by my daughter and I do not say it was not written by her. On the other hand, I say that no child of seven and a half, as you claim at that time, could possibly sit down and write a letter like that because I do not believe it. . . . Her hand was held . . . or the letters were dictated to her one by one."

"Does it occur to you that perhaps those letters that were written complaining about you were letters written by a child who might be afraid of you?"

"Her letters to me did not show that."

"The letters written to you of affection, as she said on the stand, were written because she had to write them. You know that," said Smyth.

"If she was forced to write letters of affection to me, she might be forced to write letters against me . . ." Gloria answered logically.

VANDERBILT CHILD WROTE OF HER WOE

Letters Read in Court Telling Grandmother of Unhappiness During Years Abroad.

DICTATED, SAYS MOTHER

An Adult, Maybe Former Nurse, Told Girl What to Say, She Testifies in Reply.

Mrs. Gloria Morgan Vanderbilt, who is attempting to recover possession of her daughter, Gloria, was confronted in the Supreme Court yesterday with a half-dozen letters written by the child in 1931, when she was 7 years old, expressing dissatisfaction with her life trav... with her mother fr... Paris. t...

Ex 5 M

Dear Naney

I love you so much and I love the cards that you sent me my Mother was in Paris enjoying herself while poor me was unhappy in Englan

l... r... h... is...

J... wer... of a... ...plaining to h... ...r. Mrs. Morgan has ...ady testified that she and the girl's nurse, Emma Sullivan Keislich, who was selected by Mrs. Morgan when the child was born, were the only ones who gave little Gloria any attention or maternal care.

When Justice Carew finally decided to permit the Whitney counsel to introduce the child's letters to her grandmother they were attacked by the Vanderbilt counsel, Nathan Burkan, on the same ground used by the Whitney counsel earlier in the trial when letters from the girl to her mother were introduced

NOVEMBER 15, 1934

Seven Years Apart—

Yet Both have Skin equally Young

Beautiful Vanderbilts examined by Dermatologist for Skin Age . . . *both get 20-year-old rating*

Mrs. Reginald Vanderbilt

famed for her brunette beauty. Her skin was rated by the d... tologist as being practically the same as it was eight years ago. Vanderbilt says: "The thorough cleansing Pond's Cold Cream keeps my skin clear—fine-pored—seems to wipe away tired li...

Miss Frederica Vanderbilt Webb

is an enchanting young blonde with a skin exquisitely fair. The dermatologist declares it to be "a perfect skin of twenty." She says: "I've never had a coarse pore, blackhead, or blemish. I'm sure this is due to Pond's Cold Cream."

YOUNG skin is firm and fine of texture—its color clear—glowing—radiant.

OLD skin is loose, lined, crêpy—its texture is thick and coarse—its color dull—sallow—dark.

These conditions, dermatologists report, are due to loss of tone—impaired circulation—failure of glands to produce youth-sustaining oils.

When the two charming Vanderbilts, whose portraits are shown above, were examined by a dermatologist, their rating was the same. In actual age, they are seven years apart.

Both of these two noted society beauties are faithful users of Pond's Cold Cream. Could there be more convincing proof that this cream actually keeps the skin young—the young skin at the height of its loveliness?

Cleanse your skin with Pond's Cold Cream every night. It will float away impurities—correct skin faults.

And every morning freshen your skin with this fragrant, luxurious cream. Then it will look alluringly young—silken—free from faults and age signs. Powder and make-up will smooth evenly and lastingly.

New quick-melting cream

Pond's makes a liquefying cream. It melts inst... ly on the skin. It, too, contains the specially p... essed oils for which Pond's Cold Cream is fam...

● *Pond's Cold Cream* cleanses thoroughly—corrects skin faults—prepares for powder. Preferred by 1 out of every 5 women who use cream. *Pond's Liquefying Cream* also answers these three vital needs of the skin. It is a quicker melting cream.

● ***Mail This Coupon Today***— Send coupon and 10... a generous supply of Pond's Cold Cream and 3 o... Pond's excellent beauty aids. Mail today.

Name________

Street________

City________ State____

Test your skin for these age signs. Your mirror will tell its true age. *Specially Processed Oils in this cream correct Skin Faults*

CORRECTS SKIN FAULTS USUAL *in the 20's*

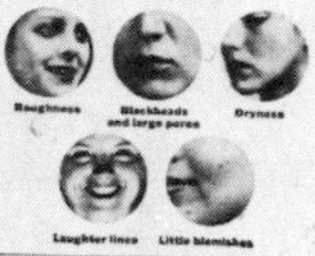

FIGHTS OFF AGE SIGNS USUAL *after 30*

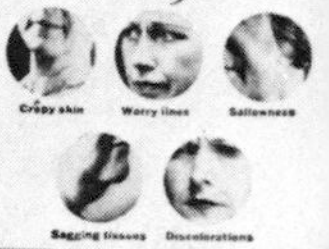

...Vitness Links Gloria-Blumey

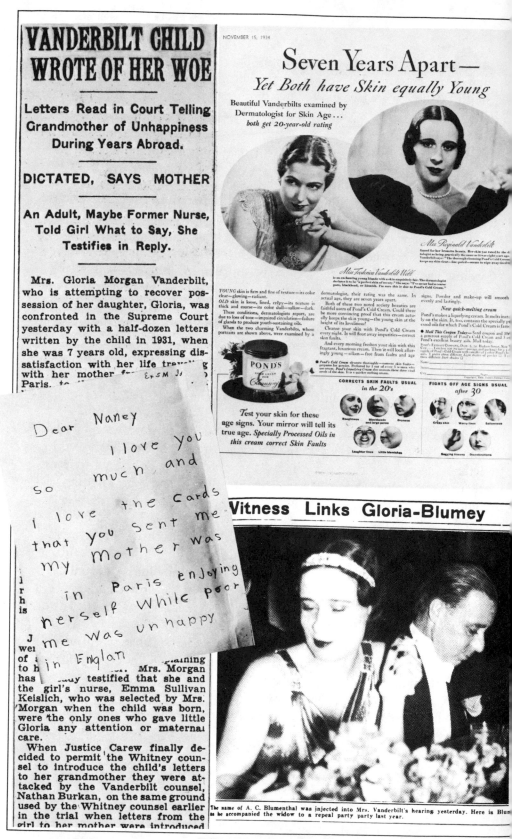

The name of A. C. Blumenthal was injected into Mrs. Vanderbilt's hearing yesterday. Here is Blum... as he accompanied the widow to a repeal party party last year.

"Do you admit the handwriting? If you do not, I will prove it, and you take the responsibility for saying it is not."

"I do not know what the responsibility is, Mr. Smyth. I am not going to acknowledge that my child *willingly* wrote that, as it is not true."

Smyth and Burkan conferred at the bench, and both declared that they would call in handwriting experts, Smyth to prove that the child had indeed written the letters, and Burkan to prove that the letters had been tampered with. Carew felt that this would "unnecessarily prolong the case," but finally gave in, saying, "I do not want you gentlemen to feel that I am overlooking any aspect of this case."

Smyth turned to the question of Gloria's alleged adulterous relationship with Blumie, asking her if she'd sailed "with a friend" on the *Europa* in June of 1933.

"I had no friends with me," Gloria replied.

Smyth produced a list headed, *No Publicity*. "Do you find your name with Mr. Blumenthal's on that list?" he inquired.

Gloria picked up the document and scanned the list. She answered, "Yes, I do, and I find Mr. Rockefeller's."

"He had nothing to do with you."

"Neither had Mr. Blumenthal."

Next Smyth produced a plan of the *Europa*, establishing that a cabin under the name of Gloria Vanderbilt's maid, Maria Caillot, connected to Blumenthal's stateroom.

"That is purely an accident, Mr. Smyth."

"I see."

"You don't think for a single moment—I know the insinuation you are trying to make—considering my friendship with Mr. Blumenthal, that I would park my maid in a cabin next door so that she could listen to everything that went on. . . . Really, you are Machiavellian in thinking that up."

Smyth introduced newspaper report after newspaper report of the midnight sailing of the *Europa* when process servers had made a futile search for Blumie and "the fair widow Vanderbilt." This was followed by photographs that had appeared in the newspapers of Blumie and Gloria (at the Baer-Schmeling fight, at the Casino in the Park, at a Repeal party, in a triangle with Peggy Fears). Smyth commented, "At the time these photographs appeared, Mr. Blumenthal was a married man. . . . He was married to Peggy Fears, and still is."

"I don't know whether he is married and had a separation—or what the arrangement was," said Gloria.

"So far as you know, he is a married man?"

"I am not answering for Mr. Blumenthal, Mr. Smyth, so I don't know."

"You know he is already married?"

"If he does not get a divorce. He is a good friend of mine."

"You know he is a married man?"

"Oh, yes, I know it!" snapped Gloria.

Carew mused from the bench, "If it appears that this lady has been in the public print with a married man, it is something for the court to consider as to whether she was leading the life that was capable of maternal solicitude."

Smyth handed Gloria a telegram she had sent in response to Gertrude's request, at the end of the summer of 1933, that she discuss the advisability of leaving the child with her. She read the telegram.

> WILL BE VERY HAPPY TO SEE YOU
> THURSDAY NOON LOVE
> BLUMIE

Gloria's hand flew to her mouth. She took a deep breath and then replied, "I am sure I don't know how that happened." After this she seemed so unnerved that her examination was postponed until eleven-thirty the following morning.

Carew returned to his chambers to find that the newspapers had printed six of the child's complaining letters. (By the following day the letters had crossed the Atlantic and appeared in the London *Daily Mail.*) In spite of this new leak, Carew still gave his own version of the proceedings. The reporters had found a clever way to exploit these bland summaries; they would print them along with the leaked testimony, pointing out the discrepancies between the two.

The New York Times stated:

> Justice Carew said yesterday that Mrs. Vanderbilt insisted that she had not neglected her child, as Mrs. Whitney charges, but, on the contrary, devoted a proper amount of time to her. She said further, according to the justice, that testimony declaring the child disliked her was false and that the child's own expressed preference for Mrs. Whitney was due simply to the influence of those now surrounding her. "The child doesn't know her own mind," said Mrs. Vanderbilt.

But the *Times* also printed the child's letters declaring, "My mother is a rare bease . . ." "My mother was in Paris enjoying herself while poor me was unhappy in Englan," and "sometimes I cry," making Carew's summary appear ludicrous.

Yet Carew persisted with his laundered versions of the testimony, and since the press obviously wanted more colorful copy, he tried to provide it as well. He said that Burkan had "produced photographs of a mural of gay life in Greenwich Village in which nudes wearing opera hats play leapfrog." Carew also invented testimony, saying that there had been a discussion concerning the distinction between art and indecent exposure which had ended "in a debate over the purity of *The Odyssey* and *Paradise Lost*." Following Carew's summary, the reporters went to the Whitney Museum and asked director Juliana Force if they could see the mural of nudes in opera hats leapfrogging. Juliana burst into laughter and answered, "The judge must have made that one up."

Thursday morning, November 8, reporters knew that something special was up. Carew was taking unusual precautions to ensure that there would be no leaks of today's testimony. He moved the proceedings from the regular courtroom to room 422, and ordered that the windows be sealed with green blotting paper. Then, as Gloria Vanderbilt's testimony commenced, he ejected Consuelo Thaw, Flora Miller, and the Harry Morgans from the courtroom. They stood in the corridor for about an hour until Carew permitted the women to return but still refused Harry Morgan entrance.

Inside the courtroom only Gloria Vanderbilt seemed unaware that something of importance was about to happen. In his cross-examination, Smyth cleverly began maneuvering to gain the opening that would legally allow him to enter the evidence that Carew's precautions clearly indicated was expected. Smyth began by asking casually, "You said something on your direct examination with regard to your father being very frequently at your house. Do you remember that?"

"Yes."

"Now did your father approve of the way that you were living?"

". . . the only thing that my father did not approve of was my engagement to Prince Hohenlohe," Gloria Vanderbilt replied. She had made exactly the slip Smyth was hoping for.

"Your mother testified that your father gave you . . . a draft of a petition to the Surrogate with a letter that would be presented to the Surrogate if you did not change your way of living . . ."

Too late, Burkan objected. "There is no evidence that such a document exists. . . . And in the event that it does, it is inadmissible evidence. . . ."

But Carew immediately jumped in, saying that Mrs. Vanderbilt had just testified that her father disapproved *only* of her engagement to Hohenlohe, and no other aspect of her life. "He is seeking to contradict her in that regard," Carew noted and overruled the objection.

Carew seemed determined to have this petition and letter as part of the record, and he presented a rationale that would allow its admission. "The point is that she says he did not disapprove of anything she did except the proposed marriage to Prince Hohenlohe. . . . I could not for a moment consider it as evidence of the truth of what is in it, but it is proof of the fact that he disapproved of what she did."

Burkan was beside himself, protesting that this constituted a flagrant violation of a privileged relationship. "Will Your Honor let these hearsay declarations destroy this woman? I say no man or woman in this country is safe if these things can be done. . . . Every mother would be in danger of losing her child by having someone write a letter about her."

But Carew cut off this discussion and directed that Mr. Morgan's petition and letter be marked as exhibits. Burkan looked at Herbert Smyth and said, "I should not want to see this published in the press." Carew then instructed that the stenographer record the name of every person in the room and said, "Each of the persons in the courtroom now whose names have just been recorded are hereby forbidden in any way, directly or indirectly, to divulge any indication of the contents of the exhibits . . . to any person whatsoever."

Harry H. Morgan's petition, written in 1928, alleged:

> . . . That the said Gloria M. Vanderbilt has maintained a large apartment consisting of fifteen to sixteen rooms, has had from twelve to fifteen servants, and has been living in a most extravagant and improper manner and has been entertaining her friends, many of them of bad reputation and improperly and illegally spending almost all of the monies which have been dispensed and directed by this Court to be used for the maintenance, education and support of the . . . infant.
>
> . . . That she is also indebted in large sums to various persons in the city of Paris which she has no independent means or income of her own to pay.
>
> . . . That many of the companions and friends whom she has been bringing to her homes in Paris and Biarritz, are of such moral character and bad habits and conduct as to endanger the moral welfare of the above named infant, Gloria Laura Morgan Vanderbilt.
>
> . . . That she failed to extend the care, kindness and solicitude for the above named infant which motherly instincts and duties should prompt. . . .

Gloria spent the afternoon trying to refute her father's petition. She insisted that the document was written "under the instigation of my mother." There were "only eight not fifteen" servants in the Charles

Floquet apartment. She was not without funds. "I had my jewelry. . . . I still have that and my furniture as well. That is something."

"But with regard to liquid assets, such as cash, stock, Liberty bonds, was that all gone?" asked Smyth.

"You mean now or then?"

"Then."

"I don't know."

"Surely you must be able to tell me something about that. You know you had at least the remainder of $150,000."

"I can't remember exactly."

"Why? Did money mean nothing to you at that time?"

"Money has never meant anything."

"You mean you spent it so freely?"

"I do not mean that. If I could help others, if I could help my father—"

"Yes. Go on."

"My father is dead now. It is a hard thing for me to say, but a large part of that went to my father. . . . I never squandered my money, but if anybody in my family asked me for help, within reason, if I could do it, naturally I was only too glad and willing to do it." Gloria explained that she had supported her mother up until the time the trial started. Why had she supported a woman who took a stand against her? "Because she was my mother," replied Gloria.

"Can you imagine any motive that your mother can have, except the welfare of the child, to say anything against you?" asked Smyth.

"Yes, I can."

"I am willing you shall state it. What motive can your mother have?"

"I am sorry to say the only motive that my mother can have is money."

"Why should money come into any motive on the part of your mother to take sides against you?"

"You'd better ask Mrs. Whitney that."

"Are you charging that Mrs. Whitney has been giving money to your mother?"

"I am charging that Mrs. Whitney has engaged a lawyer for her and is paying for it."

"You mean on this case?"

"Yes, on this case."

"I mean prior to that."

"Prior to that, I don't know anything about it."

"Well, can you imagine any motive that your mother could have prior to the time Mrs. Whitney came into this matter, in 1932, to instigate such a letter as that that your father wrote?"

"It is very simple, as I say. It is a very hard thing for me to say this, but I must say it against my mother since you are forcing me to say it, that she wants the guardianship of the child so that she would have the $48,000."

"Did she ever say that to you?"

"No, but I told her that several times."

"Then you think Mrs. Morgan's motive in taking the child away from you is that she could have the expenditure of $4,000 a month. Is that it?"

"I do."

"Do you really mean that?"

"I certainly do."

"Did you ever discuss that with anybody?"

"Yes, I have discussed it with Mrs. Whitney."

"When did you discuss that with Mrs. Whitney?"

"I discussed it several times with Mrs. Whitney. . . . I told her that the reason why Mrs. Morgan, my mother, was doing this was purely money. That she was money mad. That her god was money, money, money, and this is what made all this trouble."

"Does your mother live in any expensive way?"

Gloria hesitated. "No, she does not. . . . She is a miser."

"When did you first become possessed of this idea that your mother was a miser and money mad?"

"I have always known it."

"I ask you again, do you charge your mother now with the motive to get this child because she wanted the $4,000 a month that you are getting?"

"No, you are wrong. I did not charge her with that now. I charged her with that in 1928. Now she is being amply provided for."

"You are looking at Mrs. Whitney now?"

"Yes, I am."

"You mean by that Mrs. Whitney is giving your mother money to live on, is that it?"

"Yes."

"Let me ask you this question, and it is an important one. You know that Mrs. Whitney is a grandmother of eight grandchildren, don't you?"

"Yes, I do."

"You know that she is interested in the rearing of as many children as that?"

"I don't know what she is doing. Is she bringing up an orphan asylum? Do not their mothers look after their children?"

"You are not listening to my question."

"I will not answer such a stupid question."

"You do not know what it is going to be."

"I will answer what you said so far."

"Now, having in mind the responsibilities that Mrs. Whitney has had outside as a sculptress, and having in mind all of her activities, can you tell this court any motive that Mrs. Whitney can have, except the welfare of her brother's child?"

In what could only be a direct reference to the Evan Burrows Fontaine paternity suit against Sonny Whitney, Gloria answered, "There is a certain little child here in New York that needs Mrs. Whitney's looking after much more than mine does."

Smyth ignored the pointed reference. He dealt Gloria a blow in return. "Do you remember being told that before this court the child was asked would she go back to her mother and that she shrank in her chair and the tears came out of her eyes and she said, 'I will not go'?"

"Was that in court?"

"Yes, in court. Why were you not there?"

"What are you trying to do, break my heart!" Gloria cried out. "About the child shrinking at the very thought of me, the only thing I can say is that if she is in that state now after two years with Mrs. Whitney, it is high time the child should come away from Mrs. Whitney."

Smyth asked if Gloria Vanderbilt thought that leaving her child for extended periods of time, for a whole winter at Melton Mowbray, for example, was "taking care of your child."

Gloria answered, "I think it is just as much taking care of it as when Mrs. Whitney is never at Westbury . . . when she was in Cuba for her health or in Europe for her health."

"How much time was she in Europe?"

"I don't know and I don't care!" Gloria exclaimed. "You may smile, Mrs. Whitney. This is really true." In her inarticulate way, she was trying to bring up an important point, that actually Gertrude Whitney was no more attentive to little Gloria than she herself had been.

Smyth demanded, "How does that compare with your absences time and again with your daughter lying sick?"

"Don't give me that daughter lying sick!" Gloria lashed out, then caught herself, and turning to Justice Carew murmured sweetly, "I am sorry, Your Honor." Gloria had lost her temper, then quickly retreated into her usual defenses. She began to weep profusely and called for a glass of water, saying that she felt faint. Carew responded to this by declaring an immediate adjournment until the following Tuesday, November 13. Gloria Vanderbilt's cross-examination was abruptly ended.

Saturday, November 10, 1934: BRUNO'S FOES JOIN LITTLE GLORIA'S CASE. Albert S. Osborn and Albert D. Osborn, noted father and son handwriting experts whose testimony was a vital factor in the indictment of Bruno Hauptmann, announced that they were prepared to testify for Mrs. Harry Payne Whitney if Nathan Burkan goes through with his plan to place his own expert, Elbridge W. Stein, on the witness stand.

KIDNAP GIRL FREE TODAY, SAYS DAD. Alfred E. Distelhurst revealed that contact with the kidnappers of his daughter (the Nashville, Tennessee, child heiress who has been held prisoner for nearly two months) was to be made momentarily. Distelhurst waited at the Hotel New Yorker with a $5,000 ransom.

Sunday, November 11, 1934: LITTLE GLORIA LETTERS FORGED. Elbridge Stein told reporters, "I have examined little Gloria's letters under infrared ray and found that they have been tampered with."

DISTELHURST WAITS. At the New Yorker Hotel Mr. Distelhurst issued the following statement to his daughter's kidnappers: "To Whom It May Concern: I have followed instructions implicitly. If further instructions are necessary I can be reached safely at designated place."

Monday, November 12: BRUNO'S FOES SAY NO TAMPERING IN LITTLE GLORIA LETTERS. Osborn father and son announced that they had examined little Gloria's letters and were prepared to refute Stein's assertion that they had been altered. (Since there was no court session on Monday, the *Matter of Vanderbilt* was now clearly being tried in the press even before it reached Carew's courtroom.)

DISTELHURST EXPECTS CHILD FROM KIDNAPPER TODAY. At Mr. Distelhurst's request, federal agents and other police officials agreed to withdraw from the case, leaving the path clear for the kidnappers to collect the ransom.

Tuesday, Novembr 13: DOROTHY ANN DEAD. While newsreel cameramen photographed Alfred Distelhurst in an appeal for the return of his child, two Negro workmen digging in the flowerbed of the Davidson County Tuberculosis Hospital discovered the nude body of a girl. A rag which had been stuffed in her mouth to keep her from crying out was still in place, her skull had been bashed in with a hammer, acid had destroyed her face. Subsequently, firemen dug up two school books, the remnants of a blue and white plaid dress, and a pink lunch pail.

NEW ALL-TIME RECORD. The *Matter of Vanderbilt* entered its seventh week, setting the record for a habeas corpus proceeding. Smyth, apparently recovered from Thursday's shock, began his redirect examination by establishing that Gloria Vanderbilt had never once visited little Gloria's school, had no idea what grade she was in, had never attended a school function, was not sure who her child's playmates were, knew the name of no teacher (except for one who had been mentioned in the testimony), knew of no book that the child was reading (except *Little Women*, which had also been mentioned in the testimony).

Burkan objected that these questions were "just a repetition of the cross-examination" and protested to Carew, "This lady has not been very well. This morning the doctor was against her coming to court. I do not think this should be gone into again."

Carew cautioned Smyth to proceed hastily with his redirect examination. He did so, ascertaining that little Gloria had never received first communion. Her mother explained why this was so, but as she spoke Smyth looked away, a bored expression on his face. "Are you listening to me or are you speaking for the sole purpose of speaking?" Gloria Vanderbilt demanded.

"The stenographer is getting everything and I will read it anyway," he answered, knowing that the printed record was what mattered now. Smyth had but one devastating question left. "You did not see your child for months, did you?"

"I do not remember," Gloria answered, almost inaudibly.

Herbert Smyth excused the witness.

Lillian Fisher and Consuelo Thaw jumped to their feet to help Gloria out of the building. She walked slowly, limping badly. Outside, hundreds of mothers and children waited for her. As Gloria approached, the crowd fell back reverently: she moved like a patient leaving a hospital. One small girl rushed forward and kissed Gloria's black-gloved hand. Gloria stopped. Lena Guadagno held her baby, Adele, high up and Gloria bent to kiss the child. She turned to the assembled crowd and reporters and said, "Isn't it lovely to know that people believe in you? My ordeal has been great. At one time I did not think I could live through this. But I am hopeful. I'm so grateful for all the kindnesses that have been shown to me. I can say no more . . . I'd like to stay but I'm too tired." As Gloria Vanderbilt moved toward her limousine a rhythmic chant went up from the crowd: "Give her her baby back! Give her her baby back! Give her her baby back!"

Carew was holding his luncheon press conference in his chambers when there was a commotion outside his door. Mrs. Edith Casse barged in, waving a paper. It was headed AN HUMBLE APPEAL TO GIVE THIS MOTHER BACK HER CHILD, and bore the signatures of three hundred mothers from the Columbus Park playground and the surrounding area. Mrs. Casse read out the petition in front of the reporters.

> Your Honor, the mothers of the above playground join me in making an appeal to you re your decision concerning the custody of Gloria Vanderbilt.
>
> There is no one on earth who will do more for a child than a mother. No love like a mother's. We need not say any more. Only this: That once more we humbly beseech your discretion and decision, and appeal to you to GIVE THIS MOTHER BACK HER CHILD.

She began passing out copies of the petition. "Get this woman out of here," Carew screamed at his secretary. "You are breaking the law," he said to Mrs. Casse, but she stood firm, waving her papers in the air and yelling, "This is my law—the law of motherhood." Two bailiffs entered the chambers and forcibly removed Mrs. Casse. As the door closed behind her Carew said, "If anyone else tries a petition like that, I'll make them eat it with ketchup!"

Now that Gloria Vanderbilt had completed her testimony, the proceedings took on a desultory tone. Carew hardly seemed to be listening as Consuelo Morgan Thaw took the stand. Smyth too seemed to pay only the slightest attention, as if he were aware that the matter had already been settled. Consuelo, presented with the litany of wrongdoing of which her sister had been accused, replied that she had seen no misconduct in her sister's household; no such incident involving Prince Hohenlohe had ever occurred, nor had the incident involving Lady Milford Haven occurred. Of this she was sure because she had been staying in an adjoining room at the Miramar Hotel. Lady Milford Haven was staying in one room with Gloria. "I had another room that I was sharing with another friend of mine."

"And who was the other friend?"

"Mrs. Simpson."

Consuelo's testimony was followed by that of handwriting expert Elbridge W. Stein, who testified that he had examined little Gloria's letters and found certain erasures and alterations. But as Stein enumerated these changes, it became evident that they involved either innocuous spelling corrections or the substitution of phrases that seemed less critical than those originally written. Stein pointed to the correction of the word *Nother* to *another*, *Mormal* to *normal*, *tep.* to *Temp.* Little Gloria had changed the lower case *d* in *Dodo* to upper case.

As to changes in content, Stein asserted that the sentence "My mother is so bad to me" had originally read "My mother is a beast to me." In a sentence that had originally read "My mother was in Paris enjoying herself while poor me was unhappy in England—Oh, what a life," the child had erased the *d* in *England* and the lament, "Oh, what a life."

Stein's testimony sounded as if he were a witness for the Whitney side and Smyth cleverly declined to cross-examine Stein or to put his own experts on the stand. "I think I can shorten this," he said. "I will concede what Mr. Stein says is true." Burkan must have known that Stein's testimony would be of no help to their case. He had only one reason for placing Stein on the stand: to maintain the illusion with the press (who could not hear Stein's testimony) that Stein had proved the child's letters had been altered. Burkan gave the newspapers his own version of the proceedings, hoping that reporters would never know what Stein had actually said. The following morning the *American* reported, "Nathan Burkan contends the child's letters were tampered with after they had been sent by the child. . . . He cites certain alleged erasures, deletions and substitutions . . . found by Elbridge W. Stein." The article went on to say that "little Gloria might be recalled to the stand to determine if she is able to spell such a word as TANTAMOUNT, said to appear in one of the notes." It didn't.

Stein's appearance was followed by two more character witnesses for Gloria Vanderbilt: Consuelo Thaw's sister-in-law Henrietta Slade and her husband, Lawrence Slade, who hardly knew Mrs. Vanderbilt. Henrietta Slade testified first. She was unquestionably a lady of fine reputation, the mother of five children. She had visited Gloria Vanderbilt on the rue Alfred Roll three times—once for tea, once for a dinner party, and once when she played backgammon with Mr. Morgan. On these occasions, Mrs. Slade had observed no wrongdoing, lascivious actions, lewd and obscene pictures, lascivious literature, rats, or misconduct of any kind. Smyth declined to cross-examine.

Lawrence Slade was the next witness. His examination took five minutes. He had seen no wrongdoing when he had called on Mrs. Vanderbilt with his wife. Burkan again asked one question too many, inquiring how often Mr. Slade had visited Mrs. Vanderbilt. "Certainly on one and probably more occasions," he answered. He said he'd attended a dinner party with quite a number of people, but he'd never been upstairs in the house. Again, Smyth declined to cross-examine.

Burkan put Thelma Furness back on the stand to question her about Mr. Morgan's petition. Thelma said she'd told her father, "Daddy, how can you say that you have seen dreadful people in Gloria's house when they are all your friends too?" and that Mr. Morgan had answered, "I have been nagged so much by your mother, who has told me all these dreadful things. I really didn't mean it and let's forget about it . . . and have lunch."

Then, quite suddenly, it was over. "That is all," said Smyth.

"That is all," said Burkan. "We rest."

"He rests," said Carew.

"We rest," said Smyth.

"Both sides rest," said Carew.

Smyth moved to dismiss the writ of habeas corpus. Burkan moved to sustain it. They both waited for Carew to speak. "I will not send this child back to the life that it lived from the time that its father died until it came to New York and was delivered to Mrs. Whitney. The issue here is the best interests of this child. I cannot approve of the conduct of the mother with relation to the child, and I limit it to that because I don't want to pass upon certain aspects of the case unless I have to.

"This child is very much better off where it is than where it was. Nevertheless, this mother is a young woman. I think she is under thirty now. I don't think this child should be altogether taken from this woman. The child certainly today is very, very strongly prejudiced against the mother. I would be glad if the mother could have an opportunity, first of all, to win back the confidence and affection of the child, and, second, to show that her future conduct will not be as her past conduct has been.

"I intend in some degree now to preserve for some time to come the life which the child has now. I think the mother should have such access to the child as will not interfere with the present life of the child but will give her an opportunity to win the child back and to take care of her properly in the future. . . ."

Although Burkan had expected this decision, he felt disappointment and defeat. "As I construe Your Honor's decision, it simply means that she is deprived of her child. That is my construction of it," he said.

"To a certain extent, she certainly is. But, as I say, I want to give her an opportunity to win the child back. . . . I think that you both . . . could approximate a proper disposition of this case," Carew replied.

Burkan and Smyth argued that there was no way they could do

this. "Your Honor," explained Burkan, "we have had discussions long before this thing started. Mrs. Whitney wants this child. Your Honor, as I construe the decision, has awarded her the child. It remains there. This mother is deprived of her rights to her child. What can she do? What can she say? What is there for her to do? . . . I gather from what Your Honor has stated, that it is a complete defeat."

In the front row, Thelma Furness began to sob and Gertrude Whitney smiled. In spite of himself, Burkan's eyes filled with tears. He had pretended to himself that this was just another case; now he realized his self-deception. "I have put everything that is in me into this case," he blurted out.

Carew's manner softened. "Counselor," he declared formally, "there was never a man that worked harder or threw more of the center of his soul into a case than you did in this. And that is not flattery, and that is not said to you for the purpose of consoling you. I know that the very core of your heart and soul went into this case." Carew's speech was meant to comfort Burkan, but it was to prove a deadly accurate prediction.

"I think it would be better if you cool off for the rest of the afternoon and come and see me tomorrow," said Carew.

"Oh, I am cool, Your Honor. I didn't lose my equilibrium. I never do," replied Burkan, although his tears rendered his words a lie. "I would be a very poor lawyer if I got excited because of defeat. I usually don't," he added, trying to explain it to himself. "I am used to it. This is not the first time I have been defeated. . . . I have had a long career at the bar, and so I have had my defeats as well as my victories. . . ."

"Well, we will have one more talk, you and I and Mr. Smyth," said Carew gently. Then, turning to the stenographer, he directed: "You may transcribe from your minutes this statement: 'Mr. Justice Carew decided that the child, Gloria Vanderbilt, is not to have for the future the life that it had from the death of its father up till June 1932.' "

"That is all?" asked Burkan in astonishment.

"That is all. . . . Yes, sir," replied Justice John Francis Carew.

The Socialites' Solomon

The party I promised you will be held on the thirty-second of December. Good day, gentlemen!

JUSTICE JOHN FRANCIS CAREW

THE COURTROOM EMPTIED. The reporters and cameramen flattened themselves against the walls of the corridor. They could tell who had won by the manner in which people left the room. Thelma walked slowly, lowering her head as she wiped her tears away. Gertrude Whitney appeared jubilant, pausing periodically, waving her black-gloved hand. Nathan Burkan stared straight ahead. Smyth tipped his hat in a victorious salute.

Reporters gathered in Carew's chambers, expecting to hear the decision he'd said he would render from the bench when the trial concluded. Instead, they were given the following single sentence, typed dead center on a sheet of white paper.

> Mr. Justice Carew decided that the child, Gloria Vanderbilt, is not to have for the future the life that it had from the death of its father up till June 1932.

They were mystified, and when Carew entered the room, one reporter waved the statement in the air and demanded, "What does this mean?"

"Every word means exactly what it says and nothing else." In fact, Carew had not yet addressed himself to the practical details of the disposition of the child's custody.

"But it doesn't tell us a thing," another reporter protested.

Carew began baiting the reporters. "It was designed to keep you from finding out what it meant," he said.

"Was it designed also to keep the lawyers from finding out?"

"It was designed for what it was designed for," answered Carew angrily.

One of the reporters tried to clarify the situation by asking, "Look, what kind of a life *is* the kid to lead?"

"That will have to be worked out."

"Judge, please tell us in plain words—yes or no—is Mrs. Vanderbilt's writ of habeas corpus granted or is it denied?"

Carew flushed. "I have absolutely nothing more to say."

"But you haven't said anything."

The reporters were pushing him too hard. Carew lashed out. "Then I will say this—I never want to see you again!" With that he strode out of the room, moved rapidly down the corridor, ducked into another office, and locked the door behind him.

Carew envisioned an ideal future for little Gloria and, in a series of conferences with Smyth and Burkan, he began to devise a specific plan. Almost immediately, Smyth, on behalf of the Whitney side, offered a sacrificial lamb to finally set both parties on the track of a settlement. Choosing a lamb that, in any case, was a difficult one for them to control, Smyth volunteered, "Let me make a suggestion. So far as this nurse that they complain of is concerned, which they say is so hostile, we will change her. Your Honor can approve of the nurse."

"I do not know anything about nurses."

"Let the nurse go. We want to help . . ." said Smyth.

"Then that is settled. The nurse goes," said Carew.

"The nurse goes," agreed Burkan. They all agreed: the "hovering hen" was to be dismissed. A quarter of a century later, little Gloria Vanderbilt, still not understanding the legal maneuvering, would tell a journalist, "I couldn't understand the quarrel between my mother and my aunt. . . . I hated my mother because she'd taken away my nurse. . . . When she fired Dodo it broke my heart."

WEATHER
FAIR and WARMER.
High Tide: 3:51 A. M. 4:13 P. M.
Low Tide: 10:17 A. M. 10:33 P. M.

DAILY MIRROR

FINAL
MUrray Hill 2-1000

VOL. XI. No. 125 New York, Friday, November 16, 1934 2 cents CITY LIMITS | 3 CENTS Elsewhere

MRS. WHITNEY WON, SAYS LADY FURNESS

Story on Page 3

MOTHERS PLEAD FOR GLORIA

Continued from Page 3

affirmative of the rumor that he would be called to testify.

Mrs. Vanderbilt arrived with her usual cortege of friends, including the Prince and Princess Hohenlohe, her sisters, Lady Furness and Mrs. Benjamin Thaw, and the Harry Hays Morgans. All entered Justice Carew's chamebrs.

And all but Mrs. Harry Payne Whitney, who is seeking to keep little Gloria on the ground that her mother is not a fit custodian, were sent right out again.

To insure the last measure of secrecy, Justice Carew stationed court attendants in front of the triangular windows in the courtroom door, so that reporters could not watch Mrs. Vanderbilt's pantomime.

She was under cross-examination during most of the morning, and under re-direct examination in the afternoon. It is understood that large sums of money were mentioned during her questioning.

The usual crowd of women and children stood outside the courthouse as she came and went. One of the women thrust a note into her hand as she entered. A moment later, Mrs. Vanderbilt stumbled slightly and another woman rushed forward, kissed her hand

Justice John F. Carew

A group of mothers, bearing petitions asking that Mrs. Vanderbilt retain the custody of her child, are shown waiting outside court where the secret testimony was being heard by Justice Carew.

(NEWS photo)

ter spirits than usual, ...

RS. VANDERBILT NEAR COLLAPSE

pported by Brother and a Nurse After Testifying for Six Hours in Cou

AYS CASE IS 'GOIN

lready Planning
o Convent Whic
Attended as

Mrs. Gloria Mor
ent six hours mo
esterday in the Su
er second day as
ad been three hours
e previous day. S
aged in her direct t
ying to the witness
ehind closed doors
ourt days by Mrs. H
Whitney.

Mrs. Vanderbilt refu
ay when court adjourn
ain the idea that any c
eny her the writ of hab
which she has asked
ossession of her 10-year
Gloria. The girl has li
Mrs. Whitney for two y
as expressed a preference
ice John F. Carew for re
here.

The mother revealed that
lready planning for the chi
ure in her charge. Among
plans, she said, she intends
he child to school at the
Catholic Convent of the S
Heart in Manhattanville, where
herself went as a child.

For Mrs. Whitney, on the oth
hand, Herbert C. Smyth, her cou
sel, said "we intend to take t
very best care of the child."
child is now attending the Gr
vale private school at Rosl

until she got her child back and disposed of Mrs. Whitney's objection that she was not a good mother.

Previously she had sat in the court room with her face buried i
her hands in a complete stat
exhaustion for twenty minutes
ter the judge had left the ben
Her two sisters and her br
comforted

Justice Carew, who mu
eventual ho is to get th
child, h made clear t
the en will
contro
may b
Vand

landed at Pigou with
crew on rudely const
The captain reported h
periences and the loss
A blinding snowstor
h a thick fog and a
on Sunday nig
d responsible for
t. Roi David, Ca
of Quebec, a crew
six unidentified
wrecka
been

ouse,
ma-
often
the wel-
munity and
necessary to
He sed a one-
arliam assisted by a
jurid administrative
and nical rts to examine
and pr are bi efore their pres-
ntation to the Folketing. He further proposed abolishing the constitutional court.

"I Was Robbed of My Child", Mrs. Vanderbilt Charges

(NEWS photos by W. Hoff © 1934 by News Syndicate Co., Inc.)

"I openly charge that Mrs. Whitney has been behind this whole movement against me to rob me of my child."

"If I had wanted just an income and not my little daughter, I could have secured a good income."

". . . If need be I will go out and work at anything I can find to get back my child . . . my child that always loved me."

"I am afraid my little daughter has been very much influenced by promises of lots of things which would influence a child."

FOUR STUDIES OF MRS. GLORIA MORGAN VANDERBILT AS SHE WAS INTERVIEWED YESTERDAY IN HER 49 E. 72D ST. HOME

Carew announced that he'd decided to make no ruling on the charges of immorality leveled against Gloria Vanderbilt, but Burkan begged him to exonerate her, saying, "Your Honor, it is a very serious matter for this lady because the whole world has been apprised of these charges. . . . She may have been a neglectful mother; that is for Your Honor to find . . . but the charge of immorality and these other offenses is very serious. It is branding her down to the third generation." Then Burkan added prophetically, "I think, Your Honor, in all fairness, the day will come, it must come, when this issue must be tried out between this child and her mother, no matter what disposition Your Honor makes as to these charges."

There was a warning in Carew's voice as he answered, "I do not intend to make a finding on those specific charges. . . . And I do it out of consideration for the mother and child. . . . No matter how guilty the mother might be—and I haven't found her guilty of these things—she is a young woman, she has had a very, very severe trial and test here, and I would be very glad indeed to give her an opportunity to get this child back. . . . Even if she were a thousand times more guilty than she ever has been, I still have enough of the human in me to want to give her an opportunity for the future."

When Burkan continued to protest, Carew pronounced a moral judgment on Gloria Vanderbilt's conduct—a judgment which he considered gave her every benefit of the doubt. "It was a great mistake for this lady to take this child over to Europe. It was a great mistake ever to become interested in Prince Hohenlohe—I am speaking now entirely regarding it as an honorable courtship—a great mistake. A great mistake. Even if it were the most honorable courtship that ever was conducted, it would have been a mistake under the circumstances. . . . I think it is foolish for this young woman to be running around with Mr. Blumenthal, who is a married man. . . . I think it is very foolish for her to be doing it." Carew leaned back in his chair and concluded, "She needs a guardian pretty nearly as much as the child does!"

Carew already had decided some of the things the child needed: "I am going to see to it she [little Gloria] gets religious training in the Catholic faith," he said, and suggested that Mrs. Vanderbilt might be put in charge of this training. "I think it will be good for the mother. . . . I do feel genuine hopes that the mother might, in less time than three years, demonstrate the propriety of having the child outright."

Nathan Burkan said that before these proceedings began, his client had spoken to the mother superior of the Sacred Heart about the possibility of sending her daughter there.

"I think this child should stay in the school where it is," commented Carew. "I am coming right to the point now. . . . I think the child should stay in the school where it is and on school days—Monday, Tuesday, Wednesday, Thursday, and Friday, possibly Friday night, and Sunday night—the child should stay with Mrs. Whitney and attend that school. I have considered the possibility of letting the mother have the child for Saturdays and Sundays in order to give her an opportunity to give this child this Catholic training that she wants and we all are so anxious she should get."

The plan seemed logical to Carew, but Smyth immediately pointed out a major problem. "The only trouble about the child being sent to the mother on Saturdays and Sundays is that at the present time she is in a much worse condition than she was when Your Honor saw her, and you have pretty nearly a straitjacket proposition."

Carew's answer exposed exactly what was drastically wrong here. In his mind, he'd envisioned a happy ending—a child trained in the Catholic faith, a healthy child living quietly with her devoted aunt in the country, a child who would eventually be reconciled with a mother who had totally reformed—and he refused to acknowledge that the facts of the case totally contradicted this picture. In his consuming effort to impose his own distorted vision of reality, he could no longer even see the very child whom he was supposedly benefiting. Unaware of the shattering irony, he replied, "I'm not going to be baffled by that. If she is in such a state, she is an unfortunate child. And if she dies as a result of it—that is her hard luck!"

Ignoring the emotional aspects and possible repercussions of each new problem, Carew forged ahead with the blinkered vision that sustained him. In a private conference, Herbert Smyth told Carew that his client feared that Mrs. Vanderbilt would kidnap little Gloria as she had tried to do in the past. He asked for assurances that this would not happen, and Carew pointed out, ". . . We have in this case securities for her [Mrs. Vanderbilt's] future conduct that we ordinarily do not have. This mother has no fortune of her own . . . and she is to a very large extent dependent upon what allowances may be made to her for the support of the child." To control Gloria Vanderbilt's conduct and prevent her from kidnapping little Gloria, Carew said he'd make both George Wickersham and Thomas B. Gilchrist parties to his final order which would thereby empower him to cut off Gloria Vanderbilt's revenues on a moment's notice, if she displeased him. Gilchrist and Wickersham protested that they should not be made parties to the order, that the dispensation of monies from the child's trust rightly lay in the Surrogates' Court. But Carew responded angrily, "I will not tolerate for one moment the suggestion that the Supreme Court should go, hat in hand, to the Surrogate of New York and ask him to cut off the Relator's revenues if she kidnaps the child and removes it to Europe."

Carew felt that "Europe was not much of a journey for Mrs. Vanderbilt." Therefore he added another safeguard—little Gloria was to be made a ward of the court until she was twenty-one. That meant, in Carew's words, "that if the Relator took the child out of the jurisdiction of the State of New York that I would at once cut off her revenues" and as Smyth said, "If at any time the child is removed from New York State without permission, whoever takes her is liable to a charge of kidnapping. . . . Even if the child were taken to Europe, the person removing her could be extradited, except perhaps from Greece."

With Smyth satisfied, Burkan had two requests of his own: first, he asked Carew to incorporate into his order a provision that Mrs. Vanderbilt's income was to continue, and his final request was that Carew seal the testimony in this case so that what had been said in his courtroom would never become public!

As Carew went about drafting his final order, his behavior became increasingly erratic. Perhaps he was exerting a monumental effort to keep the painful truth of this case from his own consciousness. He began boasting of the work he was doing, telling a friend that his decision was "one of supreme genius—and will be recognized as such." The press clamored to know his decision and day after day he called press conferences—twelve within the week—but reporters never knew when they walked into his chambers if they would find a contained, affable man or an angry, disoriented one. Some days they were summoned to Carew's chambers only to be angrily dismissed. One morning they arrived and were told, "Gentlemen, my mind is still open on this settlement. . . . I will keep you informed of each and every step in this process." As they left, Carew pronounced the benediction, "*Dominus vobiscum.*" The next day, reporters arrived to find Carew's face buried in his hands, and when they asked him questions he would not lift his head or reply.

On Thursday morning, Carew's secretary called reporters up from the press room, saying that the Justice had a statement for them, but by the time they reached the sixth floor, Carew refused to see them. After lunch, Carew's secretary summoned them back to his chambers. When they arrived, an attendant apologized to them, saying that Carew was still at lunch. At three o'clock, reporters were startled to see Carew burst out of the judges' private elevator and push his way through the crowd, shouting, "I am Justice Carew of the Supreme Court. You will have to clear out of this corridor." A reporter reminded Carew that they were there because he'd said he had a statement for them. "I will not have a statement today or later. . . . I don't want to see any of you again. Ever. Clear out."

"When will the decision be filed and where?" one reporter persisted.

"It will take the usual course," Carew answered in a gruff voice.

"Our city editors will think we're lousy reporters if we don't get the decision," protested one reporter.

"Give them my regards and tell them I was very glad to have met you," snapped the judge. He yanked a cigar from his pocket, peeled off the cellophane, and jammed it into his mouth. A reporter stepped forward with a light, but Carew angrily waved him away.

"How about the party you promised us at the conclusion of this case?" a reporter asked, referring to the promise made by a Justice Carew of quite different temperament from this one.

Carew considered. "The party I promised you will be held on the thirty-second of December. Good day, gentlemen!" He walked into his office and slammed the door.

Aware of Carew's sudden shifts in mood, the reporters waited outside his door. About fifteen minutes later, he stuck his head out and screamed, "These corridors are public property," then slammed the door again. A moment later an attendant appeared and said he'd been directed by the Justice to drive the journalists back to a point exactly twenty feet from Carew's door.

At 5:30 p.m. Carew emerged from his chambers holding his hands in front of his face, as if protecting himself from blows, and repeating over and over, "I will have no converse about this case, I will have no converse about this case . . ."

On Friday, Carew called a press conference and casually remarked that his final decision would come as "a great surprise to the public." He told them that he had found it necessary to explain his decision to the lawyers for both sides and to the child's guardians because they had failed to understand his reasoning.

On Saturday, some reporters resisted visiting Carew's chambers, but were assured by his secretary that he had important news for them, and they found the Justice elated, all smiles and soft words: "I can tell you in regard to the uproar about secrecy that the eventual determination of this case will be a matter of public record and everybody can see it. . . . I have devised a plan to give the child back to her mother as soon as Mrs. Vanderbilt provides a life for the child in which the girl will be assured of happiness." Carew said he would probably sign his decision at 10:00 a.m. Monday, but when reporters came to his chambers on

Monday, he said he was unprepared to sign an order. When asked when he would sign, he replied, "At one o'clock—some day." A reporter asked if little Gloria would ever be permitted to live with her mother. Instead of answering directly, Carew began comparing his problem with that of King Solomon when two mothers claimed the same child: "My judgment will be like that of King Solomon," he declared. Reporters, filing their stories, used Carew's comparison to give him a nickname that was to identify him from that time on: "The Socialites' Solomon."

On Wednesday, November 21, 1934, Carew finally issued his decision:

FOUND, CONSIDERED, ORDERED, ADJUDGED AND DECREED:

(1) That the life led by this infant from the death of her father until June 1932, was entirely and in every way unsuitable, unfit, improper, calculated to destroy her health and neglectful of her moral, spiritual and mental education, and that it so resulted to the discomfort, detriment, damage and injury of the infant;

(2) That the life lived by the infant since June 1932, has been fit, suitable and appropriate and has resulted in a great improvement in the infant physically and mentally and has tended to promote its best welfare, comfort and happiness;

(3) That since June 1932, the conduct, mode of life, surroundings, conditions and actions of the relator have continued as prior thereto when she was in possession or custody of said infant;

(4) That the prima facie privilege of relator herein to have the custody of her infant child Gloria has been overcome by the evidence offered by both sides before me, and it is

FURTHER DECLARED AND ADJUDGED:

(5) That the following determination awarding custody is made solely for the promotion of the best interests and welfare of the infant Gloria Morgan Vanderbilt, and it is

FURTHER CONSIDERED, ORDERED, FOUND, ADJUDGED AND DECREED:

That the said writ of habeas corpus be finally disposed of as follows:

(6) That the infant Gloria Morgan Vanderbilt is hereby adjudged to be the ward of the Supreme Court of the State of New York;

(7) That Mrs. Gertrude Vanderbilt Whitney, the sister of the deceased father of said infant, is granted the custody of said infant as the representative of the Supreme Court of the State of New York and is hereby commanded to maintain the domicile and resi-

dence of said infant at 871 Fifth Ave., Borough of Manhattan, City of New York;

(8) That Mrs. Gertrude Vanderbilt Whitney as the Custodian of said infant shall provide for her a governess of the Roman Catholic faith who shall reside with her, teach her the Catechism of the Roman Catholic faith, prepare or cause her preparation for Holy Communion and Confirmation in the Roman Catholic faith, and attend with her at Mass on all Sundays and all Holy Days of Obligation of the Roman Catholic faith;

(9) That Mrs. Gertrude Vanderbilt Whitney shall cause the said infant to continue to attend the Greenvale School at Roslyn, Long Island, and while in attendance there shall cause her to live in a manner suitable to her fortune at her country home in Old Westbury, Long Island;

(10) That beginning one month after the entry of this order Mrs. Gertrude Vanderbilt Whitney as such Custodian of said infant shall cause the said infant to be delivered to the relator herein, Mrs. Gloria Morgan Vanderbilt, on each Saturday morning at 10 a.m., either at the residence of Mrs. Gloria Morgan Vanderbilt in New York or at any residence she may have within thirty miles of Old Westbury, Long Island, and the said infant will remain in the company of the relator and be redelivered by the relator to the Custodian, Mrs. Gertrude Vanderbilt Whitney, at sundown on the following Sunday at the place where she received the infant;

(11) That the infant shall be delivered (as specified in paragraph ten) to the relator herein at 10 a.m. on Christmas Day, and shall be returned at 6 p.m.;

(12) That the relator, Mrs. Gloria Morgan Vanderbilt, shall be permitted to have the uninterrupted society of the infant during the month of July unless cause shall be shown to the contrary;

(13) That Mrs. Gertrude Vanderbilt Whitney shall have the uninterrupted society of the infant during the month of August and up to the beginning of the school term at Roslyn, Long Island;

(14) That the relator and respondent are severally prohibited from taking the said infant outside of the State of New York or permitting her to be so taken without the State;

(15) That, for and upon good cause first shown, any party hereto may hereafter apply, on notice to all other parties, at the foot of this final order for other or further direction.

Enter,

Justice John F. Carew

Headlines quickly spread the news of Carew's decision across the country. MRS WHITNEY WINS GOLD CHILD . . . VANDERBILT MOTHER IN COLLAPSE . . . 78 MILLION WHITNEY WIDOW WINS . . . GLORIA VANDERBILT UNFIT . . . LITTLE GLORIA WARD OF THE STATE.

With the issuance of his final order, Carew directed that the record of the *Matter of Vanderbilt* was to be sealed. Sitting at the breakfast table, Carew's daughter Blanche asked him, "Daddy, did you really say that thing about putting ketchup on the petition and eating it?" and in answer he explained to his children that he had, and that this case was a "heartbreaking one" because he didn't believe a child should be taken away from her mother but he "did what he had to do." He said he'd barred the press because "I am an old man, and I have lived, but never have I heard such things as I have heard in that courtroom."

Carew was sure that now the trial was over, the public would recognize that he had tried to protect both the mother and the child, and he sat back and waited for the acclaim he felt was his due. It was not forthcoming. Instead, almost every aspect of his decision met with severe criticism. Asked for an analysis of his decision, Carew told reporters: "You'll have to do your own interpreting. It's in plain English." They did. They found Carew "cruel" and "unnecessarily harsh" in stating that since little Gloria had gone to live with her aunt, Gloria Vanderbilt's "mode of life had not undergone any marked reform." The press, not knowing that the Whitney side feared that Gloria Vanderbilt would kidnap her daughter, criticized Carew's point 14 which confined her to New York State: "Ten-year-old Gloria Laura Vanderbilt, child of many millions and much misery, became a ward of the state of New York yesterday, with the state ruling her life as firmly as it does the life of a foundling left on the doorstep. . . . Carew's geographic restrictions have made the child a prisoner of New York State. . . . 'Suppose,' Carew was asked, 'Gloria should want some day to go the Yale prom in New Haven, or a Yale-Harvard game at Cambridge, or to Palm Beach or to the Greenwich horse show, or to any other such affair outside the state to which a girl of her station in life would naturally be attracted?'

" 'Why, she would have to appear before a Justice of the Supreme Court to get permission,!' Carew replied."—The New York *Daily News*.

The decision was criticized on religious grounds: "Here comes a child who was baptized in the Episcopal Church and I can't see why a judge should go out of his way in a decision to compel the religious education of the child to be in the Roman Catholic Church when we have a State law which says that the first baptism of a child becomes its religion when the child becomes a State ward."—Dr. Fridolin E. Oberlander, Lutheran minister.

On moral grounds: "The mere fact that the Court believes the parent is not pursuing the wisest course in the rearing of the child does not justify taking the child from the parent."—George W. Smyth, Children's Judge.

On constitutional grounds: "The freedom of the press must be protected and preserved. . . . When the sensational details of the Vanderbilt case came to light, it became legitimate news and the newspaper had a perfect right to use it."—*Sun* editorial.

On legal grounds: "Both Wickersham and Gilchrist publicly objected to being made parties to the order, asserting that Surrogate Foley, not Justice Carew, should have complete control of the child's trust."—*United States Law Review.*

On grounds of common sense: "The order providing for five days' custody with the aunt and two with the mother may ruin the child. . . . It is easy to foresee that without coaching by psychiatrists or other competent, trained persons, Mrs. Vanderbilt may be tempted to reproach her daughter, Mrs. Whitney may be tempted to be quietly vindictive toward the mother and, since all will be trying to please the child, she is likely to have her character destroyed by getting whatever she wishes from both."—Jonah J. Goldstein, Magistrate Justice.

"What kind of provision for the child's welfare is all this, anyway? The judge has taken the child from its mother and awarded it to the woman whom the mother probably hates most in the world, and who probably returns the mother's hate with interest. How can either of these women refrain from trying to poison the child's mind against the other, and what will that do to the child?"—*Mirror* editorial.

The *American* ran a cartoon of Justice Carew sitting in the judgment seat. In front of him stood a woman, her face buried in her hands in grief. The caption read, "It is my decision that you are no longer the mother of your child."

Gertrude Whitney, who had been cast by the press in the role of a villain, now tried to handle the situation with as much dignity as possible. On Tuesday evening, November 20, while little Gloria was preparing for bed, Gertrude sat down to write a statement to present at her press conference the following day.

> My only thought since little Gloria came to live with me and throughout the court proceedings has been for the child's welfare. Her health, her happiness and what was best for her has been my only interest. It was always my hope and my desire to bring the child and her mother closer together—

Mrs. Whitney's secretary walked into the room and handed her a letter —in crude black printing on plain white paper was a threat to kill little Gloria unless Justice Carew immediately gave her back to her mother. The signature read, CATHOLIC COMMUNIST. Gertrude rushed to the phone and called the Nassau County police, who responded immediately by sending a squad of police detectives. Little Gloria was in her bedroom when the policemen flooded the house. They locked her bedroom window and posted a policeman outside her bedroom door, Another policeman kept watch in the adjoining room, and the door between the two rooms was left open. At 7:00 a.m. a fresh police squad was sent to relieve these men. Wednesday morning Gertrude Whitney made arrangements for twelve Pinkerton detectives to replace the Nassau County police detective force. The phone rang incessantly with reporters seeking statements about her victory, and she said she would answer their questions that afternoon at her press conference at 871 Fifth Avenue. She did, however, issue a brief statement to a persistent reporter, saying enthusiastically, "Gloria is very happy to continue her life in Old Westbury."

At 4:45 Wednesday, three butlers in crimson livery escorted reporters and photographers into Mrs. Whitney's drawing room, where they stood under the painted ceiling from a Roman palace, gazing at the deep-red, cut-velvet walls and drapes. Gertrude Whitney, in an effort to put them at ease, walked up to each reporter in turn and extended her hand in greeting. She motioned to a fourteenth-century refectory table which held an assortment of glasses and liquor and invited the reporters to help themselves. Then she willingly posed for the photographers, leaning against her white Italian marble mantel, smoking a cigarette. When the photographers were finally finished, she lit a new cigarette, and for the next hour chain-smoked, lighting each cigarette from the stub of the last.

Barklie Henry distributed typewritten copies of Mrs. Whitney's statement.

> . . . It was always my hope and my desire to bring the child and her mother closer together. My house was open to Mrs. Vanderbilt at all times. She could come and be with Gloria whenever she

wanted. This case was not of my making. The papers were served on me. The last thing I wanted was a court proceeding.

I am sure you all love and understand children, and I want to appeal to you on behalf of this little girl. She is the chief person in this case through no fault of her own. I appeal to you to put this case out of the public mind. I am sure you agree with me that the less said about the proceeding the better for the sake of the child.

I want to tell you all how very happy I am that Justice Carew has seen fit to give me this great responsibility. I accept it very seriously and shall do everything in my power to be worthy of his confidence in me.

Reporters read the statement while Gertrude sat on a rose-colored settee, occasionally flicking her ashes into a large ashtray.

"In your sentence, 'My house was open to Mrs. Vanderbilt at all times,' is the use of the past tense intended?" asked a reporter.

Gertrude Whitney said nothing.

"Might the 'was' be changed to 'is'?" he persisted.

"No," she replied, but then, in a typical display of manners and the suppression of emotion that characterized this woman, she added, "I hope that if there has been any antagonism, it will be forgotten in the interest of the child."

A reporter asked, "You've spoken very feelingly of your love for little Gloria. In that connection, how do you think Mrs. Vanderbilt feels now?"

Gertrude Whitney did not answer immediately. She leaned back on the settee and closed her eyes. Then she opened them, paused, and said slowly, "I have no idea."

"Do you intend to make any overtures of friendliness toward her?"

The pencil-thin woman smiled a cheerless smile. "I think the less said of personalities the better."

The questions continued for an hour. A *Times* reporter asked, "What will you do when you attempt to deliver the child to Mrs. Vanderbilt for the first weekend, if the child has another nervous frenzy, as she did when her mother attempted to visit her at your home while this case was going on?"

Gertrude Whitney answered, "I'll have to face that situation when it comes up."

When asked to describe little Gloria's interests, she said that her niece was interested in "painting and rides exceptionally well." Asked if the child would become an artist, her sculptor aunt replied, "She is too young yet to decide that. All kids go through such phases."

Gertrude Whitney explained that she wanted little Gloria to be raised as "a thorough American," and she praised her late brother Reginald Vanderbilt, saying that he "conformed to the nationalistic ideal" she sought for the child.

It was after six o'clock when Gertrude Whitney ended the conference. "I don't want to be rude, but I expect to drive out and see [little] Gloria," she said. She did not mention that Wheatley Hills was now an armed fortress.

Gertrude Whitney and Barklie Henry arrived home in time to see the Nassau County police replaced by the dozen Pinkertons. A Whitney grandchild remembers the changing of the guard and the police driving off, waving goodbye.

Gloria Vanderbilt had taken to her bed the day her testimony was completed and refused to budge. As Nathan Burkan sat by her bedside, she told him, "I can't see anybody or talk to anybody—ever again. I'm ashamed to be seen in public after the terrible things they've said about me." Gloria seemed so close to a nervous collapse that Thelma said she would return to England, get her son, and come back to stay with her sister. "I'll only be gone as long as it takes to fetch Tony," she promised.

Nathan Burkan insisted that Gloria must see the press, to counter Gertrude's press conference. "The fight is just beginning," Burkan assured her. "We'll win on appeal. I know it." Thursday afternoon Burkan welcomed the press into Gloria Vanderbilt's Japanese-wallpapered living room where a dozen photographs of little Gloria were prominently displayed. After they were assembled, Gloria Vanderbilt made her entrance, supported on both sides by Consuelo Thaw and nurse Fisher. She limped across the room wincing from the pain in her left leg, and nestled in the corner of a gold brocade sofa. Photographers moved in and snapped away from every possible angle. She was dressed demurely in a black silk, square-necked dress. Her 16¼-carat heart-shaped diamond engagement ring was the only jewelry she wore on her very short-nailed fingers. As reporters began to ask her questions, she suddenly became energized, her whole body seemed to vibrate and her dark eyes looked bright as she began an outpouring of rapid speech.

"I openly charge that Mrs. Whitney has been behind this whole movement to rob me of my child. If this case was not of her making as she says, why was her attorney securing witnesses to testify against me as early as June. . . . Mrs. Whitney some day will be shown for what she really is. At the present moment I do not know what her motives really are. I believe she has a very strong personal animosity toward me and has had for years past.

"She talks now of acting in the interests of the child . . . I do not think it fitting that a child should be brought up with hatred for the one she should love. And consider what this court decision does for her interest. She is made the center of snapshots for news cameras when she goes to school, surrounded by detectives; her little classmates talk to her about the trial; and at home she has Mrs. Whitney and my own mother and the nurse poisoning her mind."

Gloria paused for breath, took a sip of mineral water and, reverting to the theme of the poor widow fighting the whim of the high-handed rich aunt, she said, "I will fight to the last ditch, and Mr. Burkan promised me that he will stand by my side to the bitter end. This case may leave me penniless—Mrs. Whitney may try to have my allowance cut down to nothing—but if need be, I will go out and work at anything I can find to get my child—my child that has always loved me.

"It is strange, indeed, that not until the trial was it ever mentioned in my presence or hearing that my child was estranged from me. . . . I again state that I shall gladly spend all I have to hold my little girl in my arms again, and to vindicate the name that Mrs. Alice Gwynne Vanderbilt was so justly proud of . . ."

A reporter asked Mrs. Vanderbilt about Justice Carew's finding that her mode of life was so unsuitable that her natural privilege to have custody of her daughter had been "overcome by the evidence submitted by both sides."

Gloria cast a stricken look at her sister Consuelo, who answered for her. "My sister does not understand that, because there is nothing in her mode of life which could be criticized."

What of the rumor that the child had fled screaming from her mother—was she prepared to gradually win back her daughter's love?

"My child doesn't have to be brought back to love me gradually. She always did love me and she still does. That is one thing that even the Whitney money cannot buy. . . . I have gone through hell in the last weeks. I am in bed ill . . . I am afraid I shall be ill for some time. . . . It was a terrible ordeal for me, facing scorn and insult. Nobody can understand how I felt on the witness stand. . . . I was robbed of my child!"

Nathan Burkan took Gloria's hand in his. "This mother will fight this ruling to the highest courts and demand the right to regain her child and rear her a Catholic." He said that they would settle for nothing less than complete custody of little Gloria.

"Yes," Gloria Vanderbilt agreed, "I am going to appeal. . . . Mrs. Whitney shall not be permitted to keep my child. . . . I am confident that no court in this nation will sustain this fantastic and extraordinary decision." She said that Carew had promised her control of the child's religious education and had now taken even that away from her. "I will appeal Justice Carew's decision to every court in the United States. And to the highest court." She looked up at Burkan. "Whatever that is."

Gloria's denunciation of Justice Carew was printed nationwide and Carew's hate mail swelled to a torrent. "There were anonymous phone calls and vicious threats at all hours of the day and night," recalls one of Carew's children. "We changed our number practically every day, but we couldn't stop them. I don't know how they got the number."

No less than a dozen letters arrived threatening the welfare of Carew's youngest daughter, sixteen-year-old Blanche. A typical one read, "Mr. Judge—You'll see what it feels like to lose a child when Blanche dies." Carew called the police, and a guard was assigned to escort Blanche to and from classes at the Dominican Academy at Sixty-eighth Street and Park Avenue.

One morning her police escort had left her on the pavement in front of the school when a strange woman approached, called her by name, and said her father had suffered a heart attack and wanted her to come to his chambers immediately. The woman opened the door of her car and told Blanche she was going to take her to her father. Blanche ran inside the school and phoned the police. Two radio cars shrieked up, but the woman had disappeared. When the police took Blanche home, the same woman was waiting outside her apartment building. She was arrested but after a three-hour interrogation, the woman, Helen Morgan, was released. She was an *American* reporter after an exclusive story.

The critical reception to his decision, the kidnap threats, the abusive phone calls, all worked powerfully on Justice Carew's emotions. He had envisioned himself as wise as Solomon, but nothing had gone according to plan. Late the following Sunday morning, after attending church, Carew summoned reporters to his chambers yet again. He refused to sit, and paced up and down as he railed at them, saying that the criticism of his decision was "unfounded and unjust." Unable to keep quiet any longer, he breached his own ethical code as he said with bitterness, "As for the secrecy for which I have been so criticized . . . Nathan Burkan asked for that order. When he and Mrs. Vanderbilt say that they want the record made public, ask them why they asked for an order of secrecy. . . . At no time—no time—did Burkan or Mrs. Vanderbilt ask me to open the hearings to the public!"

After a few minutes, Carew picked up his black felt hat, stroked the brim, and held it out to reporters, explaining that he always wore this hat in memory of his nineteen years as the Democratic member of Congress from the Seventeenth District in New York City. "May I remind you that I served and was elected eight consecutive times by the people of New York City," he said. "They have always had confidence in my abilities." Then he raised his hat and placed it on his head and walked slowly out of his chambers.

In November of 1936, two years after this trial had ended, Gloria Vanderbilt submitted an unopposed petition to Justice Carew to amend the custody agreement. The legal papers were left at Justice Carew's chambers, but he was not there to accept them. Reporters were told that the Justice was "temporarily indisposed." Checking further, they found that although Carew had been collecting his salary, he had not appeared on the bench for several months. Two weeks later, when Carew had still not appeared, Justice Timothy A. Leary was appointed to settle the custody modification agreement.

Fifteen months later, a *News* reporter located Justice John Francis Carew. He was a patient at the Neuropsychiatric Hospital in Hartford, Connecticut, a hospital that specialized in the treatment of alcoholism and nervous breakdowns.

SINCE THEN

Rockabye Baby

Rockabye baby
Up on a writ,
Monday to Friday Mother's unfit.
As the week ends she rises in virtue;
Saturdays, Sundays,
Mother won't hurt you.

UNITED STATES LAW REVIEW

LITTLE GLORIA VANDERBILT emerged from the trial a celebrity. What an appealing symbol she was—this heiress, Vanderbilt, American princess—this child star, appearing in the poor-little-rich-girl movie scenario of her own life. But now, as in the movies, it was time for a happy ending to the story. "Little Gloria begins a new life with her wealthy aunt," said the *Sun*. Fully dressed in her Little Orphan Annie smile, little Gloria was depicted as frolicking through her troubles to a life with one of the richest people in the world—her own Daddy Warbucks—Gertrude Vanderbilt Whitney. And as the final fillip, some day she was to be reunited with her beautiful, reformed mother, who even now protested, "I will do anything to bring my baby back to my arms!"

This scenario of little Gloria's life was to cause screenwriters to resurrect a series of Eleanor Gates, Ralph Spence stories for the film *The Poor Little Rich Girl* starring Shirley Temple as a little Gloria-like "luxury laden but lonely" tyke who, in the course of her travels, is banished to a drafty attic but emerges a kinder, wiser child. Only two weeks after the trial ended (with Gertrude Vanderbilt Whitney sitting in the audience), Cole Porter, in his new Broadway musical *Anything Goes*, caught the bittersweet essence of little Gloria's appeal, epitomized in the delicious disparity of the accusation that "the tiny Vanderbilt heiress was dressed in rags."

The world has gone mad today
And good's bad today,
And black's white today,
And day's night today,
And that gent today,
You gave a cent today
Once had several châteaux.
When folks who still can ride in jitneys
Find out Vanderbilts and Whitneys
Lack baby-cloe's
Anything goes.

If, in fact, at Wheatley Hills there was a real little girl who feared her mother, kidnapping, and death, whose new life was a nightmare, no one wanted to know it.

> Little Gloria Vanderbilt yesterday started her coming life on the Harry Payne Whitney estate at Old Westbury, L.I., by taking a child's inventory of what she had gained. A pony. It is a black pony with a silky mane and he gallops up and down the estate meadows when you say "cl'k."
>
> SIX SERVANTS
>
> Six—count 'em—six special servants assigned to individual attendance on "Miss Gloria," who, in the nonlegalistic minds of the village full of servitors on the Whitney estate, now becomes the "daughter of the house" and the heiress-apparent of their world.

There was no mention that the "six servitors" were bodyguards; the newspapers consistently referred to these bodyguards as "little Gloria's retinue." When Gertrude Whitney took the child shopping the following Friday, they were followed by reporters, still photographers, and newsreel cameramen who recorded their every action.

> Surrounded by her impressive retinue, a jubilant, self-assured little Gloria called at the Best & Co. store on Franklin Ave., Garden City, and purchased numerous additions to her wardrobe.

> Clinging tightly to the arm of Mrs. Whitney, whom she addressed variously as Aunty, Darling and Sweetheart, the child stepped out of a Rolls-Royce at 2 p.m., preceded by a private detective and followed by a nurse and another private detective. All eyes were upon the child as, clad in her beloved riding habit, she made a bee-line for the misses' department. . . . Mrs. Whitney sat nearby giving advice only when requested. Standing with arms folded, the private detectives cast glowering eyes at the crowd.

On Sunday morning, in observance of Carew's edict, Gertrude Vanderbilt Whitney, for the first time, arranged to take little Gloria to St. Joseph's Catholic Church on Franklin Avenue in Garden City, Long Island. A dozen cars full of reporters waited on Whitney Lane and followed their maroon Cadillac sedan to St. Joseph's, and when they went inside, so did the reporters.

> CHILD HEIRESS GOES TO MASS
>
> Gloria Vanderbilt, the 10-year-old heiress, went to church yesterday by order of the Supreme Court of New York. Stiff as a ramrod and clutching a prayer book in one hand, she made a brave effort to observe the ritual, but two errors betrayed her. She crossed herself with her left hand instead of her right, and she failed to interpret the significance of the tinkling altar bell. . . . Episcopalian aunt, Mrs. Harry Payne Whitney, seemed a bit flustered herself. The governess who testified against Mrs. Vanderbilt in the court trial and whose dismissal the mother demands, sat on the other side of the heiress, and a private detective in the pew behind. Surrounded by her retinue . . . Gloria and her aunt sat, stood or knelt with the congregation, watching their neighbors out of the corners of their eyes, but when the bell rang for the more solemn moments of the mass, neither struck her breast, as did the rest of the congregation.
>
> Only when the 10-cent pew rent collection was taken did the presence of an heiress make itself apparent. Gloria dropped her dime on the floor and her entire retinue leaped to retrieve it. She found it herself and dropped it in the basket. Her aunt deposited a dollar bill . . .

On leaving the church little Gloria's bodyguards tried to shield her from the photographers. When Gertrude Whitney saw that they could not keep the photographers away, she reached out and took little Gloria by the arm. "Stand still and let them get one good photograph of you," she commanded the child. "Then perhaps they'll leave us alone." Little Gloria stopped and blinked into the lights. The religious upbringing so important to Justice Carew had been based on his own class and morality. In the world that little Gloria occupied, her Catholicism was mere tokenism, a humoring of this powerful man, and it had become a public spectacle. But the judgment Justice Carew had rendered was being duly observed.

Perhaps unconsciously, both Gertrude and Gloria almost immediately established a pattern of complicity with the press by using the child to gain sympathy for themselves. On Thanksgiving Day Gloria Vanderbilt, interviewed while "eating her turkey dinner all alone," reported that her daughter was leading an "unwholesome life with Mrs. Whitney." As if to counteract this assertion, Gertrude Whitney invited reporters to accompany little Gloria to the Nassau County Hospital, and *The New York Times* reported: "The ten-year-old heiress to $2,800,000 . . . accompanied by a chauffeur and a private detective . . . visited Nassau Hospital, bringing gifts to the children in the free ward . . . and invited eight small girls to a party on the estate where she is now living."

Directly after the issuance of Carew's order, Surrogate Foley announced that Gloria Morgan Vanderbilt's allowance from her daughter's trust was to continue for the balance of the year, and, in the usual manner, a hearing regarding her allowance for 1935 was scheduled early in January. Nathan Burkan then began a series of legal maneuvers to force the Justice either to sustain or dismiss the writ of habeas corpus and to stay the order giving Gertrude Whitney five-day-a-week custody of little Gloria until a Vanderbilt appeal had been decided. But the Appellate Division of the State Supreme Court upheld the form of Carew's order, declaring it final, and also unanimously denied Burkan's petition to stay the order. As a result of these proceedings, Justice Carew's opinion became public property, and, for the first time, the public realized the extent of little Gloria's hatred and fear of her mother. The *Times* printed all of the child's critical letters and excerpts from her testimony. VANDERBILT GIRL "HATED" MOTHER, SHE TESTIFIED, DESPITE LOVING NOTES. " 'I Never Want to go Back,' Carew Was Told." But even in the face of this knowledge, the public would not abandon the incredibly appealing story they'd come to believe, and Gloria Vanderbilt counteracted these revelations saying, "My little daughter has been very much influenced. You know that promises of lots of things can make a child say almost anything. There was something said not only about taking her away from her Whitney playmates and her pony, but also giving her a motorboat. . . . Miss Keislich not only tampered with the child's letters to my mother but wrote parts of them, as was proved by handwriting experts at the trial. . . . I am sure that [little] Gloria didn't mean any of the things she said to Justice Carew." The *Mirror* summed up the pervasive attitude: "Little Gloria does not realize it was her own unconscious repudiation of Mrs. Vanderbilt which separated her from her loving mother. . . ."

Saturday, December 22, was the day that Carew had designated for little Gloria's first weekend visit, and the press predicted "A Very Merry Christmas Reunion for the Glorias." Mrs. Vanderbilt told reporters that she expected "things will be much better now that I can have my baby with me. I'm very happy and I'm sure that [little] Gloria is too." She said she'd planned a weekend of shopping and Christmas festivities. Would there be a Christmas tree for little Gloria? a reporter inquired. Gloria replied, "I always have a Christmas tree, but don't ask me to tell you what Gloria will find hanging on it for herself. I don't suppose she will hang up a stocking for Santa Claus to fill. Poor child, I don't think she believes in Santa Claus anymore."

By 7:00 a.m. Saturday morning, a crowd had gathered outside the Vanderbilt town house in anticipation of the child's scheduled 10:00 a.m. appearance. A police truck pulled to the curb and wooden barricades were unloaded onto the sidewalk; then four police cars arrived and Lieutenant Cornelius Sullivan began directing his men to set up the barricades. Police officers inspected the press identifications of the eighteen cameramen and two dozen reporters before allowing them to stand in the front row of spectators. Traffic slowed to a crawl but, except for the brownstone façade with four red-and-green Christmas wreaths in the windows, there was little to see. A milkman elbowed his way through the crowd and placed three bottles of milk on the front doorstep. The *Sun* noted that "rich ladies peered as openly from their windows as Mulberry Street matrons watching a new family move into a tenement."

At Wheatley Hills, however, there was a delay—little Gloria was hysterical at the thought of being forced to see her mother. After more than an hour she was finally persuaded to leave. Gertrude Whitney wrote in her Line-A-Day diary, "G. went to town. Terrible Scenes." At 11:04 the gray Whitney Rolls-Royce pulled up in front of the house, where a crowd of about three hundred people waited. The *Sun* reported that Lieutenant Sullivan and his patrolmen "made a valiant but vain effort to hold back the crowd which quickly surrounded the machine. . . . Detectives and nurse grabbed [little] Gloria and shoved through the ring of reporters. Then the child, twisting free, ran lightly across the sidewalk and into the street-level entrance of the house. As she ran she first ducked her head at the booming of flashlights, then looked up and grinned."

The *Times* noted that "no outsiders observed the meeting between the girl and her mother." But Larry Gilman, an operative hired to guard little Gloria on the day of that first visit, witnessed the scene. He'd been waiting inside the house for more than two hours when the child arrived, and the first thing he noticed was the naked fear on her face—fear not only of the mob outside, "but also of meeting the mother she had so recently repudiated." Gilman described what happened next.

> Mrs. Vanderbilt, who'd been watching everything from an upper window, came running down the stairs. She and Gloria met in the foyer. For a moment they both halted, and looked at each other in silence, neither seeming to know just what to do, or to say, to break down the unhappy barrier between them. . . . Then suddenly, with a choked little sob, Mrs. Vanderbilt went down on her knees and held her arms out. The little girl started to cry and flew into her mother's arms. As her mother clasped her tightly and kissed her hungrily, Gloria uttered one little cry—"Mommie"—and buried her dark head against Mrs. Vanderbilt's shoulder.

But from the first, the circumstances under which the child and her mother came together precluded any possibility of a normal relationship. Little Gloria and her mother remained inside the house until the afternoon, hoping that the crowd would leave. At two-thirty Gloria gave up, and policemen and detectives broke a path to the Vanderbilt Rolls-Royce and hustled the mother and daughter inside. Gloria directed Louis to drive them to FAO Schwarz on Fifth Avenue and Fifty-eighth Street, and the chauffeur zigzagged through traffic, trying to shake off the cars full of reporters and cameramen following them. When he could not, Gloria ordered him to stop and she got out and walked back to the first of the press cars. "Please—please leave me and my child alone," she pleaded. "After all, I can only see her for a few hours a week." The newspapermen answered that they were very sorry, but they had been assigned to follow her and they couldn't afford to lose their jobs. Gloria Vanderbilt turned and walked away. Once back in the car, she directed Louis to drive normally, and he led a line of cars resembling a funeral procession to the Fifth Avenue toy emporium. Gloria and little Gloria spent the next two hours buying Christmas toys (a platinum-blond wig, a china doll, a carriage filled with five dolls—replicas of the Dionne quintuplets) while reporters followed them throughout the store. Subsequently, several newspapers noted that Surrogate Foley reimbursed Mrs. Vanderbilt $248 for her daughter's Christmas gifts.

As the year of 1934 ended, in movie theaters across the nation audiences heard the loud, urgent voice of the Metrotone News commentator:

> Here are the latest pictures of Gloria Vanderbilt, part-time mother to her ten-year-old daughter. After a sensational hearing in the New York courts—given into the custody of her rich aunt. Little Gloria, frightened by the curious crowd, flees into her aunt's car. MONEY ISN'T EVERYTHING!

On the morning before Christmas, the massive carved-mahogany doors of St. Francis of Assisi Church swung open and a crowd surged forward to the edge of the limestone steps, then parted to make a pathway as the Sunday worshippers filed out. There was a silent moment while the crowd stared at the church door, then Gloria Morgan Vanderbilt emerged. She was swathed in a massive mink coat with a cape collar that swirled below her shoulder blades, the brim of her black felt hat was tipped at a jaunty angle and highlighted by a gold-and-diamond horseshoe-shaped clip. As she walked forward, Mrs. Vanderbilt smiled wanly into the cameras. She might have been a film star on her way to a premiere, except for the dark circles under her eyes and the nervous manner in which she jammed her black-gloved hands in and out of the pockets of her coat.

At the curb a thin, middle-aged woman broke through the crowd and ran toward Gloria, grabbing her hand and kissing it; a bodyguard pulled the woman away and Gloria Vanderbilt climbed into her Rolls-Royce.

The crowd turned. A small face peeked around the church door. Little Gloria wore a tweed bonnet secured under her chin by a velvet ribbon. Her hair had been cut short like a boy's, unbecomingly exposing her ears. The crowd cheered. The face abruptly popped back out of sight. A moment later two bodyguards, one on each side, propelled the child out of the door; she moved like a wind-up toy guided by their hands. As the flashbulbs began to explode, little Gloria lifted her soft leather purse and hid her face like a felon.

The crowd pressed in on her, and the child, in desperation, turned and buried her face against the chest of one of the bodyguards. The man wrapped his arms around her. Little Gloria drew her legs up, assuming a fetal position as he carried her toward the Rolls-Royce. When they reached the curb, the bodyguard set the child on her feet. She stumbled forward, missing the step up to the running board, and pitched forward. A bodyguard caught her from behind and lifted and pushed her into the car.

The crowd pressed against the windows. Little Gloria stared straight ahead. Photographers ran forward and began photographing her through the right rear window. In front of the car five private bodyguards and a half-dozen policemen tried to force the crowd back so the car could move.

For what seemed to be an interminable time, the child sat immobile in her glass cage. The newsreel cameras ground away. Little Gloria's lips drew back over her teeth in the stretched, feral expression that, for years to come, would pass for a smile. With her right hand, she reached up high above her head. Then her hand moved slowly down, drawing with it a herringbone-patterned window shade. For several moments photographers trained their cameras on the opaque surface of the shade before they turned away. The car moved slowly as the crowd parted before it.

BUTLER PAID FOR MRS. VANDERBILT'S GIN

Nineteen thirty-five began with a fracas over money. In the public hearing before Surrogate Foley, Tom Gilchrist asserted that Gloria Vanderbilt had overdrawn her budget in the years 1931, '32, '33, and '34 and had never furnished adequate information on how she had spent the money. He said that she owed Emma Sullivan Keislich $1,500 in wages for seven months in 1931 and five months in 1932, and butler Zaug $75.83 for such items as Scotch, whiskey, brandy, and gin. Gloria countered by saying that Gilchrist was at the root of her troubles and that Mrs. Whitney was still employing detectives to follow her everywhere. Foley listened to the arguments and then awarded Gloria $750 a month for her personal expenses, $250 a month for her mother's support (putting her in the position of supporting a woman who had denounced her to the world), and ordered Gilchrist to pay the upkeep on the Seventy-second Street house. It was the old arrangement—exactly. Foley dismissed the application for co-guardianship of little Gloria's property, noting that Carew's decision had rendered it "entirely unnecessary," and Burkan withdrew the personal guardianship application, pending the outcome of the appeal for the child's custody. During the hearings Burkan told Surrogate Foley, "I want it to appear on the record that I have received no fee for my legal services. . . . She hasn't a cent of what she borrowed. . . . I have a sentimental interest in this case." Observers at the Burkan office felt that Nathan had indeed become obsessed with this case. Said Herman Finkelstein, "He knew it was his slip with the French maid that led to the accusation of lesbianism. He'd brought it out, not the Whitney side. It was a terrible error and he was determined to make up for it." Burkan began letting other cases go as he worked incessantly on the Vanderbilt appeal. At eleven o'clock one night he was sitting in his office going through the trial transcript. As he read the testimony, his rage at Justice Carew mounted. "Either he was bought, or his brain was pickled!" Burkan told Frohlich and Finkelstein. Then he complained that his chest and back hurt. His physician was called and diagnosed a severe case of indigestion or a possible heart episode. After that Burkan was unable to bend down without feeling nauseated and dizzy. His wife or the chauffeur put his shoes on for him and removed them at night, but he did not slacken his pace.

On April 25, 1935, twenty copies of the record of the *Matter of Vanderbilt* were delivered to the Appellate Division of the New York State Supreme Court. Each copy consisted of five bound volumes of approximately 5,000 pages of testimony, one volume of 1,000 pages of exhibits, and one volume of 1,000 pages of legal actions taken since the trial's end. With this appeal, the entire 7,000 pages entered the public domain. The secrecy was ended. Reporters, evidently staggered by the volume of material, made no effort to evaluate it and concentrated on printing the most sensational parts of the transcript at random. CHILD SCREAMED "DON'T LET HER KILL ME" was one headline. The *American* headline LITTLE GLORIA'S FEAR OF DEATH REVEALED ran above the obviously less important 6 NAZI U-BOATS REPORTED ALREADY AFLOAT. And again Gloria Vanderbilt countered the publicity by saying "I never touched Gloria in my life, except in love. If anything I was too gentle, I spoiled her."

Julia McCarthy also came to Gloria's defense, writing that the trial transcript provided a "complete vindication" of Mrs. Vanderbilt and calling little Gloria's testimony "childish and twisted." On the strength of her reportage of the *Matter of Vanderbilt*, Julia had staked out Society as her private preserve. She was to write about it in the *News* for the next forty years.

In spite of all evidence to the contrary, the public still clung to their original romanticized scenario. "Reunion of Two Glorias by 1938," the *News* predicted. With her appeal for her daughter's custody pending, Gloria applied to Surrogate Foley for an extra vacation allowance of $4,250, and when it was granted, she exercised her right to take little

NRA
The Weather
Today — Cloudy, probably showers.
New York American
AMERICA FIRST!
LATE CITY
TUESDAY, APRIL 30, 1935—36 PAGES
Little Gloria's Fear of Death Reveale
6 Nazi U-Boats Reported Already Afloc
CIVIL SERVICE ELIGIBLE LIST IGNORED FOR RELIEF JOBS
Finegan Tells Probers Thousands of Qualified Social Workers, Engineers Barred
BLAMES RULES OF TERA
Urges 1,000 New Investigators Asked by Corsi Be Taken from Civil Service Lists
Photo on Page 4
Yanks Defeat Senators 2-0
Gomez Allows Only Four Hits
1ST TALLY IN 4TH
Combs' Single Sends Dickey Across
FIRST INNING
SECOND INNING
THIRD INNING
DOCTOR LAYS GLORIA'S FEARS TO HER NURSE
U.S. 'MEDDLING' DENOUNCED AT C. OF C. PARLEY
THE KING'S HORSES UPSET KING'S MEN
Ready for Ma vers in North London Hea
REICH BITT
Denounces Br for 'Going Ove the Enemy'

Gloria for the month of July. In order to comply with Carew's geographic restrictions, she rented the William H. Hamilton estate in Nissequogue, Long Island. Little Gloria had no choice but to come to her. On the first day of July at 10:00 a.m., little Gloria and a bodyguard arrived in the Whitney limousine. As the child stepped from the car she was flanked by two more private detectives who had been hired by Gloria Vanderbilt and who escorted her into the house. These men were dressed in shirtsleeves, over which were leather shoulder holsters containing revolvers. Ammunition belts encircled their waists.

Machine guns were placed at many points throughout the house and around the grounds. Every gate leading to the estate had a complement of armed guards. The *Times* reported that "a number of citizens, curious to get a look at the $4,000,000 heiress, drove down to the estate, but were quickly turned back by the detectives." The private bathing beach was protected by half a dozen machine guns. A speedboat just off the beach contained more detectives and another machine gun. A few gapers who owned yachts were able to get a glimpse of little Gloria before the speedboat chased them away.

Gloria Vanderbilt invited reporters in to witness the vacation she was providing for her daughter as a tangible demonstration of why she should be granted her custody. The resulting reportage held firm to the fantasy that the child was leading a happy life. A typical report noted:

> Gloria Vanderbilt, like any other little girl of 11, played happily with her cousin, Tony Furness, yesterday, building castles of sand and paddling in the water. . . . As far as Gloria was concerned, there might have been no armed guards about, nor any speedboat idling in the inlet to prevent a possible kidnaping attempt by sea. Gloria frolicked in her swimming suit as her mother, Mrs. Gloria Morgan Vanderbilt, watched fondly.

The newspaper accounts of a happy child concealed the terrible reality of little Gloria's existence. Dodo had been torn from her; in her place was a strange governess, Mary Carney Hill, whose job it was to teach her the Catholic ritual, and all the bodyguards. The child had begun to ping-pong back and forth between her mother and her aunt, who were pulling her in two directions. Daily, Gertrude Whitney phoned little Gloria to tell her how much she missed her. Gloria Vanderbilt told reporters that Mrs. Whitney had instructed little Gloria to address her as "Mrs. Vanderbilt. . . . She has thoroughly poisoned little Gloria's mind against me." Jim Murray visited the Long Island home and found the atmosphere oppressive: "Little Gloria was running around the place and her mother had no idea what to do with her or how to entertain her. The kid was becoming an undisciplined brat and a tyrant, but Gloria felt she couldn't discipline her or they would never give her custody."

While the child was visiting her mother, Gertrude Whitney spent a great deal of her time fighting the Vanderbilt appeal. Eleanor Roosevelt invited her to spend the night of June 4 at the White House, but she declined because the following morning she was to appear at the opening day of the appeal hearings. The Vanderbilt appeal brief, written primarily by Herman Finkelstein, clearly and unemotionally contended that the accusations of neglect and immorality against Mrs. Vanderbilt had never been proven. To write and argue her brief, Gertrude Vanderbilt Whitney had selected Joseph Meyer Proskauer. Again, she had secured the best that money could buy. Proskauer had himself served as a justice of the Appellate Division and therefore undoubtedly knew exactly what arguments to present to these five justices. Furthermore, he was a brilliant writer who had composed speeches and position papers for politicians and presidents. Proskauer's appeal brief was dramatic, emotional, and brilliantly organized. He broke down the trial material into a chronology of the child's life with her mother. Each section started with a subhead of opprobrium and Victorian sentiment: "Her alleged 'engagement' broken because the baby's income cannot be used 'to finance a second marriage' (January 1929). . . . The sick child left in England for the winter (November 1929–March 1930). . . . The sick child spends another lonely winter in England (November 1931–March 1932)" were typical headings. When Gertrude Whitney took the child to live with her, the headings became more positive in tone. ". . . Improvement in the physical, mental and moral welfare of the child since June 26, 1932 when the child was delivered to the custody of Mrs. Whitney." And finally—the ultimate heading—LITTLE GLORIA . . . "HAPPY AT LAST."

Proskauer's brief detailed, over and over again, Gloria Vanderbilt's neglect and indifference toward her daughter, and indirectly reinforced the accusation of lesbianism by pointing out that Lady Milford Haven, Agnes Horter, and Helen Thomas had not come forward to refute the charges of intimacy with their good friend. Proskauer also noted that neither Constance Bennett nor A. C. Blumenthal had come forward; no doctors had appeared for Mrs. Vanderbilt, and her witnesses were family and servants who had been in her employ for brief periods of time.

In the devastating summary, Proskauer stated:

> The evidence of immorality of the mother, of her association with a certain type of woman, her reading of obscene literature, of

the unconventional friendship and intimacy for Prince Hohenlohe, of her relations with A. C. Blumenthal, a married man, of her fondness for the gayety of night life, are merely indicators of the character which has permitted her so to neglect her child and to force the child to live such a life. . . .

More than any other single document, Proskauer's brief branded Gloria Vanderbilt forever as an unfit mother. Gertrude Whitney wrote him an effusive letter expressing her gratitude. Undoubtedly unaware of the irony, her letter concluded: "I want [little] Gloria to meet you later and realize what you have done for her."

Little Gloria was still vacationing with her mother when the five justices of the Appellate Division of the New York State Supreme Court, in a unanimous decision written by Justice Irwin Untermyer, found that Justice Carew had adopted "the only possible course," and pronounced his ruling "an eminently just solution. . . ." The decision specified that the allegation of lesbian activity with Nadeja Milford Haven "is so detrimental to the Relator and the evidence to support it so insubstantial that she was entitled to unqualified and complete exoneration," but it did not encompass any of the other accusations.

Untermyer wrote that should little Gloria "desire to return to her mother" later on, and should "the court be convinced of the mother's sincerity," the custody question might be reconsidered. However, he observed that under the present ruling, Mrs. Vanderbilt would "spend more time with her child than for many years past."

Gloria's immediate reaction to the defeat was to call in the press and give a series of interviews to show that the divided custody arrangement made it impossible for her to win her child's affection, and to lash out at Mrs. Whitney. She said that the morning the Appellate decision had been reached she'd received a hand-delivered letter that had been meant for her daughter. The letter read,

Dearest Gloria:

I have told you on the telephone that everything is going well. The Appellate Division decided unanimously in our favor—that means they uphold Justice Carew's decision.

It makes me very happy to talk to you almost every day—to hear about how you are, what you do, and to hear your voice. . . .

All my love to you,
Auntie Ger

"Immediately there was a difference in her [little Gloria's] attitude toward me," Gloria said. "The barrier that I was breaking down was erected again between us. Her mother was a bad woman. Two courts had said so. . . . Do you think for a moment that a woman of Mrs. Whitney's age and experience didn't have that very thought in mind when she wrote that letter? She did that cold-bloodedly and deliberately to hurt me. . . . That letter was diabolic."

Gloria said that Justice Carew was no real Solomon: "Solomon was wise indeed when he offered to divide with a sword the baby that two women claimed—for that gave the real mother the right to show her love by exclaiming, 'Let the other woman take it,' and thus proved her own right indisputably. . . . It would be far better if my little girl was given altogether to me or to Mrs. Whitney."

But along with her criticism of Gertrude Whitney and of the custody arrangement was a violent, unconcealed anger directed publicly against little Gloria. She told the *Journal*,

> Gloria has become quite an astute little girl. If she wants to do something that I don't think she should, she tells me that her Auntie Ger would let her do it. That puts me in a fine position, doesn't it? Here I am trying desperately to regain her affections, despite the subtle, insidious undermining by Mrs. Whitney. If I refuse to let her have her own way in anything, she pouts and gives me a nasty look. Another black mark chalked up against me!
>
> For instance on July fourth, a nice day when she should have been in the country, Gloria asked me to take her to New York to see a movie. I tried to talk her out of it. I told her we had all planned to go swimming. No, she had to go to the hot city to see a movie. When I persisted in trying to change her mind, she exclaimed impetuously, "May I telephone Auntie Ger?" . . . So we all drove to town to see the movie.
>
> You ought to hear her order the servants around. . . . She's arrogant and treats them terribly. She never even thinks of thanking them for any service they perform for her.
>
> [Little] Gloria is extremely egotistical. How can she help it with all the attention she gets? And she loves to act. Her ambition right now is to be a great actress.

There was no acknowledgment that little Gloria was being subjected to inhuman pressures and divided loyalties. And there were signs that this child who had unwillingly been dragged into the spotlight of celebrity had, while hating it, begun to crave the drug of fame. Her mother told reporters that her daughter had become enamored of the publicity attendant upon her every action. When she was taken to shop in the village, little Gloria had pointed at the crowd that had gathered and exclaimed, "Look mother, my public!"

The Poor Little Rich Girl

Heiress Reported to Have Run Away
When Left Alone with 400 Servants

World Telegram, JUNE 3, 1938

"NO ONE CARED about her. No one!" little Gloria's cousin and closest friend Gerta recalls with remembered anger. "After that trial everyone simply forgot about Gloria—they let her grow up like a barbarian!" While she was depicted as a happy heiress, the reality of little Gloria's life was bleak. With the trial behind her, Gertrude Whitney began spending the week in the city, and on weekends when she came to Wheatley Hills, little Gloria was visiting her mother. Little Gloria had gone from an unfit mother, who resented her and was seldom there, to an aunt, who was unable to express affection and who also was seldom there.

Because of the publicity attendant upon the trial, little Gloria's worst hidden fears had been transmuted to reality. Some kidnap facts: Lieutenant Sullivan had no further leads on the kidnap threat against little Gloria, but by the end of the trial it was no longer unique. He'd assigned men to read the thousands of letters that poured into the Vanderbilt town house and among them were more vicious kidnap

Guards Keep Watch Over Both Glorias

By JULIA McCARTHY.

AN ARMED bodyguard, fearful of danger, has watched over the household of Mrs. Gloria Morgan Vanderbilt since last May, The News learned yesterday.

"Madame, you are in danger," he told the widow of Reginald Vanderbilt shortly after she had employed him as ... t in another capa... you to get me a ...

... whether he ... rected against ... an attempt to

... fate ... ild will be announced fo... day or tomorrow by ... Court Justice John F. ... But even though Mrs. Van... will appeal his decision awarding Gloria to Mrs. Whitney five days a week, the mother promises to fulfill in her own way his stipulation that the child be reared as a Roman Catholic.

"It was always my intention to bring up my child as a Catholic," she said yesterday. "I had her baptized, and just as soon as I get complete custody of her I shall prepare her for her first communion."

Her appeal automatically leaves the child with Mrs. Whitney seven days a week, and thus she will be unable to fulfill the unwritten request of Justice Carew that she renew the child's religious training at once.

Income Stipulated.

After the Justice received two orders, one from attorneys on each side, it was learned that Mrs. Vanderbilt's counsel had appended to theirs a stipulation safeguarding the mother's income, which now is set at $4,000 a month for

Will He Marry O[redacted] of These?

Princess Irene

Prince of Wales

...lizabeth of Greece.

Kent ... Wal... To ...

...ears, L...

When ... S... and almost ... how her d... her that ... to Ber... Jo... ink...

... she broke in ... ing after telling how her d... ter had "called me names ... can't tell," he firmly insi... she tell. Later in the ... handed him a written ... printable portion inclu... sentiments as: "You a... ant low-lifer; I hope ... dead; you old witch!"

Tells of P...

Her stories of ... Starr home in Mam... prepossessing you... her daughter, and ... pression when she sa... daughter had bragged ... how much liquor wa... failed to disturb the ...

Mrs. Josephson d... Brock, Hollywood m... in 1926. Much of the... and after that period th... at the Mamaroneck esta... Starrs, the grandmother ... Mrs. Josephson went on

MACHINE GUNS GUA... GLORIA VANDERB...

Heiress, Spending Month W... Mother on Long Island, Al... Protected by Detectives.

Special to THE NEW YORK TIMES.

...THTOWN, L. I., July 1... Vanderbilt, the 11-year-ol... ...nter of Mrs. Gloria Morga... ...nderbilt, arrived here today and ...ll spend July with her mother on ...e William H. Hamilton estate at ...sequogue, overlooking Long Island Sound.

...he month will furnish ...derbilt her first opportu... ...e time to spend more tha... ... with her daughter. Sh... ...nged for her sister ... ...y Furn... ...o op... ...ss shop ... ...his... ...he thirty... ... been ... ...y gate ... ...cted ... we... ...ge ... ...fte... ...cu... ...000

threats aimed at little Gloria. At Wheatley Hills, Gertrude Whitney employed a dozen Pinkertons to protect both herself and her niece. The Benjamin Kerin agency received the most profitable job in its history guarding little Gloria on her visits to her mother. In 1935, Gloria Vanderbilt petitioned for $3,600 to pay the Kerin agency for weekend protection alone. (For the month of July, eight extra guards were supplied.)

Little Gloria attended the Green Vale School accompanied by her bodyguards. Nedenia Hutton (daughter of Marjorie Merriweather Post and E. F. Hutton) and the Penoyer children (the grandchildren of J. P. Morgan) were also guarded. "There'd been a kidnap scare about Alfie Moore and the Taft children too," recalls Leila Burton Hadley, who was Gloria's friend and classmate at Green Vale. "When they were there they were guarded. I think Nancy Leeds (daughter of Princess Xenia of Greece) and Peter Luce (son of Henry Luce) had bodyguards, too." Leila remembers that one day on the way to school she overheard her chauffeur tell her governess ("They always spoke as if I didn't exist") that an airplane patrolled the Green Vale School yard at recess. "I noticed it that day, and every day for the rest of the school year. I never knew who the plane belonged to, but it was out there making wide circles over the play yard."

Thomas Robinson, Jr., pleaded guilty to the kidnapping of Alice Speed Stoll and was sentenced to life imprisonment. The kidnappers of little June Robles and the murderer of little Dorothy Ann Distelhurst were never apprehended, but the police did arrest Alfred Otto Wagner, who was convicted of "chiseling in" on the Distelhurst and Stoll kidnappings by writing false ransom notes that resembled the Lindbergh ransom demands. He was sentenced to twenty years in prison. Soon after, FBI chief J. Edgar Hoover told the *Times*, "Kidnapping is well in hand . . . I won't say anything about the future . . . but there's every reason to believe now that the kidnapping racket is on the decline."

On April 3, 1936, in Trenton, New Jersey, reporters, legislators, physicians, and police officials sat in the double row of wooden chairs behind the three-foot-high canvas barrier that separated them from the electric chair. At 8:39 p.m. an ashen-faced Bruno Hauptmann was led into the room. His head had been shaved and he was dressed in a gray shirt, baggy striped khaki pants, and brown carpet slippers. The Lord's Prayer and the Twenty-third Psalm were read in German. Hauptmann sat in the chair. A leather cap, equipped with an electrode which had been carefully dipped in brine, was fastened to his head; another was fastened to his leg through a slit in his trousers. A black mask was fastened over his eyes.

At exactly 8:44 p.m. executioner Robert Elliott spun the wooden wheel behind the chair. The lights dimmed, the hum of electricity rose in the chamber, the body jerked convulsively as 2,000 volts of electricity shot through it. Elliott turned the wheel again. An electrical whine rose and fell, there was a faint odor of burning flesh. At 8:47½ p.m., Dr. Howard Weisler, the prison doctor, pronounced Bruno Hauptmann dead.

On the other side of the Atlantic, Colonel Charles A. Lindbergh, his wife Anne and son, Jon, slept in their English country house in the cool spring night.

By the middle 1930s scores of famous people like the Lindberghs had left the United States to avoid kidnappers. Carew's order prevented little Gloria even from leaving New York State without special permission.

In 1936 there were two kidnap scares at Wheatley Hills: the first, when two men broke into the cottage of Thomas Griffin, the Whitney superintendent. One man held a pistol on Griffin, but they both fled when his daughter screamed, and were never apprehended. The second scare, involving a strange car parked on the Whitney grounds, turned out to be a kitchen maid enjoying a romantic moment.

In July of 1936, Frank Maseola, a fifteen-year-old boy who had written to little Gloria repeatedly during the trial, managed to get into the Nissequogue estate where the child was again vacationing with her mother. He was arrested.

Nineteen thirty-six began with another humiliating money struggle for Mrs. Vanderbilt. As if Tom Gilchrist wished to see this woman publicly pilloried, he again chose the open hearing in the Surrogates' Court as occasion to announce that in addition to her personal allowance of $9,000, Gloria had spent $34,434.95 in household expenses in 1935 for a house the child visited only on weekends, and he refused to pay $1,700 worth of Gloria's bills, saying that they had nothing whatsoever to do with the child. Among the items were ten cases of beer, three cases of ale, fifty cartons of cigarettes, fourteen dozen bottles of White Rock, and ten dozen bottles of ginger ale. Gloria's answer made headlines: LITTLE GLORIA DOES DRINK GINGER ALE, MOTHER INSISTS. Surrogate Foley ruled that the child's trust income could no longer be used to support a household in which she did not live. If Gloria Vanderbilt wished to stay in her town house after January 15, she must pay her own upkeep. Her personal allowance was again set at $9,000 a year. The rent on the house alone was $6,000 a year; Gloria moved out and rented a two-room apartment on East Fifty-second Street. Shortly thereafter, in what could only have been an act of resentment, she put all her Vanderbilt possessions on the auction block. Gertrude sent an agent to the sale, who bought nine of Reggie Vanderbilt's silver horse show trophies, including a punch bowl and a mammoth goblet, as well as five silver platters, a silver tea service, and a complete set of breakfast and dinner dishes. All of these items bore the Vanderbilt monogram or acorn crest. (They were, in fact, the same items that Alice Vanderbilt had purchased at the Sandy Point Farm auction and had given to Gloria.) In all, Gertrude bought twenty-three items for a total of $3,067, and she announced her intention "to give them to my niece at the appropriate time." She was preserving little Gloria's rightful inheritance.

Nathan Burkan was not a man to accept defeat with grace. On Gloria's behalf he'd applied to the Appellate Division for permission to appeal to the Court of Appeals, but he was unanimously refused. Still Burkan would not give up; he went to the Court of Appeals without Appellate Division sanction, but they declined to review the case. There was but one court left—the Supreme Court of the United States. Burkan submitted Gloria Vanderbilt's appeal there, on the grounds that her constitutional rights had been violated. Then in a dramatic gesture, undoubtedly calculated to demonstrate to the Supreme Court that money was not the issue, Gloria called in reporters and said that she was going to forfeit her $9,000 personal income for 1935: "I will no longer live under the curse of the Vanderbilt gold. It never brought anyone anything but unhappiness." To support herself she intended going into the dress designing business with her friend Sonia Rosenberg (the designer of her gray wedding gown). "I will be living only on the money I earn . . . in my little apartment. . . . When Gloria visits me each week I will take a hotel suite." Since Surrogate Foley insisted, according to Gloria, that her daughter "be surrounded with an entourage which would do credit to a Medici in a time of civil war," she'd petitioned for $191.10 each weekend to cover the expense of a Sherry-Netherland suite and the Kerin bodyguard service.

Now began a weekend drama that was to be repeated over and over during the next two years. On Saturday mornings, Elizabeth Wann, who had remained with Mrs. Vanderbilt after the trial, packed her mistress's suitcase and Gloria went by cab to the Sherry-Netherland Hotel and checked into a suite. Detectives Kerin and Gilman waited outside the hotel until little Gloria arrived and escorted her to the suite. Jim Murray recalls, "Gloria didn't know what to do with the kid. She'd ask me—what am I going to do with her this weekend, Jim?" Said Gloria, "There were always umpteen thousand detectives outside the door when she was here."

During the week, little Gloria remained isolated and guarded at Wheatley Hills. On weekends she became an all-American freak show exhibit. But somehow she managed to find a way to change herself to fit the image that had been thrust upon her. "Gloria's a survivor, that's how she did it," says a childhood friend. Says her cousin Gerta, "She was one person in public and another with those she trusted. When those reporters were following her around, she guarded every emotion, every reaction. Everything she did was studied. God, she hated what they'd done to her, but she learned to cope!" And Larry Gilman adds, "She became a perfect little actress in public when it came to hiding her real feelings and her true self. . . . It still seems something of a miracle that [little] Gloria's experience didn't break her."

Little Gloria's weekend performances would have done credit to the most polished of child stars, as her life became a series of headlines and feature stories. LITTLE GLORIA VISITS FAIRY CASTLE. Macy's department store opened its doors Saturday night so that little Gloria could have a private viewing of actress Colleen Moore's fairy palace dollhouse. She was taken on a special tour by Colleen's mother. The *Sun* noted that "ordinary children had waited in line several hours to see the palace." LITTLE GLORIA GOES TO CIRCUS, GUARDED. She had "a grand time . . . smiling a broad grin . . . with a toy whip in one hand and an inflated rubber giraffe in the other. . . . Two husky bodyguards stood formidably at the end of the room and frowned on reporters and news photographers." LITTLE HEIRESS ATTENDS FASHION SHOW. She "gasped at the beautiful clothes." LITTLE GLORIA RECEIVED INTO ROMAN CATHOLIC CHURCH—REGINA'S HER NEW NAME. Little Gloria, dressed in white, "smiled up at Bishop Molloy who offered his ring to the 11-year-old heiress's lips, a gesture he did not make to other youngsters." LITTLE GLORIA WORTH $4,068,593.20 SPENDS $52.99 ON HERSELF: Variations of this headline were to appear frequently over the years, providing a classic poor-little-rich-girl vignette of which the public never wearied.

For her weekend appearances, little Gloria began arriving at the Sherry-Netherland in garish outfits: once she wore white silk ankle-length socks with high-heeled patent leather shoes, her lips smeared with bright red lipstick. She began to gain weight, until she became obese, her arms and face swollen. Her fingernails were chewed ragged.

In the spring of 1936, the United States Supreme Court, without explanation, declined to review the *Matter of Vanderbilt*. Nathan Burkan had failed—it was a crushing blow. Saturday afternoon, June 6, 1936: Nathan Burkan, at his home in Great Neck, Long Island, felt an unbearable constriction in his chest. The cause of death was officially listed as "a sudden attack of acute indigestion." His funeral at New York's Temple Emanu-El was attended by hundreds of people, including Surrogate James Foley, A. C. Blumenthal, and Gloria Morgan Vanderbilt. In his eulogy, Gene Buck, president of ASCAP, said, "Underneath his force and brilliance, he was a sentimentalist. I never knew a man of greater heart." "Yes, he had a great heart," agreed Herman Finkelstein, "and I think this case broke it. He was sure he could vindicate Gloria Vanderbilt; after he'd exhausted every resource, it killed him." From the beginning, Nathan Burkan had miscalculated; his was the primary responsibility for turning the *Matter of Vanderbilt* into the most sensational custody case ever recorded in the annals of American law. But when he died, Gloria Morgan Vanderbilt felt that she had lost her greatest supporter and dearest friend.

With every legal avenue closed to her, Gloria petitioned Surrogate Foley to give her retroactively the $9,000 of "the Vanderbilt gold" she'd refused in 1936, and to pay another $12,000 worth of her bills. (In writing of this, newspapers now referred to Mrs. Vanderbilt as the identical twin of "Lady Furness, the one time pet of the former King Edward VIII," who was the world's most talked-about man, having one week previously abdicated the throne of Great Britain to marry Wallis Warfield Simpson—"the woman I love.") Foley, who had always questioned the morality of using the child's trust money as a means of badgering Gloria Vanderbilt into an acceptable form of behavior, belatedly acted on his own instincts and ruled that in the future she was to receive $21,000 annually and need not submit bills nor justify her expenses to Gilchrist. In addition, her mother's income of $250 a month would be continued. Gloria Vanderbilt would not be allowed to exceed this figure, but she could spend her money any way she desired. It seemed that, at last, she would be free to lead her own life. But in eight years little Gloria would be twenty-one and at that time the trust money would be turned over to her. The child who was growing up isolated and ignored, who "guarded every emotion" but "hated what they'd done to her," would one day be the one to hold the economic "sword of Damocles" over her mother's head.

With her income secured, Gloria Vanderbilt once again took up her restless wanderings. She missed many weekend visits with her daughter. Gertrude Whitney too began to resume her normal life, leaving little Gloria in the care of servants as she had her own children.

GLORIA CONFIRMED

Little Gloria Vanderbilt in her confirmation dress just before she was received into the Roman Catholic Church yesterday.

Regina

Her New Name

Taking the name Regina in memory of her father, the late Reginald Vanderbilt, little Gloria

Only Her Chauffeur Attends GloriaVanderbilt's Graduation

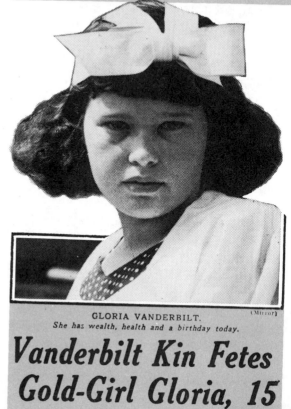

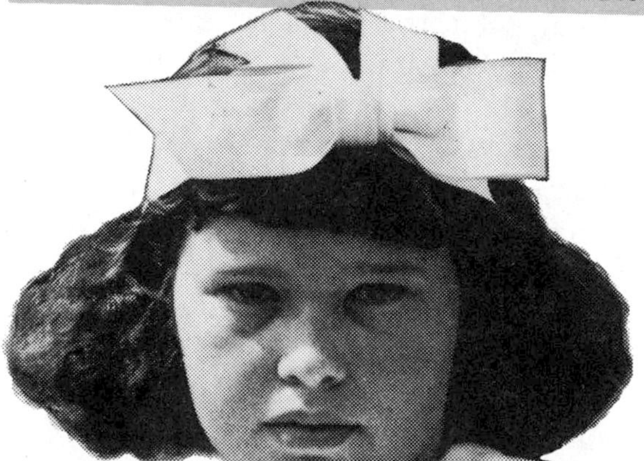

(Mirror)

GLORIA VANDERBILT.
She has wealth, health and a birthday today.

Vanderbilt Kin Fetes Gold-Girl Gloria, 15

Governess Mary Hill, little Gloria, and Gloria

"We were so much alone," recalls Gerta. "My grandmother and my parents both would leave for months at a time. Gloria and I would go to school and then we'd come home and play in my grandmother's house. We found all the dark secret nooks and we'd make up ghost stories to tell each other. For weeks at a time, we never saw anybody but servants. They just let Gloria run wild. Nobody brought her up, they didn't teach her anything: Not how to dress or how to study—nothing." In light of this, the dismissal of her beloved Dodo was all the more shattering. "She was all the world to me and surrounded me with love. . . . I felt as if the loss and the pain would never end," said little Gloria. "The trial . . . was nothing compared to being separated from Dodo." At Wheatley Hills little Gloria felt alienated, like an "imposter" who was living under "false pretenses" and "it was only a question of time before I'd be exposed." In fact, "I felt totally alone."

During the winter of 1938 (when Gertrude and Gloria were both in Europe), the loneliness became unbearable and little Gloria did run away. She got as far as Dorothy Elmhirst's house. (Mrs. Elmhirst was Harry Payne Whitney's younger sister who had a residence on the estate.) Then the bodyguards caught up with her and brought her back, providing a perfect tabloid story. HEIRESS REPORTED TO HAVE RUN AWAY WHEN LEFT ALONE WITH 400 SERVANTS. In June of 1938, when little Gloria was graduated from the Green Vale School, the headline read: ONLY CHAUFFEUR ATTENDS GLORIA VANDERBILT'S GRADUATION. Little Gloria had arrived at school in a Plymouth driven by her private chauffeur and bodyguard, Freddy Urgwig. At the time, her mother was aboard the *Queen Mary*, returning from a trip to England to comfort Nada Milford Haven on the death of her husband, George, who had died at forty-five in a London nursing home. It was said that five months previously he had slipped on the marble floor at Brook House and broken his thigh. The Second Marquis of Milford Haven was buried in Bray Cemetery, with King George VI, the Duke of Kent, George Milford Haven's brother Lord Louis Mountbatten, and his mother the Dowager Marchioness of Milford Haven among those in attendance.

Thelma Furness and Mrs. Morgan were both in New York City, but neither attended little Gloria's graduation. Gertrude Whitney, who had just returned from a forty-day cruise, did not attend either, but sent her daughter Flora Miller to represent the family; the newspapers, however, ignored her presence. The poor-little-rich-girl was too appealing a symbol to abandon.

A Great Personality

The irony . . . was that as soon as my aunt was allowed to take charge of me, she lost interest.

LITTLE GLORIA VANDERBILT AS AN ADULT

IN THE YEARS following the trial it seemed to little Gloria, alone and lonely, that the whole battle had been pointless. "The irony . . . was that as soon as my aunt was allowed to take charge of me, she lost interest." But from Gertrude Vanderbilt Whitney's point of view, the situation must have appeared quite different. She had expended a great deal of her time and money to guarantee a healthy, moral life for her niece, and she felt she had eliminated any possibility, however remote, that her niece might be murdered. Her battle was won, but she had made tremendous sacrifices in the winning: she had lost her most precious possession—privacy; her family name had been sullied; the raw exposure of the trial forced her to keep a dozen guards at her residence; her travel was curtailed, for, although not legally restricted, every time she left little Gloria for any length of time she was subjected to criticism. As Gloria Vanderbilt herself explained, "The original court order was even harder on her than it was on me. I had to be in New York every weekend, but . . . if she ever dared to set a foot out of the state I could have said, 'Oh, if the court thought I was neglecting the child, look at her!' " Which is precisely what Gloria did say repeatedly during the appeal period, inadvertently providing a portrait of the life-style of women of Society in this period:

> They've permitted Gertrude Whitney to keep [little] Gloria because I was away from her too much. Now if that be sound reasoning, then no mother on Park Avenue has any right to have her children. And that applies particularly to Gertrude Whitney. Anybody who knows anything about these things knows mothers and fathers in this position in life see very little of their children. When the babies are young they are taken care of by nurses and governesses. Mothers are busy with the duties that their social lives entail. You will usually find them out to lunch and then on to cocktails somewhere. They rush home to dress for dinner and away they go again.
>
> Their mornings are taken up by masseuses, fitters, hairdressers. Often personal financial affairs take them downtown to their bankers, brokers, or attorneys. When the children are old enough they are sent to private schools—often out of town. During the summer holidays they are off at camp. Now that is the life of ninety-nine children out of 100 whose parents are in the *Social Register*.
>
> That is exactly the way Gertrude Whitney raised her children. She saw very little of them and she sees very little of Gloria today. During the five days of the week that my daughter is in her charge down at Old Westbury, Mrs. Whitney is usually in New York. In the fall, winter and spring, she lives at her house on Fifth Avenue. You will find her out to lunch, on to cocktails and at somebody else's house for dinner day after day. If I am unfit to have custody of my own child for the reasons that the court has given, then Gertrude Whitney is equally unfit.

"But of course," Gloria added with a characteristic jab, "I have very little and Gertrude Whitney has $78 million. And $78 million couldn't possibly be wrong."

At the trial's end Gertrude was sixty years old and in failing health. "She couldn't be expected to change the patterns of a lifetime," recalls a grandson. "Her idea of child care consisted of acting in a supervisory capacity. When there was something to be done, she hired someone to do it—tutors, nurses, governesses, riding instructors, doctors. The notion that she would have to spend *time* with a child or a grandchild didn't interest her. She hadn't been brought up that way. I'm sure such things bored her."

Gertrude and little Gloria, 1938

Under a continuing barrage of public exposure and adverse publicity, Gertrude spent endless hours with Frank Crocker and his legal team, fighting Gloria's repeated custody appeals. Along with this continuing legal battle, Gertrude made an effort to return to her former life, seeing her lover Josh Hartwell "frequently" and adding yet another "admirer," George Pepper, "to an already long list." Because both of these men were married, her relationships with them were conducted in absolute secrecy. In what she termed an "orgy of creation," she resumed her sculpture, her writing, and her museum activities. In the summer of 1935, on vacation with little Gloria in the Adirondacks, she reflected her growing dissatisfaction with her custodial duties in a letter to Josh Hartwell.

> I can't tell you how the days pass here! I always *think*, now today I shall have hours to write a letter, and lo and behold . . . [little Gloria's] voice through the door, "Miss Hill says I can only stay in bathing twenty minutes." . . . It is my own fault of course, but a matriarch *is* one and prefers to remain one. Next week I go to town for a little attention to my own affairs. Does this kind of life make me a very dull person? That's what I worry about sometimes. . . .

Throughout the years 1936 and 1937 Gertrude was subjected to seemingly endless criticism by Gloria Vanderbilt—always in headlines—and everywhere she went with her "child heiress" niece, reporters followed. Every appeal, every newspaper article appeared "in Gertrude's life, as a chronic irritation." But by 1938, Gloria had no more legal measures open to her, Surrogate Foley had given her a fixed income, and Gertrude willingly agreed to a custody amendment that would no longer restrict her niece to New York State and would allow her to see her mother whenever she liked. The criticism of Gertrude ceased and she resumed her travels.

She enrolled little Gloria, now fourteen, in Miss Porter's School in Farmington, Connecticut. Gertrude seemed more able to be attentive from a distance. She wrote her niece frequently, advising her and disciplining her. Little Gloria's mother was obviously still an irritation to her. A typical letter read,

> . . . I hear you had a boy visitor. Why didn't you tell me about that?? I don't disapprove. I like you to have boyfriends so long as you are open about it. . . . You haven't answered my questions. Is your mother coming back during the holidays? If so, when do you want to go to her? (I want to make my own plans for the holi-

days.) . . . The parties you go to, you must go to from my house . . .
I insist on that. . . .

When Gloria did come home for the holidays, Gertrude engaged a chaperone to accompany her at all times. She imposed further disciplines on her niece in the form of tutors and scheduled activities. During the trial Maury Paul had written in his Cholly Knickerbocker column:

> A gay, sophisticated and cosmopolitan world lies before little Gloria if she is given into the custody of her mother. Pomp and circumstance in the old-fashioned, ultra-conservative sphere of the elder Whitneys and Vanderbilts is her lot if Mrs. Whitney triumphs. Little Gloria thinks she wants the latter regime. But she is equally the daughter of the jovial, devil-may-care Reggie Vanderbilt and the sparkling Gloria Morgan. And blood will tell. Which lot will the younger Gloria want for her own in another eight or ten years?

In the spring of 1939, little Gloria had an appendix attack, was operated on at Doctors Hospital, and missed the end of her school term. (This time the newspaper headlines read, $2,800 FOR GLORIA VANDERBILT'S APPENDIX.) Mrs. Keep, the headmistress of Miss Porter's, refused to ask her back for the following year. A classmate remembers that "when Gloria was supposedly recuperating from her operation Mrs. Keep saw a newspaper photograph of her in the Stork Club with her boyfriend Geoffrey Jones." In June her mother arrived and whisked little Gloria off on her first trip to Hollywood. B. H. Friedman, Gertrude's biographer, has observed that Gertrude's life with her niece was becoming "increasingly complicated. Where, during the custody case, the mother did accuse Gertrude of buying the child with gifts and luxurious surroundings, now Gertrude begins to feel that the mother is buying her back with a permissiveness that undermines Gertrude's strict discipline."

Among other things, little Gloria spent a weekend with her mother at San Simeon, hosted by Marion Davies and William Randolph Hearst. She recalls, "Hearst seemed to have all sorts of sorcery at his command—fairy-tale gems, Aladdin's lamps, magic carpets, and the silver screen. . . . I remember meeting Dolores del Rio and Loretta Young, surely the two most wondrous apparitions I have ever encountered. San Simeon became part of my deepest fantasies of childhood. It was a storybook castle come true, with real people living in it."

For Gertrude, visiting at the home of a man and his mistress, no matter how powerful that man might be, violated one of the rules of her social world, and she wrote to her sister Gladys, "Gloria came back yesterday but it was [July] 4 and people around all day, we have not yet had a real talk. From my standpoint it was all pretty awful. . . . A visit to Hearst & Marion Davies among other things!"

This was followed by a letter to Mrs. Keep entreating her to allow her niece to return to Miss Porter's.

> I would have written you about Gloria as soon as your letter came except that when I received it our situation was so thoroughly confused that I did not know what to say. I was very much distressed because . . . the whole influence and quality of the School as well as your personal touch had given her exactly what I had hoped for—a better comprehension of life and discipline than she had been able to grasp up to that time, by reason of her unusual circumstances.
>
> At the moment when your letter came [little] Gloria was in the throes of a number of warring interests. Her mother had arrived unexpectedly from abroad and the child was being pulled in various directions by the people whom I do not consider have her best interests at heart. . . . A hastily planned trip by Mrs. Vanderbilt took Gloria away almost immediately. The plan was to go to Catalina but they never got there and stayed in Hollywood for a month getting some rather unpleasant notoriety, from my standpoint.

On this rare occasion, Gertrude's letter failed to accomplish its purpose and little Gloria was sent to the Mary C. Wheeler School in Providence. By 1940, it was becoming increasingly clear that Gertrude's life-force, even her very world, were slipping away from her. She felt great lassitude as she struggled with her poor circulation and repeated bouts of phlebitis. Josh Hartwell became terminally ill, her only living brother, Neily, suffered a stroke, the world was again at war, the British remnant returned from Dunkirk, the triumphant Nazis occupied her beloved Paris. When her niece returned in June, she announced that she was in love with Geoff Jones and wanted her own apartment. Gertrude refused her, writing,

> . . . For a great many reasons I don't approve of the idea. I think you are in much too prominent a position. . . . The world is still full of vindictive people—and whatever you say, darling, will be heard in the world. . . . Until the time you get married it is up to me to see that you are protected against evil tongues. . . . Stories from Cal. are again appearing in the papers—lies and slander against your fam-

> ily on both sides. The dangers of another case are always hanging over our heads. That's in the background. In the foreground is your own life and . . . you are going to have your own home so soon now that for the good of everyone won't you try and see that if you were working and living home you could be getting all the things that you fundamentally want and not be putting yourself and everyone connected with you in a false position.

Little Gloria felt she was little no more. Her mother had taken a house in California the previous winter and her daughter called her up and said that "she was fed up with Auntie Ger" and wanted to live with her. Her mother told her, "If you really want to come and live with me, you'll have to make a court application through Mr. Crocker."

Gertrude Vanderbilt Whitney did not oppose her niece. Observed Mrs. Vanderbilt, "In my opinion, Mrs. Whitney was by then so fed up with Gloria, and with the whole continuing mess, that she was only too glad to wash her hands of the responsibility."

After all the pain and publicity of the custody trial, at sixteen, little Gloria chose to live in California with her mother. "I was like a bird set free," she recalls. There was no suggestion that Gloria finish high school. Her mother simply stood by as her "heiress" daughter had a telephone installed in her bathroom and sat for hours in her bubble bath talking to friends in New York (one month's bill alone was $900). She began to change her beaus and hairdos almost weekly, and most of the men she dated were old enough to be the father she had never known—Franchot Tone, Errol Flynn, Bruce Cabot, then, "I'm in love with Van Heflin and I'm going to marry him," she told her mother. When items about Gloria and Van began appearing in the newspapers, Gertrude Vanderbilt Whitney hired private detectives to report on her niece's activities. Recalls a granddaughter, "She once hired them to shadow me too. I absolutely knew she did it, but even then I couldn't believe it. There was something so strict and imposing about her—it just didn't fit somehow." It would seem that there were more direct ways of obtaining this information, but Gertrude rarely used an open path when her other personality, the secret one, manifested itself.

While the newspapers announced her impending engagement to Heflin, Gloria told her mother that she intended to marry Howard Hughes. Within a few months Hughes had been replaced by Pasquale (Pat) di Cicco, a former actors' agent on Hughes's payroll at $1,500 a month. This time, Gloria came to New York and told Auntie Ger of her romance. Her mother said, "Apparently all hell broke loose, because Gloria came dashing into my room and said, 'Mummy, I want to go right back to California. . . . Auntie Ger doesn't approve at all. But I don't care what she says. After all, you're my mother. You have a right to let me marry him.' " Looking back, little Gloria did not see herself as a giddy bubble-bath teenager. She says she rushed into marriage with di Cicco because "my mother had a great many emotional problems and I couldn't deal with them," and she didn't want "to go back to my aunt's estate on Long Island. . . . The situation with my aunt and mother was untenable. I just wanted to get out. I don't consider that a marriage."

As Reginald Vanderbilt had done eighteen years previously, Gloria Morgan Vanderbilt called upon Maury Paul to announce an engagement—this time her daughter's. This was exactly the kind of sensational Society story in which the self-proclaimed Mr. Bitch reveled: the intended bridegroom was the son of a Long Island truck farmer whose first wife, actress Thelma Todd, had been found asphyxiated after their divorce. But Maury Paul met with a tearful Gloria Vanderbilt dressed in a romantic flowing black velvet tea gown, and his friendship for her won out over his appetite for news. In his engagement announcement he referred to Pat di Cicco as "a motion picture executive" who "commands a more than comfortable salary." His assistant Eve Brown said that when people read the announcement they thought Maury was "going soft." But Eve, who knew him best, wrote, "It is quite likely that when Maury was dying, he gave his old friend, Big Gloria, some thought." Maury had experienced some heart irregularities and his doctor suggested that he take off twenty pounds to relieve the strain. He began dieting with a vengeance, never tiring of pulling his pants away from what once had been a Santa Claus tummy and jamming his arms, elbow deep, into the waistline to prove how slim he had become. But once down to an ideal weight, he could not stop losing and a hundred pounds evaporated. On July 20, 1942, his heart gave out. By then, the Café Society he had created in order to chronicle was in its twilight.

Gertrude Vanderbilt Whitney disapproved of her niece's impending marriage, but instead of getting in touch with her, characteristically she arranged for Frank Crocker to meet with Mrs. Vanderbilt to convey Gertrude's negative feelings—which really meant that if little Gloria went ahead with the marriage, she was to receive no money from Gertrude's estate when she died.

At seventeen Gloria planned for herself a Hollywood wedding far removed from the Society world into which she'd been born. At the party the night before the wedding, one of the guests, "Prince Mike" Romanoff (the "East Side Jew" who had been expelled from Gloria and Reggie's party at Sandy Point Farm) rolled on the floor with Errol Flynn and Prince David Mdivani in a wild café scuffle.

Gloria insisted that her beloved Dodo attend her wedding. Her mother objected, but was overruled. Harry J. K. Morgan had planned to give the bride away, but when he heard that Keislich was to be at the wedding he refused to attend, saying that he had not forgiven her. Gloria Morgan Vanderbilt wore the gray faille gown she had worn for her marriage to Reginald. In a ceremony replete with reporters and celebrities, on December 28, 1941, the child-woman swept down the aisle of the Mission of Santa Barbara, California. "What can one say about a first marriage," gushed the bride to the assembled press, "except that it's wonderful."

Three weeks before the wedding, the United States had entered World War II, and Gloria followed her new husband to an officers' training camp in Kansas. Interviewed there about her mother and aunt, she told *Time* magazine, "If I weren't so happy now I might hate them."

Gertrude Vanderbilt Whitney died at 2:50 a.m. on Saturday, April 18, 1942, four months after her niece's wedding. Her funeral at St. Bartholomew's Church was attended by 1,200 people. The last family member to arrive at the church was Gloria di Cicco. In her will Gertrude left her niece no money but did give her what appeared to be a token of love—a diamond and pearl bracelet, designated as "the one I almost always wear," and "all the trophies and other mementoes of her father which I have collected and preserved for her."

Within the month, workmen constructed a temporary auction platform at the east end of the largest private ballroom in New York, and Hiram H. Parke disposed of the contents of 871 Fifth Avenue: tapestries, paintings, sculpture, and furniture were dispersed to museums and private collectors throughout the world. The Metropolitan Museum of Art purchased scores of tapestries and pieces of furniture, a New England museum paid $42,000 for six Brussels Renaissance tapestries that had once been lent to King Edward VII to brighten his coronation festivities. In all, the fabulous furnishings of this American palace were sold for the knock-down price of $220,379.

Six months after Gertrude's death, on October 30, 1942, wreckers moved into the Whitney mansion. The entire grand ballroom—its floor, paneled walls, and ceiling, which were originally part of the Bordeaux château of Baron d'Albert in the time of Louis XVI—was preserved and presented to the Walters Art Gallery in Baltimore. Then a great steel ball began demolishing the Stanford White carved and gilded walls. The workers complained that the house might take two months to destroy because it was "very heavily constructed."

Gertrude Vanderbilt Whitney had been born at the beginning of an age of magnificence and splendor and when she died the age seemed to die with her. The accumulation and attrition of the great fortunes of America might well be explained in terms of the changes in the tax laws since the time of the Sixteenth Amendment and the first federal estate tax instituted in 1916. Had Gertrude died prior to 1916, and had her estate been valued at $78 million, her entire fortune would have been preserved intact. By the time she died in 1942, the federal estate tax alone on $78 million was almost $52 million. And by 1982, it will become illegal for an individual to skip a generation in his will—estates are to be taxed in every generation.

"Our heads were the first to fall," observed Grace Wilson Vanderbilt, who lived in the last Vanderbilt Fifth Avenue château to be demolished. Now on the site of 871 Fifth Avenue is a forty-five-story apartment building. Tucked into a corner of the lobby (so inconspicuously that one might easily miss it altogether) is Gertrude's twenty-one-inch bronze sculpture of the goddess Daphne. The small-breasted, beautiful nude's arms are thrown back in ecstasy. The body was modeled on Gertrude Vanderbilt Whitney's own.

In these last years of her life, Gertrude seemed obsessed with writing and rewriting a gothic story that had first occurred to her several decades earlier. It was called *The Hand*. The plot concerned a man who had lost his hand in an accident and a doctor had grafted on a new one. Soon it became evident that the hand had a life of its own, doing things that the person would never dream of doing—evil things, wild things, daring things—things totally out of keeping with the known personality of the owner.

In *The Hand* one can find the key to Gertrude's personality. "It seemed to me that there were two of me," she had written. "One the sensible middle-aged woman with a family, with ties of the most ordinary and pleasurable kind, a family whom she loved, longed to make happy; a person well dressed, normal,. healthy. But someone else was in the background, a restless person, a lonely, selfish, weak person with violent desires and wild dreams of impossible things."

This woman had confided to her journal, "I am afraid of the shadow in strange places and of the thoughts that stir me to weird actions." Yet she was a woman who insisted on discipline, an ungiving, isolated woman who observed of herself as early as age seventeen, "I have become hard inside and that hardness is spreading so that now only a little softness covers it which is the inside—beware lest the outside also harden. That curse of manners which has come to hide all things is getting to be a menace to me."

Gertrude's world has vanished, and the immutable rules that bound that world seem archaic and difficult to comprehend. Yet once it had taken ruthlessness, power, and imagination to break those rules without censure. "There is only a little while and we are given so many feelings and possibilities. Shall we die without trying all?" she had asked herself. And she had found an answer that brought her a full life, but had left her unable to express affection. The painful struggle between bohemianism and rigidity divided her essence, as well as her life.

Gertrude Vanderbilt Whitney almost always got what she wanted. Little Gloria was no exception. Yet, once winning, she moved on. Once she had evaluated herself: "You (G.W.) are a great personality," she had written. "You *must* use it. It may be rotten, but it is strong. Take it, play with it, use it lovingly and exquisitely play on the strings of it. Play havoc with all other forces. Admit no master. Get away with the things other people struggle alone to look at. . . ."

And decades later the child who had been little Gloria would mute her bitterness to say, "My aunt wanted to love me. I am sure she did. But she wasn't the kind of woman who could put her arms around a child and kiss it. There was always a wall between us. Often since her death I have thought that there was so much we might have said to each other but didn't. . . ."

Everybody's Life Is a Romance

I didn't get to know my mother until I was thirty-eight. I saw her as a pathetic woman who didn't know a single thing that had happened to her in her whole life. . . .

LITTLE GLORIA VANDERBILT AS AN ADULT

THE BLIGHT of the Vanderbilt trial had engulfed "Glorious Gloria." When it finally ended she was thirty, her income a tightly controlled $9,000 a year for personal expenses, her physical and emotional health destroyed. Branded as "unfit" for the world to see, she had slipped from celebrity to notoriety.

After the trial there were many lawsuits against her. Her Paris landlord sued for $8,993, the unpaid rent due on the rue Alfred Roll house. Nurse Keislich and butler Zaug sued for back wages. (Gloria maintained that Thomas Gilchrist had not advised her of these debts.) The Val O'Farrell Detective Agency sued Gloria Vanderbilt and A. C. Blumenthal for $4,975 in uncollected fees. California attorneys Mark M. Cohen and Irwin M. Fulop sued for $840 due for interviewing potential witnesses.

This woman who had been carefully trained to be a precious, decorative object, who had no business acumen or experience, went to work for a living. In 1935, she and Thelma started a dress business with Sonia Rosenberg.

Gloria and Thelma

Little Gloria and Gloria

Gloria envisioned working as a romantic lark. "I adore playing around with materials," she said. "I never refuse to see anyone. You can't tell what might happen. Some stranger might come here and one day help me make a million dollars." From its inception Gloria Vanderbilt–Sonia Gowns, Inc. lost money. Gloria's salary was $75 a week and she was sent on a coast-to-coast tour to promote her dresses. Reporters noted that her major contribution to the business was the use of the Vanderbilt name.

But even the great name had been tarnished. No more offers of endorsements were forthcoming, and when Gloria organized a charity ball at the Waldorf-Astoria, the attendance was so poor that the ball's deficit ran into the thousands. The twins sailed off to England where a gossip writer noted that "Thelma Furness—the former girlfriend of royalty—has lost her former glamour." Thelma sued and collected $5,000. The twins were still in the spotlight, but the glare grew harsh.

By early 1938, the debts of Gloria Vanderbilt–Sonia Gowns, Inc. had mounted to thousands of dollars and her suppliers began to sue. The twins, unbeknownst to Miss Rosenberg, abandoned the business and opened their own wholesale dress concern, Ladyship Gowns, Inc. Sonia Rosenberg sued for breach of contract, charging that Gloria and Thelma "had intoxicating liquors delivered to them during business hours. . . . They drank liquor there alone and with others. And they disposed of merchandise to their friends, fictitiously recording the transactions as sales." The twins countersued but finally both suits were dropped and Gloria filed for bankruptcy under Chapter XI. It was the first time the name Vanderbilt had ever appeared on a bankruptcy petition. On the list of her debtors was A. C. Blumenthal, who had ordered $1,000 worth of gowns for his current girl friend, actress June Lang, but had not paid for them.

After the trial Blumie had promptly dropped Gloria. A business associate summed up this pint-sized dynamo when he said: "When you're down—he's out!" Lawsuits deluged Blumie too—six in one year—but none of these legal actions seemed to slow down the nightclubbing, party-giving Blumie until the income tax evasion trial of Joseph M. Schenck. The trouble had started when mobster William (Willie) Bioff was put on trial for extorting money from four major film companies for "protection" from The Syndicate. Bioff testified that between the summer of 1935 and the spring of 1938 he had collected $1 million in cash from the film companies at the request of Nicholas M. Schenck, president of Loews, Inc., and turned the cash over to Joseph Schenck, chairman of Twentieth Century-Fox Film Corporation. Nicholas Schenck, in his testimony, said that the $1 million had gone not to his brother, but to The Syndicate, who had threatened to cripple the entire film industry with strikes. Nicholas Schenck had kept this secret because "I was afraid." Later Bioff was to say that he'd wanted to resign as shakedown man for The Syndicate, but that mob leader Louis Compagna had told him, "Anybody resigns from us resigns feet first. Understand?"

The upshot of the Bioff trial was a close examination of Joseph M. Schenck's tax records, and in March of 1941, he was put on trial for conspiring to evade payment of $412,000 in income taxes in connection with the deduction, as business expense, of one-half the cost of such items as a suite at the Ambassador Hotel shared with A. C. Blumenthal, and half the expenses of weekending in California in the company of A. C. Blumenthal and two women. Blumenthal was subpoenaed to testify about his involvement with Schenck, and to justify his own tax deductions. He fled to Mexico. Schenck went to jail. (It was a decade later when Blumenthal finally settled his affairs with the U.S. Government and was permitted to return to the United States.)

In 1940, Gloria moved to California. Her daughter joined her the next year, never leaving the celebrity spotlight—even in a Kansas officers' training camp reporters flocked to interview her, and her twenty-first birthday, February 20, 1945, was accompanied by headlines announcing:

GLORIA VANDERBILT DI CICCO COMES OF AGE

... FINAL ACCOUNTING REVEALS $4,295,628 ESTATE

> A final accounting of the estate filed with Surrogate James A. Foley yesterday by general guardian Thomas B. Gilchrist showed that . . . during the period of slightly more than eleven years in which the estate was under the stewardship of Mr. Gilchrist and the late George W. Wickersham, the estate increased in value by $488,866. . . . During the time he was guardian . . . Mr. Gilchrist had paid out $895,575. . . . Mr. Gilchrist in a recent statement formally announced the separation of Mrs. di Cicco from her husband.
>
> . . . Mrs. Gloria Vanderbilt di Cicco at the age of 21 [is] legally entitled to the proceeds of the trust . . . what provisions have been made for her mother were not disclosed yesterday. Mrs. Vanderbilt has been receiving $21,000 a year from the trust.

Gloria had come into "the Vanderbilt Gold." A relative recalls that she seemed a carbon copy of her mother at the same age. "She was totally ignorant about finances. No one had bothered to educate her.

Her grandmother, her mother, her aunt, *everybody* kept telling her how one day she'd inherit all this money, but when she did, she didn't even know the difference between a stock and a bond." For Gloria the control of her money erupted in a tangible demonstration of her childhood deprivations, needs, and resentments. Pat di Cicco received a check for $200,000 and Gloria obtained a Reno divorce. One day later, in April of 1945, she married conductor Leopold Stokowski, a man forty-two years her senior. Once they had settled in New York City she brought her beloved Dodo to live with them in private quarters in their penthouse. She lavished on Dodo a permanent annual income of $12,000 and as an added gift a $4,000 dark ranch mink coat; she continued her grandmother Morgan's yearly stipend of approximately $6,000; she bought herself $100,000 worth of jewelry. Then she cut off her mother's money, declaring (again in headlines) MY MOTHER CAN GO TO WORK OR STARVE.

There had been small signs of trouble—little Gloria's rush into marriage to get away from her mother's "emotional problems," big Gloria's mild comment about Stokowski, "Don't you think Leopold is a little old for you?"—but absolutely nothing to logically justify what seemed to be a strange, overwhelming compulsion to publicly humiliate and torture her "pathetic" mother, a sick woman who was struggling to maintain her illusions and some semblance of dignity.

In psychological terms, little Gloria seemed to be trying to recreate the childhood she'd never experienced. She had married a strong father figure who would love and protect her; she had restored the woman who had given her "mother love." Now perhaps she was paying her mother back for her desperately unhappy childhood, in the only pattern she had known, using money to control her mother's behavior and make her aware of her daughter. (Only it hadn't worked before and it didn't work now.) Years later little Gloria was to say, "I have come to see that anger is often a way to show love; those who can express anger can love more profoundly because they aren't content to keep up appearances."

Other patterns were being repeated: in typical fashion, Gloria Morgan Vanderbilt took to her bed and called in reporters to tell them that she was ill because of her daughter's "callous remarks" and that Mrs. Stokowski should remember "that charity begins at home." Her daughter called her own press conference to answer with garbled facts: "My mother should have thought of that twenty-two years ago. My mother forgets when she makes statements that when the U.S. Supreme Court in the *Vanderbilt* case judged her unfit, the Court had to be closed because some of the evidence was so terrible that it could not be made public." Then she issued a statement: "I shall always take care of my grandmother and give her everything necessary for a good life and I shall do the same for my former nurse who always gave me mother love."

Thelma Furness chimed in, saying that her twin was "very very sick" and had not slept or eaten since "my niece dealt her that cruel and unexpected blow." She chastised her niece for setting a bad example for American girls by her inhuman treatment of her own mother. Gloria Stokowski answered, "Lady Furness need not criticize and be so anxious about the American girl. The average American girl lives in a happy home and receives mother love. My mother gave me neither of these blessings. Let her Ladyship go back to England and tend to her own affairs."

In a fresh burst of publicity, Gloria Vanderbilt sold her 16¼-carat heart-shaped diamond engagement ring to diamond broker Jack M. Werst for $30,000, saying that she must have the money "in order to live." (Werst subsequently put "the Vanderbilt diamond" on exhibition across the country until it became the most displayed gem in history.) Gloria also told the press that she had decided to follow her daughter's advice about going to work and was opening a cosmetics company, Gloria Vanderbilt Ltd., bankrolled by her friend, art dealer Maurice Chalom. (Within three years, despite the $80,000 spent on advertising, the company failed.)

Gloria Stokowski's answer to the newest blast of publicity was, "The money the Court formerly gave to my mother I am now giving to blind children . . . who are homeless and starving in many countries. For this purpose I have formed a foundation . . . I am personally doing the secretarial work."

Finally, under a continuing barrage of adverse publicity, Gloria Stokowski said, "I have a natural filial regard for my mother . . . It is certain that at no time . . . will my mother suffer privation" and agreed to give her $3,000 a year. But it was four years later when she finally did so—four years of headlines. LITTLE GLORIA RENEGES ON PLAN TO AID HER MOTHER . . . CLUB REMAINS OVER MOMMY'S HEAD . . . GLORIA STOKOWSKI INSISTS MOTHER CAN SWING DINNER PAIL . . . REPORT GLORIA AGAIN AIDING MA—$250 PER MONTH.

During this period, had it not been for Thelma, Gloria might indeed have literally starved. In October of 1940, Marmaduke Furness died, and Thelma's son Tony (William Anthony Furness) inherited his father's title. When World War II ended, Thelma Furness sued her ex-husband's last wife, Enid, Lady Furness, over a codicil that cut Tony out of his father's will signed by Viscount Furness with a shaky initial *F* three months before his death. Thelma charged that her ex-husband had been a drug addict and under the influence of drugs when he'd signed the codicil. Tony Furness received an out-of-court settlement of \$6 million from the \$20 million estate, from which he helped support his mother and his aunt. Thelma, whose mansion at Melton Mowbray, along with most of her possessions, had been destroyed during World War II, came to live in California with her sister. At the very time when Gloria Stokowski announced that she was giving her money to blind children, her mother was diagnosed as having glaucoma. Thelma took her twin all over America and Europe, hoping to control this progressive eye disease. In spite of her failing sight, after her cosmetics company failed Gloria supplemented her income by manufacturing "Pooks," eighty-five-cent plastic novelty dolls that she herself painted.

During the late forties and early fifties mother and daughter were totally estranged. When Gloria was rushed to New York's Presbyterian Hospital for an emergency operation, Thelma telephoned Mamma Morgan asking for Gloria Stokowski's phone number. Although Mrs. Morgan spoke with her granddaughter almost every day, she told Thelma she didn't know the number. In desperation, Thelma got the number from a mutual friend and phoned her niece. Thelma reported that her twin had been in the operating room approximately two hours when Gloria Stokowski breezed in wearing a luxurious mink coat. Her aunt told her how worried she was and that the situation was grave. Both women waited in silence. Finally Gloria spoke, saying that she and "Stokie" were about to embark on a tour of Europe and she wanted to know what food and clothing she should take with her. An incredulous Thelma answered angrily that her twin might be dying at that very moment, and that if Gloria couldn't talk about her mother then she shouldn't talk at all. Again there was silence. Just before noon, a nurse entered the waiting room and announced that the operation had been successfully completed and that there was a good chance that Gloria would live. Thelma burst into tears of relief, while a seemingly dispassionate Gloria Stokowski stood up, wrapped herself in her long mink coat, announced that she had a hairdresser's appointment, and left. Gloria Morgan Vanderbilt remained in the hospital for three months, but her daughter never asked about her or contacted her in any way, and when her mother's hospital bills came due, she refused to pay them.

In fact, things were not going well for Gloria Stokowski, either. In her marriage she seemed to be trying to submerge herself in the role of docile child-wife. She often wore her hair in braids, she cooked and cleaned, painted, created jewelry. She had two sons, Stan (Leopold Stanislas) and Christopher, and took care of them herself. But in 1950, after five years of marriage, she suffered a nervous breakdown. Her night terrors returned, accompanied by dizzy spells and choking attacks during which she often blacked out. Her stutter grew worse. She went into psychoanalysis, and five years later left Leopold Stokowski, who swore, "If Gloria leaves me there will be a custody fight for our boys that will make the court battle her mother and aunt waged look like a picnic story." The subsequent battle echoed her own trial, the terrible patterns were again repeated. Gloria took the stand and accused her husband of overprotectiveness, saying that "he hovers over the lives of the kids like an over-anxious harassing . . . grandmother." Her critical letters to him were printed in the newspapers; she accused him of hiring detectives to follow her. She did, however, refuse to allow her sons (then seven and nine) to testify and, unlike her mother, she won their custody (with Stokowski permitted to see them weekends and for a month in the summer).

Laura Kilpatrick Morgan died in 1956, the same year Gloria divorced Leopold Stokowski. Her death provided the answer to a question that had arisen at the trial: it confirmed that Laura Morgan was a miser—her gross assets totaled $542,677. She had lived frugally in the tiny two-room apartment on East Sixtieth Street until her death. Only her twin daughters and maid Elizabeth Wann attended her funeral. Her granddaughter was bequeathed a legacy of $100,000 "in appreciation of the gifts she has made to me since she became twenty-one years of age." Laura Morgan left Gloria Morgan Vanderbilt, the daughter she had betrayed, her furs, jewelry, and $80,000, a bequest which she stated "carries with it my thanks for the time that I lived with her." When Gloria Vanderbilt received this bequest, her daughter again cut off her income on the grounds that she now had her own means of support.

Once again Gloria went to work, this time forming a perfume company with Thelma named Jumelles (the French word for twins). The company featured two perfumes: Curtain Call for winter and White Piqué for spring. The company went out of business.

By now Gloria was almost totally blind, but her twin guided her with such skill that few people knew of this. In 1956, Gloria Stokowski contracted her third marriage, to film director Sidney Lumet. At this time her mother told reporters that she hadn't seen her daughter in years and the closest she'd come to seeing her was in a television film clip of her third wedding, and added, "But I hope she's happy, that's all that matters." Gloria Vanderbilt Lumet continued her struggle for identity. She acted, making her stage debut in Ferenc Molnar's *The Swan*;

Little Gloria, at seventeen

Gloria and Elizabeth Wann

Thelma and Gloria on their fifty-ninth birthday

she wrote poetry; she made her television debut in Noel Coward's *Tonight at 8:30*. Reporters noted that when she was leaving the NBC studios, Gloria and star Ginger Rogers were mobbed by fans who grabbed at Gloria's clothing. Ginger was terrified but "through it all Gloria kept smiling," and when policemen finally came to the rescue and broke a path to her car she was "led off . . . still smiling."

After six years of marriage, Gloria and Sidney Lumet were divorced and in 1964 she married editor-writer Wyatt Emory Cooper. Seemingly desperate to earn her celebrity, she began painting and designing with furious resolve, arriving at her studio early in the morning and often working till late at night. She seemed to feel supported by Wyatt, who encouraged her, and as she began to discover her unique talents, her attitude toward her mother softened somewhat. Sometimes they would meet for lunch. In 1964, Gloria gave a birthday party for the twins. Her gift to her mother on her sixtieth birthday was a diamond bracelet (she could not see it) and to Thelma, a pair of diamond earrings.

In December of 1964, at Los Angeles' Cedars of Lebanon Hospital, Gloria Morgan Vanderbilt underwent an operation for the removal of a fusiform aneurysm, followed by extensive artery replacement. (On the same day the identical operation was performed by Dr. Michael E. DeBakey in Houston's Methodist Hospital on her former friend, the seventy-year-old Duke of Windsor.)

Gloria Vanderbilt entered the hospital again February 3, 1965, for further surgery. She died ten days later with her twin sister Thelma at her bedside. Even in death Gloria seemed to be denied her own identity. Her obituary was headlined GLORIA MORGAN VANDERBILT DIES: RAILROAD HEIRESS'S MOTHER, 60. Gloria Vanderbilt Cooper was unable to attend her mother's funeral. Less than three weeks previously she had given birth to a son, Carter Vanderbilt Cooper, and had stayed at home in New York in order to nurse her baby, an amenity of love that she herself had been denied. But her lawyer, Arnold Krakower, made sure reporters understood that the breach with her mother had been healed.

In 1958 Gloria and Thelma had written a dual autobiography, *Double Exposure*. In the photograph section of the book, fifty-four-year-old Gloria Vanderbilt is shown wearing what appears to be a shiny, strapless bathing suit with a polka-dot scarf draped over her right shoulder. There is an expression of uncomprehending pain on her ravaged face. All trace of "Glorious Gloria" has disappeared. Her left arm rests on the shoulder of a severe-faced woman in a tailored white blouse. The woman's right arm encircles Gloria's waist. She is Gloria's maid, Elizabeth Wann, who remained with her since the trial. The caption identifies her as "a faithful friend."

With the publication of this book the twins received reporters in their tiny three-room converted brownstone walk-up on East Sixty-first Street opposite the Colony restaurant. Gloria was blind and frail, but her dark hair was still shiny and pulled back in the soft waves she had worn since her youth. She saw her life in glowing romantic terms, untarnished by what actually had happened to her. "I think everybody's life is a romance. It seems to me that almost everybody I have known is a storybook," she told reporters. In her mind she recalled a time that had always been her own invention, a time that existed beautifully only in the fairy-tale myth she had created. Gloria remembered it so fondly.

> Money meant nothing; men were gallant; and women were truly feminine. . . . I think women got a lot more out of life then when they sat back and questioned wide-eyed, "Why is the world so big and round?" In those days a man never dreamed of taking a woman out to dinner unless he sent her a room full of roses. Now you have to be dead to get a single flower. . . .
>
> It was an age of splendor and extravagance, of great projects and great follies. . . . Ours was an age this world will not see again. . . .

Joy Through Pain

I think that strength of belief comes from knowing and understanding yourself and your uniqueness. I always felt incomplete because I sensed my mother felt incomplete. She felt incomplete because her mother felt incomplete, and so on. That chain of dissatisfaction is endless.

GLORIA VANDERBILT, 1979

FOR MANY YEARS, on the white wall of Gloria Vanderbilt's studio foyer was a picture of Little Orphan Annie, her curly red mop falling over a line of print that inquires, "How Does it Feel to Be Famous?" The *Matter of Vanderbilt* had thrust fame upon her and she recalls that it ripped away any "devotion," "sense of belonging," and "love" that she had known. It set her on the road to an incredible struggle for identity. Gloria says, "I don't care how rich or poor, a child without a parent is forever an orphan. The guilt—'I was so bad they left me or each other, or they died'—that never really goes away. That sense of loss is always there . . . there's something about not having that first frame of reference that one gets from a mother or a father—one's own image of oneself, of who you are. You have to get it all from yourself, and it's the most appalling, uphill battle."

Having no real people to pattern herself on in childhood, Gloria seemed to select two fictional ones, Little Orphan Annie and Jo in *Little Women.* Into adulthood Gloria surrounded herself with Little Orphan Annie paraphernalia and she admits, "I do relate to her. In a sense I was an orphan. . . . Annie inspired survival and how to go on even when grown-ups let you down. She once said, 'Remember, you're never fully dressed without a smile.' Her words have gotten me over a lot of rough spots." Gloria's childhood friend Leila Burton Hadley says, "I have a feeling Gloria may have patterned herself after Jo. Jo was a great heroine—fierce, independent, very hard working."

What seems to have sustained Gloria above all is her capacity for fantasy. If the real world became an impossible place in which to exist, Gloria carried with her another world of her own making. "Fantasy can take you anywhere. . . . It can take life and transform it," says Gloria, and she "lived in fantasy—if I hadn't, I wouldn't have survived. It's a very complicated story, my life—one I don't quite understand to this day." In her fantasy, she created a world she had never known, "with everything warm and cozy. I dreamt of painting and having lots of children and giving them all the love and attention in the world . . . something I never had when I was growing up."

As an adult, the fantasy world in Gloria burst forth and began to express itself. The way she dresses, the opulent childish fantasy of her decoration, her work, her essence, seem dedicated to creating a sense of childhood joy, of bright flowers and sunny days, of lovely carefree moments that most children remember. "I never paint from life. All joy, I think, comes out of pain. My work is filled with joy—a joy that springs from the pain of things that happened to me a long time ago, that I've spent my whole life working out. I'm now creating a joy that I never had in childhood, in recapturing something that never really happened." In Gloria's work she can go anywhere, have anything. "I began painting within myself long before I actually started painting. The canvas was a threshold that no one else dare cross. It was the door to all my possibilities. . . . There are the nestled circles made of pink and red strokes that give the illusion of the rose. . . . What garden has ever been so alive with beauty . . . ? And where, on which beach can I still find my beloved Dody? (In 1979 Gloria began referring to her nurse as Dody, not Dodo.)

"It is in surveying these secret gardens and private castles and memory faces that I have found my place. . . . My autobiography is traced in trees that merge with sky and roses that never die, eyes that smile and lips that bloom. My hand moves in time with music that I no longer hear. My canvas sings the song Dody first taught me, 'You and I together, Love . . . Never mind the weather, Love.' . . . To arrive at joy in yourself takes guts. You go through pain.' . . . Well, I have and, yes, at long last, I like being who I am," says Gloria. Her professional logo, the swan, seems an apt symbol.

In 1972, Gloria's bright fantasy would begin to be seen on a myriad of products—sheets, towels, comforters, table linen, plates, bowls, scarves, jewelry. She brought out a line of cosmetics and perfume, she began to design dresses. By 1976 she had over $3 million in sales. Interviewed that year, she said, "Sometimes I wonder, at fifty-two has success come too late? I needed it more in my 20's and 30's."

With her success, Gloria seemed free to acknowledge the positive contributions of both her mother and aunt—her mother's exquisite sense of style, her aunt's incredible drive and energy in the arts. "It has been a major triumph for me that I am able to live with all my memories and that I continue to include them more and more in my life. . . . I am grateful that my past is no longer painful for me. My work and my dreams have redeemed it." Gloria has more or less duplicated her mother's career, but has succeeded where her mother failed, and she understands a basic truth her mother could never grasp: "Women in the past have thought of money as part of masculine power, a male prerogative. Men were daddies or knights in shining armor, or Simon Legree. But often a woman's dependency on a man and his money was like living off someone else's smile. It took away a woman's responsibility for herself and made it impossible for her to control her fate."

Wyatt Cooper died in 1978, and Gloria now lives with her two sons by this marriage. She is up at five-thirty in the morning, at work by eight. Her drive and ambition seem boundless. "I want to have a Gloria Vanderbilt empire," she tells a reporter. Her latest venture, Gloria Vanderbilt Jeans for Murjani, has grossed over $160 million. Gloria is active in their promotion. Says Murjani president Warren Hirsh, "Gloria with her high level image projects beautifully for us." A Murjani television commercial begins with a brief Vanderbilt history: a photograph of Gloria's great-grandfather Commodore Vanderbilt, then one of her competitive great-aunt Alva (incorrectly identified as her great-grandmother) followed by interior views of Alva's palatial Fifth Avenue château. There is a photograph of Gertrude Vanderbilt Whitney with a glittering diamond starburst in her hair. Finally, Gloria herself appears on screen to introduce "my new status jeans," and, from a rear view, she extols the excellent fit of her product. What she is selling along with a $35 pair of pants is the nostalgia of a time when the Vanderbilt name conjured up images of American royalty, dynastic power, Croesus wealth. The vast Vanderbilt châteaux have vanished or have become curiosities. The yachts, private railroad cars, armies of domestics, pearls said to belong to empresses, diamonds the size of plover eggs—exist no more. The guidelines that clearly delineated the right people and the right places have blurred until the word Society itself has a dubious connotation.

Gertrude Vanderbilt Whitney's Wheatley Hills home is now the clubhouse of the Old Westbury Golf Club. The New York Institute of Technology occupies several other houses on the Whitney estate. Four hundred thousand tourists a year stroll through The Breakers in Newport, pausing to see a highlight of the tour, Gertrude Vanderbilt Whitney's bedroom, a young maiden's room with cabbage roses on the walls and white painted furniture. And another highlight, the small inscription over the fireplace, "What Do I Care for Riches . . ." And people have forgotten, or never knew, exactly what happened to Gloria Vanderbilt so long ago. Newspaper reports note that her father, Reginald Vanderbilt, was killed in an automobile accident. A fashionable specialty store sells ropes of fake pearls that can be cut to any length, and some customers wonder why they are called "Gloria Pearls." And when the child, little Gloria, is mentioned, it is still always in the context of "poor little rich girl . . . innocent, uncomprehending pawn" in a custody battle that took place in the dim past.

"It was the cruel lying by my daughter that hurt me most of all," Gloria Morgan Vanderbilt had said then. "I knew she was lying, but the court did not. . . . She had been influenced against me . . . during the two years I had been silly enough to leave her with Gertrude Whitney." But the child's mother did not realize that there were other elements influencing this child. And no one, except perhaps another child of the thirties, could begin to understand a fear so engulfing that it would make a little girl cry out to her own mother, "I hate you. . . . Oh, please don't take me away. . . . I hate you. . . . Don't kill me!"

The child, in the throes of a dark, unnatural dread, had repudiated her mother and had played out her role in an inexorable drama of distance and predestination. "I hate my mother. . . . As soon as I could understand things I hated her. . . . I have always hated my mother. . . . Always . . ." But did she really hate her mother?

Among the exhibits presented at the *Matter of Vanderbilt* was a photograph of a small round portrait of Gloria Vanderbilt and little Gloria when she was an infant. In Justice Carew's chambers, little Gloria Vanderbilt had sat in a large black leather swivel chair, swinging her legs, as Nathan Burkan handed her this photograph and asked, "Now, little Gloria, I show you this picture and ask you if you recognize the lady in that picture?'

"No."

"You don't recognize the woman? That does not look like your mother?"

"No."

"Just take a look at it."

"No, I don't think it is. It looks more like a painting."

"But assuming that it is a painting, doesn't the painting look like your mother? Just look at it."

"No, I don't think it does."

Before the judge and the lawyers, little Gloria had stubbornly denied that the woman in the portrait was her mother.

Forty-two years later, in December of 1976, a *Women's Wear Daily* interviewer asked the chic, talented, successful Gloria Vanderbilt di Cicco Stokowski Lumet Cooper the kind of question geared to trigger an immediate emotional response. The question was: "What if there was a fire. Suppose there was just time to take one thing—what should it be?"

And the woman who had once been little Gloria replied, ". . . The one thing I treasure most is a small round portrait of my mother and me when I was an infant. . . ."

Notes

Abbreviations of frequently used sources

CC *Champagne Cholly: The Life and Times of Maury Paul*, Eve Brown
CT Court Transcript, The *Matter of Vanderbilt*
DE *Double Exposure: A Twin Autobiography*, Gloria [Morgan] Vanderbilt and Thelma, Lady Furness
GVW *Gertrude Vanderbilt Whitney: A Biography*, B. H. Friedman
I Interview
KS *A King's Story: The Memoirs of The Duke of Windsor*
VV "The Vital Vanderbilts," Cholly Knickerbocker in *Cosmopolitan Magazine*, November 1939–January 1940
WP *Without Prejudice*, Gloria Morgan Vanderbilt with Palma Wayne

How & Why

The Visit: Gloria Morgan Vanderbilt's Version

Page
4 "I'm so glad . . ." and ff.: Court Transcript.
5 "Then . . . little Gloria will come . . ." and ff.: CT.
5 "The child has made . . ." and ff.: CT.
7 "the humiliations that grew . . .": *Without Prejudice*, Gloria Morgan Vanderbilt and Palma Wayne, p. 198.
7 "That'll be ninety-eight . . ." and ff.: *The Trial of Bruno Richard Hauptmann*, Sidney B. Whipple, ed., pps. 287, 288; *The New York Times*, Sept. 19, 1934.
8 "Oh, Mummy,": CT.
8 "If I had . . ." and ff.: CT.
10 "money mad": CT.
10 "Oh Mummy, don't go . . ." and ff.: CT.
11 "Who are these children?" and ff.: *Woman to Woman*, Gloria Vanderbilt, p. 39.
11 "the marvel of America" and ff.: *The New York Times*, March 20, 1915.
12 "Oh, Mr. Burkan, . . .": CT.
12 "She's just a little slip . . ." and ff.: Interview.
14 "Mummy, do say I can stay . . .": CT.
14 "Will you come and kiss . . ." and ff.: CT.
15 "Mummy, I have a new game . . ." and ff.: CT.
15 "Oh, yes, of course . . .": CT.
15 "Oh, Mummy, may I push . . ." and ff.: CT.
16 "My goodness, how she looks . . ." and ff.: CT.
17 "This is like a pigpen" and ff.: CT.
17 "What are you doing?" and ff.: CT.
18 "if there is any . . ." and ff.: CT.
18 "What are you doing . . ." and ff.: WP, p. 270.
18 "What have you done . . ." and ff.: CT.

p. 20 "Don't be afraid,": WP, p. 271.
20 "I will never forgive . . ." and ff.: CT; WP, p. 271; *Double Exposure*, Gloria Morgan Vanderbilt and Thelma, Lady Furness, p. 258.
20 "I hate her. . . ." and ff.: CT; WP, p. 272.
21 "Nurse, what happened? . . ." and ff.: CT.
22 "All your money, . . .": WP, p. 279.
22 "Get me that child, . . ." and ff.: I.
23 "Do you realize . . ." and ff.: WP, p. 275.

THE VISIT: GERTRUDE VANDERBILT WHITNEY'S VERSION

24 ". . . you are shy and foolish, . . .": *Gertrude Vanderbilt Whitney*, B. H. Friedman, p. 69.
25 "restless . . . a lonely, selfish, . . .": GVW, p. 431.
25 "What has happened to . . ." and ff.: CT.
26 "MRS. REGGIE VANDERBILT WILL FIGHT . . .": The New York *American*, Sept. 16, 1934.
26 "Regi was drunk . . .": GVW, p. 465.
26 "Do I have to go . . ." and ff.: CT.
27 "to keep out any mention . . .": GVW, p. 589.
28 "Oh, I can't go . . ." and ff.: CT.
29 "They're responsible for her life, . . .": CT.
29 "a wealthy child, . . .": CT.
29 "It is a terrible thing . . ." and ff.: CT.
32 "Come on and I'll show you . . ." and ff.: CT.
32 "I told her I couldn't . . ." and ff.: CT.
33 "We've gone down . . ." and ff.: CT.
35 "it would be her downfall.": CT.
35 "Don't make me go . . ." and ff.: CT.
38 "Don't let her come near me . . ." and ff.: CT; WP, p. 271; DE, p. 258.
39 "Tell Mrs. Whitney . . .": WP, p. 279.
39 "To Mrs. Harry Payne Whitney . . .": CT.

GLORIOUS GLORIA

41 "Dainty hands are a woman's . . .": WP, p. 98.
42 "I worshipped my mother, . . ." and ff.: Ibid., p. 19.
42 "I've told you a thousand . . .": DE, p. 15.
42 "The party's on me.": The New York *Sunday News*, Dec. 9, 1934.
42 "Kill-Cavalry": *Meade's Headquarters, 1863–1865: Letters of Colonel Theodore Lyman from the Wilderness to Appomattox*, selected and edited by George R. Agassiz, pps. 76, 77, 79.
43 "a hell of a damned fool, . . .": *A Diary of Battle: The Personal Journals of Col. Charles S. Wainwright*, 1861–65, Allan Nevins, ed., p. 265.
43 "a hell of a damned fool, . . .": *A Diary of Battle: The Personal Journals of Col. Charles S. Wainwright*, 1861–65, Allan Nevins, ed., p. 265.
43 "mania for titles.": CT.
43 "This is your bride's . . .": *American*, June 24, 1923.
44 "I was furious . . .": WP, p. 16.
44 "pale strong hand . . .": Ibid., p. 66.
44 "misfit . . . a bewildered, . . .": Ibid., p. 75.
44 "We speak French like Spanish . . .": *The New Yorker*, Nov. 8, 1958.

p. 45 "Thelma always leads . . .": *The New Yorker*, Nov. 8, 1958.
45 "arranged marriages tend to . . .": DE, p. 225.
45 "SON OF SOCIALITE . . .": *Daily News*, Oct. 6, 1934.
48 "light conduct": The New York *Herald*, Nov. 29, 1922 (N.Y. Herald Bureau, Paris).
48 "I am wrong to be so gentle, . . ." and ff.: *Herald*, Jan. 24, 1923 (N.Y. Herald Bureau, Paris).
50 "He was *the* social arbiter . . .": DE, p. 63.
50 "Society is not made . . .": *Ladies Home Journal*, April 1939.
50 "He understood those women . . .": I.
50 "on one morning newspaper . . .": *Champagne Cholly: The Life and Times of Maury Paul*, Eve Brown, p. 57.
51 "I think my assistant . . .": I.
52 "They are sweet, . . .": I.
54 "heir to the thirty-odd million- . . .": *Herald*, Feb. 20, 1922 (Special Dispatch, Palm Beach, Fla., Feb. 19).
54 "golden . . . wined, dined, feted. . . ." and ff.: *American*, April 12, 1923.
55 "Thelma and I let our bosoms . . ." and ff.: DE, p. 82.
55 "the nearest thing to a royal . . .": *The Big Spenders*, Lucius Beebe, p. 1.
55 "Promise me you'll let me . . ." and ff.: DE, p. 83.
56 "All my life my imagination . . .": WP, p. 90.
56 "I see you have charmed . . .": DE, p. 84.
56 "Oh look, a troika. . . .": DE, p. 84.

Reginald Claypoole Vanderbilt

59 "He has no prestige or influence. . . .": The New York *Evening Journal*, March 31, 1902.
60 "He wrote out a check . . .": *American*, June 19, 1929.
60 "So far it is very difficult . . .": *The New York Times*, Aug. 5, 1902.
61 "capitalist . . . gentleman.": *The New York Times*, April 12, 1903.
62 "full of flaming enthusiasm . . .": *The Vanderbilts and Their Fortunes*, Edwin P. Hoyt, p. 371.
62 "slipped on a banana peel" and ff.: *The New York Times*, July 14, 1915.
62 "There is absolutely no truth . . .": The New York *World*, Sept. 11, 1910.
64 "has never been interested . . .": *The New York Times*, Jan. 27, 1921.

Your Only Chance of Financial Security

67 "Oh, the troika girl. . . ." and ff.: DE, p. 85.
68 "I had known him . . .": WP, p. 90.
69 "It is pleasant, decidedly pleasant, . . .": *American*, Jan. 31, 1923, Cholly Knickerbocker.
70 "Cathleen Vanderbilt failed to arrive . . .": *Daily News*, March 7, 1923.
70 "a shock she suffered . . .": *Herald*, Oct. 25, 1923.
70 "Gloria Morgan is coming to dinner . . ." and ff.: CC, p. 105.
71 "After all, . . . I must look my best . . .": Ibid., p. 32; I.
71 "not alone a connoisseur . . .": WP, p. 91.
71 "For the first and only time . . ." and ff.: CC, pps. 106, 107; *American*, Oct. 7, 1934, Cholly Knickerbocker.
73 "But I still don't believe . . . I haven't talked this seriously . . .": DE, p. 90; WP, p. 92.

p. 74 "fragile, slim youths . . .": CC, p. 22.
74 "No *woman* is beautiful!": Ibid., p. 29.

ALICE CLAYPOOLE GWYNNE VANDERBILT

76 "Alice of The Breakers": *The Vanderbilts and Their Fortunes*, p. 378.
76 "I have never dreamed of such luxury. . . .": *The Last Resorts*, Cleveland Amory, p. 176; *The Upper Crust: An Informal History of New York's Highest Society*, Allen Churchill, p. 89.
76 "Little do I care for riches, . . .": *The Breakers: An Illustrated Handbook*, Preservation Society of Newport County, June 1953.
77 "Law! What do I care about law? . . .": *The Splendor Seekers*, Allen Churchill, p. 6.
77 "I won't sue you, . . .": *The Vanderbilt Legend*, Wayne Andrews, p. 50.
78 "Well, I don't suppose . . ." and ff.: *The Upper Crust*, p. 138.
79 "If I married her, . . .": *The Vanderbilt Legend*, p. 145.
79 "Oh no, Doctor, . . .": *The Saga of American Society*, Dixon Wecter, p. 134.
80 "Keep the money together, . . ." and ff.: *The Vital Vanderbilts*, Cholly Knickerbocker, *Cosmopolitan*, Dec. 1939.
80 "They're nice children, . . .": *The Vanderbilt Legend*, p. 30.
81 "The old man is bound to have his way, . . .": Ibid., p. 23.
82 "The haughty house of the Vanderbilt . . .": Ibid., p. 184; The Vanderbilt will case clippings, N.Y. Public Library, room 315, Nov. 1877.
82 "We cannot always control . . ." and ff.: WP, p. 162.
84 "I'm so sorry, . . ." and ff.: VV, Nov. 1939.
84 "I think that the time has come . . .": *The Upper Crust*, p. 126.
84 "a marvel of beauty . . .": *The Return of Past Glories: Beaux Arts Revivals*, The American Heritage History of Notable American Houses, Marshall B. Davidson, p. 12.
84 "I always do everything first": "The Marble Cottages," Mary Cable, *Horizon*, Autumn 1965 (Volume III, no. 4).
85 "I want to dominate the Plaza.": *The Splendor Seekers*, p. 72.
85 "Money has been expended . . .": *World*, March 10, 1895.
88 "Six windows are draped . . .": *American*, March 26, 1894.
90 "in a state of domestic prudery . . .": *The Mauve Decade: American Life at the End of the Nineteenth Century*, Thomas Beer, p. 113.
90 "I know of no profession, . . .": *The Magnificent Builders*, Joseph J. Thorndike, Jr., p. 320.
90 "drop down in harness.": *The Ultra-fashionable Peerage of America*, Rev. Charles Wilbur de Lyon Nichols, p. 32.
90 "For one to be worth . . .": *Society As I Have Found It*, Ward McAllister, p. 122.
90 "When other and later . . .": *The Big Spenders*, p. 11.
91 "The Breakers . . . was the Marble House . . .": "The Marble Cottages."
92 "I have something to tell you . . ." and ff.: VV, Jan. 1940.
93 "Inherited wealth is a real handicap . . .": *The Upper Crust*, p. 225.
96 "This is her last chance—. . .:" GVW, p. 102.
97 "desperately ill . . . he cannot endure . . .": *The New York Times*, July 15, 1896.
97 "I know my rights, . . .": *Herald*, July 17, 1896; *The New York Times*, July 18, 1896.
97 "Is he gone yet?" and ff.: *The New York Times*, July 17, 1896.
98 "Neily is to [be] married. . . .": GVW, p. 141.
98 "The ushers led the way . . .": *The New York Times*, Aug. 25, 1896.
99 "I am dying.": *World*, Sunday, Sept. 17, 1899.

p. 100 "The Germans would not dare . . .": *The New York Times*, May 1, 1915.
100 "If he gave his life . . .": GVW, p. 370.
100 "Find all the kiddies you can, boy," and ff.: *The Vanderbilt Legend*, p. 395.
101 "Don't worry, my dear lady. . . .": VV, Dec. 1939.
101 ". . . I will not marry you . . .": WP, p. 92.
101 "I have read the story . . .": *Herald*, Feb. 10, 1923.
102 "you lived your life in Macy's . . .": CC, p. 101.
102 "Dear Gloria, You will be . . .": WP, p. 93.
102 "I wish to confirm my engagement . . ." and ff.: *The New York Times*, Feb. 13, 1923.
102 "She makes Reggie . . .": *American*, Cholly Knickerbocker, Sept. 26, 1926; VV, Feb. 1940.
102 "When I am gone, my dear Gloria, . . .": "The Vanderbilt Feud," Cornelius Vanderbilt IV, *Ladies Home Journal*, July 1956.
102 "One must understand Reggie . . .". WP, p. 119.
102 "Has Gloria received her . . ." and ff.: Ibid., p. 110.

A Brilliant Marriage

104 "a brilliant marriage.": *Evening Journal*, June 29, 1926.
104 "the most eligible bachelor in town.": DE, p. 84.
104 "extraordinary.": WP, p. 119.
104 "living in some burning world . . .": Ibid., p. 98.
104 "a wonderful symbol . . .": Ibid., p 97.
105 "bear the thought of the chaos . . .": DE, p. 92.
106 "heart attacks of such virulence . . .": WP, p. 101.
106 "I watched Gloria flitting about . . .": The New York *Journal*, July 21, 1923.
106 "What do I care? . . .": *American*, April 12, 1923.
107 "A magical Morgan has done it . . ." and ff.: *World*, Sunday, July 18, 1923.
107 "If you are young, . . .": *American*, June 24, 1923.
107 "magnificently dreary and elegantly dull.": WP, p. 108.
107 " 'After all . . . you have never . . .' ": Ibid., p. 114.
108 "ran more to Rabelais . . .": *Journal*, July 21, 1923.
111 "I was subjected . . .": WP, p. 119.
111 "It was not surprising to me . . .": DE, p. 111.
111 "very hard and narrow lipped": CT.
112 "Water": VV, Feb. 1940.
116 "all personal elements extinguished . . .": WP, p. 124.
117 "It's all right, Bishop, . . .": Ibid., p. 122.
117 "The truth of the matter . . ." and ff.: Ibid., pps. 122, 123.
117 "*Everybody* was here.": DE, p. 117.
118 "My fiancée, Thelma *Vanderbilt*, . . .": *My Life with Chaplin*, Lita Grey Chaplin with Morton Cooper, p. 73.
118 "thing": Ibid., p. 83.
118 "ARE YOU OUT OF YOUR MIND?" . . . "COME HOME AT ONCE.": DE, p. 122.
119 "more than usual . . . and for the first time . . ." and ff.: *The Bennett Playbill*, Joan Bennett and Lois Kibbee, p. 88.
119 "When will you get . . .": *American*, Sept. 27, 1925.
120 "When I assured her . . .": *Herald Tribune*, June 28, 1926.
120 "slightly gassed": CT.
121 "ruddy with an alcoholic glow.": *The Vanderbilts and Their Fortunes*, p. 379.
122 "I'll see you tomorrow.": DE, p. 153.
122 "Mr. Vanderbilt died . . .": WP, p. 132.

p. 122 "sudden and unexpected . . .": *The New York Times*, Sept. 5, 1925.
123 "You are a meddlesome old . . .": WP, p. 134.

The World's Most Beautiful Widow

126 "and all appurtenances thereto": Last will and testament of Reginald Claypoole Vanderbilt.
126 "R. C. VANDERBILT LEFT . . ." and ff.: *Sun*, Sept. 25, 1925; *The New York Times*, Oct. 14, 1925; *Herald Tribune*, Nov. 1, 1925; *Sun*, Jan. 3, 1926.
127 ". . . the father of said infant . . ." and ff.: CT.
129 "a complete nervous collapse.": *World*, May 16, 1924.
130 "THE WORLD'S MOST . . .": *American*, Feb. 8, 1926.
130 "FOUR THOUSAND A MONTH . . .": *Sun*, Feb. 13, 1926.
131 "KITCHENWARE SOARS . . .": *Herald Tribune*, May 13, 1926.
132 "She's really in mourning. . . .": I.
132 "strong desire": CT.
133 "From this moment on . . .": DE, p. 165.
133 "I was never to make . . .": WP, 138.

Living at a Pretty Extravagant Rate

134 "see to it that 'the little one' . . ." and ff.: DE, p. 180.
135 "trouble: She had . . ." and ff.: Ibid., p. 180.
136 "$48,000 a year didn't go . . .": CT.
136 "What son-in-law?" and ff.: *The New York Times*, July 7, 1926.
138 "royal spasm" . . . "the richest and . . ." and ff.: "Mrs. Astor's Horse," Stanley Walker, p. 44 (from *The Evening Standard*, London).
138 "because it brings together . . .": *World*, Oct. 11, 1926.
139 "he had one of those ugly . . .": WP, p. 148.
139 "the ultimate in chic.": *Herald Tribune*, Sunday, Oct. 17, 1926.
140 "was obsessed with the belief that women . . .": *Woman to Woman*, p. 177.
140 "Your mother would be in the streets . . ." and ff.: DE, pps. 222, 223.
141 "wearing a crystal-spangled white gown . . .": *Woman to Woman*, p. 39.
141 "to finance a second marriage.": CT.
142 "She objected to my marrying . . ." and ff.: CT.
143 "*My dear Mrs. Vanderbilt*, . . ." and ff.: *Daily News*, *Evening Journal*, *American*, The New York *Mirror*, April 28, 1935–May 4, 1935; CT.
144 "I do not speak one word . . ." and ff.: The New York *Mirror*, Nov. 22, 1927.
144 "*Dear Mr. Wickersham, Enclosed* . . ." and ff.: CT.
145 "I never squandered my money . . ." and ff.: CT.
146 "CASH SMOOTHS BRIDAL PATH . . .": *American*, Feb. 2, 1929.
148 "She was my mother.": CT.

Fast Friend and Favourite Dancing Partner

150 "sudden moods of volatile hysteria . . ." and ff.: *Woman to Woman*, p. 14.
150 "would become like a vibrating . . .": WP, p. 163.
150 "I'm getting just like Dodo,": CT.
150 "spectacular spots . . . on earth" and ff.: WP, p. 164.
151 "Champagne for Marchioness . . .": *Herald*, Aug. 14, 1929.
151 "brilliant,": WP, p. 165.

p. 151 "startlingly alive.": WP, p. 167.
151 "died on a straw pallet, . . .": *Pushkin*, Henri Troyat, pps. 16–19.
152 "the Abyssinian Negro" and ff.: Ibid., p. 22, p. 13 (genealogy).
152 "Arrived Prince Hyde, . . .": *From Battenberg to Mountbatten*, Edward Spiro, p. 174.
154 "*Lady Gay: Sparkling Tales* . . ." and ff.: Research from: Private Case, Arch Room, The British Museum; *Secrets of The British Museum* (also published as *Private Case—Public Scandal*), Peter Fryer, p. 69; all titles from Album Seven; *Raped on the Railway* description from *Registrum Librorum Eroticorum*, Alfred Rose, Vol. II, p. 284; *Les Callipyges* description from Album Seven; *Memoirs of a Russian Ballet Girl* description from *Bibliographie du roman érotique du* XIXe *siècle*, Louis Perceau, Vol. I, p. 334.
155 "Mine is the story . . .": *A King's Story: The Memoirs of The Duke of Windsor*, p. ix.
155 "I have always to remember . . .": *Queen Mary, 1867–1953*, James Pope-Hennessy, p. 280.
156 "Primarily my job . . .": KS, p. 154.
156 "The world must have its heroes, . . ." and ff.: *Daily News*, Sept. 1, 1924.
157 "You must always remember . . .": KS, p. 134.
157 "But exactly who was I?" and ff.: Ibid., pps. 134, 135.
157 "What rot and waste of time, . . .": *Edward, The Uncrowned King*, Christopher Hibbert, p. 86.
157 "disapproved of Soviet Russia, . . .": KS, p. 189.
157 "I guess" and ff.: *Time*, Dec. 21, 1925.
157 "snappy.": *Time*, Feb. 16, 1931.
158 "show that, at least in matters . . .": KS, p. 196.
158 "whose pursuit of the fox . . .": Ibid., p. 195.
158 "What happened?" and ff.: "Britons Wish Their Prince Would Be More Careful," *The New York Times Magazine*, June 20, 1928.
159 "I actually possessed . . .": KS, p. 214.
159 "a ghastly mess! . . .": *Time*, Feb. 11, 1929; *Time*, April 1, 1929.
159 "And so I reluctantly . . .": KS, p. 229.

Toodles and the Teddy Bears

161 "From the moment you put . . .": DE, p. 235.
162 "Is it true what all the girls . . .": *My Life with Chaplin*, p. 166.
162 "Congratulations on the birth of your son." and ff.: DE, p. 235.
163 "She was very beautiful . . .": *The Woman He Loved*, Ralph G. Martin, p. 94.
163 "I'll give you my green one . . .": DE, p. 292.
163 "What could you possibly want . . .": KS, p. 237.
163 "pseudo-Gothic hodgepodge. . . .": Ibid., p. 238.
164 "You're not very impressed, are you . . .": "The Prince and I, Part 1, The New York *Journal American*, *The American Weekly*, June 6, 1954.
164 "hoping to keep up appearances.": *American*, June 16, 1936.
164 "a glowing radiance . . .": *The Heart Has Its Reasons: The Memoirs of The Duchess of Windsor*, p. 202.
164 "acute happiness . . . filled . . .": WP, p. 190.
165 "definitely his Royal Highness . . .": *The New York Times*, Nov. 4, 1929.
168 "No one could remain insensitive . . ." and ff.: DE, pps. 278, 279.
168 "Missing you and wanting you . . .": "The Prince and I," *American Weekly*, June 20, 1954.
169 "get-away-from-people-house,": *The Heart Has Its Reasons*, p. 181.

p. 169 "For obvious reasons . . .": *World*, May 23, 1930 (Special Correspondence from London, May 22, 1930, W. G. Marsden).
169 "Times have changed, . . .": *Time*, June 23, 1930, from London, June 16, 1930 (NANA).
169 "We entertained a great deal, . . .": DE, p. 282.
170 "You surely don't expect . . ." and ff.: *Mirror*, Barclay Beekman, March 31, 1946.
171 "the Buckingham Palace of nightclubs.": *Edward VIII*, Frances Donaldson, p. 117.
172 "Now—or so it seemed, . . ." and ff.: *Abdication*, Brian Ingles, pps. 27, 28.
172 "Gor' blime . . . it's the Queen . . .": WP, p. 207.
172 "a heightened sense of mightiness.": Ibid., p. 209.
173 "*Dear Momey, Please send me* . . ." and ff.: *The New York Times*, Dec. 19, 1934; Daily *News*, Oct. 13, 1934; *Journal American*, Oct. 20, Nov. 3, 1946, illustrated; *Daily News*, *American*, *Evening Journal*, *Mirror*, April 28–May 4, 1935; UPI News Service; UPI-Acme Photo, Daily News Photo, Wide World Photos; CT.
173 "I really have so few memories . . .": *Woman to Woman*, p. 23.
173 "no Mamma to hook onto her days . . .": WP, pps. 176, 177.
174 "that damp place" and ff.: CT.
174 "I keep account for you . . .": CT.
174 ". . . *I am very sorry about* . . ." and ff.: CT.
175 "Mrs. Simpson is fun. . . .": DE, p. 287.
175 "before our brief honeymoon . . .": *The Heart Has Its Reasons*, p. 62.
175 "The trick . . . is, or appears to be . . .": Ibid., p. 156.
176 ". . . how much like his pictures . . ." and ff.: Ibid., p. 157.
176 "A mocking look came into her eyes. . . ." and ff.: KS, p. 257.
176 "Most of all I admired her forthrightness. . . .": Ibid., p. 250.
177 "I can't write much more . . .": "The Prince and I," *American Weekly*, June 20, 1954.
177 "Pardon my breaking into Castillano, . . ." and ff.: "The Prince and I," *American Weekly*, June 20, 1954.
178 "resumed his habitual shouting . . ." and ff.: DE, p. 214.
178 "Kenya is my country. . . ." and ff.: *The Eagle*, Feb. 28, 1932 (Special Correspondence, Nairobi, Kenya, East Africa, Feb. 15, 1932).
178 "No, they are Grants. . . .": *The Eagle*, March 6, 1932.
179 "thrilled Society with . . .": *Daily News*, Feb. 30, 1931.

THE BRIDLE AND THE BIT

181 "*My dear Gloria: I have today* . . ." and ff.: CT.
182 "somewhere under his bland . . .": WP, p. 198.
182 "The bridle and the bit were constantly . . .": Ibid., p. 163.
182 "the threatening calamity . . .": Ibid., p. 198.
182 ". . . If you will make all your plans . . .": CT.
183 "Uncle Arthur, something ought to be . . ." and ff.: *The Heart Has Its Reasons*, pps. 163, 164.
183 "I lived from hotel to hotel . . .": *Women's Wear Daily*, March 4, 1976, Beverly Grunwald.
183 "*Dear Momey I have lost* . . ." and ff.: *The Upper Crust*, p. 251; UPI News Service; UPI-Acme Photo, Daily News Photo, Wide World Photos; *Journal American*, Oct. 20, Nov. 3, 1946, illustrated; *Daily News*, *American*, *Evening Journal*, *Mirror*, April 28–May 4, 1935; CT.
186 "Oh, my darling, I am sure . . .": DE, p. 301.
186 "I want to live free,": *American*, March 6, 1932 (London, Feb. 26, 1932).
186 "There is no answer!": *American*, March 6, 1932 (London, Feb. 26, 1932).

p. 186 "Mr. Andrew Rattray . . .": *The East African Standard*, Feb. 2, 1932.
187 "disheveled, unkempt," DE, p. 303.
187 "Mrs. Vanderbilt, for the past five . . .": *American*, Feb. 28, 1932, Cholly Knickerbocker.
187 "Nothing in my household ever . . .": WP, p. 198.
188 "*My dear Gloria, It just occurs to me* . . .": CT.
188 "*My dear Mr. Gilchrist, I have* . . .": CT.
189 "*Dear Naney I love you so much* . . ." and ff.: *The New York Times*, Dec. 19, 1934; *Journal American*, Oct. 20, 1946, illustrated; *Daily News*, Nov. 15, 1934; UPI-Acme Photo, Daily News Photo, Wide World Photo; *The Upper Crust*, p. 251; *Daily News*, *American*, *Evening Journal*, *Mirror*, April 26–May 4, 1935; CT.
191 "more than a casual interest," and ff.: *The Heart Has Its Reasons*, p. 161.
191 "This is my secret vice," and ff.: Ibid., pps. 172, 173.
191 "I have a poignant memory . . .": Ibid., p. 173.
192 "*Dear Naney My mother said* . . ." and ff.: *The New York Times*, Dec. 19, 1934; *Journal American*, Oct. 20, 1946, illustrated; *Daily News*, Nov. 15, 1934; UPI-Acme Photo, Daily News Photo, Wide World Photo; *The Upper Crust*, p. 251; *Daily News*, *American*, *Evening Journal*, *Mirror*, April 26–May 4, 1935; CT.

Don't Let Me Die

195 "Buy a Car Now—. . .": *Daily News*, March 31, 1932.
195 "I spent my last fifty cents . . .": *Daily News*, March 8, 1932.
195 "Abduction for ransom . . .": *The New York Times*, March 8, 1932.
195 "in a survey of 400 cities, . . ." and ff.: *Hour of Gold, Hour of Lead*, Anne Morrow Lindbergh, p. 178.
197 "*My dear Mr. Gilchrist, This* . . .": CT.
198 "the nurse seemed to be relieved . . ." and ff.: CT.
198 "Schloss *will keep in touch* . . .": CT.
199 "*Dear M., . . . The baby's body*. . . .": *Hour of Gold, Hour of Lead*, p. 209.
200 "adequate reason" and ff.: CT.
201 "needed more protection . . .": CT.
201 "sense of loss . . . at never seeing enough . . .": *Woman to Woman*, p. 62.
201 "*Dear Momey I hope that* . . .": *Journal American*, Oct. 20, 1946, illustrated; *The New York Times*, Dec. 19, 1934; UPI-Acme Photo, Daily News Photo, Wide World Photo; CT.

Gertrude

203 "The coroner established the fact . . ." and ff.: *Walking the Dusk*, L. J. Webb, a pseudonym for Gertrude Vanderbilt Whitney, p. 15. (Also available in manuscript, Archives, the Whitney Museum of American Art.)
204 "No one will ever know . . ." and ff.: I.
204 "It is evident that there . . .": *The New York Times*, Sept. 18, 1932.
204 "we played ping-pong instead of . . ." and ff.: *Walking the Dusk*, pps. 50, 196, 212.
205 "amusing places are so crowded" and ff.: Ibid., pps. 33, 35, 36, 268.
205 "We had always looked at life . . .": Ibid., pps. 42, 43.
205 "By force of circumstances . . .": Ibid., p. 18.

p. 205 "She's always been used to . . .": Ibid., p. 83.
206 "Gloria is no good. . . .": GVW, p. 465.
206 "She was a true Bohemian. . . .": I.
207 "Uptown she was very regal. . . .": Interviews with artists, Archives, the Whitney Museum of American Art.
208 "I was always reserved, . . .": GVW, p. 6.
208 "I think that in the end I will . . .": Ibid., p. 217.
208 "I have become hard inside . . .": Ibid., p. 222.
209 "My ways are deep and I cover my tracks . . .": Ibid., p. 337.
209 "Your whole life you have imposed . . .": Ibid., p. 297.
209 "to buy such unfashionable pictures . . .": Interviews with artists, Archives, the Whitney Museum of American Art.
209 "I am not exactly the same . . .": GVW, p. 42.
209 "Esther is in love with her [Gertrude], . . .": Ibid., pps. 45, 46.
210 "Come to me and lie beside me . . .": Ibid., p. 73.
210 "extreme blueness. It is Esther perhaps . . .": Ibid., p. 70.
210 "Because I don't like the way . . .": Ibid., p. 46.
210 "She was not beautiful, . . .": I.
210 "HOW THE PRETTY HEIRESS ENJOYS LIFE Miss Gertrude Vanderbilt, . . ." and ff.: *American, The Philadelphia Press*, March 25, 1895.
211 "You will always have a good time . . .": GVW, p. 66.
212 ". . . we fixed ourselves comfortably . . .": Ibid., p. 77.
213 "the union of two great American families": *The New York Times*, Aug. 26, 1896.
213 "Our American Princess": *World*, Aug. 26, 1896.
213 "It is so rarely . . .": *Who Killed Society?*, Cleveland Amory, pps. 234, 235.
213 "The house is so much Mamma's . . .": *The Whitneys: An Informal Portrait, 1635–1975*, Edwin P. Hoyt, p. 156.
214 "The $2 million Renaissance . . ." and ff.: Summary: *The New York Times*, Feb. 3, 1904; *Who Killed Society?*, p. 503.
215 "Mrs. Whitney is one of Our Set who does . . ." and ff.: The New York *Press*, Sept. 3, 1930.
215 "being fed sugar by a group of well-dressed swells.": Interviews with artist, Archives, the Whitney Museum of American Art; *Between Sittings*, p. 48.
216 "striking . . . dark and distinguished.": Interviews with artists, Archives, the Whitney Museum of American Art; *Between Sittings*, p. 49.
216 "tell him you met me . . .": GVW, p. 256.
216 "I must have it.": *Between Sittings*, p. 50; Interviews with artists, Archives, the Whitney Museum of American Art.
217 "second-rate foreign artists" . . . "uptown swillage.": Interviews with artists, Archives, the Whitney Museum of American Art.
217 "All sales in the exhibition, . . .": *John Sloan's New York Scene: From the diaries, notes and correspondence, 1906–1913*, Bruce St. John, ed., Feb. 20, 1908, p. 199.
218 "He lived for sensation . . .": *Autumn in the Valley*, Mrs. Winthrop Chanler, p. 14.
218 "The parties at the House of Fantasy . . .": Ibid., p. 18.
219 "Put aside the fact of his being a fraud and a flirt, . . .": GVW, p. 232.
220 "your spirit could play untrammeled, . . ." and ff.: Ibid., pps. 305, 306.
220 "I hate this life . . .": Ibid., p. 304.
220 "*It seems very obvious that we . . .*" and ff.: Ibid., pps. 329, 330, 331.
222 "American art will never be . . .": *The Armory Show 50th Anniversary Exhibition, 1913–1963*, p. 35.
223 "Germans will receive as much attention . . .": Juilly Hospital clip file, Archives, the Whitney Museum of American Art.

p.223 "the greater speed of the bullets, . . .": *The Evening Sun*, Nov. 4, 1914; *The New York Times*, Jan. 5, 1915, March 23, 1915.

226 "Some people took Mrs. Whitney to be shy. . . .": I.

226 "Americans love success stories . . .": Foreword: *Juliana Force and American Art Memorial Catalogue*, 1949, Forbes Watson, Archives, the Whitney Museum of American Art.

227 "You ought to round . . .": Interviews with artists, Archives, the Whitney Museum of American Art; *Sun*, Feb. 4, 1918.

227 "Mr. Luks—why do you keep following me?" and ff.: *The Improper Bohemians*, Allen Churchill, p. 247.

227 "It was the gayest place that ever was. . . .": *The New York Times*, Sept. 26, 1966, Grace Glueck.

228 "I suppose you come from below . . .": Interviews with artists, Archives, the Whitney Museum of American Art.

229 "Regi had been upsetting her . . ." and ff.: GVW, p. 465.

229 "artists for whom twelve years ago . . .": Excerpt from the Whitney Studio Club (1914–1928) *Closing Announcement*, Archives, the Whitney Museum of American Art.

229 "We don't want any more Americans. . . .": Juliana Force, "Pioneers in American Museums," Avis Berman, *Museum News*, November/December 1976.

230 "One day you can tell your . . .": I.

231 "continue the support I have . . .": *The New York Times*, Nov. 6, 1930, July 20, 1934.

231 "terribly pleased": *Sun*, Nov. 18, 1931.

A Nightmare Only Money Could Buy

232 "Why not let me take her . . ." and ff.: CT.

233 "Since the kidnaping and murder of the Lindbergh baby, . . .": GVW, p. 568.

234 "the man on the spot": CT.

234 "Are you going to marry Dr. Hartwell?" and ff.: I.

235 "were due to a considerable degree to mental . . ." and ff.: CT.

237 "I felt myself to be two people . . .": *Walking the Dusk*, p. 137.

238 "NOT GOING NEWPORT . . .": CT.

238 "a change of atmosphere . . .": CT.

238 "cheerful and bright,": CT.

239 "*Dear Momey, I am having* . . .": *The New York Times*, Dec. 19, 1934; *Journal American*, Oct. 20, Nov. 3, 1946, illustrated; Wide World Photos, UPI-Acme Photo, Daily News Photo; *Daily News*, *American*, *Mirror*, *Evening Journal*, April 28–May 4, 1935; CT.

239 ". . . one of the leading hostesses . . ." and ff.: *The People*, "Behind The Scenes," May 29, 1932.

240 "We will take only the clothes we stand . . .": *Sun*, Sept. 3, 1932.

240 "If you don't hear from us after . . .": *Sun*, Sept. 10, 1932.

240 "Our only mishap was one puncture . . .": *The New York Times*, Dec. 28, 1932 (Valletta, Malta, Dec. 27, 1932).

240 "GLORIA MUCH IMPROVED . . .": CT.

241 "frightfully backward": CT.

242 "near the surface,": CT.

242 "Dreams + + Night terrors +.": CT.

242 "God awful nurse." and ff.: CT.

243 "one, chronic constipation; . . ." and ff.: CT.

244 "in spite of her drawbacks . . .": CT.

Notes

When Will I Get My Baby Back?

p. 247 "ready money" . . . "a black speck . . .": *The New Yorker*, Profiles, Blumey, Alva Johnston, Part I, Feb. 4, 1933.

248 "the visitor is sometimes uncertain . . ." and ff.: *The New Yorker*, Profiles, Blumey, Alva Johnston, Part II, Feb. 11, 1933.

248 "you can't get classier . . .": I.

248 "somewhere between $300 . . .": *Eagle*, Aug. 21, 1932.

248 "God will strike you dead . . .": *The Tin Box Parade: A Handbook for Larceny*, Milton Mackaye, p. 274.

248 "The day we married he was flat . . .": I.

249 "WIZARD OF $500,000,000 DEALS . . .": *Sun*, July 17, 1930.

249 "worth more than any businessman in America.": *The Evening Post*, April 23, 1931.

249 "bad publicity." and ff.: *The New Yorker*, Feb. 4, 1933.

249 "benefactor,": *Gentleman Jimmy Walker: Mayor of the Jazz Age*, George Walsh, p. 322.

249 "Premier of Walker's nocturnal cabinet": *The New Yorker*, Feb. 13, 1933.

249 "the back room": *Evening Post*, March 10, 1931, Richard F. Warner.

250 "Jim looks worse . . .": *Gentleman Jimmy Walker*, p. 326.

250 "His ever changing collection . . .": *The New Yorker*, Feb. 13, 1933.

253 "gallivanting about" and ff.: CT.

253 "*Vanderbilt Guardianship Dear Mrs. Vanderbilt: . . . Your prolonged absence . . .*": CT.

254 "Oh, Mr. Gilchrist, . . .": CT.

255 "a trustworthy chauffeur,": CT.

255 "was glad that they had not been . . ." and ff.: CT.

255 "the protection of little Gloria . . .": GVW, p. 578.

255 "Rumor Hints Romance": *Mirror*, June 16, 1933.

256 "he paused in the act of signing the register . . .": *Mirror*, June 16, 1932.

257 "a swift little game of Blumey, . . .": The New York *World-Telegram*, June 17, 1933.

257 "Keeping an eye out for Mr. Blumenthal—. . .": *World-Telegram*, June 17, 1933.

257 "and for his charming wife too." and ff.: *Sunday Mirror*, June 18, 1933.

257 "BLUMENTHAL-VANDERBILT BOARD SHIP SECRETLY Denials of the yarn linking . . .": *Mirror*, June 16, 1933.

257 "unseen by a posse of process servers . . .": *Sunday Mirror*, June 18, 1933.

258 "*Dear Momey . . . If you love me . . .*": *The New York Times*, Dec. 19, 1934; *Journal American*, Oct. 20, Nov. 3, 1946; UPI News Service; UPI-Acme Photo, Daily News Photo; *American*, *Evening Journal*, *Daily News*, *Mirror*, April 28–May 4, 1935; CT.

258 "Why is she lying? . . .": I.

Possession Is Nine-tenths of the Law

259 "SHALL BE IN TOWN . . .": CT.

259 "is a fixer . . . a born ambassador": *The New Yorker*, Feb. 11, 1933.

260 "push her around.": I.

260 "WILL BE VERY HAPPY . . .": *Journal American*, Oct. 2, Nov. 3, 1946; *American*, *Evening Journal*, *Daily News*, April 28–May 2, 1935; CT.

261 "The country is so good for her," and ff.: CT.

262 "Relax dear—all married people do those . . .": *My Life with Chaplin*, p. 255; *Hollywood Babylon*, Kenneth Anger, p. 93.

p. 263 "the house goy.": I.
263 "Your tactics are a disgrace to the profession. . . .": *The New York Times*, Oct. 20, 1927 (lawyer Vincent Leisell in George and Julia M. Leary divorce case).
263 "when to require a damsel in distress . . .": *Sun*, March 25, 1930.
264 "I'm not afraid of Mrs. Whitney's money . . ." and ff.: I.
264 "We are going to Mrs. Whitney's." and ff.: WP, p. 218.
265 "I don't care what Mrs. Whitney, . . ." and ff.: CT.
265 "Mamma, my child is not for sale!": *Daily News*, Nov. 23, 1934.
265 "How would it look . . .": I.
266 "I'm being put in a very . . ." and ff.: CT.
266 "close to a criminal conspiracy.": *Herald Tribune*, Sept. 17, 1933.
266 "*My dear Gloria: Mr. Gilchrist* . . ." and ff.: WP, p. 224; CT.
267 "*Dear Mr. Wickersham, I appreciate* . . ." and ff.: WP, p. 223; CT.
268 ". . . on the question of your right . . ." and ff.: WP, p. 223; CT.
268 "to conduct nationwide warfare . . .": *The New York Times*, July 30, 1933.
269 "almost built-in . . ." and ff.: *"So the Witch Won't Eat Me,"* Dorothy Bloch, pps. 3, 4.
269 "the child's attempt to defend himself . . .": Ibid., p. 2.
269 "His 'badness' . . .": Ibid., p. 5.
269 "I am so bad,": CT.

Unfit

270 "the noble experiment": *The New York Times*, Nov. 20, 1932.
270 "I was down in Texas . . .": *The New York Times*, Jan. 26, 1936.
271 "Oh, Mrs. Vanderbilt, that was never . . ." and ff.: DE, p. 248.
271 "If we don't do something, . . .": I.
272 "moral sense was offended . . .": *The New Yorker*, Feb. 13, 1933.
272 "to be more eager to win . . ." and ff.: I.
272 "I've just had a letter from Gloria . . ." and ff.: DE, p. 306.
274 "It's from Buckingham Palace!": "The Prince and I," *American Weekly*, June 20, 1954.
274 "Who is that little boy?" and ff.: CT.
274 "Bring Miss Gloria to us at once." and ff.: CT.
274 "Tell me about Hollywood," and ff.: CT.
275 "out of the question,": *American*, Sept. 1937, Cholly Knickerbocker.
275 "Thelma Furness has captured both . . .": *The Woman He Loved*, Ralph G. Martin, p. 106.
275 "See you in London, Aly." and ff.: DE, p. 309.
276 "the Prince of Wales . . ." and ff.: *The Woman He Loved*, p. 111.
276 "to put it bluntly, he . . .": Ibid., p. 111.
276 "of romantic largesse . . .": DE, p. 310.
276 "learned to carry *Imsák* to its extreme. . . .": *Aly*, Leonard Slater, pps. 138, 139.
276 "No, darling, I can't stop. . . ." and ff.: DE, p. 310.
277 "She knew as well as everybody . . ." and ff.: Ibid., pps. 313, 314.
277 "Thelma returned in the early spring. . . .": *The Heart Has Its Reasons*, p. 184.
277 "If you had your life to . . ." and ff.: *News Review*, Dec. 10, 1936; *London Daily Herald*, March 16, 1959.
277 "Edward VIII might still be on the . . .": *R.S.V.P.*, Elsa Maxwell, p. 285.
278 "I'm not a religious man," and ff.: I.
278 "general nervous breakdown.": CT.
279 "Remember when you told me . . .": CT.
279 "Oh, I hope I can always . . ." and ff.: CT.

p. 280 "I'm tired of married life.": *American* (C. F. Bertelli, Universal Service Staff Correspondent), June 30, 1926.
280 "This winter you'll be . . .": CT.
281 "On what grounds . . ." and ff.: WP, p. 226.
281 "In the last analysis," and ff.: Ibid., pps. 227, 228.
281 "stupefied. . . . None of the . . .": DE, pps. 249, 250.
281 "It is a terrible thing to . . ." and ff.: CT.
282 "My concern is . . ." and ff.: CT.
282 "welfare-of-the-child—. . .": WP, p. 253.
282 "it was best for the child if she . . ." and ff.: CT.
283 "It is a miracle . . .": *The New York Times*, May 15, 1934.
285 "She wasn't interested in them.": CT.
285 "VANDERBILT CLAN BURIES . . . 1,000 GUNS OUT IN KIDNAPING OF CATTLE HEIRESS, 6" and ff.: *Daily News*, April 27, 1934.
285 "My child of course reads these . . ." and ff.: *American*, Sept. 29, 1935; *Sun*, Sept. 30, 1935.

DRAGGED THROUGH THE MUD

287 "THREE NOTED FAMILIES IN COURT . . .": *American*, July 25, 1934.
287 "NO AGREEMENT REACHED . . ." and ff.: *The New York Times*, July 27, 1934.
287 "never publish her disgrace.": CT.
288 "They're going to great . . .": I.
288 "a detective with class,": I.
289 "Give it lots of air. . . .": *Daily News*, Aug. 19, 1931, Snapshots, Alissa Keir.
289 " 'Sapodils'—that's what we call them . . ." and ff.: *The Eagle*, Nov. 20, 1927.
290 "Come over a little while—. . ." and ff.: *Daily News*, Feb. 5, 1938, "Own Mother's Gossip About Gloria Bared," Julia McCarthy and Neal Patterson.
290 "Mothers don't do to their children . . ." and ff.: WP, p. 245.
291 "If you can give me my check for August, . . ." and ff.: CT.
291 "Are you going against me, . . ." and ff.: WP, p. 245.
291 ". . . *there will be a hearing* . . .": GVW, p. 589.
292 "You never considered it neglect when . . ." and ff.: WP, p. 249.
292 "the welfare of the child" and ff.: WP, pps. 249, 250; CT.
292 "She is very excitable, . . ." and ff.: CT.
293 "Fourteen lawyers are . . .": *Sun*, July 27, 1934.
293 "dragged through the mud" and ff.: CT.
294 "the Whitney camp." and ff.: CT.
294 "What do you mean by giving . . ." and ff.: CT.
295 "*Dear Mumy, I am having a nice* . . .": *Daily News*, Oct. 13, 1934; *Journal American*, Oct. 20, 27, Nov. 3, 1946; Washington *Herald*, May 1, 1935; *American*, May 1, 2, 1935; CT.
295 "to kidnap her" and ff.: *Life*, March 2, 1959.
296 "My throat is so dry. . . ." and ff.: CT.
297 "there was always a wall between us.": *Daily News*, Dec. 29, 1954, Jess Stearn.
297 "Aunt Ger, I am afraid I am going to be kidnapped.": CT.

KIDNAP=MURDER=MOTHER

298 "As a result of preliminary . . .": *The New York Times*, July 27, 1934.
299 "I don't want to hurt . . .": WP, p. 253.
299 "Do you know what a trial of this caliber can do? . . .: Ibid., p. 254.
300 "my heart cut off my breath almost entirely.": Ibid., p. 256.

p. 300 "ready to use any means to put . . ." and ff.: CT.
301 "I suppose I've got to get . . .": *Sunday Mirror Magazine*, Dec. 23, 1934.
302 "without any preparation whatsoever.": CT.
302 "difficulty in using the bathroom because . . .": CT.
303 "I hate my mother." and ff.: CT.
303 "Oh, I can't go and stay with my mother," and ff.: CT.
303 "*Dear Walter Please take* . . .": CT.
304 "Take her away. . . ." and ff.: CT.

The Trial

The major part of this section is drawn verbatim from the voluminous court transcript of the *Matter of Vanderbilt*. The use of this material will be obvious to the reader, and therefore I have noted specifically only the quotations that do not fall into this category.

Dirty Linen

312 "a practical person" and ff.: *Eagle*, Nov. 25, 1934.
312 "an increasing tide of irreligion.": *The New York Times*, Nov. 3, 1930.
312 "I thought woman suffrage . . .": *The New York Times*, Nov. 13, 1915.
312 "I am an American. . . .": *The New York Times*, March 12, 1916.
312 "Free speech on the fundamental . . .": *World-Telegram*, Oct. 11, 1934.
313 "heroic pain": I.
316 "KIDNAP LADDER TRACED TO HAUPTMANN: . . ." and ff.: *The New York Times*, *Daily News*, *Mirror*, *Sun*, *World-Telegram*, Sept. 30, 1934.
317 "They've played their trump . . .": I.
317 "Watch out, Gloria," and ff.: I.
317 "the tiny heiress" and ff.: *Mirror*, Oct. 1, 1934.
318 "Gentlemen, the line forms on the right.": *Daily News*, March 19, 1976; *The Showgirl Who Shocked New York*, Anthony Burton.
325 "untenable" that "in desperation . . .": *Woman to Woman*, p. 42.
325 "love and dedication" and ff.: Ibid., p. 42.
327 "I'm going to ask Mrs. Harry Payne Whitney . . ." and ff.: *Daily News*, Oct. 2, 1934.
333 "As the only Christian . . ." and ff.: I.
333 "I'll do the work, . . .": I.
334 "Where did you find that woman? If you . . .": *Ladies of the Press: The Story of Women in Journalism by an Insider*, Ishbel Ross, p. 195.
334 "VANDERBILT BOUDOIR SECRETS . . ." and ff.: *Daily News*, Oct. 2, 1934.
334 "It is just as impossible to keep . . .": *American*, Oct. 15, 1934, Cholly Knickerbocker.
339 "These stories are so ridiculous . . ." and ff.: *World-Telegram*, Oct. 2, 1934.
340 "her expensively-coiffed head": The New York *Post*, Oct. 2, 1934.
340 "Every story they've told is a lie. . . .": *Daily News*, Oct. 3, 1934.
341 "Maid admits promise of pay for her testimony.": *Daily News*, Oct. 10, 1934.

Lies—Lies—Lies

344 "It's all a pack of malicious lies.": *Mirror*, Oct. 4, 1934.
344 ". . . A set of malicious lies.": *Sun*, Oct. 4, 1934.

p.344 "... The most monstrous criminal lie ...": *The New York Times*, Oct. 4, 1934; *Daily News*, Oct. 5, 1934.
344 "It's all so utterly false ...": *Daily News*, Oct. 3, 1934.
344 "In view of the maid's ...": *Daily News*, Oct. 5, 1934.
345 "FRENCH MAID BLURTS OUT SECRET ..." and ff.: *Sun*, Oct. 2, 1934; *World-Telegram*, Oct. 2, 1934; *Daily News*, Oct. 3, 1934.
345 "No sooner had the ..." and ff.: *Time*, Oct. 15, 1934.
346 "My mother must be mad!": *Mirror*, Oct. 6, 1934.
346 "I cannot comment on anything ..." and ff.: *Daily News*, Oct. 5, 1934.
346 "What you have heard are a set ..." and ff.: *Sun*, Oct. 4, 1934.
346 "ROYALTY OF BRITAIN FORBID ..." and ff.: *Mirror*, Oct. 5, 1934.
347 "The whole thing is disgusting ...": *The New York Times*, Oct. 4, 1934.
347 "lurid stories concerning ..." and ff.: *The Morning Post*, London, Oct. 4, Oct. 6, 1934.
347 "Mrs. Vanderbilt and a titled ...": *The Daily Express*, London, Oct. 8, 1934.
348 "I promise I'll give you ...": *Sun*, Oct. 4, 1934.
348 "I just came out to see Miss Bennett ...": *American*, Oct. 4, 1934.
348 "Of course I will testify for Gloria ..." and ff.: *The New York Times*, *American*, *Journal*, *Daily News*, *Sun*, Oct. 4, 1934.
349 "Hank has been ill ..." and ff.: *Daily News*, Oct. 5, 1934.
349 "I will insist on the fullest hearing. ..." and ff.: *Daily News*, *World-Telegram*, Oct. 6, 1934; *Mirror*, Oct. 7, Oct. 8, 1934.
351 "I am sure if my daughter ..." and ff.: *Daily News*, Oct. 6, 1934.
352 "spent a delightful Sunday ...": *Sunday Mirror*, Oct. 7, 1934.

AN EXCEPTIONALLY VIRTUOUS MAN

353 "A judge should not think of himself ...": *The New York Times Magazine*, Oct. 17, 1976.
353 "I will consider the situation ..." and ff.: *World-Telegram*, Oct. 3, 1934; *The New York Times*, *Daily News*, *Sun*, *American*, Oct. 4, 1934.
354 "disposed to admit the press ...": *Daily News*, *Mirror*, *Sun*, Oct. 5, 1934.
354 "There will be no settlement ...": *American*, Oct. 7, 1934.
354 "I have considered the situation ... so ..." and ff.: *World-Telegram*, *American*, Oct. 8, 1934; *Daily News*, Oct. 9, 1934.
355 "since it will not be sensational.": *Daily News*, Oct. 8, 1934.
356 "She prefers the front door method ...": *Ladies of the Press*, p. 195.
357 "You're not satisfied being gagged?" and ff.: *Mirror*, Oct. 9, 1934.
360 "I feel all right now,": *Daily News*, Oct. 9, 1934.
362 "a brief and spotless account ...": *Daily News*, Oct. 9, 1934.
362 "In this he was unsuccessful. ..." and ff.: *Daily News*, Oct. 9, 1934.
362 "MRS. VANDERBILT 'VINDICATED' ..." and ff.: *Daily News*, Oct. 10, 1934.
363 "My proper function as based ...": *Eagle*, Nov. 25, 1934.
363 "from mothers who have lost children ...": *Sun*, Oct. 11, 1934.
363 "right" and ff.: I.
363 "I have received a number of letters ..." and ff.: *Mirror*, Oct. 10, 1934; *News-Week*, Oct. 20, 1934.

THE LONELIEST MOTHER IN THE WORLD

364 "Mrs. Morgan turned her back ...": *American*, Oct. 15, 1934, Cholly Knickerbocker.

p. 365 "could not meet her Maker" and ff.: WP, p. 294.
368 "What right do you have to do this! . . .": *Sun*, Oct. 11, 1934.

Forbidden Fruit

374 "Mrs. Morgan gave only a brief . . ." and ff.: *Mirror*, Oct. 11, 1934.
375 "ALICE SPEED STOLL SNATCHED: . . ." and ff.: *The New York Times*, *Daily News*, *Mirror*, *Sun*, *Journal*, Oct. 12, 1934.
380 "I must decline to say . . ." and ff.: *The New York Times*, Oct. 12, 1934.
380 "BUTLER INSISTS MADAME . . .": *Mirror*, Oct. 12, 1934.
380 "Unruffled under the hammering . . ." and ff.: *World-Telegram*, Oct. 11, 1934, Denis Morrison.
381 "Someone on the Whitney side . . ." and ff.: I.
381 "concerning Mrs. Vanderbilt's nude, . . .": *Daily News*, Oct. 13, 1934.
381 "Nevertheless, cross-examination . . .": *Daily News*, Oct. 13, 1934.
382 "That nude drinking tete-a-tete . . .": *Sunday News*, Oct. 14, 1934.
382 "REINFORCEMENTS ARRIVE" and ff.: *The New York Times*, *American*, *Sun*, *Journal*, *World-Telegram*, *Mirror*, Oct. 12, 1934.
384 "GLORIA LAURA VANDERBILT, 10, . . ." and ff.: *Daily News*, Oct. 15, 1934.

Family Skeletons

385 "Here in the greatest metropolis . . .": *American*, Oct. 15, 1934, Cholly Knickerbocker.
385 "STOLL KIDNAP CAR SPOTTED" and ff.: *The New York Times*, *Sun*, *World-Telegram*, *American*, Oct. 14, 15, 16, 1934.
387 "There goes one Greek . . .": I.
389 "Instead of Ivory Soap, . . ." and ff.: *The New York Times*, *World-Telegram*, *Herald-Tribune*, Oct. 16, 1934.
393 "You've gotta see me alone," and ff.: *World-Telegram*, Oct. 15, 1934; *American*, *Journal*, *Herald-Tribune*, Oct. 16, 1934.
398 "I think you will agree . . ." and ff.: *The New York Times*, *Herald-Tribune*, Nov. 16, 1934.
398 "If you value the life of your child . . .": *The New York Times*, *Sun*, Oct. 21, 1934.
399 "is already under intensive . . ." and ff.: I.
406 "prepared to make unusual concessions": *Mirror*, Oct. 20, 1934.
407 "POLICE GUARD VANDERBILT-WHITNEY . . ." and ff.: *Herald-Tribune*, *Sun*, Oct. 20, 1934.

Little Gloria's Thrown the Key in the Fire

410 "There are cordons and cordons of them," and ff.: *Mirror*, Oct. 22, 1934.
415 "my happiest day since my baby . . .": *Mirror*, Oct. 22, 1934.
415 " 'Will you please come Wednesday, . . .": *Mirror*, Oct. 22, 1934.
415 "According to information obtained . . .": *The New York Times*, Oct. 23, 1934.
416 "There is absolutely no possibility . . .": *Mirror*, Oct. 21, 1934.
417 "Interesting. Most interesting." and ff.: *The New York Times*, *Sun*, Oct. 24, 1934.
417 "Imagine. The King's solicitor . . ." and ff.: I.

Notes

Gertrude

p.423 "Mrs. Whitney is bearing up nicely.": *Mirror*, Oct. 24, 1934.
429 "Here is Mrs. Harry Payne Whitney . . .": *Daily News*, Oct. 22, 1934.
429 "HOW U.S. APPEARS . . ." and ff.: *Mirror*, Nov. 10, 1934.
432 "They are all works of art . . .": *Mirror*, Oct. 24, 1934.
433 "You don't know art from dirt!": *Mirror*, Oct. 24, 1934.

I Have Always Been Afraid of My Mother

437 "there was always the overwhelming . . .": *Woman to Woman*, p. 17.
437 "I can remember thinking . . .": *Daily News*, Dec. 29, 1954, Jess Stearn.
438 "Court is adjourned . . .": *Herald-Tribune*, Oct. 25, 1934.
438 "smiled broadly and occasionally . . .": *Daily News*, Oct. 25, 1934.
445 "I thought they expected me to . . .": *Daily News*, Dec. 29, 1954, Jess Stearn.
454 "for a father living . . ." and ff.: *Daily News*, Dec. 29, 1954, Jess Stearn.
456 "No child should ever be brought . . .": *Daily News*, Dec. 29, 1954, Jess Stearn.
456 "Jim, start building a record for the appeal. . . ." and ff.: I.
457 "Justice Carew stated . . ." and ff.: *Daily News*, Oct. 25, 1934.
457 "NO ANTIPATHY TOWARD MOTHER" and ff.: *The New York Times*, Oct. 25, 1934.
457 "I could render a decision right now . . ." and ff.: *Herald-Tribune*, Oct. 30, 1934.

The Vanderbilt Side

460 "frequent escorts of Mrs. Vanderbilt" and ff.: *Mirror*, Oct. 21, 1934.
461 "outrageous" . . . "monstrous,": *Mirror*, Oct. 26, 1934.
466 "That woman has always had what she wants. . . .": *Sunday Mirror*, Oct. 28, 1934; *Sun*, Nov. 6, 1934.
470 "I'm not supposed to talk to you,": *Mirror*, Oct. 27, 1934.
471 "In a resolution introduced . . .": *Daily News*, Oct. 28, 1934.
471 "With grievous damage already . . .": *American*, Oct. 27, 1934.
471 "This judge is incomprehensible.": *Evening Post*, Oct. 26, 1934.

Everybody Wore Pajamas

473 "I have been summoned . . .": *Daily News*, Oct. 30, 1934.
485 "I thought it was very good." and ff.: *American*, Oct. 29, 1934; *Mirror*, *Herald-Tribune*, Oct. 30, 1934; *Mirror*, Nov. 9, 1934.
485 "What do you think of this trial?" and ff.: *Mirror*, Nov. 9, 1934.

Gloria

487 "I was walking on eggshells . . .": I.
490 "dressed all in black. . . .": *Sun*, Nov. 1, 1934.
490 "dead white and expressionless,": *Herald-Tribune*, Nov. 8, 1934.
490 "magnolia white with scarlet lips,": *Mirror*, Nov. 1, 1934.
490 "pale and drained of blood.": *The New York Times*, Nov. 10, 1934.
493 "Get back!" and ff.: *World-Telegram*, Oct. 30, 1934; *Mirror*, Oct. 31, 1934.
494 "I'm so tired. . . .": *American*, *Sun*, Oct. 31, 1934.

p.494 "I WILL COLLAPSE WHEN I . . .": *Sun*, Oct. 31, 1934.
494 "Someone has taken advantage . . ." and ff.: *Herald-Tribune*, *Daily News*, *Mirror*, Oct. 31, 1934.
495 "He's gone round the bend,": I.
495 "If there is any justice . . .": *Mirror*, Nov. 4, 1934.
495 "Mrs. Whitney has millions, . . .": *Daily News*, Nov. 1, 1934.
495 "My sister still hopes . . .": *American*, Nov. 5, 1934.
495 "I've asked Justice Carew again . . ." and ff.: *Sun*, Nov. 4, 1934.
496 "Heart attack? Gloria could always . . .": *Time*, Nov. 26, 1934.
496 "If the child said she did not want . . .": *Herald-Tribune*, Oct. 27, 1934.
496 "Obviously she was influenced. . . ." and ff.: *Mirror*, Oct. 30, 1934.
496 "God bless you, dear Mrs. Vanderbilt. . . .": *American*, Oct. 31, 1934.
496 "We're praying for you . . .": *Mirror*, Nov. 10, 1934.
496 "felt her heart break.": *Mirror*, Nov. 11, 1934.
502 "That spy! . . ." and ff.: I.
508 "Had that happened to my sister's child, . . .": WP, p. 307.
508 "Why is she doing this?": *Sun*, Nov. 4, 1934.
508 "Mrs. Whitney, elderly aunt . . .": *Daily News*, Oct. 13, 1934.
508 "Little Gloria is blissfully unaware . . ." and ff.: *Mirror*, Nov. 4, 5, 1934; *Sunday Mirror*, Nov. 11, 1934.

Give This Mother Back Her Child

510 "I picked up Gloria for Monday's . . .": I.
510 "Republicans are no longer . . .": *Mirror*, Nov. 7, 1934.
511 "LANDSLIDE FOR LEHMAN": *Mirror*, Nov. 7, 1934.
511 "LITTLE GLORIA TO BE RAISED . . .": *Sun*, Nov. 7, 1934.
514 "Justice Carew said yesterday . . .": *The New York Times*, Nov. 10, 1934.
514 "My mother is a rare bease . . ." and ff.: *The New York Times*, Nov. 15, 1934.
515 "produced photographs of a mural . . ." and ff.: *The New York Times*, Nov. 8, 1934.
515 "The judge must have . . .": *Time*, Nov. 26, 1934.
520 "BRUNO'S FOES JOIN LITTLE GLORIA'S CASE" and ff.: *Daily News*, *Mirror*, *Sun*, *American*, *World-Telegram*, Nov. 9–14, 1934.
521 "Isn't it lovely to know . . .": *The New York Times*, *Sun*, *American*, Nov. 14, 1934.
522 "Give her her baby back . . .": *The New York Times*, *Daily News*, Nov. 10, 1934.
522 "AN HUMBLE APPEAL . . ." and ff.: *Mirror*, Nov. 11, 1934.
523 "Nathan Burkan contends the child's letters . . ." and ff.: *American*, Nov. 14, 1934.

The Socialites' Solomon

526 "Mr. Justice Carew decided . . ." and ff.: *The New York Times*, *American*, Nov. 14, 15, 1934; *Mirror*, Nov. 16, 1934.
527 "I couldn't understand the quarrel . . .": *American Weekly*, Sept. 6, 1959, "Maestro vs. Millionairess," Maurice Zolotow; *Mirror*, Aug. 6, 1958, Maurice Zolotow, reprinted from *Cosmopolitan*.
531 "I will not tolerate for one moment . . .": *American*, Sept. 25, 1935.
532 "that if the Relator took the child . . .": *The New York Times*, Sept. 21, 1935; CT.
532 "If at any time the child . . .": *Daily News*, Nov. 20, 1934.
532 "Gentlemen, my mind . . ." and ff.: *The New York Times*, *Sun*, Nov. 17, 1934.

p.532 "I am Justice Carew of the Supreme Court. . . ." and ff.: *Mirror*, Nov. 15, 16, 1934; *Mirror*, *Daily News*, *Sun*, Nov. 17, 1934.
533 "a great surprise to the public.": *Sun*, Nov. 16, 1934.
534 "At one o'clock—some day.": *Mirror*, Nov. 20, 1934.
534 "My judgment will be like that . . .": *Daily News*, Nov. 18, 1934; *Time*, Nov. 26, 1934.
536 "Daddy did you really say . . ." and ff.: I.
536 "You'll have to do your own interpreting . . .": *The New York Times*, *Daily News*, *Mirror*, Nov. 22, 23, 1934.
536 "Ten-year-old Gloria Laura Vanderbilt, . . .": *Daily News*, Nov. 22, 1934.
536 "Here comes a child . . .": *The New York Times*, Nov. 24, 1934.
537 "The mere fact that the Court . . .": *Journal-American*, Nov. 23, 1934.
537 "The freedom of the press . . .": *Sun*, Nov. 23, 1934.
537 "Both Wickersham and Gilchrist . . .": *The U.S. Law Review*, Jan. 1935.
537 "The order providing for . . .": *Daily News*, Nov. 24, 1934.
537 "What kind of provision . . .": *Mirror*, Nov. 29, 1934.
537 "It is my decision . . .": *American*, Nov. 17, 1934.
538 "My only thought since . . .": *Daily News*, Nov. 21, 1934.
538 "CATHOLIC COMMUNIST.": *Herald-Tribune*, Nov. 23, 1934.
538 "Gloria is very happy . . .": *Mirror*, Nov. 21, 1934.
538 ". . . It was always my hope . . ." and ff.: *The New York Times*, *Daily News*, *Herald-Tribune*, *Mirror*, *Sun*, *American*, *World-Telegram*, Nov. 21, 22, 1934.
540 "I can't see anybody . . .": *American*, Nov. 12, 1934.
540 "I'll only be gone . . .": *Daily News*, Nov. 17, 1934.
540 "I openly charge that Mrs. Whitney . . ." and ff.: *The New York Times*, *Daily News*, *Mirror*, *Sun*, *American*, *World-Telegram*, *Herald-Tribune*, Nov. 22, 23, 1934; *News-Week*, Dec. 1, 1934.
542 "There were anonymous phone calls . . ." and ff.: I.
542 "Mr. Judge—You'll see . . .": *World-Telegram*, Nov. 22, 1934; *Daily News*, *Mirror*, Nov. 23, 1934; *News-Week*, Dec. 1, 1934.
542 "As for the secrecy . . .": *Daily News*, *Mirror*, Nov. 24, 1934.

Since Then

Rockabye Baby

547 "Little Gloria begins a new life . . .": *Sun*, Nov. 17, 1934.
548 "The world has gone . . .": "Anything Goes," Cole Porter, Copyright © 1938 courtesy of Warner Bros. Music and Chappell & Co. Ltd.
548 "Little Gloria Vanderbilt yesterday . . .": *Sunday Mirror*, Nov. 18, 1934.
548 "Surrounded by her impressive . . .": *Daily News*, Nov. 25, 1934.
549 "CHILD HEIRESS GOES TO MASS Gloria Vanderbilt . . .": *Daily News*, Nov. 26, 1934.
550 "eating her turkey dinner . . ." and ff.: *World-Telegram*, Nov. 29, 1934.
550 "The ten-year-old heiress . . .": *The New York Times*, Nov. 30, 1934.
550 "VANDERBILT GIRL 'HATED' MOTHER, . . ." and ff.: *The New York Times*, Dec. 19, 1934.
551 "Little Gloria does not realize . . .": *Sunday Mirror*, Nov. 18, 1934.
551 "A Very Merry Christmas Reunion . . ." and ff.: *American*, *Sun*, Dec. 19, 1934.
551 "rich ladies peered as openly . . .": *Sun*, Dec. 23, 1934.
551 "G. went to town. . . .": GVW, p. 598.
551 "made a valiant but vain effort . . .": *Sun*, Dec. 22, 1934.
552 "no outsiders observed . . .": *The New York Times*, Dec. 22, 1934.

p.552 "but also of meeting the mother . . ." and ff.: *Sunday Mirror*, Oct. 27, 1935, "Bodyguarding the 'Gold Child,' " Larry Gilman.

552 "Please—please leave me . . .": *Sunday Mirror*, Oct. 27, 1935, "Bodyguarding the 'Gold Child.' "

553 "Here are the latest pictures . . .": Sound track from Metrotone Newsreel.

555 "He knew it was his slip . . ." and ff.: I.

555 "LITTLE GLORIA'S FEAR OF DEATH REVEALED" and ff.: *American*, April 30, 1935.

555 CHILD SCREAMED "DON'T LET HER KILL ME": *American*, May 3, 1935; Washington *Herald*, May 2, 1935.

555 "complete vindication" and ff.: *Daily News*, July 4, 1935.

557 "a number of citizens . . .": *The New York Times*, July 2, 1935.

557 "Gloria Vanderbilt, like any other little . . ." and ff.: *American*, July 3, 1935.

557 "Mrs. Vanderbilt. . . .": *Journal*, Aug. 6, 1935; *American*, Aug. 7, 1935, Joseph Cowan.

557 "Little Gloria was running . . .": I.

559 "I want [little] Gloria to . . .": GVW, p. 601.

559 "*Dearest Gloria: I have told you* . . ." and ff.: *Journal*, Aug. 5, 1935, Joseph Cowan.

560 "Solomon was wise indeed when . . .": *American*, Sept. 29, 1935.

560 "Gloria has become quite an astute . . .": *Journal*, Aug. 6, 1935, Joseph Cowan.

560 "Look mother, my public!": *Journal*, Aug. 6, 1935, Joseph Cowan.

THE POOR LITTLE RICH GIRL

561 "No one cared about her. . . ." and ff.: I.

563 "There'd been a kidnap scare . . ." and ff.: I.

563 "chiseling in" and ff.: *The New York Times*, July 12, 1935.

564 "LITTLE GLORIA DOES DRINK GINGER ALE . . .": *Sun*, *Herald-Tribune*, Jan. 27, 1936.

565 "to give them to my niece . . .": *The New York Times*, Feb. 3, 1938.

565 "I will no longer live under the . . .": *American*, Dec. 13, 1935; *The New York Times*, Dec. 13, 1935.

565 "Gloria didn't know what . . .": I.

566 "There were always umpteen . . .": *Life*, March 2, 1959.

566 "Gloria's a survivor, . . .": I.

566 "She was one person in public . . .": I.

566 "She became a perfect little . . .": *Sunday Mirror*, Nov. 3, 1935.

566 "ordinary children . . .": *Sun*, Feb. 23, 1939.

566 "LITTLE GLORIA GOES TO CIRCUS, . . ." and ff.: *American*, April 29, 1935.

566 "smiled up at Bishop Molloy . . .": *American*, May 10, 1935.

566 "LITTLE GLORIA WORTH . . .": *Sun*, Feb. 23, 1939; *The New York Times*, Jan. 5, 1940.

567 "Yes, he had a great heart," and ff.: I.

567 "We were so much alone," and ff.: I.

570 "She was all the world to me . . .": *Woman to Woman*, p. 14.

570 "I felt as if the loss . . .": Ibid., p. 192.

570 "The trial . . . was nothing . . .": *Mirror*, Aug. 6, 1958, Maurice Zolotow.

570 "imposter" and ff.: *Woman to Woman*, p. 172.

570 "I felt totally alone.": "Gloria," Patricia Bosworth, *Town and Country*, Jan. 1978.

570 "HEIRESS REPORTED TO HAVE RUN . . ." and ff.: *World-Telegram*, June 3, 1938.

A GREAT PERSONALITY

571 "The irony . . . was that as soon . . .": GVW, p. 597.

571 "The original court order . . .": DE, p. 331.

p. 572 "They've permitted Gertrude Whitney . . ." and ff.: *Evening Journal*, Aug. 10, 1935.
572 "She couldn't be expected . . ." and ff.: I.
574 "frequently" and ff.: GVW, p. 600.
574 "orgy of creation": GVW, p. 606.
574 "I can't tell you how the days . . .": GVW, p. 605.
574 "in Gertrude's life, . . .": GVW, p. 609.
574 ". . . I hear you had a boy visitor, . . .": GVW, p. 624.
575 "A gay sophisticated . . .": *American*, Oct 14, 1934, Cholly Knickerbocker.
575 "$2,800 FOR GLORIA . . .": *Daily News*, Aug. 18, 1939.
575 "when Gloria was supposedly . . .": I.
575 "increasingly complicated. . . .": GVW, p. 634.
575 "Hearst seemed to have all . . .": *Woman to Woman*, p. 59.
576 "Gloria came back yesterday . . .": GVW, p. 633.
576 "I would have written you about . . .": Ibid., p. 634.
576 ". . . For a great many reasons . . .": Ibid., pps. 645, 646.
577 "If you really want . . ." and ff.: DE, p. 331.
577 "I was like a bird set free,": "Gloria," Patricia Bosworth, *Town and Country*, Jan. 1978.
577 "I'm in love with Van Heflin . . .": DE, p. 332.
577 "She once hired them to shadow . . .": I.
577 "Apparently all hell broke . . .": GVW, p. 653.
578 "my mother had a great many emotional . . ." and ff.: "Gloria," Patricia Bosworth, *Town and Country*, Jan. 1978.
578 "The situation with my aunt . . .": *People*, June 25, 1979.
578 "a motion picture executive" and ff.: CC, p. 111.
579 "What can one say about a first . . ." and ff.: *Time*, Jan. 10, 1955.
579 "If I weren't so happy . . .": *Time*, Nov. 19, 1942.
579 "the one I almost always wear," and ff.: *The New York Times*, May 5, 1942.
579 "very heavily constructed.": *The New York Times*, Oct. 31, 1942.
580 "It seemed to me that there were . . ." and ff.: GVW, p. 431.
580 "I am afraid of the shadow . . .": Ibid., p. 331.
580 "I have become hard inside . . .": Ibid., p. 222.
581 "There is only a little while . . .": Ibid., p. 254.
581 "You (G.W.) are a great . . ." and ff.: Ibid., p. 332.
581 "My aunt wanted to love me. . . .": *Daily News*, Dec. 29, 1945, "Gloria Vanderbilt Steps Out," Jess Stearn.

Everybody's Life Is a Romance

584 "I adore playing around . . .": *World-Telegram*, Nov. 20, 1936, "Gloria Vanderbilt 'Adores' Business: Thinks the World Replete with Romance," Sally MacDougall.
584 "Thelma Furness . . .": *Daily News*, June 2, 1937.
584 "had intoxicating liquors . . .": *Evening Post*, Sept. 13, 1938.
584 "When you're down—he's out!": I.
585 "Anybody resigns from us . . .": *Time*, Oct. 18, 1943.
585 "GLORIA VANDERBILT DI-CICCO . . .": *The New York Times*, Feb. 21, 1945.
585 ". . . FINAL ACCOUNTING REVEALS . . ." and ff.: *The New York Times*, March 1, 1945.
586 "Don't you think Leopold . . .": *Journal-American*, April 18, 1946, Cholly Knickerbocker.
586 "I have come to see that anger . . .": *Woman to Woman*, p. 192.

p. 586 "My mother should have thought . . .": *Journal-American*, March 13, 1946.
587 "very very sick" and ff.: *Mirror*, March 19, 1946.
587 "Lady Furness need not . . .": *Daily News*, March 13, 1946.
587 "in order to live.": *Daily News*, March 11, 1946; *Sun*, March 15, 1946.
587 "The money the Court formerly gave . . .": *Daily News*, March 12, 1946.
587 "I have a natural filial . . .": *The New York Times*, April 4, 1946.
588 "If Gloria leaves me . . .": *Daily News*, Dec. 31, 1954.
589 "he hovers over the lives . . .": *World-Telegram*, May 15, 1959.
589 "carries with it my thanks . . .": *The New York Times*, Feb. 17, 1956.
591 "through it all Gloria . . ." and ff.: *Daily News*, Dec. 23, 1954.
591 "GLORIA MORGAN . . .": *The New York Times*, Feb. 14, 1965.
592 "I think everybody's life . . .": *World-Telegram*, Nov. 20, 1936.
592 "Money meant nothing; men . . .": *World-Telegram*, Oct. 21, 1958.

Joy Through Pain

594 "I think that strength of belief . . .": *Woman to Woman*, p. 192; *Vogue*, Feb. 1979.
594 "devotion" and ff.: *Woman to Woman*, p. 172.
594 "I don't care how rich . . .": *Vogue*, June 1972, Edith Loew Gross.
594 "I do relate to her . . .": *Woman to Woman*, p. 3.
595 "Fantasy can take you anywhere . . .": *Woman to Woman*, p. 36.
595 "lived in fantasy—if I hadn't . . ." and ff.: "Gloria," Patricia Bosworth, *Town and Country*, Jan. 1978.
595 "I never paint from life.": *Journal-American*, Nov. 1, 1953.
595 "All joy, I think, comes out of pain. . . .": *The New York Times*, Feb. 18, 1973, "Art of Gloria Vanderbilt: Joy Born from Pain," Alden Whitman.
595 "I began painting within myself . . ." and ff.: *Woman to Woman*, pps. 255, 257.
595 "To arrive at joy in yourself . . .": *Vogue*, June 1972, Edith Loew Gross.
596 "Sometimes I wonder, . . .": *Women's Wear Daily*, March 4, 1976, "Gloria Vanderbilt Swandives into Fashion," Beverly Grunwald; *W*, March 19–26, 1976.
596 "It has been a major triumph . . .": *Woman to Woman*, p. 62.
596 "Women in the past have thought . . .": *Woman to Woman*, p. 175.
596 "I want to have a Gloria . . .": "Gloria," Patricia Bosworth, *Town and Country*, Jan. 1978.
596 "Gloria with her high level . . .": *People*, June 25, 1979.
597 "It was the cruel lying . . ." and ff.: *Journal*, Aug. 7, 1935, "Court Lies Admitted by Child," Joseph Cowan.
598 "What if there was a fire . . .": *Women's Wear Daily*, March 4, 1976, Beverly Grunwald; *W*, March 19–26, 1976.

Selected Bibliography

AARON, DANIEL, AND BENDINER, ROBERT, EDS. *The Strenuous Decade*. Documents in American Civilization Series. New York: Doubleday, Anchor Books, 1970.

AGASSIZ, GEORGE R., ED. *Meade's Headquarters, 1863–1865: Letters of Colonel Theodore Lyman from the Wilderness to Appomattox*. Boston: The Atlantic Monthly Press, 1922.

ALDRICH, MARGARET CHANLER. *Family Vista: The Memoirs of Margaret Chanler Aldrich*. New York: The William-Frederick Press, 1958.

ALEXANDER, GRAND DUKE OF RUSSIA. *Once a Grand Duke*. New York: Cosmopolitan Book Corporation, Farrar & Rinehart, Incorporated, 1932.

ALEXANDRA, QUEEN OF YUGOSLAVIA. *Prince Philip: A Family Portrait*. Indianapolis and New York: The Bobbs-Merrill Company, Inc., 1960.

ALIX, ERNEST KAHLAR. *Ransom Kidnapping in America, 1874–1974: The Creation of a Capital Crime*. Carbondale and Edwardsville: Southern Illinois University Press, 1978.

ALLEN, FREDERICK LEWIS. *The Big Change: America Transforms Itself, 1900–1950*. New York: Harper & Brothers, 1952.

———. *Only Yesterday*. New York: Harper & Row, Perennial Library edition, 1964.

———. *Since Yesterday*. New York: Harper & Row, Perennial Library edition, 1972.

AMORY, CLEVELAND. *The Last Resorts*. New York: Harper & Brothers, 1952.

———. *Who Killed Society?* New York: Harper & Brothers, 1960.

ANDREWS, WAYNE. *Architecture in New York: A Photographic History*. New York: Atheneum, 1969.

———. *The Vanderbilt Legend: Story of the Family, 1794–1940*. New York: Harcourt, Brace and Company, 1941.

ANGELL, JAMES W. *The Recovery of Germany*. New Haven: Published for the Council on Foreign Relations; Yale University Press, 1932.

ANGER, KENNETH. *Hollywood Babylon*. New York: Dell Publishing Co., Inc., A Delta Special, 1975.

ARIES, PHILIPPE. *Centuries of Childhood: A Social History of Family Life*. New York: Vintage Books, a Division of Random House, 1962.

AUCHINCLOSS, LOUIS. *Edith Wharton*. Minneapolis: University of Minnesota Press, 1961.

———. *Edith Wharton: A Woman in Her Time*. New York: The Viking Press, A Studio Book, 1971.

———. *The House of Five Talents*. Boston: Houghton Mifflin Company, 1960.

———. *Life, Law and Letters*. Boston: Houghton Mifflin Company, 1979.

BALSAN, CONSUELO VANDERBILT. *The Glitter and the Gold*. New York: Harper & Brothers, 1952.

BATTISCOMBE, GEORGINA. *Queen Alexandra*. Boston: Houghton Mifflin Company, 1969.

BEATON, CECIL. *Cecil Beaton's New York*. New York and Philadelphia: J. B. Lippincott Company, 1938.

BEAVERBROOK, LORD. *The Abdication of King Edward VIII*. Edited by A. J. P. Taylor. New York: Atheneum, 1966.

BEEBE, LUCIUS M. *The Big Spenders*. Garden City: Doubleday & Company, Inc., 1966.

———. *20th Century: The Greatest Train in the World*. Berkeley: Howell-North, 1962.

BEER, THOMAS. *The Mauve Decade: American Life at the End of the Nineteenth Century*. New York: Alfred A. Knopf, 1926.

BELL, MILLICENT. *Edith Wharton and Henry James*. New York: G. Braziller, 1965.

BENDER, MARYLIN. *The Beautiful People.* New York: Coward-McCann, 1967.
BENNETT, JOAN, AND KIBBEE, LOIS. *The Bennett Playbill.* New York, Chicago, San Francisco: Holt, Rinehart and Winston, 1970.
BERGAMINI, JOHN. *The Tragic Dynasty: A History of the Romanovs.* New York: G. P. Putnam's Sons, 1969.
BESSIE, SIMON MICHAEL. *Jazz Journalism: The Story of the Tabloid Newspapers.* New York: Russell & Russell, 1969.
BIRD, CAROLINE. *The Invisible Scar.* New York: David McKay Company, Inc., 1966.
BIRKENHEAD, FREDERICK WINSTON. *Walter Monckton.* London: Weidenfeld and Nicolson, 1969.
BLOCH, DOROTHY. *"So the Witch Won't Eat Me": Fantasy and the Child's Fear of Infanticide.* Boston: Houghton Mifflin Company, 1978.
BOARDMAN, FON W., JR. *The Thirties: America and the Great Depression.* New York: Henry Z. Walck, Inc., 1967.
BOCCA, GEOFFREY. *Bikini Beach.* New York: McGraw-Hill Book Company, Inc., 1962.
———. *The Woman Who Would Be Queen.* New York: Rinehart & Company, Inc., 1954.
BODENHEIM, MAXWELL. *My Life and Lovers in Greenwich Village.* New York: Bridgehead Books, 1954.
BOLITHO, HECTOR. *King Edward VIII.* Philadelphia: Lippincott, 1937.
BOOTHROYD, BASIL. *Prince Philip: An Informal Biography.* New York: The McCall Publishing Company, 1971.
BRANDAU, ROBERT, ED. *de Meyer.* New York: Alfred A. Knopf, 1976.
BRINNIN, JOHN MALCOLM. *The Sway of the Grand Saloon: A Social History of the North Atlantic.* New York: Delacorte Press, 1971.
BROCK, H. I., AND GOLINKIN, J. W. *New York Is Like This.* New York: Dodd, Mead & Company, 1929.
BRODIE, FAWN M. *The Devil Drives.* New York: W. W. Norton & Co., Inc., 1967.
BRODY, ILES. *Gone with the Windsors.* Philadelphia: Winston, 1953.
BROOKS, VAN WYCK. *John Sloan: A Painter's Life.* New York: E. P. Dutton & Co., Inc., 1955.
BROWN, EVE. *Champagne Cholly: The Life and Times of Maury Paul.* New York: E. P. Dutton & Company, Inc., 1947.
BRYAN, J., III, AND MURPHY, CHARLES J. V. *The Windsor Story: An intimate portrait of Edward VIII and Mrs. Simpson by the authors who knew them best.* New York: William Morrow & Company, Inc., 1979.
CABLE, MARY. *The Little Darlings.* New York: Charles Scribner's Sons, 1975.
CALVERTON, V. F., AND SCHMALHAUSEN, SAMUEL D., EDS. *The New Generation.* New York: The Macaulay Company, 1930.
CHANLER, MRS. WINTHROP. *Autumn in the Valley.* Boston: Little, Brown and Company, 1936.
CHAPLIN, CHARLES. *My Autobiography.* New York: Simon and Schuster, 1964.
———. *My Trip Abroad.* New York and London: Harper & Brothers, 1922.
CHAPLIN, LITA GREY, WITH COOPER, MORTON. *My Life with Chaplin: An Intimate Memoir.* New York: Grove Press, Bernard Geis Associates, 1966.
CHISHOLM, ANNE. *Nancy Cunard, 1896–1965.* New York: Alfred A. Knopf, 1979.
CHURCHILL, ALLEN. *The Improper Bohemians: A Re-creation of Greenwich Village in Its Heyday.* New York: E. P. Dutton & Company, Inc., 1959.
———. *The Splendor Seekers.* New York: Grosset & Dunlap, 1974.
———. *The Upper Crust: An Informal History of New York's Highest Society.* Englewood Cliffs, N.J.: Prentice-Hall, Inc., 1970.
CHURCHILL, WINSTON S. *Marlborough: His Life and Times.* London: Harrap, 1936.
COHEN, HERBERT J., ED. *One Hundred Twenty-Five Years of Famous Pages from The New York Times: 1851–1976.* New York: Arno Press, 1906–1976.

Selected Bibliography

Coles, Robert. *Privileged Ones:* Vol. V of *Children of Crisis.* Boston and Toronto: Little, Brown and Company, 1977.

Cooper, Wyatt. *Families: A Memoir and a Celebration.* New York, Evanston, San Francisco, London: Harper & Row, 1975.

Croffut, W. A. *The Vanderbilts: and the Story of Their Fortune.* Chicago, New York: Belford, Clarke & Company, 1886.

Curtis, Charlotte. *The Rich and Other Atrocities.* New York: Harper & Row, 1976.

Curtius, Frederich, ed. *Memoirs of Prince Chlodwig of Hohenlohe-Schillingsfuerst.* English edition supervised by George W. Chrystal. New York: The Macmillan Company, 1906.

Daggett, Mabel Potter. *Marie of Roumania: The Intimate Story of the Radiant Queen.* New York: George H. Doran Company, 1926.

Daniels, Jonathan. *The Time Between the Wars.* Garden City: Doubleday & Company, Inc., 1966.

Davidson, Jo. *Between Sittings.* New York: The Dial Press, 1951.

Davidson, Marshall B., author and editor in charge. *The American Heritage History of Notable American Houses.* Biographical essays by Margot P. Brill. New York: American Heritage Publishing Company, Inc., 1971.

Davies, Marion. *The Times We Had.* Edited by Pamela Pfau and Kenneth S. Marx. Indianapolis: The Bobbs-Merrill Company, 1975.

Day, J. Wentworth. *H.R.H. Princess Marina Duchess of Kent: The First Authentic Life Story.* London: Robert Hale Limited, 1962.

Dean, John. *Prince Philip.* New York: Henry Holt and Company, 1954.

Donald, David. *Divided We Fought: A Pictorial History of the War, 1861–1865.* New York: The Macmillan Co., 1952.

Donaldson, Frances. *Edward VIII.* Philadelphia and New York: J. B. Lippincott Company, 1975.

Downing, Antoinette F., and Scully, Vincent J., Jr. *The Architectural Heritage of Newport Rhode Island: 1640–1915.* Cambridge: Harvard University Press, 1952.

Drexler, Arthur, ed. *The Architecture of the Ecole des Beaux-Arts.* New York: The Museum of Modern Art, 1977.

Dupuy, I. N., and Hammerman, G. M. *Stalemate in the Trenches: Nov. 1914–March 1918.* New York: Franklin Watts, Inc., 1967.

Eisenstadt, Alfred. *Eisenstadt Album: 50 Years of Friends and Acquaintances.* New York: The Viking Press, A Studio Book, 1976.

Elliott, Maud Howe. *This Was My Newport.* Cambridge, Mass.: The Mythology Company, A. Marshall Jones, 1944.

Elsberry, Terence. *Marie of Romania: The Intimate Life of a Twentieth-Century Queen.* New York: St. Martin's Press, 1972.

Emery, Edwin. *The Press and America.* New York: Prentice-Hall, Inc., 1962.

Fels, Rendigs. *American Business Cycles, 1865–1897.* Chapel Hill: University of North Carolina Press, 1959.

Fillebrown, Charles B. *Taxation.* Chicago: A. C. McClurg & Co., 1914.

Flanner, Janet. *London Was Yesterday.* Edited by Irving Drutman. New York: The Viking Press, A Studio Book, 1975.

Folsom, Merrill. *Great American Mansions and Their Stories.* New York: Hastings House, 1976.

Fowler, Gene. *Beau James: The Life and Times of Jimmy Walker.* New York: The Viking Press, 1949.

Friedman, B. H. *Gertrude Vanderbilt Whitney: A Biography.* With the research collaboration of Flora Miller Irving. Garden City: Doubleday & Company, Inc., 1978.

Fryer, Peter. *Secrets of the British Museum.* New York: Citadel Press, Inc., 1968. Originally published in England by Martin Secker & Warburg Limited as *Private Case—Public Scandal.*

Furnas, J. C. *Stormy Weather: Crosslights on the Nineteen Thirties: An Informal Social

History of the United States, 1929–1941. New York: G. P. Putnam's Sons, 1977.

GALBRAITH, JOHN KENNETH. *The Great Crash: 1929.* Third Edition. Boston: Houghton Mifflin Company, 1972.

GATHORNE-HARDY, JONATHAN. *The Rise and Fall of the British Nanny.* London: Arrow Books, Ltd., 1974.

GESSELL, ARNOLD, PH.D., M.D., SC.D. *The Guidance of Mental Growth in Infant and Child.* New York: The Macmillan Co., 1930.

GIBBONS, HERBERT ADAMS, PH.D., LITT.D. *Venizelos.* Boston and New York: Houghton Mifflin Company, 1920.

GLACKENS, IRA. *William Glackens and the Ashcan Group.* New York: Crown Publishers, Inc., 1957.

GOODRICH, LLOYD, AND BAUR, JOHN I. H. *American Art of Our Century.* Published for the Whitney Museum of American Art. New York: Frederick A. Praeger, 1961.

GOTHA, ALMANACH DE. *Annuaire Généalogique Diplomatique et Statistique.* Gotha, Ger: Perthes, 1934.

GRAHAM, SHEILAH. *How to Marry Super Rich: Or Love, Money, and the Morning After.* New York: Grosset & Dunlap, 1974.

GRUNBERGER, RICHARD. *The 12-Year Reich: A Social History of Nazi Germany, 1933–1945.* New York: Holt, Rinehart and Winston, 1971.

GUILES, FRED LAWRENCE. *Marion Davies.* New York: McGraw-Hill Book Co., 1972.

GUSENBERG, RICHARD M., AND ULLSTEIN, DIETMAR MEYER. *Die Dreissiger Jahre.* Essay by Johannes Gross. Frankfurt/Main-Berlin-Wien: Ferlag Ullstein GmbH, 1970.

HALL, CARRIE A. *From Hoopskirts to Nudity.* Caldwell, Idaho: The Caxton Printers, Ltd., 1938.

HASKELL, MOLLY. *From Reverence to Rape: The Treatment of Women in the Movies.* New York: Holt, Rinehart and Winston, 1974.

HATCH, ALDEN. *The Mountbattens: The Last Royal Success Story.* New York: Random House, 1965.

VON HEDEMANN, BARONESS ALEXANDRINE. *My Friendship with Prince Hohenlohe.* New York: Putnam, 1912.

HEUSCHELE, OTTO. *Schönes Württemberg.* Frankfurt Am Main: Verlag Wolfgang Weidlich, 1963.

HIBBERT, CHRISTOPHER. *Edward, the Uncrowned King.* New York: St. Martin's Press, 1972.

HIGHAM, CHARLES. *Ziegfeld.* Chicago: Henry Regnery Company, 1972.

HIRSCH, MARK D. *William C. Whitney: Modern Warwick.* New York: Dodd, Mead & Company, 1948.

HOLBROOK, STEWART H. *The Age of the Moguls.* Edited by Lewis Gannett. Garden City: Doubleday & Company, Inc., 1953.

HOLLYWOOD ACADEMY OF HAIR AND BEAUTY CULTURE. *Standard Textbook of Cosmetology.* New York: Milady Publishing Corp., 1961.

HORAN, JAMES D. *The Desperate Years: A Pictorial History of the Thirties.* New York: Crown Publishers, Inc., 1962.

HORTON, GEORGE. *Recollections Grave & Gay: The Story of a Mediterranean Consul.* Indianapolis: The Bobbs-Merrill Co., 1927.

HOUGH, RICHARD (Selected and with a commentary by). *Advice to a Grand-daughter: Letters from Queen Victoria to Princess Victoria of Hesse.* With a foreword by the Princess's grand-daughter the Lady Brabourne. London: William Heinemann Ltd., 1975.

———. *The Mountbattens: The Illustrious Family Who Through Birth and Marriage—from Queen Victoria and the Last of the Tsars to Queen Elizabeth II—Enriched Europe's Royal Houses.* New York: E. P. Dutton & Co., Inc., 1975.

HOUSEPIAN, MARJORIE. *The Smyrna Affair.* New York: Harcourt Brace Jovanovich, Inc., 1971.

HOWELL, GEORGINA. *In Vogue.* New York: Schocken Books, 1976.

Hoyt, Edwin Palmer. *The Vanderbilts and Their Fortunes.* Garden City: Doubleday & Company, Inc., 1962.

———. *The Whitneys: An Informal Portrait, 1635–1975.* New York: Weybright and Talley, 1976.

Hughes, Tom. *The Blue Riband of the Atlantic.* New York: Charles Scribner's Sons, 1973.

Hugo, Howard E., ed. *Letters of Franz Liszt to Marie zu Sayn-Wittgenstein.* Cambridge: Harvard University Press, 1953.

Hunt, Frazier. *The Bachelor Prince.* New York: Harper & Brothers, 1935.

Inglis, Brian. *Abdication.* New York: The Macmillan Company, 1966.

International Who's Who. 29th edition, 1965–66, and 35th edition, 1971–72. London: Europa Publications Limited, 1971.

Jacoby, Oswald, and Morehead, Albert, eds. *The Fireside Book of Cards.* New York: Simon and Schuster, 1957.

James, Henry. *The Diary of a Man of Fifty and a Bundle of Letters.* New York: Harper, 1880.

———. *Notes of a Son and a Brother.* New York: Criterion Books, 1956.

———. *The Middle Years.* New York: Criterion Books, 1956.

Jardine, Rev. R. Anderson. *At Long Last.* Hollywood: Murray & Gee Inc., 1947.

Jonas, Gerald. *Stuttering: The Disorder of Many Theories.* New York: Farrar, Straus & Giroux, 1977.

Josephson, Matthew. *The Robber Barons.* New York: Harcourt, Brace & Co., 1934.

Judd, Denis. *The House of Windsor.* New York: St. Martin's Press, Inc., 1973.

Kavaler, Lucy. *The Astors: A Family Chronicle of Pomp and Power.* New York: Dodd, Mead & Company, 1966.

Kerr, Admiral Mark, C.B., M.V.O. *A King's Private Letters: Being Letters Written by King Constantine of Greece to Paola Princess of Saxe-Weimar during the Years 1912 to 1923.* London: Eveleigh Nash & Grayson Limited, 1925.

Ketchum, Richard M., ed. *The American Heritage Picture History of the Civil War.* (Narrative by Bruce Catton.) New York: American Heritage Publishing Co., Inc., 1960.

Kinross, Lord. *The Windsor Years: The Life of Edward, as Prince of Wales, King, and Duke of Windsor.* New York: The Viking Press, A Studio Book, 1967.

La Guardia, Mayor F. H. *New York Advancing: A Scientific Approach to Municipal Government.* New York: Municipal Reference Library, 1936.

Lane, Wheaton J. *Commodore Vanderbilt: An Epic of the Steam Age.* New York: Alfred A. Knopf, 1942.

Langer, Walter C. *The Mind of Adolf Hitler: The Secret Wartime Report.* New York and London: Basic Books Inc., 1972.

Lee, James Melvin. *History of American Journalism.* Boston and New York: Houghton Mifflin Company, 1933.

Leeds, Stanton B. *Cards the Windsors Hold.* Philadelphia and New York: J. B. Lippincott Company, 1937.

Leighton, Isabel, ed. *The Aspirin Age: 1919–1941. The great, the comic, and the tragic events of American life in the chaotic years between two world wars by twenty-two outstanding writers.* New York: Simon and Schuster, An Essandess paperback, 1963.

Lewis, R. W. B. *Edith Wharton: A Biography.* New York: Harper & Row, 1975.

Lindbergh, Anne Morrow. *Hour of Gold, Hour of Lead: Diaries and Letters of Anne Morrow Lindbergh, 1929–1932.* New York: Harcourt Brace Jovanovich, A Helen and Kurt Wolff Book, 1973.

Lipson, Milton. *On Guard: The Business of Private Security.* New York: Quadrangle/The New York Times Book Co., 1975.

Liversidge, Douglas. *Prince Philip: First Gentleman of the Realm.* London: Arthur Barker Limited, 1976.

Longstreet, Stephen. *The Young Men of Paris.* New York: Delacorte Press, 1967.

Loth, David. *The City Within a City: The Romance of Rockefeller Center.* New York: William Morrow and Company, Inc., 1966.

MacDougall, Allan Ross. *Isadora: A Revolutionary in Art and Love.* New York: Thomas Nelson & Sons, 1960.

Mackaye, Milton. *The Tin Box Parade: A Handbook for Larceny.* New York: Robert M. McBride & Company, 1934.

Mackenzie, Compton. *The Windsor Tapestry: Being a Study of the Life, Heritage and Abdication of H.R.H. The Duke of Windsor, K.G.* New York: Frederick A. Stokes Company, 1938.

Magarshack, David. *Pushkin.* New York: Grove Press, Inc., 1967.

Magnus, Sir Philip Montefiore. *King Edward the Seventh.* New York: E. P. Dutton & Co., Inc., 1964.

Malone, Dumas, ed. *Dictionary of America Biography.* Vol. X. New York: Charles Scribner's Sons, 1936.

Margetson, Stella. *The Long Party: High Society in the Twenties & Thirties.* Westmead, Farnborough, Hants, England: Saxon House, D. C. Heath Limited, 1974.

Marie, Queen of Roumania. *Ordeal: The Story of My Life.* New York: C. Scribner's Sons, 1935.

Martin, Ralph G. *The Woman He Loved: The Story of the Duke and Duchess of Windsor.* New York: The New American Library, Inc., A Signet Paperback, 1975.

Maser, Werner. *Hitler: Legend, Myth & Reality.* New York, Evanston, San Francisco, London: Harper & Row, 1973.

Massie, Robert K. *Nicholas and Alexandra.* New York: Atheneum, 1967.

Masson, Madeleine. *Edwina: The Biography of the Countess Mountbatten of Burma.* London: Robert Hale Limited, 1958.

Maurice, Arthur Bartlett, author of notes. *Magical City.* Pictures by Vernon Howe. New York, London: C. Scribner's Sons, 1935.

Maxtone-Graham, John. *The Only Way to Cross.* New York: The Macmillan Company, 1972.

Maxwell, Elsa. *The Celebrity Circus.* New York: Appleton-Century, 1963.

———. *R.S.V.P.: Elsa Maxwell's Own Story.* Boston and Toronto: Little, Brown and Company, 1954.

Mayer, Grace M., Museum of the City of New York. *Once Upon a City: New York from 1890 to 1910 as photographed by Byron.* With a foreword by Edward Steichen. New York: The Macmillan Co., 1958.

McAllister, Ward. *Society As I Have Found It.* New York: Cassell, 1890.

McGivena, Leo. *The News: The First 50 Years of New York's Picture Newspaper.* New York: The News Syndicate Co., 1969.

Middlemas, Keith, and Barnes, John. *Baldwin: A Biography.* New York: The Macmillan Company, 1970. (First published in Great Britain in 1969 by Weidenfeld & Nicolson, London.)

Miller, Francis T., ed. *The Photographic History of the Civil War*, Vol. 4, *The Cavalry.* New York: The Review of Reviews Co., 1912.

Miller, Dr. Max. *Handbuch der Historischen Stätten Deutschlands: Baden-Württemberg.* Stuttgart: Alfred Kröner Verlag, 1965.

Mitgang, Herbert. *The Man Who Rode the Tiger: The Life of Judge Samuel Seabury and the Story of the Greatest Investigation of City Corruption in This Century.* New York: The Viking Press, Viking Compass Edition, 1970.

Mooney, Michael Macdonald. *Evelyn Nesbit and Stanford White: Love and Death in the Gilded Age.* New York: William Morrow and Company, Inc., 1976.

Moore, George. *Letters to Lady Cunard, 1895–1933.* London: Rupert Hart-Davis, 1957.

Morris, Constance Lily [Rothschild]. *On Tour with Queen Marie.* New York: R. M. McBride & Company, 1927.

Selected Bibliography

Moscow, Warren. *Politics in the Empire State.* New York: Alfred A. Knopf, 1948.

Mott, Frank Luther. *American Journalism.* New York: The Macmillan Company, 1959.

Mowry, George E., ed. *The Twenties: Fords, Flappers & Fanatics.* Englewood Cliffs, N.J.: Prentice-Hall, Inc., 1963.

Munsterberg, Hugo. *On the Witness Stand: Essays on Psychology and Crime.* New York: Doubleday, Page & Co., 1913. (Copyright 1908.)

Murray, Ken. *The Golden Days of San Simeon.* Garden City: Doubleday & Co., Inc., 1971.

Myers, Garry Cleveland, Ph.D. *The Modern Parent.* New York: Greenberg, 1930.

Nevins, Allan, ed. *A Diary of Battle: The Personal Journals of Colonel Charles S. Wainwright, 1861–1865.* New York: Harcourt, Brace & World, Inc., 1962.

New York Times. *Page One: Major Events, 1920–1976.* New York: Arno Press, 1976.

New York Times. *We Saw It Happen: The News Behind the News That's Fit to Print.* New York: Simon and Schuster, 1939.

Nicholas, H.R.H. Prince of Greece. *My Fifty Years.* London: Hutchinson & Co., 1926.

Nichols, Rev. Charles Wilbur de Lyon. *The Ultra-Fashionable Peerage of America, with a Few Appended Essays on Ultra-Smartness.* New York: G. Harjes, 1904.

Nicolson, Harold. *Diaries and Letters, 1930–1939.* Edited by Nigel Nicolson. Vol. I. New York: Atheneum, 1966.

———. *The War Years, 1939–1945.* Vol. II of *Diaries and Letters.* New York: Atheneum, 1967.

———. *King George The Fifth: His Life and Reign.* London: Constable & Co., Ltd., 1952.

———. *King George VI.* London: Constable & Co., 1952.

Nicolson, Nigel. *Great Houses of the Western World.* Photography by Ian Graham. New York: G. P. Putnam's Sons, 1968. (Copyright 1968 George Weidenfeld & Nicolson Ltd.)

Noel, Gerard. *Princess Alice: Queen Victoria's Forgotten Daughter.* London: Constable and Company, 1974.

Northrop, William B., and Northrop, John B. *The Insolence of Office: The Story of the Seabury Investigations.* New York and London: G. P. Putnam's Sons, 1932.

Parish, James Robert, and Leonard, William T. *Hollywood Players: The Thirties.* New Rochelle, N.Y.: Arlington House, 1976.

Perceau, Louis. *Bibliographie du roman érotique du XIX Siècle.* Paris: George Fourdrinier, 1930. (Printed by l'Imprimerie Darantière of Dijon, France.)

Phillips, Cabell. *From the Crash to the Blitz, 1929–1939. The New York Times Chronicle of American Life.* New York: The Macmillan Company, 1969.

Pope-Hennessy, James. *Queen Mary, 1867–1953.* London: George Allen and Unwin Limited, 1959.

Robotti, Frances Diane. *Key to New York: Empire City.* New York: Fountainhead Publishers, 1964.

Rogers, Agnes. *I Remember Distinctly: A Family Album of the American People in the Years of Peace: 1918 to Pearl Harbor.* New York: Harper & Brothers, 1947.

Roosevelt, Eleanor. *This Is My Story.* New York: Harper & Brothers, 1937.

Rose, Alfred. *Registrum Librorum Eroticorum.* London: W. J. Stanislas, 1936. (Published privately by bookseller Stanislas. Rose also used pseudonym Rolf S. Reade.)

Ross, Ishbel. *Ladies of the Press: The Story of Women in Journalism by an Insider.* New York and London: Harper & Brothers, 1936.

Ross, Walter S. *The Last Hero: Charles A. Lindbergh.* New York: Harper & Row, 1968.

Ruvigny, Marquis of. *Titled Nobility of Europe.* London: Harrison & Sons, 1914.

St. John, Adela Rogers. *The Honeycomb.* Garden City: Doubleday & Company, Inc., 1969.

St. John, Bruce, ed. *John Sloan's New York Scene: From the diaries, notes and correspondence, 1906–1913.* New York: Harper & Row, 1956.

Scaduto, Anthony. *Scapegoat: The Lonesome Death of Bruno Richard Hauptmann.* New York: G. P. Putnam's Sons, 1976.

Sellman, R. R. *The First World War.* New York: Criterion Books, 1962.

Shattuck, Roger. *The Banquet Years: The Arts in France, 1885–1918.* New York: Harcourt, Brace and Company, 1958.

Shirer, William L. *The Rise and Fall of the Third Reich: A History of Nazi Germany.* New York: Simon and Schuster, 1960.

Simmons, Ernest J. *Pushkin.* Cambridge: Harvard University Press, 1937.

Sirkis, Nancy. *Newport Pleasures and Palaces.* Introduction by Louis Auchincloss. New York: The Viking Press, A Studio Book, 1963.

Slater, Leonard. *Aly.* New York: Random House, 1964.

Smith, Arthur D. Howden. *Commodore Vanderbilt: An Epic of American Achievement.* New York: Robert M. McBride & Company, 1927.

Snyder, Louis L., and Morris, Richard B. *A Treasury of Great Reporting: "Literature Under Pressure" from the Sixteenth Century to Our Own Time.* With a preface by Herbert Bayard Swope. 2nd Edition. New York: Simon and Schuster, 1962.

Spiro, Edward. *From Battenberg to Mountbatten.* New York: The John Day Company, 1968. (N.B.: Library of Congress lists author as Edward Spiro. Spine of book lists author as E. H. Cookridge.)

Stein, Harvey, and Wolner, Ted. *Parallels: A Look at Twins.* New York: E. P. Dutton & Co., Inc., 1978.

Stouffer, Samuel A., and Lazarsfeld, Paul F. *Studies in the Social Aspects of the Depression.* New York: Arno Press (New York Times Co.), 1972.

Sutton, Willie, with Linn, Edward. *Where the Money Was.* New York: The Viking Press, 1976.

Swanberg, W. A. *Citizen Hearst.* New York: Charles Scribner's Sons, 1961.

Terkel, Studs. *Hard Times: An Oral History of the Great Depression.* New York: Pantheon Books, 1970.

Thorndike, Joseph J., Jr. *The Very Rich: A History of Wealth.* New York: American Heritage Publishing Co., Inc., 1976.

———. *The Magnificent Builders and Their Dream Houses.* New York: American Heritage Publishing Co., Inc., 1978.

Time-Life Books, eds. *The Fabulous Century*, Vol. IV. New York: Time-Life Books, 1971.

Tisdall, E. E. P. *Royal Destiny: The Royal Hellenic Cousins.* London: Stanley Paul and Co., Ltd., 1955.

Tomkins, Calvin. *Living Well Is the Best Revenge.* New York: The Viking Press, 1971.

Townsend, Peter, ed. *Burke's Peerage Baronetage & Knightage.* 105th edition. London: Burke's Peerage Ltd., 1970.

Townsend, W. and L. *Biography of H.R.H. The Prince of Wales.* New York: The Macmillan Company, 1929.

Troyat, Henri. *Pushkin.* Translated by Nancy Amphoux. Garden City: Doubleday & Company, Inc., 1970. (*Poushkine.* 2 Vols., Paris: Albin Michel.)

Twain, Mark, and Warner, Charles Dudley. *The Gilded Age.* New York: Harper & Bros., 1899–1910.

Vacha, Robert, translator and ed. *The Kaiser's Daughter: Memoirs of H.R.H. Viktoria Luise, Duchess of Brunswick and Luneburg, Princess of Prussia.* London: W. H. Allen, 1977.

Vanderbilt, Cornelius, Jr. (IV). *Farewell to Fifth Avenue.* New York: Simon and Schuster, 1935.

———. *The Living Past of America: A Pictorial Treasury of Our Historic Houses and Villages That Have Been Preserved and Restored.* New York: Crown Publishers, Inc., 1955.

Vanderbilt, Gloria Morgan, and Lady Furness, Thelma. *Double Exposure: A Twin Autobiography*. New York: David McKay Company, Inc., 1958.

———. With Wayne, Palma. *Without Prejudice*. New York: E. P. Dutton & Company, Inc., 1936.

Vanderbilt, Gloria. *Love Poems*. Illustrated by Ann Bridges. Cleveland and New York: The World Publishing Company, 1955.

———. *Woman to Woman*. New York: Doubleday and Company, Inc., 1979.

Vidal, Gore; Pritchett, V. S.; Caute, David; Chatwin, Bruce; Conrad, Peter; Epstein, Edward Jay. *Great American Families*. New York: W. W. Norton & Company, Inc., 1977.

Walker, Stanley. *The Night Club Era*. New York: Frederick A. Stokes Company, 1933.

———. *Mrs. Astor's Horse*. New York: Frederick A. Stokes Company, 1935.

Waller, George. *Kidnap: The Story of the Lindbergh Case*. New York: The Dial Press, 1961.

Walsh, George. *Gentleman Jimmy Walker*. Foreword by Robert Moses. New York: Praeger Publishers, 1974.

Ward, de W. C. (photographer). *The Works of Robert Winthrop Chanler*. (An unpublished book of actual photographs which are each dated 1913. New York Public Library.)

Waters, Edward N. *Victor Herbert: A Life in Music*. New York: The Macmillan Company, 1955.

Watson, J. B. *Psychological Care of Infant and Child*. New York: W. W. Norton & Co., Inc., 1928.

Webb, L. J. [pseud. of Gertrude Vanderbilt Whitney]. *Walking the Dusk*. New York: Coward-McCann, Inc., 1932.

Wecter, Dixon. *The Age of the Great Depression, 1929–1941. A History of American Life*, Volume XIII. New York: New Viewpoints, A Division of Franklin Watts, Inc., 1975.

———. *The Hero in America: A Chronicle of Hero-Worship*. With an Introduction by Robert Penn Warren. New York: Charles Scribner's Sons, 1972.

———. *The Saga of American Society: A Record of Social Aspiration*. With an Introduction by Louis Auchincloss. New York: Charles Scribner's Sons, 1970.

Wellman, Francis L. *The Art of Cross-Examination*. London: MacMillan & Co., Ltd., 1904.

Werstein, I. *The Many Faces of World War I*. New York: Messner, Inc., 1962.

———. *1914–1918: World War I*. New York: Cooper Square Co., Inc., 1966.

Wharton, Edith. *A Backward Glance*. New York: Charles Scribner's Sons, 1964.

———. and Codman Jr., Ogden. *The Decoration of Houses*. New York: Charles Scribner's Sons, 1897.

———. *Fighting France: From Dunkerque to Belfort*. New York: Charles Scribner's Sons, 1915.

———. *The House of Mirth*. New York: Charles Scribner's Sons, 1905, 1951.

Wheaton, Eliot Barculo. *Prelude to Calamity: The Nazi Revolution, 1933–1935*. Garden City: Doubleday & Company, Inc., 1968.

Whipple, Sidney B. *The Trial of Bruno Richard Hauptmann*. Garden City: Doubleday, Doran & Company, Inc., 1937.

Whitney, C. V. *High Peaks*. Lexington: The University Press of Kentucky, 1977.

Williams, Henry Lionel, and Williams, Ottalie K. *Great Houses of America*. New York: G. P. Putnam's Sons, 1966.

———. *A Treasury of Great American Houses*. New York: G. P. Putnam's Sons, 1970.

Windsor, Duchess of. *The Heart Has Its Reasons: The Memoirs of The Duchess of Windsor*. New York: David McKay Company, Inc., 1956.

Windsor, Duke of. *A Family Album*. London: Cassell & Company, Ltd., 1960.

———. *A King's Story: The Memoirs of The Duke of Windsor.* New York: G. P. Putnam's Sons, 1947.
———. *Windsor Revisited.* Boston: Houghton Mifflin Company, 1960.
WOON, BASIL. *The Frantic Atlantic: An Intimate Guide to the Well-Known Deep.* New York: Alfred A. Knopf, 1927.
WORDEN, HELEN. *The Real New York.* Indianapolis: The Bobbs-Merrill Company, 1932.
———. *Society Circus.* New York: Covici Friede Publishers, 1936.
World Almanac & Book of Facts of 1935, The. New York *World Telegram.*
WRIGHT, WILLIAM. *Heiress: The Rich Life of Marjorie Merriweather Post.* Washington, D.C.: New Republic Books, 1978.
ZIFF, LARZER. *The American 1890s: Life and Times of a Lost Generation.* New York: The Viking Press, 1966.

CATALOGUES, PAMPHLETS

The Armory Show 50th Anniversary Exhibition, 1913–1963, Catalogue. New York: Munson-Williams-Proctor Institute, 1963.
The Art of Robert W. Chanler. Ivan Narodny. New York: W. Helburn Inc., 1922.
The Breakers: An Illustrated Handbook. Preservation Society of Newport County, June 1953.
Catalogue of the Collection. The Whitney Museum of American Art, 1934.
Gertrude Vanderbilt Whitney Collection of scrapbooks, clippings, letters and memorabilia, 1896–1942. Archives, The Whitney Museum of American Art.
Gertrude Vanderbilt Whitney Memorial Catalogue, September 24–October 30, 1949.
Interviews with artists. Archives, The Whitney Museum of American Art.
Juliana Force and American Art Memorial Catalogue, September 24–October 30, 1949.
NEW YORK COUNTY. Society of *Tammany.* New York: New York County Democratic Committee, 1928.
The Robert Winthrop Chanler Exhibition Catalogue. Introduction by Christian Brinton. New York: The Kingore Gallery, 1922.
St. Gaudens and the Gilded Era. Louise Tharpe. Boston: Little, Brown and Company, 1969.
Schloss Langenburg. Crailsheim, Ger.: Klunker & Ewald, 1973.
A Tribute to Gertrude Vanderbilt Whitney, 1964. Foreword by Lloyd Goodrich.
U.S. DEPT. OF COMMERCE, BUREAU OF THE CENSUS. *Abstract of the Fifteenth Census of the United States—1930.* Washington: United States Government Printing Office, 1933.
WORKS PROGRESS ADMINISTRATION. *New York City Guide.* Sponsored by the Guilds' Committee for Federal Writers' Publications, Inc. New York: Random House, 1939.

NEWSPAPERS

The Baltimore *American*; The Boston *Herald*; The *Daily Express*, London (*Sunday Express*); The *Daily Herald*, London; The *Daily Mail*, London (*Evening Mail*); The *Daily Telegraph*, London; The *Eagle*; The East African *Standard*; The *Evening Standard*, London; The *Globe*; The *Morning Post*, London; The New York *American*; The New York *Daily Mirror*; The New York *Daily News* (*Sunday News*); The New York *Herald*; The New York *Herald-Tribune* (after March 1, 1924); The New York *Journal* (*Evening Journal*); The New York *Journal-American* (after July 1, 1937); The New York *Post* (*Evening Post*); The New York *Press*; The New York *Sun* (*Evening Sun*); *The New York Times*; The New York *World*; The New York *World-Telegram* (after March 1, 1931); The *News of the World*, London; *The People*, London; The *Times*, London; The Washington *Herald*; *Women's Wear Daily*

Selected Bibliography

Periodicals

American Art; *Art Digest*; *Collier's*; *Cosmopolitan*; *Country Life*; *Fortune*; *Harper's Weekly*; *Horizon*; *Ladies' Home Journal*; *Life*; *Munsey's Magazine*; *The New Yorker*; *News-Week*; *Rockefeller Center Weekly Magazine*; *The Saturday Evening Post*; *The Tatler*; *Time*; *Town and Country*; *Town Topics*; *The U.S. Law Review*; *Vanity Fair*; *Vogue*

Newsreels, Photographs

Acme; Archives of the Whitney Museum of American Art; The Bettmann Archives; Compix; Culver Pictures; Fox Films; Grinberg Films; Hearst Metrotone News; Keystone; Museum of the City of New York; The New York *Daily News*; The New-York Historical Society; The New York Public Library Picture Collection; Paramount News; The San Francisco Academy of Comic Art; U.P.I.; World Wide

Libraries, Museums, Repositories

The Archives of American Art; The Avery Library, Columbia University, New York; The British Museum; The Donnell Library of the Arts, Lincoln Center, New York; The Historical Society of Newport, Rhode Island; The Humanities Research Center and Library, The University of Texas at Austin; The Museum of the City of New York; The New York Genealogical Society; The New York Historical Society; The New York Public Library; The New York Public Library Newspaper Annex; The Nineteenth Precinct Station House, Manhattan; The Ohio Genealogical Society; The Police Department, City of New York, Public Information and Personnel Records Department; The Preservation Society of Newport County, Rhode Island; The Surrogates' Office, Hall of Records, City of New York; The Whitney Museum of American Art, and archives

Acknowledgments

To my husband, Frank Perry, for being there with love, advice, and encouragement at every stage of this book, and for making the years spent on it joyous ones.

To Robert Gottlieb, my editor, for his creative contribution, and for the brilliance, wit, and protectiveness with which this was given to me.

To my literary agent, Lynn Nesbit, for her straightforward strength, acumen, and enthusiastic belief in this book.

Linda Amster, Jo Ann Goldberg, Anne Hollister, Martha Kaplan, Judith Rehak, Karen Sturges, Victoria Wilson, a special group of people to whom I am most grateful for embarking on this search with me and variously for helping with the research or contributions to the text and photographs of this book.

I wish to thank Morris Calden and Theodore Troll for guidance in my film research; Lesley Krauss, production editor; Dorothy Schmiderer, book designer; and Carole Frankel, production manager.

Each of the hundreds of people interviewed for *Little Gloria . . . Happy at Last* contributed pieces to the overall picture puzzle that finally emerged. I am especially indebted to Herman Finkelstein, whose insights, observations, total recall, and generosity over the years have vastly enriched this project. Also, to Eve Brown, an invaluable contributor her mind an encyclopedia of Society.

I wish to acknowledge the contributions of a group of lawyers who have shepherded this project: George Gallantz, Andrew Hughes, Ira Lustgarten, James A. Murray, Judge Arthur H. Schwartz, and several others who have requested that their names be withheld.

For information pertaining to Gertrude Vanderbilt Whitney, I wish to acknowledge Lloyd Goodrich and access to the archives of the Whitney Museum of American Art, which were invaluable. Also, B. H. Friedman and Mrs. Whitney's granddaughter Flora Miller Irving for the time they spent with me discussing this extraordinary woman. Mr. Friedman's comprehensive biography, *Gertrude Vanderbilt Whitney*, immaculately researched by Mrs. Irving, provides a gold mine for scholars, enriching one's knowledge not only of Gertrude Vanderbilt Whitney but of the Society in which she lived.

For information pertaining to the Hohenlohe-Langenburgs, I wish to acknowledge Prince Rainer of Hesse, Countess Rosalind Oppersdorff, and Princess Charlotte Hohenlohe-Langenburg, who has patiently answered my queries and has provided me with materials and photographs of Schloss Langenburg and Prince Gottfried and Princess Margarita, otherwise unobtainable, as well as access to Lord Mountbatten's account of the escape of Prince Andrew's family from Greece, compiled by Kenneth Rose largely from the British Admiralty files of 1922.

The following people are among the many who helped me recreate little Gloria's special world and lavished on me a wealth of information until I came to the startling realization that, although I did not interview Gloria Vanderbilt, I was in possession of crucial facts about her life that she herself could not possibly have known: Adele Auchincloss; Louis Auchincloss; Peggy Fears Blumenthal; Patricia Bosworth; Beatrice Straight Cookson; the late Dr. John Dunnington; Leila Hadley; Nedenia (Dina Merrill) Robertson; Adela Rogers St. Johns; Whitney Tower, Sr.; Whitney Tower, Jr.; Ellen Violett.

For the chapters pertaining to Newport and Portsmouth, Rhode Island, I'm indebted to the Newport Preservation Society and the Newport Historical Society but mainly to James E. Garman, a fine scholar with access to the files and photographs of these organizations. Mr. Garman has assembled an enormous collection of Vanderbilt memorabilia and served as my guide to the Vanderbilt mansions and farms of Rhode Island.

Acknowledgments

Joseph Viola and Richard Hill of the Newspaper Annex of the New York Public Library have, over the years, spent incalculable hours locating such materials as the original George Browne Post architectural plans for the Vanderbilt mansion on Fifth Avenue, plans for the Richard Morris Hunt façade of St. Bartholomew's, contributed by Alice Gwynne and Cornelius Vanderbilt II, and Vanderbilt memorabilia dating back to the early 1800's, as well as the extensive tabloid coverage of the trial itself.

The New York Society Library provided a wealth of material, and nowhere else could one find such firsthand information as Countess Gladys Széchényi's note pasted in the front of Arthur D. Howden Smith's biography of Commodore Vanderbilt, warning that the pictures that purport to be of the Commodore are of his son William Henry and saying "perhaps this extraordinary inaccuracy makes it unnecessary to go into the many inaccuracies in [the] text."

I wish to acknowledge the contributions of time and recall of staff members of the *Daily News*, the Dictaphone laboratories, the Nineteenth Precinct Station house, and Walter Brennan and Herbert Matter of the New York Studio School, which now occupies the premises of Gertrude Vanderbilt Whitney's MacDougal Alley Studio and the original Whitney Museum of American Art.

I wish to thank Mildred Newman for her insights into the lives of two children of the thirties, and for her profound understanding.

Finally, I wish to thank all those people I interviewed who gave so generously of their time and recall, especially all the children of the Thirties who confirmed my terror of kidnapping—the ones who remember the ladder.

Index

NOTE: Gloria (c.) refers to the child, little Gloria. Gloria (m) refers to her mother.

Photo Credits

PAGE i: New York *Daily News.* PAGE 19: Little Gloria, Gloria—New York *Daily News*; Gertrude—United Press International. PAGE 30: Laura Morgan—United Press International; Nurse Keislich—New York *Daily News.* PAGES 46–47: Mr. and Mrs. Morgan and Consuelo, Gloria and Thelma as children, Thelma and Gloria—United Press International; Gloria, Harry, and Thelma—New York *Daily News.* PAGE 53: Cecil Beaton. Courtesy of Sotheby's Belgravia. PAGE 63: Vanderbilt children, Reginald at horse show—United Press International; Reginald (cameo)—New York *Daily News.* PAGE 72: Maury Paul—New York *Journal-American* Morgue, Humanities Research Center, The University of Texas at Austin; Gloria—New York *Daily News*; Thelma, Consuelo, and Gloria—San Francisco Academy of Comic Art, New York *Journal-American* Morgue reproduction. PAGE 81: Alice and Commodore—The Bettmann Archive; Cornelius—New York *Daily News.* PAGE 86: Interior—The Bettmann Archive. PAGE 87: Interior—Culver Pictures, Inc. PAGES 94–95: Alice—New-York Historical Society; Alva—The Bettmann Archive; The Breakers—Rhode Island Department of Economic Development; Marble House—Nancy Sirkis; Interiors—The Preservation Society of Newport County, Newport, R.I. PAGE 103: United Press International. PAGES 108–109: San Francisco Academy of Comic Art, New York *Journal-American* Morgue reproduction. PAGE 113: Little Gloria alone and with parents—United Press International; with Reginald—New York *Daily News.* PAGES 114–115: Little Gloria, Gloria and Mrs. Morgan, Gloria and Reginald—United Press International. PAGES 166–167: Thelma and the Prince of Wales—San Francisco Academy of Comic Art, New York *Journal-American* Morgue reproduction; Fort Belvedere—United Press International; Thelma and Averill—Keystone; others—United Press International. PAGES 184–185: Little Gloria and Gloria, little Gloria and dog—United Press International; little Gloria in costume and with Nurse Keislich—New York *Daily News*; letter—Wide World Photos. PAGE 224: Gertrude and Harry, Gertrude (profile)—New York *Daily News*; Gertrude in costume and with dog—United Press International. PAGE 251: Walker and Blumie—New York *Daily News*; Repeal party—United Press International. PAGE 284: Wide World Photos. PAGE 311: New York *Daily News.* PAGES 328–329: Mrs. Morgan—Wide World Photos; others—New York *Daily News.* PAGES 390–391: Mrs. Whitney and Mrs. Morgan—New York *Daily News*; Consuelo, Gloria, Burkan—United Press International. PAGE 433: Collection Whitney Museum of American Art. PAGE 478: Hohenlohes—United Press International. PAGE 512: Letter—New York *Daily News.* PAGES 528–529: Carew—New York *Daily News*; Gloria near collapse—Wide World Photos. PAGE 556: United Press International. PAGE 562: New York *Daily News.* PAGE 569: United Press International. PAGES 573, 583: Wide World Photos. PAGE 590: Gloria and Elizabeth Wann—*Double Exposure* © 1958 by Gloria Vanderbilt and Thelma, Lady Furness; others—Wide World Photos. PAGE 593: Wide World Photos. All pictures not otherwise credited are from private collections.